GREAT LIVES
FROM
HISTORY

GREAT LIVES FROM HISTORY

Twentieth
Century
Series

Volume 1
A-Cou

Edited by
FRANK N. MAGILL

SALEM PRESS

Pasadena, California   Englewood Cliffs, New Jersey

∞ The paper used in these volumes conforms to the
American National Standard for Permanence of Paper
for Printed Library Materials, Z39.48-1984.

Library of Congress Cataloging-in-Publication Data
Great lives from history. Twentieth century series / ed-
ited by Frank N. Magill.
    p.   cm.
  Includes bibliographical references.
  Includes index.
  1. Biography—20th century. 2. Community leader-
ship. 3. World history. I. Magill, Frank Northen,
1907-   .
CT120.G69   1990
920′.009′04—dc20
[B]
[920]   90-8613
ISBN 0-89356-565-2 (set)   CIP
ISBN 0-89356-566-0 (volume 1)   AC

91-2610 WAR

PUBLISHER'S NOTE

Great Lives from History, Twentieth Century, brings to twenty-five the number of volumes in this series providing coverage of the lives, careers, and achievements of historically significant individuals from ancient to modern times. Previously published sets include the *American Series* (1987), covering 456 individuals who played key roles in the history of the United States from the time of the explorers to the late twentieth century; the *British and Commonwealth Series* (1987), representing 483 individuals from the British Isles and Commonwealth nations, from earliest times to the late twentieth century; the *Ancient and Medieval Series* (1988), whose worldwide coverage of figures not previously treated ranges from the earliest known Egyptian king to the late medieval inventor Johann Gutenberg; and the *Renaissance to 1900 Series* (1989), which extends coverage to non-American, non-British figures who flourished during the period encompassing the mid-fifteenth century through 1900.

The *Twentieth Century Series* includes 469 articles on 475 figures. Areas of achievement for these persons range from the pure sciences to social sciences, from government to the arts, including architecture, astronomy, business, diplomacy, education, government, literature, the military, music, philosophy, physics, politics, religion, social reform, and theater, among other areas. Persons represented include many who are still living at the time of publication, figures from both the Eastern and Western hemispheres, individuals who are remembered for their negative influence as well as those revered for their positive achievements. Thus, the reader will find in these pages both the famous and the infamous names of twentieth century politics—Konrad Adenauer, Yasir Arafat, Kemal Atatürk, David Ben-Gurion, Fidel Castro, Chiang Kai-shek, Chou En-Lai, Moshe Dayan, Charles de Gaulle, Alexander Dubček, Mahatma Gandhi, Mikhail Gorbachev, Haile Selassie I, Dag Hammarskjöld, Hirohito, Adolf Hitler, Ho Chi Minh, Nikita Khrushchev, Vladimir Ilich Lenin, Nelson Mandela, Mao Tse-tung, Benito Mussolini, Gamal Abdel Nasser, Jawaharlal Nehru, Kwame Nkrumah, Anwar el-Sadat, Norodom Sihanouk, Joseph Stalin, Sun Yat-sen, U Thant, Tito, Desmond Tutu, Lech Wałęsa, Chaim Weizmann—and those quieter voices that reflect and comment on the events and trends that have paved the way toward the twenty-first century: writers (from Anna Akhmatova to Elie Wiesel), musicians (From Béla Bartók to Anton von Webern), philosophers and religious leaders (Simone de Beauvoir, Martin Heidegger, John Paul II), scientists (Niels Bohr, Guglielmo Marconi, Max Planck, Konstantin Tsiolkovsky, Hideki Yukawa), dancers (Sergei Diaghilev, Vaslav Nijinsky), and students of the mind (Sigmund Freud, Carl Jung). Deliberately absent from this list of twentieth century shapers of our world are those American, British, or Commonwealth individuals who are covered in other sets in the series: *Great Lives from History: American Series* and *British and Commonwealth Series*.

The format for these articles, which average twenty-five hundred words in length, follows the easy-access standard adhered to throughout the series: Each article begins with ready-reference listings, including birth and death dates and places, areas of achievement, and a short statement on the individual's overall contribution to his or her discipline and to the world. The remainder of the article is divided into four parts. The Early Life section covers the figure's life up to the point at which his or her major work began. The Life's Work section chronologically follows the figure, relating major events and achievements. The Summary section constitutes an evaluation of the figure's contribution to or impact on history, placing the individual in context within his or her particular field. The final section is an annotated bibliography, which is intended to serve as a starting point for further research. Works are chosen for their accessibility and availability through most libraries.

Citations of books, plays, films, paintings, and other works appearing in the text include, on first mention, the earliest date of the work's first appearance (publication, if a written work). If the work is literary and was originally written in a language other than English, its English title in publication and the translation's publication date appear; where no published translation exists, a "literal" translation (appearing in lowercase letters and roman typeface) has been added where deemed valuable to the reader. Famous personages mentioned for the first time in the text of an article are identified by first and last names or the equivalent thereof. Essential facts have been systematically checked by in-house staff: birth and death dates and places, name spellings, titles and dates of literary and other written works, chronology, bibliographical information, and the like.

Volume V contains three indexes designed to aid the student: A Biographical Index lists the figures covered in the set, including cross-references from other names by which the individual may be known. An index by Areas of Achievement allows the user to gain access to historical personages by field of endeavor (art, astronomy, and so on). Finally, a Geographical Index places these individuals by nation.

Thanks are extended to our contributors, experts from fields as various as the broad array of personages covered: general historians, intellectual historians, historians of art, literature, science, and numerous other disciplines. To them we express our appreciation for their dedication to making historical scholarship available to the general reader. Their names appear at the ends of the articles and in a roster listing contributors and their academic affiliations, to be found in the front matter to Volume I.

CONTRIBUTING REVIEWERS

Michael Adams
Fairleigh Dickinson University

Patrick Adcock
Henderson State University

Bland Addison, Jr.
Worcester Polytechnic Institute

Stephen R. Addison
University of Central Arkansas

C. D. Alexander
University of Minnesota, Duluth

Arthur L. Alt
College of Great Falls

Michael S. Ameigh
St. Bonaventure University

Stanley Archer
Texas A&M University

Dorothy B. Aspinwall
University of Hawaii

Theodore P. Aufdemberge
Concordia College

Tom L. Auffenberg
Ouachita Baptist University

Mario Azevedo
University of North Carolina

Abdulla K. Badsha
University of Wisconsin-Madison

Ann Marie B. Bahr
South Dakota State University

Brian S. Baigrie
University of Calgary

Dan Barnett
California State University, Chico

Thomas F. Barry
Himeji Dokkyo University, Japan

Iraj Bashiri
University of Minnesota, Minneapolis

Erving E. Beauregard
University of Dayton

Massimo D. Bezoari
Coker College

Terry D. Bilhartz
Sam Houston State University

Cynthia A. Bily
Adrian College

George P. Blum
University of the Pacific

John H. Boyle
California State University, Chico

Michael R. Bradley
Motlow State Community College

John Braeman
University of Nebraska-Lincoln

Gerhard Brand
California State University, Los Angeles

Rennie W. Brantz
Appalachian State University

Robert Briggs
Independent Scholar

John A. Britton
Francis Marion College

J. R. Broadus
University of North Carolina at Chapel Hill

William S. Brockington, Jr.
University of South Carolina at Aiken

Alan Brown
Livingston University

Kendall W. Brown
Hillsdale College

Kenneth H. Brown
Northwestern Oklahoma State University

Robert W. Brown
Pembroke State University

Dallas L. Browne
York College of the City University of New York

David D. Buck
University of Wisconsin-Milwaukee

William H. Burnside
John Brown University

Joanne E. Butcher
University of Miami

John A. Calabrese
Texas Woman's University

Edmund J. Campion
University of Tennessee, Knoxville

Pamela Canal
Independent Scholar

Byron D. Cannon
University of Utah

P. John Carter
St. Cloud State University

Dennis Chamberland
Independent Scholar

Frederick B. Chary
Indiana University Northwest

Victor W. Chen
Chabot College

Peng-Khuan Chong
Plymouth State College

Eric Christensen
Independent Scholar

Julia A. Clancy-Smith
University of Virginia

Donald N. Clark
Trinity University

Bonnidell Clouse
Indiana State University

Robert G. Clouse
Indiana State University

Paul M. Cohen
Lawrence University

Robert Cole
Utah State University

Thomas H. Conner
Hillsdale College

Maureen Connolly
Independent Scholar

Bernard A. Cook
Loyola University

James J. Cooke
University of Mississippi

Frances A. Coulter
Ouachita Baptist University

Loren W. Crabtree
Colorado State University

David A. Crain
South Dakota State University

Frederic M. Crawford
Middle Tennessee State University

Lee B. Croft
Arizona State University

LouAnn Faris Culley
Kansas State University

Victoria Hennessey Cummins
Austin College

John C. K. Daly
Illinois State University

Donald E. Davis
Illinois State University

Nathaniel Davis
Harvey Mudd College

Ronald W. Davis
Western Michigan University

Frank Day
Clemson University

Margaret B. Denning
Sioux Falls College

Charles A. Desnoyers
La Salle University

Tom Dewey II
University of Mississippi

David R. Dorondo
Western Carolina University

Frederick Dumin
Washington State University

William V. Dunning
Central Washington University

David G. Egler
Western Illinois University

Nancy L. Erickson
Erskine College

Tom Erskine
Salisbury State University

Julia S. Falk
Michigan State University

CONTRIBUTING REVIEWERS

Stephen C. Feinstein
University of Wisconsin-River Falls

K. Thomas Finley
State University of New York at Brockport

David Marc Fischer
Independent Scholar

Robert J. Frail
Centenary College

Leslie Friedman
Independent Scholar

Peter K. Frost
Williams College

C. George Fry
Saint Francis College

Daniel J. Fuller
Kent State University

Jean C. Fulton
Maharishi International University

Jeffery L. Geller
Pembroke State University

Corinne Lathrop Gilb
Wayne State University

K. Fred Gillum
Colby College

Norbert J. Gossman
University of Detroit

Johnpeter Horst Grill
Mississippi State University

Gavin R. G. Hambly
University of Texas at Dallas

E. Lynn Harris
University of Illinois at Chicago

Fred R. van Hartesveldt
Fort Valley State College

Paul B. Harvey, Jr.
Pennsylvania State University

Robert M. Hawthorne, Jr.
Unity College

Sidney Heitman
Colorado State University

Jonathan E. Helmreich
Allegheny College

Michael F. Hembree
Florida State University

Michael Hernon
University of Tennessee at Martin

Julius M. Herz
Temple University

Fred W. Hicks
*University of South Carolina-Coastal Carolina
College*

Michael Craig Hillman
University of Texas

Shawn Hirabayashi
Independent Scholar

James R. Hofmann
California State University, Fullerton

Pierre L. Horn
Wright State University

Ron Huch
Dickinson State University

E. D. Huntley
Appalachian State University

Shakuntala Jayaswal
University of New Haven

Alphine W. Jefferson
College of Wooster

Judith R. Johnson
Wichita State University

Loretta Turner Johnson
Mankato State University

Philip Dwight Jones
Bradley University

Robert B. Kebric
University of Louisville

Karen A. Kildahl
South Dakota State University

Wm. Laird Kleine-Ahlbrandt
Purdue University

James Kline
Independent Scholar

Eve Kornfeld
San Diego State University

Arnold Krammer
Texas A&M University

Guha Krish
East Tennessee State University

Lynn C. Kronzek
Independent Scholar

Paul E. Kuhl
Winston-Salem State University

Shlomo Lambroza
St. Mary's College of Maryland

Pavlin Lange
Independent Scholar

P. R. Lannert
Independent Scholar

Karl G. Larew
Towson State University

Eugene S. Larson
Los Angeles Pierce College

Jack M. Lauber
University of Wisconsin-Eau Claire

Harry Lawton
University of California, Santa Barbara

Richard M. Leeson
Fort Hays State University

Leon Lewis
Appalachian State University

Scott Lewis
Independent Scholar

Terrance L. Lewis
Clarion University of Pennsylvania

Thomas T. Lewis
Mount Senario College

Michael Linton
Northwestern College

James Livingston
Northern Michigan University

John W. Long
Rider College

Rita E. Loos
Framingham State College

Raymond M. Lorantas
Drexel University

Donald W. Lovejoy
Palm Beach Atlantic College

David C. Lukowitz
Hamline University

Garrett L. McAinsh
Hendrix College

C. Thomas McCollough
Centre College

C. S. McConnell
University of Calgary

Mark R. McCulloh
Davidson College

Paul Madden
Hardin-Simmons University

Philip Magnier
Maharishi International University

Bill Manikas
Gaston College

Lyndon Marshall
College of Great Falls

Katherine Kearney Maynard
Rider College

Norbert Mazari
Sonoma State University

Patrick Meanor
*State University of New York College
at Oneonta*

Jonathan Mendilow
Rider College

Michael W. Messmer
Virginia Commonwealth University

L. Craig Michel
Independent Scholar

Gordon L. Miller
Independent Scholar

Eric Wm. Mogren
Independent Scholar

David W. Moore
Loyola University

Pellegrino Nazzaro
Rochester Institute of Technology

Nancy J. Nersessian
Princeton University

Brian J. Nichelson
United States Air Force Academy

CONTRIBUTING REVIEWERS

James G. Nutsch
North Carolina A&T State University

Kathleen O'Mara
State University of New York College
at Oneonta

Gary B. Ostrower
Alfred University

James Owen
Purdue University

Robert J. Paradowski
Rochester Institute of Technology

Joyce M. Parks
Independent Scholar

William E. Pemberton
University of Wisconsin-La Crosse

Nis Petersen
Jersey City State College

John R. Phillips
Purdue University Calumet

Richard V. Pierard
Indiana State University

A. J. Plotke
Cornell University

Clifton W. Potter, Jr.
Lynchburg College

Charles Pullen
Queens University, Ontario, Canada

Edna Quinn
Salisbury State University

John D. Raymer
Indiana University at South Bend

Dennis Reinhartz
University of Texas at Arlington

Rosemary M. Canfield Reisman
Troy State University

Walter F. Renn
Wheeling Jesuit College

John Neil Ries
Independent Scholar

Charles W. Rogers
Southwestern Oklahoma State University

Fred S. Rolater
Middle Tennessee State University

Hari S. Rorlich
University of Southern California

Paul Rosefeldt
University of New Orleans

Joseph Rosenblum
University of North Carolina
at Greensboro

Helaine Ross
Northwestern State University of Louisiana

Nancy Ellen Rupprecht
Middle Tennessee State University

John Santore
Pratt Institute

Stephen Satris
Clemson University

Stephen P. Sayles
University of La Verne

Nancy Schiller
State University of New York at Buffalo

Helmut J. Schmeller
Fort Hays State University

Thomas C. Schunk
Quincy College

Francis Michael Sharp
University of the Pacific

John C. Sherwood
University of Oregon

Martha Sherwood-Pike
University of Oregon

William I. Shorrock
Cleveland State University

R. Baird Shuman
University of Illinois at
Urbana-Champaign

Anne W. Sienkewicz
Independent Scholar

L. Moody Simms, Jr.
Illinois State University

Sanford S. Singer
University of Dayton

Carl Singleton
Fort Hays State University

Kyle S. Sinisi
Kansas State University

Paul A. Siskind
University of Minnesota, Minneapolis

Andrew C. Skinner
Ricks College

Genevieve Slomski
Independent Scholar

Robert W. Small
Massasoit Community College

Clyde Curry Smith
University of Wisconsin-River Falls

James Smythe
Pepperdine University

James E. Southerland
Brenau Professional College

Kenneth S. Spector
University of Massachusetts

Paul D. Steeves
Stetson University

Jean Thorleifsson Strandness
North Dakota State University

Taylor Stults
Muskingum College

Susan A. Stussy
St. Norbert College

Donald Sullivan
University of New Mexico

James Sullivan
California State University, Los Angeles

J. K. Sweeney
South Dakota State University

Glenn L. Swygart
Tennessee Temple University

Alice F. Taylor
Shorter College

Thomas J. Taylor
Independent Scholar

H. Christian Thorup
Cuesta College

David Travis
Syracuse University

Lois M. Trostle
California State University, Fresno

Spencer C. Tucker
Texas Christian University

Jiu-Hwa Lo Upshur
Eastern Michigan University

George W. Van Devender
Hardin-Simmons University

Abraham Verghese
East Tennessee State University

K. Steven Vincent
North Carolina State University

Paul R. Waibel
Liberty University

Carol M. Ward
Clemson University

James Michael Welsh
Salisbury State University

Michael J. Welsh
Illinois State University

Robert E. Whipple
Fullerton College

Kenneth Wilburn
East Carolina University

Abiodun Williams
Georgetown University

Michael W. Williams
University of North Carolina at Charlotte

William Van Willis
California State University, Fullerton

John D. Windhausen
Saint Anselm College

Thomas P. Wolf
Indiana University Southeast

Malcolm M. Wynn
Stetson University

Clifton K. Yearley
State University of New York at Buffalo

Won Z. Yoon
Siena College

Ivan L. Zabilka
Independent Scholar

LIST OF BIOGRAPHIES IN VOLUME ONE

LIST OF BIOGRAPHIES IN VOLUME ONE

GREAT LIVES
FROM
HISTORY

ALVAR AALTO

Born: February 3, 1898; Kurotane, Finland
Died: May 11, 1976; Helsinki, Finland
Area of Achievement: Architecture
Contribution: Aalto was one of the founding fathers of the so-called International Style in architecture, but he went beyond the geometrical cubism that was the hallmark of the International Style by incorporating into his mature work classical and Romantic elements. In the process, Aalto became not only Finland's most famous architect but also a national hero, even the symbol of the Finnish ideal of *sisu* (fortitude).

Early Life

Hugo Alvar Henrik Aalto was born February 3, 1898, in the small village of Kurotane in west central Finland, where his father was a land surveyor. Sometime before 1907, the family moved to Jyväskylä, the administrative/trading center for the densely forested lake region of central Finland. Aalto went through secondary school there, graduating in 1916; he served on the "White" side in the civil war that followed the declaration of Finnish independence in the wake of the Russian Revolution. He first showed his interest in and bent for architecture by his involvement in the design and construction of his parents' summer home in Alajärvi (1918). He studied architecture at the Helsinki Polytechnic Institute, graduating in 1921. There were two major influences from those years that would play a significant role in shaping his future career. One influence was Armas Lindgren, a former partner of Eliel Saarinen and, with Saarinen, a leader of the Finnish National Romantic movement. Inspired by Finland's medieval stone churches and Karelian loghouses, that movement expressed itself architecturally in a monumental rough-hewn stone style. The other influence on Aalto was the architectural historian Gustaf Nyström, Finland's leading exponent of Greek architecture and champion of the classical model as the appropriate style for the newly independent nation.

Aalto's early practice consisted primarily of designing buildings and facilities for exhibitions and fairs. His first independent architectural work was a complex of exhibition pavilions at the Tampere (Finland) Industrial Exposition in 1922. The following year, Aalto opened his own office in Jyväskylä. Probably the most important turning point in his career was his partnership with and marriage to Aino Marsio in the spring of 1924. Their honeymoon trip to Greece and Italy reinforced the attraction that classical models had for him. By the latter 1920's, Aalto had achieved a growing local reputation. His projects included the railway employees housing project (1923-1924) and Workers Club (1923-1924) in Jyväskylä; the Civil Guards' House (1925) in Seinäjoki; the Villa Väinölä (1925-1926) and Municipal Hospital

(1927) in Alajärvi; the Civil Guards' House (1926-1929) in Jyväskylä; and the Muuarame Parish Church (1927-1929).

Life's Work

The beginning of Aalto's meteoric rise from a local to an international figure dates from his winning in 1927 first place in the competition for design of the headquarters of the Southwestern Agricultural Cooperative in Turku, his accompanying relocation of his office to that city, Finland's oldest and its former capital, and his friendship (later partnership) with Erik Bryggman, one of Finland's most respected and sophisticated architects. A multipurpose structure housing a theater, offices, a hotel, restaurants, and shops whose sharp and bold exterior lines appear to have reflected the influence of the so-called *Wagnerschule* (the disciples of the Viennese architect Otto Wagner), the Southwestern Agricultural Cooperative building (1927-1928) established Aalto as an architect of the first rank. That reputation was further solidified by two follow-up Turku projects. The first was an apartment block utilizing a system of precast concrete devised by its developer, Juho Tapani. Aalto's major contribution was the façade, where broad steel window sashes provide a strong feeling of horizontality and give the appearance of a continuous glass band. Even more significant was the *Turan Sanomat* newspaper plant and offices (1928-1929), a reinforced concrete structure with a white façade marked by long strips of steel window sash, plate glass display windows, and geometrical regularity. The work was widely hailed as Finland's first International Style building and established Aalto as a leading figure in the Congrès Internationaux d'Architecture Moderne.

The most important single commission of Aalto's career was his winning first prize in the competition in 1929 for the tuberculosis sanatorium at Paimio, near Turku. The distinction of the Paimio sanatorium (1930-1933) lay not so much in its individual details—striking as each was—but rather in Aalto's success in creating a unified and integrated total environment for the comfort and convenience of the patients, including furniture, beds, lavatories, window arrangements, ventilating systems, room color schemes, and even washbasins designed to be splash proof. The international acclaim that the sanatorium attracted was reinforced by another masterpiece—Aalto's 1933 design for the Municipal Library at Viipuri (now Vyborg). The library (1933-1935, destroyed when the city and the entire province of Karelia was ceded to the Soviet Union after the Russian-Finnish Winter War of 1939-1940) strikingly demonstrated Aalto's technical virtuosity in its concealed natural-gravity ventilation, circular lightwells piercing the ceiling, and superb acoustics of the auditorium with its wavelike wood ceiling. At the same time, the work revealed Aalto's shift from the rigid and Spartan geometrical forms of the International Style to use curvilinear forms, exposed wood textures, and irregular spatial arrangements. The building represented "the most advanced fusion of aesthetic and technological considerations of any example of modern architecture of its time."

From the first days of their practice, Aalto and his wife-partner Aino were involved in the design of furniture. Aalto's first major success in this area was his folding chair; there followed his development of bent plywood chairs, culminating in the cantilevered spring leaf supported chair of 1935. From 1933 on, Aalto's furniture sold widely throughout the world. The expansion of his involvement beyond furniture to include the design of fabrics, glassware, and lighting fixtures led to the formation of the Artek Company, a partnership with Maire Gullichsen to produce and distribute Finnish-designed household furnishings.

Many of Aalto's architectural commissions in the 1930's grew out of his association with Maire Gullichsen and her husband, Harry, the heads of one of Finland's largest industrial combines. One of the most famous of those projects was the Sunila Pulp Mill (1934-1935). Aalto not only dealt brilliantly with the difficult technical problems involved—such as smoke stacks, conveyors, ventilators, processing facilities, and the like—but also achieved an aesthetic quality rarely found in industrial plants. Along with exploiting the visual contrast between the brick cubic form of the manufacturing plant and the white concrete storage sheds, Aalto successfully adapted the complex to the rough Baltic granite outcropping of the site. Further evidence of Aalto's movement from the pared-down functionalism of the pure International Style to the more Romantic use of natural materials was shown by his own home and studio in Helsinki (1935-1936) and his all-wood Finnish Pavilion for the Paris World's Fair of 1937. The masterpiece of his mature architecture, however, was the summer house he designed for the Gullichsens near Noormarkuu, approximately one hundred miles northwest of Helsinki, called the Villa Mairea (1937-1938). The L-shaped, two-story house consisted of a series of articulated rectangular volumes, accented and augmented by the free-form shape of the entrance shed, the irregular volume of Mrs. Gullichsen's painting studio, and the kidney-shaped swimming pool. To provide privacy, the interior was partitioned into living and service areas. Its most striking feature was Aalto's use of wood and natural stone to harmonize the structure with the surrounding fir forest. The house—given wide publicity by the exhibition of Aalto's architecture and furniture put on by New York City's Museum of Modern Art in 1938—became the model (lamentably watered-down in practice in most instances) for post-World War II domestic architecture throughout the world and nowhere more so than in the United States.

Aalto's first project done in the United States was the Finnish Pavilion for the New York World's Fair of 1939-1940. He was sufficiently attracted by the possibility of relocating to the United States that in 1940 he accepted a position at the Massachusetts Institute of Technology (MIT). As a Finnish patriot, however, he returned to his homeland that fall because of the threat of renewed war between Finland and the Soviet Union. At the war's end, he taught part-time at MIT until 1951. His Baker House dormitory (1946-1949) for that institution—a Z-shaped structure to maximize the number of rooms with windows facing upon the Charles River, with undulating walls, dark, rough, brick façades, and cantilevered, twin, straight-run stairways stretching the length of its main entrance (rear) façade—is the foremost example of Aalto's work in the United States.

Aalto was hit hard by the death of his wife Aino in January, 1949. In 1952, however, he married Elissa Mäkiniemi, a member of his office staff, and, like Aino, she became his partner in his architectural practice. Aalto's international reputation brought him in the 1950's and 1960's a series of major Finnish commissions, including the National Pension Bank (1952-1956), the "Ratatalo" office building (1953-1955), and Finlandia Hall (1962-1965), a concert hall and conference center complex (all in Helsinki); the main building of the Helsinki Technical University at Otaniemi (1955-1964); the Vuoksenniska Church in Imatra (1956-1958); and the Seinäjoki Civic Center (1952-1965). The masterwork of the last phase of his career was the Cultural Center (1958-1962) at Wolfsburg, West Germany. The building combines virtually every feature that had become identified as Aalto hallmarks: the fanlike arrangement of the main auditorium and meeting rooms; sunken forms or double-height spaces open to the sky or skylighted, irregular shaped volumes, undulating ceilings, and richly textured wood surfaces.

Aalto was awarded in 1957 the Royal Gold Medal of Architecture in Great Britain and in 1963 the Gold Medal of the American Institute of Architects. As he grew older, however, he became increasingly reclusive until he was inaccessible to all except a handful of longtime friends. The physical and mental impairments of age aggravated by a lifetime of heavy drinking sapped his creative energies during the last decade of his life. Aalto died May 11, 1976, in Helsinki. His death at the age of seventy-eight marked the departure of the last of the twentieth century's architectural giants.

Summary

Over the course of Alvar Aalto's fifty-four years of practice, he produced, exclusive of single-family dwellings, more than two hundred finished buildings plus the plans for scores more projects that were never built. He thus ranks second only to Frank Lloyd Wright as the most productive major architect of the twentieth century. In addition, he was highly successful aesthetically and financially in the design of furniture, home furnishings, and textiles. Until the post-World War II period, Aalto was probably more appreciated abroad than in his homeland. By the time of his death, however, his name was regarded as synonymous with Finnish architecture.

Aalto's stature as a giant of modern architecture rests upon three major achievements. The first is his technical virtuosity. Perhaps the outstanding example—one reflecting the influence of the Finnish environment with its months of limited sunlight—was his handling of site, building layout, and window and skylight arrangements to maximize the amount of natural light available. The second was his interest in, and concern for, the total environment of each building. Every detail was planned and coordinated to promote the comfort, convenience, and well-being of his buildings' users or residents. The third was his success in transcending the limitations of the International Style in which he had first made his reputation. He did so by alternating rectangular volumes with more irregular forms; by brilliantly exploiting the textural possibilities of wood, natural stone, and, in the last phase of his career thanks to the influence of Frank Lloyd Wright, red brick; and by his talent for harmonizing his structures with the natural environment of the site.

Bibliography

Dunster, David, ed. *Alvar Aalto*. New York: Rizzoli, 1979. The essay by Raji-Liisa Heinonen, "Some Aspects of 1920's Classicism and the Emergence of Functionalism in Finland," is informative. The other two main essays—Demetri Porphyrios' "Heterotopia: A Study in the Ordering Sensibility of the Work of Alvar Aalto," and Steven Groak's "Notes on Responding to Aalto's Buildings"—are murky exercises in architectural criticism. The rest of the volume consists of brief written descriptions with accompanying lavish illustrations—many in full color—of twenty Aalto buildings dating over the full span of his career.

Gutheim, Frederick. *Alvar Aalto*. New York: George Braziller, 1960. Gutheim's brief biographical sketch in this volume for the Braziller Masters of World Architecture Series, written at the height of Aalto's reputation, is adulatory, is not wholly reliable, and devotes disproportionately too much space to Aalto's experiments in large-scale town planning (none of which fully materialized) and his post-World War II Finnish commissions. The work is still a useful introduction for the layman. There are approximately eighty pages of black-and-white photographs and floor or site plans.

Pearson, Paul David. "Alvar Aalto." In *Macmillan Encyclopedia of Architects*, edited by Adolf K. Placzek, 4 vols. New York: Macmillan and Free Press, 1982. A brief but comprehensive, balanced, and judicious survey of Aalto's career and work that should be the starting point for all interested students. The major weakness—apart from the inevitable scanting on details—is that the format allows only a handful of small-sized black-and-white photographs for illustrations.

_____. *Alvar Aalto and the International Style*. New York: Whitney Library of Design, 1978. This thoroughly researched and documented account of the first half of Aalto's career, up to the death of his first wife in January, 1949, is regarded as the authoritative treatment of that phase of Aalto's life. Pearson not only analyzes in his text all of Aalto's projects, built and unbuilt, from the period, but illustrates most with reproductions of sketches/plans and photographs.

Quantrill, Malcolm. *Alvar Aalto: A Critical Study.* New York: Schocken Books, 1983. The fullest and most satisfactory one-volume account in English of Aalto's long, productive career. The first chapter examines Aalto's pronouncements on the nature of architecture; the second looks at "Modern Finnish Architecture—Background and Evolution." The remainder of the text traces the evolution of Aalto's work, with extended analyses of the more important projects and extensive photographs and copies of plans to illustrate the points made. There is, in addition, an invaluable sixteen-page bibliography of books, exhibition catalogs, and articles.

Schildt, Göran. *Alvar Aalto: The Early Years.* Translated by Timothy Binham. New York: Rizzoli, 1984. The first volume, covering up to 1927, of a projected three-volume account that should be regarded as the official biography. Schildt—who was Aalto's favorite architectural critic—tends to be hero-worshipful toward the master, but he utilizes previously untapped archival materials to shed new light on the development of Aalto's art, work style, and personality. Contains 278 color and black-and-white illustrations.

_____. *Alvar Aalto: The Decisive Years.* Translated by Timothy Binham. New York: Rizzoli, 1987. The second volume of the projected three-volume biography, covering the years from the later 1920's until 1939. This volume has the virtues and weaknesses of its predecessor but is must reading not only for serious students of Aalto but also for those interested in the development of modern architecture, at least as viewed through the eyes of one of its major shapers. Like the first volume, this one is generously illustrated.

John Braeman

FERHAT ABBAS

Born: October 24, 1899; Tahar, Algeria
Died: December 24, 1985; Algiers, Algeria
Areas of Achievement: Government, politics, and diplomacy
Contribution: Abbas was the first Premier of the Provisional Government of
Algeria (1958-1961). Regarded as the "grand old man of Algerian politics," he was an assimilationist in the 1930's and nonviolent radical nationalist in the 1940's whose so-called Manifesto of the Algerian People
marked a turning point in the development of an Algerian national independence movement. Realizing that peaceful means would not bring an
end to colonialism, Abbas became a revolutionary nationalist, joined the
National Liberation Front in 1956, and quickly became its international
spokesman.

Early Life

Ferhat Abbas was born in Tahar, Algeria, on October 24, 1899. He was
the seventh of thirteen children born to Abbas Sáid and Achoura (Maza)
Abbas. His father, a rather prosperous *cáid* (local administrative chief) in
the northern Constantine village of Chahna, who possessed clear ties to the
French government, had received the rosette and silver braid of a commander of the Legion of Honor for his service to France. Abbas received a
typical French education, attending primary school in Djidjelli and the *lycée*
at Phillippeville. After obtaining his *baccalauréat*, he did three years of
compulsory military service in a medical corps at Bône. Discharged in 1923
with the rank of sergeant, he then entered the College of Pharmacy at the
University of Algiers.

Spending eight years rather than the usual six pursuing his diploma in
pharmacy, Abbas was more interested in politics and literature than in chemistry and biology. His years at the university were an apprenticeship for his
future public life. He avidly read the works of Victor Hugo and Sophocles as
well as the Declaration of the Rights of Man and of the Citizen and began
publishing articles in *At-Takaddoun* (progress) and *Le Trait d'Union* (connecting link) that were highly critical of French colonialism. Writing under
the pseudonym Kémal Abencérages, the young Abbas argued against the
regime's systematic humiliation imposed on the Arabo-Berber Algerian population.

Elected president of the Association of Muslim Students at the University
of Algiers in 1926, Abbas appealed in his writings to young educated Algerian men like himself, but he also wrote about the discrimination endured
by muslim soldiers in the French Army, Algerian workers in France, and the
Algerian intelligentsia. His ideology at that point was assimilationist; he
argued for Algerian Muslims to be granted French citizenship with full

equality and an end to discrimination. In 1933, he opened a pharmacy in Sétif, which would be his political base for many years. The following year, he married the daughter of a wealthy landowner from Djidjelli, but the marriage, an unhappy union, did not last. With his first book, *Le Jeune Algérien* (1930; the young Algerian), a series of articles on colonial injustices, he began a career in literature and politics that would last thirty-five years.

Life's Work

The struggle for political and economic emancipation of Algerians was the major work of Abbas' life. His plans for realizing that goal and its final form were not always the same, for his ideas and strategies changed over time. In the February 23, 1936, issue of *L'Entente*, a weekly that he founded in 1933, Abbas asserted in an article entitled "Je suis la France" (I am France) that the Algerian nation had never existed, a statement that was used against him by his rivals for years to come. He also argued at that time that there could be no French Algeria without the emancipation of the indigenous people. In the 1930's, Abbas was willing to criticize the colonial system and work to dismantle it from within. He argued for assimilation, the full integration of Algerians as citizens of France. His position differed from that of the Muslim modernists such as Shaikh Abdulhamid ben Badis of the Association of Ulama (Muslim scholars), who popularized the idea of the Algerian nation, and secular nationalists such as Messali Hadj of L'Étoile Nord-Africaine (North African star), who identified with European socialists. Between 1933 and 1936 he was a town councilor from Sétif, a district representative for Constantine, and a fiscal delegate to Algiers. Early in 1938, he founded the Algerian People's Union, a party intended to mobilize the masses around a program of Algerian integration into France but with full recognition of Muslim Algerian customs, tradition, and language.

As World War II began, Abbas volunteered to serve in the French forces. Captured by the Germans after a brief period in the medical corps, he was discharged in August, 1940, and returned to political journalism and his pharmacy in Sétif. After French General Hari-Honoré Giraud rejected his appeal to enlist Muslims in the war of liberation (from German occupation), Abbas turned away from the path of assimilation. On February 10, 1943, he published the so-called Manifesto of the Algerian People, a document submitted two days later to the French administration and signed by twenty-two elected representatives of Muslim Algerians. The manifesto called for the abolition of colonialism, an Algerian constitution that would guarantee freedom and equality to all, the redistribution of settler land to Algerian peasants, the recognition of Arabic and French as official languages, the release of political prisoners, and the separation of church and state. It was an Algerian "declaration of the rights of man," a call for an autonomous Algerian state within a French Union. Several months later, Abbas was interned for nationalist agitation but then released in December prior to the governor's promulgation of a new ordinance (of March 7, 1944) granting French citizenship to an elite group of Muslims.

Opposition to the ordinance and its denial of Algerian nationhood crystallized around Abbas, who founded a new party, the Friends of the Manifesto and of Liberty, in Sétif on March 14, 1944. The party initially secured the support of Hadj's followers and the *ulama* (Muslim intelligentsia). In September, a party journal was launched, *Égalité* (equality), to promote the party's three-point program; the nonviolent struggle against colonialism, the creation of a self-governing Algerian republic in federation with France, and the elimination of special privilege. Militant nationalism, however, was developing rapidly. By March, 1945, delegates at the Congress of the Friends of the Manifesto rejected the idea of federation with France and endorsed an independent Algerian government free to choose its own alliances. Then in May, 1945, an uprising developed that permanently changed the character of the Algerian nationalist movement. It began in Sétif on May 8, 1945, with a demonstration at which police fired on placard-carrying demonstrators and quickly spread countrywide with Algerians attacking Europeans and vice versa. Algerian anticolonial protest met with fierce repression by police forces and armed settler vigilante groups. Estimates of Algerians killed during the following six weeks ranged from eight to twenty thousand.

In early 1946, Abbas formed a new party, the Democratic Union of the Algerian Manifesto (UDMA), a party of middle-class moderates and not a coalition that included Muslim factions and secular radicals. His party won eleven of the thirteen seats in the Second Constituent Assembly (an all-Muslim body) with a program calling for a secular Algerian republic secured through nonviolent means. Hadj, who had been jailed, was released in the summer of 1946 and established another party, the Movement for the Triumph of Democratic Liberties (MTLD), which won more seats in 1947 than Abbas' party. The following year, unity talks between all the nationalist groups commenced. A secret organization (OS) to prepare for armed resistance also formed and came into public view with a series of robberies in 1950, which were carried out to finance the resistance.

Abbas, who on September 17, 1945, married an Algerian-born French woman, Marcelle Stoetzel, with whom he had a son, Halim, maintained his middle-of-the-road position within the nationalist movement. His political preoccupations—equality, secularism, social justice, Algerian autonomy, and federalism—were reiterated in the pages of *La République algérienne* (formerly *Égalité*), which he edited. From 1947 to 1955, he served as a member of the Algerian Assembly, and for a time he served in the inter-colonial assembly, the French Union. Although labeled a moderate nationalist, on two occasions he was jailed by the French. The atmosphere in Algeria at the time was extremely tense, for there were trials of OS members and continued arrests of suspected militants. In 1953, the Revolutionary Committee for Unity and Action (CRUA) was formed by younger nationalists attached to the OS (Ben Bella, Muhammad Boudiaf Larbi Ben M'Hidi, Mourad Didouche) who were frustrated by Hadj's control of the Algerian Progressive Party (PPA) and MTLD. The following year, CRUA created two interlocking revolutionary organizations, the National Liberation Front (FLN) and the National Liberation Army (ALN); the latter was the military wing and the former the political wing of a national independence movement. The FLN war for national liberation began on November 1, 1954.

Abbas, essentially opposed to violence, remained aloof and even tried to act as an intermediary between the French and the FLN. French repression of the struggle and their brutal counterinsurgency strategies drew indigenous support to the FLN, including that of Abbas. He apparently joined the FLN in May, 1955, but did not publicly announce it until April 26, 1956, in Cairo. There he proclaimed that UDMA no longer existed, that the FLN represented the force for liberation, and that there would be no peace until the French were out of Algeria. With his entrance into the FLN, the party gained increased respectability, for the "grand old man of Algerian politics" had abandoned "moderation" for revolutionary violence, having lost all faith in French goodwill.

Abbas traveled often through Europe, Latin America, and the Middle East to secure support for Algerian independence. In 1957, he was appointed FLN delegate to the United Nations. The following year, he made a special appeal to the Vatican to intervene on behalf of a just peace. Shortly after the French Fourth Republic collapsed in May, 1958, and General Charles de Gaulle assumed power, the FLN based in Cairo announced on September 19, 1958, the formation of a Provisional Government of the Republic of Algeria (GPRA) with the dual purpose of intensifying the war for independence and extending the diplomatic offensive. As the most respected figure in Algerian politics, Abbas was unanimously regarded as the best choice for premier, a position he held until August, 1961, but which involved more prestige than power.

In September, 1959, Abbas responded to de Gaulle's first offer of Algerian self-determination by means of a referendum to be held four years after a cease-fire. While agreeing with de Gaulle in principle, Abbas declared that the general had to deal directly with the GPRA to obtain a cease-fire and that a free referendum was impossible with the French army in control and thousands of Algerians in prison. De Gaulle's partition plan to protect the rights of settlers, and French intentions to retain ownership of Saharan natural resources (such as oil) were rejected. Abbas issued his own appeal to European Algerians to cooperate in bringing about self-determination; the appeal met with great bitterness.

Amid continuing hostilities in 1960, preliminary negotiations for a cease-fire began in Melun, France, but quickly broke down. Later that year, Abbas visited both the Soviet Union, which granted de facto recognition to the FLN, and the People's Republic of China, which offered military aid. Following de Gaulle's referendum of January 8, 1961, in which (despite the FLN's boycot) French voters supported Algerian self-determination, talks between France and the FLN began in earnest. These resulted within a year in the Evian accords, arranging for Algerian independence on July 7, 1962. Abbas, though, was replaced as premier in August, 1961, by Benyoussef Ben Khedda, who was considered to be more sympathetic to the left wing in the FLN. With independence in 1962, Abbas became president of the National Assembly, serving one year. His commitment to liberal parliamentary politics led him to resist efforts by Ahmad Ben Bella, the first president, to have the FLN control the assembly, and in 1964 he was placed under house arrest. Released in 1965 after Ben Bella was deposed and also placed under house arrest, the "grand old man of Algerian politics" remained in retirement one of the honored leaders of Algerian independence.

Summary

The life of Ferhat Abbas, like that of his beloved nation, was a struggle for equality and dignity. His life manifested the search for identity prevalent in the politics and literature of Algeria. With his clipped mustache, avuncular features, and neatly sober dress, he epitomized the Westernized, middle-class Algerian *évolué*. His public career is key to understanding the story of Algerian nationalism and the revolution, for it was symptomatic of how the liberal moderate—through repeated disillusionment—became transformed into a revolutionary nationalist.

Abbas' life, like his father's, exemplified the way the French colonial system could work for a few. He rose successfully through the ranks of the legislative posts open to Muslims. Everything about him was oriented toward the West, France, and indeed, middle-class France. More comfortable with French than Arabic, educated and cultured, he still was not an equal citizen in his homeland. Hence, he sought equality his entire life, abandoning his integrationist views in the 1940's, endorsing nonfederalist independence and eventually armed struggle. Equality and social justice remained his goals.

Bibliography

Abun-Nasr, Jamil M. *A History of the Maghrib*. 2d ed. Cambridge, England: Cambridge University Press, 1975. A multicentury survey of the region that contains an excellent description and analysis of French colonialism and Algerian national resistance.
Clark, Michael K. *Algeria in Turmoil*. New York: Praeger, 1959. This work

includes extensive coverage of Abbas and the nationalist factions in the 1930's and 1940's. It is decidedly biased in favor of the French colonial administration.

Horne, Alistair. *A Savage War of Peace: Algeria, 1954-1962*. New York: Viking Press, 1978. The story of the Algerian war and its main players. This is probably the most readable and dramatic account of Algerian nationalism. Contains a succinct account of Abbas and his middle-class followers.

Ottaway, David, and Marina Ottaway. *Algeria: The Politics of a Socialist Revolution*. Berkeley: University of California Press, 1970. This work focuses on the final years of the liberation war and the first six years of independence. Sympathetic to the FLN, it contains valuable descriptions of the major figures including Abbas.

Quandt, William B. *Revolution and Political Leadership: Algeria, 1954-1968*. Cambridge, Mass.: MIT Press, 1969. With a focus on political leadership in the national movement, especially the FLN, Abbas is one of the more sympathetic individuals here. He was interviewed extensively by the author.

Kathleen O'Mara

CHINUA ACHEBE

Born: November 16, 1930; Ogidi, Nigeria

Area of Achievement: Literature

Contribution: Achebe was one of the first African writers to achieve international literary success. His use of a mixture of simple English and Ibo phrases reflected a uniquely African heritage and inspired many other African writers to lend their voices to different types of Western literature.

Early Life

Chinualomagu (Albert) Achebe was born on November 16, 1930, in Ogidi, Nigeria, a large Ibo village in the rainforest lands not far from the banks of the Niger River. He was the second youngest of six children born to Isaiah Achebe, a teacher-catechist for the Church Missionary Society and one of the first people of his region to convert to Christianity. Achebe's family was distinguished, as his grandfather had acquired three of the four possible titles in the village. Although as a boy he was educated as a Christian, learning to admire all things European and to reject things that were African, Achebe was still able to find beauty in traditional African culture. Since his father did not sever connections with his non-Christian relatives, Achebe established a relationship with his people's traditional world.

Achebe began his education in the Christian mission school of his birthplace. He then won a scholarship to Government College Umahia and in 1948 was chosen to be one of the first students to study at University College, Ibadan (later the University of Ibadan). While attending university, Achebe rejected his given English name (Albert) and began to use the African Chinualomagu (shortened to Chinua), which implies the meaning "God will fight for me." He also dropped his planned study of medicine and instead chose to pursue a degree in literature, receiving his B.A. in 1953. At this time, Achebe began to write short stories and essays, some of which centered on the conflict between Christian and traditional African culture, a subject that would become the focal point for much of his later works. After graduation, Achebe taught secondary school for less than a year before joining the Nigerian Broadcasting Company as "talks producer" in 1954.

Life's Work

In his first novel, *Things Fall Apart* (1958), Achebe focused on the Nigerian experience of European colonialism and dominance, developing his major themes from an African viewpoint and portraying the many aspects of the communal life of the Ibo people of Umuafia in the late nineteenth century at both the societal and individual levels. The novel is short, utilizing a close-knit style that creates an effective picture of the clash between the Ibo and European cultures at a time when white missionaries and officials were first penetrating Eastern Nigeria. The story focuses on two closely intertwined tragedies—the public tragedy of the Ibo culture as it is eclipsed by the European culture and the individual tragedy of Okonkwo, an important man of Umuafia who sees his traditional world changing and collapsing and is powerless to stop it. *Things Fall Apart* was met with wide critical acclaim and has since been translated into forty-five languages.

Achebe's second novel, *No Longer at Ease*, was published in 1960. As in his first novel, Achebe took the novel's title from a poem by T. S. Eliot. This work examines African society in the era of independence and continues the saga of the Okonkwo family with Ox's grandson Obi, an educated Christian who has left his village for a position as a civil servant in urban Lagos, Nigeria. The story deals with the tragedy of a new generation of Nigerians who, although educated and Westernized, are nevertheless caught between the opposing cultures of traditional African and urban Lagos.

In 1961, Achebe was appointed Director of External Broadcasting for Nigeria. This position required that Achebe travel to Great Britain as well as other parts of the world. During this time, a collection of Achebe's short stories entitled *The Sacrificial Egg and Other Short Stories* (1962) was published. Two years later, Achebe completed *Arrow of God* (1964). In this, his third novel, Achebe once again painted a picture of cultures in collision, and once again his novel attracted much attention, which only added to the high esteem in which he was already held.

A Man of the People, which would be Achebe's last novel for more than two decades, was published in 1966. With this novel, Achebe continued to develop the urban themes that he had presented in *No Longer at Ease*, but this time with a satirical edge, examining corrupt politicians who used to their own advantage the political system that they had inherited from the departed imperial power.

After a massacre of Ibos took place in Northern Nigeria in 1966, Achebe resigned his position with the Nigerian Broadcasting Service and moved to the Eastern Region of Nigeria, where he intended to go into publishing. When the region declared its independence as the separate state of Biafra, however, Achebe became personally involved with the ensuing civil war, serving the Biafran government from 1967 to 1970. During this period of his life, Achebe produced only one piece of work, a children's book entitled *Chike and the River* (1966).

In the years following the war, Achebe produced three collections of poetry: *Beware, Soul-Brother and Other Poems* (1971, 1972), *Christmas in Biafra and Other Poems* (1973), and *Don't Let Him Die: An Anthology of Memorial Poems for Christopher Okigbo* (1978). In addition, Achebe was a coeditor of *Aka Weta: An Anthology of Igbo Poetry* (1982). With this turn to poetry as a medium for his creative talents, Achebe was able to distinguish himself as both a great novelist and a fine poet. During this period, Achebe also wrote a collection of short stories entitled *Girls at War* (1983) and coedited another collection entitled *African Short Stories* (1984). In addition, he produced three works of juvenile literature as well as a number of essays. In the 1980's, Achebe's *Things Fall Apart* was adapted for stage, radio, and television.

In 1971, Achebe accepted a post at the University of Nigeria in Nsukka. The following year, Achebe and his family moved temporarily to the United States, where he took a position with the University of Massachusetts as a professor in its Department of Afro-American Studies. In addition, during this period, he taught at several American institutions as a visiting professor. While in the United States, he was awarded an honorary doctor of letters degree from Dartmouth College. Additionally, Achebe shared, with a Canadian, the 1972 Commonwealth Prize for the best book of poetry in his *Beware, Soul-Brother and Other Poems*. In 1976, he returned to Nsukka, where he held the rank of professor and edited *Okike*, a literary journal.

The year 1988 saw Achebe return to the novel as an expression of his now world-renowned talents. His work *Anthills of the Savannah* was very well received and earned a nomination for the Booker Prize. According to Charles R. Larson, writing for the *Chicago Tribune*, "no other novel in many years has bitten to the core, swallowed and regurgitated contemporary Africa's miseries and expectations as profoundly as *Anthills of the Savannah.*"

Summary

Chinua Achebe can be counted among the founders of the new literature of Nigeria, which has flourished since the 1950's; it is a literature that draws upon traditional oral history as well as a modern, rapidly changing African society. As a founder of this movement, Achebe has paved the way for other notable African writers such as Elechie Amadie and Cyprian Ekwensi. In addition, he has influenced an entire second generation of African writers. Achebe has also helped shape and set into place the now characteristic features of the African novel, especially the effective use of very simple language, peppered with African words and proverbs and highly reminiscent of traditional African speech patterns. As Bruce King comments in *Introduction to Nigerian Literature*: "Achebe was the first Nigerian writer to successfully transmute the conventions of the novel, a European art form, into African literature."

Achebe's novels, which comment strongly on the stages of change that have affected the entire African continent in the past one hundred years, not only are chronicles of events and trends in African history but also are extremely artistic expressions that contain a definite purpose. Unlike many novelists, Achebe rejects the notion that the writer is an individual who writes for his own personal pleasure or merely for the purpose of artistic expression. Instead, he sees the novelist as an educator. For example, in an interview with Bernth Lindfors, Achebe states: "One big message of the many that I try to put across, is that Africa was not a vacuum, before the coming of Europe, that culture was not unknown in Africa, that culture was not brought to Africa by the white world." Through his novels, his poetry, his short stories, his career as an educator, and his extension into editing the African Writers series for Heinemann Educational Books, Achebe has succeeded in founding and nurturing a major literary movement of the twentieth century.

Bibliography

Cartney, Wilfred. *Whispers from a Continent: The Literature of Contemporary Black Africa*. New York: Random House, 1969. A survey of black African writers. Contains critical analyses of *Arrow of God*, *A Man of the People*, and *No Longer at Ease* as well as a discussion of how each ties into a relationship with African culture and European colonialism. Includes discussion on other writers of the Nigerian literature movement.

Githae-Mugo, Micere. *Visions of Africa*. Nairobi: Kenya Literature Bureau, 1978. Provides original interpretations of the works of Achebe as well as four other writers and examines their various works of fiction against a sociopolitical background. Also examines Achebe's personal experiences and how they affected his writings.

Heywood, Christopher. *A Critical View on Chinua Achebe's "Things Fall Apart."* London: The British Council, 1985. A critical analysis of Achebe's first novel. Contains information on Achebe's life and work as well as his personal experiences and views on books and writing in general. Also includes selected writings from some of Achebe's critics.

Owomoyela, Oyekan. *African Literatures: An Introduction*. Waltham, Mass.: Crossroads Press, 1979. A survey of African novels, short stories, poetry, and drama. Introduces major works and their authors. Contains critical and biographical information on Achebe and his first four novels. This book is for the general reader interested in African literature.

Ravenscroft, Arthur. *Chinua Achebe*. New York: Longmans, Green, 1969. A full discussion of Achebe's first four novels, including critical and literary analysis and a brief summary of each of the four novels. Also contains biographical information on the author.

Wren, Robert M. *Chinua Achebe, "Things Fall Apart."* New York: Longman, 1980. A guide to Achebe's first novel. Each chapter in *Things Fall Apart* is summarized with questions at the end of each section. Provides a brief introduction to Achebe's life. Contains background information on the novel, the characters, and the time period covered.

Norbert Mazari

KONRAD ADENAUER

Born: January 5, 1876; Cologne, Germany
Died: April 19, 1967; Röhndorf, West Germany
Areas of Achievement: Government and politics
Contribution: Between 1917 and 1933, Adenauer served his country as Lord
  Mayor of Cologne, becoming, after 1945, founder of the Federal Republic
  of Germany and its first chancellor.

Early Life
  Konrad Adenauer was born in Cologne, Germany, on January 5, 1876.
Adenauer's family, of modest means and devoutly Roman Catholic, had
produced bakers, bricklayers, reserve army officers, and local officials. In
short, he was imbued with the ideals of hard work, self-sacrifice, and persistence. Above all, his home was steeped in the Rhenish tradition of Roman
Catholicism and moderately liberal social values. These characteristics informed Adenauer's entire life, and, like his lifelong affection for the Rhineland's hills and rivers, they never left him.
  After receiving a classical Catholic education, Adenauer took a bank
clerk's job while preparing for university studies. These studies eventually
took him to universities in Freiburg im Breisgau, Munich, and Bonn. Passing the bar in 1899, Adenauer entered civil service in the state prosecutor's
office in Cologne.
  As a Catholic Rhinelander, Adenauer lived figuratively and literally on the
periphery of the German Empire created in 1871 and was inherently suspicious of an imperial system dominated by Prussia's Protestant elite. He
treasured his region's specific cultural identity and socioeconomic evolution,
neither readily compatible with Prussia's oftentimes autocratic and militarist
virtues. While Adenauer's Rhenish homeland was an integral part of Prussia,
the Catholic western provinces had long resented distant Berlin's domination.

Life's Work
  As with most politicians of stature, Adenauer's career began locally. Establishing himself in Cologne, he joined the Center Party, a minority political party representing German Roman Catholics. Subsequently, Adenauer
became administrative assistant to Cologne's lord mayor in 1906. Hard-
working and politically loyal, he became mayoral candidate in his own right
in 1917, even as Germany collapsed at the end of World War I.
  Adenauer's steady pragmatism and determination to succeed allowed him
not only to become lord mayor but also to execute numerous major civic
improvements in the face of Germany's defeat. In the process, Cologne
became a European center of social and political progressivism. Adenauer

soon built a solid base of political support, using his genuine gifts of persuasion—"oversimplification" his detractors said—to help keep the Rhineland part of Germany at a time of rumored annexation by France or a separate Rhenish state. Expediently, Adenauer too flirted with separatism, but his political acumen cautioned that Rhenish independence was chimerical.

By 1919, Adenauer valued such caution. No longer merely Lord Mayor of Cologne, he had become a skilled and tenacious regional politician. Eliciting strong support from his followers and outwitting his less skilled opponents, he quickly established a reputation as an effective civilian leader in a country traditionally respecting only those in uniform. His reputation would carry him far in the post-1945 era.

During the interwar period, Adenauer devoted his energies to his beloved Cologne. One of Adenauer's most important early tasks was the refounding of the city's university. Utterly determined, Adenauer convinced the Prussian state government—despite budgetary difficulties and strident opposition from the neighboring University of Bonn—to reestablish the University of Cologne in 1919-1920. More immediately beneficial were Adenauer's efforts to improve Cologne's appearance and commercial accessibility. Between 1919 and 1929, he directed the razing of Cologne's outmoded fortifications. He replaced them with an extensive ring of parks around the growing metropolis. Additionally, Adenauer greatly expanded Cologne's commercial importance by modernizing the riverine harbor facilities in the city's heart. Improving and rationalizing the living conditions of the metropolitan area's population, he also directed the annexation of neighboring townships and oversaw the construction of numerous apartment projects. Adenauer greatly eased Cologne's transition from large provincial city to conurbation. More important, the office of lord mayor sharply honed his administrative and political skills, which would serve him well after the war.

With the coming of the Nazi horror in 1933, Adenauer found himself, like so many others, unable to prevent the impending catastrophe. Depression-era economic chaos had vastly exacerbated the still-nagging shock of Germany's loss of World War I and the revolution of 1918. Consequent political radicalization benefited extremists such as the Nazis and the Communists. Feeding voraciously upon the country's discontent and privation, these groups completely paralyzed Germany's democracy. The ultimate results were dictatorship and war.

On March 13, 1933, Adenauer was forced from his office as lord mayor. Failing to convince Berlin's Nazi overlords to spare him and his family from persecution, Adenauer went into secret, self-imposed internal exile in the Catholic monastery of Maria Laach in northwestern Germany. Between 1934 and 1937, fearful sojourns followed in Berlin and at Rhöndorf on the Rhine near Bonn. In Rhöndorf, Adenauer eventually built a new home for his family; the Nazis had banned him from his native Cologne.

From 1937 to 1944, Adenauer and his family lived as normal an existence as the travail of dictatorship and war would allow. A devoted father and husband, Adenauer held such normality to be critically important. In 1944, however, this normality was shattered by his imprisonment following the failed attempt by German army officers to kill Adolf Hitler. Escaping with the help of a friend, Adenauer was later recaptured and sent to a Gestapo prison. By the end of 1944, however, he had been reunited with his family, surviving both the Nazi terror and the total defeat of Hitler's Germany.

Liberating Cologne, United States forces immediately reinstated Adenauer as lord mayor. He was summarily dismissed, however, as British units assumed control of the city. Ironically, this dismissal freed Adenauer for a major role in the larger, tortured process of Germany's reconstruction. A new political party, Christian Democratic Union (CDU), served as Adenauer's vehicle. Absorbing the old Catholic Center Party, it united the middle class, a German tradition of social progressivism, and moderate political values. Skillfully outmaneuvering his Berlin rivals, Adenauer became the dominant personality of the new party by 1947. Artfully exploiting the simultaneous rift between the superpowers, he also helped to convince the United States, Great Britain, and France by 1948 that an entirely new, democratic German state should be created: the Federal Republic of Germany.

Adenauer was absolutely convinced that a Western-oriented, federated republic was Germany's sole hope for the postwar world. As head of one of the two strongest West German political parties, Adenauer assumed that he should play a leading role in that republic's formation. Throughout the difficult formative process in 1948-1949, Adenauer pursued a dual objective: to make the state-in-being acceptable to the Western allies and simultaneously to foil proposals from his domestic opposition, principally in the Social Democratic Party.

Born in May, 1949, the new German republic possessed an unmistakable Western alignment, enjoyed genuine democratic government, and operated, in nascent form, the socially responsive free-market system, which helped make the Federal Republic of Germany the economic miracle of the 1950's. As the republic's first chancellor, Adenauer would hold the office until his retirement in 1963.

Almost alone among German statesmen to 1949, Adenauer held that any new Germany must renounce nationalism for Europe's sake. Underlying the foreign policy he directed in his dual role as chancellor and foreign minister, this idea earned for Adenauer the sharp domestic criticism that such policies doomed Germany's reunification. Adenauer countered that only a federal republic, firmly anchored in a united, militarily strong Western Europe, could compel the Soviet Union to surrender its European satellites. In any case, Adenauer's anti-Prussian sentiments made accepting a supposedly temporary German division all the easier. Though this division has proven much longer-lived than Adenauer ever anticipated, his policies eliminated Germany's ancient enmity toward France and incorporated the federal republic's enormous economic potential into the growing European community. In the process, Adenauer oversaw the transformation of his country from ruined enemy of the Western world to self-assertive ally and valued friend.

Summary

Throughout his long and remarkably productive career, Konrad Adenauer maintained that the Western world is a cultural and historical community possessing fundamental and unique values not common to the East. No great theorist, he nevertheless consistently attempted, as Lord Mayor of Cologne and as Chancellor and Foreign Minister of the Federal Republic of Germany, to realize these values daily for his countrymen. Though often haughty and imperious, he possessed the unique ability to transform himself from local politician to international statesman. In doing so, he steadfastly opposed all tyrannies, even at the cost of his personal safety. Intolerant of incompetence, he earned the respect of both supporters and opponents and led much of Germany through one of her most trying periods.

While absorbed in his beloved Cologne before 1933, Adenauer transferred his public devotion to a larger cause after 1945: that of helping Germany recover from the Nazi era's shame and criminality. Shepherding the young Federal Republic of Germany through the pain of occupation and reconstruction, Adenauer saw his country reacquire full sovereignty in 1955. Furthermore, he demonstrated that his countrymen could successfully overcome past mistakes to become respected and valued allies. Though never mastering Germany's division, Adenauer's reconciliation of the federal republic with the West must be recognized as a historic achievement.

Less tangible but equally important, Adenauer represented an often overlooked German tradition of social responsibility and middle-class, liberal democracy. He guided this tradition to an unparalleled degree of popular acceptance in Germany. In a society traditionally too ready to glorify things martial, Adenauer proved decisively that civilian rule could lead effectively and provide economic success and societal well-being. In the final analysis, that accomplishment stands as his enduring legacy.

Bibliography

Alexander, Edgar. *Adenauer and the New Germany: The Chancellor of the Vanquished*. Translated by Thomas E. Goldstein. New York: Farrar, Straus, and Cudahy, 1957. In an early and enthusiastic biography, Alexander attempts to show, on two levels, Germany's objective achievements under Adenauer and Adenauer's personal development. Alexander presents an extensive section on German reunification and an epilogue by Adenauer himself.

Augstein, Rudolf. *Konrad Adenauer.* Translated by Walter Wallich. London: Secker & Warburg, 1964. The publisher of the weekly *Der Spiegel*, Augstein presents a sometimes unflattering picture of Adenauer. Augstein faults particularly Adenauer's acceptance of Germany's postwar division.

Craig, Gordon. *From Bismarck to Adenauer: Aspects of German Statecraft.* Rev. ed. New York: Harper & Row, 1965. A great American historian of Germany depicts Adenauer's statecraft in the diplomatic context, reaching back to Otto von Bismarck. In a brief, excellent account, Craig stresses the role played by Adenauer's personal characteristics in policy formulation.

Hiscocks, Richard. *The Adenauer Era.* Philadelphia: J. B. Lippincott, 1966. Hiscocks presents a rather straightforward biography of Adenauer. The work is fairly evenly divided between treatments of Adenauer's accomplishments after 1945 and a general examination of postwar Western German society and politics. Hiscocks includes a short introduction on the historical setting surrounding Adenauer's post-1945 achievements.

Prittie, Terence. *Konrad Adenauer, 1876-1967.* Chicago: Cowles, 1971. Prittie's work provides a well-written, balanced, and thorough examination of Adenauer's life and work. Adenauer's early life and services to Cologne receive fair treatment as do Adenauer's experiences during the Nazi period. A solid investigation of Adenauer's postwar career follows. Includes numerous representative illustrations.

David R. Dorondo

ALFRED ADLER

Born: February 7, 1870; Penzing, Austria
Died: May 28, 1937; Aberdeen, Scotland
Areas of Achievement: Medicine and social sciences
Contribution: Adler, the founder of individual psychology, introduced such fundamental mental-health concepts as "inferiority feeling," "life-style," "striving for superiority," and "social interest." The first to occupy a chair of medical psychology in the United States, Adler pioneered the use of psychiatry in both social work and early childhood education.

Early Life

Alfred Adler was born on February 7, 1870, in Penzing, Austria, a suburb of Vienna, the second of seven children of Leopold Adler, a Jewish Hungarian grain merchant from the Burgenland, and his wife, a native of Moravia. Though reared on a farm, Adler was exposed to the rich cultural life of Vienna's golden age. The death of a younger brother and his own bout with pneumonia at the age of five caused Adler to resolve to study medicine. He received his medical degree in 1895 from the University of Vienna. Much later, Adler would be awarded his Ph.D. from the Long Island College of Medicine in New York. In 1895, Adler married Raissa Timofejewna Epstein, a Moscow-born student. Together they had three daughters and a son. Two of his children, Kurt and Alexandra, later took up the practice of psychiatry. By 1897, Adler was practicing general medicine in Vienna, specializing in ophthalmology. His zeal for reform was indicated in articles in various socialist newspapers.

Though Adler's first professional monograph had been a study of the health of tailors, by 1900 he had become interested in neurology and in psychopathological symptoms. His review in 1902 of Sigmund Freud's book on dream interpretation led to an invitation to join the Vienna Psychoanalytic Society. Though closely associated with Freud (they attended the first International Congress on Psychoanalysis together in 1908), Adler insisted that he was neither Freud's disciple nor his student. This fact was revealed in 1907 in his *Studie über Minderwertigkeit von Organen* (*Study of Organ Inferiority and Its Psychical Compensation*, 1917). In 1911, Adler and nine others resigned from Freud's circle to found the Society for Free Psychoanalysis. Freud then launched what has been called an "almost scurrilous attack" on Adler. For his part, Adler acknowledged his respect for Freud but explained his major intellectual disagreements with him. Adler denied the dominance of the biological over the psychological in human behavior, refusing to see sex as the primary determinant of personality. Adler stressed freedom, not determinism, in conduct, believing that Freud compared humans to animals or machines, forgetting to emphasize what makes them unique, namely, concepts and values. Adler resolved to champion a holistic, humanistic psychology. By 1912, his *Über den nervösen Charakter* (*The Neurotic Constitution*, 1917) indicated the directions being taken by Adlerian or individual psychology.

During World War I, Adler served in the Austro-Hungarian army as a military doctor on the Russian front at Kraków and Brunn. Returning from three years in the war, Adler established what was probably the world's first child-guidance clinic in Vienna in 1919. Soon thirty such centers were operating in Vienna, Munich, and Berlin. Adler emerged as the first psychiatrist to apply mental hygiene in the schools, lecturing meanwhile at the Pedagogical Institute. A pathfinder of family therapy or community psychiatry, Adler involved students, teachers, and parents in treatment. Innovative counseling was done before a restricted audience as a teaching device. By 1926, Adler was much in demand as a lecturer in Europe and North America, and his work was commanding wide recognition.

Life's Work

Adler's life's work was focused on four areas. Adler was preeminently an educator. In 1926, he became a visiting professor at Columbia University, and in 1932 he became the United States' first professor of medical psychology, teaching at the Long Island College of Medicine in New York. By then his visits to Vienna were seasonal and occasional, terminating after the rise of Fascism in Austria and Germany and the Nazi suppression of his clinics. Adler's lectures were copied and published as *Menschenkenntnis* (1927; *Understanding Human Nature*, 1918), a text that is still a classic.

Second, Adler was widely read as an author. Increasingly his works were directed toward the general public, such as *What Life Should Mean to You* (1931) and *Der Sinn des Lebens* (1933; *Social Interest: A Challenge to Mankind*, 1939). Other volumes included *The Case of Miss R* (1929), *Problems of Neurosis* (1929), *The Case of Miss A* (1931), and *The Pattern of Life* (1930). After his death, Adler's papers were edited by Heinz L. and Rowena R. Ansbacher as *Superiority and Social Interest* (1964) and *The Individual Psychology of Alfred Adler* (1956).

Third, Adler was much sought as a therapist. For Adler, the psychiatrist did not treat mental disease. Rather, he discovered the error in the patient's way of life and then led him toward greater maturity. Therapy was a kind of teaching, with the emphasis on health, not sickness, and on the client's total network of relationships. Adler wanted to know the patient not simply "in depth but in context." The therapist was to be an enabler, helping the patient "see the power of self-determination" and "command the courage" to alter his entire world and his interpretation of it. In analysis, Adler relied on such diagnostic tools as dream interpretation, the meaning of early childhood recollections, and the role of birth order. Not only was therapy social as well as personal, but also it was to be preventative as well as restorative. Adler established clinics to help avoid such life failures as neurosis and psychosis. Adler was one of the first psychiatrists to apply his therapeutic techniques to the treatment of criminals, to the practice of social work, and to the education of American children.

Finally, Adler was in demand as a lecturer. The disarming gentleness that won for him acceptance from patients made him a winsome communicator to audiences. Soon as facile in English as his native German, Adler, a tenor, spoke slowly with occasional silences, pauses that were said to add to the profundity of his remarks. His was a soft voice, but one that was conciliatory and persuading in tone. His piercing eyes and friendly manner evoked a warm response. Though described as stocky and pudgy, Adler conveyed a feeling of intensity and energy with his swift movements and quickness of thought. His broad interests, cinema, cafés, music (he had a fine singing voice), drama, and hiking, established many points of contact with his auditors. It was while on a lecture tour that Adler died at age sixty-seven of a heart attack on Union Street, Aberdeen, Scotland, on May 28, 1937. His daughter, Alexandra, then a research fellow in neurology, completed the tour. Adler's teaching was institutionalized by a series of five international congresses he directed between 1922 and 1930 and since his death by the International Association of Individual Psychology.

Adler believed that the principal human motive was a striving for perfection. He argued in 1907 in *Study of Organ Inferiority and Its Psychical Compensation* that physical disability or inadequacy in the child may result in psychical compensation. Overcompensation can occur. Ludwig van Beethoven, who was losing his hearing, became a master musician. Demosthenes, a stutterer, became a compelling orator. Compensation, however, can produce not only genius but also neurotic and psychotic adaptations to life. In *The Neurotic Constitution*, Adler admitted that inferiority feeling was a condition common to all children. Children respond with an aggression drive (or, later, a striving for superiority). Adler spoke of a masculine protest (found in both males and females), which is any "attempt to overcome socially conditioned feelings of weakness" (such weaknesses being perceived as feminine).

Behavior, Adler taught, is goal oriented. For that reason, his individual psychology is teleological, not causal, as was Freud's. Adler concentrated on the consequences as much as the antecedents of actions. By the age of four or five, Adler insisted, the child has set goals for himself. These goals grow out of the self-image the child has evolved, as well as his opinion of the world. The self is a product not only of objective or external factors, such as birth order, but also of subjective or internal factors, such as interpretation and opinion. A person's creative power resides in "the ability to choose between various ways of reacting to a situation." As a person seeks maturity and wholeness, he selects goals that promise fulfillment and the means by which to attain them. A life-style becomes apparent.

Life, for Adler, consisted in meeting three main problems or fulfilling three main tasks which are "inseparably tied up with the logic of man's communal life." These tasks are occupational, associational, and sexual. A choice of work or vocation reveals the primary influences present in the child before the age of thirteen. Association with others, the development of a significant and healthy system of interpersonal relationships, is crucial. Love and marriage, or sex, is the most important of those associations, for from this relationship comes the next generation.

Failures in life, that is, neurotics (mildly dysfunctional) and psychotics (severely dysfunctional), are those who do not develop social interest. Self-bound, they are crippled with intense inferiority feelings and become obsessed with themselves. Withdrawal from life may result because of a belief that one is unable to compete. Another unhealthy adaptation is the evolving of a superiority that is useful only to themselves. Normality or health for Adler meant moving toward constructive social interest, where the person functions creatively for the welfare of all.

Adler's wide range of activities and his inclusive and practical teachings caused him to become a major new influence in psychiatry in the years following World War I. That impact has been a constant through the subsequent decades.

Summary

Through a creative career on two continents as an educator, author, therapist, and lecturer, Alfred Adler indicated new directions for the infant science of psychiatry. A contemporary of such physicians of the mind as Sigmund Freud and Carl Gustav Jung in Europe and William James in the United States, Adler became one of the founders of the science of mental health. A persuasive and popular communicator, Adler was able to involve the general public in the application of the findings of psychiatry. As a result, what once had been seen as an arcane field provided conversation for cocktail parties. Capitalizing on this widespread public interest, Adler pioneered the application of mental-health techniques to pedagogy, child psychology, school reform, and the teaching and training of an entire generation of educators. Social work in the United States is also greatly indebted to the insights of Adler. Yet it is in the field of psychotherapy that he has had his most lasting influence. Subsequent practitioners of the art of healing the mind, as diverse as Karen Horney, Harry Stack Sullivan, Franz Alexander, and Ian Suttie, have been assisted by the teachings of Adler. Alfred Adler remains one of the giants of medicine and psychiatry and of the creative thought of the twentieth century.

Bibliography

Adler, Alfred. *The Individual Psychology of Alfred Adler*. Edited by Heinz L. Ansbacher and Rowena R. Ansbacher. New York: Grove Press, 1956. This is perhaps the best single anthology of materials by Adler, culled from lectures by two of his disciples. The extracts are accompanied by a complete bibliography and critical annotations of the essays.

Bottome, Phyllis. *Alfred Adler: Apostle of Freedom*. New York: G. P. Putnam's Sons, 1939. 3d ed. London: Faber & Faber, 1957. The author's husband was Adler's secretary. For that reason, the information offered in this 315-page biography rests on eyewitness observation and access to primary papers. Bottome believed Adler to be "at once the easiest of men to know and the most difficult, the frankest and the most subtle, the most conciliatory and the most ruthless."

Dreikurs, Rudolf. *Fundamentals of Adlerian Psychology*. New York: Greenberg, 1950. This concise study initially appeared in 1933. Originally written in German, it dates from the decade of Adler's death and reflects his later thinking. It should be supplemented by more recent works.

Orgler, Hertha. *Alfred Adler, the Man and His Work: Triumph over the Inferiority Complex*. 3d rev. ed. London: G. W. Daniel Co., 1963. This classic study, first published in 1939, is a must for beginning research. Drawing on both contemporary and second-generation opinion of Adler and individual psychology, Orgler's book attempts to view the subject in the light of his own growth toward wholeness.

Rallner, Joseph. *Alfred Adler*. Translated by Harry Zohn. New York: Frederick Ungar, 1983. This work by a German scholar is concise yet comprehensive in its treatment.

C. George Fry

ANNA AKHMATOVA
Anna Andreyevna Gorenko

Born: June 23, 1889; Bol'shoy Fontan, near Odessa, Ukraine, Russian
Empire
Died: March 5, 1966; Domodedovo, near Moscow, U.S.S.R.
Area of Achievement: Literature
Contribution: Akhmatova was one of the most acclaimed and revered poets
of twentieth century Russia, struggling throughout her life to express with
intimacy and insight the plight of a woman in an adversive society. For
long periods she was forbidden to publish her works, but by the end of her
life her constant poetic inspiration of others had earned for her the International Taormina Poetry Prize (Italy, 1964) and an honorary degree from
the University of Oxford (England, 1965).

Early Life
Anna Andreyevna Gorenko was born in a suburb of Odessa, in the czarist
Ukraine, on June 23, 1889. Her father, Andrei Gorenko, was a naval officer
who left the military soon after her birth to take a position as maritime
engineer with the government. This position required him to move to Tsarskoe Selo (now Pushkin), a town near the capital city of St. Petersburg (now
Leningrad) in which one of the czar's palaces was located together with the
residences of many of the nobles and highly placed government function-
aries. This move well suited Anna's mother, the aristocratic Inna Erazmovna
(née Stogova), since her family, the Stogovs, claimed a noble heritage. She
liked to socialize with the nobility, yet she took pride in her early associations with members of the "People's Will" Party of radicals who had assassinated Czar Alexander II in 1881. This ambiguity of sympathies had the
effect upon young Anna and her four siblings, Inna, Andrei, Iya, and Victor,
of restraining them from political alignments throughout their lives.
Anna grew up in the privileged atmosphere of Tsarskoe Selo, attending
school in the same town where the great poet Alexander Pushkin had once
been a student. She was attracted to poetry and could recite both French and
Russian verse from memory. She attended poetry readings at the home of
Innokenty Annensky, an influential Symbolist poet, and began to write verse
of her own in about 1904. Through her elder brother, she met the talented
young poet Nikolai Gumilyov, who was immediately attracted to her. Anna's
slim figure and distinctive face, with its slightly humped Roman nose, gave
her a prepossessive presence which later attracted the attention of artists.
Gumilyov courted her persistently, sponsoring her into participation in the
"Guild of Poets," an organization seminal to the development of "Acme-
ism," a philosophy of poetry which demanded communicative clarity and a
sense of connection with the poetic heritage of Western Europe. In 1907,

Gumilyov was the first to publish one of Anna's poems in his journal *Sirius*. It was in this year also that Anna's father's extravagant life-style and his constant womanizing caused a separation in the Gorenko family. Anna went to Kiev with her mother, finishing her studies at the Fundukleevskaya Gymnaziya there and enrolling in the faculty of law at the Kiev College for Women. She soon withdrew from the study of law and moved back to St. Petersburg to study literature. It was at this time that she chose the pseudonym "Akhmatova," the name of her maternal great-grandmother, a Tatar princess. She took a pseudonym at the request of her father that the Gorenko family not be embarrassed by her publication of poetry.

Life's Work

In 1910, Akhmatova married Gumilyov. For the next two years they traveled abroad, spending much of the time in Paris, where Akhmatova became friendly with the still unknown artist Amadeo Modigliani, who sketched her as a dancer and as an Egyptian queen. The marriage, however, soon foundered, with both Akhmatova and Gumilyov chafing under its traditional confinements. Gumilyov traveled on his own to Abyssinia to collect African folksongs, and Akhmatova returned to stay with her mother at a cousin's estate in order to give birth to her son, Lev Nikolayevich Gumilyov, in October of 1912. In 1912 also, Akhmatova's first collection of verse, *Vecher* (evening), appeared. The collection's lyrics on a young woman's realization of love and her expectation of grief brought Akhmatova both acclaim and popularity in a degree only to be envied by Gumilyov. The subsequent successes of Akhmatova's collections—*Chetki* (1914; rosary) and *Belaia staia* (1917; white flock)—and her long poem, "U samogo morya" (1914; "By the Seashore," 1969), only served to increase their estrangement. In 1914, Gumilyov joined the cavalry and went off to fight in World War I, where he was decorated for bravery. Akhmatova stayed with a succession of friends, leaving her son to be reared by Gumilyov's widowed mother.

The social turmoil associated with the end of the war, the Russian Revolution of 1917, and the subsequent civil war effectively beheaded the country, with a great many intellectuals and people of established artistic reputations leaving to live and work elsewhere. Akhmatova, however, would not leave, even though her life became more difficult. In 1918, she divorced Gumilyov to marry Vladimir Shileiko, a scholar of Assyrian antiquity who opposed his wife's poetic activities. Nevertheless, Akhmatova managed to publish the collection *Podorozhnik* (1921; plantain), giving therein her poetic refusal to emigrate. She visited frequently with other poets, including Osip Mandelstam, and she attended the funeral of Aleksandr Blok. In 1921 she grieved over the death of Gumilyov, who was executed by the Soviet Cheka for his alleged involvement in a counterrevolutionary plot. In the 1922 collection *Anno Domini MCMXXI*, a distinctly religious dimension is evident in Akhmatova's lyric ponderings on love and human travail.

From 1922 until 1940, Akhmatova was unable to publish any new works of poetry. She was considered an "internal émigré" whose apolitical works were incompatible with the new criterion of social utility. She continued work on a collection she called *Trostnik* (1926-1940; the reed), dedicating poems to Mandelstam and to Boris Pasternak, and she wrote some scholarly articles on the life and works of Pushkin. The mass arrests of the 1930's included many people close to Akhmatova. Mandelstam was arrested, released, and arrested again, finally to perish in the labor camps. Marina Tsvetayeva, another major poetess of modern Russia and a poetic admirer of Akhmatova, was arrested soon after returning from emigration and shortly after an emotional meeting with Akhmatova in Moscow. Akhmatova's son Lev was arrested twice, the second time being released only to fight in World War II. Her companion since 1926 (she divorced Shileiko in 1928), art critic Nikolai Punin, was also arrested. Akhmatova's response to all this suffering is contained in the monumental poetic dirge *Rekviem* (1963; *Requiem*, 1964), finished in 1940 but still unpublished in the Soviet Union. In 1940 also, Akhmatova was allowed to prepare an edition of her early works entitled *Iz shesti knig* (from six books), but this edition was quickly withdrawn from publication. That same year she began work on her beautiful poetic opus *Poema bez geroa* (1960; *A Poem Without a Hero*, 1973), which she continued to perfect until her death.

World War II occasioned a relaxation of the governmental strictures on poetry, and Akhmatova, who was living in Leningrad during the early days of the terrible Nazi siege, was allowed to speak to her fellow Leningraders by radio, inspiring them with her poetry and her words of encouragement. In October of 1941, however, Akhmatova was evacuated, first to Moscow, and then to Tashkent, from which a collection of selected early verse was published in 1943. The publication of her poem "Muzhestvo" ("Courage," 1976) in the Communist Party newspaper *Pravda* in 1942 had signaled her temporary return to governmental grace, and her poems were subsequently published in several journals. After the war, however, the Communist Party decided to reimpose the former controls on literature, choosing specifically to reorganize two journals, *Zvezda* and *Leningrad*, and to denounce Akhmatova and the humorist Mikhail Zoshchenko, who had been published in them. Akhmatova, termed "half-nun, half-harlot" by Stalinist stalwart Andrei Zhdanov, was subsequently expelled from the Soviet Writers Union. Akhmatova's son Lev was arrested once more, only to be released in 1956 after Nikita S. Khrushchev's denunciation of Joseph Stalin's "cult of personality" and the associated "thaw" in the Soviet social and artistic climate. Akhmatova survived this period on a meager pension by selling translations of verse from several languages to others. Several volumes of these translations have since been published as separate imprints. One cycle of poems, *V khvale mira* (1950; in praise of peace), was ostensibly written in confor-mance to governmental canon to ease the plight of her son.

After 1958, Akhmatova was officially "rehabilitated." An edition of her earlier poetry, supplemented by more recent works, was published under the title *Beg vremeni* (1965; the flight of time). A large new collection, *Sed'maya kniga* (1965; partial translation as *The Seventh Book*, 1976), con-taining poetic musings on poetry itself, on symbolism, and on death, as well as parts of *A Poem Without a Hero*, was also published. Approaching her seventies and ailing from a weakened heart, Akhmatova was recognized as the "grande dame" of Russian letters. She began to act as a mentor to others, protesting, for example, the internal exile of the young Joseph Brodsky, a future Nobel laureate. She met the famed American poet Robert Frost. In 1964, she traveled abroad to receive the Taormina Poetry Prize in Italy, and in 1965 she was awarded an honorary doctorate at the University of Oxford in England. Her death in March of 1966 deprived Russian literature of a great poet. Her body was flown from Moscow to Leningrad, where it lay in state, visited by hundreds, in the Nikolsky Cathedral. She is buried in the town of Komarovo.

Summary

Millions of Russians know an Anna Akhmatova poem by heart, many of them committing their individual favorite to memory at a time when the poem's publication was banned. Many Russian poets have imitated Akh-matova's dirgelike recitation style. They admire her not only for the quality of her poetry but also for her lifelong advocacy of poetry as an enrichment of life, as a catalyst to sharing life's most profound values with others. Her poetry was mature from its very beginnings and is often praised for its intimacy of expression and for its touching insights into the human condi-tion. She was especially sensitive to the problems faced by women in so-ciety, and she consciously served as a role model for later numbers of femi-nist poets. Akhmatova was clearly apolitical in her achievements, appealing instead to the emotional bases of human existence, yet she remained loyal to her beloved Russian people through the sternest of its governmental trials of her. Recognizing her genius for expression of the deepest emotions and the loftiest thoughts, Akhmatova was ever true to her talent, persevering to transmit her gift to others despite the most constant and daunting of hard-ships. Her love lyrics and her poetic explorations of grief are regarded to be among the finest in any language. Translations of her verse and international scholarship concerning her verse and her life have ensured for her a promi-nent place in world literature.

Bibliography

Akhmatova, Anna A. *Poems*. Translated by Lyn Coffin, with an introduction by Joseph Brodsky. New York: W. W. Norton, 1983. Selected, high-quality verse translations of Akhmatova's poems, including several not found elsewhere. The insightful introduction by Brodsky lends the book biographical and critical significance.

_____. *Poems of Akhmatova*. Translated by Stanley Kunitz, with an introduction by Kunitz and Max Hayward. Boston: Little, Brown, 1973. A concise biographical sketch by Max Hayward, together with verse translations by Kunitz. A nice feature of this collection is that it pairs Akhmatova's Russian versions with Kunitz's translations on opposing pages.

_____. *Selected Poems*. Edited by Walter Arndt. Translated by Arndt, Robin Kemball, and Carl R. Proffer. Ann Arbor, Mich.: Ardis, 1976. This collection includes a fine article entitled "The Akhmatova Phenomenon" and a chronicle of Akhmatova's life. The translations are especially well done and well explained by notes.

Driver, Sam N. *Anna Akhmatova*. New York: Twayne, 1972. This is the first English biography, written six years after Akhmatova's death. The first third of the book deals with biographical facts and the remainder with a thematic explanation of the poetry. It is a concise yet scholarly work, still serving as the best primary introduction to Akhmatova's life.

Haight, Amanda. *Anna Akhmatova: A Poetic Pilgrimage*. London: Oxford University Press, 1976. A substantially more detailed biographical treatment of Akhmatova's life by a Western scholar personally acquainted with Akhmatova. This work is a valuable resource for the specialist as well as the layperson.

Ketchian, Sonia. *The Poetry of Anna Akhmatova: A Conquest of Time and Space*. Munich: Otto Sagner Verlag, 1986. A brilliant scholarly study of themes and method in Akhmatova's poetry. Here too is the most complete inclusion and recapitulation of recent Akhmatova scholarship, both Soviet and Western. The work, however, would appeal primarily to literary scholars.

Mandelstam, Nadezhda. *Hope Against Hope: A Memoir*. Translated by Max Hayward, with an introduction by Clarence Brown. New York: Atheneum, 1976. This memoir by Mandelstam's widow includes many a glimpse into Akhmatova's life as well and is especially valuable to those wishing to understand what a poet's life was like in the Soviet Union of the Stalin era.

Rosslyn, Wendy. *The Prince, the Fool, and the Nunnery: The Religious Theme in the Early Poetry of Anna Akhmatova*. Amersham, England: Avebury, 1984. An examination of the interplay of religion and love in Akhmatova's early collections, this book also contains considerable biographical detail. Poems are included in both Russian and English translation.

Verheul, Kees. *The Theme of Time in the Poetry of Anna Axmatova*. The

Hague: Mouton, 1971. This was one of the first English scholarly monographs devoted to Akhmatova's poetry and is still one of the most cited. The book is written for the specialist and includes many untranslated Russian citations.

Lee B. Croft

VIKTOR A. AMBARTSUMIAN

Born: September 18, 1908; Tiflis, Russia

Area of Achievement: Astronomy

Contribution: Ambartsumian developed the astrophysics of stars and stellar origins and was instrumental in the theory of gigantic catastrophe formation in galaxies related to the evolution of stars and galaxies. He was the founder of the major school of theoretical astrophysics in the U.S.S.R.

Early Life

Very few biographical details of Viktor A. Ambartsumian's childhood are known. He was born in 1908, in Tiflis, Russia (modern Tbilisi, U.S.S.R.), the son of a local teacher of literature. Early in school, he developed a passion for mathematics and physics and became extremely interested in the formation, evolution, and energy generation of stars and other heavenly bodies. Following his instincts, he went to the University of Leningrad, from which he was graduated in 1928 with high honors. He performed so well and so amazed his instructors that he was offered a position at the university, where he stayed to teach until 1944. In that year, he went to Yerevan, Soviet Armenia, to become the founder and director of the Byurakan Observatory and its subsequent permanent director.

Life's Work

Very early in his career at the Byurakan Observatory, Ambartsumian became interested in the physics of stars and nebulas, combined with a general regard for astronomical topics of all characteristics. As a by-product of his work, he became the founder of the school for theoretical astrophysics in the U.S.S.R., concentrating much of his time and effort on the cosmogony of stars and galaxies. It was his detailed work on the theory of stellar origins that brought him early recognition, particularly his explanation, derived by both reasoning and mathematics, of how gigantic catastrophic explosions had taken place elsewhere in the universe and how such explosions could take place in, or even be required for, the evolution of stars and galaxies. The idea originated from the work of Walter Baade and Hermann Minkowski, who first identified a radio source of extraordinary violence in the constellation of Cygnus. Baade had first announced that the radio source was associated with what appeared to be a closely connected pair of distant galaxies. In the photographs, it appeared that a gigantic collision was occurring, a supremely colossal event that could account for the extensive radio spectrum being emitted from that particular region of extragalactic space. Baade believed that events such as this catastrophe might even be common enough in the universe to account for the numerous extragalactic radio sources already identified by that time. Ambartsumian, however, in 1955 was able to gather enough evidence, both observational and theoretical, to show that the collision view was undoubtedly wrong. As an alternative, he proposed that vast explosions could occur within the core of a galaxy, creating a tremendous release of energy, somewhat analogous to supernova explosions, only on a galactic, rather than a stellar, scale. Mechanisms for such titanic explosions include chain-reaction supernovas erupting in the densely packed galactic core, interactions of normal matter and antimatter, the possible interactions of stars and interstellar materials with a superheavy black hole, or the total destruction of a galaxy's nucleus through some other mechanism involving fantastic releases of energy, much more than could ever be derived from simple atom bomb explosions. The discovery of other galaxies (particularly that by Allan Sandage, who worked with M-82) in the process of definitely exploding has led to Ambartsumian's hypothesis' becoming well established in current astrophysical thought.

In his role as founder of the Soviet school of combined theoretical physics and astronomy, Ambartsumian initiated the study of numerous topics, in some areas virtually inventing, redefining, and mathematically settling the field. He founded the quantitative theory for emissions of light energy from gaseous nebulas, a precursor to his ideas on how stars formed. As a method for forming such gaseous nebulas, he established a detailed synthesis for calculating the masses ejected by stars in their normal, nonstationary state, now called solar wind, and for those far enough along in their life history to become novas or exploding stars. To handle large groups of stars, such as those found in globular clusters of up to one million members, Ambartsumian developed the fundamentals of statistical mechanics as applied to stellar systems. One of the offshoots of that work was his ability to demonstrate that smaller stellar clusters, such as galactic open-star clusters, gradually decay via the loss of individual stars. On that basis, he found he could estimate the ages of the observable clusters in our galaxy.

While working as a scientist, he also performed other functions. From a role as a corresponding member in 1939, he became an academician of the Academy of Sciences of the U.S.S.R. in 1953, supplementing the position he had already held since 1943 as academician of the Academy of Sciences of Soviet Armenia. He was president of that group in 1947. Also in 1947, he became a professor at the University of Yerevan.

In the late 1940's, Ambartsumian became proficient in dealing with some fundamental problems of stellar cosmogony. In 1947, he had discovered dynamically unstable systems of a new type, called stellar associations. By studying these extremely young collections of stars, he found that light, traveling through supposedly empty space, was not being absorbed by a continuous distribution of matter in the interstellar space but rather was reduced principally by discrete dark nebulas lying between stars and the observer. He formulated a special mathematical theory for statistical research on these peculiar interstellar absorption dustballs, in the process solving numerous problems with a theory of light-scattering in dense, turbid media. His work saw the formation of stars as collapsing clouds of dust under gravity forming embryonic stars fueled by the infalling hydrogen from the dark nebula surrounding the stellar nursery. A special case he developed was the theory of baryonic stars, stars possessing a density much greater than nuclear density, which was a forerunner of the black hole idea.

Ambartsumian also had a substantial influence on the trend of dealing with the enormous activity found in central galactic areas. He proved that the nuclei of galaxies were indeed responsible for a host of recently discovered phenomena, including colossal explosions greater than anything ever before perceived, ejections of fantastic quantities of materials by both violent and quiescent means, and extremely intense emissions of radio waves, microwaves, and gamma radiation. Ambartsumian's treatment of these matters has had an impact on the new astronomy that uses the entire electromagnetic spectrum for surveying the universe.

Ambartsumian has acted as both vice president (1948-1955) and president (1961-1964) of the International Astronomical Union. He has also been a member of many different foreign academies and scientific societies. In 1968, he was elected president of the International Council of Scientific Unions. He was twice awarded the State Prize of the U.S.S.R., in 1946 and 1950, has been awarded the Order of Lenin on three separate occasions, and has received numerous other orders and medals, both within the U.S.S.R. and from foreign scientific societies.

Summary

Viktor A. Ambartsumian was one of the most visible Soviet astronomers through the early 1980's, primarily because of his frequent attendance at numerous international scientific meetings. Although he acted as member and president of the Armenian Academy of Sciences, and, since 1953, has been a member of the U.S.S.R. Academy of Sciences as a theoretical astrophysicist, he has also been an aggressive supporter of observational astronomy. Under his directorship, the Byurakan Observatory has risen to the forefront of the astronomical facilities in the Soviet Union. He has led the push to develop vast areas of astronomical research in the Soviet Union, including planetary astronomy (particularly studies of Venus), meteorites, and comets; a second major program on stellar astronomy, particularly stellar associations, flare stars, symbiotic stars, and normal stellar phenomena; and, finally, extragalactic astronomy, particularly those Markarian galaxies bright in ultraviolet light, active galaxies, and theoretical galactic studies.

Ambartsumian has been a professor at the University of Yerevan since 1947. He became a Hero of Socialist Labor in 1968 for his many contributions in science and government. He has particularly enjoyed giving public lectures, extolling an all-union society, Znanya (knowledge), which connects many outstanding scholars with adult education and helps shape policy on the numerous planetariums in the country. He is strongly in favor of the many flourishing academies established throughout the U.S.S.R. which have helped to revive the culture of particular nationalities. He has not seen this mixing of astronomy and government as a problem; rather, he sees both areas as part of his own personal search for a succinct view of the universe.

Bibliography
Asimov, Isaac. *The Exploding Suns: The Secrets of the Supernovas*. New York: E. P. Dutton, 1985. A delightful exploration of the life history of stars, emphasizing their origins and their ultimate fates as bodies destined to explode. Follows the history of various size stars to their ends as planetary nebulas, novas, or supernovas. This book is excellent reading. Well illustrated and designed for the layperson.
Mihalas, Dmitri, with Paul McRae Routly. *Galactic Astronomy*. San Francisco: W. H. Freeman, 1968. Deals with all the configurations of a normal galaxy, from stars and their origins to the gaseous contents found between the stars. Traces the evolution of stars and star clusters and discusses energy generation near galactic cores. Heavy reading with an extensive bibliography for references and some mathematics.
Murdin, Paul. *The New Astronomy*. New York: Thomas Y. Crowell, 1978. Written for the layperson, this work deals with the end of stellar evolution, when the catastrophic collapses occur. Tracing the trail of ancient supernovas, the story of the creation of the elements, black holes, and neutron stars is told, ending with the ultimate fate of the universe. Contains line diagrams.
Reddish, V. C. *Stellar Formation*. Elmsford, N.Y.: Pergamon Press, 1978. A detailed account of how stars form from the condensation of dust and gases found in the nebulas of the galaxy. The evidence for stellar birth is presented clearly, and subsequent evolution is presented in enough detail to show the resultant stages of life for different-sized bodies. Includes extensive mathematics and extra references. College-level physics is necessary for complete understanding.
Shklovskii, I. *Stars: Their Birth, Life, and Death*. San Francisco: W. H. Freeman, 1978. For the advanced layperson, an excellent summary detailing the origin of stars from dust clouds, their subsequent evolution through middle age, and their ultimate demise based on their original size. Clearly illustrated, with extensive references. Some mathematics.
Zeilik, Michael, ed. *Cool Stars, Stellar Systems, and the Sun*. London: Springer-Verlag, 1986. A collection of articles presented on star systems under various conditions of size, temperature, and activity. The evolution

of lower-temperature stars is discussed, as are the life features of multiple-star collections. The sun's history is used for comparison. Contains extensive references and heavy mathematics.

Zeldovich, Ya. B., and I. D. Novikov. *Stars and Relativity.* Vol. 1. Chicago: University of Chicago Press, 1971. A detailed treatise on the history of stars from their birth to their ultimate evolutionary stage, based on information predicted by the theory of relativity. Deals with exploding bodies, interactions of stars within galaxies, and catastrophes in nature. Extremely detailed in mathematics but possesses a tremendous amount of information.

Arthur L. Alt

ROALD AMUNDSEN

Born: July 16, 1872; Borge, Norway
Died: June 18, 1928?; Arctic Ocean
Area of Achievement: Exploration
Contribution: Amundsen was the first to navigate the Northwest Passage from Godhavn, Greenland, through the islands of Canada to Fort Egbert, Alaska. In 1911, he was the first explorer to reach the South Pole. His studies of magnetics led to major revisions of theories concerning the magnetic North Pole and greater understanding of the Arctic and Antarctic regions.

Early Life

Roald Engelbregt Gravning Amundsen was born on July 16, 1872, in Borge, Østfold, a village located southeast of Oslo, Norway. Three months after his birth, his ship-owner father moved the family to Oslo, where Roald was reared and educated. Roald was only fourteen years old when his father died. His mother, taking over the role of both father and mother, decided that her youngest son should study medicine at the University of Oslo. The young man, however, was strongly influenced by the writings of Sir John Franklin, the British polar explorer who had died attempting to navigate the legendary Northwest Passage. Franklin's crews had survived but deserted their ships and abandoned the expedition in 1848. Amundsen was fascinated by the challenge of the Northwest Passage and the Arctic Ocean. The physical hardships and suffering that he read about beckoned rather than deterred him from launching a career as an Arctic explorer himself. He neglected his studies at the university to pore over books and records of the polar explorations, secretly planning to give up medicine for a life as a professional explorer. Where Franklin had failed, Amundsen was certain that he would navigate the Northwest Passage and be the first to reach the North Pole.

Without consulting or telling his mother of his new career plans, he began a regimen of training for the Arctic hardships with unusual zeal and dedication. For the next eight years, he endured rigorous physical exercises and developed a superb physique. He became competent on skis and subjected himself to subzero temperatures in winter camping on Norway's slopes. When he was twenty-two years old, he chose a companion, and the pair began a cross-country ski trip on a high plateau near Bergen. This adventure nearly cost Amundsen his life, for the rugged terrain and the isolated plateau was caught in the grip of a terrible blizzard. The pair's supplies were lost in the snow, and without food or fuel they were stranded in subzero temperature for several days. When they finally reached a settlement eight days later, they were exhausted and nearly starved from the exertion. "The training," he said, "proved severer than the experience for which it was a preparation, and it well-nigh ended my career before it began." Amundsen's mother had died when he was twenty-one years old, and he abandoned his medical training completely.

Life's Work

Amundsen served in the Norwegian army, in which he continued his physical training. During the intervals between training, he read all available books on Arctic exploration and concluded that there was a major weakness in the earlier expeditions. Quarrels had arisen between the scientist-explorers and the captains and sailors of the ships. No explorer, he realized, was trained as a ship's captain, and he was therefore forced to rely on the judgment of someone other than an explorer during critical periods of decision. His remedy for the weakness was to gain experience both as an Arctic explorer and as a ship's captain; he would not have two leaders at cross purposes on his expeditions.

Amundsen accepted a theory espoused by Fridtjov Nansen that man could utilize the drift of the Arctic ice for the transport of ships across the Polar basin. The ice packs, he theorized, drifted poleward with a tolerable speed and ships frozen in the ice pack would continue moving across the Polar region. Adequate provisions would allow a ship and crew to reach a destination even without open water under them.

In 1894, Amundsen signed on as a crew member of a sealing ship to gain proficiency in commanding a ship for successful exploration. In 1897, he qualified as first officer and signed on as first mate of the *Belgica* with the Belgian Antarctic Expedition under Adrian de Gerlach. The expedition was en route to study the South Magnetic Pole. Gerlach knew too little about navigation in the Antarctic, however, and the *Belgica* became ice-locked for thirteen months in the Belling-Shausen Sea. The *Belgica* was the first ship to winter in the Antarctic. Amundsen not only gained polar exploration experience but also became one of the first men to survive a winter in Antarctica. The techniques of scientific research that he learned under Gerlach served him well on subsequent trips to study the magnetic fields at the North Pole.

Recognizing that magnetic study was the most likely source of funding for new exploration expeditions, Amundsen revised his well-planned personal goals. His navigation of the Northwest Passage would include finding the true location of the North Magnetic Pole. In preparation for this venture, he devoted his time to the study of terrestrial magnetism. He sought out and worked under Geheimrath George von Neumayer in Hamburg. While there, he met many scientists, and through their help and diligent study he gained a working knowledge of the theory and practice of magnetic observations. Following his studies at Hamburg, he was given access to the observatories at Wilhelmshaven and Potsdam.

In 1900, Amundsen purchased and outfitted a small ship, the *Gjøa*, for a northern expedition. It was a sailing vessel, but it was rigged with an auxiliary gasoline motor to facilitate his mastery of the Northwest Passage. He planned a year's observation of the magnetic field in the vicinity of the North Pole. He delayed two years, however, to make oceanographic observations of the North Atlantic for Fridtjof Nansen, Norway's grand old man of Arctic exploration. The delay and the costs of outfitting and provisioning the *Gjøa* proved more than his limited finances could cover, and, when angry creditors threatened to seize the *Gjøa* for payment, he sailed furtively by night on June 16, 1903, and headed toward the Arctic Ocean and the Northwest Passage.

From 1903 to 1905, he wintered on King William Island in a small, protected harbor, where he could study the magnetic field. His observations offered the first proof that the North Magnetic Pole had no exact location but constantly varied its position over a wide area. He calculated the elliptical course that it followed. During this time, he met the Eskimo of northern Canada and learned the techniques of using snowshoes and how to handle dogs and dog sledges. When his observations of the North Magnetic Pole were completed, he continued his navigation of the Northwest Passage. Pushing on through dangerous water and ice pack, he sailed to Fort Egbert, Alaska; he had mastered the Northwest Passage. From there he sailed through the Bering Strait and down the Alaskan and Canadian coasts to San Francisco. The explorers John Rae and Robert Le Messurier had discovered the Northwest Passage but were unable to get through the ice; Amundsen navigated it. Through careful planning, incredible tenacity, and unusual luck, he had accomplished his first goal. He spent 1906 and 1907 lecturing in Europe and the United States and returned to Norway with enough funds to repay all of his creditors, including the one who nearly prevented the voyage.

Amundsen now resolved to "capture" the North Pole. He borrowed the famous ship, *Fram*, from Nansen and prepared to sail for the North Pole. Before his ship and crew were ready, however, the world was told that Admiral Robert Edwin Peary had reached the North Pole in April, 1909. All that was left for Amundsen was the exploration of the uncharted Arctic Ocean by ship—or by airplane. Amundsen believed that, to regain his prestige as an explorer, he must quickly achieve a sensational success of some sort. In 1910, on board the *Fram* and using funds raised to explore the North Pole, he headed south, not north. If he had failed to capture the North Pole, the South Pole was still within reach and promised the success that he sought. From the Madeira Islands, he sent a cablegram to Robert Falcon Scott, already ahead of him by two months, advising him of his intention to join in the "race" for the South Pole. Scott's expedition included some tough Siberian ponies to pull the supplies over the ice packs. Scott also had a motor sledge; his was to be the first attempted mechanized polar exploration.

Amundsen, on the other hand, relied mainly on his men and on dogs to haul his supplies. Amundsen calculated the flesh of the dogs that carried the provisions as part of the food for the men on the return trip. The eight weeks of travel across the southern ice pack were fast-paced and fraught with danger from hidden crevasses and rifts. Amundsen pushed his men and dogs to the limit of their endurance, covering fifty miles on some days. On December 14, 1911, he snatched the prize from Scott; Amundsen was the first explorer to reach the South Pole. The disappointed Scott and his men lost more than the race to the pole, for they lost their lives on the return trip.

Exploration nearly ceased during World War I. Amundsen turned to shipping from his neutral Norway and made a modest fortune, which he invested in a North Pole drift expedition. Amundsen set sail on July 15, 1917, before the war was over, risking being torpedoed by German submarines as he sailed through the Norwegian Sea to the Arctic Ocean, but he was determined to test his theory of the drift. After two years of privation and suffering in the Arctic Ocean, he acknowledged that his Arctic polar drift theory was without basis. His goal had been completed, even if it ended in failure.

Misfortune now befell the explorer as Amundsen was preparing for a polar flight. An American promoter misused the funds that Amundsen had raised to finance a flight to the pole, another first in history, and left Amundsen penniless and discredited. It appeared as if the polar flight would be delayed indefinitely. At this point Lincoln Ellsworth offered to finance a polar flying expedition provided that he be allowed to accompany Amundsen. Readily agreeing, Amundsen accepted the offered finances, and two Dernier seaplanes were subsequently purchased. In May, 1925, Amundsen attempted to fly over the North Pole, but that early attempt ended with failure when the explorers were forced to land in the ice fields. One of the planes was lost, and the second plane was overloaded with men for a dangerous return flight to Spitzbergen. While the polar flight expedition had been delayed, it was not abandoned.

While contemplating a second flight over the North Pole, Amundsen was advised by the Italian government that a secondhand airship could be purchased from the Italian military. Interested in the offered sale, the explorer requested that Colonel Umberto Nobile, Italian officer, aviator, and designer of the airship, meet with him in Oslo to transact the sale. Finally agreeing on a price and purchasing the dirigible, Amundsen asked Nobile if he would accompany him to pilot the craft. Nobile agreed to do so, and the dirigible was taken to Spitzbergen for the polar outfitting and rigging. Ill feelings quickly arose between Amundsen and Nobile over how the airship should be prepared and handled and when it should embark. Even while they were squabbling in Spitzbergen, word was received that Admiral Richard Byrd had successfully flown to the North Pole and back on May 9, 1926. Disappointed that his plans had been thwarted, Amundsen immediately took the dirigible, renamed the *Norge*, from its moorings and began his flight across the Arctic Ocean from Spitzbergen to Alaska on May 11. The first stage of the flight was remarkably successful and three flags, American, Norwegian, and Italian, were thrown down on the tumbled sea ice around the pole. Yet during the flight onward to Alaska, the explorers were constantly in danger. They eventually made a surprisingly fortunate landfall in Teller, Alaska, after an epic flight of thirty-four hundred miles. While in Alaska, however, the dirigible deflated and sank into the sea. Nobile stepped foward and claimed all credit for the planning and piloting of the dirigible, leaving Amundsen in the background as merely one of the crew. A serious quarrel arose between the two, and Amundsen began to air his doubts and concerns over the construction and design of the dirigible.

Nobile was humiliated by the accusations of poor design, so he prepared a sister ship, the *Italia*, to make another trip and prove his design was not faulty. The *Italia* left on May 25, 1928, to journey over the Arctic. Initially successful, the *Italia* ran into difficulty and finally crash-landed somewhere on the icepack of the Arctic. Fortunately the crew survived to be rescued later, but the first reports declared that the ship was lost at sea. Amundsen shouldered the blame for the senseless flight, knowing that his quarrel had goaded Nobile into making what appeared to be his final flight (he was, in fact, rescued later). In a French seaplane, Amundsen, a pilot, and a crew of four set out to search for the downed airship on June 18, 1928, and were never heard from again. One of the greatest polar explorers of all time had died in the Arctic that he had strived all his life to understand and conquer.

Summary

Roald Amundsen belonged to the heroic age of polar exploration, when man and dogs were pitted against the frigid elements and wastes of the Arctic and Antarctic regions. His achievements were not restricted to mastering the Northwest Passage and being the first explorer to reach the South Pole; his contributions covered both exploration and scientific research. He unraveled the channels and produced a trustworthy chart of the Northwest Passage, the Arctic Ocean, and the Antarctic region, discovering islands beneath the Antarctic ice. His observations on terrestrial magnetism changed the minds of scientists everywhere. His own research added substantially to geomagnetism, oceanography, climatology, navigation of polar waters, and knowledge of the thickness of the ice caps. His determination to be first in polar exploration and discovery drove him to turn apparent defeat into new opportunities. Twice he had dreamed of being first at the North Pole, once by sea and ice, once by airplane. Both times, however, even as he was preparing his own expeditions, someone else claimed those prizes.

Man has only recently entered the polar regions, and Amundsen took part in the transition from sailing vessels to gasoline-powered ships. He was the first to sail the Arctic waters with an auxiliary motor. He saw the transition from dog sledges to mechanized sledges, and his race to the South Pole was followed by his use of both airships (dirigibles) and airplanes as the polar regions entered the air age. Unlike most explorers, Amundsen had been certain of what he wanted to do from early youth. He pursued the business of exploring in the polar regions with a single-minded concentration, undeterred by any other influence or suggestion.

Bibliography

Amundsen, Roald Engelbregt Gravning. *Roald Amundsen: My Life as an Explorer.* Garden City, N.Y.: Doubleday, Page, 1927. A firsthand account of the explorations of Amundsen in his own words. Surprisingly, only a few vital statistics are presented. He details the flight of the *Norge* and his quarrel with Nobile who claimed the honor for that flight. Published only months before the tragic death of Amundsen while seeking to rescue Nobile, it is an excellent source for the causes of their quarrel.

Bowman, Gerald. *Men of Antarctica.* New York: Fleet Publishing, 1959. The story of Antarctic exploration based on the most significant expeditions. Bowman classifies Amundsen as one of the greatest explorers. This is an excellent source for Amundsen's race to the South Pole.

Hoyt, Edwin P. *The Last Explorer: The Adventures of Admiral Byrd.* New York: John Day, 1968. While this book centers on the explorations of Byrd, it presents the competitive and cooperative relations between polar explorers such as Amundsen and Byrd. It is a good source for the cooperative spirit that allowed sharing techniques, routes, and equipment for the icelands.

Kirwan, Laurence Patrick. *A History of Polar Explorations.* New York: W. W. Norton, 1960. A comprehensive look at the history and discovery of the polar regions, from the Greeks and the Norsemen to modern times. A good exposition on Amundsen's role in the heroic age of explorers.

Neatby, L. H. *Conquest of the Last Frontier.* Athens: Ohio University Press, 1966. The "last frontier" is identified as the American Arctic, which includes the Canadian Islands and the North Pole. The book is an excellent source for Amundsen's Northwest Passage, although Neatby ranks Amundsen's efforts below those of the American explorers.

Victor, Paul-Émile. *Man and the Conquest of the Poles.* Translated by Scott Sullivan. London: Hamish Hamilton, 1963. In terms of comprehension and detail, Victor's is the best source for understanding man's interest in and knowledge of polar lands from the earliest times. An excellent source for Amundsen's Northwest Passage, Antarctic achievements, and first airship flight over the Arctic Ocean.

H. Christian Thorup

44

GUILLAUME APOLLINAIRE
Guillaume Albert Wladimir Alexandre Apollinaire de Kostrowitzky

Born: August 26, 1880; Rome, Italy
Died: November 9, 1918; Paris, France
Area of Achievement: Literature
Contribution: Apollinaire left an enduring mark on the poetry and painting of the twentieth century. He was a spokesman for the symbolists and an exponent of Surrealism; in fact, the word "Surrealist" appeared for the first time in his writing. His poem "La Jolie Rousse" (the pretty redhead) became and has remained the charter of free verse.

Early Life

The man known since his twentieth year as Guillaume Apollinaire was the illegitimate son of Angélique Alexandrine de Kostrowitzky, a member of the Polish nobility whose family had taken refuge at the papal court. She first registered her son under a false name but a month later had him baptized as Guillaume Albert Wladimir Alexandre Apollinaire de Kostrowitzky. The mystery of his father's identity lasted for seventy years; he has since been identified as Francesco Flugi d'Aspermont of a family originally from Switzerland. Wilhelm, or Kostro as he was called at different times, had a younger brother, Albert, before his mother's liaison ended a few years later. For a time, the father's brother, a member of the Benedictine Order, helped with the expenses of the boys' education. They were sent to Catholic schools in Monaco, Cannes, and Nice, where they were exceedingly devout and diligent.

In 1897 and 1898, Wilhelm became fascinated by ancient history, by magic, and by erotic literature. By that time he was apparently a militant atheist, treating religion satirically and grossly, although at times nostalgically, and steeping himself exuberantly in exoticism and obscene writings. The knowledge thus gained served as material for his poetry and stories.

By 1900, Wilhelm was living with his mother in Paris and making a precarious living in minor secretarial jobs. The following year, he went, as a tutor to the young daughter of the Viscountess of Milhau, to Germany, where he fell hopelessly in love with Annie Playden, a blonde, English governess who shared his duties. Her parents refused to allow her to marry Wilhelm, but this attachment, along with some extensive traveling in Europe, resulted in a series of stories collected in *L'Hérésiarque et Cie* (1910; *The Heresiarch and Co.*, 1965). It contained the first tale, written in 1902, that he had signed with the name Guillaume Apollinaire. His love for Annie Playden also inspired his most famous poem, "La Chanson du mal-aimé" ("The Song of the Poorly Loved"). All of his life, his love affairs were to provide inspiration for his best poetry.

Life's Work

By 1903, Apollinaire had become friends with André Salmon and Alfred Jarry. The three men founded a small review, *Le Festin d'Ésope*, which lasted for nine issues. About the same time, Apollinaire met Max Jacob and Pablo Picasso, who was to be his friend for many years. The result was a significant artistic and literary collaboration. Now too Apollinaire made the acquaintance of Maurice de Vlaminck and André Derain, with whom he drank, played cards, and visited hashish dens and brothels. He became increasingly well known in Paris cafés as a friendly and ebullient talker. The usual subjects of conversation were aesthetics and painting, and everyone was feverishly preoccupied with innovation. In 1905, Apollinaire's first writing on art appeared: two articles on Picasso.

In 1909, after a long delay, *Mercure de France* published the fifty-nine stanzas of "La Chanson du mal-aimé." Apollinaire's place in the literary world was now secure. From 1911 on, he wrote a regular column for *Mercure de France*, usually championing new painters. In addition, he had been since 1910 the regular art critic for *L'Intransigeant*. In his articles, he sought to establish his authority by discovering, explaining, and promoting the newest movements in literature and painting: He campaigned for the Fauves, the Unanimists, Henri Matisse, Picasso, Georges Braque, and Alfred Jarry. He became the principal spokesman for cubism.

In 1911, Apollinaire had the harrowing experience of being imprisoned for five days on the strength of a false accusation that he had received and hidden objects stolen from the Louvre. He was desolated. Despite his acquittal, newspapers continued to attack him; his position as leader of the avant-garde was threatened as was his legal right to stay in France. Added to these worries was his lack of funds. His spirits revived with the invitation to become associate editor of a new review, *Soirées de Paris*. His first article advised the abandonment of "likeness" and of subject matter in painting. He could not be cowed.

In the summer of 1912, Apollinaire read a nearly finished version of "Zone" to the Spanish painter Francis Picabia, and his wife. This date is important because of the resemblance of "Zone" to Blaise Cendrars's "Pâques à New York" (Easter in New York), published in 1912. Since Apollinaire regularly published Cendrars's work in *Les Soirées*, the influence may well have been mutual.

Apollinaire had for some time wanted to marry the painter Marie Laurencin, but his mother opposed the marriage on the grounds of an insufficient dowry. The liaison lasted until the fall of 1912; the breakup inspired one of the poet's best-known lyrics, "Le Pont Mirabeau" ("Mirabeau Bridge"). The climax of Apollinaire's career came in 1913: His two most important volumes appeared, *Alcools*, translated into English in 1964, and *Peintres cubistes: Méditations esthétiques* (*The Cubist Painters: Aesthetic Meditations*, 1944). The complete lack of punctuation in *Alcools*, insisted upon by the author, profoundly shocked the public.

In the spring of 1914, Apollinaire was asked to write art reviews for the *Paris-Journal*. He wrote a review daily, with three exceptions, between May and the outbreak of war, including the first *calligramme*—a poem whose words form a design. He considered the *calligramme* his most important innovation.

When Apollinaire applied for French citizenship, he was refused. He fled to Nice, where he met the aristocratic madcap Louise Coligny-Châtillon (called "Lou"), with whom he fell in love. For a brief period he gave himself up to an orgy of opium smoking and general debauchery; then suddenly he left for Nîmes and joined the artillery. Lou followed, and, although their violent love affair soon ended, it inspired many of Apollinaire's best poems in *Calligrammes* (1918; English translation, 1980).

In January, 1915, he wrote that he found the soldier's life ideal for him. He left for the front on Easter Sunday. Even from the trenches, he continued his voluminous correspondence. He wrote letters and poems to Lou and to all of his old friends and to a new love, Madeleine Pagès, to whom he became engaged. Under fire in the front line, he printed on gelatin plates twenty-five copies of *Case d'armons* (1915; a bunker), a collection of verse and drawings.

In November, he was transferred to an infantry company in the Champagne offensive, where, despite real hardship, he wrote frequently to Pagès. On March 17, he was reading *Mercure de France* in a trench, when he found that his blood was dripping onto the paper. Shrapnel had wounded his head more seriously than he at first had realized; he was moved back to Paris, where he was trepanned on May 11. While in the hospital, Apollinaire put together some unpublished stories in a volume that he entitled *Le Poète assassiné* (*The Poet Assassinated*, 1923), which was published in 1916. At the end of this year, he renewed acquaintance with Jacquelin Kolb, a redhead whom he called Ruby, and moved back to his sixth-floor apartment on the Boulevard Saint-Germain, where he found the domestic tranquillity that he had never before known.

Apollinaire's friends organized a banquet on December 31, 1916, to welcome him home and to celebrate the publication of *The Poet Assassinated*. The ninety guests included practically all the famous writers and painters of the period. One of the guests, Pierre Reverdy, founded the following March the review *Nord-Sud*, in which Apollinaire's contributions helped to open the way for Dada and Surrealism. In June, 1917, Apollinaire personally oversaw the production of his first play: *Les Mamelles de Tirésias* (*The Breasts of*

Tiresias, 1961). Its buffoonery and vulgarity excited immense interest.

With the continuing deterioration of Apollinaire's health, he relied increasingly on Kolb; they were married quietly in May, 1918. She had inspired his only important poem since his release from the hospital, "La Jolie Rousse," a summary of his attitude toward conventional and the new experimental poetry. He went on working despite depression and nagging health problems. Then, only two days before the Armistice, he died of Spanish influenza.

Summary

It would be difficult to overestimate the impact of Guillaume Apollinaire on the art and poetry of the twentieth century. Perhaps, as one of his biographers, Francis Steegmuller, claims and some of Apollinaire's painter friends hinted, the poet had no real knowledge of art, or perhaps, as Professor Leroy Breunig and numerous artists and historians have proclaimed, he was one of the greatest art critics of the century. At any rate, his vigorous and ceaseless championship of the struggling innovators of his time led to the serious acceptance of Fauvism, cubism, primitive art, abstract art, and eventually Dada and Surrealism.

Apollinaire's stories and his one play pale into insignificance by the side of his critical writings and poetry. In one article written shortly before his death, he explains that the new spirit consists largely of surprise and that poets should not abandon the traditional elements but should try to capture contemporary life. He foresaw a synthesis of the arts, aided by films and photography. In his autobiographical *ars poetica*, "La Jolie Rousse," he does not advocate the overthrow of the old "Order" but advises the acceptance of "Adventure" and leads the way. Apollinaire's numerous volumes of verse, especially *Alcools* and *Calligrammes*, place him among the masters of French lyric and elegiac poetry. His vision of poetic and artistic freedom is an enduring legacy.

Bibliography

Adéma, Marcel. *Apollinaire*. Translated by Denise Folliot. New York: Grove Press, 1955. This is the prime source of biographical material, the bible of scholars researching the poet and his epoch.

Bates, Scott. *Guillaume Apollinaire*. Rev. ed. Boston: Twayne, 1989. This book offers detailed erudite analyses of Apollinaire's major works and informed judgments on his place in French literature and in the development of art criticism. It emphasizes the importance to the entire world of Apollinaire's vision of a cultural millennium propelled by science and democracy and implemented by poetry. Included are a chronology, a twenty-six-page glossary of references, notes, and selected bibliographies of both primary and secondary sources.

Couffignal, Robert. *Apollinaire*. Translated by Eda Mezer Levitine. Tuscaloosa: University of Alabama Press, 1975. This is a searching analysis of some of Apollinaire's best-known works, including "Zone," strictly from the Roman Catholic point of view. It traces his attitude toward religion from his childhood to his death. The book contains a chronology, translations of ten texts, both poems and prose, with the author's comments, a bibliographical note, and an index.

Shattuck, Roger. *The Banquet Years*. Rev. ed. New York: Vintage Books, 1968. In the two long chapters devoted to Apollinaire, "The Impresario of the Avant-garde" and "Painter-Poet," the author gives a year-by-year and at times even a month-by-month account of his life, loves, friends, employment, writings, and speeches. The tone is judicial, the critical judgments fair and balanced. Includes a bibliography and an index.

Steegmuller, Francis. *Apollinaire: Poet Among the Painters*. New York: Farrar, Straus, 1963. This is an exhaustive, extremely well-documented, unbiased, and highly readable biography. Contains a preface, translations, numerous photographs and illustrations, two appendices, notes, and an index.

Dorothy B. Aspinwall

CORAZON AQUINO

Born: January 25, 1933; Tarlac Province, the Philippines

Areas of Achievement: Government and politics
Contribution: Aquino became the first woman president of the Philippines.
She led the revolution that ended twenty years of dictatorial rule and
restored democratic government.

Early Life

Maria Corazon Cojuangco Aquino was born on January 25, 1933, in Tarlac Province, about fifty miles north of Manila. The sixth of eight children,
"Cory," as she became known, was born with a silver spoon in her mouth.
She belonged to a wealthy and politically influential landowning family in
the Philippines. Her father, Jose Cojuangco, was a sugar baron who also
managed the family bank and later served in the national assembly. Both her
grandfathers were senators. She was educated at exclusive girls' schools in
Manila, run by Roman Catholic nuns. In 1946, when her father moved to the
United States, she continued her education at Raven Hill Academy in Philadelphia and Notre Dame School in New York, both Catholic high schools.
As a young girl, she showed deep religious conviction that would continue to
be a major influence in her life. While a student in the United States, she had
a brief foray into American politics as a member of the Junior Republicans
and supported Governor Thomas Dewey in the 1948 presidential campaign.

In 1953, Aquino was graduated from Mount St. Vincent College in the
Riverdale section of the Bronx, with a degree in French and mathematics.
She returned to Manila to study law at Far Eastern University, not because
she was contemplating a career in law but out of an interest in the discipline
of law. Soon after her return to the Philippines, she began a courtship with
Benigno "Ninoy" Aquino, Jr., a dynamic and intelligent journalist from a
well-known family in Tarlac Province. They were married in 1954, and Cory
Aquino ended her legal studies.

Life's Work

For the next thirty years, Aquino played the traditional roles of a dutiful
and loyal wife and mother. She reared four daughters and a son and supported her husband unobtrusively but effectively in his meteoric political
career. Shortly after their marriage, Ninoy was elected the youngest mayor
in the Philippines. When he became governor of Tarlac Province in 1959, he
was also the youngest in the country. He performed a similar feat in 1967 by
winning a seat in the senate and at thirty-five became the youngest senator.
As Benigno Aquino's career advanced, he became a formidable opponent of
Philippine president Ferdinand E. Marcos.

Cory Aquino's life received a major jolt in 1972 when President Marcos suspended the constitution, imposed martial law, and arrested her husband on charges of murder, subversion, and illegal possession of firearms. Marcos was seeking an unprecedented third term in the presidential elections scheduled for 1973, and it was widely believed in the Philippines that his redoubtable foe, Benigno Aquino, would defeat him. Ninoy's imprisonment was the first in a series of acts of repression by Marcos that included incarcerating hundreds of other opponents, abolishing the congress, ending the independence of the judiciary, and muzzling the press.

During her husband's seven and a half years in prison, Cory Aquino became the only link between him and the world beyond the prison gates. When Benigno Aquino went on a hunger strike in 1975, she not only solicited the help of her family to persuade him to end his fast but also tried to raise international public opinion against the conditions that had prompted his hunger strike. She regularly smuggled out messages from him to his supporters and reporters. In 1980, Benigno Aquino suffered a heart attack, and Marcos allowed him to go to the United States for a bypass operation. He subsequently became a fellow at Harvard University's Center for International Affairs. The Aquino family lived in Newton, Massachusetts, where Cory later said they spent the three happiest years of their lives.

While in the United States, Benigno Aquino further developed and refined his political philosophy. He also felt an obligation to return to the Philippines and resume the struggle against Marcos. Although aware of the risks involved, he was undeterred. On August 21, 1983, Benigno Aquino was assassinated while disembarking from a plane at Manila International Airport. Initially, the Marcos government asserted that Benigno Aquino had been murdered by Rolando Galman, who they alleged was a Communist agent and who was shot at the scene by security guards. Although the evidence pointed to a military conspiracy, the Marcos-appointed court eventually acquitted General Fabian Ver, the armed forces chief of staff, and twenty-five others who had been charged with murder.

The Philippine economy, which had been in decline since the mid-1970's, worsened dramatically after the assassination of Benigno Aquino. The gross national product declined, inflation increased, and the government was unable to make interest payments on its foreign debts. The national economic and fiscal crisis, which in part had been caused by mismanagement and corruption, had severe social costs. Unemployment rose, the standard of living of the majority of Filipinos fell, and the gap between the rich and poor widened even further. These economic and social problems fueled the Communist insurgency mounted by the New People's Army (NPA), as large numbers of people, particularly in the rural areas, became disaffected with the existing order.

The assassination of Benigno Aquino galvanized the Filipino people into action. It resulted in widespread anger and frustration, and sparked demonstrations against the Marcos regime. Benigno Aquino became a national martyr, and his widow rapidly acquired the stature of a national saint. The scale and intensity of the attacks by the Communist guerrillas also increased. The Roman Catholic church, led by the Archbishop of Manila, Jaime Cardinal Sin, became more vociferous in its criticisms of Marcos, a significant development in a country where 85 percent of the people are Catholic.

Cory Aquino, the symbol of the newly energized opposition, used her growing popularity and prestige to compaign against Marcos in the May, 1984, National Assembly elections. The opposition won a third of the seats, and although Marcos retained control of the assembly, the national consensus was that the opposition would have won a majority in a completely free and fair election. Faced with continuing calls domestically and internationally for a return to democratic government, Marcos announced on an American television program in November, 1985, that elections would be held the following February. From then on, Aquino was encouraged to run for the presidency, for many were convinced that only she commanded the support necessary to defeat Marcos and had the stature to unify a split opposition. A self-effacing and private woman who had never considered going into politics, Aquino was a reluctant presidential candidate. After receiving a petition with a million signatures and having spent a day of fasting and meditation at a convent near Manila, Aquino took up the challenge and agreed to run for president. Cardinal Sin was instrumental in persuading Salvador Laurel, who had presidential aspirations of his own, to become her running mate under the banner of Laurel's United Nationalist Democratic Organization (UNIDO).

A political neophyte, Aquino was thus pitchforked into the political arena. What she lacked in political experience she compensated for with her sincerity, forthrightness, and moral courage. Her image as a modern-day Joan of Arc bolstered her popularity. In speeches across the country, she challenged Marcos directly, holding him responsible for the political decay, social dislocation, and economic malaise that had plagued the Philippines during his long and autocratic rule. Yellow—her husband's favorite color— could be seen in the cities, towns, and rural hamlets and came to symbolize the desire for change and the aspirations of a restive populace. As her campaign progressed, Aquino became not only a symbol of opposition but also a dynamic leader, who inspired a populist movement that came to be known as "People Power."

The election, which was held on February 7, 1986, was marked by fraud and intimidation of voters by supporters of Marcos. After both candidates claimed victory, there was a stalemate that lasted for more than two weeks. On February 25, 1986, Marcos and Aquino held rival inaugurations. Faced with intense domestic and international pressures to concede defeat, and after key military officers defected to the Aquino camp, Marcos fled into exile in the United States.

Aquino inherited many daunting political, economic, and social problems from the Marcos era: promulgation of a new constitution, a foreign debt of more than twenty-seven billion dollars, land reform, endemic corruption, and a Communist insurgency. Shortly after her inauguration, she ordered the release of more than five hundred political prisoners, thus fulfilling one of her campaign pledges. She ruled by decree until a new constitution was overwhelmingly endorsed in a referendum in early 1987. The economy would show modest improvements, although many structural economic problems would remain to be corrected, in order to ensure sustained growth. The newly elected congress, dominated by landowners, passed a compromise Land Reform Bill in June, 1988, that is riddled with loopholes and falls far short of a radical redistribution of agricultural land. Although the Communist insurgency has not been overcome, the Aquino government has achieved significant gains in the war by using not only military but also public relations techniques. An interim agreement was also reached in October, 1988, with the United States, which guaranteed the operation of the United States' military bases in the Philippines until 1991. Under the agreement, the Philippines would receive $481 million annually.

Summary

Since her childhood, Corazon Aquino has possessed a strong religious faith, high ethical principles, and moral integrity. Her strength of character sustained her during the trying years of her husband's imprisonment and the arduous period following his assassination. She demonstrated the same moral and religious conviction as she mobilized the Filipino people against the Marcos regime. This essentially peaceful democratic revolution enhanced the stature of the Philippines in the Southeast Asian region and in the wider international community. She set a new standard of ethical conduct for leaders throughout the world and demonstrated that politics can be shrewd but humane.

Although naturally shy and unassuming, Corazon Aquino has grown in confidence and self-assurance as a leader. Following her speech to a joint session of the United States Congress in September, 1986, House Speaker Thomas P. O'Neill, Jr., said that hers was the "finest speech" he had heard in his long congressional career. After surviving several coup attempts and domestic upheaval, she has restored greater political stability to the Philippines. The tourist industry has been invigorated, and there has been an increase in new local and foreign investment in the economy. Aquino has shown tact, compassion, and fairness in dealing with the practical problems of politics. Under her leadership, the Filipino people have gained a new faith and pride in themselves and in their nation.

Bibliography

Burton, Sandra. *Impossible Dream: The Marcoses, the Aquinos, and the Unfinished Revolution.* New York: Warner Books, 1989. A lucid account of the Philippine revolution. It contains interesting anecdotes that throw light on the relationship between Aquino and her husband.

Haskins, James. *Corazon Aquino: Leader of the Philippines.* Hillside, N.J.: Enslow, 1988. A sympathetic biography of Aquino. Her early life is treated more briefly than her role as a political leader and public figure, which is the real focus of the study. Intended for young readers.

Johnson, Bryan. *The Four Days of Courage: The Untold Story of the People Who Brought Marcos Down.* New York: Free Press, 1987. A journalistic but thorough account of the Aquino-Marcos election campaign. Good use is made of interviews with government, military, and civilian participants in the revolution.

Karnow, Stanley. *In Our Image: America's Empire in the Philippines.* New York: Random House, 1989. One of the best historical accounts of the United States' special relationship with the Philippines. It provides penetrating insights into the circumstances that led to Aquino's rise to power. The book includes information gained from exclusive interviews with Aquino before and after she became president.

Komisar, Lucy. *Corazon Aquino: The Story of a Revolution.* New York: George Braziller, 1987. Although written without the cooperation of Aquino or members of her family, this "unauthorized biography" gives a well-rounded account of her personality. It also contains a useful background chapter on the history of the Philippines. A detailed account is given of Aquino's first year as president.

Mercado, Monina Allarey, ed. *People Power: An Eyewitness History of the Philippine Revolution of 1986.* Manila: James B. Reuter Foundation, 1986. A collection of personal accounts of events leading to the fall of Marcos, as seen from the perspectives of people from various segments of Philippine society.

Abiodun Williams

YASIR ARAFAT

Born: August 24 or 27, 1929; Cairo, Egypt, or Gaza

Areas of Achievement: Political leadership and the military
Contribution: Arafat was the founder of al-Fatah, a Palestinian revolutionary
   and sometimes terrorist organization that became the founding block of
   the Palestine Liberation Organization (PLO). A controversial figure who
   is a freedom fighter to his own people and a terrorist to Israelis and
   others, he has moved the Palestinians from near obscurity in the 1960's to
   the forefront of the world's attention.

Early Life
   Mohammed Yasir Arafat was born in Cairo or Gaza on August 24 or 27,
1929 (records are conflicting). His mother, Hamida, was a cousin of Hajj
Amin al Husseini, the Mufti of Jerusalem and Palestinian leader during the
British Mandate over Palestine. Arafat is one of seven children from his
father's first marriage. His father, Abd al-Rauf Arafat al Qudwa, was from
Qudwa family of Gaza and Khan Yunis, and a member of the Muslim Broth-
erhood. Arafat's family moved back to Gaza from Cairo in 1939, and he was
reared by an uncle after the death of his parents.
   After World War II, when Arafat was in his teens, he became active in
Palestinian student causes. He belonged to the group Futuwah, a youth organization affiliated with the Husseini clan that feuded with the rival Nash-
ashibis. In 1946, he was active in smuggling arms into Palestine from Egypt.
He fought in the 1948 Arab-Israeli war in battles south of Jerusalem. From
1951 to 1956, Arafat attended Fuad I University (now the University of
Cairo) as a civil engineering student. He underwent commando training with
a Gaza brigade in the Egyptian army in 1951 and later became involved in
groups that staged hit-and-run operations against the British around the Suez
Canal. In 1952, Arafat was elected President of the Union of Palestinian
Students.
   In August, 1956, Arafat attended the International Student Congress in
Prague and then became Chairman of the Union of Palestinian Graduates.
This position allowed him to establish contacts with Palestinians in other
countries. He began work as a construction engineer. In the October, 1956,
Suez war, Arafat fought in the Egyptian army as a bomb disposal expert.

Life's Work
   In 1956, Arafat, along with Khalid al-Wazir, formed al-Fatah (victory)
and became its spokesman. The principle of the new organization was that
its members should not belong to any Arab political party or other movement. This, he believed, was a way to demonstrate that Palestinians did not
want to interfere in Arab internal politics. During 1957, Arafat moved to

Kuwait and worked for the Kuwaiti government's department of water supply as a civil engineer; he also established a construction company that hired Palestinians. Many important Fatah contacts were made in this period. He established the first of Fatah's underground cells. In July, 1962, President Ben Bella of Algeria became the first Arab head of state to recognize Fatah. Arafat met Bella in December, 1962, and opened a Fatah office in Algiers under the name Bureau de la Palestine. Fatah subsequently developed along collective leadership lines. Arafat believed that Arab unity was key to liberating Palestine and that unity had to come from the people. His idea was to capture the imagination of the Palestinian people.

In 1964, the PLO was formed by the Arab States in Cairo, led by Ahmad al-Shuqayri but in essence controlled by Egypt. Arafat, trying to assert Palestinian independence, had many difficulties with Arab regimes that wanted to control Palestinian resistance. In May, 1966, Arafat, Abu Jihad, and twenty other Fatah members were arrested by the Syrian government on trumped-up murder charges after a Syrian plot backfired, leading to the deaths of two Fatah members.

During the June, 1967, Six-Day War, Arafat and Abu Jihad fought on the Syrian front as irregulars. Arafat's reaction to Arab defeat was despair but was also to begin a popular war of liberation. Arafat was in favor of immediate resumption of guerrilla warfare as a way to avert the psychological burden of Arab defeat. On June 23, 1967, the Fatah Central Committee confirmed the idea of returning to military confrontation, and Arafat was appointed military commander. Some small operations began in August, but Israeli security forces had uncovered most of the cells by the end of the year. Arafat believed that irregular fighting allowed the Palestinians to fix their identity. Arafat stayed in the West Bank until the end of the year and then escaped to Jordan. The years 1968 to 1970 saw Jordan used as a base for attacks against Israel.

On March 21, 1968, the Battle of Karameh occurred between Israelis and Palestinian-Jordanian forces, marking the first Palestinian military victory over Israel since 1948. Karameh was viewed as "resurrection of the Palestinian people." Many volunteers came to PLO circles. In addition, a Palestinian bureaucracy was established and intellectuals become involved in the revival of Palestinian culture. The relationship between Arafat and President Gamal Abdel Nasser of Egypt blossomed after Karameh, and Arafat became the chief spokesman for the PLO. Arafat's solution to the Palestine problem in 1968 was to espouse the idea of a Democratic State of Palestine, which from an al-Fatah perspective meant dismantling Israel by politics and nonviolence but to Israel appeared to be based on violence. The nonviolent solution was also rejected by the PLO, which sought the extinction of Israel through violent means according to its 1964 covenant.

In early 1969, Arafat took over the PLO and made it into an umbrella organization, independent of the Arab regimes. Arafat himself became a symbol of resistance, more than a freedom fighter to some. The PLO covenant bound all to "armed struggle." Arafat was elected chairman of the PLO executive committee. On November 3, 1969, the Cairo Agreement, which allowed the PLO to base itself in Lebanon, bear arms, use Lebanese territory to attack Israel, and have direct rule over the Palestinian refugee camps, was concluded. Arafat became supreme commander of the Palestine Armed Struggle Command (PASC).

During September, 1970, however, Arafat lost control of the extremists, particularly the Popular Front for the Liberation of Palestine (PFLP). Although the PFLP was suspended from the Central Committee of the Palestine Resistance, a civil war broke out in Jordan, and the PLO, including Arafat's forces, was defeated by the Jordanian army. There is some opinion that the PLO disaster in Jordan could have been averted if Arafat had used force to control the radicals. Arafat, however, seemed unwilling to restrain the leftists out of respect for the principle of national unity. Arafat also believed that use of violence against the Left would have detroyed "democracy" within the PLO.

The result was the rise of terror as a tactic by Palestinian groups after 1970. Black September, led by the PFLP, was the most violent early group, being responsible for the 1971 assassination of the Jordanian prime minister Wasfi Tal, the May, 1972, Lod Airport massacre, and the August, 1972, massacre of Israeli Olympic athletes in Munich. Arafat subsequently made a tactical alliance with the PLO Left and committed himself to armed struggle.

The first change toward moderation came in February, 1974, with a PLO working paper that indicated a willingness to accept a political settlement in exchange for a mini-state on the West Bank and in Gaza. Unofficial contacts were established with Israelis by the end of 1973, but it was not until 1977 that the Palestine National Council supported the idea of negotiations on the mini-state idea. At the Rabat Conference in 1974, the PLO was recognized as the sole legitimate representative of the Palestinian people.

On November 13, 1974, Arafat was invited to address the United Nations (U.N.) General Assembly, and he called for establishment of national authority on any land in the West Bank and Gaza. Arafat was treated as head of state. He asserted that, "Today, I have come bearing an olive branch and a freedom-fighter's gun. Do not let the olive branch fall from my hand." To critics, the gesture seemed hypocritical, while his appearance in traditional Arab dress appeared as an example of political transformation in a changing world: yesterday a terrorist, today a diplomat. U.N. General Assembly Resolution 3236 of November 14, 1974, recognized the PLO as a representative of the Palestinian people and the right of the Palestinians to self-determination, national independence, and sovereignty. Diplomatic recognition was achieved by the PLO from more than eighty states by the 1980's, as well as was observer status at the United Nations.

Arafat's 1974 successes, however, were short-lived. In 1975, the PLO became involved in the Lebanon Civil War, bringing the PLO into conflict with Syria, which did not want an independent Palestinian movement. Arafat moved in and out of Lebanon during the late 1970's, trying to position PLO forces and arrange cease-fires. The November, 1977, Sadat Peace Initiative with Israel and Sadat's historic visit to Jerusalem soured the relationship between Arafat and Sadat, as the Egyptian president appeared to usurp a role specifically delegated to the PLO.

In January, 1978, the PLO appeared to splinter further over the issue of legitimate leadership and the issue of armed struggle. Abu Nidal established a faction (Black June) and insisted that he was the real representative of al-Fatah, not Arafat. Several Palestinian supporters of Arafat were assassinated by Abu Nidal's group, and he, in turn, was sentenced in absentia to death by Fatah leadership. In April, 1978, a mutiny within Fatah was led by Abu Daoud. Arafat tried to heal the rift by integrating all militias under Fatah. Arafat, in his attempt to maintain Palestinian unity, often gave contradictory statements about what exactly was the ultimate desire of the Palestinians. In 1978, for example, in a discussion with U.S. congressman Paul Findley, he indicated that he would accept a Palestinian state in the West Bank and Gaza but "would reserve the right, of course, to use non-violent means to bring about the eventual unification of all of Palestine."

In 1982, U.S. President Ronald Regan proposed a peace plan that Arafat considered but that the Palestine National Council (PNC) ultimately rejected. This plan would have required Arafat to work jointly with King Hussein I of Jordan on Palestinian rights, which was something that President Assad of Syria did not want. Hussein desired a Palestinian state in confederation with Jordan, a situation that would narrow the independence of a PLO state. Arafat later accepted the idea of a joint Palestinian-Jordanian delegation, but Hussein insisted on including West Bank representatives in the delegation as well. Assad, in response, planned a Fatah rebellion. By 1985, Hussein indicated that the PLO would have to accept U.N. Resolution 242 of 1967, and an agreement was made between Arafat and Hussein accepting the land for peace principle. Yet PLO terrorist actions continued, undercutting Arafat's desire for moderation.

PLO leadership was caught short by the *Intifada*, the Palestinian uprising on the West Bank and Gaza that began on December 8, 1987. That uprising was begun largely because Arab states had become more interested in the Iraq-Iran war that was drawing to a close than the Palestine question. While the Intifada was spontaneous in its origins, PLO leadership moved in to control much of the activity and strikes and to provide financial support for those under Israeli occupation.

On November 15, 1988, the PNC declared an independent Palestinian state without specific borders and conditionally accepted U.N. Resolutions 242 and 338 and the 1947 Partition Plan. There was no straight answer from Arafat as to whether this meant recognition of Israel. During December, 1988, there were many clarifications, which finally led to American recognition of the PLO. In early December in Stockholm, Arafat indicated that he had accepted the existence of Israel. On December 13, he addressed a special session of the U.N. General Assembly in Geneva after having been refused a visa by the U.S. Department of State. In his address he fell short of a full renunciation of terrorism but called for peace talks. A day later, on December 14, another statement by Arafat provided another clarification on "the right of all parties concerned in the Middle East conflict to exist in peace and security . . . including the state of Palestine, Israel, and other neighbors." He also renounced all forms of terrorism. These statements satisfied the United States government and ended the diplomatic isolation of the PLO from Washington, D.C. At the same time, Arafat has been critical of what appeared to be unconditional support of Israel by the United States, which encourages hard-line positions within Israel.

Despite the recognition of Israel and renunciation of terrorism, questions still existed regarding Arafat's attitudes toward Palestinian moderates and the wishes of Palestinians under occupation. During January, 1989, threats were made by Arafat against moderates who suggested ending the Intifada. Arafat's general position by the end of the 1980's was to support the creation of a Palestinian state on the West Bank, in Gaza, and in East Jerusalem, with support from an international conference involving all parties of the Arab-Israeli conflict.

Summary

Although by the end of the 1980's Yasir Arafat had not succeeded in creating a Palestinian state, he was ultimately the symbol of the Palestinian revolution. As a world traveler and charismatic leader, he appeared to be wedded to the Palestinian revolution and was able to be all things to all men. Part of his leadership success was his ability to keep the PLO's ideology simple, especially in rejecting extraneous issues and refusing to make his organization a tool of any specific Arab regime. Ideologically, Arafat's bottom line was that Palestine was Arab land and hence Israel would never be formally recognized. Arafat was also able to obtain large financial subsidies for the Palestinian cause from oil-producing Arab regimes, which in turn increased the financial power of the PLO in Lebanon through the summer of 1982.

Arafat, however, was often said to have talked out of both sides of his mouth. His obscure statements about renunciation of terrorism and recognition of Israel did not allow him to get full support of the United States or Western European powers for the Palestinian cause. During his tenure as

PLO leader, Arafat was also criticized for his individualism—his insistence that he be free to take personal initiatives, which often led to broad promises without the support of all PLO groups. He was also criticized by other Palestinian groups for enriching himself and the leadership at the expense of those in the camps. The strategy of delaying peace until the Arabs were strong enough to dictate terms was also criticized by peace advocates outside the Middle East. Arafat's life is a testimony to the complexity of the Palestinian Arab question and the fact that it is intimately connected with Arab politics. The unanswered question is whether Arafat will become the leader of an independent Palestinian state.

Bibliography

Becker, Jillian. *The PLO*. London: Weidenfeld & Nicolson, 1984. A history of the PLO that defines the organization as terrorist and takes a negative view toward Arafat as a leader.

Curtis, Michael, Joseph Neyer, Chaim I. Waxman, and Allen Pollack, eds. *The Palestinians: People, History, Politics*. New Brunswick, N.J.: Transaction Books, 1975. A useful anthology of articles that explain the various dimensions of the Palestinian people and their political, social, and economic problems.

Friedman, Thomas. *From Beirut to Jerusalem*. New York: Farrar, Straus and Giroux, 1989. This is an exceptionally interesting examination of Israeli, Palestinian, and Lebanese politics by a Pulitzer Prize-winning bureau chief of *The New York Times* in Beirut and Jerusalem.

Hart, Alan. *Arafat: Terrorist or Peacemaker?* London: Sidgwick and Jackson, 1984. An extremely sympathetic portrait of the PLO leader and the Palestinian cause. There are many undocumented quotations from sources that are questionable and not cross-checked for accuracy.

Mishal, Shaul. *The PLO Under Arafat: Between Gun and Olive Branch*. New Haven, Conn.: Yale University Press, 1986. A structural examination of the PLO that in a scholarly way distinguishes Arafat from other Palestinian leaders and examines the mechanics of the PLO.

Rubenstein, Richard. *Alchemists of Revolution*. New York: Basic Books, 1987. A critical examination of the structure of terrorism as it developed during the 1970's and 1980's. Special attention is paid to Arafat as representative of a figure who is a freedom fighter to his own people and a terrorist to outsiders.

Schiff, Ze'ev, and Ehud Ya'ari. *Israel's Lebanon War*. Translated by Ina Friedman. New York: Simon & Schuster, 1984. An examination of the 1982 Lebanon War by Israeli war correspondents. It is fairly critical of Israeli actions during the conflict.

Stephen C. Feinstein

SVANTE AUGUST ARRHENIUS

Born: February 19, 1859; Castle of Vik, near Uppsala, Sweden
Died: October 2, 1927; Stockholm, Sweden
Areas of Achievement: Chemistry and physics
Contribution: Arrhenius was one of the founders of the interdisciplinary science of physical chemistry. He also aided in establishing the international reputation of the Nobel Prizes, clarified the physical effects of light pressure from the sun, and developed the conception, called "panspermia," that life was introduced on Earth by spores from space.

Early Life

Svante August Arrhenius was born February 19, 1859, at the castle of Vik, near Uppsala, Sweden. His family had engaged in farming for several generations and had also produced some members of at least modest accomplishment. One relative had written published hymns, an uncle was a scholar, and Arrhenius' own father had attended the University of Uppsala briefly and held a responsible position as superintendent of grounds for the university.

From an early age, Arrhenius showed skill in calculating, and at the Cathedral School in Uppsala he displayed some ability in mathematics and physics. In 1876, at the age of seventeen, Arrhenius enrolled at the University of Uppsala, the oldest and best-known Swedish institution. There to study physics, he ultimately discovered that his instructors were overly committed to experimental topics and were either unaware of or opposed to the rapid developments in theoretical physics. Thus, in 1881 he moved to Stockholm to study with Erik Edlund. By 1884, Arrhenius submitted his doctoral dissertation to the University of Uppsala, but his talent was largely unrecognized and he was granted the lowest possible honor above an outright rejection.

His thesis, built upon the work of Michael Faraday and Sir Humphry Davy, described an effective experimental method for determining the electrical conductivity of compounds in extremely dilute solutions. The thesis also included a preliminary outline of a theory of electrolytic conductivity, in which Arrhenius claimed that the salt was dissociated into two ions in the solution. This ionization increased the number of particles in a given volume, allowing Arrhenius to explain the high osmotic pressures found by Jacobus Hendricus van't Hoff as well as the decreased freezing points and increased boiling points of solutions.

Professor Per Teodor Cleve established the initial response toward Arrhenius' work by ignoring it, presuming that it was no more significant than other student theories. Fortunately, Wilhelm Ostwald recognized the significance of the work and its foundational nature for subsequent developments in the theory of electrolysis.

Life's Work

Arrhenius, disappointed by the reception of his work, began a campaign to win acceptance by sending copies of his dissertation to several scholars throughout Europe. His work was favorably received by Sir William Ramsay in England and Ostwald in Russia. When Ostwald came to Sweden to visit, his influence secured a lectureship for Arrhenius at Uppsala in 1884 and a travel grant from the Swedish Academy of Sciences in 1886 so that Arrhenius could study further in Europe.

From 1886 to 1891, Arrhenius worked with some of the finest physicists of Europe, including Ostwald in Riga and later in Leipzig, Friedrich Kohlrausch in Würzburg, Ludwig Boltzmann in Graz, and van't Hoff in Amsterdam. During this time, the ionization theory met with extensive resistance. Incomplete atomic theory contributed to the difficulty of accounting for the formation and stable existence of the ions, and certain strong solutions remained anomalous, but Ostwald advocated the fruitfulness of the new theory, demonstrating that it could account for a wide variety of chemical phenomena. When Ostwald joined with van't Hoff to found *Zeitschrift für physikalische Chemie*, Arrhenius took advantage of the opportunity to publish a revised version of his theory of electrolytic dissociation in the first issue. The three close friends thus formed a formidable association promoting the theory.

In 1891, Arrhenius refused a professorship at Giessen, Germany, to become a lecturer at the Högskola, the technical high school in Stockholm, an institution devoted to teaching research methodology in a free form without degrees. Although an outstanding faculty did genuinely creative work, the school was always underequipped. Despite opposition, Arrhenius became a professor in 1895 and later a rector. He and other leaders sought to surpass Uppsala and in the process transformed the Högskola into the University of Stockholm. Beginning in 1898, he was active in formulating the procedures governing the Nobel Prizes and served on the physics committee from 1900 to 1927.

During these years, Arrhenius continued research in electrolytic conductivity, the viscosity of solutions, the effects of temperature upon reaction velocity, and atmospheric conductivity. The results of his research appeared in *Lärobok i teoretisk elektrokemi* (1900; *Text-book of Electrochemistry*, 1902); in 1903, he published *Lehrbuch der kosmischen Physik* (treatise on cosmic physics). Also during this period, Arrhenius' interdisciplinary interests continued to expand. In 1902 and 1903, he studied in Denmark and Germany, working on physiological problems in serum therapy. In 1904, he delivered lectures at the University of California on principles of physical chemistry applied to toxins and antitoxins. In 1905, he refused the offer of a professorship and a private laboratory in Berlin in order to become the director of the Nobel Institute for Physical Chemistry, near Stockholm, a post he held until his death twenty-two years later.

Settling in Stockholm, Arrhenius began an intense period of writing. In 1906, his California lectures appeared as *Theorien der Chemie* (*Theories of Chemistry*, 1907) and as *Immunochemistry* (1907). That year, cosmologists also became aware of him through *Das Werden der Welten*, a German translation of *Världarnas utveckling* (1906; *Worlds in the Making*, 1908). The second law of thermodynamics seemed to many physicists and astronomers to point to the heat death of the universe. Arrhenius sought to discount heat exhaustion with a self-renewing model of the universe in which burned out solar objects were replaced by new stars arising from nebulas that were increasing in temperature.

In this intense period of labor, Arrhenius also published *Människan inför världsgåtan* (1907; *The Life of the Universe as Conceived by Man from Earliest Ages to the Present Time*, 1909), which represented a different approach to the older plurality of worlds (life on other planets) debate. Arrhenius supported other scientists who argued that life was universally diffused throughout the universe from already inhabited planets that gave out spores that were spread through space and reached planets that had evolved to a habitable state. Arrhenius intended this as an alternative to William Thomson's claim that meteorites were the means of seeding the planets with life. These proposals have since been given the descriptive name panspermia, and while they were high in explanatory value they have held little interest since the discovery of intense ultraviolet radiation in space.

Honors came to Arrhenius as the quality of his research was recognized. He was finally elected to the Swedish Academy of Sciences in 1901, and the widespread acceptance of his theory was recognized in 1903, when he was awarded the Nobel Prize in Chemistry. In 1902, he received the Davy Medal of the Royal Society of London and became an associate of the German Chemical Society. On a visit to the United States in 1911, he received the first Willard Gibbs Medal and became an associate of the American Academy of Sciences. In addition, he became a foreign member of the Royal Society in 1911, received the Faraday Medal of the Chemical Society in 1914, and was awarded numerous honorary doctorates.

Throughout his career, Arrhenius continued to conduct research and write. He delivered the 1911 Silliman Lectures at Yale, which were published as *Theories of Solutions* (1912). In 1915, he made a second contribution to biochemistry with *Quantitative Laws in Biological Chemistry*, and in 1918 *The Destinies of the Stars* appeared in English. Despite Arrhenius' confidence in the existence of life throughout the universe, he refrained from excesses and took Percival Lowell to task for imagining more than could be proved. In 1926, Arrhenius published his last major effort, *Erde und Weltall*, a revision and combination of his earlier books on cosmology. He died on October 2, 1927.

Summary

Ironically, Svante August Arrhenius is now most frequently cited for one of his least enduring ideas, that of life originating on planets as the result of panspermia. He is less well known for his more significant accomplishments as a founder of physical chemistry. His reach across disciplinary lines contributed to a fruitful period of research in both physics and chemistry. He strongly wished to internationalize Swedish scientific activity and saw the Nobel Prizes as a means of accomplishing this goal. His role in writing the regulations governing the administration and awarding of these prizes contributed greatly to establishing them as the most significant international scientific award. Offering a satisfactory explanation of the aurora borealis and establishing the existence of light pressure from the sun were his enduring contributions to atmospheric physics and astronomy. His good humor and command of languages (German, French, and English) made him popular wherever scholars gathered and won for him an enduring place in the memories of those with whom he worked.

Bibliography

Crawford, Elisabeth. *The Beginnings of the Nobel Institution: The Science Prizes, 1901-1915*. New York: Cambridge University Press, 1984. This significant scholarly work presents a comprehensive and detailed account of the early history of the science prizes. It also gives extensive detail of Arrhenius' involvement in the organizing of the prizes and his actions in promoting and blocking particular recipients.

Farber, Eduard. *The Evolution of Chemistry*. New York: Ronald Press, 1952. While providing minimal biographical information, this book contains a brief but clear explanation of Arrhenius' theory of dissociation. This theory was Arrhenius' most original work and the foundation of his receiving the Nobel Prize; therefore, this remains a useful source.

—————————, ed. *Great Chemists*. New York: Interscience, 1961. This work contains an abridgment and translation of an earlier work on Arrhenius. It is thorough, accurate, and one of the more authoritative English sources. As with most of the available biographical material concerning Arrhenius, there is very little about his private life in the English abridgment, a shortcoming of the book since it tends to decontextualize Arrhenius' place in the science of the day.

Jaffe, Bernard. *Crucibles: The Story of Chemistry*. New York: Simon & Schuster, 1948. One chapter of this book contains a popular and dramatic account of Arrhenius' career, depicting him as a hero who overcame great opposition from entrenched science to receive the recognition that he deserved.

Larson, Cedric A. "Svante August Arrhenius." *Science Digest* 46 (August, 1959): 83-89. This is a readily available, brief, and accurate biography.

Since this is a popular account of his life, the explanations of the science with which Arrhenius was involved are simple. The account of his life is somewhat more personal than the other available sources.

Ivan L. Zabilka

KEMAL ATATÜRK
Mustafa Kemal

Born: 1881; Salonika, Ottoman Empire
Died: November 10, 1938; İstanbul, Turkey
Areas of Achievement: Government, politics, the military, and social reform
Contribution: When the Ottoman Empire lost World War I and suffered
  Greek invasion, Atatürk created a revolutionary movement that defeated
  the invaders, overthrew the Sultan, and established the modern Turkish
  state. As president of Turkey until his death, he promoted secularization,
  industrialization, and other Western-style reforms.

Early Life

The subject of this essay received the name "Mustafa" at birth; a delighted
schoolmaster later added the name "Kemal," which means "perfection."
The surname "Atatürk," meaning "Father Turk," was bestowed on him by a
grateful nation in 1934. Indeed, the law requiring all citizens to adopt sur-
names was itself one of his many reforms. Mustafa was born to Ali Riza, a
sometime minor customs official and failed businessman, and his wife, Zü-
beyde. Although Ali died when his son was only seven, he had nevertheless
managed to instill in him a liberal and anticlerical attitude. Mustafa inherited
both a fair complexion and stubborn determination from his mother, but he
rejected her plan that he should follow a religious career. Reminding her that
his father had hung a sword by his cradle when he was only a baby, the
youngster finally obtained his mother's permission to enter a military school.
He received his commission in 1902.

The army provided Kemal with a window to the West. Sultan Abdülhamid II might suppress political reform, but he had to have a modern army,
and that meant officers who could read Western books, incidentally picking
up liberal ideas. Graduating from a staff college as a captain in 1905, Kemal
was already harboring subversive thoughts, and he soon joined the "Young
Turks," a group of reform-minded conspirators. Yet Kemal had a low opinion of some of the Young Turk leaders, and they in turn looked upon him as
a headstrong potential rival. He therefore derived scant benefit from their
successful rebellion in 1908-1909: Abdülhamid was replaced by a figurehead
sultan—a constitutional monarch—but Kemal remained on the fringes of
power.

Kemal's brilliance as an officer forced the Young Turks to give him employment. He served well in the Italo-Turkish War of 1911-1912 and in the
Balkan Wars of 1912-1913. It was in the Balkan Wars that the Ottomans lost
Kemal's hometown of Salonika to the Greeks—and much else besides. The
sultan's ramshackle, multiethnic, religious empire was proving vulnerable to

nationalism and modern technology. By 1914, Kemal was a lieutenant colonel impatient for greatness and further reform.

Life's Work

The Ottoman Empire entered World War I as Germany's ally in 1914. As a division commander in 1915, Kemal was, more than any other individual, responsible for the Turkish victory at Gallipoli, thereby preventing an Allied conquest of the Turkish Straits. As hero and general, he next fought the Russians in eastern Anatolia during 1916-1917. By the end of the war, he was a field army commander in Syria, desperately trying to counter the Anglo-Arab advance.

When the Sultan surrendered in 1918, the Allies proceeded to dismember his realm. Not only would they appropriate his Arab-speaking provinces for themselves; they would also create an independent Armenia and an autonomous Kurdistan. The Turkish-speaking heartland of the empire would be turned into a vassal state of the Allied powers. Yet the Allies, tired of war, had already begun demobilizing their armies after Germany's surrender; thus they had to count on Turkish exhaustion and docility for the realization of their plans.

Then, on May 15, 1919, the Greeks took what they considered their share by seizing the largely Greek-speaking area around Smyrna, modern-day İzmir. Turks everywhere were outraged: To submit to the great powers was one thing; to be despoiled by an ancient and despised enemy quite another. Four days later, on May 19, Kemal landed on the north Anatolian coast to take up the cause of resistance, giving organization and leadership to Turkish fury. (He would later make May 19 his official birthday.) The sultan, however, declared Kemal an outlaw, hoping to keep his throne by pleasing the Allies.

Kemal's nationalists were not without advantages. Apart from their determination and a large number of soldiers left over from World War I, they also received armaments from Soviet Russia. Kemal, anticommunist so far as his own country's politics were concerned, nevertheless welcomed Soviet assistance in a common struggle against the Western powers. Moreover, France and Italy soon became jealous of Anglo-Greek ascendancy and arranged what amounted to a separate peace with Kemal. Even Great Britain, sick of turmoil and bedeviled by the Irish problem, began to lose interest in the Hellenic cause. In the 1921 Battle of Sakarya, Kemal blocked the Greek advance on Ankara, nationalist Turkey's new capital; in 1922, he crushed the Greek army at Dumlupinar and drove the army from Anatolian soil. He then abolished the sultanate.

In the Treaty of Lausanne of 1923, the Allies recognized the new Turkish state. For its part, Turkey ceded its Arab lands. These lands had been under firm Allied control since 1918 in any case, and to reclaim them—even if that were possible—would only have meant a re-creation of the multiethnic empire that had so recently failed, a violation of Kemal's hard-won nationalist ideal. On the other hand, he would not carry that ideal to its logical conclusion by relinquishing Armenia and Kurdistan. Turkey's boundaries were thus fixed. The Turkish Straits were demilitarized and legally opened to the Allied navies—a bitter pill for the Russians, who had hoped that Turkey would be willing and able to keep the warships of Russia's potential enemies out of the Black Sea; Kemal was happy to disappoint the Soviets now that he no longer needed their supplies.

It was during the Lausanne negotiations that a sudden change occurred in Kemal's personal life. He met a woman from a well-to-do Turkish family named Latife, who had enjoyed a European education and was Western in thought and dress. She was the kind of female companion he needed, since he intended to promote equal rights for women and an end to the veil. Latife insisted on marriage, and they were wed on January 29, 1923. The marriage quickly dissolved, and they were divorced on August 5, 1925. As a substitute for marriage and a traditional family, Kemal adopted many children.

Kemal's public life was more successful than his marriage. As president and virtual dictator, he soon attained most of what he wanted. Closest to his heart was the elimination of Islamic influence over society, particularly in education and law. The symbol of this campaign was the Western hat, which he insisted must replace the fez. Although of Greek origin, the fez was cherished by practicing Muslims because it had no brim; hence the wearer could touch the ground with his forehead during prayer without uncovering himself. Like the veil, however, it had to go. Kemal also introduced the Western alphabet in place of Arabic characters, a great improvement, since the Arabic script had not been suited to the Turkish language. Government-sponsored industrialization was the remaining major item on Kemal's agenda, but the Great Depression of the 1930's hampered progress in that field.

By 1938, Atatürk (as he had now been named) was gravely ill with cirrhosis of the liver, a condition aggravated by overwork and alcohol. He would not take his doctor's advice until too late. His death that November was a great blow to the Turkish people, despite the controversy he had stirred over religion. It took fifteen years for a suitably grand mausoleum to be completed in Ankara as his final resting place.

Summary

Kemal Atatürk's reforms provoked considerable opposition during his lifetime. There were religious disturbances and a Kurdish revolt, all suppressed with a firmness bordering on ferocity. On two occasions, he tried to promote democracy by creating a party of loyal opposition, but the experiment failed, in part because he came to fear that any opposition would turn into an attack on the essentials of his movement. He was perhaps correct: Democracy would have given power to the peasant masses for whom secularism was close to blasphemy. In the years since Atatürk's death, Turkey, like many other countries, Islamic and otherwise, experienced a resurgence of religion. Turkish secularism became a conservative, establishmentarian, and endangered ideal.

On the other hand, nationalism in Turkey has prospered since 1938, as it has elsewhere. Atatürk was a pioneer in the emergence of the Third World. His movement was part of a process carried on in different ways all over the globe—for example, in Meiji Japan and in the China of Chiang Kai-shek and Mao Tse-tung. Like the Meiji reformers, Atatürk borrowed from the West what he thought appropriate, but he rejected military aggression, deciding to be a good neighbor—even of Greece—once Turkey's existence was assured.

Bibliography
Anderson, M. S. *The Eastern Question, 1774-1923*. London: Macmillan, 1966. This is a long (435-page) and detailed account of the process by which the Ottoman Empire dissolved. It is well documented and has an extensive bibliographical essay. Anderson provides the background for an understanding of Atatürk's diplomatic accomplishments.
Armstrong, H. C. *Gray Wolf*. New York: Capricorn Books, 1961. Written in a novelistic style that borders on sensationalism, *Gray Wolf* may be read for pleasure but should be tempered by the Kinross biography listed below.
Howard, Harry N. *The Partition of Turkey*. Reprint. New York: Howard Fertig, 1966. Originally published in 1931, Howard's book is still a model of scholarship, especially for its exhaustive bibliography. His approach differs somewhat from that of Anderson (see above), which also helps his book to retain its usefulness.
Kinross, Lord. *Atatürk*. New York: William Morrow, 1965. This is, and deserves to be, the standard biography. It is long (615 pages), with an extensive bibliography, a lengthy chronology, and a good set of maps, but has few footnotes. Kinross respects Atatürk but notes his less admirable traits.
Landau, Jacob M., ed. *Atatürk and the Modernization of Turkey*. Boulder, Colo.: Westview Press, 1984. This is a collection of essays, most of them highly informative and interesting, telling the story of Atatürk's reforms. The scholarship is exemplary.
Shaw, Stanford J., and Ezel Kural Shaw. *History of the Ottoman Empire and Modern Turkey*. Vol. 2, *Reform, Revolution, and Republic: The Rise of Modern Turkey, 1808-1975*. Cambridge, Mass.: Cambridge University Press, 1977. Even without Stanford J. Shaw's volume 1, this is a massive

tome: 518 pages, including a twenty-five-page bibliographical essay. It is best used as a reference work.

Sonyel, Salahi Ramsdan. *Turkish Diplomacy, 1918-1923*. Beverly Hills, Calif.: Sage Publications, 1975. Only 267 pages long, this book is nevertheless well documented and contains a good bibliography. It covers the period 1918-1923 in more detail than the other books listed here.

Tachau, Frank. *Kemal Atatürk*. New York: Chelsea House, 1987. This very brief (111-page) and profusely illustrated book is well suited to younger students. As such, it does not have much in the way of scholarly apparatus, yet it is up to date and authoritative.

Volkan, Vamik D., and Norman Itzkowitz. *The Immortal Atatürk: A Psychobiography*. Chicago: University of Chicago Press, 1984. The authors use Freudian psychoanalytical techniques to probe Atatürk's personality. It is a controversial approach, but the book will interest and challenge its readers, even if they do not agree with it.

Karl G. Larew

SRI AUROBINDO
Sri Aurobindo Ghose

Born: August 15, 1872; Calcutta, India
Died: December 5, 1950; Pondicherry, India
Areas of Achievement: Philosophy, religion, government, and politics
Contribution: Aurobindo was one of the leading politicians and great re-
ligious thinkers in twentieth century India. He was a leader of the first
national political party with a platform demanding the independence of
India from British rule. His writings and actions helped to revitalize India
politically and spiritually.

Early Life

Sri Aurobindo Ghose was born in Calcutta, India, on August 15, 1872.
His father, Krishna Dhan Ghose, was a respected physician who, after his
preliminary degree, went to England for further study. Ghose returned the
year before Aurobindo was born with not only a secondary degree but also a
love of England and an atheistic bent. In 1879, Aurobindo was taken with
his two elder brothers to be educated in England. Ghose arranged for them to
board with the Drewetts, cousins of an English friend. He asked that the
boys be given an English education without any contact with Indian or Eastern culture. Mrs. Drewett, a devout Christian, went a step further and did
her best to convert them. Aurobindo remained in England for fourteen years,
supported at first by Ghose, then through scholarships.

Aurobindo was first taught by the Drewetts. In 1884, he was able to be
enrolled in St. Paul's School in London. A prize student, Aurobindo in 1890
went to King's College at the University of Cambridge with a senior classical scholarship. In the same year, he passed the open competition for preparation for the Indian Civil Service. He scored record marks in Greek and
Latin. Praised for his scholarship in those languages, Aurobindo was also
fluent in French. In addition, he taught himself enough German and Italian
that he could study Goethe and Dante in their native tongues. He also wrote
poetry, an avocation that would lead to some published work. Other than
poetry, Aurobindo's only extracurricular activities were general reading and
membership in the Indian Majlis, an association of Indian students at Cambridge. It was in this association that Aurobindo first expressed his desire for
Indian independence.

In 1892, Aurobindo passed the classical tripos examination in the first
division. He did not, though, apply for his B.A. degree. He also completed
the required studies for the Indian Civil Service but failed to pass the riding
exam. It was suggested that his failure was the result of his inability to stay
on the horse, but Aurobindo claimed to have failed expressly by not presenting himself at the test. His reason for doing so was his distaste for an

administrative career. It happened that a representative of the Maharaja of Baroda was visiting London. He was petitioned by friends of Aurobindo, and Aurobindo was offered an appointment in the Baroda service. He left for India in 1893.

Aurobindo began with secretariat work for the maharaja, moved on to a professorship in English, and culminated his career in the service as vice principal of the Baroda College. By the time he had left Baroda, Aurobindo had learned Sanskrit and several modern Indian languages, and he had begun to practice yoga.

Life's Work

At the time of Aurobindo's return to India, the Indian Congress, presided over by moderates, was satisfied with the current state of affairs. At best they would petition the colonial government with suggestions. Dissatisfied with the effect they were having on conditions in India, Aurobindo began political activities in 1902. Prevented from public activity while in the Baroda service, he established contacts during his leaves. His original intent was to establish an armed revolutionary movement that would, if necessary, oust the English. Toward this end he helped organize groups of young men who would acquire military training.

In 1905, with the unrest caused by the Bengal Partition, Aurobindo participated openly in the political scene. He took a year's leave without pay and then, at the end of the year, resigned from the Baroda service. In his political work he met other Indians desiring Indian independence. Most notable among these was Bal Gangadhar Tilak. Eventually, with Tilak and others, Aurobindo formed the Nationalist Party. With Tilak as their leader, they overtook the congress with their demand for *swadeshi*, or India's liberty. Content to remain behind the scenes, Aurobindo concentrated on propaganda. He helped edit the revolutionary paper *Bande Matarum*, which called for a general boycott of English products, an educational system by and for Indians, noncooperation with the English government, and establishment of a parallel Indian government.

Aurobindo eventually moved into the limelight, which resulted in several arrests. Finally, in 1908, he was imprisoned for a year while on trial for sedition. Though acquitted, his and the other leaders' arrests effectively disrupted their movement. Upon his release, Aurobindo found the party organization in disarray. He tried to reorganize but had limited success. In 1910, responding to a spiritual call, Aurobindo retired from political life and went to the French Indian enclave, Pondicherry.

Aurobindo's spiritual life had a gradual growth that was marked by a few specific events. Contrary to the usual method of following a guru, Aurobindo practiced by himself, calling on masters only when he believed that he needed help. He began his practice in 1904. In 1908, feeling stifled, he consulted the guru Vishnu Lele. Following Lele's instructions, after three days of meditation Aurobindo achieved complete silence of the mind, or Nirvana.

The next event that marked Aurobindo's development occurred when he was incarcerated. He spent most of his time reading the *Bhagavad Gita* and the *Upanishads*, and meditating. The realization came to him of spiritual planes above the conscious mind and of the divinity in all levels of existence. It was at this time that the germ for the work that would consume the rest of his life took seed. It was not until 1910 that Aurobindo was told by an inner voice that he was to go to Pondicherry. In Pondicherry, Aurobindo began his work in earnest. His purpose was to cause the manifestation of the divine, via the supermind, into the lower levels of existence, and thus move mankind toward its ultimate evolutionary goal. Aurobindo did not, though, remove himself from the world. He received visitors, continued his reading, and corresponded with disciples and friends.

In 1914, Aurobindo met Paul and Mira Richard. Paul persuaded Aurobindo to write a monthly periodical that would put forth his thinking. This became the *Arya* (1916-1921). In it, some of Aurobindo's major works, *The Life Divine* (1914-1919), *The Synthesis of Yoga* (1915), and *The Human Cycle* (1916-1918), appeared serially. They were later published in book form. Mira Richard came to be Aurobindo's main disciple, then his spiritual partner. She left Pondicherry with Paul in 1915 but returned to stay in 1920. When Aurobindo and Mira met, Mira found the spiritual leader to whom she had been introduced psychically as a youth. She came to be known as the "Mother" and eventually took over the management of Aurobindo's household.

With more time to concentrate on his spiritual task, Aurobindo succeeded in penetrating the veil between the upper and lower planes of consciousness. On November 24, 1926, he accomplished the descent of what he termed the "Overmind." All that remained was for him to bring the final plane via the "Supermind" into the physical, and thus divinize, or transform, life on this plane. That India's independence came on his birthday was significant to Aurobindo: He saw it as an affirmation of his efforts.

Aurobindo, with his task not yet complete, died on December 5, 1950, in Pondicherry. His passing, though, was not like that of the average man; witnessed by outside observers, among whom were doctors, his body remained without decomposition for five days. The Mother announced that Aurobindo had come to her and explained his *mahasamadhi*, or the leaving of his body. Humanity was not ready for the descent of the Supermind because Aurobindo had found too much resistance on this plane. He explained that he would return by manifesting himself in the first person who achieved the Supermind in the physical.

Summary

Sri Aurobindo was a spiritual man driven to serve others. His success in education was largely for the satisfaction of his father. Involvement in politics was his attempt to serve his fellow Indian. He saw that for India to thrive spiritually and physically, Indians would have to throw off the yoke of the English. Aurobindo's retirement was in part the effect of a shift of focus. He no longer saw life in national terms, but universal. The development of what he saw was needed by India for true change was needed by all mankind.

Aurobindo helped organize a movement that ignited a fire in Indians and that led eventually to their independence. His spiritualism has been the subject of many religious and philosophical writings and a few international symposiums. His ashram, or commune, continued to grow after his death, and in 1968 Auroville was founded.

Bibliography

Bolle, Kees W. *The Persistence of Religion*. Leiden, The Netherlands: E. J. Brill, 1965. A study of Tantrism as a vehicle to examine India's religious history, with a chapter of its manifestation in Aurobindo's philosophy. It offers a different perspective of Aurobindo's work in an objective style.

Bruteau, Beatrice. *Worthy Is the World: The Hindu Philosophy of Sri Aurobindo*. Rutherford, N.J.: Fairleigh Dickinson University Press, 1971. A good introduction to Aurobindo's philosophy. It contains an interesting biography of Aurobindo's spiritual life and a good bibliography.

Ghose, Sri Aurobindo. *The Future Evolution of Man*. Compiled by P. B. Saint-Hilaire. Wheaton, Ill.: Theosophical Publishing House, 1974. A compilation of quotations from Aurobindo's three major works, *The Life Divine*, *The Human Cycle*, and *The Synthesis of Yoga*. A good introduction to Aurobindo's works, it contains a summary of the works, a bibliography of other Aurobindo works, and explanatory notes.

_____. *Sri Aurobindo: A Life Sketch*. Calcutta: Arya, 1937. Aurobindo's biography told in his own words in the third person. A brief overview of his life up to his days in Pondicherry.

Purani, A. B. *The Life of Sri Aurobindo*. 3d ed. Pondicherry: Sri Aurobindo Ashram, 1964. Despite its complicated organization and a devoted view, this work is perhaps the most authoritative biography of Aurobindo. It has excellent documentation of Aurobindo's early life and is filled with quotations from Aurobindo.

Radhakrishnan, Sarvepalli, and Charles Moore, eds. *A Sourcebook in Indian Philosophy*. Princeton, N.J.: Princeton University Press, 1957. A good introduction to Indian philosophy, including Aurobindo's contemporaries. It offers insight into Aurobindo's philosophy by way of contrast.

Sethna, K. D. *The Vision and Work of Sri Aurobindo*. Pondicherry: Sri

Aurobindo Ashram, 1968. The first three chapters, in which Sethna debates with a Western philosopher via correspondence, offer a good, clear explication of Aurobindo's philosophy. In later chapters there is a tendency toward proselytism.

Zaehner, R. C. *Evolution in Religion*. Oxford, England: Clarendon Press, 1971. An interesting study comparing Aurobindo and Pierre Teilhard de Chardin, a Jesuit monk. Both of the twentieth century, although they did not know of each other and had little respect for each other's religion, they are nevertheless interestingly compared. Offers a different perspective on Aurobindo's philosophy.

Shawn Hirabayashi

NNAMDI AZIKIWE

Born: November 16, 1904; Zungeru, Nigeria

Areas of Achievement: Government and politics
Contribution: Azikiwe is the father of modern Nigerian nationalism and the leader of Nigeria's independence struggle. He became the first president of the Republic of Nigeria in 1963 and retained that position until ousted during the 1966 coup. He also founded the University of Nigeria at Nsukka and was its first chancellor.

Early Life
Nnamdi Azikiwe was an Ibo who was born in Northern Nigeria and spoke fluent Hausa, the Northern trade language. Fluency in Hausa helped him become a national leader later in life. Azikiwe was educated at the Church Missionary Society's Central School at Onitsha, the Hope Waddell Training Institute in Calabar, and the Methodist Boys' High School in Lagos. While in high school, he read the work of Marcus Garvey. At age sixteen he vowed to redeem Africa. That same year, Kwegyir Aggrey spoke at his school and told the students, "Nothing but the best is good enough for Africa." Since both of Azikiwe's heroes, Garvey and Aggrey, were based in the United States, Azikiwe was determined to go there, acquire an education, and return to uplift Nigeria.

Zik, as he was known to his classmates, was graduated at the head of his high school class in 1925. Without money or backers, he decided to stow away on a ship to get to the United States. He reached Ghana before this plan collapsed. He trained for the police force in Ghana, but his parents asked that he return to Nigeria, and he obeyed. Azikiwe's father opposed his plan to study in the United States but changed his mind when he himself was insulted by a young white clerk who called Azikiwe's father an "uneducated black ape." Azikiwe's father decided that only education would ensure respect for Africans, so he decided to help his son further his education by giving him six hundred dollars.

Once in the United States, Azikiwe was helped by sympathetic Americans. He also earned money from menial jobs to help pay for his education. He remembered reading about Abraham Lincoln and James Garfield working their way up from log cabins to the White House through sacrifice, hard work, and determination. He spent every spare hour reading or playing sports. Azikiwe's first two years of study at Howard University were under American diplomat and future Nobel Peace Prize winner Ralph Bunche. Bunche said that Azikiwe had remarkable mental ability, integrity, courage, industry, and promise. In 1929, Azikiwe attended Lincoln University in Pennsylvania, earning his B.A. by 1930. Azikiwe served as a graduate in-

structor at Lincoln for two years while enrolled in Columbia University's
School of Journalism. Within two years, he had earned an M.A. in political
science from Lincoln University, a certificate in journalism from Columbia
University, and an M.A. in anthropology from the University of Pennsylvania.

While in the United States, Azikiwe gained journalistic experience writing
for the *Baltimore Afro-American*, the *Philadelphia Tribune*, and the *Associated Negro Press* in Chicago. He was awarded two honorary doctorates, a
doctorate of literature from Lincoln and an L.L.D. from Howard University.

Life's Work

In 1934, Azikiwe returned to Africa and became the editor in chief of a
Ghanian newspaper, the *African Morning Post*. Colonial authorities found
one of his articles seditious. He was charged and convicted, though later
acquitted on appeal. In 1937, he returned to Nigeria. He fought against
colonial rule and founded the *West African Pilot* and four other newspapers
in a chain controlled by Zik Enterprises Limited. His businesses were soon
worth more than two million dollars. He used this network of newspapers to
agitate for change. In his editorials he argued for one-person, one-vote,
direct elections, African control of the civil service, and the Nigerianization
of the armed forces. With Herbert Macaulay, he founded the National Convention of Nigeria and the Cameroons, or NCNC, in 1942. His papers
spread his radical political ideals to every corner of Nigeria and helped
increase the membership of the NCNC. The NCNC embraced all Nigerian
tribes and was national in scope. It fought for the working class and for self-
rule. Azikiwe by this time was the undisputed leader of the Ibo and a prominent national leader.

In the teeth of sustained agitation spearheaded by Azikiwe as president of
the NCNC, Great Britain decided to grant Nigeria self-rule in 1951. In the
subsequent elections, Azikiwe was elected to represent Lagos. The Yoruba-
dominated Action Group, under Chief Obafemi Awolowo, won control of
the legislature in the Western Region, where Lagos was located. Azikiwe
became leader of the opposition, but the Action Group blocked his election
to the federal assembly. Bitter rivalry began between the Ibo-controlled
NCNC and the Yoruba-controlled Action Group Party. Ethnic conflicts ultimately led to bloody civil war and caused the deaths of more than one and
a half million people, many of whom where children.

The NCNC controlled the Eastern Region. The British accused Azikiwe of
withdrawing $5.6 million in government funds and putting this money in his
own African Continental Bank to save it from collapse. He was tried and
found guilty of improper conduct. Azikiwe argued that this was merely a
trick to postpone independence. Nigeria's rank and file, as well as the
masses, viewed Azikiwe as their redeemer. Thus, he was able to survive the

crisis and disband the Regional Legislature without difficulty. He called elections, and he and the NCNC were swept into power. He resigned from the Western Legislature and became the Premier of Eastern Nigeria until the 1959 preindependence elections for the federal government were called. None of the major parties contesting this election won a decisive majority. Three parties contested the 1959 elections—the Northern Peoples Congress, the NCNC, and the Action Group. The Northern Peoples Congress won more seats than any other party, followed by the NCNC. These two parties decided to form a coalition government. The Action Group formed the opposition.

Azikiwe was appointed Governor-General of Nigeria and Deputy Leader of the National Peoples Congress. Abubakar Tafawa Balewa became the prime minister. Although Azikiwe often used the threat of communism to speed up independence, his vast business holdings made him favor capitalist development. This was also true of Tafawa Balewa. The fact that both men spoke Hausa drew them close together and strengthened the bond of trust between them. In October, 1963, Nigeria became a republic. It now had both internal self-government and control over its foreign affairs. Azikiwe was appointed President of the Federal Parliament because of his leading role in the independence struggle and his great popularity.

Azikiwe founded the University of Nigeria at Nsukka. This school helped unify Nigeria by expanding a common pattern of education and high levels of literacy in English, which facilitated interethnic movement and understanding. As a result, a homogeneous class of educated Africans would begin to exert considerable influence on the process of modernization and the development of a national identity.

As president, Azikiwe helped write a federal constitution that was the supreme law of the land. He fought against all forms of corruption, favoritism, tribalism, and discrimination. He stated that he wanted to build on the American model, wherein "each one cares enough to share enough so that everyone has enough." In line with this thought, he encouraged the modernization of farming, but here he encountered a serious problem that led to suffering and despair. In 1961, Nigeria's leading earner of foreign exchange was cocoa. Yoruba farmers excelled in cocoa production and were among the most efficient and prosperous cocoa producers on earth. Azikiwe asked them to pay federal taxes on the cocoa that they sold. Many balked at this request and refused to comply. Discontent mounted, and soon the federal government uncovered a plot to overthrow the government. Awolowo of the Action Group was arrested on charges of instigating the coup attempt. He was tried, found guilty, and sentenced to ten years in prison. The Yoruba were incensed that their leader had been jailed. Rioting broke out, and a state of emergency was declared in the Western Region. The Western Region became an area of chronic unrest.

To implement his plan for sharing Nigeria's resources fairly, Azikiwe called for a census. This created problems, as regions padded figures to secure more than their share of the federal budget, so a recount was mandated. Again the same problem arose. The census demonstrated that the North had an absolute majority by itself. Both Southern regions feared that this meant their eternal domination by the North. Most people in the North were Muslim and most Southerners were Christian, so this census created unmanageable tensions. Western missionaries had located most of their schools in the South. This meant that the best-educated people and those most fluent in English were mainly Southerners. Civil service examinations were written in English. Northerners went to Koran school, which emphasized Arabic, which handicapped their students in competitive national exams. The North felt discriminated against and wanted jobs assigned by quotas. Southerners wanted jobs allocated based on competition. If the census was correct, the North would win the argument based upon its numerical strength. Southerners wanted a merit system. Inability to agree on how to conduct a decisive census made sharing Nigeria's wealth problematic and inflamed passions.

The army feared general civil disorder as these problems lingered inconclusively. In 1966, the government was overthrown, and Prime Minister Abubakar Tafawa Balewa and several other prominent officials were assassinated. Azikiwe was out of the country and thus was spared. An Ibo, General Ironsi, led the coup. Since Azikiwe, who was also an Ibo, was the only major political leader spared death, Northerners concluded that the coup was part of an Ibo conspiracy to take over Nigeria and control its wealth for themselves. A general massacre of Ibos living in the North followed. Ibos who could escape streamed home to the Eastern Region of the South.

Azikiwe had long encouraged mineral exploration, and oil was discovered, by coincidence, at this time in the East. Azikiwe asked Ibo leaders to share this wealth with the nation. Ibo leaders such as Colonel Ojukwu were so distressed by the massive killing of Ibo in the North and the inability of the federal government to protect Ibo that they refused to agree to share oil revenue. They seceded instead and formed the state of Biafra. Azikiwe's counsel of calm and reason was ignored, leading to the tragedy of Nigeria's civil war.

Azikiwe isolated himself in his home at Nsukka for part of the war and devoted himself to journalism and writing. His best-known books include *My Odyssey* (1970) and *Liberia in World Politics* (1934). The burning and destruction of the library at the University of Nigeria at Nsukka was a great loss to Azikiwe.

Azikiwe joined the Biafrian government in 1967 and worked abroad to win recognition for it. After several years of carnage, it became clear that secession had failed. From this point on, Azikiwe worked for national reunification and reconciliation. He stayed overseas until 1972, when he returned to assume chancellorship of Lagos University. In 1979, civilian rule was restored and Azikiwe entered the political arena as a presidential candidate. Shehu Shagari won the election and defeated Azikiwe a second time in 1983. The military regime planned to restore civilian rule in 1991, but they have banned all former officeholders from actively seeking election.

Summary

The spirit behind the nationalist mass movement that led to independence, Nnamdi Azikiwe was the major actor in the struggle to gain independence. He embodies the bold, aggressive style of Southern Nigerian leadership. It is said that, as founder of the NCNC, he forged one of the most efficient and effective political machines in Africa. Azikiwe became the first president of the Republic of Nigeria and invited steel and oil companies to help Nigeria develop its resources. Nigeria's oil industry is one enduring monument to his enterprise and foresight.

Expansion of educational opportunities was one of his major goals. He founded the University of Nigeria at Nsukka, extended primary and secondary education, and encouraged Nigerians to seek opportunities abroad. Nigeria has more students studying in the United States than the rest of Africa combined. More than a simple story of rags to riches, Azikiwe's life embodies the ambitions and ideals of modern Africa. His inspiring rise from dusty army barracks to state house has motivated millions to improve their lives.

Bibliography
Azikiwe, Nnamdi. *My Odyssey.* New York: Praeger, 1970. A very detailed account of Azikiwe's genealogy, quest for education, trials, and successes. This book provides excellent insights into the creation of his business empire and of the preindependence struggle.
Candee, Marjorie Dent, ed. *Current Biography Yearbook, 1957.* New York: H. W. Wilson, 1957. This article discusses the machinations of the preindependence struggle. It explains the intrigue and tensions that almost sabotaged Nigeria, as well as Azikiwe's role in cementing unity.
Jones-Quartey, K. A. B. *A Life of Azikiwe.* Baltimore: Penguin Books, 1965. Written by a former student of Azikiwe, this book explains Azikiwe's fascination with Garvey and Aggrey and their significance for Nigeria. Provides a great history of the formation of the NCNC but, being written before 1966, has nothing on either of the coups that have rocked Nigeria or on the civil war.
Lipschutz, Mark, and R. Kent Rasmussen, eds. *Dictionary of African Historical Biography.* 2d ed. Berkeley: University of California Press, 1986. A brief biographical sketch. This work contains a discussion of Azikiwe's

relationship with Herbert Macaulay and a discussion of the origins of the NCNC. Briefly describes Azikiwe's role as father of the struggle for independence.

Lynch, Hollis R. "Azikiwe." In *The McGraw-Hill Encyclopedia of World Biography*, vol. 1. New York: McGraw-Hill, 1973. A brief look at Azikiwe's life up to the date of publication. Includes a bibliography and a photograph of Azikiwe.

Taylor, Sidney, ed. *The New Africans*. New York: G. P. Putnam's Sons, 1967. Excellent discussion of the tension and animosity between Awolowo and Azikiwe. This work suggests that, when one ethnic group dominates control of valued resources in a multiethnic state, the result can be extreme imbalance, exaggerated competition, conflict, and violence.

Dallas L. Browne

LEO BAECK

Born: May 23, 1873; Lissa, Germany
Died: November 2, 1956; London, England
Areas of Achievement: Scholarship, philosophy, and theology
Contribution: Teacher, author, historian of religion, philosophical-theological thinker, and outstanding articulator of modern Judaism, Baeck was the leading rabbi in Germany before World War II and one of the foremost rabbinical scholars of the twentieth century.

Early Life

One of the most important rabbinical scholars of the twentieth century, Leo Baeck was descended from a well-established rabbinical family. He was born in the Prussian town of Lissa (now Leszno, Poland) to Rabbi Samuel Baeck on May 23, 1873. Educated during the German-Jewish renaissance that produced such outstanding Jewish thinkers as Sigmund Freud, Albert Einstein, Franz Kafka, and Martin Buber, Baeck studied for the rabbinate at the conservative Jewish Theological Seminary of Breslau and the University of Breslau, where he read religion, philosophy, and languages. In 1895, he completed the Ph.D. in philosophy at the University of Berlin, where he was a student of Wilhelm Dilthey and Ernst Troeltsch. A Reform Jew, Baeck was ordained at the progressive Academy for the Study of Judaism in Berlin in 1897, where he also studied. A rabbi of the Reform wing of Judaism, he began his ministry in the Silesian town of Opole. In 1907, he moved to Düsseldorf, where his preeminence as a Jewish scholar had already brought him acclaim. In 1912, he was appointed to Oranienburger, the most prominent synagogue in Berlin, where he become the leading rabbi of the capital of Germany.

His scholarship won for him an invitation to teach homiletics and Midrash (interpretative rabbinical literature) at his alma mater, the Academy for the Study of Judaism. Though teaching was a favorite occupation, he declined the title of professor, preferring to be known as rabbi. An assimilated German Jew, he nevertheless remained fully identified with all aspects of Jewish life. His sermons were solemn explorations, painstaking "Dialogues with God," as they have been called. As an army chaplain on the Eastern and Western fronts in the 1914-1918 war, he became a pacifist. He was married and became the father of a daughter who emigrated to England before the war.

Life's Work

Baeck's first major publication was a review article responding to a provocative work by Protestant theologian Adolf von Harnack, *Das Wesen des Christentums* (1900; *What Is Christianity?*, 1901), which depicted Jesus and early Christianity as unrelated to Jewish religious and cultural tradition and

Judaic thought as inferior to Christian belief. Rejecting Harnack's conclusions and scholarship, Baeck stressed Jesus' importance as a profoundly Jewish teacher who revered the traditions of the Prophets. In his magnum opus, *Das Wesen des Judentums* (1905; *The Essence of Judaism*, 1936), Baeck defended the Jewish faith against overt or implied attacks. Basing his work on a profound knowledge of Jewish sources, deep historical knowledge, and neo-Kantian rationalism, Baeck traced the development of Judaism's central concepts—Torah, Talmud, and Halacha—from the Exodus to modern times. Interpreting Judaism as revolutionary and dynamic ethical monotheism, he stressed its development as a response to ethical demands, the categorical "ought" of the divine imperative, on generations of Jews, making Jewish history an ongoing vehicle of continuing revelation. In Judaism, he saw the highest expression of morality with a universal message. While Jewry, he argued, is unique, every people is a mystery, each "a question posed by God."

During the 1920's, Baeck expanded his studies, which led him to greater appreciation of the mystical aspects of Judaism, to which he gave place in a much-revised edition (1922) of his great work. Also in 1922, Baeck published a remarkable essay, *Romantische Religion* (romantic religion), a bold critique of the differences between Christianity and Judaism, which brought the dialogue between the two faiths to greater clarity and intensity. Baeck contrasted Christianity with Judaism, the former characterized as an emotional, sentimental, and "romantic" religion longing for redemption in the next world, the latter as a "classical," rational faith, commanded to work for the improvement of life in this world. Baeck's scholarship brought him to international prominence. During the interwar years, he became head of numerous German-Jewish organizations and was honored by many national German-Jewish groups.

His most outstanding service was rendered as the leader of German Jewry after the National Socialists came to power in 1933. So great was international respect for Baeck that the Nazis hesitated to destroy him. They offered him emigration, but, though he received attractive offers from England and the United States to take a position, he remained with his stricken community.

During the Nazi persecutions, he became the chief spokesperson for Jews in Germany. He was appointed president of the National Agency of German Jews and head of the Jewish Central Committee for Aid and Improvement. In these positions, he faced the arduous task of negotiating with the Nazi government, trying to mitigate the persecution of his people. He presided over efforts at emigration, economic assistance, charity, education, and culture with annual budgets running into millions of dollars. By prudent diplomacy he helped arrange the emigration of more than forty thousand Jews, many of them young people. He devoted his influence and diplomatic skills to defending whatever rights were left to Jews in Nazi Germany, to lessening or delaying Nazi persecution, and to upholding the morale of the beleaguered German-Jewish community. Despite the hostile environment and his many responsibilities, he continued a prodigious scholarship.

On the eve of World War II, Baeck accepted the presidency of the World Union for Progressive Judaism and was appointed as the leader of the newly formed National Organization of the Jews of Germany. Baeck was continuously endangered, arrested and released four times, and repeatedly interrogated by the Gestapo. A week before World War II began, he led a last trainload of children to safety in England, then returned. With the outbreak of the war, he was not heard from and widely feared dead, but the rabbi continued his work. His synagogue had been burned in the 1938 national pogrom, but he continued to hold services, denouncing from the pulpit the modern paganism and idolatry of the state. On one occasion, the police raided his service and sent all congregants less than sixty years of age to work as forced laborers. On the next Sabbath, he continued his services and others came.

In January, 1943, at sixty-nine, Baeck was arrested and sent to the Theresienstadt (Terezin) concentration camp in Czechoslovakia. Although millions died in the Nazi camps, including most of Baeck's family, Baeck miraculously survived. His discipline, inner strength, and vitality came to his rescue. He inspired a certain respect even among his captors, who sometimes acquiesced in his refusal to yield to their demands. In 1944, he was made head of the Council of Elders and became the center of a spiritual resistance against the Nazis. He held illegal services, led secret prayer meetings, and ran extensive educational programs in philosophy and religion, despite a Schutzstaffel (SS) ban punishable by death.

As rabbi, Baeck strengthened thousands of his people and served as pastor to many Christians, interned because of mixed heritage. He became a distributor of food to the sick and dying and ministered to those in despair. He encouraged his people to take consolation in their goodness. When all other rights were taken, he said, some yet remained: the right to be decent, self-respecting, spiritual, cultivated, and Jewish. He encouraged his people not to fear death. Reliably informed of the gassings at Auschwitz, Baeck decided not to tell his fellow inmates. Paul Tillich and others who praised Baeck have criticized him for this silence.

Despite raging typhus and starvation in the camp, Baeck remained sound. His survival seems also the result of providential mistake: In the spring of 1945, a Rabbi Beck of Moravia died, and the SS mistakenly reported Leo Baeck's death to Gestapo Headquarters. Shortly before liberation, Adolf Eichmann discovered the error and told Baeck that it would be rectified. Before that threat was fulfilled, however, the Russians liberated the camp. Baeck was one of fewer than 17,000 survivors of nearly 140,000 Jews sent to Theresienstadt. After two months, he was flown to London, where he settled with his daughter and son-in-law. At the age of seventy-two, the resilient rabbi took up his work again. A hero in the postwar world, he was elected founding president of the Society for Jewish Study, president of the Association of Synagogues in Great Britain, and chair of the World Union for Progressive Judaism.

In 1950, Baeck became a British citizen. He sought to be a voice of reconciliation with Germany, but he thought it no longer possible for Jews to live there and urged them to leave. He became president of the Council for the Protection of the Rights and Interests of Jews from Germany. At the same time, Baeck made it clear that he considered the Nazi government, and not the collective German people, responsible for the destruction of the European Jews, citing numerous acts of German-Christian assistance to Jews under the Nazis. A magnanimous man, Baeck harbored no visible bitterness toward the Germans.

Despite the loss of his personal manuscripts and library of fifteen thousand books, Baeck continued to write and publish. Some of his best works are among his final writings, notably *Die Pharisäer: Ein Kapitel judischer Geschichte* (1934; *The Pharisees, and Other Essays*, 1947), which includes writings suppressed by the Nazis. His final work, the end of forty years of adult experience, is his classic *Dieses Volk: Jüdische Existenz* (two volumes, 1955-1957; *This People Israel: The meaning of Jewish Existence*, 1964), much of which was written on scraps of paper at Theresienstadt. Monumental in scope, it covers three thousand years of Jewish history. In *This People Israel*, he emphasized the essence of Judaism as a dialectical polarity between "mystery" and "command," an eternal "thou shalt," in the form of divine instructions or commands of love and justice emanating from the divine "mystery." He interpreted "commandment" as a discipline that the Jew willingly accepts and that does not permit him to utilize emotion as the chief means of attaining grace. Piety, Baeck believed, is achieved by upholding the obligations that exist between humans, and even ritual observance is directed toward this end.

Baeck regarded the reawakening of national Jewish consciousness as one of the great signs of Jewish renaissance. Though not a Zionist, he was an early supporter of Zionist activities. With Einstein, he wrote a plea in 1948 urging Palestinian Jews and their Arab neighbors to disown the terrorists of both sides and for Jews to focus on a peaceful and democratic basis for Jewish settlement in Palestine.

In the course of his public work, he traveled throughout Europe, the United States, and Israel. He lectured at the new Hebrew University of Jerusalem, and from 1948 to 1953 was a visiting professor of the history of religion at Hebrew Union College in Cincinnati, Ohio. He lectured to audiences across the United States in behalf of Reform Judaism. He had a particular sympathy for the United States and looked there rather than to Israel for the center of Jewish religious vitality. He was received by President Harry S. Truman and, on the anniversary of Abraham Lincoln's birthday, said the prayer before the United States House of Representatives.

The Holocaust did not shake Baeck's conviction that the Jewish encounter with European culture had yielded inestimable Jewish values. He mourned the German-Jewish world that had perished and was particularly anxious that the history of German Jewry and its achievements in Jewish and general cultural life and thought should not be forgotten or falsified. In 1954, when the Council of Jews from Germany established an institute devoted to researching and writing the history of the Jews of German-speaking countries, and especially of the "Jewish renaissance," with offices in London, Jerusalem, and later in New York, it would be named the Leo Baeck Institute, and Baeck became its first president. Though he could not participate fully in its activities, Baeck expressed his full support. Also bearing his name is Leo Baeck College in London, which annually ordains rabbis who serve around the world.

Baeck died in London on November 2, 1956, after a brief illness. His death caused bereavement of Jews around the world, who counted him among their greatest figures. German Jews especially regarded him as a source of profound inspiration and their political leader during the final dark days in Germany.

Summary

Leo Baeck was one of Germany's great articulators of Reform Judaism and equal to the most sophisticated of his contemporaries on the highest level of cultural and philosophical thought. In a climate unfavorable to spiritual values and speculation about the relationship of God, man, and the world, he expounded one of the clearest expositions of liberal Jewish religious thought in the twentieth century. He raised the consciousness of modern Jewry, inspired pride in Jewish heritage, and was a strong voice against the secularizing tendencies among emancipated Jews of the twentieth century. He was the spiritual leader of German Jewry during the Nazi era and a paradigm for German-Jewish courage during the Holocaust. The last representative of a once-great community in the hour of destiny, Baeck embodied the best and perhaps some of the flaws of German Jewry, which placed its hope in German culture and civilization. Now almost a legendary figure, a saint of modern Judaism and the symbol of German Jewry, Baeck lived through the worst epoch in Jewish history with wisdom, magnanimity, and a vibrant soul.

Bibliography

Altman, Alexander. *Leo Baeck and the Jewish Mystical Tradition*. New

York: Leo Baeck Institute, 1973. A careful analysis of Baeck's growing appreciation for the role of mysticism in the Jewish religion and his reconciliation of it with Judaism as a classic, rational faith. Includes bibliographical references.

Baeck, Leo. "A People Stands Before Its God." In *We Survived*, edited by Eric H. Boehm. New Haven, Conn.: Yale University Press, 1949. Reprint. Santa Barbara, Calif.: Clio Press, 1966. An important personal memoir of the Nazi years by Baeck. A major source for some aspects of these years.

Baker, Leonard. *Days of Sorrow and Pain: Leo Baeck and the Berlin Jews.* New York: Macmillan, 1978. A well-written full-scale biography of Baeck that won the 1979 Pulitzer Prize. Illustrated with an extensive bibliography.

Bamberger, Fritz. *Leo Baeck: The Man and the Idea.* New York: Leo Baeck Institute, 1958. An insightful assessment of Baeck's contributions as teacher, thinker, and scholar.

Cohen, Arthur A. *The Natural and the Supernatural Jew: An Historical and Theological Introduction.* New York: Pantheon Books, 1962. A trenchant interpretation of Baeck's *The Essence of Judaism* and *Romantische Religion.*

Friedlander, Albert H. *Leo Baeck: Teacher of Theresienstadt.* New York: Holt, Rinehart and Winston, 1968. An intellectual biography by Baeck's student and disciple in Cincinnati. Treats Baeck's theology and development as a religious thinker from his early life to his relationship with the Nazis. Includes a critical analysis of *The Essence of Judaism* and *This People Israel*, an extensive bibliography, and an index.

Leschnitzer, Adolf. "The Unknown Leo Baeck: 'Teacher of the Congregation.' " *Commentary* 23 (May, 1957): 419-421. A valuable essay on Baeck's character and personal manner by one who worked with him from 1933 to 1939 as chief of the education division of the National Agency of German Jews.

Liebschutz, Hans. "Between Past and Future: Leo Baeck's Historical Position." In *Yearbook: Leo Baeck Institute.* New York: Leo Baeck Institute, 1966. An interpretive essay on Baeck's philosophy and theology by one of the most revered founding fathers of the Leo Baeck Institute.

Walter F. Renn

MIKHAIL BAKHTIN

Born: November 16, 1895; Orel, Russia
Died: March 7, 1975; Moscow, U.S.S.R.
Area of Achievement: Literature
Contribution: Bakhtin had an impact on literary theory, especially on point of view in the novel; on the philosophy and interrelatedness of language and society; on the extension of areas of linguistics and schools of literary theory; and on modern philosophy, presenting an alternative to systems based on Greek philosophers.

Early Life

Mikhail Mikhailovich Bakhtin was born November 16, 1895, in the provincial capital of Orel, Russia. Untitled and unpropertied, he came from a noble family who, like their city, dated back to the late Middle Ages. His father and grandfather were owner and manager, respectively, of state banks. The third of five children, Mikhail was closer to his elder brother Nikolai than to his three sisters or his parents. A German governess taught the boys Greek poetry in German translation.

When Bakhtin was nine years old, the family moved to Vilnius, the Russian-ruled capital of Lithuania. In this multiethnic center, his outlook was broadened even though the schools and church that he attended were Russian. He was influenced by new movements such as Symbolism and by the spirit of revolutionary change. A lifelong process of debate and dialogue was begun between Bakhtin and his brother and with others. Bakhtin's extensive reading included among others Friedrich Nietzsche and Georg Wilhelm Friedrich Hegel. Six years later, Bakhtin's family moved to Odessa, a major city of the Ukraine. Bakhtin attended and finished the school known as the First Gymnasium; he then attended the University of Odessa for one year, studying with the philological faculty. At sixteen, he contracted osteomyelitis.

From 1914 to 1918, Bakhtin attended the University of St. Petersburg, rooming with his brother Nikolai. Of several professors, the most influential was Faddei F. Zelinsky, credited with laying the foundation for Bakhtin's knowledge of philosophy and literature. Bakhtin's graduation in 1918, following Nikolai's departure for the White Army in 1917 and eventual self-exile to England, marked the end of the preparatory stage of his life.

Life's Work

During the years 1918 through 1929, Bakhtin established lifelong friendships with artistic and intellectual people, developed and expressed his own ideas, did extensive work on his own writings, married, and saw his first works published. He became the center of a series of informal groups comprising people from a wide variety of backgrounds, areas of achievement, and political and ideological persuasions. At Nevel, where he and his family moved in 1918, members of the Bakhtin circle included Lev Vasilyevich Pumpiansky, Valentin Nikolayevich Voloshinov, and the musician Maria Veniaminova Yudina. Bakhtin maintained his personal and philosophical commitment to Christianity at a time when all religions were suppressed in the Soviet Union. His first known publication was a two-page article in a local periodical in 1919 entitled *Iskusstvo i otvetstvennost* (art and responsibility). The ideas he expressed in this article were later developed into those of his mature works.

In 1920, Bakhtin moved to nearby Vitebsk, where the circle re-formed and expanded to include new members such as Ivan Ivanovich Sollertinsky and Pavel Nikolayevich Medvedev. In addition to writing and keeping notebooks, Bakhtin taught at Vitebsk Higher Institute of Education and held several other positions. The worsening of his osteomyelitis was complicated by typhoid in 1921, and he was nursed by Elena Aleksandrovna Okolovich; their fifty-year marriage began later that year and ended with her death in 1971.

Bakhtin spent the years 1924 through 1929 in Leningrad, where he lived on a progressively reduced medical pension. His health prohibited public activity, but he was able to meet with members of his circle and to lecture in private apartments. Works published by his friends contained his ideas but their Marxist ideology, thus making them politically acceptable for publication. Opinion varies as to authorship of these collaborative works. Some scholars believe that Bakhtin wrote them in their entirety; some believe that he composed the bulk of these texts, with his friends adding the requisite ideology; others are convinced that the works were actually written by those under whose names they were published, and merely reflect the influence of Bakhtin. One work signed by the scientist Ivan Ivanovich Kanaev questions the claims of vitalism. Of the four works attributed to Medvedev, the best known is *Formal'nyi metod v literaturovedenii: Kriticheskoe vvedenie v sotsiologicheskuyu poetiku* (1928; *The Formal Method in Literary Scholarship*, 1978). One of Voloshinov's seven titles is *Marksizm i filosofiya yazyka* (1929; *Marxism and the Philosophy of Language*, 1973). Only these twelve works are questioned; other books signed by these men are accepted as theirs, thus providing scholars with a basis for comparison.

The year 1929 was a turning point in Bakhtin's life. He was arrested and sentenced to exile in Siberia for ten years for political and religious reasons (he was never tried). Also he published his first major work under his own name (and the first since 1919): *Problemy tvorchestva Dostoevskogo* (expanded to *Problemy poetiki Dostoevskogo*, 1963; *Problems of Dostoevsky's Poetics*, 1973, 1984). Bakhtin's sentence in Siberia was reduced for reasons of health; a good review of his book by the minister of education and the fact that the questioners believed him to be the author of the disputed texts probably also helped his case.

He was allowed to go to Kustanai from 1930 to 1934, traveling without guard and choosing his own work. After a year of unemployment he was employed as an accountant for the local government, later teaching local workers his clerical skills. Here as elsewhere he was well liked. In 1934, he chose to remain for two more years; that same year he published an article based on his observations there.

In 1936, Bakhtin ended his self-exile by moving to Saransk and teaching in the Mordovian Pedagogical Institute. The next year, for political reasons, he moved to Savelovo, about one hundred kilometers from Moscow. In 1938, the first of a series of misfortunes overtook him: His right leg was amputated. An article on satire he was asked to contribute to a literary encyclopedia never appeared because the volume was canceled. As a result of the vicissitudes of wartime, several works by Bakhtin which had been accepted and were awaiting publication did not appear. In 1940, he lectured on the novel at the Gorky Institute in Moscow, writing a dissertation for that institution on François Rabelais, which was published in an expanded version as *Tvorchestvo Fransua Rable i narodnaya kul' tura srednevekov'ya i Renessansa* (1965; *Rabelais and His World*, 1968), a work rivaling *Problems of Dostoevsky's Poetics* in importance. In 1941, he began teaching German in the Savelovo schools while working on yet another important endeavor: articles about the novel, collected and translated in *Voprosy literatury i estetiki* (1975; *The Dialogic Imagination*, 1981), in which he expanded his ideas on polyphonic communication to dialogic communication, which included the self and others or the author, characters, and reader. From 1942 to 1945, he taught Russian in Savelovo.

In 1945, Bakhtin returned to Saransk, where he was promoted to the rank of docent and made department chairman. In 1946, he submitted his dissertation, defending it the following year. The committee compromised and granted him the lesser degree of candidate in 1951, precluding publication at that time. In 1957, he saw his institute become a university. The next year, he was promoted to chairman of the department of Russian and foreign literature at this newly formed institution.

Recognition came slowly. With few publications in his own name, Bakhtin was little known beyond his own circle of friends. Attention to the book on Fyodor Dostoevski marked a change: Vladimir Seduro, an American, mentioned the book in a published work in 1955; the next year, his old antagonist, the Formalist critic Viktor Shklovsky, treated the Dostoevski book in a Soviet work; in 1958, the influential Slavicist Roman Jakobson, a pioneering figure in the application of linguistics to literary study, having mentioned Bakhtin to members of the International Conference of Slavists in 1956, shared preview copies of his review of Shklovsky's book, publishing his review in 1959. Young intellectuals led by Vadim Valerianovich paid Bakhtin homage and pressed for publication of his works. The revised Dostoevski book and the revised dissertation, 1963 and 1965, established his reputation. Other works followed, some posthumously.

Poor health forced both of the Bakhtins to move to Moscow in 1969 and to nearby Grivno in 1970. Bakhtin's wife died of a heart condition in 1971. Bakhtin then moved first to a hotel for writers and in 1972 to his own apartment at 21 Krasnoarmeyskaya Street in Moscow, where he lived and, in spite of osteomyelitis and emphysema, wrote until his death on March 7, 1975. His funeral ceremonies were both civil and religious.

Summary

For much of his life, Mikhail Bakhtin was a relatively obscure figure, though in his last years he attained a measure of fame among literary specialists in the Soviet Union and saw his work begin to appear in the West. In the decade following his death, as previously unpublished works became available and early works were reissued, there was an explosion of interest in Bakhtin, to the extent that he has become one of the most influential literary theorists of the twentieth century.

In part Bakhtin's influence can be attributed to his appeal to critics and readers who value pluralism and cultural diversity. Most of the now widely used terms and concepts which Bakhtin introduced to critical discourse directly reflect his sense of literature as an interplay of voices, of meanings, of languages. "Dialogic" thinking recognizes this multiplicity (or "heteroglossia," as Bakhtin termed it); "monologic" thinking attempts to suppress it. Bakhtin's pluralism and his emphasis on the social context of meaning have made an impact not only on literary studies but also on linguistics, philosophy, theology, and the social sciences.

Bibliography

Berrong, Richard M. *Rabelais and Bakhtin: Popular Culture in "Gargantua and Pantagruel."* Lincoln: University of Nebraska Press, 1986. Reexamines Bakhtin's treatment against the backdrop of Soviet history.

Clark, Katerina, and Michael Holquist. *Mikhail Bakhtin*. Cambridge, Mass.: The Belknap Press of Harvard University Press, 1984. The standard biography and more, it traces the intellectual/political history of Russia and the Soviet Union, discusses primary works, and shares opinions about ideology and authorship. A valuable resource. The bibliography of primary works is helpful.

Kershner, R. B. *Joyce, Bakhtin, and Popular Culture: Chronicles of Disorder*. Chapel Hill: University of North Carolina Press, 1989. Applies Bakhtin's literary theories to the works of James Joyce. Discusses Bakhtin's "dialogism" in a subchapter.

Lachmann, Renate. *Bakhtin and Carnival: Culture as Counter-Culture*. CHS Occasional Papers 14. Minneapolis: University of Minnesota Press, 1987. Treats the idea of carnival in *Rabelais and His World* against the unfolding of Russian history before, during, and since the revolution.

Morson, Gary Saul, ed. *Bakhtin Essays and Dialogues on His Work*. Chicago: University of Chicago Press, 1986. Essays by the editor and others on two topics: language and literature. Extracts of two works by Bakhtin are included.

Morson, Gary Saul, and Caryl Emerson, eds. *Rethinking Bakhtin: Extensions and Challenges*. Evanston, Ill.: Northwestern University Press, 1989. This introduction to Bakhtin treats his life situation, the publishing and republishing of his works, and the disputed texts, arriving at conclusions other than those of Clark and Holquist. Essays by the editors and others develop ideas set forth in the introduction. Translations of Bakhtin's two prefaces to Tolstoy's works are included. A valuable counterpart to Clark and Holquist.

Nordquist, Joan, comp. *Mikhail Bakhtin*. Social Theory: A Bibliographic Series 12. Santa Cruz, Calif.: Reference and Research Services, 1988. An excellent bibliographic tool, more recent and fuller than the bibliography in the book by Clark and Holquist. Includes both primary and secondary works.

Patterson, David. *Literature and Spirit: Essays on Bakhtin and His Contemporaries*. Lexington: University of Kentucky Press, 1988. Essays, all by the author, relate Bakhtin to figures as diverse as Michel Foucault, André Gide, and Martin Heidegger. Patterson agrees with Clark and Holquist on Bakhtin's Christianity.

George W. Van Devender

SURENDRANATH BANERJEA

Born: November 10, 1848; Calcutta, India
Died: August 6, 1925; Barrackpore, near Calcutta, India
Areas of Achievement: Government and politics
Contribution: Banerjea's dedication to moderation in the Indian struggle for
   liberation from Great Britain served as a political focus during some of
   the most dangerous times of modern Indian history. His position as one of
   the most respected Bengali leaders helped to stabilize and concentrate
   Indian protest into the channel of the Congress Party, which was to inherit
   Indian government after independence.

Early Life

Surendranath Banerjea was born in Calcutta, a member of a respected
Brahman family that supported and believed in the British presence in India.
He was educated in local schools until about the age of ten, when he was
sent to English-language schools, including Doveton College. His education
was that of the English middle class, and, by the time he completed his
bachelor of arts degree, Banerjea was fully Westernized. It was agreed to
allow him to travel to England to study for admission to the Indian Civil
Service, although at that time, such travel over water was generally enough
to cost a Brahman caste. Nevertheless, in March, 1868, Banerjea left for
London, where, in 1869, he passed the competitive examination for entry
into the civil service. He was one of the very first Indians to do so. Before he
could be assigned, however, his name was removed from consideration on
the grounds that he was too old. This action on the part of the British
commissioners was viewed by interested Indians as clearly biased, and, as a
result of the uproar, Banerjea sued the commission. He won his suit and was
reinstated, passing the final examinations for appointment in 1871.

Banerjea returned to India in August of that year to take up his post in the
Bengal presidency at Calcutta. In 1873, he passed the departmental examination to become a First Class Magistrate, but, as a result of a clerical error,
his conduct was judged inadequate, and he was summarily dismissed. In
1874, Banerjea returned to England to pursue legal study at the Middle
Temple, but, after satisfying the requirements, he was refused entry to the
bar.

These two episodes in Banerjea's life were both, in the main, the result of
British reluctance to allow Indians to participate in the governance of their
own country. Other Indians of Banerjea's generation faced the same kind of
obstacles with the same results. In Banerjea's case, the obstacles turned his
attention toward public service of another kind. In 1876, he began a career
of public speaking among Bengali students, calling for the unification of all
Indians, appealing for Indian patriotism unrestricted by religion or local

loyalty, and urging that Indians continue to give Great Britain their loyalty and gratitude. As part of his activities he was a founding member of the Indian Association and traveled throughout India speaking on the need for greater Indian self-government within a British context.

In 1877, the Indian Civil Service renewed its attempts to stop Indians from entering the organization, and between May and November of that year Banerjea was especially active. As a result of the many political meetings that Banerjea conducted, a formal Indian protest was issued, and directed, for the first time, to the London government rather than to the government of India. This decisive move placed Banerjea in the center of the growing political activity in India.

Life's Work

In January, 1879, Banerjea became the owner and editor of the weekly journal *Bengalee*, which he developed into the semiofficial publication of the Indian Association. He used its influence to comment on current events which affected relations between the British and Indians. His editorials and reporting increasingly discomfited the British authorities, and the voice of *Bengalee* was only one of many other similarly critical journals.

It was not until the issue of April 28, 1883, that the British took decisive action against Banerjea. *Bengalee* published on that date an article which was very critical of the actions of a justice in the Calcutta High Court; as a result, Banerjea was charged with contempt of court. He was found guilty and sentenced to two months' imprisonment. Immediately, the political activists throughout India rallied in protest, culminating in an open-air meeting of more than twenty thousand held in Calcutta. The money raised for his defense later served as the genesis for the Indian "National Fund," which was used throughout India to address, through rallies and publications, urgent Indian nationalist ideas and issues. This surge in unified political action led directly to the formation of the National Conference, which was the precursor of the National Congress.

The National Congress' second annual meeting in 1885 was the first that Banerjea attended. By the Fifth Congress, he, along with two others, was selected to go to England and speak about the situation in India. The emissaries met with most of the British luminaries of the day, including William Ewart Gladstone, and continued the theme of demanding rights for Indians within the Empire. The mission was generally regarded as successful, and when the group returned in July, 1890, it was to the acclaim of the Indian nationalists.

Still, the British continued to make political errors of governance within India, and, given the temper of the times, each was more bitterly resented than the last. The partition of Bengal Province in 1905 was perhaps the final straw. The British planned to separate the administrative and political functions of the province into those of Eastern Bengal and Assam, which was to be composed of Assam, Dacca, Chittagong, Rajshahi (without Darjeeling), and Malda. The proposal made by then-Viceroy Lord George Curzon was vigorously opposed by Banerjea and the Congress Party, and the discontent it provoked led directly to the Swadeshi and boycott movements. Thus, Banerjea found himself a proponent, not of freedom within the Empire, but of true nationalism and the abolition of British influence entirely. He consistently recommended restraint, and *Bengalee* urged restraint from any kind of lawlessness, but it was becoming obvious that matters within India had passed the point of peaceful coexistence within the imperial structure.

As Indian politics grew more radical, Banerjea found his influence waning. In an attempt to regain his position, he participated in the Bengal Provincial Conference of 1906, at Barisal. Banerjea at that time spoke out in support of the patriotic Indian nationalism that had come to be represented by the shouts of "Bande Mataram," or "The Mother," which swept over the convention. This combination, not unreasonably, alarmed the British government even further.

Still, by 1907 Banerjea was no longer at the forefront of Indian politics. The struggles between "extremists," who saw India's future as one outside of Britain entirely, and "moderates" such as Banerjea, who still believed that India could flourish within a modified form of British government, could no longer be papered over. In that year, Banerjea and the moderates formally split from the extremists and, with Banerjea as chairman, held a separate convention.

This All-India Conference codified everything in which Banerjea had believed since his first return from England. It drew up a completely new constitution for the Indian National Congress that rested firmly on the ideas of gradual reform and evolution of Indian political affairs to the point where the majority of positions would be held by Indians and yet insisted that all such change would remain within the framework of the British Empire. To the degree that the formal split between the two groups was confined by the formalities of the two conferences, it may be said with reason that Banerjea and his moderates defused an increasingly dangerous political situation for a time. The moderates were never in the position of representing the majority of Indian opinion, and Banerjea himself had come to represent retrograde political beliefs.

British political attitudes toward the government of India had also been changing during the early 1900's. The adoption of the "Minto Reforms" in 1909 seemed to represent a compromise between the imperialists, who believed India should always be governed as it had been governed, and the liberals, who with some foresight believed that concessions toward participation by Indians within government were necessary. The reforms were embraced with enthusiasm by Banerjea and his wing of Indian political activists. As part of his appreciation for them, during his speech at the Imperial Press Conference, which he attended in 1909 on behalf of the Indian press, he publicly thanked Lord Gilbert Minto. This loyalty did not go unremarked in England, nor in India.

In 1913, Banerjea was elected to the Bengal Legislative Council and to the Imperial Legislative Council. These bodies were, however, the type of bodies that the advocates of complete Indian self-government most deplored. His tenure lasted until 1916, and it was during this period that he was at his most outspoken in opposition to the home rule advocates who were attempting to form their own association through congress. He was successful in resisting the formal association, but it was to be the last success of that nature in excluding the self-government representatives from positions within the party. By 1916, these representatives, including Mahatma Gandhi, Chandra Pal, and Annie Besant, had effectively taken control of the party that Banerjea had been instrumental in creating.

Still, the British were appreciative of Banerjea's efforts to maintain a balance for India within the Empire. In 1921, he was knighted and appointed Minister of Local Self-Government—unfortunately for his position within Indian politics, the appointment came at the very time that the "non-Cooperators," or self-rule proponents, were personally renouncing such honorifics and resigning from such legislative councils as a mark of their dissatisfaction. In accepting the honors, Banerjea received an enormous amount of opprobrium, and his reputation did not recover. The final humiliation came in November of 1923, when Banerjea was defeated for the Bengal Legislature by Bidhan Chandra Roy, a "Swarajist" (self-government) candidate, little known by the populace.

Summary

Surendranath Banerjea had both the fortune and the misfortune to live through the most volatile period of modern Indian politics without ever changing the political opinions he had formed as a young man. His admiration for the British Liberal tradition remained firm throughout his life, and he acted on it in the best way he could. During his youth, he had the audacity to demand full privileges with the Empire as a citizen of the Empire, and he continued to believe that that position was a profoundly important one. He was unable, however, to recognize that the mood of India and of the Empire itself had altered dramatically, nor was he able to work effectively with representatives who more fully understood that change.

When Banerjea was elected unopposed in 1920 from the Barrackpore subdivision, he believed it was a tribute to his political position—indeed, such a triumph was almost unprecedented. By subsequently accepting the ministry from Bengal's Governor Lord Ronaldshay, he placed himself firmly on the losing side of Indian political life and, thus placed, was unable to reassume his former position.

Banerjea is best viewed as a "bridge" between the traditional roles that Indians had accepted under the British and the "Non-Cooperatives," who came to be accepted as the future of India. In that sense, his early political and personal bravery in opposing British bigotry was remarkable. If, in later years, he made errors of judgment, he did so only because he refused to change the commitments to moderation and belief in the system he had made as a young man.

Bibliography

Argov, Daniel. *Moderates and Extremists in the Indian Nationalist Movement, 1883-1920, with Special Reference to Surendranath Banerjea and Lajpat Rai*. New York: Asia Publishing, 1967. One of the very few scholarly examinations of Banerjea's life, although Argov draws very heavily on Banerjea's autobiography. Its meticulous detail and analysis make it ideal for more thorough investigation of Banerjea's life in comparison to his opponents.

Banerjea, Sir Surendranath. *A Nation in the Making: Being the Reminiscences of Fifty Years of Public Life*. London: Oxford University Press, 1925. Banerjea's calm self-appraisal of his own life, detailing the turning points and mistakes as he saw them. The old-fashioned presentation is balanced by the extreme precision and detail about virtually every incident that occurred and every individual whom he met.

Chintamani, Sir C. Yajneswara. *Indian Politics Since the Mutiny*. Allahabad: Kitabistan Press, 1937. A clear presentation by this leading Indian political philosopher of the development of the Congress Party, antipartition and Non-Cooperation during 1919-1935. Chintamani devotes considerable attention to Banerjea and his pivotal role within the party.

Desai, A. R. *The Social Background of Indian Nationalism*. London: Oxford University Press, 1948. Discusses the economic importance of Banerjea to modern India, while examining the role of the Indian press in the nationalist movement. Desai particularly emphasizes Banerjea's influence on the propagation of "moral values" as part of the movement.

Philips, C. H., and Mary Doreen Wainwright, eds. *Indian Society and the Beginnings of Modernization, Circa 1830-1850*. London: School of Oriental and African Studies, 1976. A collection of articles that provide a useful background to understanding Banerjea's early influences and surroundings. J. F. Hilliker's "The Creation of a Middle Class as a Goal of Educational Policy in Bengal, 1833-1854," while very scholarly, is extremely helpful in seeing how the Indian middle class embraced Anglophilia in their lives and education.

A. J. Plotke

CHRISTIAAN BARNARD

Born: November 8, 1922; Beaufort West, South Africa

Area of Achievement: Medicine

Contribution: Barnard performed the first successful human-heart transplant on December 3, 1967, followed by his second successful heart transplant on January 2, 1968. His success opened the door for a renewed and prolonged life for many victims of heart disease and brought forth showers of applause upon South Africa.

Early Life

Christiaan Neethling Barnard was born on November 8, 1922, in Beaufort West, South Africa. His family was of Afrikaner descent. Christiaan's father, a minister, earned little money, and the family lived on the edge of poverty. Christiaan, however, enjoyed a carefree childhood and a happy family life. He often went on nature hikes with his father, who taught him the names of the trees, the wildflowers, and the plants. His mother was a very determined woman, who insisted that her sons be first in school and never admit defeat. During his high school years, Barnard was usually first in his class. By the end of his senior year in high school, still first in his studies, he was chosen by his class to give the farewell address, and, as a cadet, held the highest student rank of sergeant-major. Outside school, he formed a popular musical trio. Upon graduation Barnard left for Cape Town to study at the university there, hoping to enter the field of medicine. In Cape Town, he stayed with his brother and his wife.

Life's Work

Barnard was graduated with honors from the university and then earned two higher degrees at the University of Minnesota. Between 1953 and 1955, he studied under Owen H. Wangensteen, who described Barnard as a man with a singleness of purpose. Barnard demonstrated this when he operated on forty-nine dogs before he achieved success in an attempt to learn about an intestinal abnormality in the newborn. In three years, he completed the master of science and Ph.D. degrees in surgery.

Upon returning to Cape Town, Barnard continued his transplant research while he practiced heart surgery and supported a family. Having read about the Soviet experimentation with transplantation of a dog's head, he performed two such operations himself. He filmed the operations and took the films to Moscow, where he hoped to learn more about transplantation. He later spent time at the Medical College of Virginia.

Prior to his first successful human-heart transplant, Barnard and another brother, Marius, had performed some fifty unsuccessful experimental heart transplants in dogs in their attempt to develop a successful technique. This search for a successful heart-transplant technique was part of a worldwide ten-year study of heart transplants. The groundbreaking experimentation that led to Barnard's successful operation was performed in 1960 by Norman E. Shumway of Stanford Medical Center in Palo Alto, California. James D. Hardy of the University of Mississippi Medical Center attempted a heart transplant from a chimpanzee to a man dying of heart failure in 1964. Since then, several researchers, including Richard Laver of the Medical College of Virginia, David Blumanstock of the Mary Imogene Bassett Hospital in Cooperstown, New York, and William Likoff of Philadelphia's Hahnemann Medical College and Hospital, were ready to perform human-heart transplants at the first opportunity.

Louis Washkansky was a fifty-five-year-old wholesale grocer, who had suffered two heart attacks in a seven-year period. His diseased heart was twice the normal size and was not getting enough blood through clogged and closed coronary arteries. He also had diabetes, for which he had been taking insulin. His liver was enlarged, and increasingly his body was becoming edematous. Washkansky's doctor predicted that his patient had only weeks to live.

On November 10, 1967, Barnard consulted with Washkansky and told him about the heart-transplant technique. Washkansky agreed to the operation and signed the consent form. Barnard called in his team of thirty women and men, and they remained on a twenty-four-hour alert until a suitable donor was found.

In December, a donor was found, a woman who had been hit by a speeding car. Barnard was notified, and after obtaining consent from the victim's father, Barnard's team went to work. A team of doctors matched the blood types of Washkansky and the victim, Denise Darvall, and found them to be compatible. The transplant proceeded before the pathologist could match the white cells of the two patients to estimate how strong a rejection reaction Washkansky's system would mount against the foreign protein of the transplanted heart. Barnard cut eight blood vessels and several ligaments to free the donor heart. He then moved to an adjacent operating room to continue with the surgery. The procedure took five hours. An hour later, Washkansky regained consciousness and attempted to speak. Thirty-six hours after he awakened, he ate a typical hospital meal and soon showed improvement. He was given antibiotics to guard against infection. His heart rate soon slowed to one hundred beats per minute and his liver shrank to near-normal size. His kidneys worked so well that he lost twenty pounds of edema fluid. Washkansky died eighteen days later as a result of double pneumonia, contracted because his immune system was weakened by drugs administered to suppress rejection of his heart. By this time, Barnard had already chosen Philip Blaiberg to receive the second heart transplant. The second successful heart transplant took place on January 2, 1968, on the fifty-eight-year-old dentist.

While on a triumphal tour of the United States between the two operations, ethical questions were raised. How can one be certain that doctors would do everything to save a person's life after an accident or disease if they are considering the possible donation of organs? Marius Barnard noted that his brother had insisted that they wait to see if Darvall would survive. On his second tour of the United States, Barnard said that he followed the Hippocratic oath—"that the physician must do everything in his power to save life, to restore health, and at the very least to alleviate suffering." In the case of Washkansky, he said, life was not saved; in the case of Blaiberg, however, suffering was alleviated. Marius claimed that three criteria were used to determine death. A patient is considered dead, he said, "when the heart is no longer working, the lungs are no longer working and there are no longer any complexes" on the EEG (electroencephalogram). Another ethical question raised regarding heart transplants was, Who would decide which person should receive the donor heart if there is more than one candidate? Barnard saw no problem with this issue: The person with the most urgent need for the heart would receive it.

Summary

Christiaan Barnard's accomplishments were a milestone in medical science and in the organ-transplant field. His success was a part of the ongoing process in renewing and prolonging life. The first successful organ transplant, involving the cornea, took place in 1905. By the 1950's, doctors at Boston's Peter Bent Brigham Hospital were successfully transplanting kidneys between identical twins. By the middle of the 1960's, doctors in Colorado and Minnesota were transplanting, with success, human livers and the pancreas with duodenum attached.

In the 1960's, at least 500,000 Americans needed heart transplants, but there were not 500,000 heart donors. Michael E. DeBakey insisted that the ultimate solution was a completely artificial heart. Indeed, he and C. Walton Lillehei were already experimenting with artificial hearts. The National Institute of Health decided in 1963 that the eventual remedy for incurable heart disease would be in a complete artificial heart. Since that achievement was years away, however, human-heart transplants would be a valuable intermediate stage. Barnard predicted that the supply of heart donors would increase once the public was sufficiently educated on the subject.

Bibliography

Barnard, Christiaan. "A Human Cardiac Transplant: An Interim Report of a Successful Operation Performed at Groote Shuur Hospital." *South African Medical Journal* 41 (1967): 1271. Gives a description of the heart-transplant procedure. Discusses the circumstances of the donor and recipient of the first successful heart transplant. Lessons learned from the transplant on Washkansky are discussed.

Barnard, Christiaan, and Curtis Bill Pepper. *Christiaan Barnard: One Life*. Toronto: Collier-Macmillan Canada, 1969. Early accounts of Barnard's childhood years through his university studies are related. Conveys the drama of his first heart transplant and ends with Washkansky's death.

Beck, W., Christiaan Barnard, and V. Schrvie. "Hymodynamic Studies in Two Long-term Survivors of Heart Transplants." *Journal of Thoracic and Cardiovascular Surgery* 62 (1971): 315-320. Provides a detailed comparative study of survivors of the procedure. Cardiovascular measurements are reported to demonstrate that the transplanted heart can function at a level necessary to sustain life and can withstand various stresses.

Braunwald, Eugene, ed. *Heart Disease: A Textbook of Cardiovascular Medicine*. Philadephia: W. B. Saunders, 1980. Contains a summary of the understanding of heart disease in a comprehensive textbook. Explanations are given for the abandonment of the cardiac-transplantation procedure by 1979.

Cree, Ian Campbell. "Transplantation: Past, Present, and Future." *New York State Journal of Medicine*, 1969: 285-295. Contains a discussion of the progress in the field of transplants. It begins with the first human transplant of teeth and it continues with a detailed discussion on the transplant-rejection phenomenon. The status of using animal donors for human recipients is reviewed.

Kiley, Dennis. *South Africa*. London: B. T. Batsford, 1976. A detailed description of the geography and of race relations among the people of the different regions is given.

Lower, Richard R. "Is Heart Transplantation a Realistic Approach to Inoperable Heart Disease?" In *Controversies in Cardiology*, edited by Eliot Corday. Philadelphia: F. A. Davis, 1977. Explains why this procedure is useful only for a limited number of patients. Of the 282 cardiac transplants performed by 1975, only forty-nine patients were alive in 1977. The Stanford University team has demonstrated that totally disabled and terminally ill patients can make a spectacular recovery following this operation and achieve full rehabilitation.

Bill Manikas

KARL BARTH

Born: May 10, 1886; Basel, Switzerland
Died: December 10, 1968; Basel, Switzerland
Areas of Achievement: Religion and theology
Contribution: Acclaimed by many as the dominant theologian of the twentieth century, Barth was a Swiss Reformed pastor, professor, and writer best known for his critique of nineteenth century Protestant liberal theology.

Early Life

The eldest son of Johann Friedrich (Fritz) and Anna Katharina Barth, Karl Barth was born on May 10, 1886, in Basel, Switzerland. Both of Barth's grandfathers were ministers within the Swiss Reformed church. His father, also an ordained minister, was at the time of Karl's birth a teacher in the Evangelical School of Preachers in Basel. This conservative seminary had been founded about ten years earlier to counter the influence of Protestant liberal theology which was predominant in most of the larger European universities.

When Karl was three years old, his father accepted a position as a lecturer and subsequently as a professor of church history and the New Testament at the University of Bern. The academic environment of Bern, coupled with the conservative religious training within the Barth household, exerted considerable influence upon Karl and his siblings. From his father, Karl acquired a love for history and politics, a seriousness about study, and an appreciation for the arts, especially music. On the eve of his confirmation, Karl "boldly resolved to become a theologian." Two of his younger brothers also followed their father into academic pursuits—Peter, as an editor of a critical edition of the works of John Calvin, and Heinrich, as a philosopher who many years later taught with his brother Karl on the faculty of the University of Basel.

Young Barth began his university studies at Bern. While receiving a solid grounding in Reformed theology, he also became intrigued with the theoretical and practical philosophy of Immanuel Kant and the liberal theology of Friedrich Schleiermacher. His enthusiasm for learning made Barth anxious to continue his studies with Wilhelm Herrmann of Marburg, the leading neo-Kantian theologian of the day. In deference to his father's wish for him to remain within a more conservative academic environment, Barth postponed his matriculation at Marburg. Barth spent the following year at the University of Berlin, where he studied with the renowned church historian Adolf von Harnack; the next summer at school back in Bern; and a second year at the University of Tübingen under the tutelage of the conservative New Testament theologian Adolf Schlatter. Finally, in 1908 Barth was enrolled as a student of Herrmann at Marburg. From Herrmann, Barth learned to define faith in terms of "inner experience" which has its "ground" in the "inner life of Jesus" and is awakened in human consciousness by the influence of the Jesus of history. Three semesters later, Barth completed his formal course work, passed the theological examinations set by the Church at Bern, and was ordained. Barth never pursued doctoral studies in theology.

Life's Work

Upon ordination in 1909, Barth returned to Marburg to become an assistant editor of *Die christliche Welt* (the Christian world), a liberal periodical that concentrated upon the church's responsibility in the world. Later that year, Barth accepted a call as an apprentice pastor of a Reformed church in Geneva. At this time, Barth published an article in which he noted that theological graduates of liberal seminaries such as Marburg and Heidelberg were more reluctant to enter into practical pastoral work than were graduates of the more orthodox and pietistic institutions. Barth attributed this to the two central emphases of liberal theology: "religious individualism," which concentrated upon the subjective and personal experience of the individual Christian, and "historical relativism," which postulated that there were no absolutes in history or religion. Although still a devotee of the Protestant liberalism into which he was trained, Barth, even at this young age, was voicing a concern that contemporary Christian thought was in danger of becoming more anthropology than theology and was more a product of modern individualistic bourgeois idealism than of sound New Testament scholarship.

Between 1911 and 1921, Barth served as a pastor in Safenwil, Switzerland. It was during this pastorate that his theology underwent a gradual reorientation. The practical tasks of preparing sermons that integrated the content of the Bible with human concerns; the renewal of a friendship with Eduard Thurneysen, a neighboring pastor who seemed to have discovered the eschatologism of Christianity; and a growing appreciation for the existentialism of Søren Kierkegaard together contributed to Barth's intellectual metamorphosis. World events of the decade also influenced his theological persuasions. Following the outbreak of World War I, for example, Barth was dismayed when ninety-three scholars and artists—including his own teachers Harnack and Herrmann—signed a manifesto that supported the war policy of Kaiser Wilhelm. To Barth, this action called into question his mentors' understanding of the Bible, history, and dogmatics. Furthermore, when workers in his local parish were involved in a struggle to achieve a just wage, Barth was compelled to turn his attention to social issues. Newly sensitized to the misery and exploitative conditions of his parishioners, Barth declared himself a Christian Socialist and in 1915 joined the Social Democratic Party—an extraordinary action for a minister in that day. During this decade of disillusionment, Barth came to doubt the progressive notions of human grandeur and inevitable progress.

The work that catapulted Barth into the limelight of theological controversy was *Der Römerbrief* (*The Epistle to the Romans*, 1933), originally written in 1918, published in 1919, then radically revised and reissued in 1922. Barth's aim differed from that of other scholars of his day. While Barth did not reject the methods of biblical criticism (as conservative scholars did), he did denounce the value of commentaries that had no higher goal than to reconstruct the history of the biblical period. Barth's object, in contrast, was to let the Apostolic message of Paul's letter to the Romans break with full force upon the present age. This message, according to Barth, was in violent contradiction to the optimistic spirit of nineteenth century liberalism, which presupposed an inner continuity between the divine and the "best" of human culture. The theme of Romans, Barth insisted, is "the infinite qualitative distinction" between time and eternity, or between human and God. Thus, against liberalism's willingness to allow God and humankind to coalesce, Barth injected the demand: "Let God be God!" Although this work was more critical than constructive, Barth's concept that religion itself is under divine judgment and is a human rather than strictly a divine phenomenon had a great impact upon the future direction of Protestant thought.

On the basis of *The Epistle to the Romans*, Barth was invited to teach Reformed theology at the University of Göttingen. Leaving the pastorate for the teaching profession, Barth launched his academic career. In 1925, Barth left Göttingen to become a professor of dogmatics and New Testament exegesis at the University of Münster in Westphalia, a position he held until 1930. His publications during this period included *Die christliche Dogmatik im Entwurf* (1927; *Dogmatics in Outline*, 1949), a historically significant work because it revealed the early shape of Barth's systematic theological thinking. In this work, Barth rejected both anthropocentric and natural theology in favor of a theology grounded solely in the Word of God. For Barth, the proper subject of Christian theology is the Word of God, not the faith experience of the individual believer.

In 1930, Barth accepted a professorship at the University of Bonn. While at Bonn, Barth and his lifelong friend Thurneysen established a theological journal entitled *Theologische Existenz heute* (theological existence today). In this periodical, Barth and his associates expressed their vehement opposition to Adolf Hitler and the "German Christians" who advocated a synthesis of German National Socialism and the gospel. Barth attracted the attention of the Nazi authorities in 1934 when he wrote the famous Barmen Confession, which called Christians to obedience to Jesus Christ alone "in life and death." Later, after he refused to begin his classes in Bonn with the customary "Heil Hitler!" and to take an unconditional oath of loyalty to the Führer, he was dismissed from his teaching post and expelled from Germany. Fleeing to his original home in Basel, Barth joined the faculty at the University of Basel in 1935 and remained there until his retirement in 1962. Barth continued lecturing and writing until his death in 1968.

An indefatigable worker and prolific writer, Barth produced more than five hundred books, articles, sermons, and papers during the course of his long and illustrious career. His magnum opus, *Die kirchliche Dogmatik (Church Dogmatics*, 1936-1969, 1975), the first volume of which appeared in 1932, grew to thirteen large books totaling more than nine thousand pages in German. Barth originally designed the mammoth project as a five-volume work, although the sheer length of his study necessitated subdividing each of the sections into part-volumes. It is impossible to reduce the breadth of his theology to a few meager structural principles. It is sufficient to say that Barth's emphasis remained singularly Christocentric. His system rested upon the principle that theological understanding of any subject is fully dependent on the relationship of that subject with the Word as revealed solely in Jesus Christ.

Summary

Karl Barth's bold commentary on Paul's letter to the Romans was, in the words of a noted Roman Catholic divine, "a bombshell in the playground of the theologians." This critique of the "subjectivism" within Protestant theology was Barth's first of many statements that pointed to the dangers of allowing theology to become an ideology—that is, a creation of human culture. To Barth, liberal attempts to formulate a "reasonable Christianity" destroyed the validity of the concept of divine revelation (which, Barth insisted, was God-manifested and owed nothing to human initiatives) and weakened the prophetic function of the Church by allowing it simply to reflect rather than to critique human culture. Barth later said that in writing this book he was like the man in a dark church tower who accidentally tripped and caught hold of the bell rope to steady himself and, in doing so, alarmed the whole community. Indeed, this commentary—written to help the author clarify his own thinking—ignited a debate that significantly altered the course of twentieth century theology.

From this first book to the Theological Declaration of Barmen to his massive *Church Dogmatics*, Barth wrote with boldness and theological insight, perpetually calling the Christian church back to the Bible and to its foundation in Jesus Christ. His impact has been great, in part because he provided an outline for a theology that was thoroughly biblical, without being fundamentalist. Described by Pope Pius XII as the greatest theologian since Thomas Aquinas, Barth has been acclaimed by Catholics and Protestants alike as a "modern Church Father" who stands prominently with Saint Athanasius, Saint Augustine, and John Calvin as a defender of the transcendence and sovereignty of God.

Bibliography

Balthasar, Hans Urs Von. *The Theology of Karl Barth*. Translated by John Drury. New York: Holt, Rinehart and Winston, 1971. The best single-volume interpretation and critique of Barth's method and theology by a Roman Catholic scholar.

Barth, Karl. *Church Dogmatics: A Selection*. Introduction by Helmut Gollwitzer. Edited and translated by G. W. Bromiley. New York: Harper & Row, 1962. Selections from the thirteen part-volumes of Barth's *Church Dogmatics*. A useful introduction to the writings of Barth.

Busch, Eberhard. *Karl Barth: His Life from Letters and Autobiographical Texts*. Translated by John Bowden. Philadelphia: Fortress Press, 1976. The best and most authoritative biography of Barth. Highly recommended.

Hunsinger, George, ed. *Karl Barth and Radical Politics*. Philadelphia: Westminster Press, 1976. A collection of essays that assess Barth's relationship with radical politics. Of particular interest is Friedrich-Wilhelm Marquardt's article "Socialism in the Theology of Karl Barth," which argues that the *initium* of Barth's theology was his encounter with social struggle and socialist praxis while he was a pastor in Safenwil.

Jüngel, Eberhard. *Karl Barth: A Theological Legacy*. Translated by Garrett E. Paul. Philadelphia: Westminster Press, 1986. A lucid and readable English translation of essays by Jüngel, a scholar who served as an assistant for one of the volumes of *Church Dogmatics*. This is a sympathetic yet scholarly introduction to the major themes in Barth's theology: the otherness of God, the humanity of God, gospel, and law. Includes endnotes and a selected bibliography of the works of Barth.

Mueller, David L. *Karl Barth*. Waco, Tex.: Word Books, 1975. In Word Books' Makers of the Modern Theological Mind Series. A useful introduction to the life and thought of Barth, written by a professor of theology at the Southern Baptist Theological Seminary in Louisville.

Torrance, Thomas F. *Karl Barth: An Introduction to His Early Theology, 1910-1931*. London: SCM Press, 1962. An excellent discussion of Barth's controversial *The Epistle to the Romans* by one of the leading Barthian scholars. Includes a useful bibliography of Barth's works.

Terry D. Bilhartz

ROLAND BARTHES

Born: November 12, 1915; Cherbourg, France
Died: March 26, 1980; Paris, France
Areas of Achievement: Literature, language, and linguistics
Contribution: Barthes was one of the most important literary critics of the
  twentieth century, and he made significant contributions to semiology.

Early Life

Roland Barthes was born into the heart of the French bourgeoisie of Cherbourg on November 12, 1915. His father died in a World War I battle in
1916, leaving the family in reduced circumstances, although the mother
learned the trade of bookbinding and kept the household together for the
family. Roland's early brilliance at the *lycée* pointed to a career in the high
academic circles reserved for graduates of the École Normale Supérieure;
however, he contracted tuberculosis in 1941 and was forced to attend a
lesser institution, the Sorbonne. In 1937, he was declared unfit for military
service because of his illness, and he taught from 1939 to 1941 in *lycées* in
Biarritz and Paris. He was, however, forced to abandon teaching when the
tuberculosis flared up again, and he spent the war years in a Swiss sanatorium. After the war, he taught in Romania and Egypt before returning to
France. During this period, he became further acquainted with literary criticism and linguistics and produced his first important book, *Le Degré zéro de
l'écriture* (1953; *Writing Degree Zero*, 1967).

Life's Work

The distinguishing mark of Barthes's career was his refusal to be confined
to one field of study, one critical position, or one group. He continually
sought new areas to investigate after having made significant contributions to
areas such as linguistics or semiology. Some have accused him of not developing or testing insights or breakthroughs he made; he has left it to others to
complete systems in which he made seminal contributions. This refusal to be
restricted to one position in a period of ideological rigidity is very attractive.
A new work from Roland Barthes was always a new starting point for fresh
investigations and never a mere recovering of old ground.

Through the 1940's and 1950's, Barthes worked in a branch of the French
cultural service dealing with teaching abroad, and he was given a scholarship
to study lexicology in 1950; however, he used that time to write his first
books in the field of literary criticism. *Writing Degree Zero* is a Marxist
rewriting of French literary history that was influenced by Jean-Paul Sartre
and is, in part, an answer to Sartre's *Qu'est-ce que la littérature?* (1947;
What Is Literature?, 1949). Barthes was associated until the late 1970's with
the journal *Tel Quel*, which stood for a more formal approach to literary

works. In his first book, Barthes identifies two distinct periods of French literature. The first (or classical) runs from 1650, when the writers of that time began to see the "literariness" of language, to 1848, the year of revolution in all of Europe. The second period (or modern) began in the revolution and continues to the present; it is marked not by the representational mode of the early period but by a questioning and experimental type of literature. Later, in *S/Z* (1970; English translation, 1974), Barthes defined two types of literary writing: the readerly (or the representational) and the writerly (the experimental). In this respect, he was the champion of the new, avant-garde literature. He was a supporter of the experiments of Alain Robbe-Grillet in the novel and defended him against received critical opinion. In *S/Z*, Barthes created a critical context in which these new writers could be discussed and understood.

Michelet par lui-meme (1954; *Michelet*, 1986) and *Sur Racine* (1963; *On Racine*, 1964) show Barthes moving away from the Marxism of Sartre to seeing a literary work as a system with codes or rules for functioning. In the book on Michelet, Barthes used many of the concepts of phenomenology in which the writer's ideology is ignored, and instead Barthes discovered in Michelet the use of opposing substances, such as warm and dry. These substances show the "existential thematics" of Michelet; Michelet's thought is dismissed as of no interest. *On Racine* is more consciously structuralist and psychoanalytic, as Barthes examines the conflict between authority and the "primal horde." Barthes ignored the usual academic and historical view of the work in order to reveal its structure as composed of interior and exterior "spaces." His irreverent treatment of the most sacred of French classics engendered a challenge from the academic world. Raymond Picard accused Barthes and his criticism of being a fraud, and Barthes replied with a defense of the new criticism that won the day. Barthes has consistently opposed a merely academic view of literature. Ironically, as a result of the notoriety of the Racine book and his innovative work, Barthes was appointed to teach at an academic institution, although it was not one of the first rank. He became a full-time teacher at the École Pratique des Hautes Études in 1962.

Mythologies (1957; English translation, 1972) shows another side of Barthes; he is in this book a semiologist examining the signs and signifiers found in popular culture as well as in literature. For example, Barthes examines wrestling as a system in which spectacle outweighs sport. In a similar fashion, striptease is seen as a sport that is "nationalized" and expresses the essence of the French. The aim of the book is demystification, to show that assumptions about a practice or institution as being natural are false; they are instead strictly structured codes of culture. The book also tends to treat serious subjects in a playful way and trivial ones with great seriousness in an amusing and enlightening manner.

Mythologies was very popular, but once more Barthes refused to repeat or develop a successful mode. Next Barthes was to be a structuralist, and it is in this capacity that his greatest works were written. In *Essais critiques* (1964; *Critical Essays*, 1972), he defined structuralism as an "activity," not as a system. Its primary tools were the binary oppositions of Ferdinand de Saussure's linguistics, especially the opposition of the diachronic and synchronic and of *langue* (the language as a whole) and *parole* (the individual utterance). Perhaps the most thoroughgoing structuralist work Barthes produced is *S/Z*, in which he analyzed a story by Honoré de Balzac, "Sarrasine," in exhaustive detail. Barthes divides the analysis into codes: There is the proairetic code, which deals with plot; the hermeneutic code, which deals with suspense and enigmas; the semic code, which deals with character and other stereotypes; the symbolic code, which takes the reader from literal details to the level of symbolism; and the referential code, which deals with social and cultural aspects of the work. It is a monumental dissection of one short story, and the commentary tends to swamp the text. It does show how various types of critical apparatus can be applied to a specific literary work, but they remain fragments, as Barthes refused to combine the codes into a unified system. Some critics have seen in this refusal the seeds of poststructuralism or deconstruction. The book takes structuralism as far as it can go in revealing the "system" of a work, but it remains tantalizingly incomplete.

Barthes turned from structuralism to what is the key element of his later work, feeling. *Le Plaisir du texte* (1973; *The Pleasure of the Text*, 1975) is a discussion and description of the many ways in which the reader derives pleasure from a literary work. One of the most important ways that the reader gains pleasure is not, for Barthes, from aesthetic contemplation of the whole but by ignoring the "whole" and "drifting" to passages that catch the interest and attention of the reader. For Barthes, the pleasure of the text is equated with the body, and the pleasure derived from the text is compared to sexual bliss. It is a more personal way of looking at literature than the systems Barthes discovered earlier using linguistics as a tool.

Barthes had become an eminent figure in French intellectual life by this time, and he was appointed to a chair at the prestigious Collège de France in 1976. Barthes refused to be a traditional academic as he continued to emphasize pleasure and feeling in his critical work. In *Fragments d'un discours amoureux* (1977; *A Lover's Discourse: Fragments*, 1978), he attempts to codify the language of love by using such texts as Johann Wolfgang von Goethe's *Die Leiden des jungen Werthers* (1774; *The Sorrows of Werther*, 1779; better known as *The Sorrows of Young Werther*, 1902), and he traces the typical gestures and maneuvers of love. Each aspect of the language of love is illustrated and discussed. In "Making Scenes," for example, Barthes traces the etymology of words used in such scenes and finds that they take the rhetorical form of stichomythia. Love may have had a very defined code for Barthes, but his analysis was not merely intellectual, and it did not become more important than the object it described. *A Lover's Discourse* became Barthes's most popular book, testifying to the accuracy of his analysis and observations.

One of the last works by Barthes was *Roland Barthes par Roland Barthes* (1975; *Roland Barthes by Roland Barthes*, 1977), an autobiography done in fragments and memories. There are lists of such things as "I Like" and "I Don't Like." There are a few revealing sections in the book; Barthes includes a fragment on the "Goddess H" that speaks of the pleasures of homosexuality and hashish. There are also photographs of the young Barthes and his bourgeois environment at the beginning, but the rest of the book is arranged in alphabetical order for each topic he discusses. There is no narrative in this "autobiography," but a picture of the essential Barthes does emerge. One aspect of Barthes that is revealed in the book is his opposition to "doxa," or received opinion. He was always opposed to the rigidity of received authority.

Barthes's fertile mind continued to produce new and challenging works, such as his study of Japan, *L'Empire des signes* (1970; *Empire of Signs*, 1982), and a book on photography, *La Chambre claire: Note sur la photographie* (1980; *Camera Lucida: Reflections on Photography*, 1981). His reputation as an intellectual was not limited to France but was international. In early 1980, Barthes was tragically killed after a laundry truck struck him as he attempted to cross a Paris street near the Collège de France.

Summary

Roland Barthes is one of those rare individuals who made significant contributions to many fields. He was one of the first to see the applicability of semiology to a wide range of topics. He was not the first to discover how the structures of linguistics could be applied to all of the human sciences, but he was one of its most elegant practitioners. *S/Z* is one of the finest and fullest structuralist analyses extant. Furthermore, Barthes pointed the way for poststructuralism and showed how literary criticism could reveal not unity but fragmentation. He also never lost sight of the importance of emotion in literature and life and of the dangers of completing and fixing any system of thought. He freed criticism from a narrow academic view and led it to the multiplicity of voices it currently enjoys.

Bibliography

Barthes, Roland. *Roland Barthes by Roland Barthes*. Translated by Richard Howard. New York: Hill & Wang, 1977. A meditation by Barthes on some of the significant events and influences on his life. It is not the usual autobiography, but it is an excellent introduction to the delights and style of Barthes.

Culler, Jonathan. *Roland Barthes*. New York: Oxford University Press, 1983. The best short study of Barthes's works. Culler divides the protean Barthes into such areas as "Mythologist" and "Hedonist," which enables the reader to see the range of Barthes's mind. Contains clear, direct, and insightful discussions.

Lavers, Annette. *Roland Barthes: Structuralism and After*. Cambridge, Mass.: Harvard University Press, 1982. The most detailed study of Barthes's literary criticism. Laver discusses not only Barthes's thought but also critics who influenced and were influenced by him. Scholarly.

Sontag, Susan. "Writing Itself: On Roland Barthes." In *A Barthes Reader*. New York: Hill & Wang, 1982. Sontag provides a sympathetic and revealing introduction to Barthes's thought and an excellent selection of Barthes's writing. Students who wish to read Barthes might begin here.

Thody, Philip. *Roland Barthes: A Conservative Estimate*. Atlantic Highlands, N.J.: Humanities Press, 1977. A detailed analysis of the major works and positions of Barthes. It is not as scholarly or difficult as Lavers' book, but it is a good overall discussion.

Wasserman, George. *Roland Barthes*. Boston: Twayne, 1981. Part of Twayne's World Authors series. Begins with a brief biographical section followed by a critical overview of Barthes's works. Includes a bibliography, a chronology, and an index.

James Sullivan

BÉLA BARTÓK

Born: March 25, 1881; Nagyszentmiklós, Austro-Hungarian Empire
Died: September 26, 1945; New York, New York
Area of Achievement: Music
Contribution: Bartók was one of the great champions of Hungarian music. He was responsible for dispelling the misconceptions about Hungarian folk music which prior to Bartók had been commonly associated with Gypsy music.

Early Life

Béla Bartók was born on March 25, 1881, in Nagyszentmiklós, Austro-Hungarian Empire, which is now part of Romania. Béla was the elder of two children born to Béla Bartók and Paula Yoit. He was named for his father who was director of a government agricultural school in Nagyszentmiklós. The son suffered various illnesses throughout his growth years. He was later to suffer periodic bouts with bronchial infection and pneumonia that occasionally interfered with his musical career. Young Bartók's own natural talent and interest for music were encouraged from the earliest age. His father, active in the musical life of the community, was an amateur musician who played the piano and the cello. His mother was a teacher and a talented amateur pianist. His mother gave him his first piano lesson when he was five years old.

Bartók's father died in 1888 when the boy was only seven years old, leaving Paula Bartók to support their two children through her teaching. The family moved several times during the next few years as Paula tried to provide the best educational and musical opportunities for her son. The family first moved to Nagyszóllós, which later became part of the Soviet Union, in 1889. It was there that Bartók composed his first pieces, several short compositions for the piano. In 1892, he gave his first public performance for a charity benefit. In 1894, the family finally settled in Pozsony, which is now Bratislava, Czechoslovakia.

There, Bartók pursued his education at the *Gymnasium* and began his study of the piano with various pianists. In Pozsony, Bartók was able to attend concerts and operas and participate in public performances himself. Bartók's years at Pozsony were productive ones that saw him complete a number of works for piano and also works in the category of chamber music. During this time, Bartók fell under the influence of Ernó Dohnányi, a composer/pianist, several years his senior, who had preceded him at the *Gymnasium* and who had gone on to study at the Royal Academy of Music at Budapest.

Shortly before completing his studies at the *Gymnasium* in Pozsony, Bartók, with his mother, traveled in December of 1898 to Vienna, where he auditioned for admission to the Vienna Conservatory. Full admission and scholarship notwithstanding, Bartók elected to follow in the footsteps of his friend and role model, Dohnányi, and attend the Royal Academy of Music at Budapest. There, he studied piano with István Thomán, a former pupil of Franz Liszt, and composition with Janos Koessler. Bartók, who passed through the program with relative ease and was graduated in 1903, was viewed by the faculty as a virtuoso pianist more than as a talented and promising young composer.

Bartók became interested in the music of Liszt and Richard Wagner while he was a student at the academy, eventually turning to the music of Richard Strauss for inspiration. His interest in Strauss was the result of having heard Strauss's tone poem *Thus Spake Zarathustra* (1896) performed in Budapest in 1902. He subsequently arranged a piano transcription of Strauss's *Ein Heldenleben* (1898), which he performed for the academy faculty, and went on to compose a symphonic poem, the *Kossuth Symphony* (1903). The symphony, which is divided into ten sections, was a patriotic composition that caused quite a controversy over the composer's deliberate distortion of the Austrian national anthem found in the work. The work was first performed in Budapest in 1904.

Life's Work

Central to the development of Bartók's mature style was his study of the Hungarian folk song. He first became interested after having heard a peasant song sung by a young woman in 1904. His early study soon revealed to him a significant difference between the Hungarian folk music and the Gypsy music often mistaken as such by well-intentioned composers like Liszt and Johannes Brahms. The collection and study of Hungarian folk songs reflected, in part, Bartók's strong sense of patriotism, even as the *Kossuth Symphony* earlier had celebrated the Hungarian uprising against Austrian oppression in 1848. His research quickly led him into contact with Zoltán Kodály in 1905, a fellow Hungarian composer who was also doing research on Hungarian folk music. In 1906, the two traveled separately to remote regions of Hungary, taking down and recording folk songs, the final result being a collaboration and publication of twenty folk songs with piano accompaniment which was entitled *Hungarian Folksongs* (1907). For the next several years, Bartók continued his research of Hungarian folk songs, expanding the scope of his research to include folk songs of neighboring regions in Central Europe, including Romania and Czechoslovakia, among others. He ultimately collected thousands of songs from that general region.

His study and analysis of Hungarian folk songs led to the development of a highly personal style as he attempted to merge elements of folk music and art music together. Characteristic of his style are melodies based on modes or unusual scale structures and irregular rhythm patterns and measure groupings such as are often found in folk music. While his style is often diverse and complex, frequently utilizing much dissonance, some element of folk music is usually to be found in his works.

In 1907, Bartók's former professor, Thomán, retired, and Bartók was appointed to the faculty. The appointment provided Bartók with the financial stability necessary to pursue a career of research, performance, and composition. One of the first works to reveal Bartók's individual style was the opera *Duke Bluebeard's Castle*, which was composed in 1911 for a competition but which was not performed until 1918. The work is generally seen as the first of a trilogy, the other two works being the ballet *The Wooden Prince* (1917) and the pantomime *The Miraculous Mandarin* (1926). The first performance of *The Wooden Prince* marked Bartók's first public success, with the first performance of *Duke Bluebeard's Castle* the following year firmly establishing him as an international figure.

Included among the major works that Bartók composed are his six string quartets, which place him as the major composer in this genre in the twentieth century. He wrote extensively for the piano, frequently treating it more as a percussive instrument than a melodic one. This technique, developed by Bartók, marked a dramatic break with the way the piano had been used. The scope of his piano pieces varies from large extended works, such as the three piano concertos, to miniatures, such as the *Bagatelles* (1908). His most important work for piano is *Mikrokosmos*, which consists of 153 piano pieces in six volumes that were composed between the years 1926 and 1939. The level of difficulty ranges from the simplest pieces for beginners to works for the accomplished virtuoso.

Bartók was quite active as a concert artist and composer during the 1920's and 1930's, also continuing his work with folk-song research. In 1934, he left the teaching studio when the Hungarian Academy of Sciences commissioned him to prepare his collection of Hungarian folk songs for publication. In 1936, he composed *Music for Strings, Percussion, and Celesta*, regarded by many as his finest work. As the decade wore on Bartók became increasingly concerned as Hungary moved closer to Nazi Germany, and, when his mother died in December of 1939, he immediately began to make plans to leave the country.

He went to the United States in 1940 and settled in New York City. He was awarded an honorary doctorate in November of 1940 by Columbia University, from which he later received an appointment to continue his research in folk music. The appointment was short-lived, however, and in 1942 he found himself without a steady source of income and in poor health. His health had been steadily deteriorating for several months, and a medical examination in 1943 produced the misdiagnosis of polycythemia, a condition characterized by an excess of red blood cells. Later, he was diagnosed as having leukemia.

As Bartók's health worsened and his financial problems increased because of the illness, the American Society of Composers, Authors, and Publishers came to his assistance and provided funds for his medical care. Two of his finest works date from this period when he was fighting the disease. The *Concerto for Orchestra* was commissioned in 1943 by Serge Koussevitsky, conductor of the Boston Symphony Orchestra. Koussevitsky conducted its premier performance in 1944 with Bartók present. The other work, Piano Concerto No. 3, was completed shortly before his death in 1945, after Bartók had realized that his disease was terminal. Bartók died on September 26, 1945, in West Side Hospital in New York City. He was survived by his second wife, Ditta Pásztory Bartók, a former student who concertized in duo piano works with her husband, their only child, Peter Bartók, and a son, Béla Bartók, by his first wife, Marta Ziegler.

Summary

Béla Bartók's importance to the twentieth century is fourfold. He was a great virtuoso pianist who concertized throughout Europe and the United States. His former teacher, Thomán, compared him to Franz Liszt, perhaps the greatest pianist of the nineteenth century. Early in Bartók's career, his great talent and skill as a performer placed him in the teaching studio at the Royal Academy. There he was a great influence to many aspiring young pianists, among them Fritz Reiner, who later became a world-famous conductor. Bartók became an ethnomusicologist through his study of the folk song. He collected folk songs over the years, studied and analyzed them, published them in collections, and wrote and published articles about his research in folk music. His research in this area redefined Hungarian folk music and preserved a great body of it that probably would have been lost except for his efforts in this field. Finally, through the study of folk music, Bartók developed a highly personal and original compositional style that reflected a fusion of folk music characteristics with certain characteristics of Western art music. His music has continued to increase in popularity since his death.

Bibliography

Bartók, Béla. "Autobiography." In *Béla Bartók Essays*, edited by Benjamin Suchoff. New York: St. Martin's Press, 1976. This brief essay is by Bartók on Bartók. It provides the reader with an invaluable opportunity to see what the composer has to say about his life and works.
Griffiths, Paul. *Bartók*. London: J. M. Dent & Sons, 1984. An excellent biography. There is some technical discussion of selected works, but the book is accessible to the general reader. Appendices contain a calendar of events in Bartók's life, linking them with contemporary events and musicians. Includes a listing of his works by genre that offers such information

as dates of composition, dates of revisions, a who, when, and where of first performances, and publishers. Contains a short selected bibliography.

Lampert, Vera, and László Somfai. "Béla Bartók." In *New Grove Dictionary of Music and Musicians*, edited by Stanley Sadie, 6th ed., vol. 2. New York: Macmillan, 1980. This is the best article in English about Bartók, his works, and his musical style. A listing of his works and an excellent bibliography are provided.

Lesznai, Lajos. *Bartók*. Translated by Percy M. Young, London: J. M. Dent & Sons, 1973. The author has attempted to establish a factually accurate biography through inquiry of people who knew Bartók personally. There is little technical treatment of selected works, making it accessible to the general public. Includes some photographs and a short selected bibliography.

Milne, Hamish. *Bartók: His Life and Times*. New York: Hippocrene Books, 1982. This biography, though short, provides interesting insights into Bartók's private and professional life and attempts to put his life into perspective with the times in which he lived. Highly recommended to the general reader.

Petho, Bertalan. "Béla Bartók's Personality." *Studia Musicologia* 23 (1981): 443-458. Provides interesting insights into Bartók, the man. This short article is a good source for the reader wanting to read about Bartók's character and personality.

Stevens, Halsey. *The Life and Music of Béla Bartók*. Rev. ed. New York: Oxford University Press, 1964. Although dated, this biography remains one of the best. The book is divided into two major sections. The first section divides Bartók's life into three periods. The second section discusses Bartók's music by genre. The appendix contains a chronological list of works that includes the date of first performance when possible. Contains a good but dated bibliography. Recommended to the general reader.

Michael Hernon

NIKOLAY GENNADIYEVICH BASOV

Born: December 14, 1922; Usman, U.S.S.R.

Area of Achievement: Physics

Contribution: Basov played a key role in the invention of quantum micro-wave amplification devices (masers) and light amplifiers which operate on the principle of stimulated emission of radiation (lasers). He collaborated with Aleksandr Prokhorov, with whom he shared the 1964 Nobel Prize in Physics, to produce the first Soviet maser and did pioneering work on the use of semiconductors in lasers. In his later career, he has been a major figure in science administration and policy-making in the U.S.S.R.

Early Life

Nikolay Gennadiyevich Basov was born on December 14, 1922, in Us-man, near Voronezh in the Soviet Union, the son of Gennadiy Fedorovich Basov, a professor, and Zinaida Adreevna Basova. Russian biographical sources, which are typically reticent about the personal lives of public figures, state only that he attended primary and secondary school in Voronezh. Completing secondary school in the early days of World War II, he enlisted in the army, enrolled in the Kiev school of military medicine, and afterward served as a lieutenant in the medical corps on the Ukrainian front.

Following the war, he enrolled in the Moscow Institute of Mechanics, from which he received *Kandidat Nauka* (roughly equivalent to an American Ph.D. degree) in 1950, only five years after beginning undergraduate study. Such rapid progress on the educational ladder was not unusual at the time. Soviet science was in the process of extremely rapid expansion in response to the demands of postwar reconstruction and an effort to achieve scientific and technological parity with the West, now perceived as a threat as Cold War tensions deepened. Thinning of the ranks of older scientists by the purges of the 1930's, wartime mortality, and the diversion of scientific effort toward immediate military concerns left the Soviet Union with an acute shortage of trained scientists. Consequently, there was great pressure to rush people through the educational system and to put them to work as soon as possible. Although the educational climate of postwar Russia has been much criticized for producing mediocrity, it did enable gifted individuals to exercise their abilities at an early age. In 1948, while still a student, Basov joined the staff of the oscillation laboratory of the Lebedev Physics Institute in Moscow, first as a laboratory technician and later as a senior scientist. It was there that he began the fruitful collaboration with Prokhorov that led to their receiving the 1964 Nobel Prize in Physics for research on masers and lasers. He married Kseniya Tikhonova Nazarova in 1950, and together they had two sons, Gennadiy and Dmitri.

Life's Work

Basov's name is inextricably linked with laser research in the Soviet Union. Quantum amplification devices (masers and lasers) have been the focus of nearly all of his scientific endeavors during a long and fruitful career that began in the late 1940's with investigations on the use of microwave absorption spectra to study the structure of molecules. Absorption spectra are produced when electromagnetic radiation interacts with a substance in a low (ground) energy state. The substance absorbs certain frequencies of energy, becomes excited, and the pattern of frequencies absorbed gives important clues about the structure of the substance. To improve the sensitivity of their instruments, Basov and Prokhorov turned their efforts toward building a device, which they termed a molecular beam generator, that would produce a population of molecules all in the ground state. The design also produced a population of molecules in the excited state that could be used to amplify selected wavelengths by stimulated emission, a result which was to have far-reaching implications. A theoretical paper outlining such a device appeared in *Zhurnal eksperimentalnogo i teoreticheskogo fiziki* (journal of experimental and theoretical physics) in 1954. In the following year, Basov demonstrated the first Soviet maser (as microwave quantum amplifiers were dubbed by American workers). He received his Russian doctorate (a more advanced degree than the American Ph.D.) for this work in 1956.

This Russian maser research paralleled work being done by Charles H. Townes and others in the United States but was completely independent of it, a fact that has been well documented and was recognized by the Nobel Committee. Scientists in the U.S.S.R. in the 1940's and early 1950's were effectively isolated from their Western counterparts. Much of the research on masers came under the heading of classified information on both sides of the Iron Curtain, and the Soviets in particular regarded even routine requests for scientific information from the West as subversive. Informal exchanges at scientific meetings, an important medium of exchange between scientists, did not occur, because Soviet scientists did not travel to the West.

After the discovery of masers, Basov turned toward devising a system based on the principle of stimulated emission of visible light. The maser demonstrated that this was theoretically possible, but there were practical difficulties in producing a population of predominantly excited molecules in the optical range. The story of the invention of the laser is one of a race between several Americans, working semi-independently of one another, and the entirely separate Russian group at the Lebedev Physics Institute. The distinction of producing the first working laser belongs to an American, but the Russians were not far behind and were noteworthy in their pioneering work with semiconductor lasers. In the following years, Basov, Prokhorov, and numerous coworkers and subordinates conducted investigations into the design of a semiconductor, gas and chemical lasers, the use of lasers in controlled thermonuclear reactions, and a wide variety of practical applications of lasers in science and technology. An extensive bibliography of scientific publications from the 1970's and 1980's is testimony both to Basov's continuing activity in the field and to his prestige and influence as an academician and Nobel laureate.

In 1959, Basov and Prokhorov were awarded the Lenin Prize, the highest honor for individual achievement in the Soviet Union, for their work with masers and lasers, and in 1964 they shared the Nobel Prize in Physics with Charles Townes, the leading American laser researcher. In 1966, Basov was elected full member of the U.S.S.R. Academy of Sciences and in 1967 was elected a member of its Presidium. The Academy of Sciences is the most prestigious scientific body in the U.S.S.R., and membership in it carries with it both personal financial rewards and substantial political influence in matters such as funding of laboratories. Basov has been active in establishing and advising laser research laboratories throughout the U.S.S.R. and abroad.

Politically as well as scientifically active and ambitious, Basov joined the Communist Party in 1951 and became a deputy to the Supreme Soviet in 1974 and a member of the Presidium of the Supreme Soviet in 1982. Such active involvement in party politics is unusual for a distinguished scientist in the Soviet Union.

Summary

In his 1964 Nobel Prize lecture, Nikolay Gennadiyevich Basov characterized himself as a scientist who combined the theoretical elucidation of physical principles with their practical applications, with emphasis on the practical. This is a reasonable description of his scientific approach, but more than that it is an affirmation of his orthodoxy and adherence to the Marxist philosophy of science, which emphasizes the concrete and service aspects of science over the theoretical—sometimes to the detriment of both, particularly when the decisions as to what is practical and what is mere "bourgeois theory" are made by those ignorant of scientific methodology.

The elaboration of the theory of stimulated emission of radiation (which had been predicted by Albert Einstein on a general basis in 1917) and the development of experimental quantum amplifiers were major developments in theoretical physics; the laser itself has, in the years since its invention, become one of the most important tools of science and industry.

A brilliant and productive scientist who has devoted his career to a branch of physics with broad practical applications, Basov is patriotic, politically orthodox, politically adept, and close to being a model Soviet/Marxist scientist. Although the model may not be as appealing to Westerners as that of dissident scientists, it is an effective one, and Basov's scientific and administrative efforts on behalf of laser research have made this branch of physics one of the showpieces of Soviet science.

Bibliography

Bertolotti, M. *Masers and Lasers: An Historical Approach.* Bristol, England: Adam Hilger, 1983. A technical account of the reasoning behind the development of the maser and laser. The narrative is likely to be difficult for the average nonspecialist. The contributions made by Prokhorov and Basov are discussed in some detail and placed in the context of research being done at the same time in the United States.

Brophy, James J. *Semiconductor Devices.* New York: McGraw-Hill, 1964. A useful background reference for understanding how semiconductor lasers function. Terminology is defined and explained in nonmathematical terms; the book is aimed at the nonspecialist using semiconductor devices who wants a basic understanding of how they function. There is a brief discussion of semiconductor lasers themselves.

Hecht, Jeff, and Dick Teresi. *Laser: Supertool of the Eighties.* New York: Ticknor & Fields, 1982. The bulk of this book (nine of fourteen chapters) is devoted to uses and potential uses of lasers in medicine, communications, warfare, manufacturing, energy production, publishing, holography, and the arts. There are good nontechnical descriptions of the general principle of laser action and the design and function of various masers and lasers. The section devoted to the history of the laser concentrates on the American contribution but does include some information on Basov and Prokhorov.

Isakov, A. I., O. N. Krokhin, D. V. Sobeltsyn, and I. I. Sobelman. "Nikolay Gennadiyevich Basov, on His Fiftieth Birthday." *Soviet Physics-Uspekhi* 16, no. 1 (1973): 165-166. This testimonial, written by a number of fellow physicists, gives a chronological account of Basov's life and research. Tends to present a one-sided view of the person portrayed. Provides a good review of Basov's scientific career but contains little personal data. The Soviet view of individual effort as a part of a master plan is also evident.

Parry, Albert. *The Russian Scientist.* New York: Macmillan, 1973. This book is a good, relatively neutral account of science in the Soviet Union, beginning in czarist times and continuing to the present. Biographies of representative eminent Russian physical and natural scientists and mathematicians are given. A useful reference for a perspective on science administration in the Soviet Union and the importance of the U.S.S.R. Academy of Sciences.

Popovsky, Mark. *Manipulated Science: The Crisis of Science and Scientists in the Soviet Union Today.* Garden City, N.Y.: Doubleday, 1979. A Russian specialist in scientific journalism who emigrated to the United States,

Popovsky presents a historical overview of the practice of science in the Soviet Union. The emphasis is on failures and weaknesses of the system and the dismal record of natural sciences under Joseph Stalin.

Weber, Robert L. *Pioneers of Science: Nobel Prize Winners in Physics.* Edited by J. M. A. Lenihan. Bristol, England: Adam Hilger, 1980. Consists of brief sketches of the lives of Nobel Prize-winning physicists to 1980. Its chief use is as a source of biographical data, and it includes personal data on Soviet scientists which Soviet sources do not include.

Martha Sherwood-Pike

SIMONE DE BEAUVOIR

Born: January 9, 1908; Paris, France
Died: April 14, 1986; Paris, France
Areas of Achievement: Literature, philosophy, women's rights, social reform, and civil rights
Contribution: De Beauvoir cut across traditional academic fields to produce important works of literature, criticism, and philosophy, while her political activism made her a "pioneer" of the late twentieth century women's movement as well as a leading figure in the human rights, peace, and social reform.

Early Life
Simone de Beauvoir was born in Paris on January 9, 1908, the eldest of two daughters of Georges Bertrand and Françoise Brasseur de Beauvoir. Although her family was descended from the aristocracy, it teetered precariously on the brink of financial solvency, maintaining the status of upper-middle-class gentility with difficulty. De Beauvoir had a relatively happy childhood, which she described graphically in the first volume of her autobiography, *Mémoires d'une jeune fille rangée* (1958; *Memoirs of a Dutiful Daughter*, 1959). She especially treasured the summers that she spent at her grandfather's rambling estate at Meyrignac in Limousin, where she developed what would become lifelong passions for reading and hiking. In 1913, de Beauvoir was enrolled at the private school Cours Désir.

In her autobiography, de Beauvoir depicted herself as a precocious young girl chafing at the restraints placed upon her both by society and by other persons' wills. The personal and ideological problems in her parents' marriage, created primarily by tension between her mother's religious piety and her father's cynical agnosticism, led de Beauvoir to conclude that intellectual and spiritual life were mutually exclusive. This enabled her to reject both the Catholic religion and the social role of "dutiful daughter" imposed upon her by her parents. As de Beauvoir entered her second decade, she developed an attraction for her cousin Jacques Laiguillon. Although she had strong feelings for him, she was afraid that their love would trap her into becoming a bourgeois wife, a role that she rejected as completely as she had the life of a "dutiful daughter."

In 1928, after completing her undergraduate education, she began working at the École Normale Supérieure on her *agrégation de philosophie*, a difficult postgraduate examination for teaching positions at *lycées* and universities in France. The next year, she met Jean-Paul Sartre, a fellow philosophy student. For the first time in her life de Beauvoir found a soul mate who was her intellectual equal, a man with whom she knew she always would be compatible. In 1929, they passed the *agrégation* and began a liaison that would last a lifetime. During the same year, however, her happiness was marred by the death of her closest childhood friend, Elizabeth "Zaza" Mabille; this event marked both the end of the first volume of de Beauvoir's memoirs and her childhood.

Life's Work

Except for her work, the most important thing in de Beauvoir's life was her relationship with Sartre. Because neither of them wanted children, they rejected the notion of traditional marriage in favor of a bond that they called an "essential" love, which was to be permanent but which would not exclude what they deemed "contingent" love affairs. In 1931, Sartre did suggest that they marry, but de Beauvoir refused this proposal, arguing that they were not being true to their own principles.

In 1931, de Beauvoir was appointed to teach in a *lycée* in Marseilles. The next year she transferred to Rouen, where she was reprimanded by *lycée* authorities for questioning women's traditional role in society. Sartre, also in Rouen, met Olga Kosakievicz, a former pupil of de Beauvoir, with whom he fell in love. They experimented with a trio, which failed primarily because of de Beauvoir's jealousy; the incident furnished her with the plot for her first novel, *L'Invitée* (1943; *She Came to Stay*, 1949). In 1936, she was transferred to Paris, where Sartre was able to join her the following year.

Despite ominous clouds on the French political scene, in the prewar era de Beauvoir and Sartre remained oblivious to the world around them, burying themselves in their work, their friends, and each other. The outbreak of World War II in 1939, however, marks an important watershed in de Beauvoir's life. Sartre's induction into the army brought de Beauvoir face to face with social and political reality. They jointly adopted the philosophy of personal commitment, realizing that they had a responsibility to humanity as well as to themselves. During the German invasion of France in June, 1940, Sartre was taken prisoner, and de Beauvoir, like many other Parisians, fled the capital only to return when the reality of defeat and German occupation became obvious. On April 1, 1941, Sartre was released and returned to Paris. Although de Beauvoir and Sartre worked on the fringes of the French Resistance, they were not active participants in it.

During the war, both de Beauvoir and Sartre abandoned their teaching careers in order to concentrate on writing. Her first novel, *She Came to Stay*, was an immediate success, and from 1943 on both she and Sartre were established as major new talents on the French intellectual horizon. In 1945, de Beauvoir, Sartre, and others founded the journal *Les Temps modernes* as a vehicle for independent left-wing intellectual viewpoints. The same year, the novel that she had written during the war, *Le Sang des autres* (1945; *The Blood of Others*, 1948), was published to almost universal critical acclaim as the quintessential Existentialist novel of the Resistance.

Her philosophical treatise, *Pour une morale de l'ambiguïté* (*The Ethics of Ambiguity*, 1948), a secular breviary of Existentialist ethics, was published in 1947, the year de Beauvoir first journeyed to the United States. There she met novelist Nelson Algren and began her first serious "contingent" love affair. Her four-year relationship with Algren resulted in a proposal of marriage, which she rejected both because of her commitment to Sartre and because of her disinclination to leave France. After several transatlantic visits, the affair ended in bitterness when de Beauvoir used their relationship as a basis for her novel *Les Mandarins* (1954; *The Mandarins*, 1956), which won the prestigious Prix de Goncourt for literature in 1954.

Throughout her life, de Beauvoir, an avid traveler, visited most of the world's exciting venues, recording her thoughts and storing her memories for use in her writing. In the fall of 1949, her most famous book, *Le Deuxième Sexe* (*The Second Sex*, 1953), was published. This massive work discusses the role and condition of women throughout history from biological, psychological, historical, sociological, and philosophical perspectives. Two of its most important tenets—the concept that man has defined himself as the essential being, the subject, who has consigned woman to the subordinate position of object or "Other," and the idea that there is no such thing as "feminine nature," that one is not born a woman but becomes one through social conditioning—served as an important basis for the resurrection of the women's liberation movement in the mid-twentieth century.

In 1952, de Beavoir began her second "contingent" liaison, this time with Claude Lanzmann, an able filmmaker and journalist seventeen years her junior. This affair, which ended in 1958, was to be the last important romantic interlude in her "essential" love relationship with Sartre.

Two important changes occurred in de Beauvoir's life during the last half of the 1950's. First, her political views hardened and grew more bitter as the culpability of the French army in the torture of Algerians became increasingly obvious and the world moved closer to the brink of nuclear war. De Beauvoir's commitment to political activism intensified at this time, and she embarked on a series of public demonstrations against Charles de Gaulle, French torture in Algeria, nuclear war, and social injustice. The second major change was in de Beauvoir's writing. She all but abandoned fiction for several years in order to begin the first of what would become a four-volume autobiography and a variety of other nonfiction works. She would not return to the novel form until the publication of *Les Belles Images* (1966; English translation, 1969), which was followed in 1968 by her last major work of fiction, *La Femme rompue* (1967; *The Woman Destroyed*, 1968). These two volumes are shorter than her four earlier novels but, like them, follow in a long tradition of French women writers who have focused their work on women's lives and ambitions.

In 1967, de Beauvoir again increased her commitment to political activism, raising the issue of women's rights in Israel and taking part in Bertrand Russell's Tribunal of War Crimes, which met in Copenhagen to investigate American involvement in the Vietnamese war. The following May, she and Sartre became active supporters of the revolutionary students at the Sorbonne. During this phase of her politically active life, de Beauvoir was preparing *La Viellese* (1970; *The Coming of Age*, 1972), a lengthy but critically acclaimed study of aging that attacked modern society's indifference to the problems of the elderly.

In 1969, de Beauvoir was elected to the consultative committee of the Bibliothèque Nationale (national library) as a "man of letters." Soon thereafter she became actively involved in the women's movement, joining a series of demonstrations led by the Mouvement de la Libération des Femmes in 1970. The next year she signed the "Manifesto of 343," French women who publicly admitted to having had illegal abortions. Soon after the publication of the manifesto, de Beauvoir publicly declared herself to be a militant feminist, explaining that she had eschewed the reformist, legalistic feminism of the past but eagerly embraced the radical movement of the 1970's. In 1972, she joined street demonstrations protesting "crimes against women" and the next year began a feminist column in *Les Temps Modernes*. She renewed this feminist commitment by becoming president of the Ligue des Droits des Femmes (French league of the rights of women) in 1974, the same year in which she was selected to receive the Jerusalem Prize for writers who have promoted the freedom of the individual.

On April 15, 1980, the lifelong "essential" love of de Beauvoir and Jean-Paul Sartre ended with the latter's death. The following year, de Beauvoir published *La Cérémonie des adieux* (1981; *Adieux: A Farewell to Sartre*, 1984), a sober narrative that recorded Sartre's mental and physical decline with a brutal honesty that seemed to her to be the final tribute she could pay to him. Although de Beauvoir wrote no major literary works after Sartre's death, she remained politically active. She died of pneumonia in a Paris hospital on April 14, 1986, and was entombed with Sartre's ashes in the Montparnasse Cemetery. More than five thousand people attended the funeral to which women's organizations throughout the world sent floral tributes.

Summary

Simone de Beauvoir lived her adult life in such a way that it illustrated the most important tenets of Existentialist ethics, especially the concepts of social responsibility and commitment. Her development from a politically indifferent young woman to a socially committed adult and, finally, to a mature woman militant in the causes of women's liberation and human rights is chronicled in the four volumes of her autobiography. While de Beauvoir's Existentialist views are presented somewhat didactically in her nonfiction and philosophical essays, in her novels they are infused with nuances of ambiguity and expressed in less strident prose. She used literature to present the real world to her readers by stripping away the insulating layers of hypocrisy that she believed bourgeois society installs to obscure truth. In this way, she believed, words could be enlisted as a weapon to help obliterate selfishness and indifference in the modern world.

In the post-World War II era, de Beauvoir became one of the most visible and influential left-wing advocates of social justice, peaceful coexistence, and women's liberation. Because her life and work supported her belief in sexual and social equality, de Beauvoir contributed immeasurably by word and by example to elevating the consciousness of men and women as well as improving the quality of their lives. She is one of the most important writers of the twentieth century because of both the literature that she created and the legacy of social and political commitment that she provided.

Bibliography
Beauvoir, Simone de. *Memoirs of a Dutiful Daughter.* Translated by James Kirkup. Cleveland: World Publishing, 1959.

_____. *The Prime of Life.* Translated by Peter Green. Cleveland: World Publishing, 1962.

_____. *Force of Circumstance.* Translated by Richard Howard. New York: G. P. Putnam's Sons, 1964.

_____. *All Said and Done.* Translated by Patrick O'Brian. New York: Putnam, 1974. The best source for Simone de Beauvoir's life and works is her massive four-volume autobiography. The memoirs not only describe the events of de Beauvoir's life but also evoke both its mood and spirit.

Bennett, Joy, and Gabriella Hochmann. *Simone de Beauvoir: An Annotated Bibliography.* New York: Garland, 1988. An excellent and comprehensive bibliographical source for works written in French, English, German, Italian, and Spanish about de Beauvoir's life and literature.

Bieber, Konrad. *Simone de Beauvoir.* Boston: Twayne, 1979. Combines a lengthy analysis of her autobiography with studies of her literary works and a short biography of her life. Bieber's work is well balanced, thoughtful, and impartial. Contains a short annotated bibliography.

Cottrell, Robert D. *Simone de Beauvoir.* New York: Frederick Ungar, 1975. A good, brief literary biography of de Beauvoir that concentrates on a thematic analysis of her literary works. Cottrell is relatively critical of de Beauvoir's writing style.

Madsen, Axel. *Hearts and Minds: The Common Journey of Simone de Beauvoir and Jean-Paul Sartre.* New York: William Morrow, 1977. A provocative double biography that emphasizes the emotional, philosophical, political, and literary connection between de Beauvoir and Sartre. Madsen has some surprising and unorthodox views on the works and lives of his subjects.

Marks, Elaine. *Simone de Beauvoir: Encounters with Death*. New Brunswick, N.J.: Rutgers University Press, 1973. Perhaps the best single work on de Beauvoir's literary contribution. In addition to a brilliant and perceptive study of death in de Beauvoir's literary and autobiographical works, Marks analyzes the themes and philosophy that permeate her literary canon.

Okely, Judith. *Simone de Beauvoir*. New York: Pantheon Books, 1986. A somewhat partisan treatment of de Beauvoir that concentrates heavily upon *The Second Sex* and de Beauvoir's feminism. Contains an excellent chronology.

Whitmarsh, Anne. *Simone de Beauvoir and the Limits of Commitment*. New York: Cambridge University Press, 1981. Studies the life and works of de Beauvoir in the light of her political convictions and her relationship with Sartre. Although Whitmarsh considers de Beauvoir smug and egotistical, her work is quite informative, especially about the first half of de Beauvoir's life.

Nancy Ellen Rupprecht

MENACHEM BEGIN

Born: August 16, 1913; Brest-Litovsk, Poland

Areas of Achievement: Government and politics
Contribution: Begin placed pressure on the British Mandate government to withdraw from Palestine, enabling Israel to declare its independence and sovereignty over part of Palestine. He also served as a key opposition leader and eventually as Prime Minister of Israel from 1977 to 1983.

Early Life
"Menachem" ("one who brings comfort") Begin was born on the eve of World War I in the Polish Jewish city of Brest-Litovsk, occupied by czarist Russia. In 1918, Germany took the area from the Soviet Union in the Treaty of Brest-Litovsk, and, at the Versailles Conference in 1919, it became part of the reestablished nation of Poland. Menachem's father and mother were orthodox Jews who worked for Zionism, the return of Jews to Palestine.

As a child Menachem saw a growing anti-Semitism in Brest-Litovsk: Rocks broke windows in Jewish homes; confiscatory, discriminatory taxation on Jews was levied by the Polish government; Jewish students were beaten by their peers. Once he had to watch several leading Jewish citizens receive twenty-five lashes in a public park for alleged "sympathy with Bolsheviks." Begin decided as a youth that Jews should not take such treatment passively and helped organize resistance against unwarranted attacks by fellow students.

Early in life, Begin demonstrated a forceful and effective public speaking personality. He attended a Polish *Gymnasium* and received a good liberal arts education. He studied law in Warsaw and received the degree of *magister juris* from the University of Warsaw. Begin was greatly influenced by Vladimir Jabotinsky, an eloquent Russian journalist who preached Zionist activism and violence if necessary. Begin was a key organizer of the Polish chapter of Betar, Jabotinsky's activist youth organization, and eventually became its commander of seventy thousand.

Meanwhile, in Palestine a splinter group of young Jews broke from the Haganah (the Jewish self-defense organization), which at the time followed a passive self-restraint in trying not to alienate the British as they defended their lands against Arab terrorist attacks. The splinter group eventually adopted the name Irgun Z'vai Leumi, the National Military Organization. The new underground organization received training in sabotage and underground warfare from Polish army officers plus quantities of weapons in exchange for promises to recruit as many Jews as possible from Poland and take them to Palestine.

In the spring of 1939, Begin married Aliza Arnold, after warning her of the exceptionally difficult life she would lead as his wife. Serene and cheerful, she was one of the great strengths of Begin's life. She and Begin escaped Warsaw just ahead of the German Blitzkrieg. They went to the neutral city of Vilna, Lithuania, but Begin was arrested by the Soviet secret police and sentenced to eight years in a labor camp in Siberia. Aliza managed to escape to Palestine. After working fourteen hours a day for nearly a year in extremely cold conditions, Begin and other Polish prisoners were released to join the Polish Liberation Army. Their first assignment was Palestine, in which Begin first set foot in May, 1942.

Begin was already well known to the Irgun as the leader of the Polish Betar, Irgun's best source of recruits. Jabotinsky had recently died; many Irgun members had joined the British army; and a splinter group of the Irgun, the "Stern Gang," Lohamei Herut Yisrael (Fighters for the Freedom of Israel, or Lehi), had taken with them eight hundred Irgun members. Irgun, then, by the end of 1943, numbered scarcely five hundred members. It needed a dedicated, dynamic organizer, and Begin was chosen to lead the decimated Irgun.

Life's Work

Begin's principal purpose in life was to establish the State of Israel and build it up to survive in strength. He was willing to pay any price to accomplish that objective. "The God of Israel, the Lord of hosts, will help us," Begin declared in 1943. "[T]here will be no retreat. Freedom—or death." Begin's strategy was to demonstrate to the international community Great Britain's inability to govern Palestine—and thus hasten its departure. He did not want to destroy its ability to wage war against Germany and Japan and so did not raid British army bases or installations necessary to the war effort. Instead, Irgun sought to harass nonmilitary targets: disrupt communications; destroy records against illegal Jewish immigration; hamper the collection of taxes; and raid police stations and warehouses for weapons stockpiling. Irgun avoided killing either British or Arab—except when "necessary." Irgun raided a British army payroll train and "confiscated" banknotes amounting to thirty-eight thousand pounds.

Most members of Irgun were part-time saboteurs or propagandists (depending on the division to which they were assigned). Full-time staff of Irgun never numbered more than thirty or forty. Discipline and military training were strict. Irgun had an underground radio station begun in 1944 and the Irgun newspaper, *Herut*. (Haganah's radio station did not begin broadcasting until October, 1945.) One of Begin's strong points as a leader was the meticulous and detailed way in which he analyzed problems and planned missions for Irgun. His conduct of meetings was the same way; he even had specific questions detailed for the agenda.

Begin tried to enlist Arabs in an effort to rid Palestine of the British. Irgun leaflets distributed in Arab villages claimed Jewish willingness to see the Arabs as peaceful citizens in the future Jewish state—which was not quite the political arrangement Arabs had in mind.

In response to Irgun raids and bombings, the British in 1944 imposed a curfew on the three major cities, Jerusalem, Haifa, and Tel Aviv, and brought out an old law imposing the death penalty for possessing arms or placing explosive devices. In June, 1946, a British military court condemned to death two Irgun members for stealing weapons from a British military installation. Irgun kidnapped five British officers with the tacit warning that if the Irgun men were hanged, so too would the British die. In July, the high commissioner commuted the death sentences of the two Irgun raiders. Irgun then released the British officers, each with a one-pound note for compensatory damages. On Sabbath, June 29, 1946, the British arrested literally thousands of Jews, including members of the Jewish Agency, and even sought to arrest David Ben-Gurion.

Haganah, Irgun, and Lehi all participated in the planning of the King David Hotel bombing on July 22, 1946. Warnings were telephoned to the hotel and nearby buildings a half hour before the bomb exploded, and some escaped as a result. Nevertheless, one wing of the hotel ignored the warnings, and more than one hundred people were killed in the blast. Haganah immediately and publicly condemned Irgun and disassociated itself from the terrorist act.

Begin detested the humiliation of floggings by British authorities and warned that floggings of Jews must stop or there would be retaliation in kind. When an Irgun suspect was flogged by British police, Irgun captured a British major and three noncommissioned officers and flogged each with eighteen lashes. Then they were set free with an Irgun communiqué showing the emblem of the two banks of the Jordan River and a rifle with the slogan "Only Thus." The British flogged no more Jews or Arabs for the rest of their stay in Palestine.

Irgun's (and Begin's) greatest triumph was the successful storming of the impregnable Crusader fortress of Acre, where Jewish prisoners were kept and, in capital cases, executed. In the midst of an Arab city, Begin planned an elaborate operation that blew an enormous hole in the walls and freed 251 prisoners—131 Arabs and 120 Jews. Fifteen Jews were killed and fifteen captured. When three of those captured were executed, Irgun retaliated with the hanging of two innocent British sergeants, one of the most despicable actions ever taken by Irgun in the eyes of its critics. Equally despicable were the murders of five innocent Jews by British soldiers and policemen in Tel Aviv in retaliation for the hanging of the sergeants. No more Jewish Terrorists or British soldiers were executed in the remaining year of British occupation. After Begin became Prime Minister of Israel, he refused to permit the execution of Arab terrorists.

When the British withdrew from Palestine and the War of Independence began in May, 1948, with the invasion of Palestine by Arab troops from Transjordan, Egypt, Syria, Lebanon, and Iraq, Begin and his Irgun were a thorn in the flesh for the new government of Israel under Prime Minister David Ben-Gurion. The Haganah needed all the help it could get, but neither Irgun nor Lehi was willing to relinquish control of its organization to the new government. They were willing to fight the Arabs. The massacre of Deir Yassin remains the most notorious of uncontrolled Irgun/Lehi actions.

Begin's willingness to cooperate with the new government but not to submit to its authority led to armed conflict between Haganah and Irgun over the disposition of weapons brought in by Irgun on the *Altalena*. Of Irgun's men, fourteen were killed and sixty-nine wounded. The government ended with two killed and six wounded. Much of the desperately needed ammunition had been destroyed. To Prime Minister David Ben-Gurion, Israel could not afford to have private armies that were not under the discipline of the government. To Begin's credit, he swallowed his pride and fought the common Arab enemy and did not let the Israeli cause perish in fratricidal conflict. He refused to fight fellow Jews and accepted the authority of the government. On September 20, 1948, Ben-Gurion presented Begin with an ultimatum ordering the immediate disbandment of the Irgun. Begin accepted the order and disbanded his organization.

As the war drew to an end, Begin helped organize the opposition Herut party in Israel. Herut proposed a vigorous capitalist system instead of the labor socialism of the ruling Mapai coalition. Herut also insisted that the Land of Israel included all of biblical Palestine—on both sides of the Jordan River. In the first election to the 120-member Knesset, Israel's parliament, Herut obtained fourteen seats, including one for Begin, a post he held for thirty years.

Though usually a key opposition leader to the government, Begin closed ranks during each of Israel's wars. By 1977 Begin had formed a right-wing coalition called the Likud bloc and controlled sixty-two Knesset seats, a majority. Begin became Prime Minister of Israel. He was supported partially because of his uncompromising stance on the West Bank captured by Israel in the 1967 war. It was Prime Minister Begin who signed the Camp David agreement in an effort to normalize relations with Egypt (leading to his being corecipient of the Nobel Peace Prize of 1978 with Anwar el-Sadat), and it was also Begin who ordered the invasion of Lebanon and the war to end the Palestine Liberation Organization's attacks in Israel.

Summary

What was the historical significance of Menachem Begin? No one can doubt his dedication to the cause of Israeli independence and strength. He was a realist. He was brutal when he thought he needed to be. He suffered much. He caused much suffering. He was intensely loyal and a capable commander who tried to protect his subordinates. He brought enormous pressure on the British, who finally were almost too glad to depart Israel, thereby making it possible for Israel to win independence and prevent Arab conquest of part of Palestine. Did the British leave and the Israelis win because of or in spite of Irgun and Begin? Would the British have left anyway, or would they have left in a context more favorable to Arab Palestinians? If the Israelis had refrained from all terrorism and sabotage, would the British have cooperated more or sided with the Arabs more? These are the imponderables of history, to which no more than tentative answers can be given.

The Arabs hated the Israelis for depriving the Palestinian Arabs of the land of their fathers, but many Arabs hated the Jews long before they had such a cause. Begin played a crucial role before 1948, but the Irgun could not win the war for independence. Only the Jewish Agency and the Haganah had the resources to do what seemed impossible at the time. Begin's role as an opposition politician and later as an unpopular prime minister continues to be clouded in controversy and conflict, both of which plagued Begin all of his life.

Bibliography

Bauer, Yehuda. *From Diplomacy to Resistance: A History of Jewish Palestine, 1939-1945*. Translated by Alton M. Winters. Philadelphia: Jewish Publication Society of America, 1970. Begin arrived in Israel in 1942 and his most significant historical contributions to Israel were in the years 1942-1948. This book analyzes in detail the historical situation during the critical years for Palestine. Bauer describes the intricate interrelationships and cooperation among Haganah, Irgun, and Lehi. The ambivalent attitudes of the British government and occupying army in Palestine and their relationship to both Arab and Jew are examined.

Begin, Menachem. *The Revolt*. Translated by Shmuel Katz. New York: Schuman, 1951. In all the controversies surrounding Begin, it is only fair to hear his side of the story. Begin tells of insights and detailed facts that a sweeping narrative cannot. Begin's account, however, ends with 1948 and so is valuable only for the early period.

Bell, J. Bowyer. *Terror Out of Zion: Irgun Zvai Leumi, LEHI, and the Palestine Underground, 1929-1949*. New York: St. Martin's Press, 1977. A well-written, fascinating insight into the intrigues, mentality, and troublesome times of the Israeli underground groups and their relationships and disagreements. One hundred pages follow Begin's career, especially after his arrival in Palestine. This book was published after Begin became prime minister, giving more historical perspective to the events described.

Hirschler, Gertrude, and Lester S. Eckman. *Menachem Begin: From Free-*

dom Fighter to Statesman. New York: Shengold, 1979. A sympathetic biography of Begin with many details of his family and early life. None of the stages of his life is neglected, and, in the various controversies of his career, Begin is presented in as favorable a light as the authors can persuasively find.

Hirst, David. *The Gun and the Olive Branch: The Roots of Violence in the Middle East.* New York: Harcourt Brace Jovanovich, 1977. A sharply critical analysis of Israeli actions in Palestine, including Begin's role in "Gun Zionism."

O'Brien, Conor Cruise. *The Siege: The Saga of Israel and Zionism.* New York: Simon & Schuster, 1986. A full history of modern Israel written by an Irishman and often placing an unusual interpretation on historical events. O'Brien wrote much about Begin, including his years as prime minister. This is a balanced, scholarly account.

Silver, Eric. *Begin: The Haunted Prophet.* New York: Random House, 1984. A fascinating biography written by an Oxford-educated English journalist who lived in Israel for eleven years as a foreign correspondent. He sees Begin as the most consistent of men, unswerving in his dedication to Israeli security. He is often critical of Begin but detached in his observations and analysis.

William H. Burnside

EDVARD BENEŠ

Born: May 28, 1884; Kožlany, Bohemia, Austro-Hungarian Empire
Died: September 3, 1948; Sezimovo Ústí, Czechoslovakia
Areas of Achievement: Government, politics, and education
Contribution: Beneš helped undermine Austro-Hungarian rule in the Czech
and Slovak region during World War I and became foreign minister of the
new republic there in 1918. A brilliant statesman, he negotiated numerous
agreements, but as president he was unable to prevent the dismemberment
of his country at Munich. During World War II, he headed the Czechoslo-
vakian government in exile and after 1945 endeavored unsuccessfully to
maintain Czechoslovakia's political freedom in the face of mounting
Communist pressures.

Early Life
Edvard Beneš was born in Kožlany, Bohemia, on May 28, 1884. The
youngest of ten children, he was the son of a moderately successful farmer
who was able to send him to secondary school at Vinohrady. As family funds
were too meager to cover the cost of higher education, however, Beneš
resorted to tutoring and free-lance writing to make ends meet. In 1903, he
entered Charles University in Prague to study philology (he did become an
accomplished linguist) but switched to philosophy and came under the influence of Tomáš Masaryk, the leading advocate of Czech nationalism. At
Masaryk's urging, Beneš went to France to study at the Sorbonne and at Di-
jon, and he obtained a doctor of laws degree in political science and sociology from the latter. In Paris he met a Czech student, Hana Vlčkova, whom
he married in 1909; she was his lifelong companion and source of constant
encouragement.

In 1909, Beneš returned home, completed a Ph.D. at Charles University,
and secured a teaching post in political science at the Academy of Commerce
in Prague. He also turned away from Marxism, joined Masaryk's Progressive
Party, and wrote for its organ. In 1912, he joined the faculty at Charles
University as a lecturer in sociology. (After the war, he regularly lectured
there on sociology.) In 1913, he also became a lecturer at the Technical
College in Prague. By that time, he had become a prolific writer on politics
and international affairs and active in the national liberation movement. He
had developed a deep hatred for militarism, of both the Austrian and the
German variety, but he was not called up for army service at the outbreak of
World War I, because of a leg injury incurred in his youth when he was a
star soccer player. In early 1915, he and Masaryk (who was now in exile)
formed an underground organization called Maffia, which sought to promote
a national uprising and to aid the Allies by supplying secret information
about activities in Austria-Hungary. In September, 1915, Beneš left the

country with a forged passport to avoid imminent arrest by the Austrian police and joined Masaryk in Switzerland.

His earlier sojourn in France had imbued Beneš with Western political, economic, and cultural ideas that put him at odds with those Bohemian patriots who looked to Russia for salvation. Beneš and Masaryk became the leading spokespersons for the "Westernist" school in the liberation movement. They represented a "Europeanist" or "realist" stance; that is, they believed the nation must learn how to observe, analyze, and contemplate options carefully, rather than follow the romantic notions of nineteenth century Pan-Slavism. Through their intensive efforts in the three years that followed, Beneš and Masaryk almost single-handedly achieved their goal of an independent Czechoslovak state.

Life's Work

At their meeting in 1915, Beneš and Masaryk discussed plans for their country's future, arranged to gather funds to carry on the work, and determined that they would persuade the Allies to support their movement. Beneš functioned essentially as Masaryk's chief of staff. In February, 1916, Beneš became general secretary of the Czechoslovak National Council, which was seated in Paris, where he had extensive ties. A tireless propagandist, Beneš pounded the Allies with details about how the Czech and Slovak people were working for victory through army desertions and mutinies and civilian riots, sabotage efforts, and demonstrations against the authorities in Austria-Hungary. Their movement contributed materially to the demise of the Habsburg Empire and influenced the Allies to recognize the idea of a Czechoslovak republic. Through his French contacts, Beneš negotiated the specific mention of the liberation of the Czechoslovaks from foreign domination in the Entente's note to Woodrow Wilson in January, 1917, which spelled out their war aims, and Wilson included in his Fourteen Points in January, 1918, the demand that the peoples of Austria-Hungary should have the opportunity for autonomous development. Once Masaryk had secured the formation of the Czechoslovak Legion in Russia in 1917, the Czechoslovak National Council in Paris began to function as the government in exile of a state that had hitherto existed only in the minds of its leaders. In May and June, 1918, Beneš obtained French and British recognition of Czechoslovakia as an allied and belligerent nation, and he effectively countered Italian opposition to this recognition. He also was in regular contact with nationalist leaders in Prague, and, when the Habsburg regime collapsed, Beneš was able to secure the establishment of an independent state under the National Council on October 28. Three days later, the Slovaks proclaimed independence and joined with the Czech provinces.

On November 14, a hastily convened parliament approved the émigré committee as the constitutional government, with Masaryk as president and

Beneš as foreign minister, and the latter was commissioned to represent the new country at the Paris Peace Conference. After signing in 1919 the Treaty of St. Germain with Austria, which finalized the authority of the Czechoslovak government, Beneš returned home in triumph to take up the duties of foreign minister. He served in this post until 1935 with only a brief interlude from September 26, 1921, to October 7, 1922, as premier.

During his tenure as foreign minister, Beneš gained renown as a European statesman who was devoted to the struggle for international peace and collective security. His major achievement was the formation of the Little Entente with Yugoslavia and Romania in 1920-1921 to check Hungarian ambitions; this Little Entente, linked with the Treaty of Alliance and Friendship with France in 1924, was the foundation of the continental balance of power and the French deterrence system against Germany. Through this tie, Beneš was able to secure French assistance for construction of the Czechoslovak border fortifications, which might have saved the country from German conquest in 1938 if the Sudeten region had not been lost through the ill-fated Munich Agreement. Beneš also concluded one of the first European treaties with Soviet Russia (1922) and treaties of friendship with Poland (1921), Austria (1921), Italy (1924), and Germany (1925). He was an active participant in the Genoa Economics Meeting (1922), the Locarno Conference (1925), disarmament conferences in 1927, 1929, and 1932, and the Lausanne reparations talks (1932). In 1933, he negotiated the London Convention with the Soviet Union, Yugoslavia, Romania, and Turkey, which defined aggression and thereby applied the 1928 Paris Pact to Eastern Europe, and in 1935 he concluded an alliance (Treaty of Mutual Assistance) with the Soviet Union. He played a leading role in the League of Nations, first as acting vice president in 1920 and then as a member of the council (1923-1927), president of the assembly (1935), and chairs of various committees. In 1924, Beneš and Greek foreign minister Nicholas Politis drafted the celebrated Geneva Protocol, which was designed to prevent aggressive war by requiring that international disputes be submitted to peaceful negotiation and arbitration.

When the aged Masaryk decided to retire, the parliament named his protégé as the new constitutional head of state on December 18, 1935. Beneš tried to check Nazi expansion by means of collective security, but his efforts were torpedoed by France, which allowed Germany to remilitarize the Rhineland, cowered behind the Maginot Line, and refused to honor its treaty commitments. After the Austrian Anschluss, Adolf Hitler put pressure on Czechoslovakia to cede the area populated by German-speaking people (the Sudetenland), and when he began to concentrate troops on the border, Beneš ordered a general mobilization on May 21, 1938. By putting the country on a war footing, Beneš forced the Führer to back down, but by late summer it appeared certain that Germany would drag Europe into a general conflict over the Sudeten issue. The British and French leaders succeeded in negotiating an agreement at Munich on September 29 that allowed Germany to annex the region. Neither the republic nor its Soviet ally was consulted about the matter, and Czechoslovakia, stripped of its border fortifications, was thrown to the wolves. In response to Hitler's demands, Beneš resigned on October 5 and went into exile in London.

He traveled to the United States in February, 1939, to teach at the University of Chicago, but when Hitler seized the remainder of Czechoslovakia on March 15, he agreed to assume the leadership of his country's liberation movement. He returned to London in July, established a popular government known as the Czechoslovak National Committee, and a year later converted it into the Provisional Czechoslovak National Government. In July, 1941, the United States, Great Britain, and the Soviet Union accorded recognition to Beneš' government in exile. His wartime strategy was to pay official visits to the two men who would play the decisive roles in shaping the new order: Franklin D. Roosevelt and Joseph Stalin. He went to the United States in May, 1943, and to Moscow in December, 1943. He made it clear that Czechoslovakia would have a new and more cordial relationship with the Soviet Union after the war, and he agreed to the Czechoslovak-Soviet Treaty of Friendship, Mutual Assistance, and Postwar Cooperation that paved the way for the disaster that would befall his country after the liberation. He hoped that voluntary concessions to Stalin would make for goodwill, but his surrender of Ruthenia (Subcarpathian Ukraine), Czechoslovakia's easternmost province, gained nothing.

As the war drew to a close, the Red Army installed native Communists in Slovakia. Beneš naïvely thought that he and his government would be able to oust these Communists once he appeared on the scene, and journeyed to Russia and then to Slovakia in March, 1945, where he established provisional headquarters at Košice. He agreed to a coalition government that would include Communists, most notably the Czech party leader Klement Gottwald. On May 8, Beneš went to Prague (also liberated by the Soviets), where he was joyously welcomed.

Although Beneš set out to prevent the Communists from monopolizing power in Czechoslovakia, his program of strengthening public morale, treating the Communists evenhandedly and having them share power responsibility in proportion to their strength, yielding to their demands in social and economic but not political matters, and keeping avenues to the West open while reducing Soviet influence in the country was a failure. His position steadily eroded, and in 1948 the Communists carried off a coup. On February 25, Beneš reluctantly signed the death warrant for Czechoslovak freedom by accepting the resignation of the democratic ministers and naming a new government headed by Gottwald. By that time, Beneš was a sick man. He had already suffered a serious stroke the year before, and he resigned the presidency on June 7 and retired to his country home at Sezimovo Ústí. His physical condition deteriorated rapidly, and he died on September 3, 1948.

Summary

Edvard Beneš was the quintessential European statesman of the interwar years. Unfortunately, the times were not ripe for a person with such a commitment to international peace through collective security. Although he was a Czechoslovak patriot, he had a broader conception of the international order. He was an eternal optimist and an ineffable proponent of democracy on the international scene, and thus he was no match for dictators such as Hitler and Stalin. Although he was a brilliant negotiator and understood the art of compromise, his critics questioned whether he really had the fortitude to stand up to tyranny.

Like that of his country, Beneš' life was a tragic story. A confirmed democrat, he was forced to compromise with antidemocratic forces. His allies never came through when they were needed, and, in the crucial years of 1938 and 1948, he and Czechoslovakia were left alone and ignored as the flame of democracy was extinguished. Whether he was a victim of forces beyond his control or he had contributed to the situation by his own ineptness is a matter for historians to debate. Yet he left his mark as a statesman and fighter for a democratic nation and world.

Bibliography

Beneš, Edvard. *Memoirs: From Munich to New World and New Victory.* Translated by Godfrey Lias. London: Allen & Unwin, 1954. Reprint. New York: Arno Press, 1972. Originally published in Prague in 1947, the Czechoslovak edition was a best-seller until its suppression after the Communist coup. It was designed to justify his statesmanship after Munich and the process of undoing the agreement.

_____. *My War Memoirs.* Translated by Paul Selver. Boston: Houghton Mifflin, 1928. A detailed personal account of Beneš' activities in the Czechoslovak national movement, from the beginning of the war to Masaryk's return to preside over the new state.

Bruegel, J. W. *Czechoslovakia Before Munich: The German Minority Problem and British Appeasement Policy.* Cambridge, England: Cambridge University Press, 1973. Insightful treatment of the Sudeten German question and Beneš' efforts to deal with it. Demonstrates that he failed to grasp the significance of having such a large German minority within his state until it was too late.

Crabitès, Pierre. *Beneš, Statesman of Central Europe.* London: G. Routledge & Sons, 1935. Typical of the popular biographies that were published in the interwar years—laudatory and based on *My War Memoirs* and secondary sources.

Korbel, Josef. *The Communist Subversion of Czechoslovakia, 1938-1948*. Princeton, N.J.: Princeton University Press, 1959. Traces Communist activities in the land from Munich to the coup. Includes the efforts of Beneš to deal with the Communist exile regime and his losing struggle with Gottwald to retain democracy.

_____. *Twentieth Century Czechoslovakia: The Meaning of Its History*. New York: Columbia University Press, 1977. A historical survey that focuses on the key role of Beneš and criticizes his apparent unwillingness to exercise forceful leadership during the Sudeten crisis and the period before the Communist coup.

Mamatey, Victor, and Radomír Luža, eds. *A History of the Czechoslovak Republic, 1918-1948*. Princeton, N.J.: Princeton University Press, 1973. A collection of seventeen detailed scholarly essays on various aspects of the republic's history. The central focus is on Beneš and his leadership.

Taborsky, Edward, *President Edvard Beneš: Between East and West, 1938-1948*. Stanford: Hoover Institution Press, 1981. An account by Beneš' personal secretary and legal adviser between 1939 and 1945 who fled to America after the coup. He relates the president's deeds during the war years and defends him against his critics.

Richard V. Pierard

DAVID BEN-GURION
David Gruen

Born: October 16, 1886; Płónsk, Poland, Russian Empire
Died: December 1, 1973; Tel Aviv, Israel
Areas of Achievement: Government and politics
Contribution: Ben-Gurion dreamed of the state of Israel, then turned that
vision into reality. As Israel's first prime minister and defense minister, he
laid a solid foundation for the country's survival and prosperity; as its
leading statesman, he established the principles that continue to guide it.

Early Life
The son of Avigdor and Sheindel (Friedman) Gruen, David Ben-Gurion
was born in Płónsk, Poland, on October 16, 1886. His father was a local
leader in Hovevai Zion (lovers of Zion), a forerunner of the Zionist movement, and a product of the Haskalah (Jewish enlightenment), which sought
to fuse traditional and modern thought and to revive Hebrew as a living
language. At the age of fourteen, he and two friends organized the Ezra
Society to teach local children to speak and write Hebrew. Despite opposition from religious leaders who regarded Hebrew as too sacred for daily use,
the group attracted 150 students.

Along with his love of Israel, the young Ben-Gurion was imbibing socialist principles. Harriet Beecher Stowe, Leo Tolstoy, and Abraham Mapu
shaped his politics, and in 1905 he joined Poalei Zion (workers of Zion),
which sought to build a workers' state in Israel. A natural organizer and
orator, Ben-Gurion united the seamstresses of Płónsk to strike for a shorter
workday, and he repeatedly outdebated non-Zionist opponents who argued
for assimilation and socialist revolution in Europe.

Another lifelong belief also revealed itself in Płónsk, then ruled by czarist
Russia. The country had witnessed numerous pogroms against the Jews, who
rarely fought back against their attackers. Ben-Gurion, whose heroes were
the Maccabees and Old Testament warriors, successfully urged his core-
ligionists to arm themselves for self-defense, as later he would organize the
Haganah in Palestine to thwart Arab raids. Never a zealot, he did not want to
turn Jews into wolves, but neither did he want his people to be sheep.

In 1906, Ben-Gurion's Zionist dream took him to Petach Tikva in Turkish
Palestine, and for the next several years he worked in various settlements,
living his idea of creating a Jewish state through labor. He was never physically strong, though, and Poalei Zion recognized that he could make a more
significant contribution with his head than with his back. Appointed editor of
the organization's newspaper, *Ahdut*, he took as his pseudonym the name of
Yosef Ben-Gurion, a moderate leader of the Jewish revolt against the Romans in A.D. 66.

Life's Work

Believing that Turkey could be persuaded to grant a Jewish state, Ben-Gurion went to Constantinople in 1912 to pursue a law degree, after which he planned to enter the Turkish parliament and work for an independent Israel. The Balkan War interrupted his studies; the outbreak of World War I ended them. He returned to Palestine, where he urged support for Turkey against the Entente, fearing that if the Central Powers were defeated, anti-Semitic Russia would be awarded the ancient Jewish homeland. Indifferent to his pro-Ottoman stance, Turkish authorities arrested Ben-Gurion in February, 1915, for his Zionist activities and deported him. Together with Itzhak Ben-Zvi, later to serve as Israel's president, Ben-Gurion went to the United States to encourage Jewish immigration; throughout his life, he believed that a Jewish state would arise and prosper only if Jews settled and worked the land. He made few converts, but one of them was a young girl from Milwaukee, Goldie Mabovitch; as Golda Meir, she would be Israel's prime minister. While in the United States, Ben-Gurion published *Yizkor* (1916) and *Eretz Yisrael* (1918) to promote Jewish settlement in Palestine. These volumes did little to further that cause, but they did enhance Ben-Gurion's reputation. While in the United States, he met and married Paula Munweis (December 5, 1917).

When the United States entered World War I, Ben-Gurion realized that Turkey and the other Central Powers were doomed. His shift of allegiance to the Entente was guaranteed by the Balfour Declaration (November 2, 1917), promising a Jewish homeland in Israel; he could not know that Great Britain was also pledging to give the same territory to the Arabs and to France. Urging the creation of a Jewish Legion to support Great Britain, Ben-Gurion himself enlisted, leaving his pregnant wife. The legion saw little action, but it did return Ben-Gurion to the Middle East, where he immediately resumed his efforts to forge a united labor organization. Crucial to this goal was the Histadrut. Founded in December, 1920, with only 4,433 of the 65,000 Jews of Palestine, it grew throughout the decade, establishing its own bank, newspaper (*Davar*), construction company, and recreational facilities. Under Ben-Gurion's leadership, the various labor factions also joined politically, so that by 1930 his Mapai Party included 80 percent of the region's Jewish workers.

While Ben-Gurion's achievements and reputation grew in Palestine, he could not influence Zionist policy. The Fourteenth and Fifteenth World Zionist Congresses encouraged middle-class rather than worker immigration and favored urban instead of rural development. Ben-Gurion was philosophically opposed to this emphasis on bourgeois capitalism; he also recognized that businessmen, with no tie to the land, were likely to leave the country once prosperity ended, and so they did after 1927. Another disagreement, with Chaim Weizmann, president of the World Zionist Organization, arose over how far to press Great Britain to allow Jewish settlement in Palestine; Weizmann favored conciliation at almost any cost.

Unable to compete within the World Zionist Organization, Ben-Gurion in 1930 created a rival, the World Congress for Labor Palestine, dedicated to "a Jewish state, a laboring society, [and] Jewish-Arab cooperation." Through this new institution, Ben-Gurion hoped to enlist international Jewish support for his views, but Great Britain's efforts to placate the Arabs at Jewish expense were turning mainstream Zionists away from Weizmann. At the Seventeenth World Zionist Congress, the World Congress for Labor Palestine comprised the largest single bloc of votes, and its representatives received two seats on the executive committee. Two years later, when the organization convened again, the World Congress for Labor Palestine held 44.6 percent of the votes, thanks in large measure to Ben-Gurion's vigorous campaigning in Eastern Europe; Ben-Gurion himself was named to the Executive. By 1935, the World Congress for Labor Palestine had gained control, and Ben-Gurion became chairman of the Zionist Executive and head of the Jewish Agency.

Although he had refused the presidency of the World Zionist Organization in favor of Weizmann, the two men continued to disagree over unlimited immigration and relations with Great Britain. Realizing that Great Britain never would willingly fulfill the promise of the Balfour Declaration, Ben-Gurion in 1936 began training the Haganah, the underground Jewish army, for future conflicts with the Arabs and British. Throughout World War II, he opposed guerrilla warfare against Great Britain, but as soon as Germany surrendered he went to the United States to secure money for weapons. In October, 1945, he ordered the Haganah to use force if necessary to protect Jews entering Palestine illegally, Great Britain having refused to lift tight restrictions on Jewish immigration, and he supported a number of attacks against British installations. Great Britain responded by arresting Jewish leaders and confiscating weapons, but it also resolved to abandon its mandate, agreeing to a partition plan adopted by the United Nations on November 29, 1947.

After almost two thousand years, after a third of their number had been killed in the Nazi holocaust, the Jewish people were to have a country of their own—if they could defend it from the armies of five Arab nations poised to invade as soon as the British mandate ended. George Marshall, the American Secretary of State, urged Ben-Gurion not to declare independence but to wait five or ten years more. Instead, on May 14, 1948, in the Tel Aviv Museum, Ben-Gurion declared "the establishment of the Jewish State in Palestine, to be called the State of Israel."

Ben-Gurion had been modern Jewry's Moses, leading it to the promised land. Now he would also be its Joshua, as the army he had trained and supplied turned back the invaders. At the same time, he overcame threats

from Menachem Begin's Irgun Z'vai Leumi on the right and from the Pal-
mach on the left, each seeking to maintain autonomous military organizations. He thus established the principle of civilian control over the military.
Over the next four years (1949-1953), he led the fledgling nation as prime
minister and defense minister, doubling the nation's Jewish population and
securing international financial support.

At the end of 1953, he temporarily retired—for two years, he said—to
Sde Boker, a kibbutz in the Negev desert, fifty miles south of Beersheba. He
wanted a rest, a chance to read and write, but he also wanted to foster in
others the pioneer spirit that had brought him to Israel almost fifty years
earlier. Moreover, he regarded settlement of the Negev as crucial to the
country's security against Egypt and hoped others would follow him into this
area.

His absence from government actually lasted more than a year. A scandal
in the defense ministry led to the resignation of Pinḥas Lavon, and Ben-
Gurion replaced him. After the 1955 elections, he also resumed the post of
prime minister, leading the country to victory in the 1956 Suez campaign.
Although much of the victory was annulled by pressure from the United
States to return to prewar borders, Israel had secured freedom of navigation
through Elath. Also, France, which had helped Israel during the fighting,
agreed to build a nuclear reactor at Dimona.

At the same time that Ben-Gurion was making Israel the strongest military
power in the region, he also wanted it to be one of the world's great moral
forces. To the newly independent states of Africa and to Burma he sent
technicians and scientists, and from these countries came students who
would be doctors, nurses, and teachers in their homelands.

Well into his seventies, Ben-Gurion exemplified his definition of a leader:
"You must know when to fight your political opponents and when to mark
time. . . . And . . . you must constantly reassess chosen policies." In the
1960's, though, he became increasingly inflexible and out of touch with
reality. He refused to recognize the evidence that exonerated Pinḥas Lavon,
who had been forced to leave the defense ministry in 1955 after perjured
testimony and forged documents caused him to be blamed for terrorist acts in
Egypt. While Ben-Gurion recruited the next generation of Israel's leaders,
among them Moshe Dayan, Shimon Peres, and Abba Eban, he antagonized
many of his older colleagues, such as Moshe Sharett and Golda Meir, by
seeming to ignore them in favor of younger protégés. His close ties to
Germany brought Israel many benefits, but he failed to gauge the hostility
that many of his countrymen harbored against that country. In 1963, amid
growing opposition to his leadership, he resigned from the government; two
years later he left the Mapai Party he had done so much to create, challenging it in the 1965 elections. His faction won ten seats, Mapai forty-five.
When tension with Egypt increased in 1967, there were calls for Ben-

Gurion's return to the prime ministry, but only from those unaware that he was urging peace. It was his disciple, Dayan, who as defense minister led the nation to its swift, overwhelming victory in the Six Day War.

In 1970, Ben-Gurion left the Knesset, Israel's parliament, for what he thought was the last time, but, on his eighty-fifth birthday, he spoke to a special session called in his honor and received a standing ovation from friends and opponents alike. He then returned to the Negev, and there, after his death on December 1, 1973, he was buried, overlooking the Wilderness of Zin, where Israel's saga had begun three millennia before.

Summary

David Ben-Gurion observed that "history would have been quite different if there had been no Churchill." History would also have been different had there been no Ben-Gurion. As a young pioneer in Turkish Palestine, he had resolved, "I have but a single aim: to serve the Jewish worker in the Land of Israel." He never strayed from that purpose. When others hesitated to pressure Great Britain to declare Israeli independence and to open Israel's borders to unlimited immigration, he pressed boldly on. Though he might have shifted tactics, supporting the Central Powers and then the Entente in World War I, opposing guerrilla warfare against Great Britain and then favoring it, he never altered his goal of building a secure, moral Jewish nation.

Ben-Gurion sacrificed much for his dream. As a young man he was often ill, lonely, and hungry, as he sought work, frequently unsuccessfully, in a malaria-ridden land. Later he would have virtually no family life, traveling around Europe and the United States to cajole and coerce others into sharing his dream. His insistence on principles above politics alienated many former friends. Nor did he accomplish all that he sought, never reconciling Sephardic Jews from Africa and Asia with the European Ashkenazis, certainly not achieving peace with the Arabs. His hope of making Israel a leader among Third World nations remained unrealized.

For what Ben-Gurion did accomplish, though, he will remain, as Charles de Gaulle described him in 1960, the symbol of Zionism and "one of the greatest statesmen of [the twentieth] century." He had built his castles in the air, then had put solid foundations under them. The state of Israel is his legacy; he shaped its history and left a blueprint for its future—to do justly, to love mercy, and to walk humbly with its God.

Bibliography

Avi-hai, Avraham. *Ben-Gurion, State-Builder: Principles and Pragmatism, 1948-1963*. New York: John Wiley & Sons, 1974. This work argues that Ben-Gurion was successful in shaping modern Israel, because he could find practical ways to fulfill his ideals. It ends with Ben-Gurion's resignation as prime minister in 1963.

Bar-Zohar, Michael. *Ben-Gurion: A Biography.* New York: Delacorte Press, 1978. Bar-Zohar spent much time with Ben-Gurion and interviewed other Israeli leaders. Presents not only the public figure but also the private man behind the decisions.

Ben-Gurion, David. *David Ben-Gurion in His Own Words.* Edited by Amram Ducovny. New York: Fleet Press, 1968. Ducovny provides a brief biography of the Israeli leader and then arranges Ben-Gurion's statements under such headings as "The Philosopher" (chapter 2) and "The Scholar" (chapter 7). Includes a useful chronology through 1968.

Kurzman, Dan. *Ben-Gurion: Prophet of Fire.* New York: Simon & Schuster, 1983. Based on extensive interviews and archival research as well as published material, this work provides a comprehensive survey of Ben-Gurion's life. Contains fascinating photographs and an extensive bibliography.

Teveth, Shabtai. *Ben-Gurion and the Palestinian Arabs: From Peace to War.* Oxford: Oxford University Press, 1985. Maintains that Ben-Gurion determined Israel's attitude toward the Arabs within its borders. Traces the evolution of Ben-Gurion's thoughts on Jewish-Arab relations. Ends with the establishment of the state of Israel.

_____. *Ben-Gurion: The Burning Ground, 1886-1948.* Boston: Houghton Mifflin, 1987. A scholarly companion to Avi-hai's work about Ben-Gurion after 1948. Ben-Gurion's papers are voluminous and this work draws heavily on them. Ends at 1948 because official documents thereafter are inaccessible and because he sees Ben-Gurion as changing after Israel gained its independence.

Joseph Rosenblum

WALTER BENJAMIN

Born: July 15, 1892; Berlin, Germany
Died: September 27, 1940; Port Bou, Spain
Area of Achievement: Literature
Contribution: Unappreciated during his own tragic life, Benjamin became a
major influence upon modern cultural criticism after World War II when
former colleagues and friends began publishing his work. Using messianic
and Marxist ideas in a very idiosyncratic manner, Benjamin criticized all
attempts to mask the suffering of humanity with an aesthetic illusion.

Early Life

Walter Benjamin was born July 15, 1892, to an upper-middle-class Jewish
family living in the West End of Berlin. From his father, a dealer in art and
antiquities, he acquired an early interest in culture. While at the prestigious
Friedrich-Wilhelm Gymnasium, he was influenced by the antiauthoritarian
educational concepts of Gustav Wyneken, eventually taking on a leadership
role in the Youth Movement and publishing articles in their journal *Der
Anfang*. He separated from the group when they enthusiastically accepted
World War I, which Benjamin avoided by feigning sciatica. In Freiburg,
Berlin, Munich, and Bern, where he studied philosophy, Benjamin came
under the influence of Zionists and leftists, including Martin Buber and Ernst
Bloch. His doctoral dissertation, *Der Begriff der Kunstkritik in der deut-
schen Romantik* (the concept of art criticism in German Romanticism), com-
pleted in Bern in 1920, examined Johann Gottlieb Fichte's metaphysics and
Friedrich Schlegel's aesthetics.

In 1917, Benjamin had married Dora Pollak, their only child Stefan being born that same year. When the financial support of his parents became
strained by the mounting economic crisis in the Weimar Republic, the couple
was compelled to return to Germany so that Benjamin might seek suitable
employment.

In 1925, Benjamin submitted his manuscript *Ursprung des deutschen
Trauerspiels* (1928; *The Origin of German Tragic Drama*, 1977) as a *Hab-
ilitationsschrift* to teach aesthetics and literary history at the University of
Frankfurt. Ill suited by temperament for a university career, and with a
theoretical argument for cultural engagement that was unlikely to be appreciated by apolitical German academics, he was forced to withdraw the application. Freed from domestic responsibilities with the collapse of his marriage
after 1924, Benjamin set out to become a free-lance intellectual, hoping to
support himself with literary journalism. He also soon turned down the possibility of a teaching position in Jerusalem, obtained for him by his lifelong
friend Gershom Scholem. Ultimately he would fail in this attempt to become
an independent man of letters, his genius only being recognized after his

death. Benjamin's tragic life has come to represent the twentieth century alienation about which he so perceptively wrote.

Life's Work

Benjamin launched his career as a literary critic by publishing several major essays on ethics, violence, and Johann Wolfgang von Goethe, which appeared in journals such as the *Frankfurter Zeitung*, *Die Literarische Welt*, and *Die Gesellschaft*, and by translating works by Charles Baudelaire, Marcel Proust, and Marcel Jouhandeau. In these early essays, as in his thesis on the German drama (*Trauerspiel*), Benjamin attacked the aesthetic delusion, which covered up the tragedies of human experience by mimicking the totality of nature or by evoking a deceptive harmony of language. In one of his first essays, about Goethe's novel *Die Wahlverwandtschaften* (1809; *Elective Affinities*, 1872), Benjamin argued that criticism should reveal the calamity of the human condition by radically demolishing any symbolic representation of nature that would suggest an order to man's existence. Behind the allegorical representation of faith in the baroque tragic drama, his thesis uncovered the civilizational trauma of thirty years of war and plague. Allegory showed the importance of apprehending language in a primordial fashion, verbalizing without mediation things in themselves. For Benjamin, only a language free of human intention could reveal such metaphysical truth. The dialectical tension between all literary imagery and historical reality, which should be exposed by the critic to shock the reader or viewer, would be a recurrent theme throughout his work. Every "document of civilization" was also in some way a "document of barbarism," as were all "cultural treasures."

The complex philosophy of language by which Benjamin understood the function of words was complemented by a great mastery of his native tongue, German, allowing him to give the highest abstractions a sensuous richness. Embracing Brecht's concept of "crude thinking" by which the language of practice is used to articulate theory, Benjamin denied that the dialectician could only explain himself through arcane linguistic formulations. Both the argument and style of his writings thus brushed continually against the grain of linguistic or symbolic illusion.

As the critique of modern culture developed, Benjamin saw the fault lying less in language itself and more in the social role of bourgeois intellectuals who turned literature and art into commodities, sold and possessed rather than experienced politically. Culture should articulate the alienating and negative dimensions of human experience, thereby revealing the contradictions of industrial society. For example, the shock of Baudelaire's assaultive use of sacred images in unholy contexts exposed the social truth lying behind the trancelike pretense to normality in bourgeois art.

After 1924, Benjamin's interest in a materialistic analysis of modernity was increasingly enriched by contact with left-wing intellectuals, such as Asja Lacis, a Latvian actress who introduced him to Bertolt Brecht. He was particularly impressed with the Marxist critique of culture set forth by György Lukács in *Geschichte und Klassenbewusstein* (1923; *History and Class Consciousness*, 1971). In 1926-1927, Benjamin visited Moscow and reported enthusiastically on the wave of artistic experimentation that followed the Russian Revolution, but typically he admitted that he was too much of an "anarchist" to join the Communist Party. Nevertheless, he believed that "significant literary work" would come only from "a strict alternation between action and writing."

The Nazi takeover of the German state in 1933 forced Benjamin to Paris, where he furthered his interest in French culture, and to Denmark and Ibiza, where he enjoyed extended visits with Brecht. After 1935, there appeared in the *Zeitschrift für Sozialforschung* (journal for social research), published by the exiled Frankfurt Institute for Social Research, a number of important articles by Benjamin on nineteenth century French culture and modern urban life. A stipend from the institute had been secured for him by Theodor W. Adorno, one of its leading members.

Throughout his later essays, Benjamin defined the task of criticism as the recovery of everyday life, fragmented by the alienating and reifying forces of capitalism. The 1867 World Exhibition in Paris was, for example, a microcosm of the world of commodities wherein the emphasis on individualistic buying and selling prevented realization that production should serve human needs. The discontinuous events of modernity, experienced disjointedly through capitalistic consumerism, technological fetishes, and the crowded metropolis, estranged man from even the integral nature of his own experience.

Benjamin had hoped to bring these themes together in a masterpiece, the unfinished Arcades Project. By using the sumptuous commercial galleries of nineteenth century Paris, he wanted to write a modern allegory on the sociotechnological basis of bourgeois culture. The embodiment of modern alienation was the *flâneur* (dawdler), whose stroll past the cafés, brothels, boutiques, dioramas, theaters, newsstands, and baths that jammed the Parisian arcades represented the lonely voyeurism of the urban crowd. The luxuriousness of the shopwindows masked any understanding of the oppression required to fill them, just as exchange value obscured the intrinsic use value of capitalist production. Like the bohemian *flâneur*, bourgeois intellectuals who posed as critics in actuality legitimated the public's consumption of capitalist culture.

Benjamin, however, unlike other critics of the materialism of the modern age, such as the Pre-Raphaelites, sought no return to a simpler culture and life. He applauded, for example, advances in aesthetic techniques that might provide artists with the means of redefining the relationship between themselves and their audience. He was enthusiastic about the revolutionary potential of film. Above all else, he wanted to strip culture of the religious mystification that occurred when it was experienced passively. It was Brecht's blunt interruption of the observor's empathy with the stage that Benjamin found so enticing. As he argued in his famous and influential essay, "Das Kunstwerk im Zeitalter seiner technischen Reproduzierbarkeit" (1936; "The Work of Art in the Age of Mechanical Reproduction," 1968), the modern capability exactly to reproduce paintings fortunately destroyed their "aura," that reverential attitude of the cultivated public toward authenticity. The obsession with artistic genuineness deflected public attention away from the fact that life in bourgeois society was itself inauthentic, standardized, and unnatural. In "Der Autor als Produzent" (1966; "The Author as Producer," 1978), Benjamin suggested that literature might be politicized if the traditional ways that writers addressed their readers were overturned.

Feeling that there were "still positions to defend," Benjamin stayed in France well after many of his comrades had fled. Using the ideas of Freud, he attacked the fascist glorification of bodily discipline, sexual asceticism, and nationalistic self-sacrifice. With the Stalin-Hitler Pact of 1939, and a short internment with other German refugees at Niève, Benjamin appears to have lost some of his faith in the possibility of meaningful political engagement. Turning back to a melancholic messianism found in his own Jewish heritage, his last work, "Über den Begriff der Geschichte" (1942; "Theses on the Philosophy of History," 1968) would appear to abandon faith in historical progress. Redemption from oppression could only be found in some eschatological interruption of time, a "Now-time" or *Jetzt-zeit*, that allowed for the rediscovery of the dreams of humanity. After the Nazi invasion of France, Benjamin acquired a visa in Marseilles to enter the United States and, with failing health, tried to escape to Spain. When an official, attempting blackmail, threatened to turn him and his fellow refugees over to the Gestapo, he took his own life with a massive dose of morphine on September 27, 1940, in Port Bou, Spain. Two volumes of his collected writing appeared posthumously only in 1955. From that date, however, his work acquired an immense influence on postmodern criticism.

Summary

Calling himself the "last of the Europeans," Walter Benjamin wrote incisively about such diverse things as hashish, child toys, postage stamps, Surrealism, and Kafka. He was, as Hannah Arendt observed, a metaphysician who thought poetically. Seeing no "hermetic self-sufficiency" to any discipline, his thought allowed him to combine conservative aesthetic sensibilities with structuralist and materialist criticism. The eclectic complexity of his thought, his use of aphorism and the short essay, the density of his exposition, make a unified interpretation of Benjamin extremely difficult. As

Jügen Habermas noted, his thoughts like his friends were not always intro-duced to one another. His ultimate role was as an essayist: Opinion was like oil to a machine, he wrote; one did not dump a can on a turbine, one applied a little at a time to spindles and joints. In many ways his ideas were like the angels in the Talmudic legend, an innumerable host created in order to sing their hymn in God's presence and then cease and disappear into the void. Benjamin distrusted any limitation on a dialectical understanding of truth. His fragmentary, eclectic manner, what he called "dialectics at a standstill," well served such an understanding.

Bibliography

Benjamin, Walter. *Reflections*. Edited by Peter Demetz. New York: Schocken Books, 1986. Another diverse selection of Benjamin essays, including several autobiographical pieces (notably on his Berlin childhood and visit to Moscow), and an introduction by Demetz focusing on the different currents creating the complexity of his thought.

Buck-Morss, Susan. *Walter Benjamin and the Dialectics of Seeing: A Study of the Arcades Project*. Cambridge, Mass.: MIT Press, 1989. A penetrat-ing analysis, inspired by a New Left interpretation of Marxism, of what would have been Benjamin's masterpiece.

Eagleton, Terry. *Walter Benjamin: Or, Towards a Revolutionary Criticism*. London: Verso and New Left Books, 1981. A difficult but important work showing the influence of Benjamin on neo-Marxist and poststructuralist criticism. Eagleton explores three central themes in Benjamin—the ba-roque allegory, commodities as cultural objects, and messianic concepts of revolution.

Roberts, Julian. *Walter Benjamin*. London: Macmillan, 1982. A defense of the Marxist interpretation of Benjamin's thought, understood in the con-text of the culture and history of the early twentieth century.

Scholem, Gershom. *Walter Benjamin: The Story of a Friendship*. Translated by Harry Zohn. Philadelphia: Jewish Publication Society, 1981. An inter-pretation of Benjamin's romantic messianism by a distinguished scholar of the Kabbalah.

Smith, Gary, ed. *On Walter Benjamin: Critical Essays and Recollections*. Cambridge, Mass.: MIT Press, 1988. A useful collection of essays by leading Benjamin scholars and his friends, including Adorno, Scholem, and Habermas, with an extensive bibliography.

_____. *Thinking Through Benjamin*. Chicago: University of Chicago Press, 1989. A revised edition of essays originally appearing in *The Philo-sophical Forum*.

Wolin, Richard. *Walter Benjamin: An Aesthetic of Redemption*. New York: Columbia University Press, 1982. A defense of the position that the "dis-continuous extremes" in Benjamin's work engender its enigmatic majesty and betray its ultimate theological preoccupations, an interpretation heavily influenced by Adorno.

Bland Addison, Jr.

ALBAN BERG

Born: February 9, 1885; Vienna, Austro-Hungarian Empire
Died: December 24, 1935; Vienna, Austria
Area of Achievement: Music
Contribution: Berg was one of the pioneers in the creation of atonal and twelve-tone music. Though basing his work on the revolutionary system of his teacher Arnold Schoenberg, Berg established a link between the new style and the Romantic past and demonstrated that atonal and twelve-tone music could still be lyrical and emotionally expressive. As a result, his works gained widespread acceptance and thus encouraged a whole generation of innovative and experimental composers.

Early Life

Alban Berg was born in Vienna on February 9, 1885. His father was a prosperous businessman whose distinguished Bavarian Catholic ancestry included high-ranking military men and public servants. Even so, the Bergs were an artistic family, and Berg's brother and sister both studied music. Berg himself, however, at first seemed more interested in poetry and drama, reading Henrik Ibsen, Oscar Wilde, and the Romantic German literature common at the end of the nineteenth century. Later, as a composer of operas, Berg was to realize his literary ambitions by writing his own librettos.

Despite circumstances that were apparently comfortable, Berg's early life was not without difficulties. As a child, his health was generally frail, and, in 1900, the year his father died, he developed a severe form of asthma that plagued him throughout his life. Perhaps coincidentally, it was also in this year that he first tried his hand at composition, setting three German poems to music. From that point on, composing became his primary interest, and, over the next four years, he created some seventy works, mostly songs and piano duets. Though influenced initially by the Romantic music of Johannes Brahms, Richard Wagner, and Gustav Mahler, Berg had, as yet, no formal musical training. He was, in fact, far too high-strung and moody to be an especially good student: At age eighteen, for example, he failed his general humanities examination and then attempted suicide.

In the following year, 1904, Berg finally completed his schooling and obtained a position working for the government. After a few months at this job, he saw a newspaper advertisement for students placed by Schoenberg, a thirty-year-old composer and teacher who had already begun to rock the musical world. Berg immediately submitted several of his works to Schoenberg, who recognized Berg's talent and accepted him as a student. Over the next six years, Schoenberg became both mentor and friend to the younger man, and through patient encouragement, shaped his whole approach to composition.

Life's Work

At the time Berg became his pupil, Schoenberg was just beginning to break away from the Wagnerian Romantic tradition and would soon work out an entirely new approach to musical composition. Since the time of Johann Sebastian Bach at least, nearly all Western music had been written from the basis of tonality. Essentially, this means that the construction of a piece of music was centered on a single tone, called the "key." Tension and interest were created by moving away from the key, but, by the end, the tension was resolved by returning to the initial tone. The tools used in the tonal system were the notes of the diatonic scale (do, re, mi, fa, sol, and so on) and chords. A diatonic scale includes any seven tones in order, which are sounded by the white keys on a piano. The notes sounded by the five black keys in between are called "chromatic" tones. The twelve tones together are called a "chromatic scale." Using the chromatic notes increases the emotional energy in a piece of music.

Chords are a combination of tones played simultaneously. In the tonal system, chords are usually built of three notes (triads), each one full tone apart (do-mi-sol, re-fa-la, and so on). A chord can be made out of each note in the diatonic scale. The first chord (do-mi-sol) is called the tonic and is the chord of rest. Like tones that move away from the key, each of the other chords in the scale, which move away from the tonic, creates tension or activity. The fifth chord (sol-ti-re) is called the dominant, and it represents the most tension. Music theorists say that the dominant chord seeks to be resolved by the tonic. Moving away from the tonic chord is called "dissonance," while coming back to the tonic is "consonance."

Many composers of the Romantic period, such as Ludwig van Beethoven and Hector Berlioz, had sought to express great emotion in their music by increasing the amount of dissonance before finally returning to the tonic. Among their methods was creation of new, more dissonant chords using the chromatic notes. In the last half of the nineteenth century, Wagner had taken this technique to its logical endpoint, employing more and more "chromaticism" and delaying the return to the tonic until a nearly unbearable tension had been created. Yet Wagner had still remained within the general system of tonality, ultimately resolving the tension by returning to the fundamental key.

At the beginning of their careers, both Schoenberg and Berg wrote music within this Wagnerian tradition. By 1904, however, Schoenberg had begun to believe that the time had come to do away with consonance and the distinction beween the diatonic and chromatic tones. He wished to treat all twelve tones of the scale equally and relate them in music freely to one another, rather than to some central tone. Within a few years, Schoenberg had completely abandoned the tonal system, and his music became increasingly dissonant, always operating at a maximum level of tense, unresolved emotion. His approach became known as "atonality."

Soon, however, Schoenberg became dissatisfied with atonality, too: Abandoning the keys and consonant harmonies that were the basis of the tonal system had left nothing but musical anarchy. He now insisted that a whole new set of rules of composition had to be fashioned. Thus, he created the concept of the "tone row," any arbitrary arrangement of twelve tones. The tone row served as the unifying idea of a composition, and its tones were always used in the same order, though each new appearance of the row could start on any note of the scale. The tone row also might be turned upside down (inversion), backward (retrograde), or both (retrograde inversion), but both the melody and the harmony of a piece were always based upon the original twelve-tone pattern. This system of composition is known as the "twelve-tone" system, or the "serial technique," and has become the foundation for much of the music of the twentieth century.

The impressionable young Berg enthusiastically embraced Schoenberg's new methods, and the music he wrote under Schoenberg's tutelage followed the creative evolution of his teacher. Berg's first significant atonal work was *Five Songs with Orchestra*, written in 1912. It was first performed on February 23, 1913, in a concert of music all written by Schoenberg and his pupils. While a few of the music critics present viewed the new works favorably, the audience reacted with such violent hostility that a riot ensued. One woman fainted, and a horn player in the orchestra vowed that he would never again play such trash. While Schoenberg was apparently unaffected by these responses, this first contact with the general public made a deep and lasting impression on Berg. Though throughout his life, Berg wrote many articles praising both Schoenberg's music and the twelve-tone system, his own compositions soon began to develop a distinct style of their own.

In May, 1914, Berg saw a production of Georg Büchner's play *Woyzeck* (1836; English translation, 1927), and he resolved to create an opera out of this tragic story of a poor soldier who jealously murders his love and then commits suicide. Berg began working on the libretto immediately, but his efforts were interrupted by the outbreak of World War I. Despite his fragile health, Berg was drafted into the Austrian army for limited duty at the War Ministry. After the war, he became a teacher and finally completed *Wozzeck* in 1921. It was not until December, 1925, however, that *Wozzeck* was first performed. Scorned in Vienna, Berg arranged for its presentation by the Berlin State Opera. The performance was a tremendous success, and overnight Berg became an international celebrity. *Wozzeck* was repeated several times in Berlin and then moved on to a triumphant world tour. By 1936, it had been performed 166 times in twenty-nine cities, including Philadelphia and New York. For many years, it remained the most popular opera composed in the twentieth century.

His newfound fame seems to have had little effect upon Berg. He continued to teach and write in Vienna, despite the fact that he was largely ignored in his own country. In 1930, he was appointed to membership in the prestigious Prussian Academy of Arts, and, by 1932, he had finally gained enough financial security to purchase a small summer home on the Wörthersee, a lake in Carinthia. He was bitterly disappointed, however, when Adolf Hitler came to power in Germany, in January, 1933. The Nazis immediately branded Berg's works as "anti-German" and banned them. The growing influence of Nazism in Austria also frightened him, and he was especially disturbed when Schoenberg, whose ancestry was Jewish, was forced to emigrate to the United States.

In the last decade of his life, Berg composed a relatively small number of works, but each one was crafted with consummate skill and artistry. Shortly after the premiere of *Wozzeck*, he wrote the Chamber Concerto for piano, violin, and thirteen wind instruments. This work was dedicated to Schoenberg and written almost completely in the serial technique. In 1926, he produced the Lyric Suite, a six-movement work for string quartet that is much more expressive and lyrical and that uses a combination of atonal, twelve-tone, and even tonal methods. So popular did the Lyric Suite become that, in 1928, Berg arranged three of its movements for orchestra.

For most of his last seven years, however, Berg concentrated on the development of one work, an opera called *Lulu*. As with *Wozzeck*, he himself wrote the libretto, using material from two plays by the German writer Frank Wedekind. *Lulu* is a violent story full of murder, blackmail, sexual perversion, imprisonment, and degradation—ideally suited to the social and intellectual ferment of the 1920's and early 1930's.

In the spring of 1935, Berg was commissioned by the American violinist Louis Krasner to write a violin concerto. Absorbed by the effort to finish *Lulu*, the composer procrastinated about the concerto until the death of a young lady friend inspired him to express his grief through music. The Violin Concerto was written with uncharacteristic rapidity and was dedicated "to the memory of an Angel." This was to be Berg's last completed work and perhaps his most beautiful and gentle. In it, he successfully reconciles the twelve-tone method with traditionally tonal harmony by using an Austrian folk tune and the chorale from a Bach cantata as formative elements. Though the piece utilizes a twelve-tone row, the row itself is based on the traditional triad chord structure. The Violin Concerto was first performed in April, 1936, four months after Berg's death, and, ironically, it became his own requiem.

After completing the Violin Concerto, Berg was exhausted and went off to his summer home for a short rest. At some point in the ensuing weeks, he received an insect bite which became infected and abscessed. When he returned to Vienna to work on the *Lulu* score, he was in great pain, and, finally, on December 17, he entered a hospital, where he was diagnosed as suffering from blood poisoning. Despite several transfusions, he weakened and died on December 24, 1935. His final thoughts were given over to the unfinished *Lulu*; as he died, he went through the motions of conducting the music, and his final words instructed the orchestra to play more firmly.

Summary

Though never completed, *Lulu*, like *Wozzeck*, became a worldwide success. A suite for orchestra and soprano has been adapted from the finished portions of the score and has been performed frequently. The first two acts of the opera were presented in Zurich, Switzerland, in 1937, and the entire completed portions have been staged many times since to great acclaim. Today, Alban Berg is generally regarded as the greatest of the atonal/twelve-tone composers, and his works have influenced those of many other modern composers.

This impact has resulted primarily because Berg became the mediator between the innovative atonal and twelve-tone approaches of Schoenberg and the Romanticism of the nineteenth century. Though almost slavishly loyal to Schoenberg's overall approach, Berg's music retained much of the Romantic outlook, and he proved that atonality can express a variety of moods. His twelve-tone works are gentler and more spontaneous than those of Schoenberg. In *Wozzeck*, tonal and atonal methods are intertwined and dramtically juxtaposed. In *Lulu* and the Violin Concerto, Berg showed that the twelve-tone row could be used flexibly to create both melodic and harmonic materials with a link to the past. In all three of these works, he assimilated folk-tune elements and displayed a highly developed sense of instrumental color often reminiscent of Impressionist composers such as Claude Debussy. The success of *Wozzeck*, the Violin Concerto, and the Lyric Suite have proved that modern serious music does not have to be ugly and can appeal to the average listener. This is, perhaps, Berg's greatest contribution.

Bibliography

Deri, Otto. *Exploring Twentieth-Century Music*. New York: Holt, Rinehart and Winston, 1968. A well-written text that attempts to aid the listener in understanding and appreciating twentieth century music by explaining how its aesthetic principles and materials evolved. Contains an excellent chapter on the life and works of Berg and offers a detailed analysis of several of Berg's major works. Includes an extensive bibliography and discography.

Hansen, Peter S. *An Introduction to Twentieth Century Music*. 3d ed. Boston: Allyn and Bacon, 1971. A standard text on modern music. Presents an appreciative summary of the major movements and musical developments since 1900. Includes a separate chapter on Berg.

Lambert, Constant. *Music Ho! A Study of Music of Decline*. London: Faber & Faber, 1934. Lamberg, himself a prominent British composer before his premature death in 1951, offers a challenging view of twentieth century music. He argues that the loss of traditional values in modern society has tended to encourage composers who violate and destroy the traditional rules pretentiously and simply as a pose. He also praises Berg as a composer.

Machlis, Joseph. *Introduction to Contemporary Music*. New York: W. W. Norton, 1961. An excellent, extremely well-written text. Introduces modern music through comparison and contrast with earlier periods, creating a painless introduction to music theory. European and American composers are grouped by types; each receives a concise biographical treatment and analysis of important works. Includes an excellent bibliography and discography, and texts and translations of vocal works.

Redlich, Hans F. *Alban Berg*. London: J. Calder, 1957. Redlich has been Berg's most important biographer. His work is extremely detailed and informative, but readers unfamiliar with music theory will find his analyses of Berg's work to be very difficult. In addition, Redlich is highly opinionated, and many other critics of Berg's works have violently disagreed with Redlich's highly politicized analyses of *Wozzeck* and *Lulu*.

Reich, Willi. *The Life and Work of Alban Berg*. Translated by Cornelius Cardew. London: Thomas and Hudson, 1965. Reich is less enlightening than Redlich about Berg's personal life, but his analyses of Berg's music are both more thorough and more objective. For the advanced student, this is a superior work.

Thomas C. Schunk

FRIEDRICH BERGIUS

Born: October 11, 1884; Goldschmieden, Germany
Died: March 30, 1949; Buenos Aires, Argentina
Areas of Achievement: Chemistry, engineering, invention, and technology
Contribution: Bergius discovered how to obtain liquid hydrocarbon fuels by
   hydrogenation of coal and how to obtain synthetic sugar from wood cel-
   lulose. The fuels made by his processes aided Germany during World
   War II, and Bergius' methods form the basis for the modern synthetic
   fuels industry.

Early Life
   Friedrich Bergius was born in Goldschmieden (near Breslau), Germany,
on October 11, 1884. The son of well-educated parents, he gained early
experience in chemistry, working first in a small chemical plant owned by
his father and later in a larger plant in Mulheim/Ruhr. He studied at the
Universities of Breslau and Leipzig. At the University of Leipzig, Bergius
worked under the direction of Arthur Hantzsch, who had also influenced the
work of Nobel laureate Alfred Werner twenty years earlier. He was granted
the Ph.D. in chemistry in 1907 and proceeded to Berlin for a year of
postdoctoral work with Walther Nernst, who was one of the most prominent
physical chemists in German academic circles at that time.
   Bergius now had his first opportunity to attempt high-pressure reactions in
the laboratory. He also participated in research on the nitrogen/hydrogen/
ammonia equilibrium in Nernst's laboratory. After leaving Berlin, Bergius
spent a further semester at Karlsruhe in association with the future Nobel
laureate Fritz Haber. There, Bergius gained further experience in the application of high-pressure reaction techniques. He was not satisfied with the existing techniques and apparatus, and saw the need for improvements.
   Bergius' first-published research was a doctoral dissertation on the use of
100 percent sulfuric acid as a solvent. Bergius began his affiliation with the
Hannover Institute of Technology in 1909 and was free to pursue his developing interest in high-pressure reactions. His research was conducted partly
at the institute and partly at a private laboratory he established. As
his projects reached pilot-plant scale, further facilities were acquired. Early
work included a study of the lime/oxygen/calcium peroxide equilibrium,
which was undertaken in the hope of finding a better process for manufacturing hydrogen peroxide, but which actually was important mainly because it
required the refinement of high-pressure valves, fittings, stirred autoclaves,
and other equipment that was of great use later. Bergius and his coworkers
also patented a method of using caustic soda to convert chlorobenzene into
phenol (needed for the manufacture of plastic). This patent was one of many
German patents confiscated by the Allies after World War I and became the

basis of the manufacture of phenol by Dow Chemical Company.

As early as 1911, Bergius became interested in the nature and origin of coal—one of Germany's most plentiful natural resources. The studies that he made of the coal-forming process (the untranslatable German word is *Inkohlung*) led to the achievements for which he is most famous and for which he was awarded (jointly with Carl Bosch) the 1931 Nobel Prize in Chemistry.

Life's Work

Bergius, like Carl Bosch and Fritz Haber, sought to apply the academic principles of physical chemistry to the solution of industrial chemical problems. His goal was not only to understand chemical reactions in an academic manner but also to develop practical industrial methods for large-scale economical production. His efforts were applied mainly in three areas: the production of pure, inexpensive hydrogen, the liquefaction of coal and peat, and the conversion of cellulose-containing by-products into sugar and starch. Bergius' interests were motivated by a desire to benefit humanity in general and by a desire to help Germany end its dependence on foreign sources for food and fuel. Bergius' success in each of these areas came partly from his energy and persistence in overcoming an array of obstacles and partly from his ability to bring to bear the newest technology, particularly the use of high pressures.

The production of hydrogen from the reaction between steam and coke (the water-gas reaction) produced impure hydrogen. Bergius modified this reaction by performing the process at high pressure and developed purification methods for the hydrogen. He also found it possible to manufacture pure hydrogen by means of a reaction between water and iron. Ultimately, this proved cheaper than the use of the water-gas reaction. Modifications of the water-gas reaction and of the iron-water reaction were explored in which the use of high pressure kept the water liquid at high temperatures.

Coal hydrogenation had been performed in small laboratory experiments as early as 1869 by Marcelin Berthelot in France. Bergius improved on the earlier method by switching to high-pressure conditions instead of the relatively low pressures that were obtained by Berthelot. Using a few grams of powdered coal moistened with petroleum to form a paste and treated with high-pressure hydrogen gas, Bergius was able to obtain promising yields of liquid and gaseous hydrocarbons. Use of a rotating autoclave, which was especially developed for the purpose, permitted successful reactions on the scale of five liters, but problems remained.

The hydrogenation reaction was heat-releasing and thus needed to be conducted in a controlled manner to prevent overheating, which reduced the yield of hydrocarbons and produced useless coke. Attempts to hydrogenate coal in larger batches brought many problems. Overheating became more difficult to control in large reactors, and the batch process was inefficient and needed to be made continuous. As the size and complexity of the apparatus increased, so did the expense of the research, and Bergius sought financial backing from various industrial sources. Eventually, Bergius left his relatively small private laboratory in Hannover and began to assemble a modern high-pressure facility in Essen. By that time, he had conducted many studies on the production of hydrogen and on the hydrogenation of oil and coal and had obtained the first of his many patents. Hundreds of different samples of coal of various kinds were tested to determine which types were most suitable for hydrogenation. Soft coal and lignite (common in Germany) were well suited, but hard anthracite coal was poorly suited for liquefaction.

The coal hydrogenation reaction, when scaled up, involved formidable material-handling problems. The coal was ground to a powder and mixed with oil to form a paste. This paste was preheated and pressed into the reactor by a cylindrical ram. Products were continually removed from the reacting mixture during hydrogenation.

The development site in Rheinau/Mannheim employed about 150 workers and was exceedingly expensive to maintain. It became obvious that better capitalization was needed which could only come from affiliation with a larger company. Bergius sold his patents to Badische Anilin und Soda Fabrik (BASF), a major corporation, which continued to develop coal hydrogenation at a plant in Leuna. Much further development was needed to create the synthetic fuel industry that existed in Germany by the 1940's (twelve production facilities were eventually brought into operation), but Bergius' direct contributions were over. He turned his attention to another area: the production of synthetic food.

Chemically, starch, cellulose, and glucose (also known as dextrose) are closely related, since starch and cellulose are composed of many glucose units linked together—one pattern of linkage leading to starch and another to cellulose. Although ruminants can digest cellulose as well as starch, humans can only digest starch (or glucose). Strong acids (such as hydrochloric acid, which humans have in their digestive tracts) can eventually break down cellulose into sugar but only at high temperatures. Bergius devoted years of effort to the perfection of the method of converting sawdust, straw, or other agricultural wastes into edible material by hydrochloric acid treatment. Great care and ingenuity were needed to ensure recycling of reactants and the greatest efficiency in the use of heat. An extensive account of this work was published in 1931 as "Die Herstellung von Zucker aus Holz und ähnlichen Naturstoffen" (the preparation of sugar from wood and other natural materials). Bergius resided in Heidelberg in the late 1920's and was awarded an honorary degree by the university in 1927. In Hannover, a street was named for him, and the university awarded him an honorary degree. Even Harvard University chose to award him an honorary degree in 1936. In Heidelberg, the

Bergius household became a meeting place for artists and writers. Among those who came was Gustav Stresemann, a leader in the National Liberal Party and chancellor (1923) who had done much to rejuvenate German industry after World War I by negotiating with the Allies over the question of reparations.

Once again, however, Bergius' research began to suffer from lack of funding. He sold his home, threw all of his personal fortune into the research effort, and even made a personal appeal to President Paul von Hindenburg for support to keep his work going. Ironically, it was only the rise of Adolf Hitler and his preparations for war that finally stimulated meaningful support from the government for the so-called food from wood project. Bergius worked during the war years in Berlin but saw his facilities destroyed by air raids. At the end of the war, the Allies captured numerous documents pertaining to German scientific research. Scholars are still studying these documents, and it may be that additional details of Bergius' research activities may appear. Bergius spent the postwar years until his death in an attempt to find suitable employment and scope for his further plans. He went first to Italy, then to Turkey, Switzerland, and Spain. He left Europe in 1947 to become a scientific adviser to the Argentine government and died in Buenos Aires in 1949.

Summary

Although his life was rich in achievements, Friedrich Bergius spent the latter part of his life in circumstances that did not permit him to be as creative as he might have been. The economic chaos in Germany in the 1920's made it so difficult to obtain funding for his research that in 1925 he sold most of his patents to BASF. From that time on, Bergius was excluded from further work on coal liquefaction, the field that he had pioneered.

Turning to cellulose conversion, Bergius again did fundamental work and developed an economically viable process, but only after spending vast sums—including major amounts of his own money. Unfortunately, the commercial interest in his process did not materialize to any great extent. After World War II, having lost his laboratory and sources of funding, he became a sort of scientific refugee and traveled to many countries as a consultant until his death.

Bibliography
Bergius, Friedrich. "Die Herstellung von Zucker aus Holz und ähnlichen Naturstoffen." In *Ergebnisse der Angewandte Physikalischen Chemie*. Leipzig: 1931. One of the most complete single accounts of the cellulose conversion processes.
_____. "An Historical Account of Hydrogenation." *Proceedings of the World Petroleum Congress*, vol. 2. London: 1933. Bergius tells what

trains of thought led him to develop his coal- and oil-hydrogenation processes. There are nineteen illustrations, mostly showing diagrams of reactors or photographs of process equipment.

Nobelstiftelsen. *Chemistry.* Vol. 2, *1922-1941*. New York: Elsevier, 1966. Bergius' Nobel lecture is reprinted in this volume; it includes references to the calcium peroxide work, production of hydrogen, origin and hydrogenation of coal, hydrolysis of organic chlorides, and design of high-pressure apparatus. Contains twenty-six illustrations.

Stranges, Anthony N. "Friedrich Bergius and the Rise of the German Synthetic Fuel Industry." *Isis* 75, no. 279 (1984): 643-667. This article traces the growth of the German synthetic fuel industry, concentrating on the period 1910-1925. Includes an extensive list of references to works by and about Bergius.

——————. "Friedrich Bergius and the Transformation of Coal Liquefaction from Empiricism to a Science-Based Technology." *Journal of Chemical Education* 65, no. 9 (1988): 749-751. This article discusses Bergius' place in the application of the highly theoretical ideas of Nernst and the other founders of chemical thermodynamics.

John R. Phillips

INGMAR BERGMAN

Born: July 14, 1918; Uppsala, Sweden

Areas of Achievement: Film and theater

Contribution: Despite fluctuations in the critical appraisal of his many films, Bergman dominated the Scandinavian filmmaking industry from the mid-1940's until the early 1980's, and his films earned international acclaim. His rapport with actors and his innovative stage techniques have also earned for him a reputation as one of the world's foremost theatrical directors.

Early Life

Ernst Ingmar Bergman was born on July 14, 1918, in Uppsala, Sweden, to Erik and Karin Bergman and was reared in the country home of his maternal grandmother. A Lutheran pastor, Erik Bergman believed in strict discipline for his family. Many of Bergman's childhood memories revolve around episodes of punishment by humiliation; however, not all of his experiences were negative. His grandmother discussed important issues with the boy daily and encouraged his storytelling abilities. Though Bergman's early years were spent in relative poverty, a rich aunt did provide him with inspiration for his future career in filmmaking. She gave his elder brother a magic lantern film projector, which Bergman so coveted that he traded his collection of toy soldiers for it.

When his father became chaplain to the Royal Hospital, young Bergman was fascinated by the nearby mortuary and cemetery, gaining there a gruesome introduction to death. In 1934, Erik Bergman was appointed parish priest at Hedvig Eleonora Church and the family moved to Stockholm. As an exchange student in Germany, Bergman developed a youthful passion for Nazism. His later disillusionment with Nazi atrocities led him away from politics altogether, although his love for Berlin remained so strong that he tried several times to portray the city in film. Following a brief period of military service, Bergman attended the University of Stockholm but became involved with writing and directing plays and did not finish his degree.

After many successful stage productions for various theaters in Stockholm, Bergman became a screenwriter for Svensk Filmindustri. His first screenplay, *Hets* (1944: *Torment*), about a young student's battle with his repressive schoolmaster (based on his own experiences at Palmgren's School), was directed by his mentor, veteran director Alf Sjöberg. The best film of his early career is probably *Fängelse* (1949; *The Devil's Wanton*), which he both wrote and directed for Terrafilm, a company run by independent producer Lorens Marmstedt, to whom Bergman credits much of his own filmmaking education.

During this early part of his career, Bergman directed plays for the Helsingborg, Malmö, and Gothenburg city theaters while at the same time working on films for Svensk Filmindustri and Terrafilm. While his professional life flourished, his tumultuous personal life was marked by financial problems, illness, several marriages, divorces, and romantic affairs with his leading actresses.

Life's Work

Bergman's international reputation was established in the 1950's with a series of film dramas that explore the complexity of human relationships. The difficulty of establishing and maintaining emotional bonds inside and outside marriage is investigated in *Sommarlek* (1951; *Illicit Interlude*), *Kvinnors väntan* (1952; *Secrets of Women*), *Gycklarnas Afton* (1953; *The Naked Night*), *En lection i kärlek* (1954; *A Lesson in Love*), and *Sommarnattens leende* (1955; *Smiles of a Summer Night*). Bergman's affair with actress Harriet Andersson, who stars in several of these films, affected his early portrait of Nordic eroticism. Eva Dahlbeck and Gunnar Björnstrand, key members of Bergman's stock film/theater company, played the witty married couple in his lighter films.

In what Peter Cowie calls his "golden years," Bergman poses philosophical and moral questions about the nature of man's existence and the problem of evil. *Det sjunde inseglet* (1957; *The Seventh Seal*), a medieval allegory set during the Great Plague, contemplates the meaninglessness of life in the face of irrational death. In *Smulltronstället* (1957; *Wild Strawberries*), Bergman studies one of his favorite character types, the cold intellectual who distances himself from common humanity. Both of these films employ the journey motif favored by Bergman to chart the emotional evolution of his characters, and they feature the sunny presence of Bibi Andersson, the actress/lover with whom Bergman made his most idealistic statements. The battle of rationality and emotion, of science and art, continues in *Ansiktet* (1958; *The Magician*). One of Bergman's favorite themes during the 1950's is the conflict between what actor Max von Sydow describes as "the very sensitive, highly emotional individual who cannot bear his own feelings" and "the one who is inhibited by his intellect." After this intensely personal portrait of the artist, Bergman next adapts a fourteenth century legend about a young girl's brutal rape and her father's revenge in *Jungfrukällan* (1960; *The Virgin Spring*). Though Bergman would later criticize this film as an imitation of Akira Kurosawa's *Rashomon* (1950), *The Virgin Spring* won the Oscar for Best Foreign-Language Film. Returning to very subjective films about faith and doubt, Bergman wrote and directed what he termed his "Chamber Plays:" *Såsom i en spegel* (1961; *Through a Glass Darkly*), *Nattvardsgästerna* (1963; *Winter Light*), and *Tystnaden* (1963; *The Silence*). The bleak settings, small cast, and the spare visual/narrative style (what

Cowie calls "austere and improvisatory") underscore the themes of alienation and despair that permeate this important trilogy. Though *Through a Glass Darkly* won for Bergman another Academy Award, *The Silence* had to fight censorship boards around the world to preserve its carnal depiction of sexuality.

In 1963, Bergman was appointed as director of the Royal Dramatic Theater in Stockholm, a position he held for only three years, although he continued to direct plays there. His stark production of Henrik Ibsen's *Hedda Gabler* (1890; English translation, 1891) in 1964 was one of his most significant stage contributions. Bergman's next phase of filmmaking featured actress/lover Liv Ullmann, Max von Sydow as his alter ego, and his beloved island of Fårö, a bleak Scandinavian landscape that corresponded to his "innermost imaginings of forms, proportions, colors, horizons, sounds, silences, lights and reflections." One of his most obscure artistic endeavors, *Persona* (1966), probes the enigma of human identity through a heavily symbolic style that marks this period. Vivid hallucinations haunt the tortured artist in *Vargtimmen* (1968: *Hour of the Wolf*), blurring the boundaries between dream and reality. In his most overtly political film, *Skammen* (1968; *Shame*), war disrupts the lives of two artists who would remain detached from the events of the world. In *En passion* (1969; *The Passion of Anna*), the characters' inability to break through their essential isolation leads to frustration and violence.

After the failure of his first English language film, *The Touch* (1971), Bergman staged Ibsen's *Vildanden* (1884; *The Wild Duck*) and filmed *Viskningar och rop* (1973; *Cries and Whispers*), two of his finest artistic achievements. Filmed with the startling use of red and white images, *Cries and Whispers* powerfully recounts a family's response to a sister's agonizing death. After years of independent filmmaking, Bergman began to explore new territory in the 1970's with his lengthy productions for Swedish television. *Scener ur ett äktenskap* (1973; *Scenes from a Marriage*), Bergman's analysis of a couple's evolution through years of marriage, separation, and divorce, based on Bergman's own relationship with his third wife, appeared in six weekly episodes; *Ansikte mot ansikte* (1976; *Face to Face*), his psychological dissection of a woman's confrontation with death and madness, was presented in four parts. Bergman's lifelong love of music, inspired in part by his marriage to musician Käbi Laretei and fostered by the success of his lavish stage production of Franz Lehár's operetta *The Merry Widow* (1905) in 1954, culminated in the television production *Trollflöjten* (1975; *The Magic Flute*), an adaptation of the Mozart opera. The autobiographical study of his childhood, *Fanny och Alexander* (1982; *Fanny and Alexander*), and his portrait of a theatrical director, *Efter repetitionen* (1984; *After the Rehearsal*), both appeared first on Swedish television. All of these productions were later distributed as films, some in edited or condensed versions.

Success has not been without its costs for Bergman. Besides the physical toll that filmmaking exacted from him (chronic insomnia and nervous stomach disorders), his financial success in the 1970's led to his arrest and prosecution for tax evasion in 1976. Though he was cleared of the charges in 1979, Bergman endured public humiliation and exile from the landscape that had inspired him. Despite these personal problems, he continued his career in Germany, producing two German language films, *Das schlangenei* (1977; *The Serpent's Egg*), a pessimistic look at Berlin in transition before the rise of Adolf Hitler, and *Herbstsonat* (1978; *Autumn Sonata*), an exploration of a mother-daughter relationship starring Ingrid Bergman and Ullmann. In *Aus dem leben der marionetten* (1980; *From the Life of the Marionettes*), a psychiatrist tries to untangle the emotions that led a Munich businessman to murder a prostitute. The film remains one of Bergman's personal favorites, though it failed to receive critical or popular success. While in Germany, Bergman also successfully produced August Strindberg's *Ett drömspel* (1902; *A Dream Play*, 1912) in 1977, a provocative interpretation of Anton Chekhov's *Tri sestry* (1901; *The Three Sisters*, 1920), and his third approach to Ibsen's *Hedda Gabler*.

During the filming of *The Touch*, Bergman first announced his plans to retire from filmmaking. He reiterated his determination to restrict his creative activity to the stage after the successful production of *Fanny and Alexander*, which won for him four Academy Awards. In this joyous film, he is finally able to confront and exorcise some of the demons of childhood that have plagued him over the years; it is a fitting tribute to a lifetime of artistic experimentation and personal exploration. Though he did direct one television movie after this film, Bergman has concentrated on his theatrical productions, ignoring doctors' warnings to rest from his busy work schedule. Bergman has continued to astound audiences with his imaginative productions of William Shakespeare's classic plays *King Lear* and *Hamlet* in 1984 and 1986 respectively, of Strindberg's *Fröken Julie* in 1986, and of Eugene O'Neill's *Long Day's Journey into Night* in 1988.

Summary
Because his films are intensely personal, together forming an emotional autobiography or a cinematic spiritual odyssey, Ingmar Bergman has been appreciated as one of the true auteurs of the cinema. His influence, however, extends beyond his individual accomplishments. Grounded in the Scandinavian film tradition established by Carl Dreyer, Alf Sjöberg, Victor Sjöström, and others, Bergman has dominated the Nordic industry for more than forty years, often to the detriment of younger filmmakers trying to establish careers in his considerable shadow. Enriching that tradition, he has earned a reputation as a truly international filmmaker, bringing an artistic respectability to the film medium. Though their films differ considerably from his,

the French New Wave filmmakers were inspired by his ability to bring his personal vision to the screen with almost total control over the writing, shooting, editing, and directing. This new critical interest in film as an art form led to the serious study of film in college film programs, particularly in the 1960's and 1970's, influencing a generation of young filmmakers in the United States, especially Woody Allen. Bergman's writings about filmmaking in his published screenplays, his many interviews, and his autobiography have enhanced understanding of the creative process of the contemporary artist.

With a strong background in music, literature, and theater, Bergman has tested the boundaries between the different medium. His films employ many theatrical conventions, while his stage productions project cinematic style. Relying on familiar ensemble casts, Bergman allows improvisation from his film actors, encouraging their contributions to the development of the script; while in the theater, however, those same actors, out of respect for his favorite authors, are restricted to the original text. In each medium, Bergman has striven to achieve the ideal technical counterpart to the emotional content of the scene or shot. In film he has re-created the hallucinatory effect of dreams and extreme psychological states. Through lighting, careful shot composition, and symbolic landscapes, Bergman creates the visual equivalent of emotional states or philosophical concepts. His frequent use of the flashback technique complements his belief that confrontation of the past helps one understand the present. Not only has Bergman added to the cinematic language of film but also he has expanded, by way of his religious questionings, existential concerns, and fascination with the psychology of women, the range of appropriate subjects for film. Though his films have sparked critical debates about the intellectual interpretation of his images, narratives, and characters, Bergman's primary concern is for an emotional reaction: "I never asked you to understand; I ask only that you feel."

Bibliography
Berman, Ingmar. *Bergman on Bergman: Interviews with Ingmar Bergman by Stig Björkman, Torsten Manns, Jonas Sima.* Translated by Paul Britten Austin. New York: Simon & Schuster, 1973. Transcription of interviews with Bergman from June, 1968, to April, 1970, discussing his life, filmmaking experiences, and film theory. Includes numerous film stills, a filmography through *Cries and Whispers*, and an index.
_____. *The Magic Lantern: An Autobiography.* Translated by Joan Tate. New York: Viking Press, 1988. Conversational book arranged topically rather than chronologically (though a good chronology is included in the appendix). Includes many interesting anecdotes from Bergman's childhood and much analysis of his parents, especially his poignant discovery of his mother's diary.

Cowie, Peter. *Ingmar Bergman: A Critical Biography.* New York: Charles Scribner's Sons, 1982. An insightful, detailed biography with excellent critical analyses of films through *Fanny and Alexander*; includes film credits, or bibliography, and a list of major theatrical productions.

Donner, Jörn. *The Personal Vision of Ingmar Bergman.* Translated by Holger Lundbergh. Bloomington: Indiana University Press, 1964. Focuses on summary and analysis of films from *Torment* to *All These Women*, with simplified film credits and a good bibliography of early articles on Bergman.

Kaminsky, Stuart M., ed. *Ingmar Bergman: Essays in Criticism.* New York: Oxford University Press, 1975. General career essays on Bergman's thematic use of childhood, sex, and religion, as well as essays (sometimes pro and con) about each major film from *The Seventh Seal* to *Scenes from a Marriage.* Excellent choice of writers and topics. Includes a selected filmography.

Marker, Lise-Lone, and Frederick J. Marker. *Ingmar Bergman: Four Decades in the Theater.* New York: Cambridge University Press, 1982. A survey of Bergman's productions of plays by Strindberg, Molière, and Ibsen, including an interview with Bergman about theater. Includes a useful chronology, a selected bibliography, many production stills, and some stage blueprint sketches.

Simon, John. *Ingmar Bergman Directs.* New York: Harcourt Brace Jovanovich, 1972. Includes a short interview with Bergman, a brief overview of his major themes, detailed analyses of *The Naked Night, Smiles of a Summer Night, Winter Light*, and *Persona* (with a filmography of these four films). Contains no bibliography or index but numerous illustrations are included.

Wood, Robin. *Ingmar Bergman.* New York: Praeger, 1969. Films grouped thematically to reveal evolution of major concerns through *Shame.* Contains a chronology, a selected filmography, a selected bibliography, and numerous illustrations.

Carol M. Ward

HENRI BERGSON

Born: October 18, 1859; Paris, France
Died: January 4, 1941; Paris, France
Area of Achievement: Philosophy
Contribution: Bergson, by rejecting the mechanistic view of life held by the noted positivists of his day, focused renewed attention on the importance of the human spirit, its creative potential, and its inherent freedom, thereby opening new intellectual vistas to many creative artists.

Early Life

Henri Louis Bergson was born into a sophisticated, multinational family in the year that Charles Darwin published *On the Origin of Species* (1859), a book that profoundly affected Bergson's thinking and against whose dispassionate view of human existence he reacted significantly. Bergson's father, Michel, studied piano under Frédéric Chopin before leaving his native Warsaw to pursue a career in music elsewhere in Europe and in Great Britain. There he met Katherine Levinson, a beauty of Irish-Jewish lineage. He soon married her and took British citizenship.

Henri, although born in Paris, was taken to London as an infant and remained there until he was eight, whereupon the family resettled in Paris. There Bergson spent most of his remaining years, taking French citizenship as soon as he turned twenty-one. He attended the Lycée Fontane, later renamed the Lycée Condorcet, from the time he was nine until he was nineteen, the year in which he published his first article, a prizewinning solution to a problem in mathematics, in the *Annales de mathématiques* (*Annals of mathematics*).

Equally gifted in the sciences and the humanities, Bergson decided upon entering the École Normale Supérieure to concentrate on philosophy. Earning his degree and license to teach in 1881, he taught first at the Lycée D'Angers, then at the Lycée Blaise Pascal in Auvergne. His first book, *Essai sur les données immédiates de la conscience* (1889; *Time and Free Will: An Essay on the Immediate Data of Consciousness*, 1910), appeared when he was thirty, at which time he also completed his doctoral dissertation, in Latin, on Aristotle, which won for him a Ph.D. from the University of Paris.

Returning to Paris in 1891, he married a cousin of Marcel Proust, Louise Neuberger. Bergson taught at the Lycée Henri IV until 1900, when he was appointed to the chair in Greek philosophy at the prestigious Collège de France. Before assuming this position, he had published *Matière et mémoire*; (1896; *Matter and Memory*, 1911), which was concerned with how the brain's physiology is related to consciousness. He found neurophysiological explanations of consciousness frustratingly limited because they failed to explain satisfactorily the roots of recollection.

Life's Work

Bergson had gained considerable attention and some celebrity through his early publications, but his *Le Rire: Essai sur la signification du comique* (1900; *Laughter: An Essay on the Meaning of the Comic*, 1911), a short study of the essence of the comic, placed him in the company of the more significant thinkers of his day. Bergson's theory is that people laugh as a result of a mechanistic impediment, physical or mental, to the usual progression of any activity in life. Using such classic writers as Jonathan Swift, Charles Dickens, and Molière to support and illustrate his contentions, Bergson considered laughter a release of tensions caused by a situation in which the flow of life is impeded by the mechanical.

Following this book was *Introduction à la métaphysique* (1903; *An Introduction to Metaphysics*, 1912), in which Bergson defends intuition against the analytical approach of science, which had been adopted by many humanistic disciplines in an attempt to make them seem more scientific and therefore more credible. Bergson considers analysis, dependent on abstract symbols for its expression, to reside outside humans and outside knowledge, whereas intuition resides within them. It is through intuition, Bergson contends, that humans approach reality in the Platonic sense.

The study for which Bergson is best known is *L'Évolution créatrice* (1907; *Creative Evolution*, 1911) a work that changed the thinking of a whole generation of creative people. Bergson accepts Darwin's evolutionary theory but interjects into it the notion of the *élan vital*, the life energy that Darwin in his mechanistic, analytical approach denies. Perhaps the most influential concept in Bergson's thought at this time was that humans do not exist in time, but rather that time exists in humans, a notion with which William Faulkner experimented in his writing.

This distinction is at the heart of Bergson's departure from that considerable legion of intellectuals that was in his day trying to apply scientific method to all intellectual concerns. Never antiscientific, Bergson insisted, nevertheless, that science must be kept in a proper relation to human intuition and that humans must revere it less than intuition, the quintessential humanizing element in all intellectual processes.

Creative Evolution, widely read by intellectuals, also had considerable appeal to a more general reading public, largely because of Bergson's clarity of expression and overall persuasiveness. Bergson departed from Darwin in postulating that human evolution was not simply a routine, mechanistic alteration of the species but that inherent in it was a creative process that had purpose. Obviously, Bergson was moving away from science toward religion, and he was embraced happily by Roman Catholic and other Christian thinkers of his time.

Immediately before World War I, Bergson was at the peak of his influence, lecturing in Europe, Great Britain, and the United States. As war encroached upon Europe in 1914, he was inducted into the French Academy. In that year, he was the Gifford Lecturer at Scotland's University of Edinburgh. He gave his first series of lectures, "The Problem of Personality," in the spring, but he could not return to give his final lectures in the fall because war had erupted.

Rather, he wrote two thoughtful essays, "The Meaning of War" and "The Evolution of German Imperialism," in both of which he tried to analyze according to his own philosophy the reasons for the conflict. He cast the French as those who represented individual freedom and their opponents as those who venerated the masses rather than the individual. During the war, Bergson served as a French diplomat to Spain and the United States, and, at the war's end, he embraced Woodrow Wilson's League of Nations, becoming president of its Commission on Intellectual Cooperation.

Shortly after the end of the war, Bergson's health began to fail. Badly crippled with arthritis that occasionally caused paralysis of his limbs, he was unable to go to Stockholm in 1928 to receive the 1927 Nobel Prize in Literature that had been reserved and that he was awarded the following year. The award speech in Stockholm stressed Bergson's role in freeing the creative imagination and indicated his profound influence on artists of his day. He was praised for breaking out of the stultifying mold in which he was educated, for forging beyond it to celebrate the greatness of the human spirit and for realizing its creative potential.

Bergson's last book, *Les Deux Sources de la morale et de la religion* (1932; *The Two Sources of Morality and Religion*, 1935), completed at a time when he was extremely ill and suffered from blinding migraine headaches, has to do with his conception of God. This conception was largely Christian, although Bergson remained a Jew. In a will that he executed in 1937, Bergson indicated that he would have become a Roman Catholic at that time had he not felt compelled to support his fellow Jews at a time when their futures and their very lives were being seriously threatened by the Nazi incursions.

Because of Bergson's international celebrity, his age, and his membership in the French Academy, which he once served as president, France's Vichy government excused him from resigning his official offices and registering with the government as Jews were required to do. To show his support for his Jewish compatriots, however, Bergson, then eighty-one years old, resigned his honorary chair in philosophy at the Collège de France. He registered with the government as a Jew, having to stand in line on a bitterly cold, damp day, when he was already ill, until he was served. In consequence he developed a lung inflammation that resulted in his death on January 4, 1941.

Summary

Henri Bergson sought to free his fellow intellectuals from the constricted scientific approach to learning that dominated much of the philosophical thinking of his day and that has since continued to dominate intellectual circles. Frequently accused of being antiscientific, Bergson, who understood the sciences well, wanted merely to control the extent to which scientific method was used in pursuits that were essentially nonscientific.

Bergson's most appreciative audience was found among graphic artists, composers, and writers, many of whom felt constrained by the scientific bias of contemporary society. Thinkers such as Bertrand Russell complained that much of Bergson's work was based on opinion rather than on hard research data; it is hard to deny that such was the case. One cannot ignore, however, the incredible promise that Bergson's writings and his idea of the creative force, the *élan vital*, stirred in a broad range of writers who derived from his writing precisely the kind of justification they required to validate their activities.

Writing about consciousness, Bergson outlined a methodology for many modern writers who were grappling with the stream-of-consciousness as a method. Writers such as Thomas Mann, Marcel Proust, Virginia Woolf, and Paul Valéry, as well as painters such as Claude Monet and Pablo Picasso, imbibed the spirit that emanated from Bergson's writing and translated it into their own media, thereby creating challenging art forms. It is for this kind of contribution that Bergson will be remembered.

Bibliography

Alexander, Ian W. *Bergson: Philosopher of Reflection*. New York: Hillary House, 1957. This book provides an introspective look into Bergson's theories of knowledge and consciousness. It is lucid and direct in presenting the salient parts of Bergson's philosophy and theology, noting the effects of his thinking on creative artists.

Čapek, Milič. *Bergson and Modern Physics: A Re-interpretation and Re-evaluation*. Dordrecht, The Netherlands: D. Reidel, 1971. The three portions of this book deal with Bergson's biological theory of knowledge, with his notion of "intuition," and with his theory of matter and its relationship to modern physics. An interesting book to read in tandem with Gunter's study below.

Gunter, Pete A. Y., ed. *Bergson and the Evolution of Physics*. Knoxville: University of Tennessee Press, 1969. Gunter and his contributors try to show that Bergson was not antiscientific and that his emphasis on the *élan vital* and on intuition is positive for science rather than negative as it has often been portrayed.

Hanna, Thomas, ed. *The Bergsonian Heritage*. New York: Columbia University Press, 1962. The eleven essays in this collection, drawn from a convention held at Hollins College to commemorate the centennial of Bergson's birth, present assessments of Bergson's impact on theological thought and on literature. The book also contains reminiscences by people who knew him at the Sorbonne and the Collège de France.

Mullen, Mary D. *Essence and Operation in the Teaching of St. Thomas in Some Modern Philosophies.* Washington, D.C.: The Catholic University Press, 1941. Mullen shows the effect that Bergson had on the developing Thomism of Jacques Maritain, a debt that Maritain acknowledged. The portions of this book that deal with Bergson are chronicles of a spiritual journey that caused Bergson to see the Church as a creative force.

Pilkington, Anthony Edward. *Bergson and His Influence: A Reassessment.* Cambridge, England: Cambridge University Press, 1976. This five-chapter book presents an initial overview of Bergsonism, then devotes one chapter each to Bergson's influence on Charles Péguy, Valéry, Proust, and Julien Benda. The chapter on Benda contains interesting insights into Bergson's theory of mobility.

Russell, Bertrand. *The Philosophy of Bergson.* Cambridge, England: Cambridge University Press, 1914. Russell, more devoted to an undeviating scientific method than Bergson, looks with considerable skepticism on Bergson's theories of knowledge and dependence on intuition in shaping arguments. He particularly questions Bergson's *Creative Evolution*, in which the theory of the *élan vital* is fully expounded.

R. Baird Shuman

EDUARD BERNSTEIN

Born: January 6, 1850; Berlin, Prussia
Died: December 18, 1932; Berlin, Germany
Area of Achievement: Social reform
Contribution: Bernstein, a German political theorist, socialist politician, and historian, was the originator of Revisionist Socialism. He tried to modify the traditional Marxian prediction of the imminent collapse of capitalism and the subsequent rule of the proletarian class by proposing a theory according to which social-reformist social change would lead to the realization of socialism.

Early Life
Eduard Bernstein was born in Berlin on January 6, 1850, into a lower-middle-class family of German Jewish ancestry. His father was originally a plumber but later became a railroad engineer. Since there were many children in the family—Bernstein was the seventh of fifteen born—his opportunities for a formal education were limited. At age sixteen, he left the *Gymnasium*, an academic secondary school, and became first an apprentice and then a clerk at a bank. After his apprenticeship, his interests began to reach beyond his daily employment. He engaged in working-class political activity and joined the German Social Democratic Party in 1872, devoting occasional evenings and entire weekends to political agitation. He also continued his self-education by developing his public speaking skills and his notable intellectual talents, which brought him to the attention of socialist party leaders.

In 1878, Bernstein gave up his secure employment at a bank and moved to Switzerland to become secretary to Karl Höchberg, a wealthy socialist idealist whom he helped edit a socialist periodical and other publications. While engaged in these journalistic pursuits, he read and digested the recently published *Herrn Eugen Dührings Umwälzung der Wissenschaft* (1877-1878; *Herr Eugen Dühring's Revolution in Science*, 1934), by Friedrich Engels. According to Bernstein's recollection, it was this powerful book that converted him to Marxism. The enactment of the anti-Socialist law under Otto von Bismarck in the same year prompted the German Social Democratic Party to issue its principal newspaper, *Der Sozialdemokrat*, in Zurich for secret distribution in Germany. Bernstein became an early contributor to the party organ and, having earned the confidence of the party leadership, was appointed its editor late in 1880. During the following decade, he turned this newspaper into an effective instrument of agitation as well as a teaching tool for Marxist orthodoxy. In 1888, pressured by Bismarck, the Swiss government expelled Bernstein, who now moved to London. He continued to edit the party newspaper there until the lapse of the anti-Socialist law in 1890.

There Bernstein not only rounded out his own ideological education under the watchful eye of Engels but also was exposed to different socialist groups in England, including the Fabians.

Life's Work

Although the repeal of the anti-Socialist legislation restored more normal conditions for political agitation in Germany and permitted socialist exiles to return to their homeland, the imperial government barred Bernstein from returning until 1901. All of his major publications relating to Revisionist Socialism were thus written abroad but published in Germany. After his work with the party newspaper ended, he edited Ferdinand Lassalle's works, published a historical study of the English Revolution, and contributed to socialist publications in Germany. As he studied Marxian writings more closely, especially the first two volumes of *Das Kapital* (1867, 1885; *Capital*, 1886, 1907, 1909) and the third, issued by Engels in 1894, Bernstein became increasingly disturbed by the gap between Marx's predictions and societal reality as he observed it. Marx had forecast the intensified centralization of capitalism and the advancing impoverishment of the proletariat, whereas British and German economic and social conditions indicated no such trends. The 1890's brought, especially in Germany, increasing prosperity, which improved the condition of the proletariat and moderated the violence of the class struggle. A catastrophic change in the near future appeared to be unlikely. If anything, the British historical developments and the German Social Democratic experience pointed toward a process of evolutionary change.

Bernstein first expounded his new ideas in a series of articles entitled "Probleme des Sozialismus," which appeared in *Neue Zeit* between 1896 and 1898, the main German socialist periodical, edited by Karl Kautsky. One year later, his book *Die Voraussetzungen des Sozialismus und die Aufgaben de Sozialdemokratie* (1899; *Evolutionary Socialism*, 1909) expanded the theme that he had outlined in the earlier articles. Bernstein rejected Marx's concept of the apocalyptic end of capitalism and the attendant immiserization of the working class. According to Bernstein, Marx had underestimated the economic, social, and political factors that stabilized the capitalist system and led to expanded production that also brought increase in mass consumption and a rise in the workers' real income. He demonstrated that Marx's prediction that in a capitalist society the rich would become richer and the poor, poorer was not borne out by the facts. Rather, Bernstein found that the class structure under capitalism was becoming more differentiated. Rising income levels improved the condition of many workers, and the traditional middle class, instead of shrinking, as Marx had anticipated, was being expanded by a new middle class of white-collar workers and civil servants. Bernstein also raised serious questions about Marx's theory of historical materialism, or economic determinism. In Bernstein's view, noneconomic factors were often as important in determining historical processes as productive forces and relations of production. Lastly, the most heretical departure from Marxian orthodoxy was Bernstein's contention that the realization of socialism would not come about within the scheme of inexorable determinism that Marx had borrowed from Georg Wilhelm Friedrich Hegel but within a critical intellectual framework informed by the rational principles of Immanuel Kant. In short, he implied that socialism would be attained not as a natural development of history but must be worked for as an ethical goal.

Bernstein's propositions for the revision of Marxian theory created a controversy that lasted for years and resulted in a more rational basis for reformist politics in German Social Democracy, much of which had been in vogue since the founding of the party in Bismarck's time. In contrast, the 1891 Erfurt Program of the German Social Democratic Party, the theoretical part of which had been drafted by Kautsky and its tactical section by Bernstein, was based on Marxist formulations. Doctrinaire Marxists such as Kautsky, the more eclectic August Bebel, and the radical Rosa Luxemburg all felt threatened by Bernstein's new challenges to party dogma. They wanted to uphold the revolutionary party program in combination with moderate reformist practice, and they strongly objected to broadening reformist politics by collaboration with non-Socialist parties as the theory of Revisionist Socialism suggested. Bernstein's ideas were hotly debated at party congresses in Germany between 1898 and 1903 as well as at the International Socialist Congress in 1904. Even though Revisionist Socialist theory was repeatedly rejected by action of the party congresses, it refused to die.

After his return to Germany in 1901, Bernstein was elected to the German Reichstag in the following year and served in the parliamentary body with no interruptions until 1928. His life as a party politician was never as significant as that of a political theorist and journalist. Moreover, in the political arena he was by no means a consistent supporter of right-wing German Social Democracy. As a pacifist and internationalist, Bernstein quite often dissented from his reformist party colleagues on issues of foreign policy and militarism. His most notable break with the majority of the German Social Democratic Party came in 1915 during World War I. After reluctantly voting for war credits at the beginning of the war, he joined, late in 1915, a minority of largely left-wing party members, who refused to lend further financial support to the imperial government. First organized as a dissenting group, the defectors formally established the Independent Socialist Party in 1917. At the end of the war, Bernstein, however, returned to the majority German Social Democratic Party and even briefly served in a ministerial position in the government. Yet he always spoke out courageously on controversial issues despite hostility from party and public audiences. He defended many provisions of the Treaty of Versailles and even asserted that imperial Germany was guilty of causing the war. Some of his sharpest attacks were directed at the Russian revolutionary left, the Bolsheviks. He contended that in the Bolsheviks' lust for power they had barbarized Marx's evolutionary teachings, resorted to ruthless violence, and disregarded Marxist economics by leaping into socialism from a lower capitalist base than that of any Western country. These polemical controversies and frequently unpopular stands were not helpful to restoring Bernstein's influence of earlier times. He came to be seen more as a party curiosity than a leader. At the same time, even his enemies granted that he was a man of unimpeachable integrity and intellectual honesty. In the last decade of his life, Bernstein concentrated on writing his memoirs, a party history, and journalistic articles; he also gave lectures before university audiences. He observed with concern the revival of anti-Semitism and the worsening of economic conditions not only in Germany but also throughout the world. His death in December, 1932, spared him the pain of experiencing the advent of a brutal dictatorship.

Summary

The significance of Eduard Bernstein's contribution lay in his sharp criticism of orthodox Marxian theory and the introduction of an eclectic array of doctrines that provided a theoretical foundation for socialist reformist practice. He was not noted for great philosophical originality, and his ideas made only a modest contribution to socialist thought. The basic assumptions of Revisionist Socialism were not grounded in hard philosophical principles, nor were they, for that matter, always very clear. Common sense and empirical observation of facts were what often informed the philosophy of Revisionist Socialism and infused it with a rational optimism. Nevertheless, Revisionist Socialism provided a clear-cut direction for political action that was particularly relevant to the state and society of Germany. Bernstein regarded, above all, the democratization of political and economic institutions as a prerequisite for the realization of a socialist society. In the German Empire, he considered the immediate tasks of the German Social Democratic Party to be the struggle for political rights of the working class and the struggle for all reforms in the state that were likely to improve the conditions of the working class and to transform the state in the direction of democracy. In theory and practice, he reinforced an absolute commitment to a form of socialism that was, above all, democratic. During the Weimar Republic, the German Social Democratic Party program, adopted at Görlitz in 1921 under his influence, gave recognition to Revisionist Socialist principles which sharply differentiated this party from the German Communist Party. It was not until after the defeat of Hitler that the German Social Democratic Party threw overboard the remnants of tradition-honored Marxist dogmas and, in the Bad Godesberg program of 1959, declared many Revisionist Socialist principles to be the prevailing orthodoxy.

Bibliography

Bernstein, Eduard. *Evolutionary Socialism: A Criticism and Affirmation.* Translated by Edith C. Harvey. Reprint. New York: Schocken Books, 1961. This readable exposition is a full statement of Bernstein's critique of Marxism and his formulation of the tasks and possibilities of Social Democracy.

——————. *My Years of Exile: Reminiscences of a Socialist.* Translated by Bernard Miall. Reprint. Westport, Conn.: Greenwood Press, 1986. This reprint of Bernstein's autobiography, which was first published in English in 1921, covers his years in exile in Switzerland and England. It provides insights into his personality and the milieu of socialist friends and associates, including Engels and Marx.

Fletcher, Roger, ed. *Bernstein to Brandt: A Short History of German Social Democracy.* Baltimore: Edward Arnold, 1987. A group of British and German historians summarize the history of German Social Democracy from its beginning to the present. Good for a quick overview and a short summary on Bernstein in particular. Contains a very good bibliography.

Gay, Peter. *The Dilemma of Democratic Socialism: Eduard Bernstein's Challenge to Marx.* New York: Columbia University Press, 1952. A classic intellectual biography of Bernstein. Even though it is dated, it remains very useful for an understanding of Revisionist Socialism and the way stations of its originator.

Hulse, James W. "Bernstein: From Radicalism to Revisionism." In *Revolutionists in London: A Study of Five Unorthodox Socialists.* London: Oxford University Press, 1970. Secondary material is combined with original research in this biographical chapter on Bernstein. It provides a good introduction to his life and ideas and is particularly suitable for mature high school students and undergraduates.

Lichtheim, George. *Marxism: An Historical and Critical Study.* New York: Frederick A. Praeger, 1961. An excellent treatment of Marxism as a historical and theoretical body of thought that shows the interconnection between events and ideas. The emergence of Revisionist Socialism is succinctly analyzed in the broad spectrum of European socialism.

Lidtke, Vernon L. *The Outlawed Party: Social Democracy in Germany, 1878-1890.* Princeton, N.J.: Princeton University Press, 1966. The standard study of the German Social Democratic Party during the "heroic epoch" when Bismarck attempted to suppress it. Bernstein's role as editor of *Sozialdemokrat* and his involvement in party politics before 1890 are well described and judiciously interpreted.

Schorske, Carl E. *German Social Democracy, 1905-1917: The Development of the Great Schism.* Cambridge, Mass.: Harvard University Press, 1955. A classic study of the genesis of the factional split that destroyed the unity of German social democracy. Though it tends to favor the left in the party,

Bernstein and Revisionist Socialism are also placed in their historical context.

Tudor, H., and J. M. Tudor, eds. *Marxism and Social Democracy: The Revisionist Debate, 1896-1898*. New York: Cambridge University Press, 1988. A judicious selection of articles, speeches, and letters illustrates the early debate on Revisionist Socialism by juxtaposing the orthodox Marxist Bernstein and the revisionist Bernstein as well as his Marxist opponents. An informative introduction by H. Tudor traces the evolution of the revisionist debate. A good bibliography of the primary and secondary publications is also provided.

George P. Blum

VILHELM BJERKNES

Born: March 14, 1862; Christiania (modern Oslo), Norway
Died: April 9, 1951; Oslo, Norway
Areas of Achievement: Physics, oceanography, and meteorology
Contribution: Bjerknes made some advances in early radio-wave theory, but
he is recognized primarily for his extensive work on the formation and
behavior of cyclones, polar fronts, squall lines, and other weather phenomena. Under his direction, the Norwegian Weather Forecasting division at Bergen became the world center for meteorological study between
1918 and 1930.

Early Life
Vilhelm Frimann Koren Bjerknes was born in what is now Oslo, Norway,
on March 14, 1862. His mother Aletta Koren, a lively and highly practical
woman, had married in 1859 the rather absentminded and highly impractical
C. A. Bjerknes, a mathematician of some renown who liked to dabble in
physics, conducting experiments on the kitchen table. As Vilhelm grew up,
he spent much of his time with his father, preferring parental company to
that of other children. Bjerknes began his university studies in science at
Christiania in 1880, entering the same class as Fridtjof Nansen, who would
later become known as an explorer of the polar regions and whose collected
data on weather and ocean currents would later be invaluable to Bjerknes in
his meteorological investigations. Prior to graduation, Bjerknes collaborated
with his father on a number of hydrodynamic projects. At the age of twenty,
he published his first minor article. In 1889, he received his degree and
determined to go his own way for a time.

Bjerknes' first advanced research was not in the field of meteorology or
oceanography but in electrodynamics under the tutelage of the great German
physicist Heinrich Hertz. The young Norwegian's interest in electrodynamics had been prompted, as he notes in *C. A. Bjerknes: Hans liv og arbeide*
(1925; *C. A. Bjerknes: His Life and Work,* 1932), by his father's own fascination with the eighteenth century scientist Leonhard Euler. Euler's *Lettres
à une princesse d'Allemagne sur divers sujets de physique et de philosophie*
(3 vols., 1768-1774; *Letters of Euler to a German Princess, on Different
Subjects in Physics and Philosophy,* 1795) contained a nontechnical discussion of corpuscular and wave theories of light as well as the phenomenon of
action at a distance, that is, the extension of forces such as gravity through
allegedly empty space. Euler's development of the idea of a space-filling
medium through which light waves could theoretically propagate themselves—a luminiferous ether—impressed C. A. Bjerknes, and he spent
much of his career investigating the similarities between the wave properties
of electricity, magnetism, and hydrodynamic phenomena.

This devotion to ether theory and electromagnetic undulation in electro-dynamics was, for the younger Bjerknes, both an impetus and a kind of nemesis. Earnest and determined, Bjerknes journeyed to hear the Maxwell lectures of Henri Poincaré in Paris in 1889 after finishing his university degree, then to Bonn to study with Hertz in 1890. His experimental and theoretical collaboration with Hertz was highly productive, especially on subjects such as electric resonance, which made possible the later development of the radio. Yet Albert Einstein's radical new theory of relativity was looming on the scientific horizon, and nothing but obsolescence was in store for the mechanical approach underlying Bjerknes' ideas on electromagnetism and ether, not to mention his father's ambitious attempt to unite the methodologies of hydrodynamics and electrodynamics. Unfortunately, the young Bjerknes would spend many years trying to complete his father's doomed project after taking a position in mechanics at the Högskola in Stockholm in 1893, the year Hertz died. On the other hand, his work in this period had the salutary result of guiding him, by means of his hydrodynamic and thermodynamic investigations, into speculations about the atmosphere and the oceans, on which he published a significant paper as early as 1898. This interest doubtlessly grew and was nourished by Bjerknes' collaboration with Hertz, who had himself written on the origin of the winds. Bjerknes, like his father, saw the central question of both electrodynamics and hydrodynamics as the question of action at a distance, that is, What is the nature of the medium (ether or water, respectively) through which moving bodies execute an effect on one another?

Life's Work

The originality of Bjerknes' work lay in applying paradigms, metaphors, and analogies from one field to the conceptual apparatuses of another. It was this approach, familiar to him from the work of his father, that led him to impose the models and concepts of thermodynamics, hydrodynamics, and other fields of physics on the data of meteorology, and to apply ideas on fluid strata and waves to the atmosphere. This syncretizing attitude allowed him to envision such things as fronts (by analogy to military conflict), where warm and cold masses of air clash and converge, tending to create swirling vortices not unlike those of rotating objects and gases in the heavens. Bjerknes' ideas put weather forecasting on scientific ground; indeed, he is best remembered for the fundamental constructs he devised for modern meteorological science.

Bjerknes' first practical contributions were, however, in the field of radio science. He wrote several important articles on electromagnetic wave resonance during and shortly after his time in Bonn, Germany, where he served Hertz as research assistant from 1890 to 1892. Upon returning to Norway, he completed a doctoral thesis on electrodynamics and began to work on a field of great interest to his father—hydrodynamics. Bjerknes developed two famous circulation theorems for fluids of varying densities in the late 1890's, during his studies of barotropy and vorticity based on earlier work by Hermann von Helmholtz and Lord Kelvin. As a professor of physics at Stockholm (first at the Högskola in 1893, then at the university in 1895-1907), he continued to develop these ideas, including the proposition, independently discovered by another scientist, that movements in the atmosphere are stimulated by heat from the sun while at the same time these motions radiate heat as the result of friction of air masses rubbing against one another. The novelty of Bjerknes' theorems was that they went beyond the immediate description of the physics of circulation, accounting as well for the formation and decay of circulations such as vortices within fluids and—by analogy—within the atmosphere. His notions captured the attention of the Carnegie Foundation during a sojourn in the United States in 1905, and he would receive considerable research support from the foundation for the next thirty-six years.

Bjerknes' theoretical work on hydrodynamics and the application of its principles to meteorology continued after his return to teach at the University of Christiania in 1905, leading to the publication of the two-volume *Dynamic Meteorology and Hydrography* (1910-1911) in collaboration with Johan Wilhelm Sandström and others. In 1912, Bjerknes accepted a chair at the University of Leipzig and took over direction of the newly founded Geophysical Institute. Physical privations caused by World War I, the conscription of most German research assistants, and Fridtjof Nansen's efforts to secure a new position for Bjerknes were developments that finally convinced the aging scientist to return to his own country and pursue his research in Bergen. The stormy Norwegian coast proved an excellent meteorological laboratory, and Bjerknes was spurred on by the need for improved weather prediction for agriculture and the fishing industry in the light of the wartime restriction of imports and communications. It was here that the idea of the weather front emerged.

Beginning in 1919, in a time when studies of the upper atmosphere were limited by the primitive state of aeronautics and the lack of such things as radar images, Bjerknes was able to conceive, on the basis of information collected at hundreds of weather stations in Norway and on the Continent, a comprehensive scheme of atmospheric process. Assisted by his son Jacob and others, Bjerknes showed once and for all that the atmosphere was no homogeneous or continuous system as such but should be viewed as a composition of distinct masses of air, converging here and there to produce various meteorological effects, depending on conditions. Along with his several collaborators, he proposed the now-familiar idea of perpetual polar fronts, which was soon empirically confirmed. Bjerknes' efforts at a synoptic meteorology, represented in the classic paper *On the Dynamics of the*

Circular Vortex with Applications to the Atmosphere and Atmospheric Vortex and Wave Motion (1921), made much use of concepts from electrodynamics as well, describing the genesis of cyclones in terms of wave motion and amplitude disturbances within atmospheric layers of varying density.

Bjerknes spent nine years analyzing data, drawing maps, and synthesizing information into a comprehensive picture of weather dynamics. In 1926, he accepted an extraordinary professorship in mechanics and mathematical physics at the University of Oslo, formerly Christiania, and immersed himself in his lectures and colloquia. While he did publish a book on kinematics and the relatively new field of vector analysis in 1929, his other effort—a theoretical development of his father's ideas on hydrodynamics—did not bear fruit.

Summary

Vilhelm Bjerknes' lasting achievement lies in establishing modern meteorology as a dependable forecasting tool with a sophisticated theoretical apparatus. While much of his scientific career was devoted to enlarging on his father's already outdated ideas on electrodynamics, he nevertheless managed, through tireless empirical investigation as well as the highly creative manipulation of known concepts, to put dynamic meteorology and physical oceanography on firm scientific footing. In this lengthy effort he had the help of many assistants and collaborators and was admired and respected as a collegial leader and an excellent lecturer.

In fact, his cultural sensitivity formed a large part of his scientific motivation, particularly for his later work in weather mapping and prediction. When he left Leipzig during World War I, he returned to Norway in order to assist his neutral and isolated homeland in surviving the privations of war. His so-called Bergen school of meteorology soon established a comprehensive system of practical weather forecasting in collaboration with Norwegian agriculture and the supremely important national fishing industry. He was no nationalist as such, however, but a cosmopolitan thinker. He envisioned the rise of civil aviation, such as transatlantic flight, and its coming dependence on meteorology. He also insisted on the expansion of the radio communications network for the exchange of meteorological information.

Bjerknes' greatest strides in geophysics began with the formulation of his circulation theorems in 1897, which provided a physicomathematical description of the behavior of real fluids and, by extension, atmospheric phenomena. The vortex was the central dynamic form of his system. Much of his work in the intervening years involved exhaustive empirical description of the state of the atmosphere, calculating humidity, pressure, density, velocity, and temperature. Applying the concept of the wave as well as lines of force from electrodynamics, he developed a global model in which cyclones emerged and traveled a wavelike path along the surface of discontinuity formed by warm and cold fronts. Data amassed by the Bergen school suggested that polar air masses form permanent fronts in conflict with equatorial air masses. The atmospheric struggle conceived and described by Bjerknes and his coworkers forms the basis of all modern meteorology.

Bibliography

Devik, Olaf, Carl Ludvig Godske, and Tor Bergeron. "Vilhelm Bjerknes: March 14, 1862-April 9, 1951." *Geofysiske Publikationer* 24 (Spring, 1962): 6-25. A biographical sketch combined with an examination of Bjerknes' contributions, written by colleagues who knew him well. The first article by Devik treats Bjerknes' relationship with his father at length, while Bergeron's essays on the Stockholm period and the Bergen school provide a good overview of Bjerknes' most productive period.

Friedman, Robert Marc. "Constituting the Polar Front, 1919-1920." *Isis* 73 (Fall, 1982): 343-362. A thorough bibliography is contained in the footnotes that accompany Friedman's historical essay on a central concept in Bjerknes' dynamic meteorology. The author takes the deconstructionist standpoint that Bjerknes and his followers were motivated largely by a desire for authority within their field.

Jewell, Ralph. "The Meteorological Judgment of Vilhelm Bjerknes." *Social Research* 51 (Autumn, 1984): 783-807. This article traces the evolution of Bjerknes' preoccupation with reforming meteorology. An excellent discussion of his ideas and portrayal of the man in his pursuit of scientific advancement and the common good. The author discusses Bjerknes' connections with the Carnegie Institution of Washington in some detail.

Süsskind, Charles. "Hertz and the Technological Significance of Electromagnetic Waves." *Isis* 56 (Fall, 1965): 342-345. This article gives a brief description of Hertz's thinking on the technical possibilities for wireless telegraphy and telephony during the period when Bjerknes was his assistant.

Mark R. McCulloh

LOUIS BLÉRIOT

Born: July 1, 1872; Cambrai, France
Died: August 2, 1936; Paris, France
Area of Achievement: Aeronautics
Contribution: Blériot completed the first overseas flight in a heavier-than-air craft in 1909 and later became a pioneer in the fledgling aeronautics industry. He played a critical role in the French war effort during World War I and the subsequent establishment of commercial aviation.

Early Life
Louis Blériot's youth and the infancy of aviation go together. In other times, Blériot, the son of a local merchant in Cambrai, might have contented himself with a business career. He supplemented a basic education in the French system with a deep practical intuition that earned for him quick success in the business world. By the time Blériot was thirty, he had amassed a modest fortune in manufacturing as a leading producer of headlights and other accessories for the rapidly growing automobile industry. Blériot's first love, however, was always aviation, and once independently wealthy he developed what started as a hobby into a lifelong avocation.

Many governments were slow to realize the possibilities of military and civil aviation; not so the French. Almost from the moment that Wilbur and Orville Wright successfully flew a heavier-than-air craft at Kitty Hawk in December, 1903, French military officers in the diplomatic corps, as well as journalists and amateur aviators, inundated the country with information. Shortly after their epochal achievement, the Wright brothers themselves came to France to demonstrate their technology to an enthralled government and public.

Blériot was among many Europeans for whom Kitty Hawk seized the imagination. As early as 1899, he had experimented with flying machines, including an ungainly—and unsuccessful—device called an ornithopter, which tried to mimic the flapping wings of birds. He corresponded actively with the Wrights and other experimenters.

Blériot's earliest successful flight tests in 1907 were with gliders towed by power boats on the Seine River, near Paris. Their design immediately revealed Blériot's pragmatism and imagination. The gliders imitated the biplane and forward elevator configuration used by the Wrights but also kept the boxkitelike tail assembly preferred in Europe. The result was an aircraft as maneuverable as the early Wright machines but much more stable. Blériot also exhibited an early preference for aircraft launched from water rather than land, a penchant followed by many other European aviation pioneers.

Blériot's first original aircraft design was a leap into the unknown: a monoplane equipped with large forward wings, an enclosed fuselage, and a tail assembly with rudder, elevators, and ailerons. This formula would become fundamental to virtually all aircraft designs in the twentieth century. It was, however, somewhat ahead of the times. Blériot's monoplane crashed on its fifth test hop. Nevertheless, despite widespread criticism of his radical designs, Blériot persisted. Among the few who encouraged such daring were Gabriel and Charles Voisin, generally recognized as the leading authorities on aviation in France at the time.

Life's Work

The name of Louis Blériot acquired worldwide fame in 1908 and 1909, when he recorded a pair of spectacular breakthroughs. In the early years of flight, philanthropists and newspaper publishers prodded aviators with trophy cups and cash prizes for specific achievements. On October 31, 1908, Blériot captured a prize of five hundred pounds sterling for the first successful round-trip flight, with landings, between two prearranged points, the French towns of Toury and Artenay, which were a bare fourteen kilometers apart.

In 1909, The London *Daily Mail* offered a prize of one thousand pounds for the first person to pilot a heavier-than-air craft across the English Channel, in other words, to complete the first—and about the shortest possible—overseas flight across open water. Several aviators already had tried the Channel and failed, but Lord Northcliffe, the visionary patron of the *Daily Mail*'s prize offer, wanted to convince colleagues in the British government that aircraft would soon change the character of European geopolitics.

Blériot made his Channel crossing on July 28, 1909, in Monoplane 11, which he designed and built himself. It was a spidery craft with an engine that produced barely twenty-five horsepower. Taking off from a field outside Calais, Blériot landed in England, near Dover, after about a thirty-minute flight. His aircraft flew a modest eighty meters or so above the water and averaged just over seventy kilometers per hour. Perhaps the most breathtaking aspect of the brief flight was that Blériot, relying only on dead reckoning, became the first human being to pilot a heavier-than-air craft out of sight of land: for ten minutes.

Blériot's Channel crossing, modest though it seems in the annals of flight, electrified Europe. It meant that, in the future, England would no longer be insulated from Europe by the Channel. (Legend has it that the British government did not immediately sense this; Blériot contends that he was met at the field in England by a customs officer who merely asked him if he had anything to declare.) The plodding pace of Monoplane 11 cut by half the crossing time of the fastest mailboat; perhaps more ominously, it left its French destroyer escort far behind. The Channel crossing showed that aircraft engines were light and powerful enough to contemplate even more daring ventures.

The broad enthusiasm for aviation symbolized by Blériot's achievement led briefly to the emergence of France as the world leader in the field. The government bestowed upon Blériot the Cross of the Legion of Honor. It sponsored the first international air meet at Reims in 1909, where, although Blériot had engine trouble, French aviators reaped awards and set many new speed and distance records.

World War I was the first international conflict in which aircraft played a significant role, and Blériot became deeply involved in the French war effort. When the war began in 1914, lighter-than-air vehicles were still masters of the skies. The first reconnaissance craft designed by Blériot differed little from Monoplane 11. At first, these aircraft were not even armed. The French pilots had instructions to ram German Zeppelins headed for the front. Yet it is doubtful whether they had the speed or power necessary to catch the dirigibles.

During the war, Blériot submitted design after design to the French government. Yet technology was moving rapidly beyond the perspective of individual inventors, and his greatest success in military aviation came after joining forces with a team of experts. One result was the famous SPAD fighter, the equal of anything in its class for the duration of the conflict.

After World War I, Blériot's interest returned to commercial aviation. Although large companies increasingly dominated the development and utilization of aircraft in the 1920's and 1930's, Blériot never lost his admiration for individual achievement, even as it reduced his once awe-inspiring flight across the English Channel to relative insignificance. When Charles Lindbergh landed at Orly Field outside Paris on May 21, 1927, having completed the world's first solo flight across the Atlantic Ocean, Blériot was there with a French delegation to receive him. Nor did his vision for the future know any bounds. In 1931, Blériot himself offered a cash prize for the first supersonic aircraft, years in advance of any such prototype.

Blériot's own designs also continued to be at the forefront of commercial aviation. In August, 1933, he shipped a giant monoplane to New York to attempt from there a new world distance record. Loaded with some seven thousand liters of fuel, the aircraft, like Lindbergh's much smaller *Spirit of St. Louis*, had such large tanks that there was no forward vision: The pilot had to use mirrors to take off and land. This behemoth of the times completed a record nonstop flight from New York to Rayak, Syria, a distance of more than 6,250 kilometers. Blériot died in August, 1936, in Paris.

Summary

Louis Blériot belonged to a generation of daredevils and tinkerers who made heavier-than-air aviation a practical reality. He flourished at a time when accumulating knowledge about powered flight was in the public domain, and the applications of that knowledge were widely acclaimed. Thus,

Blériot and others could innovate quickly, using the work of recent pre-decessors. The technological challenges of early aviation were amenable to the solutions of pragmatists and often yielded to intuition.

Blériot was a leader, even among these early pioneers who usually were anxious to share their knowledge, in disseminating as widely as possible not only the technology of aviation but also the basic knowledge of flying skills accumulated by trial and error. Aviators all over the world, including the United States, got their start in the flying schools he established in more than a dozen countries.

Blériot's early career also demonstrates the level of risk involved in air-craft development. Generally, he and his colleagues flight tested their own designs. Blériot himself was in more than fifty accidents, including a near-fatal crash in 1907 and one in which his aircraft plunged through the roof of a building during a demonstration in Constantinople. During his epic flight across the English Channel, Blériot was in serious pain from leg burns re-ceived in a gasoline explosion only the previous day. Louis Blériot was a man whose bravery and imagination, as much as the engines on his aircraft, powered the early development of aviation.

Bibliography
Collier, Basil. *A History of Air Power*. London: Weidenfeld & Nicolson, 1974. Broad, incisive coverage of aviation technology, especially inter-relationships between military and commercial developments.
Gollin, Alfred M. *No Longer an Island: Britain and the Wright Brothers, 1902-1909*. Stanford, Calif.: Stanford University Press, 1984. An impor-tant study that places Blériot's Channel crossing in broader historical per-spective. Gollin shows that British concern over the potential of aircraft to alter strategic planning began very early, and that Blériot's achievement had a much greater public impact because there was already open debate in Great Britain about the implications of air power.
Josephy, Alvin M., Jr., ed. *The American Heritage History of Flight*. New York: American Heritage, 1962. Typical of many general histories of aviation organized to emphasize the overall development of industry and technology rather than the careers of individuals.
McFarland, Marvin W., ed. *The Papers of Wilbur and Orville Wright*. 2 vols. New York: McGraw-Hill, 1953. Volume 2, covering the period from 1906 to 1948, contains numerous references to Blériot, suggestive of how closely early aviators followed the exploits of their colleagues.
Sunderman, James F., ed. *Early Air Pioneers, 1862-1935*. New York: Franklin Watts, 1961. Deals with the careers of many early aviators, again arranged so that the interconnections among these figures are stressed. Particularly useful for its international perspective on technological devel-opments.

Taylor, John W. R., and Kenneth Munson. *History of Aviation*. London: New English Library, 1972. Heavily illustrated and detailed accounts both of major milestones in the history of flight and of contributors to early aviation. One of the best organized sources of biographical accounts.

Ronald W. Davis

EUGEN BLEULER

Born: April 30, 1857; Zollikon, Switzerland
Died: July 15, 1939; Zurich, Switzerland
Area of Achievement: Psychiatry
Contribution: Bleuler's major achievements were in the study and treatment of schizophrenia, a term he coined in 1908 to denote the splitting of psychological functions that he observed in many of his patients. He also introduced the related terms "autism" and "ambivalence" into psychiatry. He has been admired as much for his tireless and uncompromising devotion to his psychiatric patients as for his important contributions to psychiatric theory.

Early Life

Eugen Bleuler was born on April 30, 1857, in Zollikon, which was then a farming village and is now a suburb of the city of Zurich, Switzerland. His father was a merchant and local educational administrator, but his ancestral roots reached deeply into the Swiss farming tradition. It is quite significant for Bleuler's personal and professional development that during the 1700's the farmers and their families living in the countryside around Zurich were governed by the aristocrats living in the city. These city authorities restricted the access of the country people to educational opportunities and to certain professions, a state of affairs that caused great resentment among the peasants. Thus, in 1831, they overthrew the aristocracy and established a democratic form of government. The Bleuler family participated in this social and political movement, one of the primary goals of which was to create a university open equally to all citizens. The University of Zurich was founded in 1833 in the hope that the children of the farm families could gain the advanced training necessary to serve the legal, educational, religious, and medical needs of the population, and to do a better job of it than had been done by the officials appointed for this purpose by the aristocracy.

Bleuler was a beneficiary of this democratic revolution in nineteenth century Zurich. One problem with the new educational system, however, was that, since Zurich did not have a strong academic tradition, many of the teaching posts had to be filled by Germans, who did not speak the Swiss dialect. Bleuler was well aware of the long-standing social and interpersonal difficulties brought on by this language gap. During his college years, a young village girl was taken to the university psychiatric clinic with a serious psychological disorder, and the girl's relatives were frustrated by the communication difficulties they encountered with the clinic's German director. The belief among the peasants was that psychiatrists who were attentive to the needs and conversant in the dialect of the Swiss people would be able to provide much more effective treatment. Sentiments such as these influenced Bleuler's decision to devote his life to the practice of psychiatry among his native people. After obtaining his M.D. from the University of Zurich, he served as a resident at Waldau Mental Hospital near Bern and later went to Paris to study briefly with the great French neurologist Jean-Martin Charcot at the Salpêtrière clinic. He also traveled to London and Munich and then returned to Switzerland to begin in earnest his professional psychiatric career.

Life's Work

In 1886, Bleuler, at age twenty-nine, became medical director of the mental hospital in Rheinau, a secluded town on the Rhine River. This large institution housed 850 patients and was badly in need of rehabilitation and administrative reorganization. Bleuler threw himself into this task and, being a bachelor, lived in the hospital and devoted countless hours to his patients. He participated in all aspects of their treatment and organized a system of occupational or work therapy, which was designed not only to encourage the patients to engage in productive and creative activity but also to provide regular occasions for the patients and the staff to come into close personal contact. It is significant that Bleuler considered work therapy the most essential aspect of psychiatric treatment, for it reveals his firm conviction that, though his mental patients were torn and troubled, they nevertheless remained human beings with hopes, fears, needs, and possibilities. During his years at Rheinau, Bleuler became convinced that, while the neurological aspects of psychiatric disorders and treatment were of great importance, the practice of communicating with the patient in a caring and familiar manner in an effort to understand the real meaning of his expressions, symptoms, and behavior was of even greater therapeutic significance. Bleuler thus replaced the microscope, which he had learned to use so well during his medical training and which was still the primary instrument of psychiatric research among his contemporaries, with the human ear and human voice as the most essential tools of such research. In addition to being a faithful friend to his patients, Bleuler was also a sympathetic father figure to his staff. He worked alongside them, ate meals with them, arranged for and participated in their social gatherings, and sometimes assisted them in financial matters. The structure and sensitive style of therapy, as well as the democratic manner of dealing with coworkers, that Bleuler developed at Rheinau would characterize all of his subsequent psychiatric work.

In 1898, the Zurich government honored Bleuler by offering him the opportunity of succeeding Auguste Forel as head of the Burghölzli Mental Hospital and professor of psychiatry at the University of Zurich. He accepted the offer, in part to be closer to his aging parents and to his boyhood home, and thus became the first professor of psychiatry in Zurich who spoke the local Swiss dialect. He accepted the teaching aspect of the position with some reluctance, knowing that he would no longer be able to devote his time and attention exclusively to his patients. He came, nevertheless, to view his professorial responsibilities as an important opportunity for conveying to his students the insights he had drawn from his wealth of clinical experience.

Bleuler's lectures eventually grew to form the core of his influential book entitled *Dementia praecox: Oder, Gruppe der Schizophrenien* (1911; *Dementia Praecox: Or, The Group of Schizophrenias*, 1950). He first presented the term "schizophrenia" in a 1908 article in which he said that "dementia praecox," the older and widely accepted term promoted by Emil Kraepelin and meaning "premature dementia," was not accurate, because simple dementia was not universally observed in these patients and because the disorder did not always appear at an early age. Bleuler suggested that "schizophrenia," a coinage derived from Greek words meaning "split mind," was a better term, because he had discovered through extensive clinical observations that the most common characteristic of his schizophrenic patients was the dissociation of different aspects of their personalities—of thoughts from emotions, or of words and intentions from behavior. He distinguished between primary symptoms, those arising directly from the unknown organic process, and secondary symptoms, those involving psychological reactions to the primary symptoms. Bleuler thought that the lack of integration in his patients' personalities caused them to lose contact with reality, a state for which he invented the term "autism." He also noticed that many patients experienced the simultaneous presence of opposite or conflicting thoughts or emotions concerning a particular object, idea, or person, and he described this condition as "ambivalence."

Bleuler's new theory of schizophrenia not only was a terminological and descriptive innovation but also implied new forms of treatment. While most psychiatrists of his day were convinced that hope for those afflicted with mental disorders would have to await the discovery of effective physiological treatments, Bleuler was the foremost proponent of the optimistic idea that the symptoms of schizophrenia could be alleviated through psychological forms of therapy. At the Burghölzli Mental Hospital, he continued the therapeutic measures instituted at Rheinau but supplemented them with psychoanalytic techniques being developed by Sigmund Freud and Carl Jung. Bleuler had become acquainted with Freud through discussions of the latter's early neurological research on aphasia, and this relationship formed the basis for years of productive interaction between Freud and several of the Zurich psychiatrists. Jung became a resident at the Burghölzli Mental Hospital in 1900, and he and Bleuler were the first to employ word-association tests in modern psychiatric research.

The first decade of the twentieth century was a critical period in the development of the emerging discipline of psychoanalysis, and Bleuler collaborated with Freud and Jung, along with other Swiss and Austrian psychiatrists, in various intellectual and organizational endeavors during these early years. They were all present in Salzburg in 1908 for the first international meeting of psychoanalysts, and the first psychoanalytic journal appeared in the same year as a joint venture of the three. By the time of the second congress of the International Psychoanalytic Association in 1910, however, disagreements concerning the structure and purpose of the association had arisen between Bleuler and Freud, and Bleuler decided to resign. Because Bleuler was the most prominent representative of academic psychiatry, his resignation served to weaken the link between psychoanalysis and the larger field of psychiatry. Bleuler continued the teaching and practice of psychiatry at the university and hospital in Zurich for many years and died there in 1939.

Summary

Eugen Bleuler's passion was to understand and to heal the victims of severe mental disorders, particularly schizophrenia. Bleuler's new theory of schizophrenia recognized the importance of underlying organic factors but is significant in that it was not a purely organic theory but was instead the most successful nineteenth century attempt to recognize and to deal with psychological factors as well. In his efforts to introduce psychological understanding and treatments into the care of psychiatric patients, Bleuler initiated a way of thinking and style of therapy that has come to be known as the existential approach, which emphasizes the importance of finding meaning in life. It is not surprising that Ludwig Binswanger, a major twentieth century exponent of this approach, was a student of Bleuler in Zurich.

Bleuler's selfless and uncompromising search for psychiatric truths motivated every aspect of his professional life. It led him to criticize many of his colleagues for engaging in what he called "the autistic-undisciplined thinking in medicine"—a form of thinking in which the physician or psychiatrist is entrenched in his own conceptual system and, therefore, does not make full contact with the reality of the patient. A similar criticism was the basis of Bleuler's disagreements with Freud, for Bleuler believed that both Freud and the International Psychoanalytic Association were becoming overly intent on the simple advancement of psychoanalysis and were sacrificing open-minded evaluation of the theory in the service of this sectarian cause. He also disliked the rigid hierarchical structure the association was assuming and would have preferred a more flexible, democratic organization. Bleuler, it seems, retained the spirit of his Swiss peasant heritage throughout his life and could not rest easy in the face of splits in humanity, neither those between human beings nor those within.

Bibliography
Alexander, Franz G., and Sheldon T. Selesnick. *The History of Psychiatry.*

New York: Harper & Row, 1966. A study of psychiatric theories and therapies from ancient through modern times. Contains several chapters on the emergence and development of psychoanalysis and on the relationship and friction between Bleuler and Freud. Includes references to the Freud-Bleuler correspondence, selections from which have been edited and published by the authors.

Bleuler, Eugen. *Dementia Praecox: Or, The Group of Schizophrenias*. New York: International Universities Press, 1950. Discusses the history of research on schizophrenia and numerous theoretical and therapeutic issues concerning it.

_____. *Textbook of Psychiatry*. Translated by A. A. Brill. New York: Dover, 1951. Contains a biographical sketch of Bleuler by Jacob Shatzky as well as a bibliography of Bleuler's writings.

Bleuler, Manfred. "Some Aspects of the History of Swiss Psychiatry." *American Journal of Psychiatry* 130 (September, 1973): 991-994. This article, written by Bleuler's son (who was also to become a professor of psychiatry at Zurich and director of the Burghölzli Mental Hospital) outlines some of the historical and cultural factors that, in the author's view, have shaped the contributions of Swiss psychiatrists.

Brome, Vincent. *Freud and His Early Circle*. New York: William Morrow, 1967. Discusses the formative years of the psychoanalytic movement and deals with the relationships between the major centers and pioneers, including Bleuler.

Ellenberger, Henri F. *The Discovery of the Unconscious: The History and Evolution of Dynamic Psychiatry*. New York: Basic Books, 1970. A substantial and detailed study of the development of dynamic psychiatry. Deals with Bleuler's life and influence in a number of instances and contains many illustrations of the players in this drama.

Zilboorg, Gregory. "Eugen Bleuler and Present-day Psychiatry." *American Journal of Psychiatry* 114 (October, 1957): 289-298. This article, originally an address delivered to the American Psychiatric Association on the centenary of Bleuler's birth, is an appreciative survey of his personal convictions and professional achievements, and an appraisal of their enduring relevance.

Gordon L. Miller

ALEKSANDR BLOK

Born: November 28, 1880; St. Petersburg, Russia
Died: August 7, 1921; Petrograd, U.S.S.R.
Area of Achievement: Literature
Contribution: Blok is one of Russia's greatest poets. He was called the "last
   Romantic poet," and his work in literature and drama reflected the pro-
   found changes that his country and its people experienced during the era
   of World War I and the Russian Revolution.

Early Life

Aleksandr Aleksandrovich Blok was born in St. Petersburg, Russia, on
November 28, 1880, into a family of the gentry. His father, Aleksandr L.
Blok, was a jurist, a professor of law at Warsaw University, and a talented
musician. His mother, the former Aleksandra A. Beketova, was a writer.
Blok's parents divorced soon after he was born, and he spent much of his
childhood in the family of his maternal grandfather, Andrei Beketov, a bota-
nist and rector of the University of St. Petersburg, in St. Petersburg and at
his estate, Shakhmatovo, near Moscow. Blok rarely saw his father. In 1889,
Blok's mother married an officer, F. F. Kublitsky-Piottukh, and the family
moved back to St. Petersburg. After graduation from the *Gymnasium*, Blok
entered the law school at the University of St. Petersburg, but in 1901 he
transferred to the historical philology faculty. He was graduated in 1906.
Blok had an early interest in drama and in becoming an actor, but by the age
of eighteen he had begun to write poetry seriously and was almost immediately successful.

In 1903, Blok married Lyubova D. Mendeleyeva, the daughter of the
famous chemist Dimitry Mendeleyev. She inspired much of his early poetry,
but their marriage was always a turbulent one. In his later years, for example, Blok also developed strong relationships with the actress Natalia Vol-
okhova and the singer Lyubov Delmas, who together inspired much of his
work at the time.

Life's Work

Blok's first published poetry appeared in the literary journal *Novyi put'*
(new path) in 1903, and his first volume of poetry, *Stikhi o prekrasnoy dame*
(verses on a beautiful lady), appeared in 1904. These early works reflected
the influence of the philosopher Vladimir Solovyov, his nephew and Blok's
cousin Sergei Solovyov, Andrei Bely, and other Symbolists, and they were
well received by them. Blok already showed some innovation by giving new
meaning to old symbols. It was his second book of poems, *Nechayannaya
radost* (inadvertent joy), in 1907 and his lyrical drama *Balaganchik* (*The
Puppet Show*, 1963) in 1906 that first gained for Blok real fame.

At this time his poetry was profoundly lyrical and deeply interwoven with mysticism and religious decadence. Blok can thereby also be linked to the tradition of Afanasy Fet. Consequently, some literary critics have called him the "last Romantic poet" for his work during this early period, but it is a label that might also be applied to his entire career.

Yet, *Nechayannaya radost* and another volume, *Zemlya v snegu* (1908; land in snow), also heralded a change coming about in Blok's worldview, brought on in part by the so-called Revolution of 1905 in Russia and its eventual failure. His classical mystical symbolism was beginning to collapse, and the breakdown of rhyme in these works anticipated Futurism.

Symbolism had its origins in France and had ramifications in several national literatures. It flourished in Russia in the first decade of the twentieth century, contributing significantly to what is known as the "silver age" of Russian poetry (as opposed to the "golden age," presided over by Alexander Pushkin in the nineteenth century). Symbolism exhibited a resurgence of idealism and aestheticism and represented a neo-Romantic reaction against positivism and realism. Most Russian Symbolists were liberal supporters of reform and revolution. In the post-1917 era, the Futurists (who also drew inspiration from their counterparts in Italy) rejected the mysticism of the Symbolists but readily accepted their technical innovations.

In 1909, Blok traveled to Italy, and he also made a rare visit to Warsaw on the occasion of his father's death. Italy and Warsaw both gave impulse to his writing as his fame grew. His later work came more and more to reflect the influence of the post-Romantic poet Apollon Grigoryev. World War I came, and Blok was drafted in 1916. He used his reputation to secure a desk job near Pskov, which he held until March of 1917.

Blok was a member of the left wing of the Socialist Revolutionary Party and in 1917 welcomed the February Revolution. In May, 1917, he took on the job of editing the testimony of former czarist government ministers to the Extraordinary Investigative Commission to the Provisional Government. He also initially welcomed the October Revolution and tried to cooperate with the Bolsheviks after they came to power. As a "Left SR" he was briefly arrested in 1919 as part of the aftermath of the so-called Conspiracy of the Left SRs against the new revolutionary Soviet government. Nevertheless, in 1920 he was elected chairman of the Petrograd of the officially sponsored new All-Russian Union of Poets.

Blok's two most famous and controversial works were of this later period: the poems *Skify* ("The Scythians") and *Dvenadtsat* (*The Twelve*, 1920), both of which appeared in the crucial year of 1918. In "The Scythians," "Scythian" comes to symbolize both the restless duality of Russian existence between East and West and the artist as eternal nomad. With "The Scythians," Blok also reopened the nineteenth century debate between Slavophiles and Westernizers on Russia's heritage and future. In his own way,

Blok came down firmly on the side of the more mystical Slavophiles.

The Twelve vividly and insightfully tells the story of a platoon of the Red Army during the Russian Civil War. Some Soviet critics have contended that in addition to being the last gasp of Blok's poetic genius, these poems mark his final reconciliation with Bolshevism. In fact, however, during the last two years of his life, Blok was deeply disillusioned with the Bolsheviks and pessimistic about Russia's future. He also was not well enough, physically or mentally, to continue to protest. Blok died on August 7, 1921, in Petrograd.

Summary

In addition to being an important dramatist, essayist, and critic, Aleksandr Blok was the most important Russian Symbolist poet. He was the lord of the silver age of Russian literature, and he epitomized the Symbolist movement in Russia better than any other member. In the process, he drew on, reflected, and drew together much of Russia's rich poetic heritage. A profound mystical Russian nationalist, Blok too was deeply moved by the events of World War I, the Russian Revolution, and the Russian Civil War, and he was intimately involved in them.

Blok's language, themes, and images affected later Russian poetic schools, including some of those to which he was opposed, such as Futurism. He also had a direct influence on some of the most important poets of the Soviet period, such as Vladimir Mayakovsky and Anna Akhmatova. Blok can justly be considered one of Russia's greatest poets.

Bibliography

Chukovsky, Kornei. *Alexander Blok as Man and Poet*. Translated and edited by Diana Burgin and Katherine O'Connor. Ann Arbor, Mich.: Ardis, 1982. A very good Soviet monograph, equally divided between biography and critical analysis of Blok's work. Best known as a scholar of children's literature, Chukovsky was a friend of Blok, and his account is enriched by personal reminiscence.

Hackel, Sergei. *The Poet and the Revolution: Aleksandr Blok's "The Twelve."* Oxford, England: Oxford University Press, 1975. This book-length study of Blok's most celebrated poem explores his ambivalent responses to the Revolution. Includes a bibliography.

Mochulsky, Konstantin. *Aleksandr Blok*. Translated by Doris V. Johnson. Detroit: Wayne State University Press, 1983. First published in 1948 and only recently translated into English, this lengthy critical biography is still worth consulting.

Pyman, Avril. *The Life of Aleksandr Blok*. Vol. 1, *The Distant Thunder, 1880-1908*. Oxford England: Oxford University Press, 1979.

_____. *The Life of Aleksandr Blok*. Vol. 2, *The Release of Harmony,*

1908-1921. Oxford, England: Oxford University Press, 1980. On its completion, this two-volume critical biography was hailed as the definitive study of Blok's life and works. Pyman's narrative combines a novelistic richness of detail with a mastery of the literary and historical background. Illustrated, with extensive notes, a selected bibliography, and an unusually ample index.

Dennis Reinhartz

LÉON BLUM

Born: April 9, 1872; Paris, France
Died: March 30, 1950; Jouy-en-Josas, France
Areas of Achievement: Government and politics
Contribution: As prime minister of France's Popular Front government in 1936-1937, Blum was responsible for the adoption of landmark social legislation that has permanently affected French political and economic life.

Early Life

Léon Blum was born in Paris on April 9, 1872, and enjoyed a happy and healthy middle-class childhood. His father, an Alsatian Jew, was a successful manufacturer of silks and ribbons. The Blum family placed a premium on reading and education, and they expected Léon to become a writer or lawyer. His early education took place at the prestigious Lycée Henri IV, where he studied philosophy under Henri Bergson. He studied for two years at the École Normale Supérieure before being enrolled in law school at the Sorbonne in 1891. He earned his law degree with highest honors in 1894. Shortly thereafter, Léon passed the appropriate examination and became a civil servant for the Conseil d'État; his principal tasks included drafting legislation for the state and settling the claims of private individuals against the state. During a civil service career that lasted twenty-six years, Blum rose to the top rank of *maître de requêtes* (solicitor general).

Blum's intellect, however, drove him well beyond the practice of law. He frequented the literary salons of Paris and by his early twenties he was recognized as a key figure in the literary world. From the age of nineteen, he became involved with the enterprising, durable, and pretentious *La Revue blanche*, a journal in which all forms of art were discussed and analyzed. Blum served as the journal's literary critic from 1894 to 1900, when he was succeeded by André Gide. He then wrote drama criticism for *Comoedia*, *La Petite République*, and *Le Matin* and contributed articles on law and literature to other publications. Blum's best work on literature and society was *Stendhal et le Beylisme*, published in 1914.

While a student at the École Normale Supérieure, Blum was introduced to socialist thought by the school's librarian, Lucien Herr. Yet it was only in the wake of the most intense stage of the Dreyfus affair (1898-1899) that Blum became actively interested in politics. Through Herr, he met Jean Jaurès and quickly became an apostle of the great socialist leader, sharing his vision of a unified socialist movement in France.

The outbreak of World War I and the assassination of Jaurès in July, 1914, persuaded French socialists to end their traditional boycott on governmental participation. Blum accepted an invitation to become chief of staff in the

Ministry of Public Works, where he remained until 1917, when he resigned in protest over the government's denial of permission for French socialists to attend an international congress in Stockholm. Shortly thereafter, Blum published *Lettres sur la réforme gouvernementale* (1918), in which he analyzed French governance and expressed the need to give the prime minister executive authority. By the end of World War I, it was clear that Blum would pursue a career in politics. He was drawn, at the age of forty-seven, to active political life at the moment when Jaurès' dream of a unified socialist party was about to be shattered by the revolutionary events of 1917-1919.

Life's Work

Early in 1919, Blum was made chairman of the executive board of the Socialist Party and elected to the Chamber of Deputies. At that time, the party was split between those who wanted to emulate the Russian Bolsheviks and join the Third (Communist) International and those who, like Blum, believed in the republican, liberal, reformist socialism of Jaurès. Blum's view was in the minority at the annual Socialist Party congress at Tours in 1920. The majority voted to join the Third International and to expel dissidents such as Blum. They adopted the name of French Communist Party and took over the machinery and treasury of the old Socialist Party.

Blum remained an authentic spokesman for reformist socialism. To him fell the enormous task of reconstructing the party, financing it, and winning mass support away from the Communists. Blum's political philosophy was based on a distinction between the "conquest of power," the "exercise of power," and "participation" in a nonsocialist government. The first was the revolution itself and could occur only when the socialists took over the state and put their programs into place. The exercise of power, however, could occur only if the socialists became the largest party in the chamber and were invited to form a government. This possibility justified working legally within the constitutional framework.

Blum, however, adamantly opposed participation in a nonsocialist government, which he could justify only in a national emergency. He thus declined an invitation to join the government in 1924 and maintained this stance into the mid-1930's. Denounced by some as a doctrinaire theorist, Blum believed that he had to avoid appearing as an opportunist. He was successful. In 1920, the Socialist Party had been left with only 30,000 members as opposed to 130,000 for the Communists. By 1932, the Socialist strength was more than three times that of the Communists. The rise of Adolf Hitler in Germany and the violent tactics of domestic right-wing organizations during the mid-1930's made it desirable for the left-of-center parties to close ranks. In January, 1936, an electoral coalition known as the Popular Front emerged among the Communist, Socialist, and Radical Socialist parties. Elections in May and June, 1936, produced an overwhelming victory for the Left, and on

June 4 Blum became premier of France's first Popular Front government.

The Popular Front was greeted immediately by a wave of demonstrations and strikes among French workers and trade unionists. Blum immediately invited representatives of the unions and employers' organizations to meet together in his official residence, the Matignon Palace. The result was the Matignon Agreements, by which workers agreed to end the strikes and return to work. In exchange, they won recognition of their right to be represented by unions and to collective bargaining over wages and working conditions. With the domestic turmoil assuaged, Blum pushed the Popular Front program through the legislature in little more than two months. The major pieces of legislation, destined to have a permanent impact on French national life, provided for the following: a forty-hour work week, paid holidays, a central marketing organization for grain, a public works program, reform of the Bank of France, nationalization of the armaments industry, and dissolution of armed fascist-style leagues.

It was in foreign policy where the coalition among the leftist parties began to collapse. No issue proved more troubling to Blum than the Spanish Civil War. General Francisco Franco began the military revolt against the Spanish Popular Front government in Madrid in July, 1936, barely a month after the French Popular Front had been installed. The cornerstone of Blum's foreign policy was solidarity with Great Britain. After consulting with the British, Blum decided to follow their lead by observing strict neutrality, or nonintervention, in the Spanish Civil War—even when it became apparent that Germany and Italy were violating their pledges of nonintervention by sending military aid to the Franco rebels. Frequently denounced as typical of Blum's nonactive intellectualism, the policy of nonintervention was not one that Blum desired but rather one forced upon him by circumstances. His immediate reaction to the outbreak of the civil war had been to aid the Spanish loyalists with war material and money. The Radicals, however, opposed involvement in Spain. In addition, British leaders let it be known that if war erupted between France and Germany over the Spanish issue, England would not feel bound by her earlier guarantees of French security. Blum's only choice, therefore, was nonintervention, since party solidarity was necessary to launch the Popular Front social program.

As the conflict over Spain intensified, the Communists and left wing of the Socialist Party grew more dissatisfied with the policy of nonintervention. In addition, a serious financial crisis resulted in devaluations of the franc in 1936 and 1937. The crisis forced the prime minister to ask the legislature for emergency powers. When these were denied by the senate in June, 1937, Blum resigned, thus putting an end to the one-year rule of his government. The government fell largely because of weaknesses inherent in the French political system, which Blum had analyzed about twenty years earlier in *Lettres sur la réforme gouvernementale*—the lack of executive authority and the dependence of the government upon unstable party coalitions.

In the succeeding Popular Front government headed by the Radical, Camille Chautemps, Blum served as vice premier. Chautemps resigned on March 12, 1938, following Adolf Hitler's invasion of Austria. Once again Blum was asked to form a government. Unsuccessful in building a broad-based coalition, his cabinet rested solely on the Socialist/Radical alliance. It was clearly a transition government, which remained in power for only three weeks. With Blum's second resignation, the Popular Front era came to an end in France.

Although Blum had been unenthusiastic about military expenditures, his first term in office had witnessed the highest level of appropriations for national defense in the peacetime history of France. Yet his detractors on the Right accused him of misappropriation. He was subsequently brought to trial by the Vichy regime in 1942 and accused of squandering the nation's military resources, thus leaving France unprepared for war. The trial was blatantly unfair, and Blum used the opportunity to embarrass his accusers with an eloquent defense. The record shows that he became convinced after Germany's absorption of Austria in March, 1938, that war was likely and that France must be prepared. He therefore offered his support, in the interest of national unity, to the more conservative government of Édouard Daladier. When World War II began in September, 1939, Blum supported its vigorous prosecution; after the defeat of France, Blum was among the minority in the National Assembly who voted against turning over all power to Marshal Philippe-Henri Pétain. The Vichy regime retaliated by taking Blum into "administrative custody." His trial resulted in imprisonment, first at Bourassol in France and then, from March, 1943, until the liberation, at Buchenwald in Germany. During this period of captivity, Blum wrote one of his most moving books, *À l'Échelle humaine* (1945; *For All Mankind*, 1946), which, despite his personal circumstances, brims with optimism and hope about the future.

Blum's last experience of exercising power came in late 1946 and early 1947. It was a moment of parliamentary crisis. The constitution of the Fourth Republic had been voted but had not yet come into operation. The leaders of the largest parties to emerge from the elections of 1946, the Communists and a Catholic faction, were unsuccessful in forming a government. In this unpromising situation, Blum was asked to take office for one month, until the constitutional framework could be set in motion. His cabinet was composed entirely of Socialists. With such a thin base of support, Blum harbored few illusions about what could be accomplished. The last Blum government succeeded in temporarily halting price rises, but Blum's efforts at governing were hamstrung by the same party irresponsibility that had contributed to the collapse of the Third Republic.

Following his final resignation, Blum retired at the age of seventy-five to what he loved best—solitude and books. He died at his home in Jouy-en-Josas on March 30, 1950. The public mourning on the Place de la Concorde in Paris and the flood of condolences from around the world provided eloquent testimony that Blum was indeed one of the preeminent men of twentieth century France.

Summary

Léon Blum first made his name not as a politician but as a literary critic and man of letters. His subsequent political career can be understood only in relation to the beliefs and standards of this intellectual youth. Through his education, Blum acquired a sense of moral rigor and an appreciation of intellectual honesty and consistency—qualities evident in his published work but which frequently clashed with the compromises necessary in the political world. In 1936, for example, he was forced to abandon his moral inclination to aid the Spanish Republic in its struggle for survival against General Francisco Franco in order to save the political coalition necessary to pass the Popular Front's social and economic reforms through the French legislature. These reforms—including the forty-hour week, the right to collective bargaining, and the right to paid vacations—stand as Blum's most important political achievement. His moral rigor was again challenged in 1946, when he was compelled to abandon his admiration for Charles de Gaulle as a resistance leader in a dramatic confrontation with the general over the nature of postwar French democracy. Blum's career is a classic example of the dilemmas to be faced by an intellectual with his qualities of mind in the compromising and dissembling world of politics.

Bibliography

Alexander, Martin S., and Helen Graham, eds. *The French and Spanish Popular Fronts: Comparative Perspectives*. Cambridge, England: Cambridge University Press, 1989. This book is a collection of essays, many of which are useful in understanding the Popular Front phase of Blum's life.

Colton, Joel G. *Léon Blum: Humanist in Politics*. New York: Alfred A. Knopf, 1966. This is a full-scale political biography of Blum, which treats the literary years before 1914 only as a prologue to his career in politics. It is especially useful for the period from 1936 through World War II and contains a full bibliography.

Dalby, Louise Elliott. *Léon Blum: Evolution of a Socialist*. New York: Thomas Yoseloff, 1963. This study concentrates on the development of Blum's political thought from anarchism to Marxism to humanist socialism.

Dreifort, John E. *Yvon Delbos at the Quai d'Orsay: French Foreign Policy During the Popular Front, 1936-1938*. Lawrence: University Press of

Kansas, 1973. Although the author focuses on the foreign minister of the Popular Front, this book is especially useful for understanding Blum's ideas on the formulation and practice of foreign policy.

Joll, James. *Three Intellectuals in Politics*. New York: Pantheon Books, 1961. This volume contains an interesting short analysis of Blum's career with an emphasis on the travails of an intellectual in political life. Blum's career is compared with those of Walther Rathenau in Germany and Filippo Tommaso Marinetti in Italy.

Lacouture, Jean. *Léon Blum*. New York: Holmes & Meier, 1982. Translated by George Holoch. This translation from French concentrates on the political side of Blum's life. Unlike earlier biographies, however, such as those by Colton and Joll, which portray Blum as a nonactive intellectual beset with indecision, Lacouture depicts Blum as a "realist" concerned with the safety of his party and country.

William I. Shorrock

UMBERTO BOCCIONI

Born: October 19, 1882; Reggio di Calabria, Italy
Died: August 17, 1916; Sorte, near Verona, Italy
Area of Achievement: Art
Contribution: Boccioni is the foremost painter and sculptor of the Italian
    Futurist movement, which developed in the years immediately preceding
    World War I. Besides producing paintings and sculptures, Boccioni was
    the leading technical theorist of the movement. His principles of sculp-
    ture, in particular, shaped the mixed-media and dynamic productions of
    the twentieth century.

Early Life

Umberto Boccioni was born on October 19, 1882, in Reggio di Calabria,
at the toe of Italy's boot, but his family moved often as his father, Raffaele,
a minor civil servant, was transferred. The Boccioni family, including Umberto's mother and his sister, Amelia, moved shortly after his birth to Forli;
subsequently, they lived in Genoa, Padua, and Catania, at the latter of which
Umberto attended the Technical Institute. Apparently he was interested in art
even as a child. While in school, he also contributed critical articles to a
local newspaper.

Just before the turn of the century, Boccioni moved to Rome, where he
divided himself between commercial work and art study. At the insistence of
his father, he studied with a sign maker, and at least part of his income was
derived from commercial advertising work. He also studied at the Free
School of Nude Painting, but the most significant event of his stay in Rome
was his acquaintance with another painting student, Gino Severini, and his
introduction through Severini to the older painter Giacomo Balla, who taught
the younger men modern painting techniques and with whom Boccioni studied until 1902. The young artist traveled extensively, spending time in Paris,
Munich, and St. Petersburg, and studied in Padua and Venice before settling
in Milan in 1907 with his mother, who served as a model for his work
through most of his short life, and his sister. His earliest paintings show
influences as disparate as the medieval artist Albrecht Dürer and the Art
Nouveau movement. He seems to have been most significantly affected by
the work of the Impressionists and the Symbolists. Although those influences
remain in his later works, Boccioni's aims and his methods were dramatically changed by his meeting in 1910 with the writer Emilio Filippo Marinetti, the originator of Futurism.

Life's Work

Marinetti was an avant-garde poet and critic who had spent time in Paris,
where he was exposed to the sparks that would ignite the efflorescence of
modern art. While publishing a literary magazine, *Poesia*, in Milan, Mari-

netti wrote the first Futurist manifesto, published February 20, 1909, in the French newspaper *Le Figaro*, for which he was the Italian literary correspondent. Drawing on such sources as the German writer Friedrich Wilhelm Nietzsche and the French philosopher Henri Bergson, Marinetti constructed a purposely offensive and radical anthem for a new movement that turned its back on the past subjects and techniques of art. In place of homages to the great artists, Marinetti extolled the portrayal of speed, machismo, and violence. Although some of the Futurist rhetoric may have been an Italian nationalist reaction against the European perception of Italy as backward, many critics have found affinities to Fascism in some tenets of the Futurist movement.

Within a year, Marinetti's ideas for a nationalist art movement that would include disciplines as diverse as music and fashion design had begun to gain adherents, including Boccioni. He was one of five painters to sign the first manifesto of the Futurist painters on February 11, 1910. On April 11 of the same year, the group issued the *Manifesto tecnico della scultura futurista* (technical manifesto of Futurist painting); as usual with this movement, theory preceded practice. Although five names, including those of Severini and Balla, are affixed to these documents, Boccioni is thought to be largely responsible for them. The first painting manifesto echoes Marinetti's ideas, placing science above nature and arguing for the replacement of traditional static human or natural representations with the symbols of technology, such as oceanliners and automobiles. The technical manifesto is more specific, as Boccioni had begun the work of transforming words into new, or recycled, techniques. The painters vowed to abandon traditional forms and colors, but the Impressionist and Symbolist painters had already begun that task. Most significant for the new Futurist movement was the interest in dynamism: the representation of the multiplication of images caused by the speed of modern life.

A prime example of Futurist dynamism in painting is Boccioni's *Città che sale* (1910-1911; the city rises), which is typical in its urban subject: a construction site. Despite the Futurist celebration of technology in the manifestos, Boccioni chose to depict horses rather than machines at work. The painting's glowing colors and elongated brushstrokes create a violent and vibrant sense of action; in fact, the horses seem to drag their masters into a vortex of movement that may seem as much destructive as constructive. Another major painting by Boccioni, the triptych *Stati d'animo: Gli Addii, Quelli che vanno, Quelli che restano* (states of mind: the farewells, those who go, those who stay), painted and repainted in 1911-1912, also reveals an interest in action unfolding over time. The triptych depicts expressionistically the departure of a train and the feelings of those described in the subtitles. The source of the main title is the work of Bergson; his interest in the relativism of human perspective and perception as well as contemporary

experiments with time-lapse photography and film influenced Boccioni's efforts. Also, perhaps surprisingly, there seems to be an affinity between Boccioni's theories of dynamism and Albert Einstein's theory of relativity; for
both theorists, matter and energy are related states of being.

The repainted version of *Stati d'animo* includes numerals that reflect the
influence of the cubists, particularly Pablo Picasso and Georges Braque.
Boccioni's friend and fellow Futurist, Severini, had returned from a stay in
Paris to report that the Italians were out of touch with the latest artistic
developments. Thanks to financial support from Marinetti, Boccioni visited
Paris in 1911 and 1912. Cubist works he saw there supplemented the reading
he had done in Italy. After exhibiting several times in Italy, the Futurists
finally mounted an exhibition in Paris in 1912 at the Bernheim-Jeune Gallery. This exhibition toured Europe, and only a denial of the Futurists' request for separate gallery space blocked their participation in the historic
Armory Show in New York in 1913, the show that introduced European
modern art to the United States.

Included in the Bernheim-Jeune catalog for the Futurist show is a discussion of "force-lines," or the idea that objects contain unique and characteriz-
ing lines of emotion. Boccioni and other Futurists combined the cool of
analysis of the cubists and their dismemberment of subjects into their parts
with the Italian movement's expressionistic dynamism, the representation of
movement over time. This Futurist interest in all four dimensions as well as
the beginnings of cubist sculpture may explain Boccioni's shift to a new field
to which he would make his most important contributions: sculpture.

In 1912, Boccioni published his *Manifesto tecnico della scultura futurista*.
Perhaps the two most significant elements are a focus on a new relation
between the art object and its environment and a call for mixtures of unconventional sculptural materials. His suggestions for materials include glass,
cardboard, concrete, and even electric lights. In 1913, Boccioni first exhibited in Paris sculptures intended to illustrate his techniques; the ten pieces
and twenty drawings shown survive in photographs, but only four or five
pieces of Boccioni's sculptural output still exist (one is of questionable authenticity). Conflicting stories have circulated about the loss or destruction
of most of his pieces, after a posthumous exhibition in 1917. They may have
been thrown in a stream by a distraught or jealous friend; they may have
been exposed accidentally to the elements.

Fortunately, one of the surviving sculptures is the 1913 bronze *Forme
uniche della continuatà nello spazio* (unique forms of continuity in space),
the last of three striding figures that Boccioni created. Although the energy
and sense of a figure caught in time suggest the influence of Rodin, Boccioni's figure is mechanical as well as romantic. It seems to be a form rather
than a body, and Boccioni has attempted to break up the form according to
the theories most clearly enumerated in the book *Pittura scultura futuriste*

(dinamismo plastico) (Futurist painting and sculpture [plastic dynamism]), published in 1914.

Artistic, personal, and political differences soon sundered the Futurist movement. Boccioni joined Marinetti in 1914 in supporting the Fascist call for Italian intervention in Eastern Europe. Their opposition to Italian neutrality and their romanticization of war made them ripe for service. Boccioni joined the cycling unit of the Italian army; he eventually landed in the artillery. The horrors and the nuisances of war cured Boccioni of his romanticism, but there was little time or opportunity for producing art. A leave in the summer of 1916 did allow him to produce a few paintings. Although they seem to suggest that he was abandoning Futurist methods in favor of an exploration of Paul Cézanne's geometric techniques, the change may be attributable to the fact that these paintings were commissioned.

In August, after returning to his unit in Sorté, near Verona, Boccioni fell from a horse during military exercises and died the next day, August 17. Despite the loss of most of his sculpture and the relatively short duration of his career, Boccioni's reputation has been enhanced by exhibitions of the remaining sculptures and of his paintings. His theoretical concerns have also proved to be wider than imagined. Besides his manifestos on painting and sculpture, an unpublished manifesto of Futurist architecture was rediscovered in 1971. His fascination with the interplay between object and space might have led him in other directions as well, if not for his early death.

Summary

Although Umberto Boccioni is the best known of the Italian Futurist painters, his influence through the rest of the twentieth century is primarily in sculpture and in the application of his dynamic theories. Despite the loss of most of his sculptural pieces, Boccioni's insistence on merging sculpture and environment can be recognized in works as diverse as Alexander Calder's giant mobiles and Robert Smithson's environmental sculptures, which mold the landscape itself.

Boccioni is open to charges that he never fully succeeded in transforming his theories into art that faithfully represented them. His embrace of Fascism has also made him the object of criticism. Yet his work in paint, words, and shapes remains an enduring contribution to the erasure of traditional artistic boundaries and the rise of modern art.

Bibliography

Coen, Ester. *Umberto Boccioni*. Translated by Robert Eric Wolf. New York: Metropolitan Museum of Art, 1988. Produced in conjunction with a 1988-1989 exhibition at the Metropolitan Museum of Art, this is the only book-length work in English on the artist. Includes lavish illustrations and supporting materials.

Golding, John. *Boccioni's Unique Forms of Continuity in Space*. Newcastle upon Tyne, England: University of Newcastle upon Tyne, 1972. A transcription of a lecture exploring the evolution of Boccioni's most famous sculpture and his ambivalence about his sources.

Hultén, Pontus, organizer. *Futurism and Futurisms*. New York: Abbeville Press, 1986. A monumental resource on all forms of Futurism, including a dictionary of Futurist terms and personalities and illustrations of the exhibition that the book documents.

Martin, Marianne W. *Futurist Art and Theory, 1909-1915*. Oxford, England: Clarendon Press, 1968. Reprint. New York: Hacker Art Books, 1978. Perhaps the seminal work in English on Futurism, this book documents the rise of the movement and its influences from such French artistic movements as Surrealism and cubism.

Perloff, Marjorie. *The Futurist Moment: Avant-Garde, Avant Guerre, and the Language of Rupture*. Chicago: University of Chicago Press, 1986. Labeling a whole cavalcade of prewar radical artistic movements Futurist, Perloff insists that they all tore down barriers, both in art and between the art object and the world.

Soby, James Thrall, and Alfred H. Barr, Jr. *Twentieth Century Italian Art*. New York: Museum of Modern Art, 1949. Published in conjunction with an exhibition, this books remains valuable for its clear exposition and its early bibliography.

Taylor, Joshua C. *Futurism*. New York: Museum of Modern Art, 1961. A good introduction to the Futurist movement, including translations of four Futurist manifestos, illustrations, and a bibliography.

Helaine Ross

NIELS BOHR

Born: October 7, 1885; Copenhagen, Denmark
Died: November 18, 1962; Copenhagen, Denmark
Areas of Achievement: Physics and chemistry
Contribution: Bohr discovered the fundamental structure and character of the atom, its components and how they interact. For this discovery, he won the Nobel Prize in Physics in 1922. Bohr also made significant contributions to the understanding of how quantum and classical physics unify as a single philosophy in his principle of complementarity.

Early Life

Niels Henrik David Bohr was born in Copenhagen, Denmark, on October 7, 1885. Bohr's early environment invited genius; his father, Christian Bohr, was a professor of physiology at the University of Copenhagen, and his mother, Ellen née Adler, came from a family of eminent Danish educators. Bohr's younger brother, Harald, would become a professor of mathematics.

Bohr attended Gammelholm Grammar School and entered the University of Copenhagen in 1903. Bohr studied under the tutelage of C. Christiansen, a prominent physicist and an original, creative educator. At the University of Copenhagen, Bohr took his master's degree in physics in 1909 and his Ph.D. in 1911.

Bohr published his first scientific work in 1908. The opportunity arose as a result of a prize offered to the individual who solved an investigation of surface tension by means of oscillating fluid jets. Bohr won the gold medal, and his piece appeared in the *Transactions of the Royal Society.*

In the fall of 1911, Bohr studied abroad at the University of Cambridge, pursuing largely theoretical studies under Sir J. J. Thomson. Yet he had not been at Cambridge long before he realized that the true frontier work in theoretical physics was occurring at the laboratories of Nobel laureate (1908) Ernest Rutherford at the nearby University of Manchester. Bohr also was drawn by Rutherford's dynamic personality. Before Bohr arrived at Manchester in the spring of 1912, Rutherford had already deduced the structure of the atom experimentally, although the concept's theoretical foundation still held significant flaws. Bohr, however, was about to uncover an idea that would forever change the face of physics and the very concept of the physical world itself.

Life's Work

As Bohr pondered the beauty of the emerging picture of the atomic structure, he, like Rutherford, was perplexed by the evident contradictions in theory. Rutherford's atomic model held that the atom was made of a very dense, positively charged central core surrounded by a cloud of negatively charged particles. Yet, based entirely on Newtonian, classical physics, such a structure could not exist, becoming unstable and falling apart. It was no wonder that Rutherford's peers held that the theory was fatally flawed. Yet Bohr had an almost heroic faith in Rutherford's insight and experimental proficiency, so he stubbornly clung to the idea that the experimental evidence had only to be matched with the appropriate theory.

In 1911, the infant science called quantum mechanics had found few applications. Bohr recognized that by linking the statistical methods of quantum mechanics with an invariant number called Planck's constant, for Max Planck, he could theoretically vindicate Rutherford's experimental evidence. Bohr reasoned that energy from the atom, emitted only in well-defined energy levels, was related to electrons falling or rising into stable orbits around the nucleus, a concept somewhat alien to Isaac Newton's classical notions of cause and effect. Using Planck's constant, he was able to derive the calculations necessary to describe the stability and transitions of the electrons, thus defining precisely the nature of the atom itself. The results of his work were ultimately verified by experimental evidence. He published these results in 1913 and for them would win the Nobel Prize in Physics nine years later.

From this work, Bohr reasoned that the model for the atom described in quantum terms must join smoothly with classical physics when the dimensions become larger than atomic size. This logic vindicated Rutherford's physical, experimental evidence as essentially correct. Yet in a larger sense, the idea enabled a philosophical justification of using the quantum set of scientific rules to describe the atomic world and the classical set to describe the larger universe. He called this fusion of ideas the principle of correspondence.

In 1916, Bohr returned to Copenhagen an acclaimed physicist. By 1920, Bohr was named the director of the Institute of Theoretical Physics at Copenhagen. It would later be renamed the Niels Bohr Institute. By this time, Bohr had continued his investigations and uncovered evidence that the active properties, degree of stability, and character of all matter itself were largely dependent on the arrangement of the electron shells of the elements. Yet all the ongoing descriptions of the atomic character were being almost wholly defined in quantum terms, many being derived from a form of statistical probability. Albert Einstein was dissatisfied with this state of affairs, which violated his sense of universal simplicity, and stated, "God does not play dice with the universe."

Bohr recognized that this debate was threatening the very foundation of theoretical physics. He used the example of two experiments to deliver what he called the principle of complementarity. The experiments he referenced were ones that unambiguously showed the electron to be a wave form and another that showed it in equally definitive terms to be a particle. Bohr said that one observation necessarily excluded viewing results that only the other could obtain and vice versa but that one did not necessarily disprove the other. Together, however, the concepts were complementary proofs of each other. It was all a matter of philosophy, as was the foundation of science itself. The principle of complementarity stood as a brilliant turning point in physics. With it, the dominance of classical physics was ended and the new insights of the surreal quantum world were engendered.

Bohr's reputation attracted physicists the world over to Copenhagen to study and discuss the direction of modern physics. Bohr and Einstein frequently debated the consequences of quantum mechanics and the effects of this science on the perception of causality.

Denmark was taken by the Nazi stormtroopers in 1940. Bohr was an outspoken anti-Nazi and his mother was Jewish. Under the threat of imminent arrest, Bohr and his family escaped Copenhagen in 1943 on a fishing boat to Sweden. They eventually traveled to the United States. Bohr worked with the Allies' most influential physicists under the direction of J. Robert Oppenheimer, and they succeeded in building the nuclear bomb that would end the war. Indeed, it was Bohr who first predicted that the isotope uranium 235 would be the element of choice for a nuclear weapon.

After the war, the golden age of physics was irrevocably ended for Bohr. He set about at once to convince both Franklin D. Roosevelt and Winston Churchill of the immediate need to control nuclear weapons. Failing this, he helped establish the First International Conference on the Peaceful Uses of Atomic Energy, eventually winning the first Atoms for Peace Award in the United States (1957). Bohr died in Copenhagen on November 18, 1962.

Summary

Using the concept of complementarity, Niels Bohr forged the link between quantum mechanics and classical physics. This linkage enabled science to move deliberately ahead into subatomic research using a philosophy that was both unique to the atom's peculiar interior and relative, in a complementary sense, to a larger world. Bohr was a restless scientist who believed that there was an innate unity to many aspects of the physical world, expressed in the abstractions of complementarity, yet he was also practically oriented.

Bohr's creation and forceful leadership of the Institute of Theoretical Physics in Copenhagen served as a wellspring of emerging knowledge about the atom to scientists worldwide. Yet to Bohr it also represented an undisguised empire, directing the pace and direction of atomic science. From Copenhagen, Bohr would personally coordinate and trace the direction of theoretical physics as his institute became the center of world attention to this strange, new science.

His empire would both collapse and race out of his control with the ascension of Adolf Hitler's war machine and his consequent contributions to the development of the atom bomb at Alamogordo, New Mexico. Bohr was one of the first scientists to grasp fully the aggregate implications of the bomb to humanity, *ex post facto*. When Bohr returned to postwar Copenhagen, the impetus of theoretical physics had shifted to the United States. Bohr's own energy would be devoted to attempting somehow to repair the damage or at least to slow the proliferation of the nuclear bomb. Yet Bohr's influence on modern physics will profoundly overshadow the misfortunes of war and the misapplication of science. The ability of one man logically to unite the seemingly disparate worlds of quantum and classical physics in a philosophical, mathematical unity called complementarity stands as one of the most important and astonishing intellectual triumphs of science.

Bibliography

Asimov, Isaac. *Understanding Physics*. Vol. 2, *Light, Magnetism, and Electricity*. New York: Walker, 1966. This book is written for the general reader with some acumen in the sciences. Explains Bohr's work through a chronological accounting of modern physics. Written in a historically relevant style, setting Bohr and his peers against the background of a developing science.

Crease, Robert P., and Charles C. Mann. *The Second Creation: Makers of the Revolution in Twentieth Century Physics*. New York: Macmillan, 1985. An altogether exquisite work that tells Bohr's story to the general reader like perhaps no other. It gives an easy-to-read, personal, even charming account of Bohr's early professional life, while detailing the science, woven into the fabric of an emerging picture of the bizarre world of the atomic interior.

Folse, Henry J. *The Philosophy of Niels Bohr: The Framework of Complementarity*. New York: North-Holland, 1985. This work details complementarity as a philosophical orientation along with its broad views and many applications. It is written for a college-level audience and superbly details the later, postwar applications of Bohr for the wider views of complementarity.

French, Anthony P., and P. J. Kennedy, eds. *Niels Bohr: A Centenary Volume*. Cambridge, Mass.: Harvard University Press, 1985. A book of essays about Bohr and his ideas, this work varies widely in appeal and depth. Many of the articles are written by those who knew him. The approaches vary from the highly technical to personal treatments.

Lamont, Lansing. *Day of Trinity*. New York: Atheneum, 1965. This is a historical narrative, setting Bohr in the middle of the development of the atom bomb. He and his son are integrated into the Manhattan Project after escaping from Denmark. It links Bohr with Oppenheimer and Einstein in a completely enthralling and true wartime thriller.

Moore, Ruth. *Niels Bohr: The Man, His Science, and the World They*

Changed. New York: Alfred A. Knopf, 1966. If there is a definitive, English-language sketch of Bohr's life, it is probably Moore's sketch of the physicist. Details Bohr's life from birth to his fight for peaceful applications of nuclear power. It is written for all readers, even those without a background in physics.

Dennis Chamberland

HEINRICH BÖLL

Born: December 21, 1917; Cologne, Germany
Died: July 16, 1985; Merten, West Germany
Area of Achievement: Literature
Contribution: Böll, who was awarded the Nobel Prize in Literature in 1972, remains one of the greatest German authors of the postwar era. His works evince a keen moral sense and a sincere commitment to social change.

Early Life

Heinrich Böll was born in the city of Cologne on December 21, 1917. Cologne is a strongly Catholic city located on the banks of the Rhine River in central Germany, and this religious heritage is evident in the author's liberal and humanitarian themes. Böll attended elementary and secondary schools in Cologne and was graduated in 1937. He entered an apprenticeship in a bookstore and began to study German literature. During World War II, he served in the German army and was wounded four times. He was finally captured by the Americans near the end of the war. Böll had married Annemarie Cech in 1942, and they eventually had three sons. She often served as his collaborator in the numerous translations of English and American literature that he later published.

After the war, Böll returned to his studies of German literature and began to write his first fictional works. Although still unknown as a writer, he was invited to the 1949 meeting of the Group 47 circle of German writers, who gathered together once a year to read and evaluate one another's texts. Böll's narrative skills earned for him the respect of his peers, and, in 1951, he won the award for the best work read that year. From that point on, he wrote prolifically and won a number of prestigious awards. Throughout his life, he remained in the Cologne area.

Life's Work

Böll's first works deal with his personal experiences during and in the immediate aftermath of World War II. The major theme of virtually all of his writings—the alienation of the individual at the mercy of vast and impassive social and religious institutions—also becomes evident in these initial texts. The novel *Der Zug war pünktlich* (1949; *The Train Was on Time*, 1956) examines the brutal operations of the Nazi government bureaucracy that utilized the efficient German train system to transport millions to their deaths in concentration camps. He also assails the passivity and lack of compassion of the countless Germans who witnessed these events. His second novel, *Wo warst du, Adam?* (1951; *Adam, Where Art Thou?*, 1955), also takes up the strong antiwar themes of his first works. The main character, a soldier named Feinhals, must passively observe the terror of the Nazi era but serves, as do many of Böll's characters, as a kind of moral "witness" figure whose testimony of the horrible events of that time forces the society of postwar Germany to remember a dark past that it would prefer conveniently to forget. This strong sense of social and moral conscience prevails in all Böll's writings. These novels also suggest the sharply dualistic moral vision of the world that characterizes many of the figures in his works. Individuals are portrayed as either good or evil, as the helpless victims of persecution or the ruthless executioners of the innocent.

The novel *Und sagte kein einziges Wort* (1953; *Acquainted with the Night*, 1954) was an international success and illustrates Böll's attempts to employ the techniques of modern narration. In alternating first-person accounts, he tells the story of Fred and Käthe Bogner, a married couple who lived in poverty and desperation in Cologne during the years immediately following World War II. Their marriage is falling apart, and, as a result of the stresses of their impoverished life, Fred has become alienated, unable to keep a job and given to drinking heavily. This novel takes up one of Böll's more controversial themes: the hypocrisy of the Catholic church. Although it professes the love and compassion of Christ, the established Church with all its power, wealth, and influence does nothing to alleviate the very real sufferings of its followers. Böll remains deeply suspicious of social and religious institutions that have come to value their power and authority rather than the individuals whom they are presumably committed to serving.

Das Brot der frühen Jahre (1955; *The Bread of Our Early Years*, 1957) and *Billard um halbzehn* (1959; *Billiards at Half-Past Nine*, 1961) both examine from a critical perspective the postwar years of Germany, its rapid economic recovery, and its new spirit of materialism and prosperity. The latter novel remains one of Böll's most famous texts. It presents the story of the Faehmels, a family of architects in the Cologne area, and chronicles several generations of their involvement in German history in the period from 1907 to the 1950's. Böll is extremely critical of postwar German society and its apparent attempt to forget the Nazi past. As in his other novels, he tends to characterize individuals in this novel in terms of a somewhat dualistic "good/bad" schema. In *Billiards at Half-Past Nine*, he also experiments with more complex modes of narration by having the various family members present their perspectives in different chapters. In 1962, Böll visited the Soviet Union for a brief period.

Böll's next novel, *Ansichten eines Clowns* (1963; *The Clown*, 1965) is one of his most popular and most controversial works. It continues the strong criticism of social and religious institutions found in his earlier texts. Hans Schnier, a satirical pantomime artist now drunk and unemployed, tells in a series of narrative flashbacks the story of his family and his failed marriage to his beloved Marie. Böll assails the hypocrisy of postwar German society in the figure of Schnier's mother, a former racist Nazi who denies her deplorable past and now heads a group promoting intercultural harmony and understanding. Schnier is a typical Böll character who refuses to let postwar Germany forget its participation in the Nazi era. The hypocritical and insensitive stance of the Catholic church destroys his genuinely innocent but "unlawful" relationship to the woman he truly loves. Schnier is another of those alienated "outsider" figures who provide a critical perspective on society. At the time Böll was working on this text, he and his wife were also translating the well-known American novel *The Catcher in the Rye* (1951), by J. D. Salinger, and the character of the alienated adolescent Holden Caulfield clearly informs that of Hans Schnier. Because of the rather negative view of the Catholic church presented in this novel, its initial publication generated a rather heated debate in the press. With Böll's increasing prominence, his marked liberal views on social and religious issues began to invoke the wrath of the more conservative elements in German society. Böll also served as a guest professor in the mid 1960's at the University of Frankfurt.

In 1972, Böll was awarded the Nobel Prize in Literature. The novel *Gruppenbild mit Dame* (1971; *Group Portrait with Lady*, 1973) was a decisive factor in the Swedish Academy's selection. The story of a poor woman, Leni Gruyten-Pfeiffer, the novel spans most of twentieth century German history. Leni represents one of the author's "innocent" figures, a generous and deeply spiritual person who dedicates her life to the poor but who is scorned by a materialistic and uncompassionate society. Böll's selection for the Nobel Prize evoked a barrage of negative reactions from the conservative German press, which maintained that the prize was awarded only to liberals and left-wing radicals.

The 1970's were a difficult time for German society. Left-wing terrorism—kidnappings, assassinations, bombings—conducted by the well-known Baader-Meinhof group of radicals polarized public opinion. Many conservatives, especially the right-wing Springer publishing concern, advocated measures that would seemingly compromise democratic rights of civil liberty. Although Böll deplored acts of violence committed by the terrorists, he spoke out for the rights of the individual and as a result was often attacked in the press. His novel *Die verlorene Ehre der Katharina Blum* (1974; *The Lost Honor of Katharina Blum*, 1975) deals with the fate of a young woman who, because of a love affair with a suspected terrorist, is viciously slandered in the popular conservative newspapers. The work is a thinly veiled polemic against the Springer press. This novel was made into a popular film version in 1975 by the German director Magarethe von Trotta and Volker Schlöndorff.

The novel *Fürsorgliche Belagerung* (1979; *The Safety Net*, 1982) also deals with issues concerning the terrorism of the 1970's and presents the author's criticism of modern Germany's social values. Böll maintained this aggressive stance with regard to human rights in both his literary works and his public speeches throughout his later life. In 1974, he acted as host for the expelled Russian novelist Aleksandr Solzhenitsyn.

One of Böll's last published works recalls the subject matter of his works written at the beginning of his career in 1947. Entitled *Das Vermächtnis* (1982; *A Soldier's Legacy*, 1985), the novel is set during the German occupation of France in 1943. The narrator, a soldier named Wenk, is an alcoholic who drinks to numb the pain he feels at the horror of the violence around him. His superior officer, Schelling, is a moral individual who tries to unmask the black market corruption of the troop. They are the typical Böll characters who represent the "good" people who suffer at the mercy of those who are "evil." Captain Schnecker is one of the latter type, and he eventually has Schelling murdered so that the profiteering can continue.

Although best known for his novels, Böll was also a master of the short story form, a genre which became popular in Germany after World War II as American literature was more widely read. During his life, he published a number of short story collections. Böll died on July 16, 1985, in the town of Merten, not far from his beloved city of Cologne. His last work, the novel *Frauen vor Flusslandschaft. Roman in Dialogen und Selbstgesprächen* (*Women in a River Landscape*, 1988), was published in 1985, after his death.

Summary

In the era after the end of World War II, Heinrich Böll assumed an important role in the history of German literature, and, as winner of the 1972 Nobel Prize, his place in the canon of world literature has been assured. Although there are some critics who find his technique of stark "good/evil" characterization simplistic, his talent as a traditional narrative artist established him as a popular author, and his works have been well received throughout the world.

Böll's literary career as well as political pronouncements had often been regarded as controversial, but he remained consistently true to his moral vision of society. Böll's relentless championing of the individual's rights in face of the impersonal authority of societal institutions and his rigorous efforts to examine the moral guilt of Germany's involvement in the horror of the Nazi period made him a spokesperson for the moral conscience of his wartime generation. His criticisms of the materialistic values of Germany's postindustrial society and his radical espousal of humanitarian and compassionate social values suggest his strongly spiritual and religious vision of the world. In a sense, he can be regarded as a radical Catholic who takes the Christian message of love and charity in its purest form and who deplores the seeming inertia and conservatism of the established Church. Throughout his life, Böll remained a committed writer who believed that it was the moral duty of the artist to address the social and political issues of his time.

Bibliography

Burns, Robert A. *The Theme of Non-Conformism in the Work of Heinrich Böll*. Coventry, England: University of Warwick, 1973. This volume is a scholarly dissertation that presents a detailed discussion of the "outsider" theme in Böll's major texts up to the early 1970's.

Conrad, Robert C. *Heinrich Böll*. Boston: Twayne, 1981. This well-written and extensive book offers the reader an excellent survey of Böll's works up to *The Lost Honor of Katharina Blum*. It contains a selected bibliography of secondary works (in both German and English) as well as listings of published interviews with the author.

MacPherson, Enid. *A Student's Guide to Böll*. London: Heinemann Educational Books, 1972. This rather slim volume is part of the publisher's Student's Guides to European Literature series and presents a well-written and informative introduction to the author's major themes and works. It should be supplemented with more extensive secondary sources.

Reid, James Henderson. *Heinrich Böll: Withdrawal and Reemergence*. London: Wolff, 1973. A brief but useful introduction to Böll's works for the beginning student.

Thomas, R. Hinton, and Wilfried van der Will. *The German Novel and the Affluent Society*. Manchester, England: Manchester University Press, 1968. This volume deals with Böll directly in only one section, but it presents a good portrait of the German literary scene in the 1950's and in the 1960's in which Boll's writing is to be situated.

Thomas F. Barry

DIETRICH BONHOEFFER

Born: February 4, 1906; Breslau, Germany
Died: April 9, 1945; Flossenbürg, Germany
Areas of Achievement: Philosophy, religion, and theology
Contribution: Bonhoeffer defined the concept of Christian discipleship, especially as it related to the Church in Germany during the 1930's. He provided a unique combination of theology and political ethics that made him a leader in German resistance to Adolf Hitler and also led to his untimely death in 1945.

Early Life

Dietrich Bonhoeffer was born in Breslau, Germany (now Wrocław, Poland), on February 4, 1906. His father was Karl Bonhoeffer, a well-known physician and psychiatrist. There were eight children in the family, of whom Dietrich and his twin sister, Sabine, were the sixth and seventh, respectively. The family soon moved to Berlin, where Karl Bonhoeffer became professor of psychiatry at the University of Berlin. It was there that Dietrich spent his childhood.

The realism that later characterized the philosophy and theology of Bonhoeffer was imparted to him by his father and through the influence of his mother, who was from one of the leading intellectual families in Germany. The family home became a meeting place for friends and neighbors representing some of the most brilliant minds of the day. Included were Adolf von Harnack, an eminent historian of Christian doctrine, and Ernst Troeltsch, a philosopher and theologian. The influence of these men helped place Bonhoeffer in the liberal spectrum of Christian theology as well as at the forefront of the ecumenical movement.

At the age of sixteen, Bonhoeffer dedicated his life to the study of theology and to service in the Lutheran church. He entered the University of Tübingen in 1923 and was matriculated at the University of Berlin the following year. He remained in Berlin for the completion of his formal education. During his years at the university, Bonhoeffer became a follower of the post-World War I theology of Karl Barth, soon to become known as neo-orthodoxy. These ideas enhanced Bonhoeffer's realism and helped him to accept the tremendous suffering and destruction of the recent conflagration, as well as Germany's lowered status in the community of nations.

When Bonhoeffer was twenty-one, he presented his doctoral dissertation to the faculty at Berlin. It was entitled *Sanctorum Communio: Eine dogmatische Untersuchung zur Soziologie der Kirche*. After it was published in 1930, the work was praised by such men as Barth.

Bonhoeffer left Berlin in 1927 to serve two years as an assistant minister to a German-speaking congregation in Barcelona, Spain. He proved to be a tremendous help and encouragement to the church and its elderly pastor. Back in Berlin in 1929, Bonhoeffer soon became a lecturer in systematic theology at the university. Before settling into the routine, however, he went to the United States for a year of additional study at Union Theological Seminary in New York City. Somewhat surprised by the lack of interest in serious theology on the part of American students at the seminary, Bonhoeffer was impressed by their social concern for the poor and needy. Bonhoeffer was well prepared for his life's work when he returned to Berlin in 1931. He was ready to face the challenges to Germany and the world in the person of Hitler.

Life's Work

By the time Bonhoeffer began his full-time lecturing, he was identified with the ecumenical movement, seeking to unite Christians around the world, and also with the ideas of Barth, whom Bonhoeffer soon met at a seminar in Bonn. At first, the students at the university were skeptical about the youthful professor but were soon drawn to him by the depth and relevance of his views. Bonhoeffer's first book, *Schöpfung und Fall* (1937), was an outgrowth of these early lectures.

Bonhoeffer's rising popularity in Berlin coincided with the rising popularity of the National Socialist German Workers' (Nazi) Party throughout the country. The Bonhoeffer family had been deeply affected by the defeat of Germany in 1918 and by the humiliation of the nation in the Treaty of Versailles, but they strongly opposed the ultranationalistic philosophy and the superior race ideology of the Nazi Party. Even while outside the country, Dietrich was kept informed about the growing Nazi influence, particularly as it related to the Jews. His twin sister, Sabine, was married to Gerhard Leibholz, whose father was a Jew, although Gerhard had been baptized as a Lutheran.

Bonhoeffer was soon dismayed by the paralysis of the German Christians regarding Nazi ideology. His realism, as well as his theology, compelled him to speak out against that ideology. On February 1, 1933, two days after Hitler had become Chancellor of Germany, Bonhoeffer addressed the German public on radio and urged them not to adopt an ultranationalistic leader who could easily become a national idol. The broadcast was cut off the air before the speech was completed. In the minds of Nazi leaders, Bonhoeffer was already a marked man.

Most Lutheran leaders succumbed to Nazi pressure and formed the German Christian Movement, a vital part of German nationalism. Bonhoeffer and a minority formed what became known as the Confessing church, seeking to purify the church through discipline. These leaders were shocked by parallels being drawn between Jesus and Hitler. Unable to accept such ideas, Bonhoeffer went to Great Britain in the fall of 1933, answering the call to pastor two German-speaking congregations in South London. During his eighteen months there, he studied the Sermon on the Mount and the idea of Christian discipleship. The result was his best-known book, *Nachfolge* (1937; *The Cost of Discipleship*, 1948). In this absorbing volume, Bonhoeffer criticized what he called the cheap grace being preached in many churches. He defined cheap grace as "the preaching of forgiveness without requiring repentance." Bonhoeffer then advocated costly grace which "is costly because it costs a man his life, and it is grace because it gives a man the only true life. . . . Above all it is costly because it cost God the life of his Son."

In 1935, Bonhoeffer was called back to Germany by the Confessing church to lead a clandestine seminary, eventually located in Finkenwalde, Pomerania. This seems to have been a profitable and pleasant time for Bonhoeffer and the small group of students; in 1937, however, the seminary was closed by the Gestapo. Following the closing, Bonhoeffer became active in the resistance movement dedicated to the overthrow of Hitler. From 1937 to his arrest in 1943, Bonhoeffer lived in temporary places of refuge, such as the Benedictine Abbey at Ettal. His spare time during these years was used to write *Ethik* (1949; *Ethics*, 1955). He regarded this work as his greatest contribution as a theologian.

As the clouds of war began gathering over Europe, Bonhoeffer's friends urged him to leave Germany and continue his work abroad. He did return briefly to London and in June, 1939, visited the United States; he soon felt constrained to return to his homeland. Before leaving, Bonhoeffer wrote to Reinhold Niebuhr, an American neo-orthodox leader, and declared, "I shall have no right to participate in the reconstruction of Christian life in Germany after the war if I do not share the trials of this time with my people." Taking advantage of one of the last opportunities to do so, Bonhoeffer returned to Berlin on July 27, 1939.

In the spring of 1941, a major conspiracy was organized to assassinate Hitler and overthrow the Nazi government. Bonhoeffer's role in this plot was to use his ecumenical contacts in Great Britain and the United States to convince the allies to stop fighting while the overthrow was in progress. The unsuccessful attempt was made in July, 1944, but by then Bonhoeffer had been in prison for more than a year. He was arrested on April 5, 1943, at his parents' home in Berlin, along with his sister Christel and her husband, for helping smuggle fourteen Jews into Switzerland.

For the next two years, Bonhoeffer wrote and ministered from various German prisons. The writings were later edited and published by his close friend, Eberhard Bethge, under the title *Widerstand und Ergebung* (1951; *Prisoner for God*, 1953; also as *Letters and Papers from Prison*, 1958).

Bonhoeffer's final days were spent in the concentration camp at Flossenbürg. On April 9, 1945, by a special order from Nazi Schutzstaffel leader

Heinrich Himmler, Bonhoeffer was hanged. About the same time, his brother Klaus and two brothers-in-law were executed elsewhere for resistance activities.

Summary

Dietrich Bonhoeffer had a clear understanding of the relationship between church and state. He first clarified the difference between state and government. By state, Bonhoeffer meant an ordered community; by government, he meant the power which creates and maintains order. The Nazi system, therefore, was government representing only the rulers and not the full German state. Bonhoeffer believed that the New Testament teaches that the basis of government is Jesus Christ and that only from Christ does government have authority on earth. By this simple concept, Bonhoeffer destroyed the foundation of Nazi ideology, including the exaltation for the German state and the attempt to use the Church as an instrument of governmental power.

This Christocentric view of government was also used by Bonhoeffer to justify the involvement of the Confessing church in the Resistance. He declared this involvement to be the responsibility of the church because of "the persecution of lawfulness, truth, humanity and freedom" that permeated the Nazi system. Although he was basically a pacifist, this combination of theology and ethics made Bonhoeffer a leading spokesman for the Resistance. Behind all that Bonhoeffer preached and practiced was his emphasis on discipline, which he urged all Christians and all Germans to follow.

Bibliography

Bethge, Eberhard. *Dietrich Bonhoeffer: Man of Vision, Man of Courage*. New York: Harper & Row, 1970. Written by a friend, relative, and associate of Bonhoeffer, this volume and others by Bethge comprise the basic authority for any study of Bonhoeffer.

Bonhoeffer, Dietrich. *Ethics*. Translated by Neville Horton Smith. New York: Macmillan, 1964. Edited and first published by Bethge in 1949, this book is taken from essays written by Bonhoeffer between 1940 and 1943. It is the best source of why Bonhoeffer became involved in the Resistance.

──────────. *Life Together*. Translated by John W. Doberstein. New York: Harper & Row, 1954. This is an outgrowth of Bonhoeffer's life in the close-knit seminary community at Finkenwalde between 1935 and 1937.

──────────. *Prisoner for God: Letters and Papers from Prison*. Translated by Reginald H. Fuller. New York: Macmillan, 1953. This book gives valuable insights into the life of Bonhoeffer during his last two years.

Bosanquet, Mary. *The Life and Death of Dietrich Bonhoeffer*. New York: Harper & Row, 1968. Perhaps the clearest and most objective biography. Much information is from Bonhoeffer's twin sister and from Bethge.

Ott, Heinrich. *Reality and Faith: The Theological Legacy of Dietrich Bonhoeffer.* Translated by Alex A. Morrison. Philadelphia: Fortress Press, 1972. This is an exhaustive study of Bonhoeffer's theology and its impact on the future.

Rasmussen, Larry. *Dietrich Bonhoeffer: Reality and Resistance.* Nashville, Tenn.: Abingdon Press, 1972. This is a good summary of how Bonhoeffer's theology shaped his political ethics and led him into the Resistance.

Robertson, Edwin. *The Shame and the Sacrifice: The Life and Martyrdom of Dietrich Bonhoeffer.* New York: Macmillan, 1988. An excellent and later evaluation of Bonhoeffer's influence. It includes some interesting insights into the Resistance and those who survived.

Glenn L. Swygart

PIERRE BONNARD

Born: October 3, 1867; Fontenay-aux-Roses, France
Died: January 23, 1947; Le Cannet, France
Area of Achievement: Art
Contribution: One of the most independent of Postimpressionist artists, Bonnard created a style and an artistic vision of art as an enchanting celebration of life which, at one and the same time, freed him from his Impressionist predecessors and carried on their tradition of art as a loving record of human and natural beauty.

Early Life

Pierre Bonnard was born in an exclusive suburb of Paris at the home of his father, who was an important official in the French war ministry. He was sent to expensive private schools and began his senior studies in the classics and philosophy. He was not a particularly good student, but his father had ambitions for him to enter the civil service. He studied law, as his father wished him to do, but he was interested in art and registered as well in a private art school, the Académie Julian. He also studied for a time at the École des Beaux-Arts, but he proved too undisciplined and spent much of his time sketching in the Paris museums with another young man, Édouard Vuillard, whose career was to be closely tied to that of Bonnard. In 1899, he failed his oral law exams, but his father retrieved him by arranging employment for him in an office. Only his sale of a poster for a champagne advertisement persuaded his reluctant father that he should have a chance to become a professional artist. He continued to work at the Académie Julian, where he developed associations with other young artists, including Vuillard, and the group were to form themselves, somewhat informally and very loosely, into an association which came to be known as the Nabis (a lighthearted word meaning "prophets"), who discussed and began to experiment with new ways of painting and drawing. In 1890, Bonnard took his turn, as was the law of the day, in the French army, but he returned to Paris to begin his career as an artist in earnest, sharing a studio with Vuillard and other Nabis at 28 rue Pigalle.

Life's Work

The Nabis believed that the Impressionist revolution in French art, which had been in force through the 1860's, 1870's, and 1880's, was inadequate for their needs as young artists. The Impressionists had felt the same about their predecessors, repudiating the high finish and restricted subject matter of early nineteenth century painting for a loose, vivacious, improvisatory recording of day-to-day life. Their battle for recognition was still going on in the early 1890's, but Bonnard's associates were strongly influenced by Paul Gauguin, who had turned away from his Impressionist contemporaries to painting in which the message became important, in which works carried spiritual or social symbols, and in which the spontaneous recording of minute-to-minute reality, rapidly painted with deliberately loose draftsmanship and visible brush marks (the common marks of Impressionism), were rejected for a deliberate patterning, a determination to flatten the canvas in ways that were strongly influenced by Japanese drawing and painting. The more serious members of the group followed Gauguin zealously into what he called "Symbolist" painting.

Bonnard, however, stubbornly hung back from total commitment to Gauguin's preaching of the new faith. A tall, slender, wispy man, who was to look very much the same until his death, Bonnard seemed anything but the wild romantic figure of the artist, and he was noted for his whimsical sense of humor and good nature. He was not, however, easy to convince, and he never gave way on his own ideas about how he wanted to paint. He picked up the enthusiasm for Japanese art, and it began to show up immediately in his work; yet he never seemed interested in using his painting for the purpose of portentous symbolic comment on life.

Always modest about his talents, Bonnard accepted the Nabis' idea that the painter was not to record the minute details of reality but to represent on canvas his personal, imaginative response to that reality. The message that came through in Bonnard's case was a tender celebration of ordinary, mundane life, which linked him to the Impressionists, even if his style was clearly much more rigorously patterned than was the Impressionist inclination. He was, in that sense, the most Impressionist of the Postimpressionists. He was not reluctant to use his gift in minor ways; he continued to do posters and design covers for sheet music, and he became particularly successful as a book illustrator. Tiffany's of New York asked him to design a stained glass window. He knew Henri de Toulouse-Lautrec, who was doing similar work, and there is often a similarity in their posters, although Bonnard's rendering of Paris night life is less intimate and less melancholy. He had his first one-man show in 1896; during this time, his color range was rather narrow, strongly leaning toward low-keyed blacks and blues. The double influence of Gauguin and the Japanese was very strong, particularly in his lack of bright, natural colors and in the flatness of his design, but his own charmingly innocent humor pervades his work.

By the late 1890's, he was established, and he entered a loose contractual arrangement with the dealer Bernheim-Jeunes, which provided him with a steady income. At the turn of the century an obvious change occurred in his work: There was an explosion of color, in the tradition of the Impressionists, and a similar flooding of incident and detail into his paintings of common life. The Japanese habit of "layering" their works, putting one subject over another with little concern for the European habit of connecting the subject lines with careful perspective gradation, was particularly attractive to Bonnard. His paintings are often difficult on first viewing to understand, since background, middle ground, and foreground subjects seem to be equally important and often on the same plane.

Without much theorizing, Bonnard continued to break the rules of painting in several ways. He often deliberately broke perspectival obligations, distorted, and used a kind of flicking painterly shorthand to suggest objects in his works. He rejected the Impressionist insistence upon working from real life; even his landscapes, seemingly so immediate and improvisatory, were painted in the studio, an act of supreme Impressionist heresy. He was to say that the presence of a subject intimidated him and prevented him from expressing himself freely.

In the first decade of the century, Bonnard began to spend more time in the country, in the first instance in a group of villages outside Paris. In 1910, he went to the south of France and was deeply moved by its brash, lush fecundity, a perfect mirror image of the rich density of his paintings. From that time forward, he moved on a regular basis between Paris, a house outside Paris on the Seine very near Claude Monet's studio at Giverny, and a small house in the south, near Cannes.

He was always inclined to pick at his work, never entirely confident of his technique. There was a period in which he concentrated on drawing, bringing a linearity back into his work, but by the 1920's his softening of the line, his natural inclination to blur outlines, and a new spurt of ebullient color took over and established his final stylistic position.

There was about Bonnard's work, particularly in the later years, a kind of shambling tenderness and sweet-natured charm that worked even in his long series of intimate paintings of nudes, which are often compared to those of Edgar Degas. Like Degas, Bonnard catches his subjects at intimate moments and at odd angles, but his nudes seem less sexually vibrant, less erotically charged with voyeurism. There is a gentleness about his work, a modesty even in his wittiness, which is all of a piece with his peculiar habit of being able to paint anywhere. Often in hotel rooms, he would simply pin a canvas on the wall and set to work.

Bonnard was admired from early in his career but not considered a major figure, and his international reputation began substantially only in the 1920's. He lived a quiet life, working steadily through the 1930's, moving back and forth between the north and the south of France. He avoided Paris during World War II and produced a considerable number of watercolors and gouaches during that period, since oils were hard to obtain during the war. In 1925, he had married Maria Boursin, who had been his companion since their youth and was often a subject of his paintings; in 1940, she died. He continued to work steadily, the work becoming, if possible, more richly colorful than ever. He died in his house at Le Cannet, near Cannes, on January 23, 1947.

Summary

Pierre Bonnard began his career with a group of young rebels determined to free themselves from the powerful influence of Impressionism, and that impetus was to explode into several different ways of painting in the twentieth century, many of serious consequence to the history of painting. Bonnard, however, made his own way, not through any group or any particular theoretical structure but through a fastidious picking and choosing of those aspects of the new ideas and the old that were consistent with his own character as an artist. He, in a sense, invented himself as an artist by developing a private style quite unlike that of anyone else, which included touches of Gauguin's Symbolist theory, large swatches of Japanese design, the Impressionist love for the mingling of nature at its most beautiful and human beings at their moments of quiet innocence, and his own very subtly sophisticated amusement at life. Bonnard was not a member of any school or the leader of any group but was a kind of odd man out who developed a personal style that is immediately recognizable as beholden to many but peculiarly his own. He proved that the single artist could resist the power of movements and make his own way in the face of enthusiasms that demanded attention if he had talent and an idea of what art was meant to be, however individual. In the practice of his singularity, he produced some of the best paintings of the twentieth century.

Bibliography

Callen, Anthea. *Techniques of the Impressionists*. London: New Burlington Books, 1987. The best introduction to Bonnard is through an understanding of technique, particularly that of the Impressionists, since he is so like them in the way he uses paint. This book has an excellent layman's introduction to the subject.

Farr, Dennis, and John House. *Impressionist and Post-Impressionist Masterpieces from the Courtauld Collection*. New Haven: Yale University Press, 1987. An exhibition catalog that contains an interesting discussion of three works by Bonnard.

Rewald, John. *Pierre Bonnard*. New York: Museum of Modern Art, 1948. Prepared for a Bonnard exhibition, this work contains an excellent, short critical biography of the painter and generous illustrations of Bonnard's drawings, paintings, lithographs, and photographs of Bonnard and his surroundings.

_____. *Post-Impressionism from Van Gogh to Gauguin*. New York: Museum of Modern Art, 1962. Bonnard is only a minor figure in this work, but it is an intensive study of how the major painters of the late nineteenth century resisted the Impressionists and established themselves as something else, often of equal importance. Helps to show how individual Bonnard was.

Soby, James Thrall, et al. *Bonnard and His Environment*. New York: Doubleday, 1964. Another good short critical biography and a rich full-color
selection of his paintings.

Charles Pullen

BJÖRN BORG

Born: June 6, 1956; Södertalje, Sweden

Area of Achievement: Sports
Contribution: Borg is the only man to win five consecutive Wimbledon championships. He also captured a host of other honors, including six French Open championships.

Early Life

Björn Rune Borg was born on June 6, 1956, the only child of Rune and Margaretha Borg. He spent his childhood in a Stockholm suburb (Södertalje) noted for producing automobile parts and hockey stars. In fact, Borg's first love was ice hockey. At the age of nine, he was the starting center for Södertalje's junior team, with visions of one day playing for the Swedish national team. Borg's father, however, was one of the country's leading table-tennis players. In 1966, after winning the city championship, the elder Borg selected a tennis racket as his prize.

Björn was elated at his father's choice. Even though he continued to play hockey, it was immediately obvious that tennis would become his sport. Unable to be enrolled in the beginners' program at the Södertalje Tennis Club because it was overcrowded, Borg spent the next six weeks attacking the family garage door. Finally, a vacancy occurred in the junior program, and Borg was able to practice in more formal surroundings.

In 1967, a nationally known tennis coach (Percy Rosburg) came to Södertalje to scout another player for Sweden's Davis Cup team. Rosburg was amazed by the ability of the young Borg, especially by his uncanny facility to return almost any ball hit to him. Borg was, therefore, asked to train with Rosburg at the Salk Tennis Club in Stockholm. The invitation meant a ninety-minute train ride one way, but Borg seized the opportunity.

From the beginning, Borg was an unorthodox player in that he used a two-handed grip at all times. This resulted from the fact that his first racket was simply too heavy. As his strength developed, he began to hit his forehand shots with one hand, but he retained, despite substantial criticism, a two-handed backhand. The consensus in the tennis world was that no male tournament player could succeed with a two-handed backhand. Borg was convinced he knew better. Indeed, despite his apparent handicap, he won his first tournament at eleven and followed that the next year with a victory in his age division in the Swedish National School matches. At age thirteen, he was triumphant in both the thirteen and fourteen age divisions in the Swedish National Junior Championships.

While it was obvious the young man was a tournament contender, a substantial obstacle loomed in his path: school. It was not that Borg was a bad student, but the time required for effective tournament play had a deleterious effect on his academic standing. In fact, several of his teachers suggested that he should complete his education before undertaking a career in tennis. Borg's reaction was to suggest to his parents that the most sensible course was to leave school instead. Borg's decision was heartily supported by the Swedish Tennis Association. Faced with such pressure, the school system capitulated.

Borg promptly competed in the Madrid Grand Prix (March, 1972), where his victory over Jan Erik Lundquist allowed him, at age fifteen, to qualify for the Swedish Davis Cup team. In addition, Borg captured the junior crowns at Berlin, Barcelona, Milan, Wimbledon, and Miami. He was, in consequence, considered the junior world's champion.

Borg's debut in Davis Cup competition was quite spectacular. He won both his singles matches against New Zealand and became a national hero. Borg's participation in Davis Cup competition brought him into contact with Lennart Bergelin, the leader of the Swedish Davis Cup team. It was Bergelin, after Rosburg, who was most responsible for Borg's development as a tournament player. Bergelin insisted not only that his players should develop a considerable degree of mental toughness but also that intensive daily practice was essential. In Borg, he found an individual who was more than willing to subordinate everything to the game of tennis. In 1972, Borg turned professional. His career was under way, and his childhood, such as it was, came to an end.

Life's Work

Turning professional involves more than a simple act of will and a public announcement. Most important, the individual competitor must secure financial resources sufficient to meet considerable expenses. Fortunately for Borg, the Swedish Tennis Association was so desirous of keeping him available for Davis Cup competition that they arranged for him to be employed by Scandinavian Airlines as a public relations officer. Borg was thereupon obligated to play in all major Swedish tournaments and the Davis Cup for a salary of $400,000 a year, plus free air travel anywhere. With his immediate financial needs satisfied, Borg could concentrate on becoming the best tennis player in the world.

Borg's performance on the tennis circuit in his first years was somewhat erratic. Nevertheless, he acquired an increasing confidence in his game and refined his already impassive on-court demeanor. Indeed, reporters and fans alike were astonished at his ability to ignore distractions that elicited vitriolic displays from other players.

Borg was particularly fortunate in that his appearance at the 1973 Wimbledon tournament coincided with a boycott of the competition by the Association of Tennis Professionals. In consequence, the appearance of the young, blond, teenage Borg provided the tennis media, in the absence of other possible stories, with an opportunity to create an overnight sensation. Borg soon found himself surrounded by adoring, vocal, youthful fans whenever he ventured beyond the confines of the tennis pavilion.

Although Borg had yet to win a major tournament, he was successful in defeating several of the reigning luminaries of the game, such as Roscoe Tanner and Arthur Ashe. On June 3, 1974, Borg disposed of Ilie Nastase in the Italian Open, becoming the youngest player to win a major international tournament. Borg followed that impressive performance within two weeks in Paris, becoming the youngest player ever to win the French Open. Unfortunately, his efforts in the French and Italian tournaments exhausted his physical and mental resources, so much so that he was destroyed in the third round of the 1974 Wimbledon competition.

Borg quickly rallied, however, to win a tournament in Sweden as well as the U.S. Professional Tennis Championship. In consequence, the commercial endorsements became so numerous that Borg found it necessary to employ an agent to supervise his burgeoning financial empire. Borg undertook so many endorsements, in fact, that he became the object of numerous humorous asides. In this, as in so many instances, Borg went his own way— even to the extent of moving his mother and father to Monaco when he determined it was necessary to avoid the exactions of the infamous Swedish tax collector.

Borg continued to play on the international circuit, winning the French Open again (1975) as well as the U.S. Professional Tennis Championship (1975). In addition to his tournament play, Borg undertook a series of exhibitions that afforded him publicity and substantial revenues. Nevertheless, despite considerable improvement in his game, he failed to advance to the Wimbledon final round.

The year 1976 opened auspiciously for Borg with a financially rewarding victory over Guillermo Villas in the World Championship of Tennis. Unfortunately, this triumph was followed by a devastating loss during the opening rounds of the French Open. This defeat proved a blessing in disguise, however, as Borg gained an unexpected respite before Wimbledon. He used the occasion to develop a powerful, accurate first serve, a deficiency that had proved his undoing in the past. Borg then proceeded to astonish the tennis world by defeating the heavily favored Nastase for the Wimbledon championship. Borg, at twenty, was the youngest Wimbledon champion in forty-five years and the first in twenty-three years to survive the tournament without the loss of a single set. Still, Borg followed his victory at Wimbledon with yet another loss in the U.S. Open. Despite Borg's truly impressive effort, including one of the most spectacular tiebreakers in history, Jimmy Connors frustrated Borg's attempt to win the only major tournament to escape his grasp.

Indeed, such was to be the pattern for the remainder of Borg's career. He won the Wimbledon championship on an unprecedented five occasions, the French Open six times (four in succession), and a host of exhibition matches and invitational tournaments. Yet he never captured the U.S. Open—a prerequisite for the coveted Grand Slam of tennis.

Borg's approach to tennis required not only an awesome mental commitment but also rigorous and lengthy daily practice to keep his mind and body in near-perfect union. Not surprisingly, therefore, in 1983, after fifteen years of competition, Borg announced his retirement at the age of twenty-seven. The all-consuming demands of the game had taken their toll, and what was fun became a chore, a duty, and an obligation that had to be abandoned if he were to avoid collapse in the face of the mental and physical stress that his playing style demanded.

Summary

Björn Borg was not, by conventional standards, a great tennis player. His famous two-handed backhand and his consummate mastery of the topspin forehand never found favor with other professionals. Still, he was a superb athlete whose absolute concentration allowed him to tire his opponents. His most impressive victories were the result of exhaustive campaigns of attrition, in which Borg systematically blunted his opponent's offensive with a consistent counterattack that made a virtue of monotony.

Aside from his many accomplishments, Borg's impact on the game of tennis was quite profound. He dramatically affected recreational tennis in that his use of heavy topspin on ground strokes spawned millions of imitators. Moreover, he was the first legitimate international tennis superstar. The attention lavished on the young phenomenon by fans and the sports media was largely responsible for catapulting the game into the big business it has become. Equally important, Borg's performance on the international circuit galvanized the Swedish Tennis Association's program of junior education, so much so that in 1985, Sweden had as many players among the top sixteen seeds at the U.S. Open as did the United States—despite the enormous disparity in terms of population. Borg never joined the select company of Don Budge or Rod Laver insofar as the Grand Slam of tennis was concerned, but his impact on the game was quite exceptional, if not unequaled.

Bibliography

Amdur, Neil. "A Breakdown." *World Tennis* 36 (April, 1984): 28-29. Written after Borg's retirement, this article discusses the tennis star's life and mental state.

Borg, Björn. *The Björn Borg Story.* Translated by Joan Tate. Chicago: Henry Regnery, 1975. This is a very slim volume (ninety-six pages) which was supposedly written without benefit of a ghostwriter. There is little in the way of personal biography beyond what appeared in the press, but much information concerning the matches played to that point.

Borg, Björn, as told to Eugene L. Scott. *My Life and Game.* New York: Simon & Schuster, 1980. Only half of this as-told-to work involves Borg's autobiographical comments—none of which disputes the picture painted by the media, save his assertion that he did have emotions. Of particular interest are assessments of Borg by various rivals and his rebuttal.

Borg, Mariana. *Love Match: My Life with Björn.* London: Sidgwick & Jackson, 1981. This work provides candid photographs of Borg interspersed with anecdotes by his first wife designed to demonstrate the human side of her husband. The couple were divorced shortly after Borg's retirement.

Moritz, Charles, ed. "Björn Borg." In *Current Biography Yearbook, 1974.* New York: H. W. Wilson, 1975. This entry is a fairly detailed account of Borg's life up until the year it was published. Includes a brief bibliography.

Phillips, B. J. "The Tennis Machine." *Time* 115 (June 30, 1980): 54-59. Provides a good overview of Borg's life and career, from childhood to his fifth Wimbledon championship.

J. K. Sweeney

JORGE LUIS BORGES

Born: August 24, 1899; Buenos Aires, Argentina
Died: June 14, 1986; Geneva, Switzerland
Area of Achievement: Literature
Contribution: Author of an important body of stories, poems, and essays,
  Borges has influenced modern fiction and criticism in both South and
  North America.

Early Life

The son of Jorge Guillermo and Leonor Alcevedo de Borges, Jorge Luis
Borges was born in Buenos Aires on August 24, 1899. His ancestors had
been involved in Argentina's history, having fought for the country's independence and later against various dictators; these ancestors would serve as
subjects for some of Borges' poems. So, too, would his childhood home in
Palermo (a working-class neighborhood on the north side of Buenos Aires),
with its windmill to draw water, its garden, and its trees and birds. A frail
child who did not enter school until he was nine, Borges spent much time in
his father's extensive library, an activity that he later called "the chief event
of my life." There he read many of the works that would inform his writing,
by authors such as Mark Twain, Charles Dickens, Lewis Carroll, Miguel de
Cervantes, Percy Bysshe Shelley, John Keats, and Algernon Charles Swin-
burne. He read their works in English because his paternal grandmother,
Frances Haslam, had come from Great Britain and "Georgie," as he was
called at home, learned her language before he knew Spanish. Even *Don
Quixote de la Mancha* (1605) he first encountered in English. When he later
read the original, he felt that he was reading a translation. From Haslam, he
also heard stories about the Argentine frontier of the 1870's; one of these
stories, about an Englishwoman abducted by Indians, provided the basis of
"Historia del guerrero y la cautiva" (1949; "Story of the Warrior and the
Captive," 1962).

His literary vocation, along with his weak eyes, he inherited from his
father, a lawyer and man of letters who had published some poetry and a
novel. Borges claimed that his father taught him that language could be
magical and musical, and from his youth Borges was destined to fulfill the
literary dream that failing sight denied his father. Certainly he came to
writing early: At six, he produced a short summary of various Greek myths,
anticipating his lifelong interest in minotaurs, labyrinths, and the fantastic.
About three years later, *El País*, a Buenos Aires daily, published his Spanish
translation of Oscar Wilde's "The Happy Prince"; the translation was so
mature in style that the work was attributed to Borges' father.

In 1914, the family went to Europe so that the elder Borges could be
treated for increasing blindness. Borges enrolled at the College of Geneva,

and, unable to return to Argentina because of World War I, he spent the next several years in this Swiss city. There he learned French, Latin, and German, and he read voraciously. When travel was again possible, the Borgeses moved to Lugano and Majorca before settling temporarily in Spain. In Seville, Borges published his first poem (in *Grecia*, December 31, 1919), a Whitmanesque hymn to the sea, and joined a group of avant-garde writers who called themselves ultraístas. Their emphasis on metaphor and rejection of the psychological, realistic novel would influence Borges' views of literary composition.

Life's Work

Upon returning to Argentina, Borges organized a number of young poets under the banner of ultraísmo and published the short-lived *Prisma* (December, 1921, and May, 1922), dedicated to their vision of literature. He would edit two other magazines, both called *Proa*, in the 1920's, and he contributed to almost a dozen others. In addition, he published seven books during this decade, four volumes of poetry and three of essays. In many ways, these are apprentice pieces—Borges said that later he sought out copies and burned them—but they reveal a number of interests that underlie his mature work. Commenting on his first collection of poetry, *Fervor de Buenos Aires* (1923; translated in *Selected Poems, 1923-1967*, 1973), he stated, "I think I have never strayed beyond that book. I feel that all my subsequent writing has only developed themes taken up there. I feel that all during my lifetime I have been rewriting that one book." Much of the volume, like his others of this period, is devoted to local color, for Borges was discovering his native city and country for the first time. While much of his later work is less regional in flavor, Borges remained a literary nationalist. In 1950, he published an essay on the literature of the Argentine frontier (*Aspectos de la literatura gauchesca*) and ten years later another on gaucho poetry, having co-edited an anthology of such works in 1955 (*Poesía gauchesca*).

More characteristic of Borges' best-known writing are the discussions of time and space. In "El Truco," which describes a Latin American card game, Borges notes that, because the number of possible combinations of cards is finite, players must repeat hands that others held in the past. Not only are the hands the same, though; the players, too, according to Borges, become their predecessors. "Caminata" (stroll) claims that, if the viewer stops looking at the street, the scene vanishes. Borges is herein playing with George Berkeley's idealism and challenging the conventional notion of reality. If what seems real may be obliterated with a blink, that which is "False and dense/ like a garden traced on a mirror" can become real ("Benarés"). Already, too, one finds the learned allusions, the depth of reading so typical of Borges.

Although Borges is best known as a writer of short stories, he came to this genre slowly, hesitantly. According to Borges, he began writing short stories after an accident in 1938 left him uncertain of his mental abilities. Fearing that failure with a poem or essay would be too devastating, he turned instead to a new form and produced "Pierre Menard, autor del *Quijote*" (1942; "Pierre Menard, Author of the *Quixote*," 1962). Actually, he had been thinking about, even writing, prose fiction well before this. In *Discusión* (1932), he had included an essay that anticipated his practice, commenting in "El arte narrativo y la magia" (narrative art and magic) that the novel should resemble "a precise game of staying on the alert, of echoes, and of affinities." Rejecting supposedly realistic, psychological narratives, he praises the work of Edgar Allan Poe, Herman Melville, and William Morris, for whom plot rather than character is primary. In addition to theorizing, he began publishing a number of short stories, thinly disguised as essays; many of his later pieces, including "Pierre Menard, Author of the *Quixote*" wear a similar mask.

In August, 1933, he accepted the editorship of *Revista Multicolor de los Sábados*, a Saturday supplement published by *Critica*, Argentina's most popular newspaper. Borges contributed about thirty original pieces and a number of translations. Among the former was "Hombre de las orillas" (September 16, 1933; "Streetcorner Man," 1970), a short story camouflaged as reporting and published under the pseudonym Francisco Bustos, indicating Borges' reluctance to be associated with the work. Here, too, he presented a series of six fictionalized biographies of malefactors; these were later collected as *Historia universal de la infamia* (1935; *A Universal History of Infamy*, 1972). In 1936, "El acercamiento a Almotásism" ("The Approach to al Mu'tasism," 1970) appeared in a collection of essays, *Historia de la eternidad*; this short story was disguised as a book review. Frequently Borges subsequently assumed the role of a reader of extant works rather than the creator of new ones. While "Pierre Menard, Author of the *Quixote*" was thus not Borges' first short story, it did signal a willingness to admit to himself and others that he was turning his attention to another genre. His production of poems was already diminishing: Between 1929 and 1943 he published only six.

His life was changing in another way also. Until 1937, he had refused regular employment, living off the irregular income he earned by writing and allowances from his father. In that year, he took the post of first assistant at the Miguel Cané Library. Seemingly, such a job would have been ideal for the bookish Borges, but he despised his nonliterary colleagues (whose only interests were gambling and women), the pay was poor, and fifty people had been hired to do the work of fifteen. "La biblioteca de Babel" (1942; "The Library of Babel," 1962) reflects the boredom, even horror, that Borges felt. Because there was little to do and he could not converse with his coworkers, he spent five or six hours daily reading and writing, producing a stream of translations and stories, among them the first Spanish version of Franz Kafka's *Die Verwandlung* (1915; *The Metamorphosis*, 1936) in 1938, an anthology of fantasic literature (edited with his close friend Adolfo Bioy Casares), and two volumes of fiction that shun the realism prevalent in Latin American literature of the period. Young authors such as Octavio Paz and Julio Cortázar were deeply influenced by this new approach that Borges was advocating in his essays and demonstrating in his books.

Borges' politics were as atypical as his writing style in the 1940's, for he supported democracy and the Allies when Argentina was ruled by a military regime friendly to the Nazis and Fascists. When Juan Domingo Perón came to power in 1946, Borges was "promoted" from librarian to inspector of chickens and rabbits. In choosing this post for Borges, the dictator was demonstrating his dim view of intellectuals. Borges resigned immediately, but he needed to replace the salary on which, limited as it was, he had come to depend. Despite an almost pathological fear of speaking in public, he began lecturing on British and American literature at various private schools in Argentina and Uruguay. At first he wrote out what he wanted to say, then sat silently while another read the lecture; but soon he overcame his phobia and delivered his learned talks himself. He also continued to write, publishing one of his best collections of short stories, *El Aleph* (1949, 1952; translated in *The Aleph and Other Stories, 1933-1969*, 1970). If Perón had meant by his appointment that Borges was as timid as a chicken or a rabbit, he mistook his man, for, as president of the Argentine Society of Writers, he repeatedly spoke out against the regime.

With the fall of Perón, Borges' fortunes improved. In 1955, he was named director of the Argentine National Library, where he initiated a series of lectures and revived its defunct journal, *La Biblioteca*. The following year, he received the first of what would prove to be a number of honorary doctorates when the University of Cuyo (Argentina) presented him with the degree on April 29, 1956. In 1956, he also received the National Prize for Literature and was appointed professor of English and American literature at the University of Buenos Aires.

Borges' sight had been failing for a long time: He had had the first of eight eye operations in 1927. Immediately after he became head of the Argentine National Library, he lost his vision. In "Poema de los dones" (1960; "Poem About Gifts," 1964), he comments on the irony of gaining so many books just when he could no longer read them. While his blindness did not prevent him from writing, it did return him to poetry, and, because he found formal verse to be easier to compose mentally than free verse, he became especially fond of the sonnet. He also abandoned fiction for a time, writing no short stories between 1953 and 1970.

As early as 1928, Borges had won a literary award for *El idioma de los argentinos* (1928; the language of the Argentines), and by the 1940's many of his countrymen recognized him as Argentina's leading writer. International appreciation came slowly, though. Not until 1961, when he shared the first Fomentor Prize with Samuel Beckett, did he become known widely in Europe and North America. *Ficciones, 1935-1944* (1944; English translation, 1962) appeared simultaneously in six languages, and he made the first of several visits to the United States as a visiting professor and guest lecturer. Further honors came to him, among them the Jerusalem Prize (1971), the Gold Medal from the Académie Française (1979), the Miguel de Cervantes Award (Spain, 1980), and the Balzan Prize (Italy, 1980).

Borges, who had opposed military dictatorships throughout his life, in his last years came to support the junta ruling Argentina. When it collapsed after the Falklands war with Great Britain, Borges left his native land for Geneva, where he died of cancer on June 14, 1986. He was buried at Plainpalais, Switzerland, close to John Calvin.

Summary

Jorge Luis Borges' labyrinthine body of work traces the image of his mind—learned, profound, philosophical, questioning, and often laughing. As recondite as he could be, he nevertheless did much to shape contemporary literature. Indeed, Carlos Fuentes has said that without Borges modern Latin American literature could not exist, for he made possible its flight from nineteenth century realism. In the United States, Robert Coover, Donald Barthelme, John Gardner, and John Barth are among his disciples, and Vladimir Nabokov's *Pale Fire* (1962) reveals a Borgesian influence. Borges' view that each author alters the reading not only of works that come after him but also of his predecessors' writings has affected Harold Bloom's literary criticism.

Borges was especially fond of the detective story and wrote a number of orthodox works in this genre. In a larger sense, everything he wrote seeks to resolve a mystery, the mystery of existence. Language and things are metaphors, vehicles for that unknown tenor, reality, that Borges continually sought. In his quest, he commented upon the library of Babel that is the world, at the same time that he was creating an ordered, alternate universe of literature more enduring than its vexed double.

Bibliography
Borges, Jorge Luis. "Autobiographical Essay." In *The Aleph and Other Stories*. New York: E. P. Dutton, 1970. A modest but essentially accurate chronological account, particularly useful for understanding the early influences on the writer and for his assessment of his various works.
Cheselka, Paul. *The Poetry and Poetics of Jorge Luis Borges*. New York: P. Lang, 1987. Concentrating on the poetry that Borges wrote before 1964, Cheselka undertakes a chronological survey of the verse, examining

its themes and the way that Borges presents them.

Christ, Ronald J. *The Narrow Act: Borges' Art of Illusion.* New York: New York University Press, 1969. Among the first book-length studies of Borges in English and one of the best. Looks at Borges' use of British and American authors to understand how and why he chooses these sources.

Cortinez, Carlos, ed. *Borges, the Poet.* Fayetteville: University of Arkansas Press, 1986. Based on a symposium at Dickinson College in April, 1983. Begins with three conversations with Borges—on Emily Dickinson, Hispanic literature, and North American writing—followed by twenty-four essays that explore such matters as oriental influences on Borges' poetry, Borges' use of imagery, and the relationship between the poetry and various nineteenth and twentieth century works.

Rodríguez Monegal, Emir. *Jorge Luis Borges: A Literary Biography.* New York: E. P. Dutton, 1978. A detailed account of the life and works by a close friend and admirer. Despite the wealth of detail, the book reads well and is indispensable for an understanding of the writer.

Stabb, Martin S. *Jorge Luis Borges.* New York: Twayne, 1970. A good general introduction to the works, with limited attention to the life. Devotes a chapter each to the poetry, essays, and short stories, and another to Borges' critical reception. The annotated bibliography of primary and secondary sources, though dated, is useful.

Sturrock, John. *Paper Tigers: The Ideal Fiction of Jorge Luis Borges.* Oxford: Clarendon Press, 1977. Concentrates on the stories in *Ficciones, 1935-1944* and *El Aleph* because they are the most enigmatic and hence most fascinating of Borges' prose fiction. Sturrock maintains that these works are reflexive critiques of how stories should be told, and he sets the fiction in its cultural and philosophical context and offers close readings of themes, images, and techniques.

Updike, John. "Books: The Author as Librarian." *New Yorker* 41 (October 30, 1965): 223-246. A key article in the development of Borges' reputation in the United States and an incisive analysis of his work. Discusses Borges' economy of language, imagery, and use of the imagination. Updike suggests that Borges' approach to literature may provide an escape from the dead end that the novel seemed to have reached. The essay includes a careful analysis of "The Waiting" and "The Library of Babel." Available in book form in Updike's collection *Picked-Up Pieces* (New York: Alfred A. Knopf, 1976).

Joseph Rosenblum

LOUIS BOTHA

Born: September 27, 1862; near Greytown, Natal
Died: August 27, 1919; Pretoria, Transvaal, Union of South Africa
Areas of Achievement: Diplomacy, government, politics, and the military
Contribution: During the Boer War, Botha fought valiantly to preserve the
  independence of the Transvaal. When the war was lost, he worked suc-
  cessfully for a united South Africa under the Crown.

Early Life

When Louis Botha was born in 1862, the territory that was later to become
the Union of South Africa consisted of four distinct entities: two British
possessions, Cape Colony and Natal, and two independent Boer republics,
the Orange Free State and the Transvaal. Botha was born in Natal but grew
up in the Orange Free State and was associated during his public life with the
Transvaal. Reared on an isolated farm in a typically large Boer family, he
received little formal schooling but learned much about human nature, white
and black. When only eighteen, he was entrusted with the sheep and cattle
that the family pastured on the borders of Zululand. After his father's death,
he joined a party of Boers who were taking part in a civil war among the
Zulus and was rewarded with a farm in the district of Vryheid; he took part
in the government of the small republic that was organized there, and, when
Vryheid was merged with the Transvaal, he became active in this larger
sphere. Farming remained his chief interest, however, and he rapidly expanded his holdings in land and livestock. In 1888, he married Annie Emmett, a relative of the Irish patriot Robert Emmett, and lived happily with
her until his death.

In the meantime, tension between the Boer republics and the British Empire was growing. The discovery of gold on the Rand had brought a stream
of immigrants, chiefly British, into the Transvaal; The Boers called them
"Uitlanders," and, although they brought prosperity with them, the government of President Paul Kruger was careless of their rights, taxing them
heavily and denying them the franchise. They in turn were supported by Sir
Alfred Milner, the governor of Cape Colony, who pressed the Boers to
recognize British suzerainty. Botha, now a member of the Volksraad or
legislature, favored concessions to the Uitlanders, as did Jan Christiaan
Smuts, who later became Botha's loyal ally in peace and war. Both Kruger
and Milner were stubborn, however, and Kruger precipitated a war on
October 11, 1899.

Life's Work

The war began with a Boer invasion of Natal, intended to overwhelm the
British troops there before reinforcements could arrive. Initially the invasion

was a success; the British were cut off at Ladysmith, while the Commandos—mounted infantry organized into regional units—swept around them and far into Natal, at one point capturing Winston Churchill, who was covering the war as a journalist. Botha at first served as a simple field cornet—a local commander—under Petrus Joubert, but his natural aggressiveness and the illness of his superiors made him practically second in command on the Natal front; later he became commander, and finally, after the death of Joubert, Commandant General of the Transvaal. As British reinforcements poured in, the Boers found it expedient to retreat to the Tugela River, where they could block any British advance into the Transvaal while still keeping the Ladysmith garrison under siege. Botha fortified the line with a series of nearly invisible trenches, hoping to lure the British into a trap. Sir Redvers Buller was repulsed at the Battle of Colenso but evaded the trap. On his second try, at Spion Kop, he was foiled only by a heroic counterattack organized by Botha himself. At Pieter's Hill (February 27, 1900), Buller finally broke through and relieved Ladysmith. On the same day, Boer resistance on their other front in the west collapsed. Botha, now in supreme command, could only fight delaying actions before Johannesberg and Pretoria were occupied and the Transvaal government fled eastward toward the Mozambique border.

Some thought the war had ended, but Botha simply shifted to a guerrilla campaign, in which the Boers won many small victories and even penetrated the Cape Colony. Horatio Kitchener, now the British commander, responded ruthlessly, devastating Boer farms and herding women and children into concentration camps. By May, 1902, Botha and Smuts were ready to make peace and to dissuade those among the Boers who wished to fight to the death. The Boer republics became British colonies, but otherwise the terms were mild.

Following the peace, Botha and two other generals went to Europe to try to raise money for the relief of Boers impoverished by the war. They got little from private sources but did get an appropriation of eight million pounds from Parliament after Botha had argued the case in a magazine article. Back in Africa, Botha, having skillfully repaired his own shattered fortunes, returned to politics. His main objects were to effect a reconciliation between Boers and Britons (and also between the "bitterenders" and the "handsuppers," the patriots and the quislings among the Boers) and to obtain self-government within the Empire for the former republics, perhaps eventually as part of a unified South Africa. He began by founding Het Volk (the people), an association through which the Boers could assert themselves and recover their self-confidence. The Transvaal attained self-government in 1907, and Botha became its first prime minister. Among other problems with which he had to deal were the related problems of language and education. The peace treaty had guaranteed equality for English and Afrikaans, the

Boers' Dutch dialect. Many English speakers expected Dutch to die out, while some Boers expected the English to learn Dutch; Botha and Smuts simply wished children to be instructed in the language they already knew. Botha naturally was much interested in farming; he established a land bank, and he hoped to make the Boers somewhat primitive farming methods more scientific, even if it meant keeping on English-speaking experts originally appointed by Milner. Already popular in England, he confirmed that popularity by presenting King Edward with a typical South African product, the largest diamond in the world, for the crown jewels.

Meanwhile sentiment had been growing for a union, or at least a federation, of the four South African colonies under the Crown, and in 1908 a national convention was called. Botha and Smuts had little difficulty in persuading the other delegates to support a close union rather than a loose federation and to accept English and Afrikaans as equally official languages. More difficult was the question of a capital. In the end, Botha's compromise was accepted: Pretoria was to be the seat of the executive, Cape Town the meeting place of the Parliament, and Bloemfontein the seat of the supreme court. The constitution was ratified by the British Parliament, and Botha was invited to become the first prime minister; this post he held until his death.

The last period of Botha's life brought for him a whole series of triumphs in peace and war, but it was also a period of almost intolerable emotional strain, caused by the opposition of the bitterenders, some of whom had been his comrades in the war. Somewhat reluctantly he had taken General Jan Hertzog into his cabinet, but Hertzog was so violently opposed to Botha's policy of reconciliation and so vocal in expressing his hatred of the British that he had to be maneuvered out again. The outbreak of war in 1914 produced an inevitable crisis. Botha thought that both duty and self-interest obliged South Africa to support Great Britain, but the bitterenders wished to stay neutral or even to seize the opportunity to restore the republics. An armed rebellion erupted, which Botha put down easily and mercifully. Botha could then answer Great Britain's request that he occupy German Southwest Africa with South African troops. Like the Boers in 1899, the Germans were vastly outnumbered but had geography on their side. Botha himself led the invasion, moving swiftly and efficiently, and giving the Germans no time to organize a guerrilla campaign. He was also merciful, even letting the German reservists keep their rifles for defense against the natives. Later he sent South African troops under Smuts to fight in German East Africa. At the end of the war, Botha and Smuts participated in the Versailles Conference, where both enjoyed considerable prestige and influence; they were unsuccessful, however, in moderating the terms that were to be imposed on the Germans. Botha, moreover, was in ill health and died on August 27, 1919, soon after his return to South Africa.

Summary

In contemplating Louis Botha's career, one is struck by the number of fields in which he achieved success without any formal training and sometimes without a meaningful apprenticeship: farming, stock breeding, business speculation, war (regular and guerrilla, including fortification), statecraft, and diplomacy. Smuts spoke of Botha's intuition, which may be a fair term, for Botha often reached appropriate conclusions in a short time and without communicating the thought processes that led to them. Smuts also spoke of Botha's sympathy, his ability to place himself in the position of another, whether to win his friendship or defeat him in battle. The great theme that ran through his life was the theme of reconciliation: of Botha with Kitchener, of bitterenders with handsuppers, of Boer with Briton, of Germany with the allies. One would like to add "of black with white," but Botha, though he spoke several African languages and was fair enough in specific dealings, was never willing to share power with the colored races. Basil Williams called Botha "a simple, God-fearing man, not clever, but with the immense wisdom of the patient and loving." Smuts called him "the greatest, sweetest, cleanest soul of all my days." These pronouncements may seem extravagant, but they find confirmation in the facts of his life.

Bibliography
Davenport, T. R. H. *South Africa: A Modern History.* London: Macmillan, 1977. A highly condensed and detailed history written from a liberal, African point of view. One can trace the events and policies of Botha's career back to their sources in the past and forward to their often disastrous consequences in the future.
Engelenburg, F. V. *General Louis Botha.* Introduction by J. C. Smuts. London: George G. Harrap, 1929. Originally written in Afrikaans by a journalist who knew Botha well, the book has much interesting detail. It is better on the politics than on the military aspects.
Garson, N. G. *Louis Botha or John X. Merriman: The Choice of South Africa's First Prime Minister.* London: Athlone Press, 1969. A brief but thorough piece of research. Perhaps the choice of Botha was inevitable, for Merriam's support came chiefly from the bitterenders.
Pakenham, Thomas. *The Boer War.* New York: Random House, 1979. Thoroughly researched, massively annotated and detailed, equally good on the political and military aspects. Pakenham goes beyond previous histories in his coverage of civilian sufferings and of the part played by blacks. Includes a bibliography and illustrations.
Warwick, Peter, ed. *The South African War.* London: Longman, 1980. A well-edited anthology of essays on all aspects of the war: "Women in the War," "The Poetry of War," and so forth. Especially relevant to Botha's career are "Military Aspects of the War" and "Reconstruction in the

Transvaal." The book has extensive bibliographies and lavish illustrations.

Williams, Basil. *Botha, Smuts and South Africa*. London: Hodder & Stoughton, 1946. Written by a distinguished British scholar, this book covers a large body of material in a compact and readable form. Includes maps and a brief bibliography.

John C. Sherwood

WALTHER BOTHE

Born: January 8, 1891; Oranienburg, Germany
Died: February 8, 1957; Heidelberg, West Germany
Area of Achievement: Physics
Contribution: Bothe was awarded the Nobel Prize for his invention of the coincidence counting technique and for discoveries made using it, including the nature of cosmic rays and the fashion in which X rays interact with electrons. He was one of Germany's leading atomic scientists and constructed their first cyclotron.

Early Life

Walther Wilhelm Georg Bothe was born at Oranienburg, Germany, on January 8, 1891. He was the son of Fritz (a merchant) and Charlotte Bothe. Walther studied physics, chemistry, and mathematics at the University of Berlin. As a graduate student, he became one of the few ever to study under the famous Max Planck. After obtaining his doctorate in 1914, he began to work for Hans Geiger in the radioactivity laboratory of the Physikalische-Technische Reichsanstalt (physical-technical institute).

World War I soon intervened, and Bothe became a machine gunner in the German army. Captured by the Russians in 1915, he spent the next five years as a prisoner of war in Siberia. While there, he was able to continue his studies in mathematics and physics as well as learn Russian. He married a Russian woman, Barbara Below, in 1920 and returned to the Reichsanstalt in Berlin. He and his wife had two daughters.

While performing research at the Reichsanstalt, Bothe began a simultaneous teaching career at the University of Berlin. It was an exciting, if somewhat confusing, time for anyone in the field of physics. The nature of radioactivity and the structure of the atom were two topics which defied understanding within the confines of the familiar (classical) rules of physics.

Among the most accurate measurements of the day were those of the spectroscopists, those who measured the various colors of light emitted by atoms. Niels Bohr had proposed a very curious model of the atom in order to explain these measurements. In Bohr's model, electrons orbited a nucleus of protons (neutrons were yet to be discovered). Strangely, the electrons could have only certain specific values (quanta) of energy or angular momentum. For unknown reasons, other values were not allowed. Bohr's conjectures were accepted only because they worked, not because they made sense in terms of known physics.

To extend the theory, Bohr and others calculated how an X ray and an electron would interact. It was supposed that since X rays are electromagnetic waves, the energy and the momentum of the wave would be spread out all along the wave. It was at this point that Bothe and his coworker, Geiger, entered the picture.

Life's Work

Bothe and Geiger decided to test Bohr's new theory. They wanted to compare it with a theory of Arthur Holly Compton. In the Compton effect, an X ray (treated as a particle) strikes an electron with the result that the electron recoils in one direction while the X ray scatters in a different direction and also has less energy.

According to Compton, the total energy of the electron and incident X ray (before the collision) should be the same as that of the recoil electron and scattered X ray (after the collision). This is called conservation of energy and momentum and is believed to be fundamental in nature. Yet according to Bohr, the energy and momentum of the X ray are spread all along the wave and are not localized at the site of the electron. Bohr predicted energy and momentum would be conserved only on the average and for a large number of collisions. A recoil electron might have absorbed some energy from many X ray waves and would therefore not be related to any specific incident X ray.

In the experiment of Bothe and Geiger, X rays struck gas atoms inside a Geiger counter tube. The tube was connected to a pointer which moved when a recoil electron was detected. A second counter tube was placed beside the first with the hope that it would detect the scattered X ray. If it did, its pointer also moved. Both pointers were continuously photographed on film moving through a camera at about ten meters per minute. Many hundreds of meters of film had to be developed, hung from the ceiling to dry, and then painstakingly inspected.

Bothe and Geiger were able to show that the tubes did indeed record coincident events, two events occurring at essentially the same time. The conclusion was that the recoil electron and the scattered X ray were produced simultaneously, and, hence, Bohr's latest theory was wrong. In fact, energy and momentum were conserved in individual collisions.

In 1926, Bothe joined many other physicists in studying radioactivity. Heavy elements such as radium and uranium were known to emit alpha particles. These particles were allowed to strike targets of carbon, boron, or some other light element. Bothe was keenly interested in any radiation that the target might now emit, hoping that it would give him some insight into the structure of the atomic nucleus.

Some of these reactions emitted protons, and Bothe was among the first to use electronic counters to detect them. In 1930, Bothe and H. Becker studied the radiation from a beryllium target. They found it to be surprisingly penetrating and assumed that it consisted of high-energy gamma rays. They missed another major discovery, for not long after Sir James Chadwick showed that this radiation must consist of neutral particles, which he named neutrons.

At about the same time as his work with beryllium, Bothe worked with Werner Kolhörster in analyzing cosmic rays. Using Bothe's coincidence method, they placed one counter tube above a second counter tube and placed absorbing material between the tubes. If both tubes signaled a count at the same time, it was assumed that a single cosmic ray had gone through both tubes and had not been trapped in the absorber. Somewhat to their surprise, their results were not those expected from high-energy gamma rays. Instead, their experiments implied that cosmic rays are charged particles. Bothe pointed out that in order to penetrate the earth's atmosphere, these particles would need to have an energy equivalent to being accelerated through a thousand million volts. Since this was a thousand times more energy than any process known then could produce, it was a very radical suggestion. History, however, has shown it to be correct.

During the 1930's, Bothe continued his studies of multiple scattering of electrons and began similar studies with neutrons. An article by him on both the experimental and theoretical aspects of scattering appeared in the 1933 edition of the *Handbuch der Physick* (handbook of physics).

When the Nazis came to power, they urged that the scientific theories of Jews, such as Albert Einstein, no longer be taught. Bothe could not agree with the restriction, and in 1932 he moved his work to the politically more tolerant Heidelberg, eventually becoming a professor at the university and simultaneously the director of the Physics Institute of the Max Planck Institute for Medical Research.

Bothe's reputation for excellence was such that in 1939 he was called to be one of the chief scientists in the German atom bomb project. One road to the bomb was to construct a nuclear reactor in which to make the element plutonium. Bothe was called upon to decide the key issue of whether carbon could be used to slow neutrons in the nuclear reactor. According to Bothe's measurements, carbon would absorb too many neutrons and was unsuitable. This result was in error, and it is very curious that someone of Bothe's ability would have made this mistake. Bothe had no liking for Hitler, and it may be that he purposely reported the wrong results, for this became one of the key reasons for Hitler's failure to develop the bomb.

In order better to study nuclear reactions, Bothe needed a cyclotron, a machine that can accelerate particles, such as protons, and cause them to collide with target nuclei. Bothe supervised the construction of the first cyclotron in Germany, completing it in 1944. After the war, Bothe used the cyclotron he had constructed at Heidelberg to produce radioactive isotopes for medical studies. He continued his work with cosmic rays and was senior author of *Nuclear Physics and Cosmic Rays* (1948) as well as of many scientific articles.

Bothe devoted the same intensity to his hobbies that he gave to his scientific studies. He was an excellent pianist and took special pleasure in playing the works of Johann Sebastian Bach and Ludwig van Beethoven. On holidays he liked to go to the mountains and paint. His oil and watercolor paintings were quite professional looking. Bothe is described as being a strict taskmaster in the laboratory but hospitable and relaxed at home. He was awarded the Nobel Prize in Physics in 1954 and died on February 8, 1957.

Summary

Walther Bothe was a physicist's physicist. Other physicists consulted his works for definitive statements of a problem, its current status, and experimental techniques for studying it. As such, his influence among physicists was great although he was little known to the public. Perhaps it was the growing awareness and acknowledgment of this influence that led to his somewhat belated award of the Nobel Prize. When it came, Bothe was in failing health and unable to attend the ceremony, but at least he had the satisfaction of living to see his work widely recognized.

The coincidence method pioneered by Bothe is now a common and widely used technique in nuclear physics. Electronic counters are used instead of film to record the results, and it was Bothe who pioneered the use of these electronic counting circuits. Among his other achievements, he was the first to show that high-energy cosmic rays are particles and the first to introduce a widely used notation for nuclear reactions. In addition to the Nobel Prize, Bothe was decorated a Knight of the Order of Merit for Science and Arts (1952), awarded the Max Planck Medal (1953), and awarded the Grand Cross of the Order for Federal Services of Germany (1954).

Bibliography

Beyerchen, Alan D. *Scientists Under Hitler: Politics and the Physics Community in the Third Reich*. New Haven, Conn.: Yale University Press, 1977. This excellent work describes the political involvement (or noninvolvement) of many of Germany's top scientists. Nobel laureates become public figures and are often pressured into some kind of political action.

Goudsmit, Samuel A. *Alsos*. New York: Henry Schuman, 1947. Reprint. Los Angeles: Tomash, 1983. Alsos was the code name for the intelligence mission to discover the status of the German atom bomb project. Includes Goudsmit's interview and appraisal of Bothe at the war's end. The reader should be cautioned that Werner Heisenberg believed that Goudsmit undervalued the German achievements. Keeping this in mind, the reader will find the book quite useful.

Irving, David. *The German Atomic Bomb*. New York: Simon & Schuster, 1967. A fascinating and easily read account. Details Bothe's work on the project from start to finish. Gives an exciting account of how the Allies sabotaged German efforts to procure heavy water and explores other reasons for the lack of success of the German project. Highly recommended.

Nobelstiftelsen. *Physics.* Vol. 3, *1942-1962*. New York: Elsevier, 1964. This work is among the very few which describe Bothe's Nobel work in a manner at all accessible to the layperson. As an added benefit, the reader will note Bothe's clarity in writing.

Rhodes, Richard. *The Making of the Atomic Bomb.* New York: Simon & Schuster, 1986. One of the most comprehensive books on the subject that is readily accessible to the lay reader. Includes references to Bothe from his production of neutrons in 1930 to his completion of Germany's first cyclotron in 1944.

Weart, Spencer R. *Scientists in Power.* Cambridge, Mass.: Harvard University Press, 1979. Weart describes the French World War II atom bomb project and follows its postwar development to the first plutonium production in 1949. He discusses Bothe's use of the French cyclotron as well as Bothe's error in measuring the absorption of neutrons by carbon. For the layman.

Charles W. Rogers

PIERRE BOULEZ

Born: March 26, 1925; Montbrison, France

Area of Achievement: Music
Contribution: Boulez's compositions, essays, and lectures have changed the direction of Western music. Though he emerged from the French tradition of Debussy, Ravel, and Messiaen, he rejected his roots and redirected his spiritual allegiance to the Austro-German tradition as embodied in Schoenberg, Berg, and Webern. He also became one of the most influential conductors of modern music in both Europe and the United States.

Early Life
Pierre Boulez was born in the town of Montbrison, in the Loire section of the southeastern part of France, in 1925. He came from a respectable middle-class, Roman Catholic family. His father was an engineer and technical director of a local steel company, while his mother, who tended to be freethinking, fulfilled her role of the energetic housewife. He was introduced to orchestral music on a radio that his father had brought back from the United States. An elder brother of the same name, Pierre, had died in infancy, and the death of that brother confirmed Boulez's Darwinian and, therefore, deterministic view of existence. As he himself has stated, "I believe I survived because I was the stronger. He was the sketch, I the drawing." These two modern strains, Darwinism and electronic technology, provide the backdrop for Boulez's spiritual evolution.

Because Montbrison had no *lycée*, the young Pierre attended the best school in the area, which happened to be the Roman Catholic seminary Institut Victor de la Prade. An extremely devout daily communicant, he remained there until he was fifteen, taking first honors in chemistry and physics. He also sang in the choir and took piano lessons privately in the larger nearby town of Saint-Étienne. By the time he was sixteen, he was unalterably dedicated to music, a fact that disturbed his father greatly, since it was assumed that young Pierre was to pursue an engineering career, as his father had. Although deferring to his father's wishes and studying mathematics at the University of Lyon with the hope of entering the École Polytechnic in Paris, he spent most of the year practicing the piano and studying musical theory. In direct conflict with his father's wishes, he entered in 1943 not the École Polytechnic in Paris but, rather, the famous Paris Conservatoire, where he excelled in all of his courses. He received excellent instruction from Olivier Messiaen, the deeply religious visionary composer and organist. Messiaen was a maverick professor and performer, and he introduced his students to the exotic sources of his own music: Gregorian chant, Asiatic rhythms and techniques, and the actual songs of hundreds of birds. It was during Messiaen's class that Boulez discovered the genius of Claude Debussy, Igor Stravinsky's *The Rite of Spring*, and the early works of Arnold Schoenberg.

In 1945, Boulez heard a performance of Schoenberg's Woodwind Quintet under Leibowitz's direction, and the performance became a revelation to him of a whole new set of musical possibilities. He asked Leibowitz to teach him the rules of this new musical aesthetic. Boulez found in twelve-tone music a completely new musical language, a language that freed him from the past clichés and exhausted formulas of a long dead but unburied Romanticism. He adopted Leibowitz as his new mentor and began an allegiance to the Austro-German tradition, a much more stringently intellectual and analytical approach to music. The composers who grew out of this tradition were the classic moderns of twentieth century music: Schoenberg, Alban Berg, and, most important, Anton Webern.

By 1948, after working as the musical director of the new Compagnie Renaud-Barrault under his only conducting teacher, the distinguished composer-conductor Roger Désormière, he produced two pieces of music that gradually drew the interest of the French musical establishment: his Second Piano Sonata and his cantata, *Le soleil des eaux* (the sun of the waters). It was, however, the stunning performance by Yvonne Loriod (Messiaen's wife) of the Second Piano Sonata at the Darmstadt Festival in 1952 that propelled the young Boulez into the international musical spotlight, a position that he would occupy for the next forty years or so.

Life's Work

Boulez's career began its complicated odyssey in 1948 with his Second Piano Sonata and, therefore, as the composer of what many critics saw as a French expression of the Austro-German school of compositional style. In keeping with his consistent pattern of rejecting his actual father and other father figures such as Messiaen, Leibowitz, and Stravinsky himself, his first works were grounded not in a French tradition that started with Jean-Philippe Rameau and flowered with Debussy and Messiaen, but paid homage to his native country's avowed enemies, Germany and Austria. He even attributed the German presence in France during the occupation as the occasion that brought high culture to his homeland.

From Schoenberg's introduction of a serial or twelve-tone system of composition, he found the possibility of breaking away from the exhausted forms of a late and decadent Romanticism as found, for example, in composers such as Johannes Brahms or Peter Ilich Tchaikovsky. He wished to move away from the concept of tonality (that is, music written in a certain key or tonal center that remains the same throughout the piece) to atonality, in which there is no tonal center dictating the rules of composition. Schoenberg had invented a system that not only eradicated stale musical habits from the past but enlarged the parameters of musical expression by extending the range of musical possibilities from the standard seven tones to all twelve tones of the chromatic scale. For Boulez, these radical new forms meant that he had found a musical grammar that successfully replaced tonality by expanding the limits of musical expression but remained rooted in a mathematical system that kept it from collapsing into mere emotional declamation. The new musical aesthetic could save music from the pathos of old Vienna and its counterpart, the cult of personal stylistic evolution.

Once he detected the truth, Boulez rigidly adhered to any and all ramifications of that revelation. He promoted the composers who had engendered his own stylistic developments: Schoenberg, Berg, and Webern. These composers were responsible for purifying the language that moved music into new possibilities. To remain consistent, Boulez also promoted those earlier composers who influenced these three classic moderns, such as Richard Wagner, Gustav Mahler, and Ludwig van Beethoven. Boulez himself summed up the significance of serial or twelve-tone music: "With it, music moved out of the world of Newton and into the world of Einstein. The tonal idea was based on a universe defined by gravity and attraction. The serial idea is based on a universe that finds itself in perpetual expansion."

Out of Boulez's newfound dogma came what has come to be regarded as his masterpiece. Indeed, some scholars find *Le Marteau sans maître* (1954, revised 1957; the hammer with no master) worthy of comparison to Stravinsky's *The Rite of Spring* or Schoenberg's *Pierrot Lunaire*, two benchmarks of the modernist movement of the twentieth century. As he did with his earlier *Le soleil des eaux*, Boulez utilized sections of another of René Char's brilliant but complex poems. He attempted to follow the accents and meters of Char's poetry with the rhythms and dynamics of his own music. The piece is scored for seven instruments: alto voice, viola, guitar, vibraphone, xylophone, flute, and percussion. There are nine movements, but only four contain parts of Char's poems. Over the years, numerous imitations of the exotic instrumentation have been attempted by many young composers. The music embodies the tonal equivalent of the message of Char's apocalyptic poem—that is, civilization is mechanistically moving toward its own doom. It has no master to guide it, and Boulez is calling the attention of the world to its condition.

Because of the quickly spreading fame of Boulez as a composer, he came into considerable demand as a teacher and conductor all over Europe but particularly in Germany and Paris itself. With the support of the wealthy widow of the French Fascist author Pierre Drieu la Rochelle, Suzanne Tezenas, and of the Compagnie Renaud-Barrault, he founded the famous Domaine Musical series of concerts at which he lectured on and presented the works of contemporary composers and neglected works of the past that he considered to be especially relevant to modern sensibilities. The concerts became an important part of the musical life of Paris from 1954 until 1967. He also began to accept academic positions in universities in both Europe and the United States. He lectured at the University of Darmstadt for twelve years and was professor of composition at the University of Basel from 1960 to 1963. He delivered his now famous lectures at Darmstadt, which were subsequently published as *Penser de musique aujourd'hui* (1964; *Boulez on Music Today*, 1971).

There seems to be a direct correlation between Boulez's increasing demand as a conductor and lecturer and the decreasing number of compositions he was producing in the 1960's and 1970's. His compositional style did, however, change dramatically because of the influence of the American composer John Cage. Boulez had actually met Cage years before in Paris, had become fast friends, and then, consistent with his rejection of father figures, had had a falling out. Yet Cage's experiments with aleatory (chance) music and open form became major influences on Boulez's work. With Boulez's *Deux Improvisations sur Mallarmé* (1953), *Strophes* (1957), and his Third Piano Sonata (1958), he moved into an exploration of the possibilities of open form, which meant that the work is, theoretically, never finished. All works become works in progress and, therefore, are open; they are treated as if they possess an organic life of their own and are permitted to join themselves with larger entities as later works emerge. All during the late 1950's and 1960's, Boulez followed this aleatory or chance model, believing that the composition of a particular piece was primarily a process rather than a product. Both *Deux Improvisations sur Mallarmé* and *Strophes* eventually became part of his next great work, *Pli selon pli* (1962; fold by fold). In his Third Piano Sonata, which is still unfinished, the pianist has the choice of arranging the order of the piece's five movements and also may choose within movements to play or omit certain sections. The performer is given alternative paths or options.

Boulez's later work moved his attention into spatial explorations. In *Domaines for clarinet alone or with twenty-one other instruments* (1968), he experimented with the physical distribution of the players themselves with the clarinetist actually moving within the various instrumental groups. In . . . *explosante-fixe* . . . (1971), the players involved have a wide range of forms on which to decide as well as the task of determining how many and specifically what instruments will be used. He returned to his longest-standing work in progress, *Livre pour quatuor* (1958) and arranged it for full string orchestra, changing the title, appropriately, to *Livre pour cordes* (1968).

Boulez has moved in the same direction in which many modern poets and novelists such as James Joyce, Marcel Proust, and his beloved Stéphane Mallarmé moved—that is, to the subject of poetry as the making of poetry, or, for Boulez, to the subject of music as the making of music. Authentic contemporary aesthetics always produces some version of a portrait of the artist. Modern art is always about itself, and the only operation that saves it from becoming an empty act of solipsism is the act itself. The imaginative energy of the creative artist is, in Boulez's view, the sole creator of meaning in a deterministic and violent universe.

Boulez's later career, although he has never stopped composing music, has been spent in becoming one of the most influential and controversial conductors both in Europe and in the United States. In 1963, he returned to Paris after a long and bitter hiatus to conduct triumphantly the first French performance of Berg's *Wozzeck* at the Paris Opéra, an accomplishment that garnered for him numerous invitations for conducting engagements. His performance of his own piece, *Pli selon pli*, at the Edinburgh Festival became an international musical event. It was his invitation to conduct Wagner's *Parsifal* at Germany's most sacred musical shrine, Bayreuth, which catapulted him into the front rank of major conductors. His brilliant performances, characterized by the utmost lucidity and coherence, captured the attention of the great conductor of the Cleveland Orchestra, George Szell, who subsequently engaged him for a number of performances with his orchestra during the late 1960's. Boulez's recordings with the Cleveland Orchestra, particularly his stunning interpretation of Stravinsky's *The Rite of Spring*, won for him worldwide recognition as one of Western music's most accomplished conductors. His association with Szell also brought him into proximity with the New York Philharmonic Orchestra, since Szell had been a musical adviser and frequent conductor of the philharmonic for many years.

The climax of Boulez's conducting career came in 1970-1971, when he became the musical director of both the British Broadcasting Company Symphony in London and America's most renowned orchestra, the New York Philharmonic. His tenure at the Philharmonic was marked by controversy and innovation, because he considered the primary mission of a major orchestra to be the education of the public. Unfortunately, the board of directors lost its nerve after ticket sales plummeted as a result of Boulez's intellectually stimulating but unpopular programming. He also inaugurated a series of informal "Rug Concerts," which were similar to his highly successful Domaine Musical concerts in Paris during the late 1950's. These concerts were widely attended by young people who wished to hear and understand the latest in contemporary music. He was determined to teach the younger generation the language of twentieth century music by connecting it to its sources and inspirations in both the eighteenth and nineteenth centuries. It worked superbly.

In 1974, Boulez relinquished his position at the Philharmonic and moved back to Paris, where he has resided as the director of France's most sophisticated musical research facility, the Institut de Recherche et de Coordination

Acoustique/Musique, or IRCAM. Music critic Peter Heyworth, of the London *Observer*, calls IRCAM a "milestone in the history of Western music as crucial as the advent of the airplane has been in the field of transport." It was only a figure like Boulez, with his international reputation as a great composer, conductor, and writer, who could have marshaled the financial support for such an enormous enterprise.

Summary

Pierre Boulez is one of the twentieth century's most brilliant and controversial musical figures. He is one of the most influential composers of the modern era; *Le Marteau sans maître* probably has as many imitators as Schoenberg's *Pierrot Lunaire*, and Boulez's Second Piano Sonata has become a staple in the repertoire of pianists who are seriously devoted to contemporary music. No major composer of the twentieth century is so consistently literary both in his texts and in his role as possibly the most compelling writer on music in the second half of the century. By choosing the complicated texts of René Char, Henri Michaux, and Stéphane Mallarmé, he demonstrates not only his authenticity as a genuine modernist but also that, in music as well as poetry, form is never more than an extension or revelation of content. He characterized his own style as "organized delirium," which would certainly apply to the poets listed above and place him firmly in the tradition of the great French dramatist Antonin Artaud. His project as a composer has been, however, to externalize his interior conflict and embody it in forms appropriate to its expression. When that expression and attention change, it is incumbent on him to generate new forms. Yet those forms must come only out of musical materials, a lesson he learned well from the composer he most admired and imitated, Anton Webern. It would be difficult to locate a composer, conductor, and writer in the second half of this century as influential as Pierre Boulez.

Bibliography

Boulez, Pierre. *Notes of an Apprenticeship*. Translated by Herbert Weinstock. New York: Alfred A. Knopf, 1968. A collection of eighteen of some of the most brilliant utterances on music in the twentieth century. Boulez lays out quite clearly the major musical developments and schools of the modern era. The profundity of his insights combined with the security of his rhetoric seems, at times, to constitute a final statement on whatever he may be discussing. Unrelentingly provocative and bursting with insights.

Machlis, Joseph. *Introduction to Contemporary Music*. New York: Norton, 1961. Machlis, the author of the clearest and most intelligent introductory text on music, *The Enjoyment of Music*, makes even the complexities of modern music understandable. His lengthy chapter on Boulez and a highly

readable analysis of *Le Marteau sans maître* serve as an excellent introduction to the difficulties of Boulez's musical ideas and procedures.

Peyser, Joan. *Boulez*. New York: Schirmer, 1976. The definitive work on
Boulez as a composer, conductor, and human being. Peyser writes with
great honesty and insight on the personal coldness of Boulez and his
inability or unwillingness to participate in even the most common forms of
social intercourse. Highly readable and a required book for a full understanding of this enigmatic genius.

_____. *Twentieth Century Music: The Sense Behind the Sound*. New
York: Schirmer, 1970. The most accessible book on the complexities of
modern music. Peyser's short chapter on Boulez places him squarely
within the Schoenberg, Webern, Austro-German tradition, but the author
also shows how his roots were originally those of Debussy and Messiaen.
Highly informative.

Thomson, Virgil. *A Virgil Thomson Reader*. Boston: Houghton Mifflin,
1981. There are many references to Boulez throughout this wonderfully
witty and brilliantly written collection of essays and reviews that cover a
fifty-year life in music. Thomson's review of both of Boulez's books constitutes the single most intelligent short piece written in English on him.
Thomson's honest admiration for Boulez as a composer, conductor, and
writer vivify his comments and honor its subject.

Patrick Meanor

HABIB BOURGUIBA

Born: August 3, 1903; Monastir, Tunisia

Areas of Achievement: Government and politics
Contribution: Bourguiba organized Tunisians to confront French rule and was the catalyst for independence, leading his people to nationhood in 1956. For thirty-one years, Bourguiba served as Tunisia's only president, until he was toppled from power in a bloodless *coup d'état* in Tunis.

Early Life

Habib Bourguiba was born in Monastir on August 3, 1903. Monastir, located on the north-central coast of Tunisia, was the site of a large, ancient Islamic fortress that was a constant reminder of Tunisia's ties to Islam. Bourguiba's family was one of modest means, being members of the lower-ranking civil service. When Bourguiba was five, his mother died, and his father then sent him to Tunis to reside with his elder brother Muhammad. There was no question about the young Bourguiba's intelligence, and, after training in the local Koranic schools, he went to the elementary school of Sadiki College. Later, he attended the college itself, an important center of Tunisian learning, as well as the Lycée Carnot. It was at Sadiki College and the Lycée Carnot that Bourguiba learned the best of both the French and the Tunisian worlds. Sadiki College would prove to have a profound impact on the young Habib Bourguiba and a dramatic impact on the course of Tunisian history.

Founded in the 1860's, Sadiki College trained generations of Tunisians who would become the leaders of the nationalist movement. These young Tunisians sought to blend a modern Tunisian nationalism with old Arab, Islamic values, and with the best that France had to offer. It was into this environment that Bourguiba entered as a student. Never in good health, Bourguiba had bouts of illness that slowed his studies, but eventually he went on to Paris to study law in 1924.

While in Paris, Bourguiba saw and adopted many French and Western European ideas, and before returning to Tunisia in 1927 he married a French woman. As a young intellectual, deeply impressed by life in the sophisticated French capital, Bourguiba was not simply content to practice law in Tunis. In 1922, he joined the Tunisian Destour (constitution) Party. While composed of forward-looking Young Tunisians, the Destour Party did not have a coherent program or specific ideology. While it admired things French and modern, praising traditional French ideals (which were so often forgotten in the imperialist scheme of things), Destour looked backward to a supposed golden age of reform before the establishment of the 1881 protectorate.

Life's Work

Bourguiba and his circle of friends rejected the program of the Destour Party as the way to independence, and in 1933 they prepared the groundwork for the establishment of a new organization, the Neo-Destour Party. In 1933, Bourguiba and others founded the newspaper *L'Action tunisienne*, which was highly critical of the Destour leadership and which called for stronger action to end the French protectorate, an action designed to provoke the French. At Kasr Hillalin in March, 1934, the mavericks formed a vigorous new party, the Neo-Destour, with Bourguiba as its leading light. Many of the Neo-Destourians were from small towns, and a high number were from the ranks of Sadiki College graduates. From 1934 to 1936, Bourguiba and many of his Neo-Destour colleagues found themselves in jail for anti-Protectorate agitation. From 1938 to 1943, Bourguiba was again in jail. Following a series of riots in Tunis in April, 1938, the Neo-Destour was outlawed, and its leadership was arrested and incarcerated by the French.

The French Republic had good reason to fear unrest in Tunisia. Fascist Italy, with which France had had decent relations up to 1938, began a concentrated effort to extend its control over several French holdings, including Tunisia. Italian colonial claims to Tunisia in 1881 were substantial, and the young Italian government suffered a deep humiliation when Tunisia was added to the French Empire. The issue surfaced again in 1896 and, again, briefly, after the end of World War I. Benito Mussolini, with his dreams of a revitalized Roman Empire and feeling secure in his newfound friendship with Adolf Hitler, began to pressure the much-weakened Paris government over Tunisia. The result was a panic in Paris and repression in Tunisia.

That Bourguiba regarded Fascism as he did Marxism there can be little doubt, and the shrewd North African could see no future with either the Roman fasces or the Russian hammer and sickle. Pressured by the Fascists during his incarceration in Rome in 1942 and 1943, Bourguiba continued to urge support for France but warned that support did not mean an end to Neo-Destourian agitation for an end to the Protectorate. Once liberated from Fascist imprisonment, Bourguiba went back to work as an organizer.

By 1948, Bourguiba was perhaps the most popular nationalist leader in Tunisia, with a great following among those Tunisians who had served in the allied armies against the Axis and among young, well-educated Tunisians in general, but there seemed to be no relief from the short-lived de Gaulle government (1944-1946). The change finally came in 1954, when France, reeling under the Indo-Chinese War and facing continual problems (but not yet revolution) in Algeria, changed its imperialist policy. In that year, French Premier Pierre Mendès-France visited Tunisia and on July 31, 1954, proclaimed the self-government of Tunisia within a French union. Even Bourguiba, back in prison, hailed the French move and praised the French as keeping faith with their own revolutionary heritage. For two years, negotiations took place between Tunisia and the French, looking forward to the 1956 target. In 1955, Bourguiba returned to Tunis and was given a hero's welcome by the people. By the time of independence in 1956, there was no more popular figure in Tunisia than Bourguiba.

Bourguiba's tenure as Tunisia's first president represented moderation. He rejected virulent Arab nationalism, cautioned against Tunisia's being too deeply embroiled in the Arab-Israeli conflict (even though that conflict had not yet drawn distinct lines), urged nonalignment, promoted a Tunisian brand of Arab socialism (the Neo-Destour Party changed its name in 1964 to the Parti Socialist Desturien), encouraged French help (assistance among equals), and tried to come to grips with the thorny and ever-present problem of state-Islam relations. Bourguiba did give sanctuary to the Algerian rebels, who were locked in a bloody life-and-death struggle with France, but he feared the rampant nationalism of the Algerians; he worried lest the Algerians infect Tunisian youth who saw the Algerian Front de Libération Nationale and their army as a set of true North African heroes.

Bourguiba's relationship with Islam was a rocky one. While the 1956 constitution proclaimed Islam as the religion of the state, there was a quiet contest between Bourguiba and Islam. In 1960, this contest came to a head when Bourguiba prescribed the dates for Ramadan, the month of fasting, one of the five great pillars of the Muslim faith. The month of Ramadan tries the patience of the believers, and it can seriously hinder commerce and industry. Also, the end of Ramadan is marked by *al-Futur*, a feast of celebration which can also tax the faithful. Bourguiba, citing national goals, tried hard to curtail Ramadan, without success. Bourguiba had shown, however, a tendency to interpret Islam in the context of the modern nation-state. In 1960, this was an issue, but by the 1980's, with Islam flexing a strong and militant muscle, the picture would be different indeed.

As early as 1957, Bourguiba officially began to address the needs of Tunisian women in the modern world. He personally attacked the veil as a relic of the past that was not rooted in Islam. In 1957, over strong objections by traditionalists, he encouraged the formation of the Union des Femmes de la Tunisie (UNFT), and he continued his support of Tunisian women by assuring them the vote in municipal elections in 1957 and in all subsequent national and local elections. More than forty thousand women were enrolled in the UNFT by 1960, and the future seemed quite bright for Tunisian women. By the 1980's, however, the bright banner of the UNFT had become tarnished, as had many once so promising national institutions, because of the lack of direction from the rapidly aging Bourguiba.

In creating Tunisia, Bourguiba built a one-party state with power resting mainly in his hands and, to a much lesser extent, in the hands of the Neo-Destour cadres. If Bourguiba had had to rely only on his own position as president or on his role as head of the party, it is doubtful that he could have lasted thirty-one years. His charisma, his role in Tunisian independence, and his basic moderation, keeping Tunisia relatively free of embroilment in the ongoing Arab-Israeli conflict and stemming the tide of Islamic revivalism and fundamentalism, made Bourguiba the figure of stability and continuity for Tunisia.

Bourguiba never did come to grips with the question of an orderly succession, nor did he, throughout the 1970's and early 1980's, encourage the emergence of new leadership within the party. While the future looked good for Tunisia, there were troubling signs, such as rising unemployment and an economic slowdown. Four major problems would come to plague Bourguiba's last few years in power: Bourguiba's health and the succession issue, the atrophy of the one-party state, Islamic revivalism and fundamentalism, and relations with Tunisia's North African neighbors, Algeria and Libya.

In the early 1980's, rumors emanated from Tunis that Bourguiba was suffering from a number of ailments and that old age had begun to take its toll on the leader. Bourguiba's son had been named as a likely successor, but this was destined not to be. No one seemed to be sure what Bourguiba had in mind, and there were reports that his behavior was becoming more erratic. This had its impact on the political faithful who saw their position challenged by more youthful political aspirants.

In 1983, the Bourguiba government froze wages, but inflation continued until, in 1984, there were severe food riots which shook the foundation of the government. There were signs of an Islamic revival. The Movement de la Tendance Islamiste became something of a force in the towns and on campuses. Labor problems beset the government. Muhammad Mzali, the prime minister and the man selected by Bourguiba to succeed him at some unspecified time, found it difficult to deal with the rising tide of religious, political, and economic discontent.

Libya continued to be a clear threat to Tunisia, and neither Bourguiba nor Mzali seemed able to curb the open enthusiasm for Libya's anti-Western posturing. Libya's position fitted well with the Muslim revivalists and with those who called for radical change in Tunisia.

In November, 1987, in a bloodless coup, Tunisian security chief (appointed by Bourguiba), Zin al Abidin bin Ali, removed the ailing, eighty-four-year-old president. The new leader simply stated that Bourguiba was "mentally unfit" to remain in power, and he was placed in house arrest near Tunis. For all practical purposes, Bourguiba, a sick, aged man, passed from the political scene.

Summary

Despite Habib Bourguiba's removal from power there remained his legacy: an independent Tunisia. His accomplishments were many, and will, in the long run, overshadow the last years of his rule. Bourguiba's first and greatest accomplishment was the nurturing of the ideal of independence, which grew into the reality of a bloodless transition from colonial status to new nationhood. He helped bring Tunisia to independence without the bitter ideological baggage that weighted down so many new states of the Third World. Bourguiba's second feat was to steer a moderate course when other African and Arab states were mired in wars and successive, destructive *coups d'états*. It was always clear that Bourguiba led an Arab, Islamic state, but his reasonable approach brought him respect from all sides, and he was able then to suggest answers and compromises to feuding factions.

In the late 1970's and early 1980's, however, Bourguiba, frustrated with the course of Arab-Israeli relations, did involve Tunisia more and more with the Palestine Liberation Organization, allowing them to maintain offices and camps, especially for orphaned and traumatized children, in the Tunis area. Ironically, it was this evidence of Tunisia's Arab status that brought violence in the form of an Israeli air raid and assassinations. As Bourguiba reasoned, it was perhaps inevitable that the conflict would touch even the most moderate Arab state.

Bourguiba also left behind one of the most prosperous North African states, with concrete achievements in education, wage earning levels, and women's rights. By the last half of the 1970's Bourguiba's prestige was at its highest, but as he aged this prestige began to slip away. Perhaps Bourguiba believed that only he, the man who gave life to independent Tunisia, had the insights to keep it on its course. As Bourguiba's force waned so did the basic direction of the state, and this led to his removal in 1987. Despite the inglorious end to his career, his achievements cannot be tarnished.

Bibliography

Brown, Leon Carl. *The Tunisia of Ahmad Bey, 1837-1855*. Princeton, N.J.: Princeton University Press, 1974. This is a study critical to understanding the reform period which deeply affected the Tunisian nationalists of the twentieth century.

Micaud, Charles A. *Tunisia: The Politics of Modernization*. New York: Praeger, 1964. Despite its date, this work contains valuable information on the course of Tunisian politics and society after independence.

Moore, Clement Henry. *Politics in North Africa: Algeria, Morocco, Tunisia*. Boston: Little, Brown, 1970. This useful volume compares the politics of the three former French North African states since independence. It is detailed and makes serious comparisons.

——————. *Tunisia Since Independence*. Berkeley: University of California Press, 1965. This book remains one of the better studies on the emergence of Tunisian elites after independence.

Sylvester, Anthony. *Tunisia*. London: The Bodley Head, 1969. Sylvester's work is a serious study of the entire fabric of Tunisian history. What this work does is to relate the developments of the twentieth century to Tunisia's past. Well written, this book helps the reader to see the whole history of Tunisia in a usable, compact form.

Zartman, I. William, ed. *Political Elites in Arab North Africa*. New York: Longman, 1982. This important work includes the former French colonies and also Libya and Egypt. The scholarly, well-researched articles by leading authorities tie together all of Arab and Islamic North Africa, regardless of former colonial status. While focusing on the elites, this book sheds great light on the complexities of inter-North African diplomacy and relations.

James J. Cooke

CONSTANTIN BRANCUSI

Born: February 19, 1876; Hobitza, Romania
Died: March 16, 1957; Paris, France
Area of Achievement: Art
Contribution: A craftsman and a poet of forms, Brancusi carried abstraction to its utmost limits, often far beyond the material's own representational element. Renouncing the traditional form, he attempted to extract from the material—whether marble, metal, or wood—its maximum effect. His major contribution to modern sculpture was his unique capacity to render meaning through sheer form.

Early Life
Constantin Brancusi was born on February 19, 1876, in the small Romanian village of Hobitza, hidden in the foothills of the legendary Transylvanian mountains. Both of his parents were of peasant stock. A small parcel of land provided their rather large family—Brancusi had three half brothers, besides two brothers and a sister—with its daily bread. Young Brancusi idealized the pastoral life in the remote Transylvanian village. From his early years, he felt a strong attachment to his land. The native landscape influenced the youngster and provided him with unusual spiritual intensity that later characterized the artist and his work. Brancusi's communion with nature kept his sanity intact, while his mother's love alleviated the burden of poverty and the harshness of everyday life in Hobitza.

In 1887, Brancusi left his family and went to find his fortune in the small provincial town of Tîrgu-Jiu. There, for five years, he was compelled to earn his own living toiling at painful and hard, if varied, work. At the end of 1892, Brancusi went to Craiova, the capital city of the province of Oltenia. Although he had no previous formal schooling, his voracious intellectual curiosity, as well as an inherent ability to learn quickly, helped him to be accepted into the School of Arts and Crafts in the fall of 1895. Brancusi, being much older than all of his classmates, became noteworthy for his seriousness and diligence. The high grades he received represented the recognition of his assiduity. He excelled in woodcarving and, on the advice of his teachers, specialized in sculpture.

In 1898, at the age of twenty-two, he was graduated with honors from the School of Arts and Crafts. To overcome his youthful appearance, Brancusi, who was short yet strongly built, grew a small beard that he wore with open pride. After graduation, the artist's peasant character helped him overcome the difficulties of a rather penniless existence. Brancusi supported himself by working on non-art-related jobs that he found tedious and even hateful. During his last year of study at the school in Craiova, with the aid of a small, locally administered grant, he produced one of his first recognized works: the head of the roman emperor Aulus Vitellius. Modeled with an unusual psychological subtlety and constructed with the vigor of an antique sculpture, the bust brought him the recognition of his artistic talent. It also provided him the opportunity to receive additional grants that enabled him to leave for the capital city of Bucharest and become enrolled at the famous School of Fine Arts, an equivalent of the École des Beaux-Arts in Paris. From 1898 to 1902, Brancusi worked relentlessly to refine his talent and to improve his skills.

As during his early years in Craiova, Brancusi's unusual talent and hard work won for him the recognition of his teachers and the admiration and envy of his classmates. Brancusi won a number of prizes, notably for his *Antinous of Belvedere* and for a life-size anatomy figure that revealed an unusual knowledge of the human anatomy. During his last schooling year, Brancusi studied human anatomy. He performed numerous dissections under the direct supervision of doctor Dimitrie Gerota, a renowned Romanian professor of anatomy. For his final examination, Brancusi presented a study of the now-famous Écorché—a life-size plaster of a nude man. Early in 1903, as a recognition of his talent, Brancusi was commissioned to create a bust of General Doctor Carol Davila, the founder of the modern Romanian School of Medicine. At the end of the year 1904, after a lengthy trip through Europe and a short stay in Munich, Brancusi arrived in Paris. The French capital became his adoptive city.

Life's Work

For more than half a century, from 1904 to 1957, Brancusi worked and lived in Paris. Life in the French capital was different from the easygoing life-style in Bucharest. After a long journey of more than a year across Europe, most of it made on foot, Brancusi arrived in Paris with very little money. The young Romanian sculptor had to endure a lengthy period of financial difficulties. For almost a year and a half, he was unable to use his artistic skills. During this time, Brancusi earned his living by washing dishes and by working and singing in a Romanian church in Paris. Nevertheless, after a year of hardships and numerous painful adjustments to the fast-paced Parisian life, Brancusi's determination to succeed finally paid off. With the help of some of his Romanian friends, Brancusi began to receive commissions for a number of busts. Although done from live models, most of the portrayals do not reflect the sculptural flamboyance that characterized Brancusi's later works. At the end of 1905, Brancusi produced several busts, this time done from photographs. Worth mentioning are *Portrait of a Concierge* and *Portrait of Dr. Zaharia Samfirescu*. Two other works, *Portrait of Restaurant Owner* and *Portrait of Mrs. Victoria Vashide*, earned for the sculptor a modest sum that enabled him to meet his daily expenses.

In 1905, Brancusi was enrolled at the famous École des Beaux-Arts, at that time holding its classes in the studio of Antonin Mercié. The school, which had students from all over the world, emphasized the work on sculptural details of old French churches, Gothic cathedrals, and Baroque ornaments rather than on live models. Brancusi, who felt no desire to follow the school's rigidly imposed curricula, worked assiduously, making new sculptures almost daily—but destroying every single figure he made.

The year 1906 marks Brancusi's first participation in the famous Salon d'Automne. At the Salon he exhibited the head of a girl in bronze entitled *Pride*. The sculpture was made by Brancusi in 1905 while he was still a student at the École des Beaux-Arts. Two other works, *Bust of a Boy* and *Portrait of G. Lupescu*, both plaster, were done from photographs. At the exhibit, Brancusi had the chance to meet August Rodin, at whose studio he would soon be working. The beginning of 1907 appears to have been a critical time for Brancusi. At thirty-one, he had to leave the École des Beaux-Arts because of the school's rigid age limitations. For two months, in March and April, he worked for Rodin. Soon, however, he left the master's studio because of their opposite views on art. At this time he made his famous remark: "Nothing can grow in the shadow of the great trees."

On April 18, 1907, Brancusi received his first big commission. He was to make a funerary monument for the grave of Petre Stanescu, but the monument was to be erected in Buzău, Romania. With only five hundred francs advance money, Brancusi rented his first studio at 54 rue du Montparnasse. In the summer he journeyed to Romania to begin his work on the monument, which, according to the agreement, was to have a portrait of the deceased and a figure of a kneeling body in prayer. The portrait, done mainly from family photographs, is one of Brancusi's most eloquent sculptures. The figure represents a nude of a young woman with her arms over her chest in a gesture of crossing herself; its attitude alternates between rest and tension, between restrained dignity and an expression of private yet strong emotion. Brancusi started his work on the *Prayer* in 1907. When it was finished at the end of 1909, it marked the end of Rodin's influence on Brancusi. From then on, the Romanian sculptor was his own master. Brancusi's fame grew steadily. The Romanian press began noticing the impressive artist from Hobitza. The art critics remarked on the sculptor's ability to render the magic of sheer form without distorting its content.

Most of the earliest works of Brancusi are now lost, and in most cases knowledge of his sculptures is fragmentary. Brancusi's artistic output is relatively small. In 1913, Brancusi had five works displayed in the Armory Show in New York; at the end of the same year he had only three works exhibited in London. In February, 1914, five of his sculptures were shown at a cubist exhibit held in Prague. Brancusi's first one-man exhibition was held at the Alfred Stieglitz Gallery in New York, marking the beginning of the sculptor's long and lasting relationship with the American public and collectors. In both Europe and the United States, Brancusi's work was steadily gaining critical recognition.

Although Brancusi had his "artistic and social roots" in Paris, he often traveled to his native Romania. Before World War I, he made two trips to Bucharest, where he participated in nine exhibitions. After the war, he also returned to the United States, where in 1926 he opened a one-man show at the well-known Wildenstein Galleries in New York City. At the end of the same year, he was back in New York to participate in his third one-man exhibition, opened this time at the Brummer Gallery. During this trip, Brancusi got involved in lengthy litigation with the United States Customs Office. The Customs Office claimed that Brancusi's bronze sculpture *Bird in Space* was not a work of art but an "object of manufacture." After an unpleasant trial, at the end of 1928, the tribunal finally decided in the artist's favor. Overnight the solitary Romanian sculptor had become a public figure.

While in Paris, Brancusi was a regular of the small, family cafés of Montparnasse. He became a friend of many other artists, poets, and writers who frequented the same establishments. Among his numerous friends were Amedeo Modigliani, Guillaume Apollinaire, Jean Cocteau, Henri Matisse, Pablo Picasso, and Fernand Leger. A shy and solitary man, Brancusi liked to take long walks through the woods of Clamart, near Paris, to escape the often suffocating Parisian summers and to be alone with nature. In his studio, Brancusi re-created some of the familiar surroundings of his native Oltenian village. A wooden gate adorned the entrance; a millstone surrounded by four wooden stools occupied the middle of the room. In this small Romanian universe, Brancusi liked to entertain his friends with Romanian folk music played on his guitar and with Romanian dishes that he had prepared himself. Brancusi's best friend, however, was his sheepdog, Polar, who accompanied him during long walks in the woods. Brancusi's last trip to his native country took place in the summer of 1937, when he was commissioned to do an ensemble of sculptures for a park in Tîrgu-Jiu. The monument was to commemorate the Romanian resistance to the Germans during World War I. The result was a large public conception. It was a group of sculptures composed of *Table of Silence*, a travertine-like stone called bampotoc encircled by twelve round stone stools, and *Gate of the Kiss*, constructed of a number of blocks and slabs of stone. Both the Table and the Gate, located in the public park, are connected by an alley lined by square stone seats, also designed by Brancusi. In line with the Table stands his famous *Endless Column*. The Column, designed by Brancusi, was built under the technical supervision of the Romanian structural engineer Stefan Georgescu-Gorjan, a friend and an artist in his own right, the Column's repeated elements extending to the sky create a sensation of upward flight, of infinity. Its decorative elements in diamond shape are similar to those found in the borders of Romanian peasant rugs and on the carved capital posts of wooden Oltenian houses.

Before the beginning of World War II, Brancusi made his last trip to the United States to participate in the celebration of the tenth anniversary of the Museum of Modern Art in New York City. During the German Occupation of France, Brancusi stayed in Paris, working on a monumental version of one of his early sculptures, the well-known *Cock*. The first study, done in clay, reveals the bird's nervous energy. The second, large-scale version of *Cock* is considered to represent an expression of the sculptor's art and craft in rendering the boldness and the strength of a cock crowing. This was one of the last large sculptural works done by the artist. Brancusi, in poor health, was unable to attend the 1955 one-man exhibit of his works organized at the Solomon R. Guggenheim Museum in New York. One year prior to his death, to celebrate Brancusi's eightieth birthday, the Art Museum in Bucharest held an exhibition of works from Romanian collections. Brancusi died on March 16, 1957. He was buried in the Cimetière Montparnasse, in Paris. His studio and all of its contents were willed to France, whose citizen he had become shortly before his death.

Summary

Recognition came rather late to Constantin Brancusi, after World War II. The Parisian literary and artistic world rapidly adopted the shy Romanian peasant, whose childlike simplicity charmed everyone who knew him. Famous himself, he knew almost every prominent artist in Paris. His private life, however, remained a mystery even to his closest friends. During his long and productive artistic life, Brancusi produced a relatively small number of works. The extant works, excluding numerous plasters of objects in stone, bronze, and wood, slightly exceed two hundred. All, however, are overpowering in their perfection. He was against the empty grandiloquent and the fake monumental. Clarity and simplicity are the trademarks of his sculptures.

A fine artistic intuition helped Brancusi assimilate the forms and the shapes of the mythic world of Romanian folklore. Brancusi in his pursuit of essence also succeeded in assimilating the shapes of the natural world around him to the extent that he was able to produce forms that seem to be free from their reliance on nature. Nevertheless, his synthesis did not lead to a simplistic system of forms. The shapes of his sculptures always carried a meaning and a hidden intimacy of expression.

Bibliography

Brancusi, Constantin. *Constantin Brancusi*. Edited by Carola Gideon-Welcher. Translated by Maria Jolas and Anne Leroy. New York: George Braziller, 1959. One of the most authoritative works on the Romanian sculptor. It includes an in-depth analysis of his work. The volume is

268   *Great Lives from History*

illustrated with numerous photo-documents.

Comarnescu, Petru, Mircea Eliade, and Ionel Jianu. *Témoignages sur Brancusi*. Paris: Arted, 1967. Three essays written by three of the artist's Romanian friends. Each essay presents Brancusi from a personal viewpoint, yet all essays are unified by the strong bonds of the same cultural milieu.

Geist, Sidney. *Brancusi: A Study of the Sculpture*. New York: Grossman, 1968. A solid and well-documented monograph of Brancusi's work and life. The volume provides an extensive description of the artist's major works and how they related to various stages in Brancusi's life.

_____. *Constantin Brancusi, 1876-1957: A Retrospective Exhibition*. New York: Solomon R. Guggenheim Foundation, 1969. The listing of Brancusi's works is accompanied by a pertinent presentation of each individual work. The book explores Brancusi's artistic universe and provides valuable insights into his manner of work.

Lewis, David. *Constantin Brancusi*. New York: Wittenborn, 1957. Richly illustrated, this relatively small book contains one of the best accounts of Brancusi's themes and techniques.

Selz, Jean. *Modern Sculpture: Origins and Evolution*. Translated by Annette Michelson. New York: George Braziller, 1963. The book contains a good analysis of Brancusi's life and work. The author emphasizes the modernity of the artist's works.

Spear, Athena T. *Brancusi's Birds*. New York: New York University Press, 1969. One of the best summaries of Brancusi's recurrent theme: the bird. The author discusses the bird motif in Brancusi's work and its folkloric implications.

Hari S. Rorlich

WILLY BRANDT

Born: December 18, 1913; Lübeck, Germany

Areas of Achievement: Government and politics

Contribution: Brandt was awarded the Nobel Peace Prize (1971) for his efforts in improving relations between West Germany and Eastern Europe. He was instrumental in creating a competitive political party system in West Germany. In 1985, Brandt received the Albert Einstein Peace Prize and the Third World Prize.

Early Life

Willy Brandt, who never knew his father, was the son of an unwed salesclerk who gave him the name Herbert Ernst Karl Frahm. His maternal grandfather, Ludwig Frahm, upon returning from service in World War I, became the principal influence in Brandt's childhood. When he was five, Brandt went to live with his grandparents and subsequently saw his mother regularly but infrequently. As had his father, Ludwig had been a farm laborer. Dissatisfied with those working conditions, he took a factory job and, after the war, was a truck driver. Even before leaving farm work, he was a socialist, one who read widely the works of leading socialist thinkers. Young Brandt picked up this political orientation, which not only was unpopular then but also was considered to be subversive by many.

Unlike many socialists who denounce religion, the Frahms were Protestants, who baptized their children but did not let them attend religious classes in public school. Brandt continued to follow the Christian ethos as an adult but rarely in a conventional fashion, as set out in a strict denominational way. A bright pupil, he won a scholarship to a prestigious *Realgymnasium* (college preparatory high school). There, he had a difficult time as one of the few students from a working-class family. This disparity was compounded by his outspoken political views and his occasional attire, the uniform of the Socialist youth organization.

At this time, Brandt's active career as a Socialist began. First, he wrote pieces for the Lubeck Social Democratic newspaper. Its editor, Julius Leber, a Social Democratic Party (SPD) member of the *Reichstag*, offered encouragement and advice to the young man, who adopted the pen name Willy Brandt. Although the required age was eighteen, with Leber's endorsement, Brandt became a member of the SPD in 1930 at the age of sixteen. The next year, the close tie between Leber and his protégé was severed. Considering the SPD insufficiently radical and indecisive toward the Nazi threat, Brandt joined the Socialist Workers Party (SAP), an offshoot of the SPD but which pursued direct action, taking on the Nazis in street fights.

When the Nazis came to power in 1933, leftist parties, such as the SPD and the SAP, prepared to go underground. SAP plans included establishing centers abroad in key cities. Brandt was sent to Oslo for this purpose when the man initially selected to head that activity was arrested by the Nazis. Thus, when only nineteen, Brandt was in a leadership post that permitted him to travel across Europe, in Belgium, in Berlin, and in Spain, covering the Civil War in 1937 as a correspondent for Scandinavian newspapers. He also briefly attended a Norwegian university. In 1941, he married a Norwegian socialist, Carlota Thorkildsen, whom he divorced in 1947, after a 1943 separation. He later married Rut Hansen, a member of the wartime resistance in Norway. They were divorced in 1980. The first marriage produced a daughter; the second, three sons.

Brandt had not yet been granted Norwegian citizenship when the Nazis invaded Norway in 1941. Wearing a friend's army uniform, Brandt was captured with the friend's unit. His fluent Norwegian enabled him to deceive the Nazis, who released him with other members of the unit. Then he went across the border to Sweden, a neutral nation where he spent the rest of the war, receiving his Norwegian citizenship and writing or coauthoring six books. His principal activity at that time was journalism.

As soon as hostilities ceased, he returned to Norway, before departing in October, 1945, to cover the Nuremberg War Crimes Trials. In 1946, Brandt became press attaché with the Norwegian military mission in West Berlin.

Life's Work

Now Brandt's life came to a crossroads. At both Nuremberg and Berlin, he had met several figures who hoped to, and in many cases would, shape postwar Germany. After some hesitation, he decided to renounce his Norwegian citizenship and resumed that of Germany in 1947. At that time, he legally became Willy Brandt, the name that he had used for years.

On the recommendation of Kurt Schumacher, leader of the SPD, Brandt became a party official in Berlin, where he came under the tutelage of Mayor Ernst Reuter, whose aide he was during the dramatic Airlift of 1948-1949. In addition to offices within the SPD, Brandt continued his journalistic career and was elected to local and national legislatures. He emerged as a national, perhaps international, figure in 1956, when he quelled an unruly Berlin rally protesting the use of Soviet troops to crush the Hungarian Revolution.

The next year, Brandt was elected Mayor of Berlin, a post he held during two key events in postwar Germany: the 1959 Bad Godesberg SPD conference, at which he played a minor role in the party's renunciation of three historic goals—pacifism, anticlericalism, and nationalization of the economy—and the erection of the Berlin Wall in 1961. He was disappointed by what he considered an inadequate U.S. response to the Berlin Wall, but international attention focused on Berlin thrust him into the spotlight: He emerged as the leading figure in the SPD, a role magnified by his fluent English.

Brandt was the SPD chancellor candidate in the September, 1961, 1965, and 1969 *Bundestag* elections. Although the SPD increased its share of the vote in each successive try, it did not become the largest *Bundestag* party until 1969 and even then needed the support of the small Free Democratic Party (FDP) to form a government. The stage was set for this success in 1966, when the Grand Coalition was created. This arrangement between West Germany's two largest parties was precipitated by the nation's faltering economy and what was regarded as the weak leadership of Ludwig Erhard, who had led the Christian Democratic Union (CDU) to its fifth successive headship of a coalition government in 1965. Following negotiations between the CDU and the SPD, Erhard resigned, and a CDU/SPD government, with Brandt as vice chancellor and foreign minister, took office.

With his foreign policy portfolio, Brandt first strengthened West Germany's links with the Western Alliance, especially France. Then he turned to Eastern Europe, cautiously reinstating diplomatic ties with Romania and Yugoslavia. His efforts to create closer ties with Eastern Europe accelerated when he became chancellor and were supported by his foreign minister, Walter Scheel, head of the FDP. In a series of negotiations, Brandt pursued his *Ostpolitik*, or Eastern policy. In a relatively short period, treaties were signed with East European Communist nations, most importantly the Soviet Union, Poland, and East Germany. These treaties produced more normal relations with these nations; especially key were easier trade, relaxed travel restrictions on West Germans to East Germany, and West Germany's pledge not to use force to seek return of the Oder-Neisse territories, which were parts of pre-1939 Germany that had been placed under Russian and Polish "administration" in 1945.

Ostpolitik was the high point of Brandt's career. His efforts to achieve modest domestic goals were frustrated: SPD radicals, seeking more purely socialist programs, diluted his support within the party; members of the FDP, opposing his economic policies or questioning his conciliatory overtures toward the Communist Bloc, defected from the governing coalition; and voters wanted more government services but no higher taxes to fund them. To compound the situation, the West German economy stagnated.

With the coalition's majority down to one vote, Brandt used the unique "constructive vote of nonconfidence" of the Basic Law (constitution) to force a *Bundestag* election, the first in which the parliament had not lasted its maximum four-year term. In the November, 1972, election, the SPD with a plurality of seats formed another coalition with the FDP. Despite the coalition's comfortable majority, Brandt faced more obstacles: public workers' strikes, SPD losses in state elections, continued SPD factionalism, and Communist governments that delayed implementing *Ostpolitik*.

In April, 1974, the final act of Brandt's chancellorship began with the arrest of his close aide, Günter Guillaume, who was charged with being an

East German spy over a period of eighteen years. Amid rumors about his personal life and doubts about his leadership, Brandt resigned on May 7, 1974. Brandt was involved with women before and after his first marriage, a practice not uncommon in Europe. The women with whom he was closely associated tended to be active in public life. Susanne Sievers, whom he met in Bonn in 1951 while he served in the Bundestag and she was a Bundestag employee, was said to be one reason for his 1974 resignation. Rumors purported that she was about to release details of their affair or had been paid a large sum of money not to reveal their former relationship.

This event did not end Brandt's public career. He served in various capacities, often in the international arena, including an unsuccessful effort to mediate the 1984 election in Nicaragua. He was chairman of the Independent Commission on International Development Issues (the Brandt Commission), a body of fifteen distinguished statesmen from across the globe. Appointed by Robert McNamara, President of the World Bank, the commission issued a lengthy document, the North-South, or Brandt Report, in 1980 that called for extensive economic aid from the industrial nations to the Third World. Despite a generally favorable reception and its inclusion on the agenda of the 1981 Cancún (Mexico) economic summit conference, the report was not acted upon. In 1983, he married his third wife, Brigitte Seebacher.

When he resigned as chancellor, Brandt retained his post as chairman of the SPD, a position that he held while his successor, Helmut Schmidt, was chancellor. This position gave Brandt a platform from which he could speak out within and beyond the party. Often he seemed to be undercutting Schmidt. Brandt continued as party leader under the CDU chancellor, Helmut Kohl, until 1987, when he abruptly gave up the party leadership. Brandt's resignation as SPD chairman was also the result of his association with a woman. He stepped down amid the clamor over his intention to appoint Margarita Mathiapoulos, a friend of his wife, to be press spokesperson for the SPD. Critics of his decision noted that his choice was neither a German citizen nor an SPD member and was not familiar with the party organization. Moreover, her fiancé was a prominent CDU official. Yet, after the tumultuous events in the two Germanys in late 1989, Brandt once again rose to prominence and was even elected in February, 1990, honorary president of the East German Social Democratic Party.

Summary

Willy Brandt's personal and public lives cannot be separated. In the aftermath of defeats, and sometimes victories, within the SPD and in his public official roles, he frequently manifested an indifference or malaise, if not depression, that might occupy him for days or weeks. He has also been criticized for being indecisive. Brandt, however, illustrates the complexities that may be found in the makeup of a prominent national and world leader:

impressive qualities of command but also traits of weakness. Yet there is a persistent pattern in his life of seeking a better life for the oppressed and impoverished, whether victims of Adolf Hitler's Third Reich, East Germany's Communist regime, or economic adversity in the Third World.

Bibliography

Barnet, Richard J. *The Alliance: America-Europe-Japan, Makers of the Postwar World*. New York: Simon & Schuster, 1983. Chapter 7, "The Double Detente: Mr. Nixon and Herr Brandt Look East," focuses on Brandt's *Ostpolitik* in the context of general East-West relations.

Binder, David. *The Other German: Willy Brandt's Life and Times*. Washington, D.C.: New Republic Book Co., 1975. Completed shortly after Brandt's resignation as chancellor; one of the few works that comments on the Brandt-Sievers affair.

Brandt, Willy. *Arms and Hunger*. Translated by Anthea Bell. New York: Pantheon, 1986. Examines the issues and politics that the Brandt Commission faced.

_____. *My Road to Berlin*. Garden City, N.Y.: Doubleday, 1960. Brandt's account of his life up to the time that he became Mayor of Berlin.

_____. *People and Politics: The Years 1960-1975*. Translated by J. Maxwell Brownjohn. Boston: Little, Brown, 1978. The second installment of Brandt's memoirs, covering the zenith of his career. Includes an index.

Braunthal, Gerard. "Willy Brandt: Politician and Statesman." In *Government and Leaders*, edited by Edward Feit et al. Boston: Houghton Mifflin, 1978. Brief, analytic work that concentrates on factors affecting Brandt's personality. A companion piece to the Kellerman article on Brandt.

Drath, Viola Herms. *Willy Brandt: Prisoner of His Past*. Radnor, Pa.: Chilton, 1975. Bibliography of both English- and German-language sources. More on the Guillaume affair than most sources have.

Gress, David. "Whatever Happened to Willy Brandt?" *Commentary* 76 (July, 1983): 55-58. Unlike most biographical pieces on Brandt, this one focuses on his flaws.

Harpprecht, Klaus. *Willy Brandt: Portrait and Self-Portrait*. Translated by Hank Keller. Los Angeles: Nash, 1971. Largely composed of excerpts from Brandt's writings. Not analytical but illustrates Brandt's views and impressions on some issues and events.

Homze, Alma, and Edward Homze. *Willy Brandt: A Biography*. Nashville: Thomas Nelson, 1974. Brief, complimentary biography, mentions Brandt's resignation as chancellor in only one paragraph.

Kellerman, Barbara. "Mentoring in Political Life: The Case of Willy Brandt." *American Political Science Review* 72 (June, 1978): 422-433. Assesses the impact of three key mentors—his grandfather, Julius Leber, and Ernst Reuter—on Brandt's life.

Prittie, Terence. *Willy Brandt*. New York: Schocken Books, 1974. The Standard biography on Brandt. Finished before Brandt's 1974 resignation, but a postscript comments on that. Contains a very extensive bibliography in English and German.

Wechsberg, Joseph. "The Outsider." *The New Yorker* 49 (January 14, 1974): 35-40, 42, 44, 46-50, 52-57. This gives an impression of Brandt's managerial style with civil servants, other politicians, and the public. Also offers observations on *Ostpolitik*.

Thomas P. Wolf

GEORGES BRAQUE

Born: May 13, 1882; Argenteuil, France
Died: August 31, 1963; Paris, France
Area of Achievement: Art
Contribution: Braque cofounded cubism with his friend, Pablo Picasso. Braque is best known, however, as a master of the still life, which constituted approximately two-thirds of his output. His paintings are famous for their discipline, rationality, classical lines, and subdued colors.

Early Life

Georges Braque was born May 13, 1882, into a family of decorators and "Sunday painters" in Argenteuil. In 1890, the family business was moved to Le Havre. Braque attended the local *lycée* in 1893 and by 1897 took classes at the École des Beaux-Arts. In 1899, he was apprenticed to a decorator and in 1900 sent to Paris to get a craftsman's diploma. After completing military service in 1902, he enrolled in the Académie Humbert, where he was influenced by the Fauves. After two years at the Académie Humbert, he set up his own studio.

Few of his earliest paintings survive, yet in *Ship in Harbor, Le Havre* (1905), he turned from imitating Impressionism to a geometric consideration of shapes. In 1906, he allied with the Fauves and contributed seven paintings to their exhibition at the Salon des Indépendants. In the summer of 1906, he painted in Antwerp with a boyhood friend, Othon Friesz, and produced some lovely Fauvist works, for example, two brilliantly colored pieces, *The Bay at Antwerp* (1906) and *Landscape Near Antwerp* (1906), both with a linear structure. He then set out for L'Estaque on the Mediterranean, passing through Paris to see the Paul Gauguin exhibition. During the winter of 1906-1907, he captured the blinding colors of Provence. Yet his paintings from the south also show an uncharacteristic structural rhythm, patterned shapes, and a formal order, for example in *L'Estaque, Road with two Figures* (1906).

When Braque returned to Paris in October of 1907, he saw the great Paul Cézanne exhibition. Cézanne's works emphasized their creator's famous maxim: Treat nature in terms of the cylinder, sphere, and cone. Within a few months, Cézanne's influence replaced that of Gauguin and Henri Matisse. This influence is particularly noticeable in two of Braque's paintings, *View from the Hôtel Mistral* (1907) and *Houses at L'Estaque* (1908), where Cézannian blues, greens, and browns replaced bright Fauvist colors, and geometrical patterns took over from pointillist and speckled and dotted areas.

In October, 1907, Braque's dealer, David Henry Kahnweiller, introduced him to the poet Guillaume Apollinaire, who took him to meet Pablo Picasso. Here Braque saw Picasso's *Les Demoiselles d'Avignon* (1907). As a result, in the winter of 1907-1908, Braque painted the large *Standing Nude*, with its broken and tilting planes and parallel brush strokes. Because of Braque's discovery of Cézanne and Picasso, he now realized that his own approach to painting would be conceptual rather than perceptual. The Fauvist colors were forever gone in favor of subdued greens, browns, blues, and grays. Also, he raised or tilted his picture's view so as to cut out the horizon. His pictures appeared suspended and with multiple viewpoints. By 1908, he had established the grammar of cubism with its enclosed and definable spaces and still lifes done on interlocking planes. That year he painted what he called his first cubist picture, *Still Life with Musical Instruments*, in which the illusion of perspective has been eliminated by tilting the picture's plane like a solid wall until there is no horizon. The picture's curved and angular forms are rendered in ochers and greens. The picture is considered Braque's first unquestioned masterpiece.

When Braque submitted six of his L'Estaque paintings to the Salon d'Automne, the Fauvist jury rejected them. Matisse used the derisive word "cube," and the art critic Louis Vauxcelles borrowed this word in a review of Braque's new style: "He despises form and reduces everything, landscapes and figures and houses, to geometrical patterns, to cubes." Vauxcelles had unknowingly labeled the most important art movement of the twentieth century.

Life's Work

A new pictorial language had made its appearance, one of volume, tactility, enclosed space, and interlocking planes. One can see that Braque's lighthouses depicted on a flat plane in the painting *Harbor in Normandy* (1909), called "cubic oddities" by Vauxcelles, could have been salt and pepper shakers, and the picture itself is full of greens, buffs, and bluish-grays in a constructionist landscape where sea, land, and sky are fragmented and geometrical forms occur in a dense network of vertical, horizontal, and diagonal lines.

When Braque returned to Paris in the fall of 1909, his friendship with Picasso ripened, and together they developed "analytical" cubism. One of the earliest works illustrating this phase of Braque's development is *Guitar and Fruit Dish* (1909). It is both the last work in Braque's Cézannian period and the first in this phase. In this painting is the basic grammar of Cubism. Objects—musical instruments and fruits—are seen from all different angles simultaneously. All objects are brought to the very surface of the picture by the use of tilted planes. It is a work almost entirely in buff with some soft grays and a darker shade outlining each object. There is an immense scaffolding of diagonal lines built up of parallel brushstrokes which move from dark to light, and each flat surface slightly tilts. The lighting in this picture appears to be playing from several sources at once in a neutral color scheme, or grisaille palette. For the presence of all these elements, the term "analytical cubism" was coined by a fellow cubist, Juan Gris, to describe just such a painting of fragmented images as if these images were reflected in shattered glass.

In 1910, Braque executed two paintings to emphasize his two-dimensional interpretation of space through fragmentation and the "analysis" of the resulting volumes entitled *Violin and Pitcher* and *Violin and Palette*. Each painting is a highly vertical and slender arrangement of forms suspended from the top rather than built up from the bottom. In each, the instrument has been taken apart "analytically" and, then, reassembled from rectangular or irregularly shaped pieces. The instruments actually merge into the background. A nail complete with its shadow is painted at the very top as if to emphasize that the whole hangs suspended. The brushstrokes have been sharply reduced to short stabs, and the colors no longer have specifically descriptive functions.

In 1911, Braque's analytical phase reached high tide. It tended dangerously toward pure abstraction. For example, in such paintings as *The Portuguese*, almost entirely in buffs and black-grays, Braque dissociated both color from description and planes from physical volumes. Only the lettering "BAL" and some numbers save this picture from pure abstraction; there is no other way to reassemble the world except through these plain bits of reality. This painting is the Siamese twin of Picasso's *Ma Jolie* of the same year. Braque, like Picasso, was not interested in any abstract ideal; rather, he was opposed to it. Braque wanted to approach the real world and, thus, took steps to avoid complete abstraction. Hence, the "hermetic" phase of analytical cubism, from which the famous *The Portuguese* comes, remains the closest approach to abstraction for Braque, and this phase ended in 1911.

In the new "synthetic" cubism of 1912, Braque introduced more elements of reality while simultaneously simplifying structure. Along with lettering and numbers, Braque innovated with imitated wood paneling, marbling, cutout paper, and oilcloth, and added bits of sand, metal filings, sawdust, ash, or even tobacco to his paints for greater tactility. Already in the bottom left corner of *Homage to Bach* (1912), the first imitated wood paneling appears along with the lettering BACH and J. S. in the painting's center. It is a painting that is quite emptied of space and very flat. In the same year, in *Fruit Dish and Glass*, Braque used separate areas for a black charcoal drawing on white and extended over the pasted areas of wallpaper. Braque now totally dissociated color from form and made it entirely independent. Braque did additional works remarkable for their simplicity, penciled outlines, and charcoal lines forming a light scaffolding with some dark cutout areas, such as *Aria de Bach* (1913) or *Still Life with Playing Cards* (1913). In the latter painting, the black edge of a table, oak panels, and cards make a first showing in cubist iconography.

In 1914, Braque served in the French army and was seriously wounded. After convalescing, he began painting again in 1917. *The Musician* (1917), in which both form and color are dissociated, looks like a typical Gris or Picasso of that same period. By 1919, Braque was moving away from cubism, as in *Café-Bar*. In this work, Braque uses the three-dimensional technique of light areas for the table and dark areas for its background. It is painted mainly in greens with some sparse white, as in the lettering for which the picture is named. The picture is also noteworthy for its heavy black outlining of objects. This picture looked forward to the 1920's and 1930's, especially to the *guéridons* (pedestal tables), with their vertically arranged objects on high stands.

Braque's *guéridon* series, done from the 1920's through the 1940's, were paintings executed essentially in a high and narrow vertical format. They often use texture and color to enrich the sensuous tactility of the objects cluttering the high tables or mantles. In each of these paintings, the viewer's eyes follow the vertical line upward until it can look down at the clustered objects on the table or mantel—a bottle, fruit, a glass, a knife, and so forth. This double viewpoint is a quintessential Braquian technique. Braque's first painting in this series, *Le Guéridon* (1921-1922), shows a very shallow room with a flow of light brightening the colors. The green table is painted in a slender vertical fashion with its top tilted toward the plane of the picture where a series of white objects lie. The pedestal is a realistic and heavy yellow tripod, resting on a marble checkered floor. The viewer's eyes move upward from the thickish base to the musical score and the impasto-painted stringed instrument, even higher to the grapes and vase, and ever onward to a black folded screen, it would appear, just behind the table. This screen serves to amplify the curvature of various objects on the tabletop. The whole composition is surrounded by a sense of space. Part of the wall paneling recedes downward. In later paintings, Braque enlarged the interior space and used a sand and plaster mixture to obtain a grainy background, which he then covered thinly with paint applied in smooth plains so as to give the whole work the impact of a fresco.

His wartime *guéridons*, painted in occupied Paris, have a realistic tone and severity usually achieved by the simplicity of a few objects. His most popular wartime canvases are *Black Fish* (1942) and the austere *Interior: The Grey Table* (1942), which is also referred to as *Interior with Palette*. In these two magnificent paintings, the objects are now dispersed broadly across the horizontal plane of the picture. The depth of color determines each object's distance from the viewer. Braque lays two crossed fish along the horizontal plane on a grayish plate, which rests on a black table. On the left, balancing the black fish, are two pieces of fruit, one a dull orange and the other a soft yellow. The background wall has the long horizontal lines of rectangles and, acting as a counterpoint to the fish, black pictures in gray frames. *Interior: The Gray Table* is distinguished by rectilinear forms and two transparent volutes superimposed on the soft browns of the composition. Likewise, there are grays and greens laid over the picture's solid black background. In these two paintings, the force and elegance of simplicity mark the culmination of the entire *guéridon* series. An extension of the *guéridons* was a series of billiard tables emphasizing rectangular forms and focusing on the playing table from various angles simultaneously. The largest and most dazzling of the so-called billiards dates from 1947 to 1949 and shows a pinched table with flared raised ends done in lavish greens.

In 1949, Braque started his famous studio series, the apogee of his art. It is a series of eight large canvases that represent the metaphysical aspects of the artist's own studio. Each is meditative and atmospheric. The first is the most realistic and direct in design: A large white pitcher in the upper canvas stands in its own canvas against a black background and below it, to the left, is another smaller canvas with a black pitcher contrasted on the left beside a plate of fruit on a white tablecloth.

Braque's last works have an extreme simplicity of design and color, such as his birds for the ceiling in the Etruscan gallery of the Louvre or his *Doves* (1958). At the very end, he returned to the landscape theme of his youth. These are paintings such as *The Boat* (1958), *The Plough* (1959-1960), and *The Weeding Machine* (1961-1963). The last one was his final work. It is deeply impressionistic and atmospheric. The weeding machine stands deserted in the light and shadow of an approaching storm, and the sky is dotted with a small white cloud, as brown birds fly near the old weeder on the just-harvested field. It is a deeply nostalgic piece. Braque died on August 31, 1963, after completing this work.

Summary

Georges Braque rejected the notion of the realistic relationship between the actual and the painted object. Instead, he made it clear that the painted apple never was supposed to represent a real apple. Its reality, rather, was the fact that it is a painted apple and not a painting of an apple. This meant that a painting was the artist's two-dimensional interpretation of reality. Braque rejected the Renaissance notion of perspective, which gave the illusion of a third dimension to a flat surface. He did not want to create this false notion. Art, according to him, is an autonomous reality. Still lifes allowed Braque to limit his experimentation to a small number of objects but to know that range thoroughly. It was this purposeful limitation that determined his style. These still lifes became his microcosm of the universe and allowed him the use of familiar things in their own natural environment. From them he could create universal and archetypal shapes, particularly transforming birds into metaphysical creatures in flights of fancy to the world of imagination. In the end, he succeeded in making the simplest objects believable by lifting them from the ordinary and everyday to the signs and symbols of his own puristic art.

Bibliography

Braque, Georges. *Georges Braque*. Edited by Jean Leymarie. Munich: Prestel, 1988. This is an excellent work with important contributions by Carla Schulz-Hoffmann and Magdalena M. Moeller. Especially important is the analysis, painting by painting and in chronological order, of the main works of Braque. The color plates are magnificent.

Hope, Henry R. *Georges Braque*. New York: The Museum of Modern Art, 1949. This is one of the earliest and best monographs on Braque. Unfortunately, its color plates are of very poor quality. Nevertheless, its analysis of Braque's art forms the basis of all later criticism.

Leymarie, Jean. *Braque*. Translated by James Emmons. Cleveland: World Publishing, 1961. Leymarie is the French expert on Braque and knew the artist. His view of Braque's art gains from this acquaintance, because he was able to ask a very private and quiet person about important aspects of his art. The color plates are average.

Mullins, Edwin B. *The Art of Georges Braque*. New York: Harry N. Abrams, 1968. This is a thoughtful analysis of the man and the artist with reasonably good illustrations. The author's four digressions in chapters 6, 8, 10, and 11 are the best and most provocative parts of this book.

Richardson, John. *Georges Braque*. Harmondsworth, Middlesex, England: Penguin Books, 1959. This is the best introduction to Braque. It is brief and understandable and has many illustrations at the back, though of poor quality.

Zurcher, Bernard. *Georges Braque: Life and Work*. New York: Rizzoli, 1988. To date this is the best and most comprehensive work on Braque as man and artist. It is a rewarding reading in art appreciation, and its color plates are excellent. It approaches the artist's works in topical groups. Especially noteworthy is the inclusion and analysis of the artist's sketches.

Donald E. Davis

FERNAND BRAUDEL

Born: August 24, 1902; Lunéville, France
Died: November 28, 1985; Paris, France
Areas of Achievement: Historiography, geography, and social sciences
Contribution: Braudel expanded significantly the nature and scope of historical research by reintegrating history with the social and behavioral sciences and by devising a distinctive analytical theory and methodology to justify and make possible a major shift in the ways in which historical research was conducted.

Early Life

Fernand Braudel, born in a village in eastern France, received his early education in Paris, where his father taught mathematics in a secondary school and became a headmaster. Young Braudel's interest in history was first aroused by an instructor who taught the history of France as high drama. Later, at the Sorbonne in Paris, Braudel specialized in historical studies, partly as an adolescent revolt against his father's desire that he become a mathematician like himself. Braudel completed his undergraduate education in 1923, still undecided in his vocation.

Over the next decade (1923-1932), he taught history at the secondary level in French Algeria, following closely the prescribed curriculum based on the history of politics and of great men. Having decided as early as 1923 to pursue doctoral studies, Braudel chose as his dissertation topic the policies of the sixteenth century Spanish monarch Philip II. Subsequently, from 1935 to 1937, he taught at the University of São Paulo in Brazil.

Braudel's sojourn in the New World, coupled with his long residence in North Africa, contributed to a gradual broadening of the scope and focus of the dissertation topic. He found himself drawn increasingly to the history of the whole Mediterranean basin. The years 1927-1933 proved to be critical for the final transformation of Braudel's original concept. When in 1927 he informed the eminent French historian Lucien Febvre of his project on Phillip II, Febvre had responded: "Why not the Mediterranean *and* Philip II?" From this point, Braudel became aware that Philip II attracted him less and less, and the Mediterranean more and more.

Meanwhile, Febvre, with his renowned colleague Marc Bloch, had in 1929 founded in France a new historical journal, called *Annales*, devoted explicitly to countering the long-prevailing view of history as consisting primarily of politics and great men. The editors hoped to promote through their new journal the cultivation of what Bloch described as "all the sciences involved in the study of man and society," especially the interaction of history with sociology, economics, and geography. This is the vision of a new interdisciplinary approach to history that Braudel imbibed while still teaching in Algeria. Henceforth he sought consciously to transcend the political, diplomatic, and military focus of conventional narrative history. In the process he would become for a time the most influential historian in the Western world.

Life's Work

At first, however, Braudel was discouraged by the predominantly political and diplomatic character of the archival sources he found in Spain and elsewhere around the Mediterranean. He recalled vividly the deep satisfaction and joy he felt when in 1934 he discovered in the Dubrovnick archives in Yugoslavia the stuff of the new history he hoped to write. There were the names and precise routes of hundreds of commercial ships, along with their cargoes, the prices of the various commodities, and associated details of maritime commerce ranging over most of the sixteenth century. In these masses of economic and social data, Braudel says, he "saw the Mediterranean of the sixteenth century for the first time." To duplicate these and similar documents elsewhere, he had adapted an old motion picture camera to provide him with up to three thousand manuscript pages a day. This is the first known use of the microfilm technique for scholarly purposes.

By the fall of 1939, Braudel, having mastered the sources necessary to complete his task, had devised a full outline of a panoramic study of the Mediterranean in the sixteenth century. Before he could begin the writing, however, the horrors of World War II enveloped most of Europe, including his native France. Mobilized as an officer in the French army, Braudel was captured early in 1940 and found himself confined for the remainder of the conflict in a German prisoner-of-war camp. It was partly to distance himself from the bitter reality of the fate of France and partly to occupy the long hours of forced inactivity that Braudel decided to write his history of the Mediterranean.

Over the five years of his imprisonment, Braudel wrote slowly, from memory, without a single note, the first draft of the book. While this feat was remarkable by any standard, he had immersed himself in the archival and other sources of his great subject and pushed the project doggedly to completion. Released at war's end, in 1945, Braudel polished his draft, filled in the references, and in 1947 submitted the result to the Sorbonne to satisfy the requirements for the doctorate in history. It was published in 1949 in two volumes under the title *La Méditerranée et la monde méditerranéen à l'époque de Philippe II* (*The Mediterranean and the Mediterranean World in the Age of Philip II*, 1972). Twenty-six years had elapsed from conception to completion of the project.

The book was immediately hailed as a masterpiece of historical scholarship, the closest and most impressive realization thus far of the *Annales* ideal of a "total history" that sought to encompass all the major facets of human experience. Braudel's originality lay not only in his formulation of a new paradigm for understanding human history but also in his coining of a special terminology to express his insights.

In *The Mediterranean and the Mediterranean World in the Age of Philip II*, Braudel distinguished three main levels or layers of temporal experience to be found in history: the geographic, the socioeconomic, and the individual. Of these he clearly regarded the geographic component as most important. Braudel described this "geohistorical" layer as consisting essentially of the enduring major physical features of the Mediterranean basin: its mountains, plains, valleys, climate, and, above all, the great sea itself. Change in these phenomena was only very gradual, almost imperceptible, over millennia. The "long duration" that characterized the temporal dimension of these environmental factors effectively dwarfed the particular human activities that occurred in and around the Mediterranean, including the political and military conflicts of Spain's Philip II with the Turkish sultan in the sixteenth century.

A second, more superficial, level of temporal experience lay for Braudel in slow-changing economic and social movements, rhythmic patterns discernible in human "economies, societies, and civilizations" that formed, in turn, collective trends of "intermediate duration," able to be reckoned in cycles of five to fifty years and more. Finally, like "crests of foam on the waves" were the comparatively short-term events of conventional political and diplomatic history, the transient phenomena of daily life that depended for their significance on the broader geohistorical and socioeconomic contexts within which they occurred.

Braudel defined the relationship among the principal temporal levels of his paradigm as a dialectic process marked by the continual interaction of the natural and human dimensions of experience. The fundamental problem, in his view, was "how to convey simultaneously both the surface history [of events] that holds our attention by its continual dramatic changes and that other, submerged history."

The history that Braudel described in his book on the Mediterranean world took place at three distinct hierarchical levels, of which the most meaningful by far was the deep structural base composed of the geographic and climatic features complemented by the socioeconomic cycles and other patterns found in human societies and subject to quantitative analysis. He consistently minimized the significance of the third level of individual people and events, regarding them as locked inexorably within the iron frame of their physical and socioeconomic environments. Braudel alludes to this determinist theme in the concluding words of the book: "When I think of the individual I . . . see him imprisoned within a destiny in which he . . . has little hand. . . . In historical analysis . . . the long run always wins in the end."

This was the chief conclusion that Braudel conveyed to his readers and especially to dozens of younger scholars coming to professional maturity after mid-century. After 1950, he deepened and extended his thesis through further publications as well as in seminars conducted at the College of France in Paris, where he assumed an endowed professorship in history. In 1956, Braudel succeeded Lucien Febvre as president of the prestigious "Sixth Section" (history) of the School of Higher Studies (École Pratique des Hautes Études). The following year he became sole editor of the journal *Annales*. These positions not only assured a permanent institutional base for the new French history but also placed Braudel at the very center of it over the next quarter century and beyond. His reputation and influence spread across the Western world. He was elected to the French Academy in 1984.

Braudel's other major work was a social and economic history of the world from the late Middle Ages to the Industrial Revolution. He entitled this trilogy *Civilisation matérielle et capitalisme, XV-XVIII siècle* (1967-1979; *Civilization and Capitalism, Fifteenth to Eighteenth Century*, 1982-1984). In it he traced the gradual emergence of the market economy of modern capitalism out of the age-old agricultural subsistence economy of the Middle Ages. He left unfinished at his death a history of France.

Summary

Fernand Braudel's most notable achievements lie not only in the theory and methodology of his approach to history but also in the institutional base that he provided for the *Annales* movement that he personified for nearly two generations. Braudel sought to reenergize historical studies by effecting a fresh synthesis of the perspectives and methods of history with those of related disciplines such as sociology, economics, and human geography. He was convinced that the resulting cross-fertilization would allow historians to deepen and enliven their understanding of the past, far beyond the narrow political and diplomatic frame of "great events" history.

Closely related to this belief is Braudel's contention that the standard descriptive history of persons and events can be meaningful only against the backdrop of the environmental structures that surround it. It is the mountains, the oceans, and the long-term patterns of climate that shape and constrain human life with binding force across the centuries, effectively supplanting the human agent as the chief element in social explanation. Braudel considered his most important innovation to be the uncompromising shift away from the individual and the event of short-term history through primary concentration on the long and intermediate perspectives.

Finally, Braudel, in advocating a "total" or "global" history, extended permanently the scale of the historical enterprise, in space as well as time, in methodology as well as subject matter. He urged historians to take for their proper study not only human life in all its rich diversity but also, in particular, the close analysis of those large impersonal forces of history that most affected the human condition. In the process, and above all through his majestic history of the Mediterranean, Braudel profoundly changed the ways in which students of the human past now approach their subject.

Bibliography
Braudel, Fernand. *The Mediterranean and the Mediterranean World in the Age of Phillip II.* 2 vols. New York: Harper & Row, 1972. Translated by Siân Reynolds. The classic work on which, above all, the *Annales* paradigm of history rests. Any serious attempt at assessing Braudel's achievement as historian should begin here.

—————. "Personal Testimony." *Journal of Modern History* 45 (Fall, 1972): 448-467. Braudel's own account of the genesis of his historical theories. Particularly illuminating for the early career and the strong encouragement he received from his friend and mentor Febvre.

Cannon, John, ed. *The Historian at Work.* London: Allen & Unwin, 1980. Contains a clear, very informative discussion of the leading features of Braudel's thesis by the noted British social historian Peter Burke. Most valuable for the careful examination of the more serious criticisms leveled against Braudel.

Hexter, Jack. *On Historians: Some Reappraisals of the Masters of Modern Historiography.* Cambridge, Mass.: Harvard University Press, 1978. A probing, detailed analysis of Braudel's leading ideas and contributions to the "new history" by an eminent American scholar. Balances a thorough critique with full appreciation of what Braudel achieved. The best brief examination of the subject in English.

Iggers, Georg G. *New Directions in European Historiography.* Rev. ed. Middletown, Conn.: Wesleyan University Press, 1984. Sets Braudel's achievement firmly in the context of the vigorous intellectual debates on the nature of history and society that flourished at the turn of the century. Traces the specific influences on Braudel's thought.

Stoianovich, Traian. *French Historical Method: The Annales Paradigm.* Foreword by Fernand Braudel. Ithaca, N.Y.: Cornell University Press, 1976. The major work in English on the *Annales* theory of history. Braudel's work receives major attention throughout. A generally sympathetic account by an American scholar with close ties to the *Annales* school.

Wallerstein, Immanuel. "Braudel." In *Twentieth Century Supplement: Encyclopedia of World Biography,* edited by David Essenberger, vol. 13. Palatine, Ill.: Jack Heraty, 1987. A brief biographical essay on Braudel that sums up the major events of his life and highlights his historical theories. Includes a short list of recommended reading.

Donald Sullivan

BERTOLT BRECHT

Born: February 10, 1898; Augsburg, Germany
Died: August 14, 1956; East Berlin, East Germany
Area of Achievement: Literature
Contribution: Brecht is generally considered not only Germany's leading dramatist but also one of the central influences on Western theater since World War II.

Early Life

Even though Eugen Berthold (later Bertolt) Brecht composed several ballads in his early twenties that told of his having been descended from shrewd, ruthless, guileful peasants, his genealogy was solidly middle-class and could be traced back to the sixteenth century. His father, Berthold Friedrich Brecht, was the managing director of a paper mill in Augsburg, a sleepy town of ninety thousand, forty miles northwest of Munich. He was Catholic, and his wife Sophie was Protestant; both Berthold and his younger brother, Walter, were reared in their mother's faith and primarily by her—the father was a workaholic. Brecht's boyhood and adolescence were marked by self-confidence, quick-mindedness, cunning, and vitality—all characteristics that stood him in good stead throughout his life. His skill in manipulating people and suppleness in pursuing his goals were also evident from his youth.

During World War I, Brecht began medical studies at the University of Munich to delay an early conscription; however, the only medical lectures he attended were those dealing with venereal diseases. Instead, he studied theater history with a Professor Artur Kutscher and made an idol of Frank Wedekind, who not only wrote notorious, Expressionistic plays advocating sexual liberation but also composed and sang ballads with aggressive bravado. Imitating Wedekind, Brecht created and bawled out his own ballads, performing in the coffeehouses and cabarets of Munich. In 1918, he wrote his first play, *Baal* (English translation, 1963), about an amoral bohemian bard-balladeer who cruelly exploits and then discards friends and lovers of both sexes. Baal's only care is for the natural world, whose beauty he celebrates in rawly eloquent lyrics. That same year Brecht began writing *Trommeln in der Nacht* (*Drums in the Night*, 1961), a powerful pacifist drama whose protagonist is a disillusioned veteran returning to a Berlin dominated by war profiteers.

Perhaps the best of Brecht's early works was *Im Dickicht der Städte* (1923; *In the Jungle of Cities*, 1961), in which two men engage in a seemingly motiveless duel of wills. Shlink, a Malaysian lumber dealer, seeks to buy Garga's soul but is himself shown to be a victim—one whose skin has been so toughened by life that he can no longer feel; he stages his battle with Garga to penetrate his own shell of indifference.

Life's Work

Moving to Berlin in 1924, Brecht became a celebrated personality in that city's culturally brilliant postwar jungle. He shortened his first name to "Bert" and established for himself a part-intellectual, part-proletarian persona. His trademarks were a seminarian's tonsorial haircut, steel-rimmed spectacles, two days' growth of beard, a leather jacket, a trucker's cap, a cheap but large cigar, and chronic rudeness. People found him either charismatic or repulsive; many women found him irresistible. He charmed the beautiful singer-actress Marianne Zoff in the early 1920's. They married in November, 1922, had a daughter in 1923 but separated that year, and divorced in 1927. Brecht was to have many mistresses, of whom the most cherished were Elisabeth Hauptmann, Margarete Steffin, and Ruth Berlau.

The most significant woman in Brecht's life was the Vienna-born actress Helene Weigel, who was Jewish, strongly Marxist, and staunchly feminist. They met in 1923, married in 1929, and had a son, Stefan, in 1924 and a daughter, Barbara, in 1930. Weigel's marvelously expressive face and superbly disciplined acting skills caused many theater critics to consider her the finest actress of her time on the German-speaking stage. Her greatest successes were in the title roles of Brecht's *Die Mutter* (1932; *The Mother*, 1965) and *Mutter Courage und ihre Kinder* (1940; *Mother Courage and Her Children*, 1941).

A central problem for students of Brecht is his adherence to Communism and its effect on his work. What is clear enough is that, from youth on, he revolted against the middle-class values that led Germany to a wasteful war, bitter defeat, extreme socioeconomic disorder in the 1920's, and the National Socialist ascension to power, under Adolf Hitler, by the early 1930's. What is also certain is that Brecht read Karl Marx's writings with close attention in the middle-to-late 1920's. What attracted him to Marxism was largely its hostility to the selfishness and arrogance of Germany's business and military circles. The anarchic individualist in him delighted in this bitter opposition to the ruling classes, and, though Brecht's membership in the Party remains uncertain—did he join it in 1930? later? never?—one cannot doubt his commitment to Marxism from the late 1920's until his death. His adherence to Communism remained, nevertheless, consistently idiosyncratic and equally indigestible to the official Soviet cultural apparatus, to the House Committee on Un-American Activities (before which he testified on October 30, 1947), and to the rigid party-liners who ran East Germany after World War II.

What does seem fundamental to Brecht's vision and work is his derisive, cynical perspective on human nature. He is fascinated by human cruelty and sharklike bestiality, often depicting man as a predator motivated chiefly by his economic needs. Should a Brechtian character speak of love, loyalty, friendship, honor, progress, or religion, the chances are that he is merely masking a corrupt deal. Brecht's Joan of Arc is an evangelical Salvation Army lassie in *Die heilige Johanna der Schlachthöfe* (1931; *Saint Joan of the Stockyards*, 1956). She tries to soften the heart of a Chicago meat magnate (well-named Pierpont Mauler) toward the plight of exploited stockyard workers; he tries to convince her of their alleged wickedness. In the end, starved and dying, sold out by her organization, she converts to the class struggle: "Those who are below are kept below/ so that those above may stay above/ and the vileness of those above is measureless."

In his best plays, Brecht manages to rise above his mixture of cynicism-cum-Communism. In *Der gute Mensch von Sezuan* (1938-1940; *The Good Woman of Setzuan*, 1948), the heroine, Shen Te, is naturally loving, kindly, selfless, and motherly; she fulfills herself by giving and thrives on sharing her feelings and goods. Unfortunately for her, the world repays her virtues with greed, betrayal, envy, spite, and ruthless exploitation. Hence, she must with increasing frequency call on the services of her calculating male "cousin," Shui Ta, who meets the world on its own level of meanness and deception. Shui Ta turns out to be Shen Te masked, the other half of her personality that she needs to protect her interests, yet also the half that denies Shen Te her essential identity.

Brecht's persistent return to characters of goodness, compassion, and vulnerability is perhaps illustrated in another parable play, *Der kaukasische Kreidekreis* (1944-1945; *The Caucasian Chalk Circle*, 1948). Its coprotagonists are Gruscha, a kitchen maid in the mansion of a rich governor in Russian Georgia, and Azdàk, an alcoholic village scribe. Both perform impulsive deeds of kindness: Gruscha adopts the abandoned son of the governor's wife when she flees during an uprising: Azdàk shelters a grand duke who has become an abject refugee in the same revolution. The scampish Azdàk is rewarded with a judgeship, which enables him to render verdicts combining the biting wit of Groucho Marx with the proletarian bias of Karl Marx. In the concluding courtroom scene, Azdàk awards Gruscha permanent custody of the boy, then flees the powerful vengeance of the boy's birth mother. His brief days of judgeship are celebrated in a closing ballad as a "Golden Age when there was almost justice"—as happy a period, Brecht indicates, as man can realistically achieve in a society plagued by the defeat of decency.

In *Mother Courage and Her Children*, his most famous work, Brecht seeks to present a relentlessly Marxist indictment of the economic causes of war. In the drama's atmosphere of rape, pillage, and meaningless murder, where Protestants and Catholics slaughter one another in the Thirty Years' War, all human ideals degenerate into hypocritical cant, while heroism shatters into splinters of cruelty, madness, greed, or absurdity. The protagonist, owner of a canteen wagon who follows the close-to-endless war, is a shameless profiteer who cashes in on the troops' needs for alcohol and clothes;

repeatedly she is called "a hyena of the battlefield."

Leben des Galilei (first version wr. 1938-1939; *Life of Galileo*, 1947) is in some respects a companion piece to *Mother Courage and Her Children*. Both dramas have protagonists who, like their creator, are egotistic opportunists, canny, shrewd, sometimes unheroic, and consistently self-divided. Brecht's Galileo is not only a self-indulgent sensualist who loves to gorge himself with food and wine but also a masterly researcher and teacher, an intellectual locksmith picking at encrustated concepts as he elucidates his proof that the earth revolves around the sun. After the nuclear explosions over Hiroshima and Nagasaki, Brecht revised Galileo's last long speech so that he would revile himself (that is, physics) for having failed to fulfill his/ its duty to society, by having recanted his discoveries in fear of the Inquisition.

This altered ending may carry an autobiographical charge: The Galileo who lashes himself for his cowardice and lack of integrity may also be Brecht condemning himself for his foxy, slippery ethics. After all, Brecht usually put self-interested opportunism ahead of all other values. He spent his last years living affluently in East Berlin, presented by the Communist regime with his own theatrical company, the Berliner Ensemble, and with virtually unlimited time and means to stage his own plays. Concurrently, he was shrewd enough to place the copyright of his works with a West German publisher, to provide himself with ample Western currency and to obtain Austrian citizenship so he could travel freely to and from the East. Like Galileo, Brecht insists on defying easy categories of understanding.

Summary

Like his greatest characters—Shen Te, Gruscha, Azdàk, Courage, Galileo—Bertolt Brecht was a survivor. He survived fifteen years of exile in the 1930's and 1940's; he survived harrowing stresses of migration, poverty, personal crises, grubby internecine rivalries, the whole bitter pathos of Hitler's demonic enmity to culture and Joseph Stalin's betrayal of left-wing idealism. Wherever he was, however sour his circumstances, he managed to pour out an impressive volume of distinguished plays, poems, and provocative essays on dramaturgy at full pressure. Like his literary/scientific alter ego, Galileo, he employed his sly tenacity to persist in his work.

No theatrical practice since Henrik Ibsen's, August Strindberg's, and Anton Chekhov's has achieved as many masterpieces as that of Brecht: *The Good Woman of Setzuan*, *The Caucasian Chalk Circle*, *Mother Courage and Her Children*, and *Galileo* are assuredly among modernism's dramatic peaks. The brilliant waywardness of *Baal*, profundity of *In the Jungle of Cities*, and poignancy of *Saint Joan of the Stockyards* are not far behind. Brecht's only rival for reigning as the leading Western playwright of the middle and late twentieth century is Samuel Beckett.

Bibliography

Bentley, Eric. *The Brecht Commentaries, 1943-1980*. New York: Grove Press, 1981. Bentley is both the leading American drama scholar and the leading authority on Brecht in the United States. This anthology of his essays assembles articles from various periodicals, from several other Bentley books, and introductions to several plays.

Demetz, Peter, ed. *Brecht: A Collection of Critical Essays*. Englewood Cliffs, N.J.: Prentice-Hall, 1962. This collection, in the distinguished Twentieth Century Views series, includes several articles translated from the German and concerns itself with Brecht's poetry and theories of drama as well as his plays.

Esslin, Martin. *Brecht: The Man and His Work*. Garden City, N.Y.: Doubleday, 1960. Esslin is a solid and diligent scholar who has assembled an enormous amount of information which he organizes clearly. Particularly valuable is a long reference section which includes a descriptive list of virtually all Brechtian works, a comprehensive bibliography, and a detailed list of all productions of Brecht's plays in the United States up to the time of his death.

Hayman, Ronald. *Brecht: A Biography*. New York: Oxford University Press, 1983. Hayman's text is painstaking and comprehensively researched. While valuable for its multitude of facts, this book unfortunately blurs the dimensions of Brecht's complex character and is generally unable to bring much light to an understanding of his works.

Lyons, Charles R. *Bertolt Brecht: The Despair and the Polemic*. Carbondale: Southern Illinois University Press, 1968. While Lyons' style is sometimes opaque, he does demonstrate a trenchantly perceptive understanding of the Brechtian dramas he closely analyzes.

Gerhard Brand

ANDRÉ BRETON

Born: February 19, 1896; Tinchebray, France
Died: September 28, 1966; Paris, France
Area of Achievement: Literature
Contribution: A novelist, poet, and founder of the Surrealist movement,
Breton embodied the principle that the imagination is the center of man's
definition of reality and that his creativity must be permitted to emerge
unencumbered by the constraints of logic and reason.

Early Life

André Breton was born in Tinchebray, Normandy, on February 19, 1896.
His family came, though, from Brittany and Lorraine, and he spent his youth
in Lorient on the Brittany coast. In 1907, he was sent to the prestigious
Lycée Chaptal in Paris, from which he was graduated in 1912. His parents
then sent him to the University of Paris to begin his medical studies. Although he was a respectable student, his interests lay elsewhere, specifically
in the latest productions of the emerging modernist poets such as Arthur
Rimbaud, Le Comte de Lautréamont, Paul Valéry, and especially Guillaume
Apollinaire. His formal medical studies were interrupted by World War I,
and he found himself serving in the ambulance corps and the neuropsy-
chiatric wards for the war-injured in Nantes, at Saint-Dizier in the Marne
and at the Val-de-Grâce in Paris, where he became an intern.

Three important events happened to Breton during these difficult times.
One was his participation in the trauma of the war in which he witnessed the
slaughter of young men and their precipitation into "a cloaca of blood,
stupidity, and mud." The other was his meeting with two men who became
seminal influences in not only the direction of his professional life but also,
more important, the formation of his general attitudes toward life itself. The
first important influence on Breton was his meeting the poet-dramatist whom
he most admired, Apollinaire. Indeed, Breton became this young poet's
protégé in spite of the fact that Apollinaire lay wounded and dying as a result
of his war injuries. Although a leading avant-garde figure, Apollinaire tried
to move the young Breton away from his innate pessimistic view of life and
encouraged him to examine the philosophical relationship between poetry
and painting. He also helped him to view the commonplace as an avenue to
adventure by encouraging him to walk randomly the streets of Paris.

The other major influence was Jacques Vaché, who could not have been
more different from Apollinaire. Vaché was another young soldier dying in a
hospital as much from wounds received in battle as from his addiction to
drugs and alcohol. He urged the young Breton not only to become more
pessimistic but also to approach the absurdity of life with iconoclastic scorn
and ridicule; the only approach to the lunacies of the world, according to

Vaché, is violence. Vaché became for Breton the embodiment of nihilistic self-destruction, an image that haunted him for the remainder of his life. Apollinaire became a precursor to Surrealism. In fact Breton first heard the word "Surrealist" in Apollinaire's play *Les Mamelles de Tirésias* (1918; *The Breasts of Tiresias*, 1961) and used it as the name of the movement he founded in memory of Apollinaire. Vaché became the embodiment and, in a sense, a precursor of the Dada movement even before its inception.

Besides the major influences of these two men, Breton, as a medical doctor and psychiatric student, studied the psychological works of both Jean-Martin Charcot and Pierre Janet. Charcot's studies of hysteria became primary texts for the Surrealists in their search for valid expressions of the unconscious, while Janet's work in automatic writing became a channel of therapy and a medium of exploring the deepest parts of the psyche. Janet, who was one of Carl Jung's teachers, treated the writing process as a medium or mediator between the conscious and the unconscious but only if logical rationality were sublimated. Once the logical was deactivated, real progress could be made into the world of dreams, and the energies of the primordial imagination could be tapped.

As a result of the influence of Janet's pioneering studies in automatic writing, Breton and the young writer Philippe Soupault wrote the first pre-Surrealist automatic text, *Les Champs magnétiques* (1921; magnetic fields), a work that purported to use Rimbaud's "derangement of the senses"— without using drugs or alcohol—in permitting random expressions to form themselves into their own kind or order. The imagination had to be left completely free and open so the hand could write whatever the words dictated, an exercise that Rimbaud called the "alchemy of the Word." They published their findings in a journal they founded called *Littérature*, using that word in an ironic sense because the texts they published challenged conventional literature of all kinds. With the publication of *Les Champs magnétiques* in his Surrealist journal Breton took full command of the formulation and development of the Surrealist movement, a movement that revolutionized both the writing and the visual arts and brought them into the modern era.

Life's Work

Although Breton and his disciples became briefly enamored of the emerging Dadaist movement founded by the charismatic Tristan Tzara, the Surrealists disapproved of the Dadaist's brand of nihilism primarily because they did not view the imagination as the sacred source and energizing force of human expression, an expression that could only take place once the life-denying force of logical reasoning was displaced. The Dadaists proved too iconoclastic and negative for the serious artists of the Surrealist movement. They preferred to record their automatic writing in perfectly correct syntax;

the world, not the sentence, was in need of an enfreshened vision.

To clarify the distinction between the aims and purposes of the Dada movement and the Surrealist project, Breton set down in writing in 1924 the text that subsequently made him famous, *Manifeste du surréalisme* (1924; *Manifesto of Surrealism*, 1969). In this document, he articulated in marvelous aphoristic maxims the major tenets of the movement whose enemy was rationalistic constraint of any kind. Reason had led mankind to the brink of planetary destruction and had to be replaced with methods and techniques that possessed the ability to tap the energies of the unconscious, the seat of the imaginal realm, and release its healing powers. What is most important, the vehicles for entering into that realm were automatic writing and the dream world. From 1924 on, Breton took formal control of the Surrealist movement he had founded, publicly defending its philosophical and aesthetic purposes and procedures and producing works that adhered to its principles with dogmatic consistency.

With the publication of the *Manifesto of Surrealism*, Surrealism became not only the first anti-intellectual intellectual movement but also, and more important, a way of life for the select members of his coterie, which included such writers as Louis Aragon, Paul Éluard, Antonin Artaud, Robert Desnos, and Benjamin Crevet. Many notable artists also participated in the strange exercises that Breton devised to help them free themselves from the chains of logical training. These activities consisted of, besides automatic writing, dream interpretation and transcription, hypnosis, aleatory (random) walking through the streets of Paris, psychic automatism in both painting and writing, and attempts at accurate simulation of verbal communication of the insane. Some of these artists eventually attained worldwide fame and became synonymous with the avant-garde of the 1920's and 1930's: Max Ernst, Salvador Dalí, René Magritte, Marc Chagall, Mata, and Yves Tanguy among others. For writers and painters alike, these spiritual exercises became attempts on their part to return to a form of radical innocence that viewed the world with a childlike sense of the marvelous. The purpose of such Surrealist activities was a revitalization and recuperation of the redemptive powers of the imagination that had been displaced by the abstractions of rationality. They viewed the imagination not as the opposite of the real but, rather, as its center.

Breton himself began a series of books that demonstrated his absolute adherence to these principles and beliefs. Surrealism may be a composite of a number of mysterious traditions, but there is no question that Breton was reformulating also the basic tenets of Romanticism at its most basic level— that is, that human utterance and expression, unencumbered by societal rules, is at all times "truth" in its purest form. So-called objective truth is a fiction, and the only truth available since Immanuel Kant's *Kritik der reinen Vernunft* (1781; *The Critique of Pure Reason*, 1838) is subjective truth.

Breton began a six-year unsuccessful flirtation with Communism that ended in the mid-1930's. His first major text, *Nadja* (English translation, 1960), appeared in 1928. The work is unapologetically autobiographical; it studiously avoids plot in any traditional sense. Indeed, Breton hoped that new works such as *Nadja* would destroy the traditional novel, which nurtured logical and naturalistic techniques and overly descriptive styles. The technique used not only in this novel but also in his other three major prose works is that of the interior monologue. The autobiographical elements are portrayed by actual photographs of sites where the action takes place. He used photographs because he wanted to eliminate any form of extraneous description. He also wanted to rid his novels, as he states in his first *Manifesto of Surrealism*, of all situations that do not directly influence the destinies of the characters' souls or the meaning of their lives.

Breton's next prose works, *Les Vases communicants* (1932; communicating vessels) and *L'Amour fou* (1937; mad love), explore further and in more detail the topics that he had theoretically proposed in the first *Manifesto of Surrealism*. In *Les Vases communicants*, Breton analyzes his own dreams and their relationship to the waking state in the hope of establishing some sort of "conducting wire" between them. For him the unconscious and its spokesman, the dream, do not consist of bipolar opposites or mutually exclusive polarities. The dream establishes a relationship or communication between the interior and exterior worlds, extinguishing dichotomies such as "real" and "imagined" or "subject" and "object."

In *L'Amour fou*, Breton continues his journey into the possibilities that life offers him and their relationship with what he calls "objective chance." He finds, by chance, the great love of his life, Jacqueline, who in real life was Jacqueline Lamba, who became Breton's second wife and mother of his only child, Aube. These forces of the marvelous depicted in this trilogy of antinovels were consistently favorable toward its searching protagonist, Breton. Indeed, the energies of the unconscious as presented by Surrealist artists were usually benign, whereas the Dadaists preferred to demonstrate their destructive and nightmarish aspects, a philosophical orientation that separated these two schools early in their development.

In *Arcane 17* (1944), Breton moved from Europe to western Canada, specifically the Gaspé Peninsula. He attempted to play down any novelistic techniques in this work and stressed a documentary format intermingled with fairly obvious mythological patterns. Elisa Bindhoff, the woman whom Breton subsequently married, is viewed as a modern embodiment of the Celtic Goddess, Melusine, but she also mirrors his own alienated condition from his European roots. This antinovel is Breton's most alchemical work and takes its title from the seventeenth card of the Hebraic-Egyptian tarot pack representing the reign of love and intelligence that takes place after the fall of Lucifer. This is Breton's most consciously mystical book, but his mysticism is grounded in the optimism of the redemptive and transfigurative power of love itself, the greatest of all mysteries. Love, as embodied in the form of Melusine-Elisa, succeeds in the alchemical reconciliation of opposites, turning darkness into light by its power. Ironically, the years in which this strange work was written were not only his own but also Western civilization's darkest.

True to Breton's penchant for formulating his philosophical ideas prior to specifying them in his literary work, his *Second Manifeste du surréalisme* (1930; *Second Manifesto of Surrealism*, 1969) had reoriented his prose works toward conception of the world as a monistic entity rather than a battleground of dualistic, or bipolar, opposites. In the *Second Manifesto of Surrealism*, he quite consciously sought models or analogies taken from classic studies of the occult and the alchemical, as Jung himself had done in the mid-1930's. Indeed, his poetry had always presented love as the unifying point of vision and desire, but it is in his later and more structured long poems that clearly articulated alchemical motifs are used as both metaphors and physical entities. In *L'Union libre* (1931; *Free Union*, 1982), *L'Air de l'eau* (1934; the air of water), and *Fata Morgana* (1941; English translation, 1982), he intermixes romantic-erotic love and the four elements into a hermetic-alchemical text that only the initiates of love can decipher.

In his last major poem, *Ode à Charles Fourier* (1947; *Ode to Charles Fourier*, 1970), he moved away from the difficult hermetic texts of the war years and turned toward the figure of the Utopian sociologist Fourier as an example of a conciliator of opposites in a very literal sense. He also abandoned his adherence to free verse and unashamedly produced an ode, which he justified by stating that its subject, Fourier, was worthy of such a dignified literary form. After the war, Breton returned to France and found himself hopelessly out of style and replaced by the dark existentialism of Albert Camus and Jean-Paul Sartre. His brand of optimism and Romanticism held little or no interest for a Europe that had been nearly decimated by the war and the holocaust.

Summary

Although renowned for his many innovative prose manifestos and anti-novelistic novels, André Breton will be remembered most for founding the last clearly defined artistic and literary movement, Surrealism. He is certainly one of the last great spiritual leaders in the history of Western aesthetics. In short, his philosophical works, novels, and poems became artistic embodiments of the theoretical discoveries of two of the twentieth century's most original thinkers, Sigmund Freud and Carl Jung. His application of automatic writing and dream material evolved directly from Freud's pioneering research into the unconscious, while his later attempts at an archetypal and alchemical reconciliation of opposites and a redefinition of reality as a monistic entity rather than a dualistic contest were a direct result of Jung's lifelong study of occultism and alchemy.

Because of Breton's influence on virtually all the major visual artists and many writers of the 1920's and 1930's and their utilization and adaptation of the principles of Surrealism as a viable aesthetic program, the entire intellectual thrust of Western thought was redirected away from the cold abstractions of logical positivism and reformulated according to a new and deeper consideration of the tenets of Romanticism. Because of Breton, the imagination as central to man's attempt to define reality was once again restored to its primary position.

Bibliography

Balakian, Anna. *André Breton: Magus of Surrealism*. New York: Columbia University Press, 1971. The most intelligent, comprehensive, and scholarly treatment of Breton's entire career. Balakian treats all aspects of Breton's intellectual and spiritual development, stressing his romantic roots and orientation. Her superb explication of the highly complex hermetic-alchemical motifs in his later work are especially helpful. All of the French quotations are translated.

Caws, Mary Ann. *André Breton*. New York: Twayne, 1971. Caws brings the full force of her considerable intelligence to bear on Breton alone in this work. Though not as philosophically acute as Balakian, her emphasis on practical analysis of individual works makes this book an excellent beginner's text. The French is ably translated into readable English.

_____. *Surrealism and the Literary Imagination: A Study of Breton and Bachelard*. The Hague: Mouton, 1966. Caws' study is limited because it stresses the literary and philosophical affinities between these two intellectual giants so that only their common interests are highlighted. The advantage to this approach is that her perceptive comments on Bachelard often uncover aspects of Breton normally left unexamined. The French texts are left untranslated.

Gershman, Herbert S. *The Surrealist Revolution in France*. Ann Arbor: University of Michigan Press, 1969. The treatment of Breton is not flattering, but Gershman does place him within an intellectual context. His history is accurate and his discussions of the aesthetics and philosophical underpinnings of Surrealism are cogent.

Matthews, J. H. *André Breton*. New York: Columbia University Press, 1967. Although very short, this book pulls together in a very readable way a coherent reading of Breton's major prose and poetry. Matthews places Breton within a tradition of Romantic and modernist aesthetics and presents him as a genuine hero of the modern sensibility.

Patrick Meanor

JOSEF BREUER

Born: January 15, 1842; Vienna, Austria
Died: June 20, 1925; Vienna, Austria
Areas of Achievement: Psychiatry, physiology, and medicine
Contribution: Breuer was one of the foremost physiologists of the nineteenth century and made major contributions to the understanding of the process of respiration and the function of the inner ear. Yet he is remembered primarily for his discovery of the cathartic or "talking out" method of treating neurotic disorders, a discovery that led, through Sigmund Freud, to the development of psychoanalysis.

Early Life

Josef Breuer was born at a time when the Jews of Eastern Europe were beginning to reap the fruits of their emancipation from years of social and political oppression. Josef felt deeply indebted to his father, Leopold, and others like him who, through replacing Yiddish with standard German and the customs of the Eastern ghettos with the culture of the Western world, effected the assimilation of the Jewish population. Leopold, a teacher of religion who also wrote a much-used religious textbook, obtained an appointment from the official Jewish Community of Vienna in 1836. Josef was born into this milieu in the year 1842.

Breuer's mother died during the birth of his younger brother, so the role of mother was assumed by his grandmother. He did not attend public school but was tutored at home by his father and was able to read perfectly at the age of four. When he was eight, he entered the *Gymnasium* and enjoyed his eight years of study there, especially the higher grades, in which intellectual curiosity and critical thinking were encouraged. Breuer's critical or skeptical turn of mind would become evident later in his departure from orthodox Judaism and his adoption of more liberal Jewish views.

For quite some time prior to his graduation in 1858, he had been planning to become a physician, and in 1859 he entered the medical school of the University of Vienna. Breuer's interests during his first year of medical studies centered on chemistry and anatomy, but during his second year he discovered his lifelong love, physiology. The emerging interests and skills of the budding physiologist blossomed under the tutelage of Ernst Brücke, in whose laboratory Sigmund Freud would also spend formative years in physiological and histological research. Breuer received his medical degree in 1867 and in the following year married Matilda Altmann; they had five children.

Life's Work

Immediately after his graduation from medical school, Breuer became an assistant in the clinic of Johann Oppolzer, a Viennese internist whom Breuer came to admire and to emulate. When Oppolzer died in 1871, Breuer resigned his position and went into private practice. During this period, Breuer also made his first historic contribution to the study of physiology. He had been conducting research on the self-regulation of respiration at the Josephinum, the military medical school of Vienna, with professor Ewald Hering, and they published the results of their work in 1868. They had discovered that there are receptors in the lungs that sense the degree of expansion. Thus, when the lungs are inflated during inhalation, these receptors send impulses along the vagus nerve to the brain, which then triggers a reflex for exhalation. Following exhalation, other receptors stimulate impulses that trigger inhalation, and so on in an alternating cycle. This automatic regulatory process of respiration, one of the first biological feedback mechanisms discovered in mammals, is known as the Hering-Breuer reflex.

Breuer's other major contribution to physiological research arose from a series of investigations into the fine structure and function of the inner ear. He first focused his attention on the semicircular canals, which are filled with a fluid called endolymph. He theorized that the control of head movements is based on impulses generated by the flow of the endolymph in the canals, and he presented the theory and supporting evidence, which had been arrived at independently and almost simultaneously by Ernst Mach and Crum Brown, in 1874 and 1875. Breuer also showed that sensations of bodily posture are connected to another inner ear structure called the otolith. Although his findings were not accepted immediately, they have come to be considered basic for modern physiological research on the perception and control of bodily equilibrium and movement.

Breuer was appointed lecturer in internal medicine at the University of Vienna in 1875 but resigned in 1885 following a disagreement with the medical faculty concerning teaching policies; he also declined an offer to be nominated as an extraordinary professor. Yet his knowledge and expertise as both a scientist and a clinician were well known, as evidenced by his election in 1894 to the Viennese Academy of Sciences and by the fact that many influential citizens of Vienna, including not only Brücke and numerous other medical faculty members but also Freud, chose him as their personal physician. His humanitarian impulses are revealed by the fact that he offered his services free of charge both to the poor and to his colleagues and their families.

In 1880, Breuer began treating a twenty-one-year-old female patient who was suffering from severe hysteria. Her name was Bertha Pappenheim, but she is known in the annals of psychiatry as "Anna O." This patient, after becoming physically and mentally exhausted through months of nursing her seriously ill father, began to suffer from a variety of troubling and remarkable symptoms. These included occasional paralysis and loss of sensation in the extremities on the right side, and sometimes on the left side, of her body, disturbances in eye movement, restrictions in visual perception, difficulties with the posture of her head, a severe nervous cough, and aversion to nourishment. She would also lose her ability to speak her native German language from time. to time and was subject to daily periods of "absence" or clouded confusion associated with alterations of her entire personality.

When Anna O. was in her more normal psychological state, she was typically unable to remember the disturbances and hallucinations of her confused state. Breuer discovered that if, while his patient was under hypnosis, he repeated to her words she had said during her periods of delirium, she was enabled to remember and to relate the content of her hallucinations. This process, which Anna O. termed the "talking cure," was found to alleviate her symptoms and calm her mind. Breuer also discovered that if she would methodically relate her memories of a particular symptom back through time until she unearthed her memory of the traumatic circumstances surrounding its first appearance, the symptom would quite dramatically disappear. Breuer referred to this therapeutic method as catharsis, and he employed it in the successful treatment of each of Anna O.'s symptoms.

Breuer conducted regular sessions with Anna O., often for several hours each day, for a two-year period ending in June, 1882. In November of that year, he told his close friend Freud, whom he had met a few years earlier in Brücke's laboratory, about this intriguing case. Freud was extremely interested, and Breuer shared with him many of his detailed and systematically recorded case notes. Although Breuer abandoned psychotherapy at that time, at least in part because of his concern over the strong sexual attachment Anna O. developed toward him near the end of her treatment, Freud revived the cathartic method in his own practice, in consultation with Breuer, some seven years later. Freud repeatedly confirmed the therapeutic effectiveness of the cathartic method during the following four years, and the insights and experiences shared by Breuer and Freud during the twelve years from 1880 to 1892 form the foundation upon which psychoanalysis was built. They published their findings in article form in 1893, and in a much expanded book form in 1895, as *Studien über Hysterie* (*Studies in Hysteria*, 1936).

Based on his treatment of Anna O., Breuer had concluded, first, that neurotic symptoms arise when emotions or "affective ideas" are deprived of normal expression and thus remain unconscious, and, second, that these symptoms disappear when their sources are uncovered and consciously verbalized. Breuer and Freud then hypothesized that the basic process underlying these psychodynamics is the effort of the nervous system to keep its overall quantity of excitation at a constant, and preferably low, level—a process they claimed is governed by the "principle of constancy." When psychic pressures grow and normal outlets or avenues to consciousness are not available, these unconscious conflicts erupt through inappropriate channels into a diversity of symptoms. In this way, the overexcitation or imbalance of the nervous system is at least temporarily alleviated. Since Breuer and Freud considered an overly or suddenly excited nervous system to be the source of unpleasant sensations and the discharge of this energy to be the source of pleasure, the constancy principle is intimately tied to the pleasure principle. The method of catharsis thus came to be understood as functioning in the service of these principles.

For almost two decades, beginning in the late 1870's, Breuer and Freud were firm friends. Breuer, fifteen years Freud's senior, served as fatherly adviser, cherished companion, and, sometimes, financial supporter of his less-established colleague. Yet their close collaboration on the personally and professionally sensitive issues relating to their research on hysteria put a severe strain on their relationship, which was thus severed, rather sadly and bitterly, in 1896.

Summary

Josef Breuer's research on the reflex regulation of respiration and on the labyrinth of the inner ear were sterling achievements in the field of physiology. Yet these accomplishments have sometimes faded from historical consciousness, and Breuer's subsequent fame has centered primarily on his seminal studies of psychopathology. This has occurred partly because, although Breuer's published articles on purely physiological subjects span forty years and total more than five hundred pages, he had no permanent institutional affiliation and no intellectual disciples. The fact that Breuer is recognized first for his relatively brief research and publications on hysteria is also the result of the enormous historical impact of Freud and psychoanalysis. Although Anna O.'s cure was not complete during the two years she spent with Breuer (she continued to suffer relapses for several years thereafter), the systematic "talking out" of her unconscious conflicts can be regarded as the first instance of a sustained attempt at deep psychotherapy, a form of treatment that has flourished during the twentieth century.

Breuer's training and research in physiology cannot, however, be separated from his study of psychopathology. On the contrary, his early insights into physiological processes apparently had a major formative influence on the theory of hysteria that he and Freud developed, an influence particularly evident with regard to the principle of constancy. This principle, used to describe the self-regulatory activity of the nervous system, is strikingly similar to the self-regulatory reflex of respiration and the mechanisms of bodily equilibrium that Breuer had discovered in his early physiological research. The fact that he and Freud (who was trained for years in neurology) thought that the psychological processes of neurosis could be described adequately by reference to an essentially physical principle, based on quantities and currents of energy, is evidence of the influential role that mechanistic and materialistic explanations, which excited the psyches of so many nineteenth century scientists, played in the creation and evolution of psychoanalysis.

Bibliography

Breuer, Josef. "Autobiography of Josef Breuer (1842-1925)." Edited and translated by C. P. Oberndorf. *International Journal of Psychoanalysis* 34 (1953): 64-67. Brief autobiographical comments, first published in Vienna in 1925, on Breuer's family, cultural background, inspirational acquaintances, and major professional achievements.

Breuer, Josef, and Sigmund Freud. *The Standard Edition of the Complete Psychological Works of Sigmund Freud*. Vol. 2, *Studies on Hysteria*. Edited by James Strachey. London: Hogarth Press, 1955. The standard English translation of the authors' 1895 book. This edition also contains the 1893 article known as the "Preliminary Communication" and an informative introduction by the editor dealing with the publications' historical background and their influence on psychoanalysis, as well as the scientific differences between Breuer and Freud. Freud's numerous references to Breuer, scattered throughout the twenty-four volumes of this set, can be located via the index.

Cranefield, Paul F. "Josef Breuer." In *Dictionary of Scientific Biography*, vol. 2. New York: Charles Scribner's Sons, 1970. An excellent biographical article covering Breuer's physiological and psychological research. Contains a bibliography of scholarly works by and about Breuer.

_____. "Josef Breuer's Evaluation of His Contributions to Psychoanalysis." *International Journal of Psychoanalysis* 39 (1958): 319-322. An analysis of the contributions that Breuer and Freud made to the creation of psychoanalysis, containing a letter from Breuer evaluating his own contributions.

Ellenberger, Henri F. *The Discovery of the Unconscious: The History and Evolution of Dynamic Psychiatry*. New York: Basic Books, 1970. A substantial and detailed study of the development of dynamic psychiatry. Deals (in various locations indicated in the index) with Breuer's life, his work with Freud, and his formative cultural influences. Also contains many illustrations of the major players in this drama.

_____. "The Story of 'Anna O.': A Critical Review with New Data." *Journal of the History of the Behavioral Sciences* 8 (1972): 267-279. Ellenberger provides a thorough examination of this famous case, gives biographical information about Anna O., and discusses two previously unknown case histories of her, one written by Breuer in 1882, discovered by the author.

Jones, Ernest. *The Life and Work of Sigmund Freud*. New York: Basic Books, 1953. This classic, three-volume biography of Freud, written by one of his leading disciples, is noted for its richness of biographical data, although it also suffers from some factual inaccuracies. Volume 1 describes the personal relationship between Breuer and Freud and includes references to Freud's expressions of delight at being in Breuer's "sunny" presence.

Sulloway, Frank J. *Freud, Biologist of the Mind: Beyond the Psychoanalytic Legend*. New York: Basic Books, 1979. A groundbreaking book that not only deals with the details of Freud's and Breuer's lives and work but also places it all in the context of nineteenth century science. Chapter 2 discusses the evolution of the theory of hysteria; chapter 3 examines the reasons for the estrangement of the two men.

Gordon L. Miller

HENRI-ÉDOUARD-PROSPER BREUIL

Born: February 28, 1877; Mortain, France
Died: August 14, 1961; L'Îsle-Adam, France
Area of Achievement: Anthropology
Contribution: A major figure in prehistoric archaeology, Breuil specialized in prehistoric art, opening new vistas of understanding and establishing the first useful chronologies for this crucial facet of early human cultural activity.

Early Life

Henri-Édouard-Prosper Breuil came from a family with generations of deep ties to Normandy and northern France. His father practiced law in his hometown of Mortain, but when Henri was still an infant the family moved to Clermont de l'Oise, where his father had been appointed public prosecutor. Henri's father was a stern, orderly individual, though not unkind. Throughout his life, Breuil remained more devoted to his mother, to whom he wrote nearly every week, regardless of where he was at the time.

At age ten, following elementary schooling in Clermont, Breuil went to the Collège Saint-Vincent in Senlis, run by Marist fathers. Breuil apparently was not in the best of health as a child and had difficult times with larger, more robust boys. He was also a rather solitary and deeply contemplative child. Breuil did not take well to the unimaginative rote-learning methods of the school, and he had to start in the lowest class. He spent much of his free time alone, walking in the forests and meadows around Senlis, where he developed a lifelong passion for the natural sciences, particularly entomology.

In 1894, Breuil passed his baccalaureate examinations, without any particular distinction except in the natural sciences. By this time, he was in such poor health that doctors prescribed an entire year of rest. During this period, Breuil began exploring the hundreds of caverns in the Somme country, where he heard tales of fossils and strange drawings to be found in some of the caves. He also briefly considered a career in medicine, as well as one as a missionary. Breuil's twin avocations for science and theology led him to enroll in October, 1895, in the seminary at Issy-les-Moulineaux, in a suburb of Paris. There he was fortunate to encounter as an instructor the Abbé Guibert, an avid evolutionist and naturalist, who convinced Breuil that the priesthood and a scientific career were not incompatible. In particular, Guibert encouraged Breuil to turn his attention to the fascinating and controversial finds just beginning to sketch out the world of prehistory.

Life's Work

Breuil was ordained a priest in June, 1900, and obtained a degree in natural sciences from the University of Paris in 1903. He was never to occupy a clerical post. With approval from the sympathetic Bishop of Soissons, Breuil obtained an extended leave from religious duties to pursue research in prehistory. Already reputed to be an expert draftsman and artist, in 1901 Breuil got his first opportunity to investigate systematically and record prehistoric art at La Mouthe cave in the Dordogne, at the request of its discoverer, Émile Rivière.

Breuil's unique blend of artistic talent and scientific rigor was useful for the study of prehistoric cave art. In the early twentieth century, photographic technology was not sophisticated enough to record the frequently enormous expanses of artwork on the walls of dimly lit or even pitch-black caves, work which often was in a terrible state of preservation. Breuil approached this grueling task with unbridled enthusiasm. Maneuvering himself through long, restricted passages of rough, damp rock, spending long hours in a crouch or on his back to render his copies, Breuil suddenly liberated himself from his chronic frail health.

Even Breuil, however, could not have foreseen the magnitude of the task. He had barely begun at La Mouthe when news came in September, 1901, of sensational discoveries in two caves in the Vézère Valley, each of which contained hundreds of meters of paintings. Among the paintings were hosts of animals either extinct or no longer found in Europe, a few depictions of humans, and groups of mysterious symbols. They were so extensive that there could no longer be serious doubt of their prehistoric origins, despite claims of detractors that they were forgeries, hoaxes, or simply modern renderings by unnamed hands. In 1902, Breuil, Rivière, and a team of French archaeologists, having examined La Mouthe and the Vézère Valley finds, officially declared them the work of prehistoric artists. No one, however, yet had any idea of the time period into which these works fell.

At the suggestion of colleagues, Breuil prepared for an expedition to examine the cave paintings at Altamira in Spain. These had been discovered as early as 1868, but after early excitement, dismissed as, at best, a few hundred years old. By 1890, Altamira had been forgotten by all but a few prehistorians. Breuil and a colleague, Émile Cartailhac, spent weeks at Altamira in painstaking copywork. With the environment too damp for watercolor, Breuil retrained himself on the spot in pastels. In 1903, Breuil read two papers to scientific congresses testifying to the prehistoric authenticity of Altamira. Publication of his results in 1906 by the Institut de Paléontologie Humaine in Paris created a storm of controversy. Many were convinced, but opposition to the idea continued.

In 1906, Breuil commenced a five-year stint as lecturer in prehistory and ethnography at the University of Fribourg in Switzerland, punctuated by numerous trips to France and Spain to explore more caves. In 1910, he became professor of prehistory at the Institut de Paléontologie Humaine, expanding his lecture circuit to include all of Western Europe. Two years later came another sensational discovery of cave paintings in the Tuc d'Audoubert, near Toulouse on the river Volp. Breuil and his companions broke into a chamber unoccupied for millennia, covered with animal bones and human footprints. Tuc also revealed a clay bison, the first evidence of prehistoric sculpture in this medium.

During World War I, Breuil interrupted his scientific career to serve as an Allied intelligence agent in Spain. The work allowed Breuil many chances to explore more caves, and in 1916 associates excitedly called him back to Tuc d'Audoubert, where a narrow connection had been found leading to a whole new series of caverns. The new discovery, Trois-Frères, was a half-mile-long cavern covered with animals and humans in strange, ritual costumes, symbols of reproduction and sexuality, and even musical instruments. In numerous episodes during succeeding years, Breuil was to spend nearly a year in Trois-Frères copying the work. These reproductions are regarded as among the best executed and most significant of his career.

By the 1920's, despite continued criticism, the sheer quantity of cave paintings, becoming ever more obvious at Breuil's artistic hand, decisively turned the academic tide. It was now possible for Breuil to distinguish artistic styles and motifs which clearly belonged to different periods of prehistory and, from there, to begin constructing prehistoric sequences and relating them to the other material remains, such as fossils and stone tools. Evolutionary change could be discerned in the paintings, indications of new concepts of the human relationship to the animal and spiritual world, the development of central elements in human consciousness. Although absolute dates were still a matter of speculation, it was clear that human prehistory in Europe covered tens of thousands of years.

Breuil began to climb rapidly in academic circles and soon acquired international renown. In 1926, he lectured on prehistory at Oxford, two years later became a professor at the Sorbonne, and in 1929 was appointed to the faculty of the Collège de France. During the 1930's, he traveled extensively to prehistoric sites in Europe and made two visits to China, where scholars were just beginning to suspect that the antiquity of human occupation might even antedate that of Europe.

By chance, Breuil went to southern France to spend the winter of 1939-1940 with a colleague. Thus he escaped the German invasion of France and the fall of Paris in the spring of 1940. In September, 1939, two young boys brought Breuil some drawings they had made of animals on the walls of a cave they had discovered near Montignac, a small town on the Vézère. The place was barely accessible by a small hole and exceedingly dangerous, as Breuil discovered upon entering. What he saw, however, dispelled any concern for safety. It was the fabulous art of Lascaux.

Even during World War II, Breuil's sensational discovery stirred Vichy

France. Sealed for thousands of years, Lascaux's paintings, richly engraved, appeared almost as they had in Paleolithic times. Some scholars have speculated that the artists constructed scaffolding to reach the higher points of the vaulted roof. By 1940, Breuil's artistic renderings were no longer needed; the wonders of Lascaux were photographed in breathtaking detail.

In 1941, Breuil was invited to take up a professorship at the University of Lisbon. Seizing the opportunity to get away from the war, he escaped once again, this time from the German Occupation of southern France. In 1942, Breuil embarked on a three-year expedition to southern Africa. There good fortune followed him as he was able to locate animal bones which forced redating of an Australopithecine or early hominid site to more than one million years in—of all places—a jewelry store. He also examined South African rock paintings, including the famous White Lady of Tsisab in Southwest Africa.

Breuil returned to Africa in 1947 to attend the first Pan-African Congress on Prehistory, and again in 1951 for more exploration of sites. Now retired from the Collège de France, he nevertheless continued to write and do research. In the last decade of his life, as the work of Louis Leakey and Mary Leakey and other paleontologists began to come to light, it dawned on Breuil that southern and eastern Africa might well be the site of human origins, and that, for all the difficulty his generation faced in convincing skeptics that human prehistory spanned tens of thousands of years, the real saga might be far longer than even Breuil had once imagined. He died on August 14, 1961, in L'Îsle-Adam.

Summary

Henri-Édouard-Prosper Breuil was a seminal figure in the emergence of the discipline of prehistory. He formulated a descriptive language for style and elaborated sequences and chronologies which became canons for the study of prehistoric art in the Old World. His academic training and incalculable physical labor allowed him to bring to light the achievements of Paleolithic culture as no other person could. As a scholar, his work was unsurpassed in the field.

Unlike many others, however, Breuil had the capacity, through his writing and his artistic talent, to transmit his discoveries to a fascinated public. His paintings and commentaries invited Europeans, Asians, and Africans to contemplate the genius of their forebears across hundreds of generations and thousands of years, and to balance the evidence against traditional religious and prescientific canons regarding human origins. In this respect, Breuil contributed mightily to the intellectual ferment of the twentieth century.

Bibliography
Brodrick, Alan Houghton. *Father of Prehistory, the Abbé Henri Breuil: His*

Life and Times. New York: William Morrow, 1963. This is the only biography of Breuil in English, a somewhat rambling narrative composed by a personal friend that is obviously a labor of love. A chronology of Breuil's life is included.

Burkitt, Miles Crawford. *Prehistory: A Study of Early Cultures in Europe and the Mediterranean Basin*. Reprint. Freeport, N.Y.: Books for Libraries, 1971. Contains a preface by Breuil and is a useful summary of the state of prehistory after Breuil's major cave art discoveries.

Leroi-Gourhan, André. *The Art of Prehistoric Man in Western Europe*. Translated by Norbert Guterman. London: Thames & Hudson, 1968. Leroi-Gourhan was instrumental in spreading word of Breuil's discoveries to the English-speaking world. This work summarizes the state of knowledge at the time of publication with particular emphasis on the contributions of Breuil and his contemporaries.

Marshack, Alexander. *The Roots of Civilization: The Cognitive Beginnings of Man's First Art, Symbol, and Notation*. New York: McGraw-Hill, 1972. A groundbreaking, controversial synthesis of Paleolithic art and symbol, valuable not only for its imaginative hypotheses but also for extensive illustrations of cave paintings. Extensive bibliography.

Ruspoli, Mario. *The Cave of Lascaux: The Final Photographs*. New York: Harry N. Abrams, 1987. A poignant look at these famous paintings before the French government permanently closed Lascaux to the public to prevent further deterioration of the paintings from human atmospheric disturbance. Good bibliography on cave painting and preservation issues.

Ronald W. Davis

LEONID ILICH BREZHNEV

Born: December 19, 1906; Kamenskoye, Ukraine, Russian Empire
Died: November 10, 1982; Moscow, U.S.S.R.
Areas of Achievement: Government and politics
Contribution: Brezhnev directed the Soviet Union for nearly two decades (1964-1982). His administrative record as party chief and head of government was characterized by emphasis on continuity and the status quo in domestic policy, an increase in military strength, and a mixture in foreign policy of cautious adventurism, arms control agreements with the United States, and military intervention in two neighboring states.

Early Life

Leonid Ilich Brezhnev was born in Kamenskoye (now Dneprodzerzhinsk), Ukraine, on December 19, 1906. Of ethnic Russian background, Brezhnev was the son and grandson of factory workers in the local steel mill. He began work in the same plant at age fifteen. As a young boy at the time of the 1917 revolutionary period and the following civil war, he recalled the strikes and turmoil in his native town. Brezhnev joined the Komsomol in 1923 at age seventeen. He was graduated (1927) from an institute in Kursk as an agricultural specialist and moved to the Urals region to work as an economic administrator and a local government official. He joined the Communist Party in 1931 at age twenty-five and entered a metallurgical institute in Dneprodzerzhinsk the same year. Graduating in 1935, he entered a Red Army training school for tank drivers. In 1937, Brezhnev became the vice chairman of the Dneprodzerzhinsk soviet but soon after moved into administrative work in the Communist Party.

He became (February, 1939) secretary of the regional party committee in Dnepropetrovsk, a major industrial center in the Ukraine. After the start of the war in Europe, Brezhnev was selected for the newly created post of Secretary for the Defense Industry in the region, responsible for overseeing the transition of local plants for possible war production. In 1941, following the Nazi invasion of the Soviet Union, he volunteered for military service and served in the role of a political officer. By war's end, he was a major general and Chief of the Political Department of the Fourth Ukrainian Front. He saw some limited military combat service in the Black Sea, Caucasus, and Ukraine regions. Following the war, he became party head of the Zaporozhye region in the Ukraine (1946-1947) and then held the same post in the Dnepropetrovsk region of the Ukraine. His primary task was to oversee economic reconstruction of the areas damaged by the war.

Life's Work

Brezhnev made his record as a loyal party administrator who provided steady leadership and fulfilled the responsibilities assigned to him. He slowly but steadily rose in the Communist Party apparatus to higher positions, eventually culminating with his selection as First Secretary of the Communist Party in October, 1964, replacing Nikita S. Khrushchev. (The office was retitled "general secretary" in 1966.)

At age forty-three, Brezhnev was selected to be First Secretary of the Moldavian Republic Communist Party and worked there from 1950 to 1952. He then rose to national party positions in late 1952, with his election to the Communist Party Central Committee, the Party Secretariat, and (as a candidate member) the Communist Party Presidium. Scholars interpret this advancement as part of Joseph Stalin's preparations to purge the older party leadership in favor of new and younger subordinates. Brezhnev, in his midforties, apparently was being groomed for new leadership responsibilities, but, with Stalin's death in March, 1953, Brezhnev lost his secretariat and presidium positions.

During 1953-1954, Brezhnev worked in the Ministry of Defense as the first deputy chief of the main political administration with the rank of lieutenant general. His responsibility was to ensure ideological and political loyalty to the party and government. He returned to direct party service in early 1954 as Second Secretary of the Kazakh Communist Party and was later promoted to First Secretary in August, 1955. During the mid-1950's, Brezhnev implemented Khrushchev's "Virgin Lands" scheme and won more fame for the initial success of this ambitious agricultural undertaking. He was reelected to the Central Committee of the Party in 1956, as well as returning to both the Secretariat and the ruling Party Presidium as a candidate member. He was raised to full membership in the Presidium in June, 1957. These promotions marked Brezhnev as a Khrushchev associate who benefited from loyalty to his chief.

By 1960, Brezhnev's relations with Khrushchev seem to have weakened, as Khrushchev was entering the final period of his rule. Brezhnev again gave up his Secretariat position in 1960 and was elected Chairman of the Supreme Soviet Presidium (the titular head of state or "president"), with primarily ceremonial functions. He resumed duties in the secretariat in mid-1963 and relinquished the head of state position in June, 1964. Khrushchev's ouster as party head in October, 1964, immediately resulted in Brezhnev's selection as First Secretary, and he held that responsibility until his death in November, 1982. It was in this office that he made his mark and left a mixed legacy to his successors.

The years of collective leadership—Brezhnev as party head and Aleksei Kosygin as government head—worked reasonably well until the latter's resignation in October, 1980, and death soon after. In fact, Brezhnev steadily expanded his influence and visibility over the period. During the Brezhnev years, the Soviet Union saw a number of achievements: continued manned space efforts, growing emphasis on military strength, the celebration of the fiftieth anniversary of the Bolshevik Revolution, expanded relations with other world Communist parties, and the holding of important party congresses. Brezhnev expanded his functions and titles, becoming Marshal of the Soviet Union in May, 1976 (the only party leader besides Stalin to hold that rank) as well as Chairman of the Defense Council. In 1977, he became Chairman of the Supreme Soviet Presidium and held that position until his death.

On the domestic scene, the Brezhnev era soon developed a reputation as a conservative and status quo administration. The Party apparatus was more tightly controlled, and few significant changes in the Communist Party Presidium (renamed the "Politburo") and other agencies occurred until the early 1970's. Literary dissidents felt continued harassment, beginning with the arrest of Andrei Donatovich Sinyavsky and Yuli Markovich Daniel in 1965 and their trial in early 1966. The problems with Aleksandr Solzhenitsyn, which led to the author's forcible deportation in February, 1974, are widely known. Andrei Sakharov's human rights activity from 1968 onward eventually led to his banishment to the city of Gorky in 1980. Despite promises of domestic reform and human rights, as specified in the 1975 Helsinki Accord, repression continued throughout the Brezhnev years as a dominant motif.

Economic policies returned to the more centralized system, as the later Khrushchev experiments were terminated. Virtually no innovations appeared during the Brezhnev years after 1965, and the economy suffered as a result of the old ideological priorities and institutional administrative structure. Improved relations with the United States in the early 1970's permitted substantial imports of grain to cover shortages in Soviet agriculture. Industrial growth rates fell, and both quality and quantity suffered. This was especially true in the late 1970's and early 1980's during the remaining years of the Brezhnev leadership.

In foreign policy, the Soviet Union showed a diversity of options and tactics. Military buildup in conventional and nuclear systems dominated the budgetary priorities for the period. The Party's tough and uncompromising attitude can be seen in the military intervention in Czechoslovakia in August, 1968, to oust the reform movement of Alexander Dubček, in what came to be known as the "Brezhnev Doctrine." In the Western Hemisphere, the Soviet Union continued its role as the major patron of Fidel Castro's Cuba and also began the penetration of Central America by its support of the Sandinista movement in Nicaragua. The Soviet decision to shape events in Afghanistan eventually led to the introduction of Soviet troops in December, 1979, and the emergence of a full-scale war, which lasted a decade in that neighboring state.

Soviet relations with the United States varied widely, affected by the

Glassboro Summit (1967), the Czech intervention (1968), the era of détente in the early 1970's with the Strategic Arms Limitation Treaty (SALT) I (signed 1972), a cooling in the mid- and later 1970's, and the signing of SALT II (1979). Throughout the Brezhnev era, Soviet foreign policy remained in the hands of the experienced and competent Andrei Gromyko as foreign minister. Relations with the People's Republic of China remained poor, including Sino-Soviet skirmishes on the Ussuri River frontier in 1969. Soviet influence in the Middle East fluctuated, especially in Egypt in the early 1970's. Brezhnev traveled widely in the 1960's and 1970's to both Communist and non-Communist nations.

By the time of the Twenty-fifth Party Congress in 1975, Brezhnev's health and abilities began a marked deterioration. This decline continued for the remaining years of his life, until his death in Moscow on November 10, 1982, at the age of seventy-five.

Summary

The latter years of Leonid Ilich Brezhnev's life gave ample evidence of his faltering leadership and the problems he was not able to face and resolve. Since his death, the deleterious effects of his rule have become all too painfully evident. During the era of Mikhail Gorbachev, the inadequacies and damage of the Brezhnev perod were widely publicized as what is called the "era of stagnation." Economic problems were the usual focus along with the Brezhnev "command" system of decision making, the existence of cronyism, and corruption within the Communist Party. The attacks on Brezhnev, who was given an official state funeral in 1982, affected members of his immediate family even to the imposition of jail sentences. Brezhnev's name was also removed from towns, schools, and streets that had been named in his honor.

On the positive side, Brezhnev's leadership reveals strengths and positive attributes. He ended Khrushchev's increasingly desperate efforts to find a "quick fix" for domestic and foreign problems. Brezhnev provided stability and a sense of continuity in both domestic and foreign policy. The Soviet economy grew during his years in office, although not at rates sought. The standard of living for many Soviet citizens improved, and construction of new housing was an ongoing priority. Food prices were kept low by heavy state subsidies. Medical care was expanded, and educational programs absorbed large numbers of Soviet youth. Space technology efforts had extensive funding and successes. No one doubts that the Soviet Union became militarily stronger and more formidable under Brezhnev's efforts to provide greater national security, but an unfulfilled agenda remained at his death to challenge his successors.

Bibliography

Academy of Sciences of the U.S.S.R. *Leonid I. Brezhnev: Pages from His Life*. New York: Simon & Schuster, 1978. This revealing Soviet biography of Brezhnev is notable for its omissions of important information, excessive praise, and overstated ideological fervor. It does cover the main outlines of his life and presents Brezhnev as an excellent leader and world statesman.

Breslauer, George W. *Khrushchev and Brezhnev as Leaders: Building Authority in Soviet Politics*. London: Allen & Unwin, 1982. A carefully researched study of Brezhnev's leadership since 1964, with penetrating assessment of the results as affected in three time periods, by economic concerns, and by Party issues. Portrays Brezhnev as a "consensus" leader. Provides alternative interpretations of Brezhnev's policies but indicates the author's own preference.

Dornberg, John. *Brezhnev: The Masks of Power*. New York: Basic Books, 1974. Readable account of Brezhnev's background, rising career in the Communist Party, and first decade as general secretary. Portrays him as an ideological and political conservative who brought stability to his nation. Anecdotes reveal Brezhnev's personality in the period before the onset of the "era of stagnation" and other problems in the later Brezhnev era.

Gelman, Harry. *The Brezhnev Politburo and the Decline of Detente*. Ithaca, N.Y.: Cornell University Press, 1984. Gelman effectively studies the objectives and techniques underlying Soviet foreign policy in the Brezhnev era. He includes the external and domestic factors. Factions and disputes within the Politburo and the Party apparatus are reviewed. The author sees the Soviet Union seeking foreign policy opportunities but not according to a "master plan."

Murphy, Paul J. *Brezhnev: Soviet Politician*. Jefferson, N.C.: McFarland, 1981. This straightforward political biography gives a detailed account of Brezhnev's early Party career and rise to power in 1964. Provides good coverage of his political maneuvering and leadership from 1964 to 1980. Portrays Brezhnev as capable, shrewd and scheming, and essentially a Stalinist in outlook.

Smith, Hedrick. *The Russians*. New York: Ballantine Books, 1984. A well-known account by a Pulitzer Prize recipient describing the Soviet Union in the 1970's. Excellent balance of anecdotal description and careful analysis of the nation's people, leaders, ideology, and daily life. Brezhnev's leadership and influence are assessed, especially for his last years.

Taylor Stults

LOUIS DE BROGLIE

Born: August 15, 1892; Dieppe, France
Died: March 19, 1987; Louveciennes, Yvelines, France
Area of Achievement: Physics
Contribution: Through his theory of the wave-matter composition of electrons, Broglie introduced a major and necessary component to quantum theory.

Early Life

Louis Victor Pierre Raymond de Broglie took his name from a small town in Normandy, France. He belonged to an ancient and famous family. From the seventeenth century on, this family produced several religious leaders, two Marshals of France and two prime ministers. As the head of an aristocratic family, Louis' father held the title of *duc*, which was passed on to Louis' older brother Maurice and to Louis in 1960. In taking an active interest in science, both brothers broke from family tradition. Maurice was the first to do so, suggesting to his family in 1898 that he resign his commission in the navy and follow a career in physics. The family objected to such an undertaking and a compromise was achieved: Maurice took a leave of absence from the navy and converted a room in the family estate into a laboratory. During this time, Louis began attending the Lycée Janson-de-Sailly in Paris, where his academic interest was in history. Louis continued to pursue this interest in history at the Sorbonne in the University of Paris, where he earned his bachelor's degree in 1910. Sometime before completing this degree, Broglie had become drawn to both theoretical physics and the philosophy of science. While his brother played a role in this shift of interest, Broglie also stated that the works of French mathematician Henri Poincaré were decisive in changing his mind. After three years of intensive work, Broglie completed a science degree from the faculty of science at the University of Paris.

In the year that he completed his science degree, Broglie was drafted into military service. During World War I, Broglie was stationed in Paris in the Eiffel Tower, working as a wireless operator. After the war, in 1918, Broglie continued his study of physics in his brother's private laboratory. During this time, Maurice was working on the nature of charged particles in an electric field; he found that small particles became charged when exposed to X rays. This led to further work in nuclear physics. Louis benefited by the experimental work with Maurice, and they shared an interest in the nature of the atom.

Life's Work

As a theoretical physicist, Broglie's contribution to science was to provide a different way of thinking about physical phenomena. Unlike experimental scientists, who can demonstrate their results, Broglie analyzed the contributions of physicists undertaken over many years and provided a new interpretation of the physical world. By the end of the nineteenth century, classical physics, which explained physical activity as the interaction between discrete particles or corpuscles of matter or by wave activity, seemed to have answered all the significant problems of physics. One problem, which was first posed in 1900, involved the exchange of energy between electrons and the walls of a container that enclosed the radiation. Max Planck discovered that these exchanges occurred in bursts of energy rather than a continuous flow of energy. This marked the beginning of the theory of quantum mechanics, a theory that states that electromagnetic waves come in discrete units of energy rather than one continuous flow of wave action. As an idea, quantum theory violates one of the most rigorously established notions of physics—that light, or radiation, as a wave spreads in a continuous and unbroken manner throughout space. This difference marks the dividing line between classical physics and the modern world of quantum mechanics. For the next quarter of a century, there would be vigorous and bitter debate between physicists who held the classical view and those who began to shift to the quantum description of the universe. Even Planck was not convinced that his own discovery was a conceptual break of such magnitude.

Broglie was discharged from the army in 1918 and returned to the family estate to continue his education in physics. Two years later, he joined his brother on X-ray research. Their work dealt with the spectrum of electrons released by X rays at given frequencies and was directly related to the new model of the atom developed by Niels Bohr. By 1924, the brothers became intrigued by a discovery of Arthur Compton. When a quantum of light, which Compton called a "photon," struck an electron, the photon would lose some of its energy and would become a light wave of longer wavelength. Thus, the light photon acted more like a particle than a wave. All the components for a new view of the physical world were now available, and Broglie proposed the wave-particle duality: Not only could waves act like particles but also particles could act like waves. For twenty years, evidence had been gathered that, under certain circumstances, light waves or electromagnetic waves functioned like particles. Yet the electron in the Bohr atom acted like a wave when it was pushed to a higher orbit. If there was a dual character to light, then perhaps there was also a dual character to electrons. Broglie presented the idea that an electron in orbit around a nucleus represented a specific wavelength. When energy was applied to the atom, the electron would jump to a higher orbit that was equal to an integral number of the electron wavelength. When an electron returned to a lower orbit, the excess energy would be given off as one photon of light.

In 1924, Broglie presented this analysis as his doctoral dissertation, entitled "Research on the Quantum Theory," to the University of Paris. The faculty viewed his idea with skepticism, since there existed no experimental evidence to support his view. With the support and encouragement of Albert Einstein, however, Broglie was awarded his degree and went on to publish his work. Einstein also began actively to promote this analysis among other physicists. Erwin Schrödinger used this idea of the dual nature of matter to develop a theory of wave mechanics. By 1927, Clinton Davisson and Sir George Paget Thomson, working independently, were able to demonstrate that electrons could be bent, focused, and diffracted like waves. As a result of this experimental confirmation and for his contribution to quantum mechanics, Broglie was awarded the Nobel Prize in Physics in 1929.

For several years, Broglie continued this line of research while looking for a foundation of quantum mechanics based on classical physics. Yet quantum mechanics would not operate on the simple cause-and-effect model of classical physics but rather on a statistical probability. In 1933, Broglie was elected a member of the French Academy of Sciences and in 1945 served with his brother as a counselor to the French High Commission on Atomic Energy. Broglie was awarded a number of prestigious prizes, including the first Henri Poincaré Medal of the French Academy of Sciences (1929) and the Grand Prize of the Society of Engineers of France (1952). He held honorary degrees from a number of universities and was a member of many scientific societies, including the Royal Society of London, the American National Academy of Sciences, and the American Academy of Arts and Sciences. On the death of his brother in 1960, he assumed the family title. He died in Louveciennes in 1987.

Summary

There were two breakthroughs in physics at the turn of the century: the theory of relativity and the theory of quantum mechanics. While the term "relativity" has entered the general vocabulary, quantum mechanics remains obscure to the general public. Yet many scientists in a variety of areas— chemistry, astronomy, biology, and other disciplines—regularly use the quantum theory in their daily work. Louis de Broglie was able to join a number of perplexing and anomalous experiments and theories into a single grand insight into the nature of the physical universe. Waves are part of every moving physical object, such as a thrown baseball. The wavelength of a moving baseball is insignificant compared to the size of the ball. Yet the wavelength of an electron is significant when compared to the size of the electron and results in a wave-particle duality. By bringing together wave and particle, Broglie helped to produce a fundamental change in the way scientists understood the physical world.

Bibliography
Broglie, Louis de. *Matter and Light: The New Physics*. Translated by W. H.
    Johnson. New York: W. W. Norton, 1939. Broglie was a prolific writer
    and wrote a number of books on quantum mechanics and wave theory.
    This volume is the least technical of his scientific works, but large sec-
    tions are probably beyond the scope of the general reader.
    _____. *The Revolution in Physics: A Non-Mathematical Survey of
    Quanta*. Translated by Ralph W. Niemeyer. New York: Noonday Press,
    1953. A highly recommended text for those seeking nontechnical informa-
    tion on quantum mechanics. The reader can also capture a sense of Bro-
    glie's writing style and his thought process.
Einstein, Albert, and Leopold Infeld. *The Evolution of Physics: The Growth
    of Ideas from Early Concepts to Relativity and Quanta*. New York: Simon
    & Schuster, 1938. One of the most accessible one-volume histories of the
    development of modern physics available to the general reader. There are
    virtually no technical terms, and no knowledge of mathematics is re-
    quired. The final section of this book is on quanta.
Flato, M., et al., eds. *Quantum Mechanics, Determinism, Causality, and
    Particle: An International Collection of Contributions in Honor of Louis
    de Broglie on This Occasion of the Jubilee of His Celebrated Thesis*.
    Boston: D. Reidel, 1976. One of several volumes that celebrated Broglie's
    part in the formulation of quantum mechanics. While the articles in this
    collection are varied in their quality as well as their difficulty, they do
    provide an overall view of the significance of quantum mechanics to
    science.
Jammer, Max. *The Conceptual Development of Quantum Mechanics*. New
    York: McGraw-Hill, 1966. Traces both the physics and the conceptual
    framework of quantum theory. The sections dealing with the formative
    development of quanta are moderately accessible to the general reader.
Stuewer, Roger H. *The Compton Effect: Turning Point in Physics*. The
    Compton effect was a critical experiment for Broglie that led him toward
    the insight of the wave-particle duality. The author covers the historical
    background and describes the significance of this effect for the future of
    physics.

Victor W. Chen

EMIL BRUNNER

Born: December 23, 1889; Winterthur, Switzerland
Died: April 6, 1966; Zurich, Switzerland
Areas of Achievement: Theology, church reform, and religion
Contribution: A leading and articulate exponent of the "new theology" or
"dialectical theology" movement that dominated European theology dur-
ing the 1920's and 1930's and profoundly influenced American theology,
Brunner lectured widely, published frequently, and was an influential and
respected theologian, especially in English-speaking religious circles. His
work on behalf of such international organizations as the Young Men's
Christian Association (YMCA) and the Ecumenical Movement earned for
Brunner the reputation of a world Christian theologian.

Early Life
One of the twentieth century's noteworthy and influential religious thinkers, Heinrich Emil Brunner was born in Winterthur, Switzerland, on
December 23, 1889, the descendant of generations of Swiss farmers. Brunner himself has noted, in autobiographical sketches, the influence of his
background and ancestry in the value that he placed upon personal life, in
his emphasis upon direct, interpersonal relationships, and in the precedence
given in his writings to the orders of marriage and family in society.

Emil Brunner was graduated from the *Gymnasium*, a prestigious boys'
high school in Zurich, in 1908 and was educated at the Swiss University of
Zurich and at the German University of Berlin. He was awarded his doctorate in theology from the University of Zurich in 1913, and during the following year his doctoral dissertation was published: *Das Symbolische in der
Religiösen Erkenntnis* (the symbolic element in religious knowledge).

During his formative years, Brunner and his family had been drawn into
the Religious Socialist Movement, the founders of which were a Swiss activist named Hermann Kutter, pastor of the Neumünster Church in Zurich,
under whom Brunner was catechized (and whom he regarded as "the gentlest
man" whom he had known), and Leonhard Ragaz, who was one of Brunner's teachers at the University of Zurich. With the outset of World War I in
1914, however, Brunner's faith in progress was shattered, and his religious
socialism, he reflected, began "to look suspiciously like a beautiful illusion." During the years 1913-1914, Brunner spent several months in England teaching languages at a high school in Leeds and becoming proficient
in the use of English. When the war began in Europe, he returned to his
native Switzerland and served for a time in the militia.

Brunner's pastoral experience began with a six-months' service as vicar in
Hermann Kutter's Neumünster congregation. In 1916, Brunner, a minister in
the Swiss Reformed church, received the call to become pastor of a small

congregation in Obstalden in Canton Glarus. He was to serve the congregation as pastor for eight years. In 1917, he married Margit Lauterburg from
Bern, Switzerland, a niece of Kutter. To the Brunners were born four sons,
three of whom served with the Swiss Army during World War II.

It was during his pastorate in Obstalden that Brunner wrote and published
his first two important books. The year 1921 saw the publication of his
inaugural thesis, *Erlebnis, Erkenntnis, und Glaube* (experience, knowledge,
and faith), in which he attacked modern theology, dominated as it was by
historicism (a product, Brunner believed, of the prejudiced idea that every
given reality can be understood from the standpoint of its historical development) and psychologism (religion understood as experience). Three years
later, he published his first major contribution to the "dialectical theology
movement" (a circle of thinkers including Karl Barth, Eduard Thurneysen,
Friedrich Gogarten, George Merz, and Rudolf Bultmann), a critical examination of the theology of the German Romanticist Friedrich Schleiermacher,
entitled *Die Mystik und das Wort* (1924; mysticism and the word). This work
represents a search for what Brunner himself has called "a scientifically
satisfying formulation" of his faith. It was written at a time when he was
reacting to the ideological framework of Religious Socialism and when
Brunner himself was deeply engrossed in the study of philosophy. It was the
second edition of the Schleiermacher book, considerably modified and expanded (published in 1928), that brought Brunner, now a college professor,
to center stage in the theological struggles that were engulfing European
theology and thought.

During the academic year 1919-1920, Brunner studied at Union Theological Seminary in New York City, the "first Swiss fellow" to be chosen; there
he began to make contacts with religious thinkers, institutions of learning,
and churches in the United States. In 1922, he became a privatdocent in
Zurich and two years later was called to the Chair of Systematic and Practical Theology at the University of Zurich, where he was to teach for thirty-
one years until his retirement in 1955. Brunner continued to live in Zurich
until his death there on April 6, 1966.

Life's Work

Brunner's theological writings have been called, by German theologian
Christof Gestrich, an accompanying phenomenon to the development of dialectical theology (new theology). They may be described more accurately
as lucid, articulate, sometimes controversial (in choice and development of
themes), not always original attempts to develop and to defend basic theological themes in the post-World War I era. Brunner is often compared,
rather unfavorably, with his Swiss contemporary, the theologian Karl Barth,
as the spirit of water over and against Barth's fire, as lucidity to depth, as
conventionality to creativity. Brunner contended, however, that from the

beginning he had taken a position independent of that of Barth. Like Barth, Emil Brunner had been a child of nineteenth century Liberalism, and, like Barth, he had passed through the ashes of liberal thought to erect a new theology, primarily by a return to the Reformers Martin Luther and John Calvin. From his early acceptance of "experience" as the basis of religious beliefs and actions, Brunner moved to a rejection of experience as "mysticism" and to placing his emphasis upon faith, *sola fide* (by faith alone), as the basis and path of belief.

Brunner's major theological writings demonstrate a faith that is at once biblical in its basis, strongly reformational in its accent, and independent in its direction. His extensive writings cover the entire range of theology and social ethics and include such notable and widely read books as *Der Mittler: Zur besinnung über den Christusglauben* (1927; *The Mediator: A Study of the Central Doctrine of the Christian Faith*, 1934), on the doctrine of reconciliation, in which book Brunner accepted the idea of a general revelation, his widely admired book on Christian ethics, *Das Gebot und die Ordnungen: Entwurf einer protestantisch-theologischen Ethik* (*The Divine Imperative: A Study of Christian Ethics*, 1937), published in 1932; and a powerful treatise of humanity, sin, and reconciliation, *Der Mensch im Widerspruch: Die Christliche lehre vom wahren und vom wirklichen menschen* (1937; *Man in Revolt: A Christian Anthropology*, 1939).

Brunner's career was marked by many series of well-received lectures, beginning with a tour of Holland in 1923, which was followed in 1928 by an extensive tour of the United States, where his lectures, delivered mainly in Reformed and Presbyterian colleges and seminaries, were published, in 1929, as *The Theology of Crisis*. In 1931 Brunner lectured in London, Glasgow, and Edinburgh, and in 1947-1948 he delivered the prestigious Gifford Lectures in Scotland, which resulted in a two-volume work published as *Christianity and Civilization* (1948-1949). Brunner also accepted invitations to lecture in Hungary, Denmark, Finland, and Sweden.

Of particular importance to Brunner in the 1930's were two "spiritual factors" which, despite their apparent diversity, were to be closely connected in their contribution to his theological thought and method. The first was the Oxford Group Movement, which reached Switzerland in 1931, with its relationship between spiritual reality and fellowship or communion. The second spiritual factor that influenced Brunner was the "I-Thou philosophy" of Ferdinand Ebner, whose approach to personal and interpersonal relationships was given a powerful statement by the Jewish thinker Martin Buber in his 1922 book *Ich und du* (*I and Thou*, 1937) and subsequently by the prominent European thinkers Friedrich Gogarten and Paul Tillich. These writers in their turn owed insights to the Bible and to the profoundly original Danish thinker Søren Kierkegaard, one of the founders of existentialism. This I-Thou philosophy helped Brunner to expound his anthropology on a plane above the traditional rationalistic thought scheme of subject and object and enabled him to understand the biblical concept of humanity as human responsibility before God. The I-Thou philosophy also aided Brunner in understanding "truth as encounter," which he characterized as the "lodestar" of his theological thinking from the year 1938 onward.

Shortly before the outbreak of World War II, Brunner had been offered a combined professorship at Princeton University and at Princeton Theological Seminary. Although he declined, citing the needs of his native Switzerland and of the European Church and civilization during the coming time of darkness, Brunner did remain in the United States for one year as a guest professor at Princeton Theological Seminary. In 1946, he returned to the United States for another lecture tour, this time traveling through the eastern states and the Midwest.

Emil Brunner's various contributions to the Christian church and to world Christianity were not limited to his lecturing, teaching, and writing. From 1930 on, he worked intensively with study groups in the framework of the emerging ecumenical movement as a member of the study commissions on "life and work" and "faith and order." Upon invitation from John R. Mott, American YMCA leader and pioneer in the ecumenical movement, Brunner served as theological adviser to the YMCA, helping in the Christian training of YMCA secretaries. In 1949, he traveled to the Far East, where for several months he was involved in lecturing and in leading training courses in Japan, Korea, India, and Pakistan. Prior to his retirement from the University of Zurich, Brunner spent the years 1953-1955 in Japan, where he helped to build the new International Christian University in Tokyo. He interrupted his sojourn in Japan long enough to return to the United States one final time to deliver the Earl Lectures on faith, hope, and love. It was during his return from Japan to Switzerland that Brunner suffered a stroke from which he would never fully recover and which limited his writing but not his strong personal faith and his commitment to the work of Christian theology in the ecumenical age.

Summary

Among the system-builders of Christian theology in the twentieth century, Emil Brunner holds a deserved place of unquestioned eminence. It was Brunner who first introduced the "new theology" to the English-speaking world, and it was Brunner and his theology that influenced generations of pastors, teachers, and theologians in Europe and especially in the United States, where his importance was felt until the early 1960's. In his development of a Christian anthropology during the 1930's and in his presentation and defense of "truth as encounter" as biblical and as opposed to the subject-object antithesis that he rightly regarded as a legacy of Greek thought, Brunner changed the face of European and American theology and redirected religious thought and action toward personal encounter, human responsibility, and intersubjective relationships. Brunner's entire theology was set within the framework of "the divine self-communication," which he developed and stated with clarity and conviction in his three-volume *Dogmatics* (1949).

During the years of his distinguished academic career, Brunner was perceived by his students from many countries as a lucid, cogent, friendly teacher. These students remember Brunner's opening early morning classes with a rousing hymn, his orderly, clearly-written lectures delivered with passion, his wise counsel in courses of pastoral care, and the hospitality of the Brunners' home in Zurich and the countless evenings of discussion there. These personal influences, which were consistent with his emphasis upon the I-Thou relationship, and his fondness for personal encounters are as important and as lasting as his published works. Through his writings, however, Brunner was, and still is, a very lucid, occasionally profound, and always stimulating Protestant theologian.

Bibliography

Brunner, Emil. *Our Faith*. Translated by John W. Rilling. New York: Charles Scribner's Sons, 1936. Short writings that cover the scope of the Christian faith. This book, which has been translated into nineteen languages, remains the best introduction to Brunner's theology.

Humphrey, J. Edward. *Emil Brunner*. Waco, Tex.: Word Books, 1976. For the student this is the clearest and most comprehensive introduction to Brunner's theology and writings. Humphrey skillfully develops the foundation of Brunner's theology and the Christian doctrines. Includes a selected bibliography.

Jewett, Paul K. *Emil Brunner: An Introduction to the Man and His Thought*. Chicago: Inter-Varsity Press, 1961. Part of the IVP series on contemporary Christian thought. A brief but readable study of Brunner and his theology; focuses upon Brunner himself, upon the place of reason in his thought, and upon his views of faith and the Bible. Includes a selected bibliography.

Kegley, Charles W., ed. *The Theology of Emil Brunner*. New York: Macmillan, 1962. Includes an intellectual autobiography of Brunner, seventeen essays of interpretation and criticism of Brunner's work, Brunner's personal and social ethic, and Brunner as apologist for the Christian faith, with a reply by Brunner. Contains a bibliography of Brunner's writings to 1962.

Nelson, J. Robert. "Emil Brunner." In *A Handbook of Christian Theologians*, edited by Dean G. Pearman and Martin E. Marty. Cleveland: World Publishing, 1965. Contains a brief biography, a sketch of Brunner's theology, and an assessment of Brunner's influence on Christian thought.

Van Til, Cornelius. *The New Modernism: An Appraisal of the Theology of Barth and Brunner*. Philadelphia: Presbyterian and Reformed Publishing, 1947. A well-known and provocative study that accuses both Barth and Brunner of building their theologies upon the same principle that governs modernism, it attempts to compromise the divine by means of argument. Van Til treats critically various aspects of Brunner's theology.

L. Craig Michel

MARTIN BUBER

Born: February 8, 1878; Vienna, Austro-Hungarian Empire
Died: June 13, 1965; Jerusalem, Israel
Areas of Achievement: Philosophy, religion, and literature
Contribution: One of the greatest Jewish philosophers of the twentieth cen-
    tury, Buber postulated an interpersonal relationship between God and
    man. This theoretical relationship, which he called I-Thou, profoundly
    affected diverse thinkers of all faiths.

Early Life
    Mordecai Martin Buber was born in Vienna on February 8, 1878, the son
of Carl and Elise (née Wurgast) Buber. When Martin was only four years
old, his mother mysteriously disappeared. (It was discovered later that she
had eloped with another man.) The motherless boy was sent to Lemberg
(now Lvov, Ukrainian Soviet Socialist Republic) to live with his paternal
grandparents. His grandfather, Salomon Buber, was a landowner, grain merchant, mine operator, and philologist. He was also one of the last great
scholars of the Jewish Enlightenment, responsible for authoritative critical
editions of the Midrash, a special class of Talmudic literature comprising
interpretations of the Bible, wise sayings, and stories.
    Buber's grandmother, Adele, was also a lover of words. A rebel who
taught herself to read and write in an era when such things were proscribed
for the women of her class, she arranged for young Martin to be tutored at home until he was ten years old. Because the household of Salomon
and Adele Buber was one in which many languages were spoken, Martin
learned the integrity of the "authentic word," the word that cannot be para-
phrased. The boy, not having many playmates, made a game of creating
conversations between people of different languages, imagining what a German would think when talking with a Frenchman, or a Hebrew with an ancient Roman.
    When Buber was nine, his father remarried, and the boy began spending
summers on his father's estate. There he learned to love horses. More important however, he learned to relate to the world in a way which became the
basis for his most famous work, *Ich und du* (1922; *I and Thou*, 1937). He
later credited his father, a farmer who knew how to relate directly, one-on-
one, both to animals and to his fellowman, with teaching him to practice
"immediacy."
    At the age of ten, Buber was enrolled in the local *Gymnasium*, where he
studied until he was eighteen. The school was primarily Polish; Jews were
the minority. At the school, Christians and Jews alike were obliged to participate in daily devotional exercises. Buber would later recall that he and
the other Jewish children would stand through these prayers, head bent,

feeling only that the services meant nothing to them. The experience left the man with a lifelong antipathy toward missionary work.

Buber moved from his grandparents' home into his father's townhouse at the age of fourteen. At eighteen he finished his studies at the *Gymnasium* and entered the university.

Life's Work

Buber spent his first year of university study in Vienna, a city of mixed German, Jewish, and Slavic influences. In Vienna, Buber discovered the living theater and became acquainted with many contemporary writers. At the University of Vienna, he studied literature, art history, and philosophy, and wanted to become a poet.

In the winter of 1897-1898, the young man studied at the University of Leipzig, and in the summer of 1899 at the University of Zurich. His subjects included philosophy, history of art, literary history, psychiatry, Germanics, classical philosophy, and national economy. Buber soon discovered a preference for seminars over lectures. He worked in a psychological seminar and was the only nonmedical student in the physiological institute. He belonged to a number of intellectual and social clubs, including the literary society.

Buber met two people in 1899 who would change his life forever. One of these was Gustav Landauer, a socialist who led and taught a group known as the Neue Gemeinschaft, or New Community. Founded by Heinrich and Julius Hart, the New Community believed in divine, boundless moving upward, as opposed to comfortably settling down. It saw in the ideal future a communal settlement in a new age of beauty, art, and religious dedication. Buber's relationship with Landauer prompted him to change his major course of study from literature and the history of art to German mysticism.

Even more important than his friendship with Landauer, though, was Buber's marriage to Paula Winkler, a fellow student in Zurich. One year his senior, Paula was probably his superior intellectually when the two met. That meeting was to have inestimable meaning for Buber, compensating as it did for the "mismeeting," a word coined by Buber, between his unforgotten mother and himself. Reared as a Roman Catholic, Paula converted to Buber's faith before the two were wed, giving up her earlier life and family for him. It has been said that the existential trust that underlies *I and Thou* would not have been possible without Buber's relationship with Paula.

It was Paula's strength which enabled Buber to be decisive about the direction of his life. With her help and encouragement, he found his path through Hasidism, a form of Jewish mysticism. Paula also increased his self-confidence. Buber believed marriage to be the life-style most suitable for man. He dedicated his books to his wife, as in this poem from *Tales of the Hasidism* (1949):

Do you still know, how we in our young years
Traveled together on this sea?
Visions came, great and wonderful,
We beheld them together, you and I.
How image joined itself with images in our hearts!

Paula and Martin had two children, Rafael and Eva. Paula was a writer of fiction who published under the pseudonym of George Munk.

Buber joined the Zionist movement in 1898, and was a delegate to the Third Zionist Congress in 1899. Although he addressed the congress on behalf of the propaganda committee, he stressed the importance of education over propaganda. He became editor of the Zionist movement's *Die Welt*. He wrote his doctoral dissertation on German mysticism and received his Ph.D. from the University of Vienna in 1904, then withdrew for five years to concentrate on the study of Hasidism, long regarded as occult and disreputable by most modern thinkers. Hasidism had flourished in the isolated villages of Poland during the mid-eighteenth century. While the movement stressed inward renewal, it was also characterized by exuberant manifestations of spiritual experience. Buber's study ultimately resulted in three books on Hasidism, *Gog u-Magog* (1941; *For the Sake of Heaven*, 1945), *Or ha-ganuz* (1943; *Hasidism and Modern Man*, 1958), and *Pardes ha-Hasidut* (1945; *The Origin and Meaning of Hasidism*, 1960).

At the start of World War I, Buber founded the Jewish National Committee, which was devoted to wartime work on behalf of Eastern European Jewry. In 1916, he started a monthly magazine called *Der Jude*, for eight years the most important organ of the Jewish renaissance movement in Central Europe. Buber believed strongly in Utopian socialism and envisioned a world in which people would live communally and in direct personal relationship with one another. From 1926 to 1930, he coedited another journal, *Die Kreatur*.

In 1922, Buber published *Ich und du*, a basic formulation of his philosophy of dialogue. He published in 1925, in collaboration with Franz Rosenzweig, a German translation of the Bible, in which the translators attempted to preserve the original literary character of the Hebrew Bible as a work meant to be spoken rather than simply read silently. Buber held the only chair of Jewish philosophy at a German university when he became professor of comparative religion at the University of Frankfurt (1925-1933). In 1933, he became director of the Central Office for Jewish Adult Education in Germany after Jews were barred from all German educational institutions. In 1935, he was finally forbidden to speak at Jewish gatherings in Germany.

Buber moved his family to Palestine in 1938 and became professor of philosophy at the Hebrew University. Not surprisingly, he was very active in public affairs in Israel. He pressed for a peaceful settlement of the Arab-

Hebrew disputes and was a strong advocate for rapprochement and a joint Arab-Israeli state. He was the first president of the Israel Academy of Sciences and Humanities (1960-1962). In his later years, Buber lectured outside Israel, widely influencing Jewish and Christian thinkers alike. He served at the end of his life as a counselor for kibbutz members. Buber died in Jerusalem on June 13, 1965.

Summary

Martin Buber's beliefs often ran contrary to contemporary thought. His interpretation of Hasidism, for example, came under fire again and again, and his interpretation of the revelations in the Bible is still controversial. His study of Hasidism changed scholarly opinion about the subject; it is now considered one of the great mystical movements of the world. As a member of the Zionist movement, he favored a renewal of Jewish culture over the creation of a Jewish state, an unpopular stand among his peers. In Israel, he argued for the peaceful coexistence of Hebrews and Arabs.

Buber believed that the only real evil is refusing direction, because the only possible direction is toward God, the theme of *Good and Evil* (1953). He believed strongly in a "living God," one with whom it is possible to have a direct personal relationship. He wrote of the inseparability of man's relationship to God and to his fellowman. The old theory of the duality of existence was reinterpreted. Rather than two worlds, the sacred and the profane, there are, according to Buber, two ways to respond to the mundane world. The world may be perceived as a thing to be experienced, a distant thing, or the individual may enter into direct relation with the world and experience the immediacy of God. In this immediacy is the key to eternity, because time becomes meaningless and the relation is all. For Buber, faith becomes an entrance into the whole of reality, because when one stands in direct relation to the world, one speaks the words "I-Thou." Buber believed that dialogue with God, not monologue about God, is the root of the Hebrew faith.

Bibliography

Bach, H. I. *The German Jew: A Synthesis of Judaism and Western Civilization, 1730-1930.* Oxford: Oxford University Press, 1984. This volume in the Littman Library of Jewish Civilization touches on Buber's work in the context of a history of German Jewry. An excellent survey, providing valuable background for an understanding of Buber.

Diamond, Malcolm L. *Martin Buber: Jewish Existentialist.* New York: Oxford University Press, 1960. A discussion of Buber's work in the context of Jewish thought. Indexed. College-level material.

Friedman, Maurice. *Martin Buber's Life and Work.* Vol. 1, *The Early Years, 1878-1923.* New York: E. P. Dutton, 1981.

_____. *Martin Buber's Life and Work*. Vol 2, *The Middle Years, 1923-1945*. New York: E. P. Dutton, 1983.

_____. *Martin Buber's Life and Work*. Vol. 3, *The Later Years, 1945-1965*. New York: E. P. Dutton, 1984. Based in part on personal acquaintance, Friedman's three-volume biography provides by far the fullest available account of Buber's life and work. Included are extensive discussions of the revival of Hasidism and other relevant subjects.

Streiker, Lowell D. *The Promise of Buber*. Philadelphia: J. B. Lippincott, 1969. One professor's response to a study of Buber's philosophy of dialogue. Provides many valuable insights. Contains a suggested reading list of Buber's works and an index.

Vermes, Pamela. *Buber*. New York: Grove Press, 1988. This volume in the Jewish Thinkers series provides a concise and well-informed introduction.

Joyce M. Parks

NIKOLAI IVANOVICH BUKHARIN

Born: October 9, 1888; Moscow, Russia
Died: March 15, 1938; Moscow, U.S.S.R.
Areas of Achievement: Government and politics
Contribution: Bukharin was a leader of the Bolshevik Revolution of 1917 and the foremost theoretician of the Soviet Communist Party during its early formative years. In 1924, after the death of the Party's founder, Vladimir Ilich Lenin, Bukharin became his heir and successor until he was forced from power by Joseph Stalin in 1928.

Early Life

Nikolai Ivanovich Bukharin was born in Moscow, Russia, on October 9, 1888. He was a precocious child who could read and write by age four, and he was educated at home by his parents, who were both schoolteachers. He early developed a lifelong interest in art, nature study, and science and read widely in the Russian and European classics of literature. Later he attended a public *Gymnasium* (high school), where he became acquainted with Marxist ideas, which were spreading through Russia as a form of revolutionary protest against the tyrannical conditions of the czarist regime.

When revolution broke out in 1905-1907, Bukharin led workers' strikes and organized student demonstrations, and in 1906, he joined the Bolshevik faction of the Russian Social Democratic Workers' Party led by Lenin. In 1907, he entered the University of Moscow to study economics, and he continued his illegal party activities, for which he was arrested in 1910 and exiled to the north of Russia as punishment. He soon escaped abroad, where he remained for the next decade, working with radical socialist organizations in Europe and the United States. In New York, he met another future leader of the Party, Leon Trotsky, edited a socialist Russian-language newspaper, and helped to found a revolutionary Marxist organization that later became the American Communist Party.

When the czarist government of Nicholas II was deposed by revolution in March, 1917, Bukharin returned to Russia and joined Lenin's followers in planning the overturn of the Provisional Government that had succeeded the monarchy. When the Bolsheviks struck for power in November, 1917, Bukharin led the struggle to win Moscow for the Party. Though still in his twenties, he was entrusted by Lenin with many important party and government posts, and he was elected to leading positions in various political, economic, scientific, and cultural organizations seeking to create a new Marxian-socialist order in Russia.

In 1919, Bukharin helped to organize the Third (Communist) International, which united all Communist parties in the world for the purpose of carrying out international proletarian revolution, and he later became its chairman. He also edited the influential newspaper *Pravda*, which was the ideological arm of the Russian Communist Party.

Life's Work

Although Bukharin attained some of the highest positions in the Russian and international Communist hierarchy of his day, his most important and enduring impact on the early history of Soviet Communism stemmed not from the manipulation of the instruments and symbols of power but from the force and influence of his thought. A dedicated and learned Marxist, Bukharin believed that the struggle for worldwide revolution and communism had to be waged not only on the barricades but also in the minds of men, and it was to this effort that he devoted his main energies. Accordingly, he set for himself the formidable task of providing the international and Russian Communist movements with a comprehensive theoretical rationale by reformulating the classical nineteenth century Marxian doctrines to accommodate developments in the world since the deaths of Karl Marx and Friedrich Engels.

Bukharin was well endowed for this effort, for he was extremely intelligent, familiar with foreign languages, well read in the classical and current literature of the West, and adept at writing and public speaking. He was also very prolific, and his written works and public speeches would, if collected in one place, fill many large volumes. These qualities led Lenin to characterize Bukharin as the "most valuable and biggest theoretician" of the Soviet Communist Party and its personal "favorite" and darling, testifying to Bukharin's ideological influence and great popularity, particularly among the young people of Russia. Bukharin's many theoretical works helped to shape the official doctrine of the Soviet and international Communist movements. By 1925, Bukharin had written several important works, including *Mirovoe khoziaistvo i imperializm* (1918; *Imperialism and World Economy*, 1929) and *K teorii imperialisticheskogo gosudarstva* (1925; the theory of the imperialist state), which were two pioneering studies of how world capitalism was expected to bring on inevitable proletarian revolution leading to ultimate world communism. He had also written, with Evgeny Preobrazhnesky, *Azbuka kommunizma* (1921; *The ABC of Communism*, 1921), which was a widely circulated popular explanation of the theory and practice of Bolshevism that was translated into twenty foreign languages.

As a result of his high positions, prolific pen, and wide influence, Bukharin became the most prominent leader of the Russian Communist Party after Lenin's death early in 1924 and was generally viewed within the Soviet Union and abroad as Lenin's legitimate heir and successor, though the struggle for succession was not immediately resolved. By virtue of his authority as the foremost figure in the Soviet Union, Bukharin was able to persuade the Party to follow a gradualist, humane policy of building socialism and eventually communism in Russia and to defeat the opposition of Trotsky and his followers, who advocated forceful, coercive measures against the workers and peasants to speed up the process of revolutionary transformation. Bukharin, in alliance with Stalin, led the ideological struggle against Trotsky and had Trotsky purged from the Party and exiled from Russia in the late 1920's.

By defeating Trotsky, however, Bukharin left himself exposed, and in 1928 Stalin turned against him. Differences between the two men concerning Party policies and practices reached a crisis, and in a series of moves in 1928-1929, Stalin had Bukharin removed from power because Stalin controlled the membership and apparatus of the Party. Having earlier helped to remove others from competing positions in the leadership, and having failed to build a political base himself, Bukharin was easily defeated and pushed into the shadows while Stalin launched his Five Year Plans of rapid industrialization and enforced agricultural collectivization at great costs in human life and suffering. Bukharin waged a rear-guard struggle in the Party against Stalin's brutal policies, but, in 1936, Stalin launched the infamous purge trials intended to rid himself of his rivals. Two years later, Bukharin was accused of treason and placed on public trial. Though he was innocent, he confessed to the charges in order to spare his wife and son, who were promised safety if Bukharin would plead guilty. On March 14, he was declared guilty, and the following day he was executed. After his death, Stalin ordered the history of the Party to be rewritten to eliminate any traces of the achievements of Bukharin and hundreds of other victims of Stalin's terror, who became "unpersons" in the official annals of Soviet Communism.

Summary

For more than thirty years following his demise, Nikolai Ivanovich Bukharin's name and accomplishments were obscured and repressed in the Communist world, and his important contributions to the early history of the Bolshevik movement were arrogated by Stalin as his. Only since the advent of *glasnost* and *perestroika* in the Sovet Union under Mikhail Gorbachev has the historic record of Soviet Communism been rectified and the record of Bukharin's life and career cleared of the Stalinist distortions. In 1988, Bukharin was posthumously exonerated of the charges of treason and restored to honor in the annals of the Party, and his writings were again circulated in the Soviet Union. Many of his prescriptions for developing socialism gradually by means of a mixed collectivist and private system of enterprises acquired new relevance when Gorbachev came to power in 1985 and initiated his radical reforms of the highly centralized command economy inherited from the Stalinist and Brezhnev eras. There has also been renewed interest in Bukharin's philosophical and theoretical ideas, which mark him as one of the most original thinkers of the twentieth century and one of the most important and influential disciples of Marx and Engels.

Bibliography

Cohen, Stephen F. *Bukharin and the Bolshevik Revolution: A Political Biography, 1888-1938.* New York: Alfred A. Knopf, 1973. This book is the only full-scale biography of Bukharin in any language. It is a masterful study of Bukharin's life and thought viewed against the background of Soviet and international events of his day, on which he exercised a major influence.

Heitman, Sidney. *Nikolai I. Bukharin: A Bibliography.* Stanford, Calif.: Hoover Institution Press, 1969. This is the most comprehensive guide to Bukharin's numerous written works and speeches, published in twenty languages throughout the world. It also includes notations and the locations of each item in major Western libraries.

Katkov, George. *The Trial of Bukharin.* Briarcliff Manor, N.Y.: Stein & Day, 1969. This book is an account of Bukharin's life and career leading up to his infamous treason trial in 1938. It reveals, among other things, the inner workings of the Stalinist regime by focusing on the power struggles in the Soviet Communist Party culminating in the purges of the 1930's.

Medvedev, Roy A. *Nikolai Bukharin: The Last Years.* Translated by A. D. P. Briggs. New York: W. W. Norton, 1980. This account deals with the hitherto little-known last decade of Bukharin's life and thought, when he was relegated by Stalin to obscurity and disgrace in the Soviet Communist Party. It is written by a leading Soviet dissident historian, who had access to documents and witnesses unavailable to Western writers.

Nicolaevsky, Boris I. *Power and the Soviet Elite.* Edited by Janet D. Zagoria. New York: Frederick A. Praeger, 1965. A collection of essays by an émigré Russian scholar who knew Lenin, Bukharin, Stalin, and other Soviet leaders personally. One of its main thrusts is to show that the policies advocated by Bukharin in the 1920's were those Lenin would have followed, had he lived past 1924, contrary to the claims of Stalin.

Tarbuck, Kenneth J. *Bukharin's Theory of Equilibrium: A Defense of "Historical Materialism."* London: Pluto Press, 1989. This study by a British Marxist examines Bukharin's interpretation of classical Marxian philosophy and refutes the claim that Bukharin held unorthodox or incorrect views, as claimed by Stalin and some non-Communist writers. The book is one example of the renaissance of interest in Bukharin's life and thought since his rehabilitation.

Sidney Heitman

BERNHARD VON BÜLOW

Born: May 3, 1849; Klein-Flottbeck, Holstein
Died: October 28, 1929; Rome, Italy
Areas of Achievement: Government, politics, and diplomacy
Contribution: During twelve years of high office, first as foreign minister
and then imperial chancellor, Bülow virtually shaped the expansionism
that Emperor William II of Germany embraced as the guiding principle
for both foreign and domestic policy. Bülow believed in *Weltpolitik* as the
guarantee of German national security and interest. He acquired the sobriquet "the Eel" for his skill in forwarding this policy.

Early Life

Bernhard Heinrich Martin Karl von Bülow was born May 3, 1849, in
Klein-Flottbeck in Holstein to a prominent Prussian Junker family with connections across northern Germany and Denmark. His father was a distinguished diplomat, much acclaimed for his handling of the Schleswig-
Holstein Question after 1850. Young Bernhard was much influenced by his
father and bowed to his wishes in most things, including following in his
footsteps to an even more distinguished career as diplomat and statesman.

Bülow grew up in Frankfurt in the 1850's and 1860's, living a few streets
away from Otto von Bismarck, whom Bülow came to admire and regard as
the greatest statesman in German history. The families were friends. The
Bülows played host to many notable personalities, German and other. In
1861, Bülow entered the nondenominational Frankfurt Gymnasium, where
he was taught by Catholic, Protestant, and Jewish masters. The headmaster
was Tycho Mommsen, younger brother of Theodor Mommsen, the great
classical scholar. The Bülows had many Jewish friends in Frankfurt, including banker Mayer Rothschild, who could recall the time when Frankfurt
Jews were locked up in the ghetto at night. Bülow gained an appreciation of
diversity from such connections. He eventually married an Italian Catholic—even as he shared the evangelical Pietist tradition that characterized
much of the Prussian aristocracy and regretted that his Jewish friends would
not see the light and become Christian.

Frankfurt was an important influence. In the romantic atmosphere of pre-
unification Germany, the city represented "the grandeur, but also the tragedy
of German history." From growing up there he acquired the nationalist beliefs that became the central philosophy of his intellectual and professional
life. In his mind these beliefs connected directly to the tradition that German
imperial unity began with Charlemagne more than a thousand years before.

Bülow wanted to enter the university in Bonn after passing matriculation
examinations in 1867. His father feared the influence of the Student Corps in
that Rhenish setting and directed his son to Lausanne, Switzerland, instead.

The following year, Bülow entered the University of Leipzig, and in 1870, Berlin, where he remained. During those student years, he undertook walking tours of Germany, the Austrian Empire, and Italy, acquiring an abiding affection for both regions in the process.

In 1870, Bülow joined the Royal Hussar Regiment on the outbreak of war with France. He served with courage, if not distinction, and was commissioned a second lieutenant in 1871. "Oh, glorious, splendid days!" he recalled near the end of his life. "My heart bleeds when I think of them now, and then remember the wretchedness and shame of the present."

The war ended with France humiliated by defeat and German unification declared in a ceremony at Versailles outside Paris. Bülow's German nation was reality at last, and he devoted his life to its service. Bismarck was architect of the new Germany and its first chancellor, and worked to establish its place in Europe. In his turn, Bülow would work to make the German Empire a colonial world power. A career that spanned the great age of European imperial expansion convinced Bülow that a centuries-old Prussian dictum applied equally to the larger German stage: that in order to survive and prosper, the German Empire must become a world power. He worked toward this end from the moment he began his diplomatic career right through his nine years as imperial chancellor.

Life's Work

Bülow left the hussars at his father's insistence to enter the foreign service. His career followed conventional patterns. Between 1875 and 1897, he served successive diplomatic posts in St. Petersburg, Vienna, Athens, Paris, and Bucharest, each with success, and gained increased respect with each experience. He ended this run with an ambassadorship in Rome, which led directly to the Wilhelmstrasse as secretary of state for foreign affairs in 1897 and to the chancellery three years later. There were several amorous adventures along the way (but without scandal), until he met, and in 1886 married, an Italian aristocrat with an annulled marriage, Marie Anna Zoe Rosalia Beccadelli di Bologni, Princess Camporeale. Meanwhile, Bülow expanded his range of acquaintances among Europe's great statesmen, including Benjamin Disraeli and William Gladstone of Great Britain. Prince Aleksandr Gorchakov of Russia, a pivotal diplomatic figure in the middle third of the century, he knew from his Frankfurt days.

In 1897, Bülow was relatively unknown outside diplomatic circles, and it was widely speculated that his appointment as foreign secretary was a foreign-policy move. This might even have been true. Relations among the Triple Alliance members, Germany, Austria, and Italy, were slipping. Bülow had been a very popular ambassador in Rome, and his elevation to the Wilhelmstrasse would be read in Rome as a positive move to strengthen the alliance. Moreover, he was known to have been a longtime admirer of Bismarck, the alliance architect, a fact that increased the symbolic importance of his appointment. Regardless of whether it was his doing, the alliance continued to hold together, at least long enough to allow Germany to stumble into a general European war in 1914.

As foreign secretary and chancellor, Bülow pressed forward with Kaiser Wilhelm's *Weltpolitik*, specifically through pressuring the other colonial powers to grant Germany access to overseas colonies. During Bülow's time, German overseas interests expanded into Asia and further into Africa. In 1899, he successfully negotiated acquisition of the Caroline Islands, for which he was made a count. In 1900, he was named Minister-President of Prussia and Chancellor of the German Empire, from which position he pushed *Weltpolitik* even harder.

Upon his appointment as chancellor, speculation was again rife as to why he had been chosen to replace the aging Prince Chlodwig Karl Viktor Hohenlohe. It was not enough that William II was pleased with Bülow's work in the Wilhelmstrasse. Remembering Bismarck's conflict with the young emperor and subsequent abrupt dismissal by him, the *Berliner neueste Nachrichten* reckoned that a "cautious and versatile diplomatist such as Bernhard von Bülow appears to be best adapted" to dealing with the temperamental William, who would not tolerate a rival in the formation of foreign policy. More than once over the next nine years, Bülow was accused of being merely executor of the emperor's will.

Of course Bülow was an executor, but not merely. In defending himself against the charge, Bülow argued simply that emperor and chancellor must trust each other and agree on a common policy. Failure to do this (plus the monumental egos involved) had driven Bismarck from office. The defense was simple enough to be correct, and simple enough also to be dissembling. It more than justified Bülow's sobriquet as "the eel." Actually, Bülow and William believed equally that the growth of Germany as a world power was necessary to preserve and expand German national interests. Delivering a skillfully compelling and ultimately successful justification before the Reichstag of Germany's actions in China was among his early achievements in promoting *Weltpolitik* and was but one instance when he spoke for the emperor and for himself.

As chancellor, Bülow was responsible also for domestic policy. He was accused of being an "agrarian," of structuring domestic policies that favored the landed Junker aristocracy at the expense of the nation. He responded that he was an agrarian only in being himself a landowner, and that as chancellor his duty was to all sections of the nation, social and economic. Historians do not agree that he practiced very assiduously what he preached, and his book *Imperial Germany* written during this period contains some rather strikingly "agrarian" arguments in the sense implied by his critics. All the same, some credit is due Bülow for the rapid expansion of material Germany during the first decade of the twentieth century. Also he did rise above domestic particularism sufficiently to hold together the diverse elements that composed the government's Reichstag majority.

Throughout his chancellorship, whether on foreign or domestic issues, Bülow was William's partner (critics naturally preferred "servant," and indeed William took this view in his more pompous moods). At the same time, Bülow's dedication to state interests compelled him to disagree with his sovereign when conscience deemed it necessary. This was in the best Junker tradition, and, despite frequent rumors to the contrary, William allowed Bülow's disagreement so long as it was not substantive, as Bismarck's had been.

In 1905, Count Bülow was raised to the rank of prince in part as a reward for success in dealing with the French. The title left no doubt that Bülow was in favor with William. In 1906, on the occasion of the passage of a finance bill that Bülow shepherded through the Reichstag, the emperor publicly backed his chancellor against public speculation that he was to be fired.

The test of Bülow's independence came over the Kaiser's infamous *Daily Telegraph* "interview," published in London on October 28, 1908, in which William made many ill-considered remarks. Both British and German opinion was aroused. Bülow loyally took responsibility for the interview and tendered his resignation. William would not accept it. Bülow then let it be known in a Reichstag speech that the emperor was not persuaded of the disastrous consequences of the interview, had learned his lesson, and in future would "observe that strict reserve, even in private conversations, which is equally indispensable in the interests of a uniform policy." Bülow emerged from the incident both unscathed and appearing to have chastened his sovereign. He was worthy of being named "the Eel" and had proved to be the man to handle William. No other chancellor came close to him in this regard.

Bülow, however, was not so adroit in evading the consequences of a disastrous budget proposal laid before the Reichstag the following year. The liberal-conservative bloc that sustained him broke up, and he remained in office only long enough to shepherd a mutilated budget through the assembly. In July, 1909, he left office, his public career ended.

Summary

Bernhard von Bülow was a cultured, sophisticated aristocrat with more than mere pretensions of intellectuality. His knowledge and grasp of German literature, philosophy, and political thought were considerable, and his marriage to the Italian Princess Camporeale, at one time a piano student of Franz Liszt, indicated a cosmopolitan outlook as well. Beneath all of this ran the deeply German nationalist and imperialist sympathies that both informed and directed his work and career, and indeed his life, making it both possible and inevitable that his contribution to German history would be the enhancement of an eventually destructive power. To the extent that Germany was responsible for World War I, the fault lies as much with Bülow as with his imperial master.

Bibliography

Barkin, Kenneth D. *The Controversy over German Industrialization, 1890-1914*. Chicago: University of Chicago Press, 1970. Includes a fairly involved discussion of Bülow's tariff legislation and his effect on Germany's industrialization.

Bülow, Bernhard von. *Letters of Prince von Bülow*. Translated by Frederic Whyte. London: Hutchinson, 1930. This work presents letters from Bülow's period as chancellor. The selection is reasonable, but it was not Whyte's purpose to praise Bülow.

_____. *Memoirs*. 4 vols. Boston: Little, Brown, 1932. Extremely informative but self-justifying, as such memoirs frequently are. Yet no more detailed account exists of Bülow's life, and a full appreciation of the man and his historic role is impossible without these memoirs.

Kitchen, Martin. *The Political Economy of Germany, 1815-1914*. London: Croom Helm, 1978. Provides a good overview of Bülow's role in the economy of Germany during the time he was in office.

Mommsen, Wolfgang J. "Domestic Factors in German Foreign Policy Before 1914." *Central European History* 6 (March, 1973): 3-43. Sets forth some of the complications in German foreign policy arising from expanding industrialism, internal political conflict, and the emotional surge toward colonialism.

Steiner, Zara. *The Foreign Office and Foreign Policy, 1898-1914*. Cambridge, England: Cambridge University Press, 1968. A useful analysis of European relations balanced on the fulcrum of Anglo-German rivalry during Bülow's time as foreign secretary and chancellor.

Turner, L. C. F. *Origins of the First World War*. New York: W. W. Norton, 1970. Another general work on the period that focuses on the causes of World War I. Bülow's role is discussed throughout.

Robert Cole

RUDOLF BULTMANN

Born: August 20, 1884; Wiefelstede, Germany
Died: July 30, 1976; Marburg, West Germany
Areas of Achievement: Religion and theology
Contribution: Bultmann's contributions to New Testament research and
    Christian theology significantly shaped the methodology and content of
    both endeavors in the twentieth century. Bultmann's concept of demyth-
    ologizing and his argument for an existential reading of the New Testa-
    ment continue to influence much modern discussion about the Bible.

Early Life

Rudolf Karl Bultmann was born August 20, 1884, in Wiefelstede, a village near Oldenburg in the Lower Saxony region of Germany. Bultmann was
born to a family of Lutheran clergy; his father and maternal grandfather were
Lutheran pastors, while his paternal grandfather was a missionary. From
1892 to 1895 Bultmann attended the humanistic *Gymnasium* in Oldenburg,
where he initiated his study of religion and the Greek language. In 1903, he
commenced his university studies, beginning at the University of Tübingen
and then moving to the University of Berlin and finally to the University of
Marburg. It was at Marburg in 1910 that Bultmann completed his doctoral
dissertation, comparing the preaching style of the apostle Paul with the di-
atribe of Hellenistic moral philosophy. In 1912 Bultmann completed his
research and writing on the exegetical method of Theodore of Mopsuestia,
the late fourth century and early fifth century bishop and biblical scholar who
played an important role in the theological controversies of the period.

In this period of university training, Bultmann was deeply influenced by
the work of his mentors Johannes Weiss and Wilhelm Hermann. Weiss, a
New Testament scholar, employed a "history of religions" approach to the
study of early Christianity and led Bultmann to see the New Testament and
the early Christian community in the context of the larger social and religious world of the ancient Mediterranean.

From the systematic theologian Wilhelm Hermann, Bultmann inherited an
approach to Christian theology that emphasized the priority of the self as the
means for knowing and understanding God. God is known as God acts on
and transforms the self and makes possible authentic existence. As Hermann
would say and Bultmann would later repeat, "[W]e can say nothing about
what God is in himself, but only what he does for us."

In 1916, Bultmann assumed the position of assistant professor at Breslau
and remained there until 1920, when he was called to succeed Wilhelm
Bousset at Giessen. Bultmann left Giessen the next year to return to Marburg
as professor of New Testament studies. He remained at Marburg until the
end of his academic career in 1951.

Life's Work

Bultmann's research and writing continued to reflect the twofold emphasis of his mentors. Indeed, one of the more lasting contributions of Bultmann was his integration of New Testament scholarship with constructive contributions to Christian theology. Bultmann's pioneering work in New Testament scholarship was persistently welded to reflections on the importance of these advances for Christian theology and human self-understanding.

In 1921, Bultmann published his seminal work on the New Testament, *Die Geschichte der synoptischen Tradition* (1921, enlarged 1931 and reprinted with a supplement 1957; *The History of the Synoptic Tradition*, 1963). The book identified traditional material in Matthew, Mark, and Luke and traced the history of the transmission of this material from its origins to its use by the Gospel writers. This book displayed Bultmann's skepticism regarding the recovery of the historical Jesus and laid the foundation for his later efforts at offering a program for "demythologizing" the New Testament message. Bultmann argued that the whole framework of the central message of Jesus (the "kerygma") was wrapped in ancient Jewish and Hellenistic Gnostic mythology. The description of Jesus' ministry and the stories about Jesus presupposed a conception of the universe as a three-storied structure (heaven, earth, and underworld) in which creatures from the upper and lower levels were constantly intervening in the lives of those living on earth. This conception, Bultmann argued, was no longer meaningful and thus must be removed (demythologized) in order for the kerygma to maintain its relevance for human existence.

The brutal realities of Germany during the two world wars pushed Bultmann to find an adequate description of the human condition. The idealism and romanticism of nineteenth century German philosophy seemed entirely unfit for the first half of the twentieth century. Bultmann discovered the answer in the work of the philosopher Martin Heidegger, who became his colleague at Marburg in 1922. Heidegger described the human condition as indeterminate and stressed the critical role of decision making at each moment in history for giving shape to one's being and for making possible authentic or genuine existence. For Bultmann, this emphasis on the critical role of decision and the polarity between unauthentic and authentic not only mirrored historical experience but also found its correlate in the description of human existence in the letters of Paul. Paul had described the conversion or turning of a life conditioned by sin and death to a life free from sin and opened to the path of obedience to God. The transition from the old (unauthentic) to the new (authentic) rested on the human response (decision) to the kerygma, that is, to the proclamation of God's love and forgiveness and to obedience to God's claims on one's life.

This formulation of theological anthropology figured prominently in many of Bultmann's writings. Bultmann had consistently emphasized that the knowledge and description of God must begin with God's action on humans; thus any work on theology must begin with and constantly return to anthropology. In *Jesus* (1926; *Jesus and the Word*, 1934) Bultmann described the kerygma as the call to humans to a decision to accept the demand for radical obedience to God. This idea was further clarified in his commentary on the Gospel of John, *Das Evangelium des Johannes* (1941; *The Gospel of John*, 1971), and his principal work of biblical theology, *Theologie des Neuen Testaments* (3 vols., 1948-1953; *Theology of the New Testament*, 2 vols., 1951-1955).

Unlike a number of his colleagues, Bultmann remained in Germany during the Nazi regime. From the outset of the Nazi takeover, Bultmann sided with the Confessing Church, which opposed Nazi church policy. At the same time he never participated actively in resisting or overthrowing the Nazis. In his own words, he "never directly and actively participated in political affairs." At the end of the war, Bultmann's reputation as a scholar attracted a number of gifted students who later held important positions in European and American universities. He also traveled to the United States in 1951 and Great Britain in 1955 for extensive lecture tours. Aside from these travels abroad, Bultmann's later life was spent almost entirely in Marburg, where he died in 1976.

Summary

Rudolf Bultmann was a gifted scholar and teacher whose influence on New Testament scholarship and Christian theology has been exceptional. This has been the consequence not only of the insightful and provocative character of his writings but also of the ongoing work of his students.

Bultmann's scheme for demythologizing the New Testament has been attacked as draining the text of its revelational power and denying any importance to the historical person Jesus. It is certainly the case that to follow Bultmann is to shift the emphasis of Christian theology from the person of Jesus to the message of Jesus and the early Church and to insist that the message be presented in a manner that is relevant and meaningful for the present. For many, this seemed not only a proper but also a necessary shift. At a time when it appeared that the entire biblical and theological endeavor would collapse under the weight of historical-literary critical scholarship and the tragic events of the early twentieth century, Bultmann forged a path that was constructive and profoundly meaningful.

Bultmann's ability to wed New Testament scholarship and theological analysis seems to be a lost art. The tendency to academic specialization has left the academy and the Church with few if any who can make original contributions that bridge the two fields. Bultmann may be not only one of the greatest of the New Testament theologians but also perhaps one of the very last.

Bibliography
Bartsch, H. W., ed. *Kerygma and Myth*. Translated by R. H. Fuller. Rev.
    ed. New York: Harper & Row, 1961. The first volume of a series con-
    taining essays that respond to Bultmann's concept of demythologizing and
    three essays by Bultmann in which he answers significant questions raised
    by his critics.
_____. *Kerygma and Myth II*. Translated by R. H. Fuller. London:
    S.P.C.K., 1962. The second volume in the series, it includes the critical
    essay by Karl Barth entitled "Rudolf Bultmann—An Attempt to Under-
    stand Him."
Kegley, Charles W., ed. *The Theology of Rudolf Bultmann*. New York:
    Harper & Row, 1966. A fascinating and insightful collection of essays in
    which Bultmann engages in dialogue with his major American and Euro-
    pean critics.
Neill, Stephen, and Tom Wright. *The Interpretation of the New Testament
    1861-1986*. Oxford: Oxford University Press, 1964, 2d ed. 1988. This
    updated edition of a classic survey of New Testament criticism places
    Bultmann's work in its historical context. An excellent introduction.
Perrin, Norman. *The Promise of Bultmann*. Philadelphia: J. P. Lippincott,
    1969. An overview of Bultmann's work by a renowned New Testament
    scholar. Perrin's own work both championed and criticized Bultmann, and
    this critical engagement makes this brief work unusually penetrating.
Smart, James D. *The Divided Mind of Modern Theology: Karl Barth and
    Rudolf Bultmann, 1908-1933*. Philadelphia: Westminster Press, 1967. A
    description of the education and early careers of these two major figures.
    Smart analyzes the various factors that led to the breakdown in the al-
    liance which initially existed between these influential scholars.

C. Thomas McCollough

LUIS BUÑUEL

Born: February 22, 1900; Calanda, Spain
Died: July 29, 1983; Mexico City, Mexico
Area of Achievement: Film
Contribution: With his first three films, Buñuel virtually defined the genre of Surrealist cinema. The thirty-two films that he directed (and often co-scripted) establish him as one of the century's most gifted film auteurs.

Early Life

The eldest of seven children, Luis Buñuel was born in Calanda, Spain, on February 22, 1900. His father, Leonardo, was a landowner with intellectual interests who died in 1923; his mother, Maria, was a well-educated, devout Catholic. Although Buñuel soon moved with his parents to Zaragoza, he regularly revisited Calanda for Easter weekend, when he would join hundreds of other males in a two-day drumming ritual called the Procession of the Drums. Buñuel received top marks as a student; among his interests were music and zoology. Following his father's urgings, he entered the Students' Residence in Madrid to become an agricultural engineer; in 1920, however, he surreptitiously began a two-year course of studies in entomology. A sports enthusiast, he also became the amateur boxing champion of Spain in 1921.

By the early 1920's, Buñuel had become acquainted with a group of friends that included Federico García Lorca and Salvador Dalí. Increasingly involved in literary and theatrical pursuits, he began the study of philosophy and letters at the University of Madrid, receiving his degree in 1924. He moved to Paris in 1926 with a letter of introducton to the pianist Ricardo Viñas, who soon assigned him to act as scenic director in the 1926 Amsterdam production of Manuel de Falla's *El retablo de Maese Pedro* (1923) under the musical leadership of Willem Mengelberg.

Soon afterward, a viewing of Fritz Lang's *Der müde Tod* (1921; *Destiny*) awakened Buñuel to the possibilities of film as an art form. After receiving an introduction to Jean Epstein, he spent the following two years working as assistant director on *Mauprat* (1926) and *La Chute de la Maison Usher* (1928; *The Fall of the House of Usher*), as well as the Josephine Baker vehicle *La Sirène des Tropiques* (1927; *Siren of the Tropics*). Buñuel also partook of more personal endeavors, enjoying some recognition as a writer, organizing screenings in Spain, and trying to initiate a number of film projects. Besides writing fiction and poetry, he edited the cinema page of *La Gaceta literaria hispanoamerica*, writing eight articles that reflected his commitment to Surrealism. In 1928, he helped to organize the Cineclub Español, the second such organization in Spain. That same year, he completed *Un Chien andalou* (1928; *An Andalusian Dog*), a collaboration with Dalí.

Life's Work

The seventeen minutes of *An Andalusian Dog*, among the most unforgettable and widely analyzed in cinema, provided both Buñuel and Dalí with their entry into the Surrealist circle. Buñuel's savage slicing of an eyeball comprises the film's most emblematic moment, for, with its revolutionary mixture of brutality, sexuality, and *amour*, Buñuel's first film opened Surrealist eyes to the potential of cinema to provoke the public into confronting previously unexplored truths.

Insisting that *An Andalusian Dog*, with its violent succession of titles and sequences, was "a desperate and passionate appeal to murder," Buñuel voiced dismay upon discovering that some had found beauty in it. Though *L'Âge d'or* (1930; *The Golden Age*) utilized a more coherent story line, it nevertheless sparked one of Paris' great controversies. An irreverent examination of the tension between human passions and social mores, the film opens with a documentary sequence about scorpions and proceeds to launch stinging attacks on a number of institutions, Catholicism among them. After Fascists and anti-Semites interrupted one of the film's first screenings, vandalizing the theater, *L'Âge d'or* was banned in France.

Buñuel left the Surrealist movement in 1932 but remained very sympathetic to its spirit. His documentary *Las Hurdes: Tierra sin pan* (1932; *Land Without Bread*), narrated in bitter, sardonic tones, was a landmark study of life in an impoverished region of Spain. As in his previous films, Buñuel used lush classical music, in this case excerpts from Johannes Brahms' Fourth Symphony, as his score.

Over the following years, Buñuel worked as a dubbing director in Paris and Madrid and oversaw the production of four comedies for the Spanish company Filmófono, leading crews with characteristic discipline and financial restraint. After the outbreak of the Spanish Civil War, he assisted the Republican government in Paris, where he supervised the production of a documentary about the conflict.

Following the war's cessation, Buñuel went to New York, where he worked at the Museum of Modern Art Film Department from 1939 to 1941. There he created documentaries from previously existing footage until anti-Communist paranoia and Dalí's comments regarding Buñuel's religious views precipitated his resignation. After a brief stint as a commentator for United States Army Intelligence films, Buñuel lived with his wife, Jeanne, and their two sons, Juan Luis and Rafael, in Hollywood. Backed by producer Oscar Dancigers, he began his directing career anew in Mexico with *Gran Casino/En el Viejo Tampico* (1947) and *El gran calavera* (1949; *The Great Madcap*, 1949).

Buñuel returned to international prominence with *Los olvidados* (1950; *The Forgotten Ones*). Winner at the 1951 Cannes Film Festival of the Jury Prize for best direction, the film depicts the lives of Mexico City slum youth with startling, unsentimentalized imagery. In the ensuing years, the director worked at a quick pace, creating profitable low-budget films with varying degrees of artistic success. *Susana* (1950; *The Devil and the Flesh*) and *La hija del engaño* (1951; *Daughter of Deceit*) were followed by *Una Mujer sin amor* (1951; *A Woman Without Love*), a melodrama that he considered his worst effort. More intriguing were the award-winning *Subida al cielo* (1951; *Mexican Bus Ride*), *El Bruto* (1952; *The Brute*), and *Las aventuras de Robinsón Crusoe* (1952; *The Adventures of Robinson Crusoe*), his first use of color. He made several more commercial films in the 1950's, including *Nazarín* (1959), a tale of a priest's attempt to emulate Christ's ideals, which won the 1959 Special Jury Prize at Cannes, and, to the anticlerical Buñuel's amusement, almost received the Prix de l'Office Catholique as well.

Despite his commercial orientation in the 1950's, Buñuel developed a manner of storytelling distinguished by its moral integrity, quasi-documentary realism, and iconoclastic incorporation of the incongruous. After making the political thriller *La Fièvre monte à El Pao/Los Ambiciosos* (1959; *Republic of Sin*) and *La Joven* (1960; (*The Young One*), he inaugurated a new phase of his career with *Viridiana* (1961), the official Spanish entry at Cannes. The spectacle of Buñuel the iconoclast collaborating with the Francisco Franco regime surprised many, but ultimately the brilliance of his direction vindicated Buñuel, who kept the censors from "supervising" his production by arranging for final mixing to occur in France just before *Viridiana*'s festival premiere. The film won for Spain its first Palme d'Or, but the final cut's treatment of sexuality and presentation of beggars mimicking *The Last Supper* were among the elements that led to *Viridiana*'s being vilified by the Vatican and banned in Spain.

For the next two decades, Buñuel enjoyed greater financial support and increasing control over subject matter. *El ángel exterminador* (1962; *The Exterminating Angel*) finds a group of people unable to leave a room in which they have just eaten their dinner. An updating of the Octave Mirbeau novel, *Le Journal d'une femme de chambre* (1964; *Diary of a Chambermaid*), Buñuel's first film with producer Serge Silberman and writer Jean-Claude Carrière, climaxes with a searingly personal indictment of French bigotry at the time of *L'Âge d'or*.

In 1966, Catherine Deneuve appeared as the bourgeois wife/prostitute in the 1967 Venice Film Festival winner *Belle de jour*, a treatment of the 1929 Joseph Kessel novel. After Buñuel made *La Voie lactée* (1969; *The Milky Way*), an anachronistic pilgrimage through Christian heresy, Deneuve returned alongside Fernando Rey in *Tristana* (1970), the director's second adaptation of a Benito Perez Galdos novel.

In the 1970's, Buñuel became increasingly subject to deafness and other problems of advanced age. If his first three films had established him as a fiery young iconoclast, his final three revealed him to be a matured master, able to enhance his Surrealist sensibility with an exceptionally profound understanding of human foibles. *Le Charme discret de la bourgeoisie* (1972; *The Discreet Charm of the Bourgeoisie*), winner of an Academy Award for best foreign language film, revolves around a group of well-to-do friends who continually arrange dinner appointments but hardly manage to eat anything. *Le Fantôme de la Liberté* (1974; *The Phantom of Liberty*) presents a series of bizarre vignettes in a free associational manner. *Cet obscur objet du desir* (1977; *That Obscure Object of Desire*) dramatizes the perverse relationship between a flirtatious young woman and an older gentleman who wishes to possess her.

In 1983, the year of Buñuel's death, the English translation of his autobiography, *My Last Sigh*, was published. He died in Mexico City at the age of eighty-three.

Summary

Although Luis Buñuel's early films represent a fraction of his entire output, they have often served as a pretext for categorizing him merely as an anti-Catholic provocateur with a predilection for scandalously violent imagery. While the significance of those works is incontestable (*An Andalusian Dog* and *L'Âge d'or* in particular were of paramount importance to the Surrealists), the entirety of his oeuvre, reflecting a level of wisdom and craftsmanship attained by few artists, is worthy of close consideration as reflecting the genius of one of cinema's great masters.

Buñuel deliberately cultivated a "flat" camera technique that focused attention on his enigmatic imagery and captivating scenarios, in which fanaticism, passion, and pathos often come to the fore. Slow motion and fading are used to imbue sequences with dreamlike qualities; montage is used sparingly. Music, used with irony in Buñuel's first films, faded further into the background as the director's career progressed (indeed, many of his later works lack scores). Also used sparingly are naturalistic sound effects, sometimes employed to suggest mental states or, notably, to obscure dialogue (a device that approximated Buñuel's own hearing difficulties). An underappreciated aspect of his directorial style is his treatment of actors; having been weaned during the silent era, Buñuel seems to have placed great stock in the histrionics often seen in silent melodramas.

Notwithstanding his iconoclasm, Buñuel was a creator rather than a destroyer, a moralist whose art arose from a deep appreciation of existential mystery and the human condition. At all points in his career, the director remained faithful to an aesthetic dictate predicated on "awakening" audiences by depicting authentic social relations. In many respects, he can be considered a forerunner of filmmakers such as Pedro Almodóvar, the members of Monty Python's Flying Circus, and John Waters. His achievements continue to have a profound influence on world cinema.

Bibliography

Aranda, Francisco. *Luis Buñuel: A Critical Biography.* Translated by David Robinson. London: Socker and Warburg, 1975. A valuable source of rare primary materials in English translation, this survey emphasizes the relationship between Buñuel's career and Spanish culture, and details some of his childhood experiences.

Bazin, André. *The Cinema of Cruelty.* Translated by Sabine d'Estrée. New York: Seaver Books, 1982. Introduced by François Truffaut, this collection of essays includes critiques of seven Buñuel films as well as an interview with the director.

Buache, Freddy. *The Cinema of Luis Buñuel.* Translated by Peter Graham. New York: A. S. Barnes, 1973. An admirer offers an impressionistic appreciation of Buñuel's films in a book that suffers from its awkward translated prose.

Buñuel, Luis. *My Last Sigh.* Translated by Abigail Israel. New York: Alfred A. Knopf, 1983. Assisted by Jean-Claude Carrière, Buñuel drolly reflects on his exploits.

Durgnat, Raymond. *Luis Buñuel.* Rev. ed. Berkeley: University of California Press, 1977. An unexceptional guide to Buñuel's films through *The Phantom of Liberty.*

Edwards, Gwynne. *The Discreet Art of Luis Buñuel.* London: M. Boyars, 1982. This book contains clearly written summaries of selected Buñuel films.

Higgenbotham, Virginia. *Luis Buñuel.* Boston: Twayne, 1979. A chronology and filmography help to distinguish this thorough study from Buache's and Durgnat's books.

Mellen, Joan, ed. *The World of Luis Buñuel.* New York: Oxford University Press, 1978. This most useful collection of essays includes Henry Miller's famous "The Golden Age" from *The Cosmological Eye* (1939) and pieces by Bazin, Vincent Canby, Carlos Fuentes, Ado Kyrou, and Andrew Sarris.

Sandro, Paul. *Luis Buñuel and the Crises of Desire.* Columbus: Ohio State University Press, 1987. A professor of French offers a scholarly, jargon-ridden look at the psychology of Buñuel's films.

Williams, Linda. *Figures of Desire.* Urbana: University of Illinois Press, 1981. Written with an obvious appreciation of Buñuel's subtleties, this book offers an invaluable, highly sophisticated look at *An Andalusian Dog, L'Âge d'or, The Phantom of Liberty,* and *That Obscure Object of Desire.*

David Marc Fischer

PLUTARCO ELÍAS CALLES

Born: September 25, 1887; Guaymas, Mexico
Died: October 19, 1945; Mexico City, Mexico
Areas of Achievement: Government and politics
Contribution: Calles was a member of the Sonoran Dynasty, which dominated Mexico's political life between 1920 and 1934. As president and *jefe maximo* (1924-1934), he institutionalized the Mexican Revolution and embarked upon a reform program that laid the foundation for modern Mexico's economic and political growth.

Early Life

Plutarco Elías Calles was born into a family that had lived in the Mexican province of Sonora for generations. His ancestors had founded towns, fought against American filibusters and French invaders, and served as governors of the province. His parents were Plutarco Elías and Maria Jesus de Calles, and he was orphaned at an early age. He was educated in the Guaymas public schools and at the State National School in Hermosillo. As a teenager he taught school in Guaymas and at the Escuela de la Moneda in Hermosillo.

His family connections served him well. He served as treasurer of the Guaymas Teaching Association, bartender, hotel manager, operator of a hacienda and flour mill, and newspaper editor. During this period, Calles had become an alcoholic, and, as a consequence, most of his positions were plagued by irregularities, firings, and bankruptcies. Calles also married twice, once during this period to Natalie Chacon in Sonora, who gave him seven children, and later to Leonor Llorente, with whom he had two children.

Life's Work

Calles' real interest, however, was in politics. He supported the Mexican Revolution (1910-1917) and fought for Francisco Madero and Venustiano Carranza. In 1911, he lost a campaign for Congress, but in 1912 he became police chief of Agua Prieta. At this time, he attached his political star to the Sonoran caudillo Álvaro Obregón and over the next few years emerged as part of the Sonoran Triumvirate (Obregón, Calles, and Adolfo de la Huerta). In 1917, following Carranza's triumph, Calles became constitutional governor and military commander of Sonora.

Calles' complex character emerged during this period. On the one hand, he posed as a reformer with socialist and anticlerical biases. As a reformed alcoholic, he promoted a prohibition campaign against the sale, manufacture, and use of alcohol, and he established Cruz Galvez Industrial School for orphans. On the other hand, his rule reflected ruthless intolerance for political opposition, including jailings, beatings, firing squads, and *ley fuga* as well as self-aggrandizement. These contradictory impulses remained a constant feature of Calles' career.

In September, 1919, Carranza made Calles secretary of industry, commerce, and work. In February, 1920, however, Calles resigned in order to support the presidential aspirations of General Obregón against Carranza's hand-picked successor. On April 23, 1920, the Sonoran Triumvirate pronounced the Plan de Agua Prieta and drove Carranza from office.

Calles served briefly as secretary of war in the interim government, and, when Obregón assumed the presidency in December, 1920, Calles became secretary of the interior (1920-1923). The Obregón government made a determined effort to implement the principles of the Mexican Revolution, especially in education, land, and economic programs. In 1923, Obregón tilted in favor of Calles as his successor, forcing conservatives and anti-Obregónistas to rally behind the aspirations of Huerta. A brief and bloody revolt occurred late in 1923, and Huerta was compelled to flee to the United States. Calles then easily won the presidential election and assumed office on December 1, 1924, the first peaceful transfer of power in Mexico since 1884.

President Calles proved to be a tough, no-nonsense leader. He was a tall, solidly built man with a short mustache and a dour demeanor. His features earned for him the nickname "El Turco." His cabinet was filled with cronies who became wealthy by looting the treasury. The most notorious of these so-called "forty thieves" was Luis Morones, head of the Confederacion Regional Obrera Mexicana (CROM), whom Calles made secretary of labor. Morones used his position to bring all recalcitrant labor groups under his control. For his part, Calles became a large landowner near Cuernavaca and ruled with an iron fist, adding *ley de suicidio* to his list of repressive measures.

Even so, Calles' record was filled with accomplishments. He had come to power at a moment when the Mexican economy was expanding and there were revenues available to finance his modernization program. He placed Mexico's finances in order with the creation of the Bank of Mexico, and he initiated Mexico's first income tax. He instituted a massive public works program to build Mexico's infrastructure: railroads, roads, bridges, dams, canals, and air service. He sent teachers into isolated rural areas, and he began national public health and inoculation campaigns. Agricultural schools were established to improve farming techniques.

Calles was aggressive in other areas as well. In land reform, he distributed eight million acres to fifteen hundred *ejidos*, and then plots were distributed to individual farmers. Agricultural banks were established to provide credit, but this proved to be a major source of corruption as most of the loans went to *Callistas* and *hacendados*. Calles used his relationship with Morones to keep labor strikes down while modestly increasing wages and other benefits.

One of Calles' great achievements was to tame the Mexican Army and subordinate it to civilian control. This enabled him to reduce the military budget and transfer money into his public works program.

The opposition of the Catholic church to the Mexican Revolution and the Constitution of 1917 proved to be one of the gravest challenges to the Calles government. Calles precipitated the crisis by banning all religious processions, closing church schools, and exiling foreign priests. The Church responded by going on strike, and the Cristero War (1926-1929) was quelled only with great difficulty. In 1929, with unofficial mediation from the United States, the Church and the government agreed to a *modus vivendi* in which the government promised not to destroy the Church and the latter would submit to registration of its priests with the government.

Calles also zealously enforced the constitution's provisions regarding state control over natural resources. In 1925, Calles ordered all domestic and foreign oil companies to exchange their titles for fifty-year leases. Consequently, United States-Mexican relations became strained. In 1927, Ambassador Dwight M. Morrow arrived in Mexico City to resolve the crisis. Morrow exhibited sensitivity toward the Mexican people and their culture, and he developed a close working relationship with Calles. At Morrow's suggestion, Calles worked out a compromise. In 1927, the Mexican Supreme Court ruled that the oil companies had to comply with the law, but the leases would not be terminated in fifty years.

By 1927, it was clear that no *Callista* could succeed to the presidency, and Calles decided to allow Obregón to return to power. He amended the Constitution to allow six-year presidential terms and to allow former presidents to serve nonconsecutive terms. Political enemies censored this move as violations of the principles of the Revolution and launched a brief and unsuccessful revolt. This left Obregón without significant opposition in the 1928 presidential campaign. Unfortunately, Obregón's victory was short-lived, because he was assassinated on July 17, 1928, by a Catholic fanatic.

Obregón's murder was Calles' great opportunity. He decided not to take the presidency himself and appointed General Emilio Portes Gil of Tamaulipas as provisional president until an election could be held. On September 1, 1928, he declared that the era of the caudillo was over and that the Revolution would be dominated by institutions, not by men. To achieve this, he met in February, 1929, in Querétaro with state governors, generals, and influential politicos to create a national political party, the Partido Nacional Revolucionario (PNR). This party represented the various sectors of the Mexican economy as well as politicos and military officers. The PNR then proceeded to nominate General Pascual Ortiz Rubio of Michoacán, as the next president.

Calles' great achievement was tarnished by his desire to rule behind the scenes as *jefe maximo de la revolucion* (supreme leader of the revolution), thus making the presidency a satellite of his power. This era is known as the *maximato* (1928-1934). Calles changed presidents at will: Ortiz Rubio was replaced in 1932 by General Abelardo Rodriguez. The *maximato* reflected a significant shift to the right as Calles lost much of his reforming zeal, especially in agrarian and labor matters. Instead, the era saw the consolidation of national power under the PNR and corruption at all levels of government.

As the *maximato* concluded, Calles became concerned over the drift of the revolutionary program, and he made an effort to move to the left with a six-year plan designed to promote further reform and stimulate the economy. He also selected General Lázaro Cárdenas, Governor of Michoacán, to be the next presidential candidate. Upon Cárdenas' victory in 1934, however, Calles was dismayed to find the president unwilling to take orders. Cárdenas moved rapidly to isolate Calles from the power elites of the party and the military. When Calles criticized the government's handling of labor unrest, Cárdenas exiled him on April 11, 1936, to the United States. Calles remained in exile until May 5, 1941, when President Manuel Ávila Camacho allowed him to return in peace. In 1942, Calles was given his old position in the Mexican Army, and on Independence Day, 1942, Calles joined Avila Camacho and all living former Mexican presidents on the balcony of the National Palace to symbolize Mexican unity during World War II. Calles died in Mexico City in October 19, 1945.

Summary

Plutarco Elías Calles' record is a mixture of dedication to public service and to self-interest. As a result, his place in Mexican history remains controversial. Whatever his motivations, he unquestionably helped to bring an end to the cycle of revolutionary violence that had characterized Mexican politics between 1910 and 1928. The creation of the PNR was statecraft of the highest order—it brought political peace to Mexico at long last; and it represented a successful experiment in authoritarian, one-party democracy that has continued into the 1980's. That act was tarnished by Calles' lust for power and his intention to govern Mexico as *jefe maximo*.

Calles did much good. His public works program broke down the isolation of Mexico's agrarian poor, and his public health campaigns improved their general standard of health. He distributed more land to peasants than any other president before him, but he failed to increase agricultural production, leading to food shortages in the 1930's. In the end, Calles was forced to declare that the Revolution had failed and needed to be reinvigorated by a bold new plan for economic development.

At heart, Calles was one of the last caudillos, not a democrat. He believed in force and power, and he devoted his political life to the institutionalization of power and to making it work for the common good and for himself. He also defended Mexican nationalism and independence from foreign, particularly United States', encroachment. For all of his flaws as a political leader, Calles was a giant of the Revolution whose impact, for good or ill, is still felt in Mexico.

Bibliography

Alba, Victor. *The Mexicans: The Making of a Nation*. New York: Pegasus, 1967. A balanced overview of Mexican political history, emphasizing the Mexican revolutionary era. A generally positive interpretation of Calles' career.

Brenner, Anita. *The Wind That Swept Mexico: The History of the Mexican Revolution, 1910-1942*. New York: Harper and Brothers, 1943. Combined with George R. Leighton's photographs, this is an interesting, if jaundiced, view of the revolutionary era. Calles' career is emphasized.

Callcott, Wilfred Hardy. *Liberalism in Mexico, 1857-1929*. Stanford: Stanford University Press, 1931. A well-researched analysis of liberalism's impact on Mexico. Very good description of Calles' reform program.

Calles, Plutarco Elías. *Mexico Before the World: Public Documents and Addresses of Plutarco Elías Calles*. Translated by Robert Hammond Murray. New York: Academy Press, 1927. Consists of addresses made by Calles relating to Mexican problems, including personality portraits and biographical data provided by Calles' supporters.

Cline, Howard F. *The United States and Mexico*. Cambridge, Mass.: Harvard University Press, 1963. Excellent analysis of United States-Mexican relations from the 1800's to the post-World War II era. The section on the Sonoran Dynasty is very scholarly and filled with detail.

Dulles, John W. F. *Yesterday in Mexico: A Chronicle of the Revolution, 1919-1936*. Austin: University of Texas Press, 1961. An excellent review of the Sonoran Dynasty, with emphasis on the Calles era. Well written and balanced in discussing political movements and personalities.

Magner, James A. *Men of Mexico*. Milwaukee: Bruce Publishing, 1943. Consists of a series of small biographies of men who made Mexico a nation. Harshly critical of Calles.

Stephen P. Sayles

ALBERT CALMETTE

Born: July 12, 1863; Nice, France
Died: October 29, 1933; Paris, France
Areas of Achievement: Biology and medicine
Contribution: Calmette, working with Camille Guérin, was the first to introduce vaccination against tuberculosis. In 1894, he improved the serum
used to treat patients with plague that was first prepared by Alexandre
Yersin. Calmette was one of the first to introduce a single antiserum
against snake venom that was effective against many different types of
snakes. His work in public health extended to the introduction of sewage
purification as well as the control of many infectious diseases.

Early Life

Albert Calmette was born in Nice, France, on July 12, 1863. He had two
brothers, one of whom became an army physician, and the other, a journalist. When he was only two years old, his mother, Adèle Reine Charpentière,
died, and his father, Guillaume Calmette, remarried; Calmette was reared by
his stepmother, Marie Quiney. When Albert was ten years old, the family
moved to Clermont-Ferrand and, three years later, to Saint-Brieuc in Brittany. It was in Brittany that Calmette obtained his *baccalauréat* at Saint
Charles College. In 1881, Calmette entered the Naval Medical College at
Brest. Two years later, he was sent as part of his training to the Far East,
where he was greatly influenced by the work of Sir Patrick Manson, a pioneer in tropical diseases.

With this newfound knowledge, Calmette returned to France in 1885 and
completed the requirements for the M.D. degree by 1886, working on the
disease filariasis. Between 1886 and 1888, Calmette studied sleeping sickness and blackwater fever in the French Congo, in Gabon. On his return to
France, he married Émilie de la Salle, who bore him two sons. Subsequently, he was stationed at Saint Pierre and Miquelon, which were French
islands off the coast of Newfoundland. There he studied the red spotted
condition of salted cod, establishing this strange condition as being a result
of infection and demonstrating that it could be prevented by the addition of
sodium sulfate to the salt. In 1890, Calmette joined the French Colonial
Medical Service to pursue a research career in the study of tropical diseases.

Life's Work

The turning point in Calmette's career was the year 1890, when he attended a course in microbiology given by Pierre-Paul-Émile Roux at the
Pasteur Institute in Paris. The course not only captured his interest and
imagination but also allowed him to distinguish himself as an outstanding
pupil with the capacity for clear thinking. When the Undersecretary of State
for the French colonies sought the help of Louis Pasteur to study the prob-

lems of smallpox, rabies, dysentery, and cholera in Indochina, Calmette's name was immediately suggested for this position. On December 10, 1890, Calmette sailed to Saigon, where he established a Pasteur Institute with the primary aim of locally producing needed vaccines. Substituting young water buffalo for the young calves usually used in the West, Calmette was able to mass-produce smallpox vaccines and a half million people were soon inoculated against the deadly disease. In initial studies, Calmette was able to demonstrate that the disease *choi-ghai* in dogs was in fact a manifestation of rabies. Subsequently, he used the spinal cords of rabid rabbits as a storage reservoir for the virus and used the vaccine successfully in forty-seven out of forty-eight animal-bite victims.

About the same time, the high mortality of cobra-bite victims caught his attention, and he embarked on a study of the venoms of these reptiles. He painstakingly categorized and classified them, and compared them to toxins produced by bacteria. His studies revealed that the toxic effects of cobra venom on the brain could be neutralized by gold chloride solution. He also discovered that the venom could be attenuated (and made less toxic) by calcium hypochlorite solution, laying the basis for the production of anti-venom serum in animals by injecting increasing doses of the venom into these animals and after a few weeks removing serum from these animals that was now rich with protective antitoxin.

During his stay in Saigon, Calmette refined the processes of alcohol and opium fermentation. He also made attempts to define Asiatic cholera, using fresh cultures of the organisms from patients who had died of the disease. He described in detail the toxic effects of the organisms as well as his attempts at immunization and his recommendations for treatment, including peritoneal dialysis with saline solution. In 1893, two years after his arrival in Saigon, Calmette was recalled to France, having accomplished a prodigious amount of work in that short period of time. Riddled by bouts of dysentery and exhausted by the intense rigors of his work in Saigon, Calmette moved to the Pasteur Institute in Paris, where he continued his research efforts in antivenom therapy. In 1893, he was awarded the Cross of the Legion of Honor for his efforts in Saigon. In 1894, Calmette, using some of the expertise he had gained working with snake venom, worked to improve the anti-plague serum developed by Yersin and thus helped to quell the plague epidemic in the Far East that year. In 1896, he was appointed director of the Pasteur Institute at Lille, France, a position he was to hold for twenty-four years.

At this time, the main public health problem facing Lille was a high incidence of tuberculosis, the death rate being in the region of 300 per 100,000. Calmette approached the problem systematically, in the same manner that he had tackled other problems that he encountered in the Far East. He began the first antituberculosis dispensary at Lille in 1901, and, subsequently, a tuberculosis sanatorium at Montigny-en-Ostrevant in 1905. In 1907, he introduced the conjunctival tuberculin test that was used to demonstrate whether a patient had tuberculous infection; this test was soon replaced by the more convenient intradermal tuberculin test which was devised by Charles Mantoux.

Observing the validity of Marfan's law, which proposed that progressive lung tuberculosis was rare in patients who had previously developed tuberculosis lymph-node infection, Calmette attempted to develop a vaccine against tuberculosis along the lines of the antirabies vaccine pioneered by Pasteur. The major problem in the development of the vaccine was creating a strain of tubercle bacillus that would not cause clinical disease in persons vaccinated and yet retain enough similarity with the native tuberculous bacillus that the patient's immune system would be stimulated to develop resistance against the tuberculous infection. Serendipitously, Calmette and Camille Guérin noted that subculturing tubercle baccilli in ox bile led to a lowering of the ability of the organism to cause disease. They therefore proceeded to grow the bacillus originally provided them by Edmond Nocard (an aggressive strain isolated from the udder of a tuberculous cow) in this medium. Interrupted in their attempts to initiate animal experiments with this attenuated strain by World War I, they continued to subculture the bacillus until 1919, when they were able to demonstrate that the strain no longer produced tuberculosis in animals. This bacillus was named Bacille Calmette-Guérin (popularly referred to as the BCG vaccine).

Between 1921 and 1928, several thousand infants were given the BCG vaccine by the oral route without adverse effects. The statistics provided by Calmette and Guérin demonstrated a significant reduction in death from tuberculosis among susceptible, vaccinated infants. Except for sporadic skepticism in Great Britain and the United States, the BCG vaccine was well received and tested. Yet in 1930 disaster struck: A scheme to vaccinate newborn babies was undertaken by a team of doctors in Lubeck, Germany, and of 250 babies vaccinated, 73 died and another 135 developed tuberculosis but recovered. Much criticism was raised about this issue, which was traced to contamination of the vaccine by a virulent strain of tubercle bacillus in the Lubeck laboratories. At the Oslo meeting of the International Union Against Tuberculosis, Calmette defended the vaccine and was received with great appreciation. Yet the Lubeck disaster was forever to affect his sense of optimism and cheerful disposition.

Following a short illness, Albert Calmette died in Paris on October 29, 1933, at the age of seventy. He was buried in the Pasteur Institute in Paris. During his productive lifetime, many honors were bestowed on Calmette. He was elected to the French Academy of Sciences in 1907 and the French Academy of Medicine in 1919. In 1928, he was elevated to the Grand Cross of the Order.

Summary

Born into an era that boasted such renowned scientific figures as Élie Metchnikoff, August von Wassermann, and Louis Pasteur, Albert Calmette rose to distinction by hard work, dedication, and a passion for detail. In a career that spanned fifty years, he was able to make substantial contributions to preventive and therapeutic medicine. Besides initiating several Pasteur Institutes in needy places, he expended great effort in quelling epidemics of ancylostomiasis, typhoid, plague, and tuberculosis. The creation of the BCG vaccine for tuberculosis has earned for him a place in medical history. A cheerful optimist and a born administrator, he was revered by all with whom he came into contact. His outstanding abilities to adapt laboratory techniques to a sweltering tropical climate and produce vaccines on a large scale were impressive. By his ceaseless endeavor, curiosity, and industriousness, Calmette has left behind him a legacy for humankind.

Bibliography

Calmette, A. *Venoms, Venomous Animals, and Antivenomous Serum-Therapeutics.* Translated by Ernest E. Austen. New York: W. Wood, 1908. This book by Calmette, complete with detailed illustrations, is an example of the meticulousness with which he approached different tasks. The book reveals Calmette to have been a talented naturalist; this work alone would have ensured his renown. His achievements in BCG control overshadowed his work with cobra venom.

Calmette, A., et al. *A Series of Public Lectures, Specially Prepared for the Sixth International Congress on Tuberculosis.* Philadelphia: W. F. Fell, 1908. Contains the transcripts of a series of public lectures given by Calmette (and others) describing the rationale, development, and application of the BCG vaccine.

Gelinas, J. A. "Albert Calmette: The Saigon Years." *Military Medicine,* 1973. Provides photographs of the locale and architecture of the Pasteur Institute in Saigon and a description of Calmette's work environment and achievements in Saigon. His work on the smallpox and rabies vaccines and the method by which he overcame the problems of inadequate refrigeration by using animal reservoirs is a fascinating story in itself. His work with dysentery, cobra venom, Chinese yeast (which he refined so that it doubled its yield of alcohol), and opium is also described.

Sakula, A. "BCG: Who Were Calmette and Guérin?" *Thorax* 38 (1983): 806-812. This article, written on the fiftieth anniversary of the death of Calmette, briefly reviews the lives of both Calmette and Guérin and their association to produce the BCG vaccine. Includes a photograph from the Pasteur Institute in Paris and a reproduction of the French postage stamp issued on the occasion of the First International BCG Congress in 1948, with Calmette's likeness on it. The article also provides a background of the stages in the development of the BCG vaccine. Details of the tragic Lubeck disaster are also described.

Wallgren, A. "Value of Calmette Vaccination in Prevention of Tuberculosis." *Journal of the American Medical Association* 103 (1934): 1341-1345. A scholarly survey on the efficacy of BCG vaccination tested in Göteborg, Sweden. Out of 355 children who were vaccinated with BCG, 230 of them were subsequently exposed to tuberculous infection after being vaccinated, and only one developed probable pulmonary tuberculosis. The review was strongly in favor of the vaccination.

Abraham Verghese
Guha Krish

ALBERT CAMUS

Born: November 7, 1913; Mondovi, Algeria
Died: January 4, 1960; near Villeblevin, France
Areas of Achievement: Literature and philosophy
Contribution: Camus's philosophical and literary writings established his
    reputation as the moral conscience of France during the 1940's and
    1950's. With understated eloquence, he reaffirmed the intrinsic values of
    individual freedom and dignity in the face of such evils as Nazism, Stalin-
    ism, and colonial exploitation.

Early Life

Albert Camus had a very difficult childhood. When he was born on November 7, 1913, his parents Lucien and Catherine were living in the small
Algerian city of Mondovi, where his father worked for a vineyard. His
parents were very poor. The very next year, Lucien was drafted, and he died
in October, 1914, as a result of wounds received during the Battle of the
Marne. His widow Catherine, already partially deaf, suffered a stroke soon
after Lucien's death, and this stroke permanently affected her speech. She
moved to Algiers with her two sons, Albert and Lucien. They lived with her
domineering mother, Catherine Sintes, in the working-class neighborhood of
Belcourt. The harsh conditions of Camus's youth taught him to value independence, personal responsibility, and human dignity.

Camus did very well in grammar school and earned a scholarship to the
prestigious Grand Lycée of Algiers, where he developed a profound interest
in philosophy and literature under the guidance of his teacher, Jean Grenier,
to whom he would later dedicate both a volume of essays, *L'Envers et
l'endroit* (1937; *The Wrong Side and the Right Side*, 1968), and a philosophical essay, *L'Homme révolté* (1951; *The Rebel*, 1956). At the age of seventeen, however, he became gravely ill with tuberculosis, from which his
lungs never fully recovered. Camus did, however, resume his studies, and in
1936 he defended his master's thesis on the problem of evil in the writings of
Plotinus and Saint Augustine. Although his mother was Catholic, Camus
was an agnostic. His medical problems prevented him from being offered a
teaching position in Algeria.

Between 1935 and his move to France in 1942, he worked as a journalist
in Algiers. He also became involved with a theatrical troupe there, first as an
actor and then as a playwright and director. He wrote his first play, *Caligula*
(English translation, 1948), in 1938. He temporarily joined the Algerian
Communist Party, but he soon became disillusioned with communism. His
distrust of communism greatly influenced his political opinions. In 1940, he
married Francine Faure. Two years later, he moved permanently to France in
order to join the French Resistance. Francine stayed in Algeria from 1942

until 1944. She rejoined Camus in 1944 after the liberation of Paris. Camus
and Francine had two children—twins, Catherine and Jean, born in 1945.

Life's Work

Although Camus did publish in Algiers two well-crafted volumes of short
stories, *Betwixt and Between* and *Noces* (1938; *Nuptials*, 1968) in the
1930's, his work was then appreciated only in Algeria. His international
reputation as a writer and philosopher dates from the publication in occupied
Paris of *L'Étranger* (1942; *The Stranger*, 1946) and *Le Mythe de Sisyphe*
(1942; *The Myth of Sisyphus and Other Stories*, 1955).

The *Stranger* is a first-person narrative whose principal character, Meursault, does not even have a first name. Meursault, an Algerian office worker,
is alienated from society. He is incapable of expressing strong emotions even
at his mother's wake and burial. He has no real ambition or sensitivity to the
feelings of his lover Marie. Meursault does not truly respect the dignity of
other people. Raymond, a close friend, is a pimp, and Meursault sees nothing wrong with this amoral profession. Meursault kills an Arab who has been
following Raymond. Although Meursault is clearly guilty, he still should
receive a fair trial. Impartial justice, of course, no longer existed in occupied
France. The presiding judge overtly favors the prosecutor, who is allowed to
introduce numerous irrelevant and damaging remarks about Meursault,
whose incompetent or corrupt lawyer never protests effectively. Nazi collaborators in France denounced *The Stranger* as a dangerous novel because it
held the French judicial system up to ridicule. In an early essay on *The
Stranger*, Jean-Paul Sartre noted perceptively that these collaborators had not
fully understood *The Stranger*. This novel clearly condemns the legal injustices committed by the Nazis and their collaborators, but it also reaffirms
the French republican ideals of "Liberty, Equality, and Fraternity." The
Nazis wanted nothing to do with the moral values of the French Third Republic, which they had destroyed in 1940.

Camus's next major work was his 1942 philosophical treatise *The Myth of
Sisyphus*. According to Greek mythology, Sisyphus was condemned for eternity to push a large rock to the top of a mountain. Every time he reached the
summit, his rock rolled back into the valley. Despite the apparently absurd
nature of his task, Sisyphus never gave in to the forces that were trying to
destroy his spirit. Camus imagines that Sisyphus was being punished because he had rebelled against the arbitrary power of the gods. Camus transforms Sisyphus into a moral hero who resists evil. Many readers have interpreted *The Myth of Sisyphus* as an ethical defense of the French Resistance.
In the last paragraph of this work, Camus describes Sisyphus at the bottom
of his mountain. Sisyphus must decide whether it is worth the effort to
continue his fight for human dignity. Sisyphus will not give in to evil. Camus
ends *The Myth of Sisyphus* with the thought-provoking remark, "We must

imagine Sisyphus to be happy." Sisyphus realizes that he is morally superior to the evil forces that seek to destroy him.

Three years after the liberation of France, Camus published his most extended reflection on the evil of Nazism. His powerful 1947 novel *La Peste* (*The Plague*, 1948) takes place in the walled Algerian city of Oran. *The Plague* is technically a series of diary entries, but readers do not discover until the very last chapter that Dr. Bernard Rieux kept this diary. Camus describes Oran as a typical modern city with which any reader can identify. The plague suddenly breaks out and the walls of Oran are closed in order to prevent this epidemic from spreading to other cities. For the inhabitants of Oran, this plague symbolizes the absolute evil against which they must fight. The political and moral implications of *The Plague* were clear to Camus's contemporaries. The closed walls of Oran may represent the closed frontiers of those countries occupied by the Nazis or they may refer more directly to the walls around the Nazi death camps. In plague-ridden Oran, crematoria are used to dispose of the numerous corpses. This clearly reminds Camus's readers of the crematoria used by the Nazis in their concentration camps.

For highly diverse reasons, characters such as the agnostic Dr. Rieux, the journalist Rambert, and the modest civil servant Joseph Grand all decide to fight the plague. The incredibly destructive power of evil is illustrated when Camus describes the painful death of Judge Othon's young son. The screams from this dying child cause Father Paneloux to question his belief in a just God, and they almost destroy Judge Othon's will to live. The gruesome death of his young child is reminiscent of the millions of equally innocent children and adults whom the Nazis murdered. At the end of this novel, the plague itself is over but its effects will last for years and generations to come. Camus ended this powerful novel by reminding his readers that evil can never be permanently eradicated, because a plague may break out at any time in another "happy city." *The Plague* was such an extraordinarily effective novel that the members of the Swedish Academy seriously considered giving Camus the Nobel Prize in 1947. Camus was then only thirty-four years old, and the youngest previous Nobel laureate had been Rudyard Kipling, who was forty-three years old when he received his Nobel Prize in Literature in 1907. In 1957, the Swedish Academy would honor Camus with the Nobel Prize in Literature.

During the last twelve years of his relatively short life, Camus became very involved in the theatrical life of France. His plays stressed both the absolute need to respect human life and the danger of political theories that try to justify the use of violence as a means of changing society. Among his most important contributions to the theater were *L'État de siège* (1948; *The State of Siege*, 1958), *Les Justes* (1950; *The Just Assassins*, 1958), and his 1956 adaptation of William Faulkner's *Requiem for a Nun* (1951). His major philosophical work from this period was his 1951 book *The Rebel*, in which he argued against all uses of violence as a technique for social change. *The Rebel* provoked an extremely negative reaction from Jean-Paul Sartre, who believed that violence was sometimes justifiable. Camus considered Sartre's arguments to be both specious and dangerous. The rupture between Camus and Sartre would be permanent. In 1956, Camus published his last complete novel, *La Chute* (*The Fall*, 1957), a marvelously ironic book about an amoral lawyer named Jean-Baptiste Clamence. During the last year of his life, Camus worked on a novel entitled "Le Premier Homme" (the first man) about his own youth. When he died in an automobile accident on January 4, 1960, the unfinished manuscript of "The First Man" was found in Camus's attaché case. Although he died at the relatively young age of forty-six, Camus was a very prolific writer with extremely varied interests.

Summary

Albert Camus was an eloquent "man of letters" in the finest sense of the term. His intelligence, modesty, and fierce commitment to moral values created a very favorable impression on contemporaries from Africa, Europe, and other continents as well. Since his death in 1960, his writings have continued to inspire much creative scholarship, and his analysis of the human condition still fascinates readers from around the world.

His refusal to propose simplistic answers to complex moral and social problems alienated Camus from many French intellectuals on both the political Left and Right. He refused, however, to compromise his ethical beliefs in order to placate even influential critics such as Jean-Paul Sartre and François Mauriac. Personal integrity was indispensable for Camus. He courageously resisted all attempts to limit basic freedoms. He fought in the French Resistance; he was once expelled from his native Algeria because of newspaper articles he had written to denounce the mistreatment of Arabs by the French colonial authorities, and he frequently criticized political abuses in such countries as Francisco Franco's Spain and communist Hungary and East Germany. When he received the Nobel Prize in Literature in December, 1957, his acceptance speech stressed that a conscientious writer should convey to others the interrelated values of truth and liberty. His profound insights into the human condition have enriched the lives of readers from many different cultures.

Bibliography

Brée, Germaine. *Camus and Sartre: Crisis and Commitment*. New York: Delacorte, 1972. This book accurately describes similarities and differences between Camus and Sartre. Brée disagrees sharply with O'Brien's contention that Camus was insensitive to the situation of Arabs in Algeria.

Fitch, Brian T. *The Narcissistic Text: A Reading of Camus' Fiction*. Toronto: University of Toronto Press, 1982. This creative book examines

Camus's major works of fiction from the perspective of reader-response criticism. Fitch stresses the numerous ambiguities in *The Stranger, The Plague*, and *The Fall*.

Lazere, Donald. *The Unique Creation of Albert Camus*. New Haven: Yale University Press, 1973. This fascinating psychoanalytic reading of Camus's works also enriches our appreciation of Camus's style. Lazere's final chapter summarizes well American critical reactions to Camus's works.

Lottman, Herbert R. *Albert Camus*. Garden City, N.Y.: Doubleday, 1979. This is an extremely well-documented biography of Camus. Lottman based this book on extensive interviews of people who knew Camus well.

Merton, Thomas. *Albert Camus' "The Plague": Introduction and Commentary*. New York: Seabury Press, 1968. This book proposes a profound theological interpretation of *The Plague*. Thomas Merton, a Trappist monk and a famous writer, shows that the two sermons delivered by Fr. Paneloux in this novel distort the traditional Christian concept of grace.

O'Brien, Conor Cruise. *Albert Camus of Europe and Africa*. New York: Viking Press, 1970. This very controversial book argues that Camus was insensitive to the plight of Arabs in French Algeria. Brée and other critics have questioned the validity of O'Brien's thesis.

Rhein, Phillip H. *Albert Camus*. New York: Twayne, 1969. This excellent general study of Camus's works defines well the originality of his contributions to French literature and philosophy.

Edmund J. Campion

FELIX CANDELA

Born: January 27, 1910; Madrid, Spain

Area of Achievement: Architecture

Contribution: Candela specialized in thin concrete shells as an architectural form. Although not the first to use them, he carried them to new artistic heights, while maintaining their practicality and economy.

Early Life

Born in Spain and descended from Galician, Basque, and Moorish blood, Felix Candela later preferred to emphasize his Moorish ancestry partly because of the Mediterranean tradition of building. Upon the death of his father in 1929, the burden of supporting the family fell upon Candela's shoulders. Needing a vocation, and feeling no particular calling, he heeded the advice of a friend and took up architecture. He enrolled at the Escuela Superior de Arquitectura in Madrid, where the curriculum included highly theoretical courses such as geometry, structural theory, and the theory of elasticity. Although Candela did well in his studies, he was not particularly taken with the theory of structures, other than for an intense interest in geometry.

Candela was an accomplished athlete as a youth. In 1932, he became the Spanish national champion skier; in 1934, he led his rugby team to the Spanish national championship; and he also excelled at mountain climbing, the triple jump, pole vaulting, and the hurdles. His athletic experiences, he once related, helped sharpen the mind and build self-confidence.

While still a student, Candela developed a strong interest in thin concrete shells and began to compile an extensive bibliography on the subject, including articles in German, French, and English. Upon being graduated from the Escuela Superior de Arquitectura in 1935, Candela opened a small studio in Madrid with two other architects. There Candela and his associates tutored students and took in drafting and calculating work from other architects. In 1936, Candela won a travel scholarship to study thin concrete shells in Germany, but the outbreak of the Spanish Civil War prevented him from using it. Instead he joined the republican army, eventually being promoted to captain of engineers. With the Franco victory, he fled to France, where he was held in a concentration camp for four months, and later sailed to Mexico. He arrived in Vera Cruz in 1939 and shortly thereafter resumed a practice in architecture.

Life's Work

Candela's first few years in Mexico were not entirely successful. First, he became the architect for a colony of Spaniards near the city of Chihuahua. After building several residences and starting a municipal building, the colony dissolved and Candela returned to Mexico City. For a short time he worked as a draftsman for a small construction firm, but in 1941 he moved to Acapulco. Entering into a partnership with a contractor, Candela built several residences, an apartment building, and a series of bungalows for a hotel. Returning to Mexico City in 1942, he joined the architectural office of José Marti, where he spent the next four years. By his own description, the time in Marti's office finished what he saw as his apprenticeship. He then joined forces with his brother Antonio, an engineer, and built more apartments and a hotel. All the projects from his first decade in Mexico, however, were nondescript. Only in his last year with Marti did Candela rediscover his fascination with thin concrete shells.

Once again, Candela began compiling a reading list of works on thin shells, using foreign-language dictionaries to translate them. This renewed interest in thin concrete shells represented a renewal of his career as well. He saw, as a result of his wide reading on the subject, a new approach to building thin shells, one which relied less on scientific theory and more on aesthetic concerns and the designer's intuition. He continued to think and write about the design of thin concrete shells, and in 1953 (1954 in English) he published in *Progressive Architecture* an article entitled "Stereo-Structures," which attacked the indiscriminate use of scientific theory by architects and engineers. He pointed out that there was nothing inherently wrong with modern structural theories, but he did not think they applied to reinforced concrete. In 1954, at a conference at the Massachusetts Institute of Technology (MIT), he presented a paper on his method of designing thin concrete shells. When a member of the audience expressed skepticism about one of his equations, he pointed out that perhaps it was better to look at his structures, which were standing, than to rely on equations.

By the mid-1950's, Candela had established a firm reputation on the basis of his shells and the many uses for them. After some early experimentation, Candela settled on the hyperbolic paraboloid shape (also known as a hypar) for virtually all of his shells. He considered it the easiest and the most practical to build, an assertion supported by the economy of many of his projects. Aesthetically, the designer could accomplish much with these shells, since they were usually only one and a half inches thick and could be shaped in a great variety of ways. Another attractive feature of the hypars was the relative ease (compared to many other types of structures) with which the shell's stresses could be calculated, thus giving the designer greater artistic license. In designing these shells, Candela began with an artistic shape, then determined its dimensions (based on his previous experience), mentally estimated the stresses of the shell, and finally checked his work with mathematical analysis.

A hypar shell is a doubly curved shape (in conventional configurations it resembles a saddle), which can be "distorted" by lengthening one side, by squaring the edges, leaving the edges curved, or using many other variations of the basic form. One particularly useful form that Candela exploited is known as the umbrella. Usually rectangular in plan, it consists of four hypars and actually resembles an umbrella blown inside out. When supported on a single central column, an umbrella can function as a roof over an entrance to a building or as a shade in an outdoor work area. A series of interconnected umbrellas becomes an inexpensive means of putting a roof over a large floor area. It is not surprising, then, that Candela's umbrellas were used in many factories and warehouses throughout Mexico.

In contrast to the flattened hypars of the umbrellas, Candela also employed more daring forms of hypars in his structures. One of his best-known churches, the Iglesia de la Virgen Milagrosa (Church of the Miraculous Virgin), has a sharply sloped roof, sixty-five feet at its highest point, made up of series of hypars that extend from the peak of the roof almost to the floor. Candela actually derived the hypars in this structure by elongating and bending umbrella shapes.

Candela departed from the angular edges of his umbrellas and modified umbrellas in designing the shells that enclose the main hall of Mexico's stock exchange. A Mexican architectural firm, in early 1954, wanted to build a doubly curved, groined vault for the stock exchange but was unable to find an engineer who could design such vaults. When the firm approached Candela, however, he thought it was a beautiful and logical idea and began studying the problem. These vaults differed from his other shells because they had curved edges, rather than the straight edges of the umbrellas—a whole new structural problem. Candela found the solution, however, and successfully built the vaults.

In El Altillo Chapel, Candela created yet another form of hypar. The roof for this chapel, rhomboidal in plan, was a relatively flat hypar with a slightly tilted vertical axis—this was the first time Candela tried such a hypar (it greatly complicates stress calculation). The lower two corners of the "saddle" were supported, allowing the other two corners to be cantilevered (with only minimal support, in order to check deflection caused by temperature changes). This particular hypar has been likened to a sheet of paper twisted gently in the wind.

Most of Candela's shells were only one and a half inches thick, but it is often difficult to judge the thickness, because of beams or framework that added strength in critical areas. Candela saw these additions, as many engineers might not have, as impediments to the beauty of the shell. He viewed it as a special challenge in his work to remove the edge beams from his shells, thus expressing visually the strength and beauty of the shell. This type of shell is known as a free-edge shell, the best example of which is found in the restaurant at Xochimilco. It is one of Candela's best-known works and the one which he considers to be his most significant. The restaurant is an octagonal groined vault made up of four hypars rotated about a common center. The structure is the shell, and its thinness is apparent even to the layman's eye, since there is quite literally no other supporting structure. In this way, Candela achieved the uncompromised shell—its shape is its strength.

Summary

Felix Candela's impact lies in the originality and variety he brought to thin concrete shell construction, especially in hyperbolic paraboloid shells (hypars). In fact, in Mexico, Candela's name is synonymous with hypars, such is the extent of his work with them. Candela is not an architect per se; rather, he considers himself a contractor, looking after architecture, structure, and construction all at once. This combination of roles is the result of his work with hypars in the sense that the building materials and techniques create an architectural shape that provides its own structural strength. Candela places artistic creativity before engineering as he designs his shells. He uses calculations to check that which his artistic sense and his engineer's intuition tell him is right.

Economy is also extremely important to Candela. This concern for economy follows naturally from his affinity with shells, in which he believes shape, not mass, gives strength. A major consideration, then, is to be as economical as possible in the design of a shell, in both appearance and material. The free-edge shells, such as the restaurant at Xochimilco, carry these ideals to new limits. By finding new solutions to old architectural problems and by taking a new approach, freed from the fetters of theory, Candela has made his mark on architecture and on structural engineering.

Bibliography

Billington, David P. *The Tower and the Bridge: The New Art of Structural Engineering*. Princeton, N.J.: Princeton University Press, 1983. A very readable and informative monograph on structural engineering from the Industrial Revolution to the 1980's. The author clearly shows how Candela and his ideals fit into the historical context of structural engineering. Written for the general reader, with sufficient illustrations to make the point.

Faber, Colin. *Candela: The Shell Builder*. New York: Reinhold, 1963. The most complete book on Candela and his work. Thoroughly illustrated with photographs and line drawings (many of the former by Antonio Candela and the latter by a member of Candela's office). In addition to illustrations, the book contains a brief biographical sketch, a general discussion of his work, a discussion of hypars and their technical details, and bibliographies of works by and about Candela.

"Recent Work of Mexico's Felix Candela." *Progressive Architecture* 40

(February, 1959): 132-141. This is actually a collection of three short articles: one on Candela's work at a Bacardi rum distillery, one on the restaurant at Xochimilco, and an analytical piece entitled "Can a Man Be Architect, Engineer, and Builder?" The latter article concludes that Candela is not always successful in combining the three roles, since his shells are often obscured when "architecture" is added (often by collaborating architects).

"Shell Concrete Today." *Architectural Forum* 101 (August, 1954): 157-166. A report on the MIT conference on thin concrete shells. It defines all types of concrete shells, from flat slabs to domes to hypars, and then discusses the major types of shells in some detail, including illustrations. Candela's work figures prominently in the article.

Smith, Clive Bamford. *Builders in the Sun: Five Mexican Architects.* New York: The Architectural Book Publishing Co., 1967. As the title implies, this book treats five architects, one of whom is Felix Candela. It is well illustrated, with simple explanations of Candela's work. One particularly good feature is the use of extensive quotes from Candela—they give the reader an interesting view of his work and motivations.

Brian J. Nichelson

KAREL ČAPEK

Born: January 9, 1890; Malé Svatoňovice, Bohemia, Austro-Hungarian
Empire
Died: December 25, 1938; Prague, Czechoslovakia
Area of Achievement: Literature
Contribution: Čapek, a practicing journalist, is best remembered as a dramatist who also wrote children's stories, short stories, and novels, many of
them satirical. An early master of science fiction, Čapek's most famous
play, *R.U.R.: Rossum's Universal Robots* (with Josef Čapek, 1921; English translation, 1923) popularized the word "robot," invented by his
brother Josef.

Early Life
    Karel Čapek, the last of Antonin Čapek and Božena Čapková's three chil-
dren, was born on January 9, 1890, in the country town of Malé Svatoňovice, situated in the Krakonose Mountains a few kilometers from what
later became Czechoslovakia's border with Austria and Germany. Antonin, a
physician, had far-ranging interests and led a local amateur theatrical group.
Božena Čapková was a cultured woman with a particular interest in regional
folklore. She knew the folk songs and legends of her area, and her children
were steeped in folk culture from their earliest recollections. Karel and
Josef, his brother and lifelong companion, imbibed these early influences,
and the writing of each reflects them. Karel was a sickly child. His mother, a
neurotic, was distrustful of men, including her husband, and was hypochon-
driacal. She was abnormally concerned about the health of her children,
especially Karel, whose lungs were weak.
    Karel and his brother were seldom apart until 1910, when Karel, having
studied at the *Gymnasium* at Brno in Moravia and having then completed his
secondary education in Prague, went to Berlin to study further, while Josef
went to Paris. Before he went to Berlin, however, Karel studied philosophy
for one year at Charles University in Prague, where he met Thomas G.
Masaryk, a professor of philosophy who was President of Czechoslovakia
from 1918 until 1935 and was intimate with the Čapek brothers throughout
their lifetimes. Before they went their own ways in 1910, Karel and Josef
had collaborated on a folk play, *Lásky hra osudná* (wr. 1910, pr. 1930), but
they were to collaborate on nothing more until they published *Krakonošova
zahrada* (1918; the garden of Krakonos), a collection of their early sketches.
Their most thoroughgoing collaboration, *Ze života hmyzu* (1920; *The Insect
Play*, 1923), followed it.
    Karel became interested in the pragmatism of William James, and, in
1911, while visiting Josef in Paris, he broadened his interest in art and
aesthetics, becoming aware for the first time of the writings of Henri

Bergson and of Bergson's concept of the *élan vital*, which was to influence Karel's future writing greatly. He completed his doctoral dissertation in aesthetics in 1915, probably led to this topic by the experience of his Parisian summer.

Because chronic spinal problems caused Karel agonizing pain, he had to seek employment that would not overtax him. He served for a year as tutor to the son of Count Vladimír Lažanský, then returned to Prague to become a journalist for *Národní listy*, for which he became a literary and art editor before leaving in 1921 to accept a position with *Lidové noviny*, a newspaper for which Josef also worked.

Life's Work

Throughout his adult life, Čapek had abiding political concerns. His overtly political books include his three-volume *Hovory s T. G. Masarykem* (1928-1935; *President Masaryk Tells His Story*, 1934; also as *Masaryk on Thought and Life*, 1938), his *O věcech obecných: Čili, Zóon politikon* (1932; on public matters), and his posthumously published collection, *Věci kolemnás* (1954; the things around us).

Čapek honed his thinking skills through his extensive study of James's pragmatism, which resulted in his publishing *Pragmatismus* (1918) early in his career. This philosophical exploration combined with his delving into aesthetics, which resulted in his publishing his doctoral dissertation as *Musaion* (1920-1921) and led him to understand specific ways in which art can affect and influence a whole society.

His early employment as a journalist gave Čapek the fluency required to write voluminously. It taught him as well some of the investigative techniques that would help to shape his later writing, particularly his political satires. The Čapek brothers received international attention for two of their collaborations, *R.U.R.* and *The Insect Play*, both plays that deal with the question of a technology that gets out of control. The plays are not anti-progressive so much as they are anti-utopian. They question the wisdom with which humankind will deal with the technological advances of a mechanistic age. Karel's play of the same period, *Věc Makropulos* (1920; *The Makropulos Secret*, 1925), is in a similar philosophical vein. From 1921 to 1923, Čapek served as director of the City Theater of Prague, directing thirteen plays during his tenure. Ironically, although he is best known as a playwright, most critics consider Čapek's science-fiction novels, particularly *Krakatit* (1924; English translation, 1925) and *Válka s mloky* (1936; *The War with the Newts*, 1937), stronger literarily than his better-known plays. Čapek himself far preferred to write as a journalist or novelist than as a playwright because of the lack of control that playwrights have when their plays are produced by others.

The Insect Play is essentially a latter-day medieval morality play in which each character is consciously intended to represent some generalized vice or virtue, clearly defined and presented unilaterally. The play sounded dire warnings to those in the post-World War I years who were moving toward the kind of totalitarianism that was to result in the rise of the Axis powers during the next decade. This play is an early warning, whereas Čapek's 1936 novel, *The War with the Newts*, is an anguished cry against the rise of Nazism. The latter work was directly responsible for Čapek's being denied a Nobel Prize in Literature in 1937 or 1938. At that time, Sweden was still trying to appease Adolf Hitler. To have honored Čapek, whose name was under serious consideration by the Nobel Committee, would have been to offer a direct challenge to Germany's all-powerful Führer.

From the time the Treaty of Versailles established Czechoslovakia as a discrete political entity in 1919, Čapek worked to make his country a democracy. His close and sustained friendship with President Masaryk took the form of weekly meetings every Friday night in the double house that Josef and Karel built in 1925. Josef lived in one side of this house, Karel in the other.

In 1925, Karel was elected president of the PEN Club of Prague but soon resigned, because he feared his personal political utterances might be attributed to the club and construed as PEN policy. A decade later, H. G. Wells persuaded Čapek to succeed him as international president of the PEN Club, and Čapek agreed. He was not able, however, to attend the annual meeting in Latin America, so his candidacy did not materialize.

Čapek's political concerns led him in the early 1930's to overcome his inherent shyness and take to the radio in an attempt to solidify the Czech people against totalitarianism. His eventual support of Edvard Beneš for the presidency and his attempts to bring about a peaceful coexistence between the Czechs and the southern Germans of Bavaria in the mid-1930's shocked and irritated many Czechs. It was clear that Čapek had greater public impact through his writing than through his more direct personal appeals, as the reception of *The War with the Newts* illustrates.

As Adolf Hitler's influence grew, Čapek's distress increased. The Munich Pact of 1938 appalled Čapek. He sank into a spiritual decline and his lungs, always weak, became inflamed. On Christmas Day, 1938, nine months before the beginning of World War II, he died in Prague of pneumonia. When Nazi troops swarmed into Prague less than three months later, Čapek's widow, Olga, destroyed all of his papers, fearing that these writings might incriminate Čapek's friends and associates. Shortly thereafter, the Nazis, unaware that Čapek had died, appeared at his house with a warrant for his arrest.

Summary

Only history will tell what Karel Čapek will be remembered for. He was an Olympian in many respects. He had a total devotion to democratic principles and was fearless in advancing the cause of political self-determination. Leaving such considerations aside, however, Čapek towers as a giant in the field of modern science fiction. Much of his work was satire, one of the most difficult literary forms to master. Čapek was totally in control of satire, applying it to novels, short fiction, and drama.

Čapek learned much about literature from the folktales to which he was regularly exposed during his youth. He also understood the dynamics of medieval morality plays and used many of their techniques to promote his ideas subtly and indirectly. His early appreciation of the writing of Wells made Čapek aware of the potential for using science fiction satirically, and he became a master of this technique, some of the technical flaws of his plays notwithstanding. Čapek's philosophical engagement with the writing of James and with the aestheticism of Henri Bergson provided a sound intellectual overlay for his own writing. His work as a journalist helped him to perfect many of his writing techniques, and directing plays for the City Theater of Prague provided him with insights into the practical aspects of play-making.

If he has not received the full recognition that seems his due, this is attributable in part to the fact that he wrote in a language spoken by relatively few people. Although his work was translated into other languages, the full impact of his writing is best appreciated by the limited audience that is able to approach it in its original language.

Bibliography

Bradbrook, Bohuslava R. "Chesterton and Karel Čapek: A Study in Personal and Literary Relationship." *Chesterton Review* 4 (1977-1978): 89-103. An interesting assessment of the continued relationship between Čapek and British author G. K. Chesterton, which began when Čapek was an emerging author and continued until Chesterton's death in 1936.

_____. "Karel Čapek's Contribution to Czech National Literature." In *Czechoslovakia Past and Present*, edited by Miloslav Rechcigl. The Hague: Mouton, 1968. Identifies Čapek as being clearly among Czechoslovakia's leading writers and shows the strong influence that his writing had upon the culture of the country. Comments on the author's inventiveness and on his ability to work in several genres. One of the better short treatments of the author.

Harkins, William E. *Karel Čapek*. New York: Columbia University Press, 1962. The most dependable critical biographical source on Čapek. This book considers the whole of Čapek's literary production and relates it to his life and to the social milieu in which he was working, particularly to the onset of Nazism in Czechoslovakia. An indispensable book to Čapek scholars yet easily accessible to those new to him.

Mann, Erika. "A Last Conversation with Karel Čapek." *The Nation* 149
   (January 14, 1939): 68-69. Erika Mann, daughter of German Nobel Prize
   laureate Thomas Mann, relates her interview with Čapek shortly before his
   death in 1938, at about the time of the Munich Pact. She attributes his
   death to a sickness of the spirit, to Čapek's unwillingness to go on in the
   face of Hitler's threat to the Czech nation.
Matuška, Alexander. *Karel Čapek: An Essay.* Translated by Cathryn Alan.
   London: Allen & Unwin, 1964. This extensive study considers the artistry
   of Čapek's writing, emphasizing such matters as thematic development,
   characterization, plot development, and method of handling detail. An
   important book for students of Čapek.
Wellek, René. *Essays on Czech Literature.* The Hague: Mouton, 1963. Wellek's essay, "Karel Čapek," which originally appeared in 1936, is one of
   the most searching pieces written about the author during his lifetime.
   Wellek comments on Čapek's relative youth and considers him at the
   height of his powers. When these words were written, Čapek had less than
   three years to live.

R. Baird Shuman

LÁZARO CÁRDENAS

Born: May 21, 1895; Jiquilpan, Mexico
Died: October 19, 1970; Mexico City, Mexico
Areas of Achievement: Government and politics
Contribution: The energetic and controversial President of Mexico from 1934 to 1940, Cárdenas carried out bold policies intended to benefit peasants and workers. In 1938, he posed a major challenge to the United States and Great Britain by his nationalization of their Mexican oil properties. His assertion of the authority of the Mexican government left an indelible imprint on his times and provided precedents for other developing nations after World War II.

Early Life

A humble son of provincial Mexico, Lázaro Cárdenas had few of the characteristics associated with success in Mexican politics. The eldest male among eight children, he grew up in the household of a struggling merchant in the town of Jiquilpan in the state of Michoacán. He was a solemn youth who took his six years of schooling seriously and developed strict views on moral issues, particularly gambling and the use of alcohol. After the completion of grammar school, Cárdenas worked as an assistant to the local tax collector.

As the thirty-four-year-old dictatorship of Porfirio Díaz collapsed in 1911, sixteen-year-old Cárdenas was drawn to the excitement and idealism of the revolutionary movement led by Francisco Madero. Although the overthrow of Madero's presidency in 1913 greatly disappointed him, he joined the forces of Venustiano Carranza, who carried on in the deposed president's name. A courageous and at times impetuous field commander, Cárdenas rose to the rank of brigadier general by 1920. During these years of combat, he developed an awareness of social and economic issues. The Indian part of his ancestry (he was a mestizo, or a person of mixed Indian and European descent) gave him a special sensitivity to the needs of the rural poor.

Although increasingly involved in politics, Cárdenas decided to remain in the army as zone commander of the units stationed in Tamaulipas from 1925 to 1927. The young general quickly learned that United States and British oil companies expected him to accept expensive gifts in exchange for special favors, a common practice among zone commanders in the oil region. Cárdenas also saw that Mexican laborers received a fraction of the pay of their foreign counterparts for doing the same work. Oil company managers and engineers lived in the comfort of segregated compounds while Mexican workers endured in makeshift housing in the hot, humid coastal environment. Cárdenas rejected the bribe offers but retained a vivid memory of the difficulties faced by his fellow Mexicans.

Life's Work

In 1928, Cárdenas left active military service to become governor of Michoacán. After fifteen years on the battlefields of the revolution and in the command centers of the army, he ventured into the arena of politics with a combination of idealism and determination that was unusual in Mexico of the late 1920's. He pursued a vigorous policy of distributing farmland to the peasants while improving public education throughout the state. He led in the mobilization of peasants and workers in a statewide political party with a broad platform that included prohibition and women's rights. Although these efforts did not always bring the results he wanted, Cárdenas built an impressive image as governor and began to gain national attention.

One of the effects of the worldwide economic depression in Mexico was to make an already uncertain political situation even more unstable. Cárdenas emerged in this environment as a competent state governor who had a brief tenure as head of the recently formed Partido Nacional Revolucionario (PNR, or National Revolutionary Party). In 1933, Plutarco Elías Calles, Mexico's dominant politician, approved of Cárdenas as the PNR's presidential candidate for the election of 1934. This nomination virtually ensured victory, but Cárdenas chose to conduct a strenuous campaign anyway. In the process, many residents of isolated villages saw a presidential candidate for the first time. The man they saw was, at a glance, hardly an imposing personality. He was not a fiery public speaker, and the receding chin beneath his fleshy cheeks, along with a quiet manner, created an impression of reserve. Cárdenas, nevertheless, managed to generate excitement. He relished his personal meetings with the common people, and his simple life-style with his new bride, Amalia Solórzano of Michoacán, won for him the admiration of peasants and workers. After easily winning the election, Cárdenas converted his popularity with the voters and his respect among generals and politicians into a major coup—the peaceful expulsion of the nation's political boss, Calles, not only from Mexican politics but also, in 1936, from Mexico itself.

In spite of his limited formal education, Cárdenas had an awareness of the importance of ideas in shaping a presidential administration. The PNR had adopted a six-year plan as a campaign platform. A conglomeration of Western liberalism and Soviet economic planning grafted onto Mexico's Constitution of 1917, the six-year plan was both a help and a hindrance to the new president. It established a central goal of massive social and economic change, a goal that Cárdenas readily accepted. It also contained vague Marxist slogans and made socialist theory the main doctrine in education. Such radicalism caused widespread protests from irate Catholics. Although he was anticlerical, Cárdenas backed away from strict enforcement of socialist education and eventually moderated the government's commitment to Marxist ideas.

By contrast, Cárdenas ventured far to the Left in land reform. The heavy concentration of land in a few large estates, or haciendas, was the product of centuries-old traditions in Mexico. Since the early years of the revolution, leaders such as Emiliano Zapata had made clear the importance of the breakup of the haciendas for the benefit of the peasants. After twenty years of rhetorical promises, however, land reform had made little progress. An impatient Cárdenas quickly implemented controversial policies: government expropriation of haciendas, which were then converted into collective farms, or *ejidos*, for the peasants. Yet the young president realized that this transfer of property was only the first step. If the *ejidos* were to be successful, they needed credit to support their large-scale operations and technical skills to cultivate and market their products. Consequently, the Cárdenas government provided loans and technical training for the *ejidos*. In spite of this comprehensive approach, the farmers brought more enthusiasm than expertise to their work. Widely hailed as a political success by the peasant farmers and a daring innovation by leftist observers, the *ejidos* did not achieve sufficient levels of productivity.

The rise of Cárdenas to the presidency coincided with the appearance of a new labor organization known as the Confederación de Trabajadores de México (CTM, or Mexican Confederation of Workers). Numerous spontaneous and disruptive strikes testified to the dynamism of the movement, but the Cárdenas administration established more orderly procedures through its close relationship with the CTM. Under the constant urging of the president, the CTM expanded to include many small unions and eventually reached a total membership of 600,000. In return for the allegiance of the CTM, Cárdenas transformed some benefits for the working class from theory into practice, particularly in technical education and government support in strike settlements.

The greatest challenge faced by Cárdenas came when the oil workers of the CTM struck for better wages and working conditions against United States and British petroleum corporations. The dispute went to the Mexican supreme court, which ruled in favor of the union. The corporations refused to comply and thereby openly defied not only the court but the entire Cárdenas government as well. Cárdenas responded with his own defiance: the nationalization of the oil corporations' properties on March 18, 1938. Faced by aggressive Fascism in Europe, the British wanted military seizure of the oil fields, but the United States was committed to its Good Neighbor Policy. Presidents Franklin D. Roosevelt and Cárdenas initiated negotiations that resulted in a settlement for all parties in 1942. Cárdenas confronted the two foreign powers with the largest investments in Mexico and won a signal victory.

With these accomplishments in oil nationalization, labor organization, and land reform, Cárdenas obligated his government to expensive programs that weighed heavily on Mexico's limited financial resources. The complex process of land reform reduced agricultural production, which combined with higher wages for workers to create inflation. United States and British oil companies refused to purchase Mexican oil, which cut into the government's tax revenues. Plagued by this economic crisis, Cárdenas took a more moderate course after 1938.

Cárdenas left the presidency in 1941, but he continued to exercise influence in Mexican affairs until his death in 1970. He was especially active in regional economic development in Michoacán and in commentary on international affairs, in which he was a consistent opponent of imperialism. He and his son Cuauhtémoc came to symbolize the independent Left in twentieth century Mexico.

Summary

The legacy of Lázaro Cárdenas contains the contradictions and disappointments of a political leader who attempted to change a nation's entrenched hierarchical economic structure by peaceful methods. In order to deal with this structure, Cárdenas relied on a powerful government bureaucracy which, after he left the presidency, stressed stability and security over experimentation and change. The government and political party that Cárdenas helped to build for the benefit of the masses came to dominate them and eventually came to stifle local initiative.

Yet Cárdenas did make significant contributions to Mexican history in terms of the principles he espoused. He aroused Mexican peasants and workers in the name of peaceful social and economic change and, within limits, oversaw the early stages of land reform and labor organization for their benefit. He accumulated extraordinary personal power but willingly relinquished the presidency to his successor. He chose not to meddle in politics theareafter, thereby breaking with the authoritarian tradition of the imposition of continued influence by extraconstitutional means.

Caught between the world of his roots, the isolated mountain village, and the world of power politics, the intermeshed international economic system, Cárdenas used decisive if controversial methods to meet the challenges of modernization that have confronted most developing nations in the twentieth century. He committed Mexico to the adoption of modern technology and values in agriculture, industry, and education. He sought to redistribute wealth in his country through the nationalization of the property of foreign-owned corporations, a path that other nations would follow. In the process, he maintained a course independent of both communism and liberal capitalism. Operating in the context of the 1930's, Cárdenas underwent experiences that anticipated struggles elsewhere in Latin American, Africa, and Asia later in the century.

Lázaro Cárdenas

Bibliography

Ankerson, Dudley. *Agrarian Warlord: Saturnino Cedillo and the Mexican Revolution in San Luis Potosí.* DeKalb: Northern Illinois University Press, 1984. This book is a valuable account of the rise and fall of one of the Cárdenas administration's main antagonists. Provides a careful explication of Cedillo's point of view.

Ashby, Joe C. *Organized Labor and the Mexican Revolution Under Lázaro Cárdenas.* Chapel Hill: University of North Carolina Press, 1963. The author focuses on the expansion of organized labor and its participation in politics and the oil expropriation.

Carr, Barry. "Crisis in Mexican Communism: The Extraordinary Congress of the Mexican Communist Party." *Science and Society* 50 (Winter, 1986): 391-414; and 51 (Spring, 1987): 43-67. Penetrating analysis of the internal and external problems of the Mexican Communist Party during the last years of the Cárdenas presidency.

Daniels, Josephus. *Shirt Sleeve Diplomat.* Chapel Hill: University of North Carolina Press, 1947. Daniels was United States ambassador to Mexico from 1933 to 1942. His sympathies for Cárdenas were evident in the resolution of the oil expropriation controversy and also in this account of his years in the United States embassy in Mexico City.

Hamilton, Nora. *The Limits of State Autonomy: Post-Revolutionary Mexico.* Princeton, N.J.: Princeton University Press, 1982. Hamilton explains the origins and weaknesses of Cárdenas' political alliance and the limits of its power within the context of national and international economic structures.

Michaels, Albert L. "The Crisis of Cardenismo." *Journal of Latin American Studies* 2 (May, 1970): 51-79. While this article concentrates on the crisis after the oil expropriation, it also provides an evaluation of the entire six-year presidency.

Prewett, Virginia. *Reportage on Mexico.* New York: E. P. Dutton, 1941. Prewett, a conservative journalist, was generally skeptical and at times critical of the Cárdenas administration in contrast to Daniel's *Shirt Sleeve Diplomat.*

Tannenbaum, Frank. "Mexico's Man of the People." *Reader's Digest* 31 (October, 1937): 43-44. A brief but insightful portrait by a Columbia University historian who knew him well.

Townsend, William Cameron. *Lázaro Cárdenas, Mexican Democrat.* 2d ed. Waxhaw, N.C.: International Friendship, 1979. This highly laudatory study of Cárdenas and his presidency is the only biography available in English. Useful because of the author's long-term personal relationship with Cárdenas.

John A. Britton

RUDOLF CARNAP

Born: May 18, 1891; Ronsdorf, Germany
Died: September 14, 1970; Santa Monica, California
Area of Achievement: Philosophy
Contribution: Carnap is recognized as a leading figure in the philosophy of logical positivism and made significant contributions to logic, the theory of probability, philosophy of science, and linguistic analysis.

Early Life

Rudolf Carnap was born in Ronsdorf in northwestern Germany on May 18, 1891. His parents were deeply religious and did not want to expose their children to secular influences. Consequently, both Rudolf and his sister were educated by their mother at home. His father died when Rudolf was seven years old, and his mother continued to supervise his education until he left for the Universities of Jena and Freiburg in 1910. For four years, Carnap studied physics, philosophy, and mathematics. While studying at Jena, Carnap attended the lectures of Gottlob Frege, widely acknowledged as the most eminent logician of his time. Frege deeply influenced Carnap's future work, although at that moment, Carnap's interest lay in the physics of electrons. Carnap began his doctoral dissertation in physics when World War I began. He spent three years at the front and, in 1917, was transferred to Berlin to work on developing wireless communication for the army. For Carnap, the period of the war created an awareness of his pacifism and the irrationality of violent human conflict, and confirmed his belief in the values of rationality and science.

Carnap returned to philosophy in 1919 and at the same time encountered the works of Bertrand Russell. Frege had earlier sparked an interest in logic, and now Russell renewed that interest. The idea that symbols could take the place of sentences and that sentences operate with each other in a limited number of ways led Carnap to write a dissertation on an area that bordered both philosophy and physics. In 1921, he completed his work and received his Ph.D. from Jena with a thesis that compared the concepts of space used in physics, mathematics, and philosophy.

For several years, Carnap was content to work independently in areas of logic and physics. He wrote a number of articles on space, time, and causality, and began work on a textbook on symbolic logic. In 1926, he was invited to teach at the University of Vienna, and this turned out to be the decisive step toward an important career in philosophy.

Life's Work

When Carnap was invited to become an instructor at the University of Vienna in 1926, he was ready to begin a unique exploration of one philosophical area. Moritz Schlick, who had arranged the invitation to Vienna, also formed the Vienna Circle that year by bringing together philosophers, mathematicians, linguists, and other scholars. Schlick wanted to develop a system of philosophy in which all statements could be rigorously verified by logic. Carnap became a leading member of the Circle and from their discussions shared in the initial ideas of logical positivism or logical empiricism.

Before going to Vienna, Carnap had begun to organize his interest in mathematical logic. Frege recommended a reading of *Principia Mathematica* (1910-1913), a masterful work on logic by Russell and Alfred North Whitehead which attempted to derive all of mathematics from a set of premises. Deeply influenced by this work, Carnap in 1924 completed a first draft of a textbook on mathematical logic entitled *Abriss der Logistik mit besonderer Berücksichtigung der Relationstheorie und ihrer Anwendungen*. It was first published in 1929 and later translated into English from a considerably different version in 1958 as *Introduction to Symbolic Logic and Its Applications*. Carnap arrived in Vienna in 1926 and began his duties as an instructor at the university. During the next five years, he actively participated in conversation with the members of the Vienna Circle, taught, and wrote.

During this period in Vienna, Carnap became one of the leading advocates for a philosophical position called logical positivism or logical empiricism. This school of thought synthesized the empiricism of David Hume and, combined with the revolution in modern physics, attempted to create a precise and rigorous philosophy that claimed all human knowledge originated from immediate experience. For Carnap, the culmination of these five years was the publication in 1928 of *Der Logische Aufbau der Welt* (the logical construction of the world). Carnap organized all the objects of the world into four main types: socio-cultural objects, others' minds, physical objects, and personal experiences. By accepting the human ability to remember similarities, Carnap built a system of knowledge where comparison between similarities would lead to the creation of a temporal order. Carnap believed that a person's experience at any given moment was created from a series of elements and that these series were constructed over time. Those remembered similarities provided the initial store of experiences that led to the definition of a person, perception, and the world.

In 1930, Carnap and Hans Reichenbach published a periodical called *Erkenntnis* for the purpose of promoting and discussing the issues of the Vienna Circle. Published for ten years, this journal contains central ideas of the school as well as controversies and points of difference. In 1931, Carnap accepted the chair of natural philosophy at the German University in Prague, Czechoslovakia. While continuing his close relationship with the Vienna Circle, Carnap turned his attention more narrowly to problems of logic and language. This work resulted in the publication in 1934 of his second major work, *Logische Syntax der Sprache* (*The Logical Syntax of Language*,

1937). In this book, Carnap attempted to formulate the logical syntax of any language in terms of rules of formation and transformation. Also during the Prague period, Carnap moved away from the rigorous demands of his earlier empiricism, in which sentences that cannot be tested by observation were regarded as empirically meaningless. Carnap devised a means by which those sentences unable to be checked directly may be reduced in such a way as to be testable.

With the rise and threat of National Socialism in Germany, Carnap decided to leave Europe in December, 1935. Upon arrival in the United States, he received an appointment as professor of philosophy at the University of Chicago. He spent seventeen years at Chicago and, during this period, engaged in several revisions of *Logical Syntax of Language* and shared the editorial responsibilities over the publication of *The International Encyclopedia of Unified Science* (1938). The overall purpose of the encyclopedia was to unify scientific terms with a series of articles devoted to general problems in the philosophy of science and specific disciplines in science. In his own work, Carnap shifted his emphasis toward problems in semantics, which resulted in three books: *Introduction to Semantics* (1942), *Formalization of Logic* (1943), and *Meaning and Necessity* (1947). Although his concern with semantics was new, the problem for Carnap originated with his first work. He wanted to rid philosophy of metaphysics, or "pseudoproblems." He believed that much of the difficulty in philosophy was the result of a misunderstanding or misuse of language. With an artificial language, set according to specific rules and regulations, he believed that it would be possible to communicate more directly and clearly. Along this same path, Carnap took an avid interest in artificial languages such as Esperanto and Interlingua.

After 1945, Carnap shifted to the final phase of his philosophical life and worked on problems of probability and introduction. The publication of his third great work, *Logical Foundations of Probability* (1950), was the result of this effort. The core of Carnap's philosophy lay in the belief that the meaning of a sentence lay in its ability to be tested or verified. Although deductive logic was a well-defined and complete system, inductive logic was not. Carnap attacked the problem by the claim that a close parallel existed between inductive and deductive logic. Through the construction of a formal system of inductive logic, which corresponded to deductive logic, Carnap led to the conclusion that if the process of deduction was valid, then by implication so was the process of induction.

In 1952, Carnap received an appointment at the Institute for Advanced Studies at Princeton. There he was freed from academic duties and devoted his time to research. Upon the death of Hans Reichenbach in 1954, Carnap decided to accept the chair in philosophy at the University of California at Los Angeles vacated by his friend. He remained there until his retirement in 1961. At Los Angeles and during his retirement, Carnap continued to work on various refinements of his philosophical interests. Carnap became an American citizen in 1941. He received a Rockefeller Fellowship in 1942 and was a Fellow of the American Academy of Arts and Science. He was awarded honorary doctorates from Harvard University (1936), the University of California (1963), the University of Michigan (1965), and the University of Oslo (1969). Carnap died in Santa Monica, California, in 1970.

Summary

Rudolf Carnap enjoyed a long and productive intellectual life that spanned almost half a century. He brought together several major stands of Western philosophy, including the empiricism of Hume, which exerted a powerful influence throughout the nineteenth century, and blended this tradition with the revolutionary advances in modern logic developed during the early part of this century. During his formative years, he was influenced by several of the greatest thinkers of the twentieth century, including Bertrand Russell, Gottlob Frege, and Ludwig Wittgenstein. During his productive years, Carnap maintained an active dialogue with individuals from a variety of academic disciplines. He became the best-known member of the Vienna Circle and provided the seminal works that proved invaluable in creating a modern philosophy of science. In 1940-1941, when Carnap was a visiting professor at Harvard University, he became a part of a discussion group that included Russell, Alfred Tarski, and W. V. O. Quine. Students privy to those discussions must surely have been aware that they sat at the feet of intellectual giants.

At the beginning of his career, Carnap committed himself to the position that a viable empiricism needed to be wedded to logic. Although his original position was characterized by an unprecedented rigor, throughout his life he modified this position in favor of greater flexibility. Along with his contributions to probability, it could be said that he placed one cornerstone in the study of the philosophy of science.

Bibliography
Ayer, Alfred Jules. *Philosophy in the Twentieth Century.* New York: Random House, 1982. This book covers the major philosophical developments in the twentieth century. Chapter 4 covers the beginning of the Vienna Circle and the following chapter deals in some detail with Carnap's contribution to logical positivism. Accessible to the general reader.
_____, ed. *Logical Positivism.* Glencoe, Ill.: Free Press, 1959. A thorough and comprehensive review of the philosophy of logical positivism. There are lengthy sections on Carnap and on the central figures of the Vienna Circle.
Buck, Roger C., and Robert S. Cohen, eds. *Boston Studies in the Philosophy of Science.* Vol. 8. Dordrecht, The Netherlands: D. Reidel, 1971. A

collection of articles written on the occasion of Carnap's seventieth birthday. The subjects of these articles cover the range of Carnap's life and philosophy: from personal qualities of the man, his influences as a teacher, to the quality of his philosophical thought.

Kraft, Viktor. *The Vienna Circle, the Origin of Neo-Positivism: A Chapter in the History of Recent Philosophy.* Translated by Arthur Pap. New York: Philosophical Library, 1953. This book is recognized as the standard work on the members of the Vienna Circle. Kraft covers in some detail the major contributors to the circle and Carnap receives a significant amount of attention. A good place to begin.

Passmore, John Arthur. *A Hundred Years of Philosophy.* Rev. ed. New York: Basic Books, 1967. Passmore's book provides a very readable and comprehensive text for recent developments in philosophy. Although the section on Carnap is brief, logical positivism is described in language that is relatively easy to understand.

Schilpp, Paul Arthur, ed. *The Philosophy of Rudolf Carnap.* La Salle, Ill.: Open Court, 1963. An excellent source for an overview of Carnap's philosophy. It is possible to pick and choose among the sections and critical essays and to gain some insight into how Carnap proceeded in his thinking. Contains a complete bibliography.

Victor W. Chen

HENRI CARTIER-BRESSON

Born: August 22, 1908; Chanteloup, France

Area of Achievement: Art

Contribution: Cartier-Bresson, whose photography is acclaimed for both its immediacy and its human authenticity, has contributed a body of work unique in the history of the craft. Aside from his emphasis on the typical and ordinary in his choice of subjects, his use of the new, smaller hand-held camera and faster films defined the ideas of "the decisive moment" in photography.

Early Life

Henri Cartier-Bresson's father, André Cartier-Bresson, a Parisian, was a wealthy textile manufacturer descended from a family who had been in the thread-making business since the mid-nineteenth century. His mother, Marthe Leverdier, came from a family of Norman landowners who had entered the cotton industry in the 1840's. His younger brother eventually took over the family business; his sister became a poet.

Throughout his early years, Cartier-Bresson spent a considerable amount of time in the Norman countryside but was educated in Paris at the École Fénelon and then at the Lycée Condorcet, from which he was graduated in 1927. Drawn to a life of adventure, he had little interest in the family textile business. Consequently, with his father's approval and encouragement, he set out to realize a long-standing and passionate desire: to become a painter. He traveled to Paris and studied painting with the cubist painter André Lhote from 1927 to 1929 and then with Jacques Émile Blanche, a noted portraitist. The pervasiveness of Surrealism in French art and literature during Cartier-Bresson's youth inevitably affected his aesthetic development and reinforced his strong belief in the power of the imagination.

In 1929, during eight months of study at Cambridge, England, Cartier-Bresson explored both English literature and painting. Returning to France in 1930 for compulsory military service, he continued painting while stationed at Le Bourget near Paris. It was about that time, using a Brownie box camera, that he renewed an earlier interest in photography.

Life's Work

In 1931, after his release from the army, Cartier-Bresson spent about a year in Africa hunting wild game and selling the meat to earn a living. A severe case of blackwater fever, a form of malaria, that he contracted while living in a native village on the Ivory Coast, compelled him to depart for Marseilles to convalesce. There, through experiments with a Leica camera, which he had acquired in 1930, he became more fully aware of the artistic potential of the photographic medium. Combining that newly discovered creative outlet with his adventurous and independent spirit, he became a free-lance photojournalist.

Over the next few years, Cartier-Bresson traveled widely throughout France, Germany, Austria, Italy, Poland, Czechoslovakia, Mexico, and the United States, selling his photographs to magazines and newspapers whenever possible. Because of the relatively small market for photographs at that time, he was forced to frequent cheap hotels and restaurants. Gradually, however, Cartier-Bresson began to win recognition for his photographic expertise and especially for his unique ability to photoreport powerful, concrete images of ordinary people engaged in typical, rather than unusual, activities.

His first works were exhibited at the Gallery Julien Levy in New York in 1932, followed by presentations of his first great reportage photos by Ignacio Sanchez Mejias and Guillermo de Torre at the Club Atheneo in Madrid in 1933. In 1934, he had a joint exhibition with a Mexican photographer at the Palacio Bellas Artes in Mexico City. Some of his finest early pictures were taken while living in that city's slum district after the demise of the photographic exhibition that had brought him to Mexico.

He spent the following year in the United States, where he met the renowned American photographer Paul Strand, who was then devoted to film-making and who aroused in the French visitor some of his own interest in motion pictures. The next year, back in France, Cartier-Bresson worked for the film director Jean Renoir as his second assistant director on *Une Partie de campagne* (*A Day in the Country*, 1950), produced in 1936 and released in 1946. Cartier-Bresson later helped to direct the masterpiece *La Règle du jeu* (1939; *The Rules of the Game*, 1950). His association with Renoir was an exceedingly rewarding experience for Cartier-Bresson, who later maintained that Renoir, along with Lhote, had taught him everything he knew. So powerful was Renoir's influence that Cartier-Bresson abandoned still photography almost entirely for a while, devoting himself instead to motion pictures, even though he later acknowledged his limited ability in the latter medium. His early artistic influences also included the photographs of Eugène Atget, Man Ray, and later André Kertesz.

In 1937, Cartier-Bresson married the Javanese dancer Ratna Mohini (a marriage which eventually ended in divorce) and directed his own first film, *Victoire de la vie* (victory of life), a documentary about medical aid to the Loyalists during the Spanish Civil War. Assigned to report on the coronation of King George VI in London, he returned to his true talent later that year. By ignoring the pageantry of the coronation itself and photographing instead the anonymous ordinary people in the crowds lining the route of the royal procession, he produced a remarkable series of pictures that is still regarded as classic. This oblique approach to historic events, typified by his treatment of the coronation, is considered to be one of the hallmarks of his work.

With the outbreak of World War II in 1939, Cartier-Bresson was drafted into the army and served as corporal in the Film and Photographic Unit. Taken prisoner by the Germans in 1940, he spent thirty-six months in prisoner-of-war camps but managed to escape on his third attempt. On a farm in Touraine, he hid out as a laborer until he could acquire false papers that allowed him to return to Paris. There he photographed artists such as Henri Matisse and Georges Braque and writers for the publisher Pierre Braun. During this time, he joined an underground resistance movement created to aid other prisoners of war and escapees. In 1944, he organized an underground photographic unit, consisting mainly of French press photographers, for the purpose of providing pictorial documentation of the German occupation, the Allied invasion of France, and the subsequent German retreat.

At the request of the United States Office of War Information, in 1945 Cartier-Bresson directed his second film, *Le retour* (the return), a documentary about the homecoming of French prisoners of war and deportees. This film has been described as one of the most moving documents to have emerged from World War II. Cartier-Bresson returned to the United States in 1946 to complete a "posthumous" exhibition at the Museum of Modern Art in New York; the exhibition began in the mistaken belief that Cartier-Bresson had disappeared in the war.

In 1947, Cartier-Bresson, along with Robert Capa, David Seymour, and George Rodger, founded a cooperative agency called Magnum Photos. These men had first met in Spain during the days of the Spanish Civil War and met later in Paris. Their agency was created in order to realize their common goal of taking photographs that were restrained, soft in contrast, accidental, and gently lyrical while also being harshly real. Not only historical events but also everyday life became their subject matter.

In the three decades following the founding of Magnum Photos, Cartier-Bresson traveled throughout the world in search of new subjects, traversing Europe and America repeatedly and also visiting many countries of Asia and Africa, especially China, Japan, and India. Equipped with his favorite camera, a vintage Model-G Leica, he assumed the role of photoreporter without assignments, occasionally using the pseudonym "Hank Carter" in an effort to protect the anonymity that he believed was vital to capturing his subjects unaffected and unposed.

The individual shots and photographic essays resulting from Cartier-Bresson's journeys have appeared in most of the world's leading magazines and have also formed the basis for several impressive volumes of work. More than a hundred of his most memorable early photographs are contained in *Images à la Sauvette* (1952; *The Decisive Moment*, 1952). In this work, Cartier-Bresson wrote thirteen pages of text that one photographer has called some of "the most intelligent and lucid writing about photography" that he has encountered.

Major exhibitions of Cartier-Bresson's work in museums and galleries have also made him internationally recognized. In 1954, the Louvre in Paris abandoned a long-held prejudice against photography by making his pictures the subject of its first photographic exhibition. Honored once again in 1966, he became the first photographer in history to have a second one-man show at the Louvre. The 270 prints of the second exhibition drew record-breaking crowds in Japan at a duplicate show called "Henri Cartier-Bresson: Exhibition of Photographs after the Decisive Moment." The Museum of Modern Art in New York also gave him two noteworthy one-man shows, in 1947 and 1968. A 1969 exhibition of his work in England opened at London's Victoria and Albert Museum in the early spring and toured the museums and galleries of major British cities until the end of November. Cartier-Bresson had occasionally worked in films since the early 1960's, producing such documentaries as *Impressions of California* (1969) and *Southern Exposure* (1971). After 1973, Cartier-Bresson began photographing less frequently, concentrating instead on drawing and painting. In 1970, he married the photographer Martine Franck.

When viewed superficially, Cartier-Bresson's photographic technique appears to be simple and casual. Avoiding elaborate equipment, color film, filters, and posed shots taken from unusual angles or perspectives, he almost always used his Leica's standard fifty-millimeter lens, almost always holding his camera at eye level. Instead of cropping his negatives, he relied on his personal vision to give his pictures their structure and organization.

Although some critics have argued that his approach may result in amateurish photos no different from those taken by any well-equipped tourist, most feel that the unique quality of Cartier-Bresson's photographs derives from his compassion for the people he has photographed. His work is characterized by both an intuitive grasp of the essence of human nature and a profound respect for people—as indicated by his assertion that there are photographs he would never take, regardless of the circumstances, because of the possibility of intruding on feelings or experiences too intimate to be shared with the world at large. Photography, for Cartier-Bresson, was a way of understanding what he saw. Maintaining that pictures took him rather than vice versa, he preferred to choose his subjects spontaneously, unlike those photographers who prefer assignments planned in advance. He patiently awaited what he called "the decisive moment," or the moment when the exterior and interior visions merged in the single eye of the camera lens. It was only then, almost automatically and without awareness of the physical process of adjusting his equipment, that he snapped the picture.

Among Cartier-Bresson's many honors and distinctions are the 1948 award of *U.S. Camera* for his photographic essay on the death of Gandhi, the 1953 American Society of Magazine Photographers' award for most contributions to the progress of magazine photography, the 1958 award of the Photographic Society of America for international understanding through photography, and Overseas Press Club awards for his reportage from China, the Soviet Union, and Cuba. From 1952 to 1953, he worked in Europe, and in 1954 he became the first foreign photographer to be admitted to the Soviet Union after the end of the Stalin era. In 1975, he received an honorary doctorate of letters from the University of Oxford in England.

Summary

Although he rejected the label of "photojournalist," proclaiming that he had no interest in documentation, Henri Cartier-Bresson has had, nevertheless, a great impact on an entire generation of photojournalists and documentary photographers. During a career spanning more than four decades, Cartier-Bresson has captured an era on film. While formed by the values of the nineteenth century, he recorded the twentieth century—not in all its historical detail but in its significance and emotional essence. His ability to perceive and capture the essential is perhaps partly the result of his early training in painting and composition and possibly also his interest in Zen, but it is as much the result of a personal desire to appreciate life in all its manifold forms. Although Cartier-Bresson's photographs are characterized by their simplicity and understatement, as the famous photographer Ernst Haas has noted, commenting on the work of Cartier-Bresson, "there is nothing more difficult than to be simple. It is the highest abstraction in life and in photography."

Bibliography

Beaton, Cecil, and Gail Buckland. *The Magic Image*. Boston: Little, Brown, 1975. In this well-written 304-page book on the history of photography from 1839 to the time of publication, replete with appendices on various types of photography, a glossary, and an index, the authors include a concise but informative overview of Cartier-Bresson's career along with a brief biographical sketch in the entry devoted to this photographer.

Cartier-Bresson, Henri. *The Decisive Moment*. New York: Simon & Schuster, 1952. Containing some of his most memorable photographs, this collection of Cartier-Bresson's work in China, Java, India, and North Africa is equally noteworthy for its thirteen-page introduction, written by Cartier-Bresson himself, on his theory of photography.

Haas, Ernst. "Henri Cartier-Bresson: A Lyrical View of Life." *Modern Photography* 60 (November, 1971): 88-136. Haas, widely recognized as one of the world's outstanding contemporary photographers, gives an insightful and interesting inside view of the life and work of his colleague. Haas offers personal anecdotes, biographical information, as well as a guide to

Cartier-Bresson's theory and practice of photography.

Hofstadter, Dan. "Stealing a March on the World." Parts 1/2. *The New Yorker* 65 (October 23/October 30, 1989): 49-72, 59-93. This detailed article on Cartier-Bresson provides good biographical information as well as a close-up look into the artist's daily activities.

Newhall, Beaumont, and Nancy Beaumont. *Masters of Photography.* New York: Time-Life, 1958. This book, containing many color and black-and-white plates accompanying the text, includes essays on the great photographers in history. In the brief but informative section on the life and work of Cartier-Bresson, the authors stress Cartier-Bresson's style and personal philosophy and also offer some pertinent biographical information.

Schwalberg, B., D. Vestal, and M. Korda. "Cartier-Bresson Today: Three Views." *Popular Photography* 60 (May, 1967): 109-142. In the days when there were very few critics of photography, this is an invaluable source of information about Cartier-Bresson's technique. Schwalberg and Vestal, both photographers themselves, discuss Cartier-Bresson's aesthetic and intuitive grasp of the photographic medium; Korda, primarily a writer, compares Cartier-Bresson's work with the great nineteenth century novelists, such as Honoré de Balzac and Victor Hugo, in its charting of the broad sweep of human emotions.

Genevieve Slomski

PABLO CASALS

Born: December 29, 1876; Vendrell, Spain
Died: October 22, 1973; San Juan, Puerto Rico
Area of Achievement: Music
Contribution: Although recognized as a conductor and composer, Casals is best known for his sensational mastery of the cello. He evolved systems of fingering and bowing that are the source of modern playing technique, and his musical interpretation greatly enhanced international appreciation of the cello as an instrument of artistic expression.

Early Life

Pau (Catalan for Pablo) Casals was born on December 29, 1876, in Vendrell, a small town in the Catalan region of Spain. The second of eleven children of Carlos Casals and Pilar Defilló de Casals, he received his first music instruction from his father, the local church organist and piano teacher. By the time young Casals was five, he sang in the church choir; at six, he studied organ and piano; at seven, he studied violin and also composed and transposed music. He was substituting at the organ for his father when he was eight and, at ten, collaborated on the musical score for the town's Christmas play. The first cello Casals saw—a makeshift instrument—was played by a group of wandering minstrels. Soon after, he attended a performance of prominent cellist José García and, at age eleven, asked his father for lessons on the instrument which was to be his specialty. In 1888, at his mother's insistence despite the opposition of his father, Casals went to the Municipal Music School in Barcelona and became a pupil of García. He also studied piano and composition with José Rodereda. Casals made very rapid progress, winning prizes and assisting with classes. He rebelled against the conventional techniques—the stiff right arm and restricted left-hand fingering—and his early experimentation with bowing and fingering produced his unique style. In order to support himself while in school, Casals organized a trio and performed at the Café Tost. He incorporated classical music into the café repertoire, attracting the attention of the intellectual elite in Barcelona; among these listeners was the well-known composer Isaac Albéniz, who quickly became Casals' friend and adviser. It was also during these years that Casals discovered Johann Sebastian Bach's unaccompanied suites for cello, which helped launch his career of serious study and through which he later popularized the cello in solo performance.

After graduation, armed with letters of introduction from Albéniz, Casals left for Madrid in 1893. There, he met Count de Morphy, an adviser to the queen regent and an avid music enthusiast. De Morphy helped Casals obtain a scholarship to the Royal Conservatory of Music in Madrid, where he studied under Tomás Bretón (composition) and Jesús de Monasterio (chamber music). In 1895, Casals went to Brussels to study at the conservatory there. After only one day, he left abruptly—disturbed by the response to his cello audition—and went to Paris, where he played at the Folies-Marigny music hall. After a short time, Casals returned to Barcelona and accepted the position held by his former teacher, García, at the Municipal Music School. Casals threw himself into his teaching and also played in churches and the Opéra orchestra. He joined a piano trio, founded a string quartet, and even played in a casino in Portugal during the summers. After several years of such hard work, Casals had saved enough money to launch his career as a virtuoso.

Life's Work

Carrying letters of introduction to Charles Lamoureaux, the famous conductor, Casals went to Paris in the fall of 1899. His playing so impressed Lamoureaux that his Paris debut was arranged with Lamoureaux's orchestra on November 12, 1899. Casals was an instant sensation and became in great demand all over Western Europe. He toured in the United States from 1901 to 1902 and then again in 1903-1904. In 1903, he also played concerts in South America, and it soon became clear that Casals was one of the greatest cellists of all time. In 1906, Casals married one of his pupils, the Portuguese cellist Guilhermina Suggia. After a divorce, he was married again in 1914, to the American singer Susan Metcalfe. By 1914, Casals' international reputation had already reached its height, and it was sustained during the 1920's and 1930's by his extensive and extremely successful concert tours. Casals was also active as a conductor and performed as guest conductor with leading orchestras in cities such as Vienna, Paris, Rome, London, New York, Zurich, Prague, Berlin, and Buenos Aires. While not traveling, Casals divided his residence between Paris and Barcelona. In Paris, in addition to playing recitals and concerts, he formed a noted trio ensemble with violinist Jacques Thibaud and pianist Alfred Cortot, and these three men helped Auguste Mangeot found the Paris Normal School of Music in 1914. During these years, Casals had close friendships with musicians such as Fritz Kreisler, Maurice Ravel, and Camille Saint-Saëns.

After World War I, Casals turned his attention to his homeland. Because he believed Barcelona needed a first-class symphony orchestra, Casals founded his Pau Casals Orchestra there in 1919, despite great obstacles and friends who tried to dissuade him. On October 13, 1920, the first concert of the Pau Casals Orchestra was performed in the Music Auditorium of the Catalan Palace. As Casals had been warned, the city was apathetic, but he continued to give magnificent concerts, and eventually his audiences grew until the hall was regularly full. When the orchestra became established, Casals developed another goal. He wanted the working people of Barcelona—those who could not afford to buy concert tickets—to have good music. Once again, through great personal commitment and effort, Casals established the Workingmen's Concert Association, through which working people could, for a small fee, attend various musical events, including the Sunday-morning concerts of the Pau Casals Orchestra.

In 1936, the life of Casals and the life of his country were interrupted by civil war in Spain. Casals was an ardent supporter of the Loyalist government that was fighting against the forces of General Francisco Franco. Despite the pleading of his friends, Casals stubbornly refused to leave Barcelona; he believed that an artist who tries to ignore political actions that deny human rights is degrading his art. Casals insisted that, during times of great trouble, great music was all the more important for the Spanish people. So, in the midst of war, he continued to conduct his orchestra and give cello performances. He also played some concerts in England and France, contributing his earnings to support the Loyalists. When Franco emerged victorious, Casals left Spain and went into voluntary exile in Prades, a small Catalan village on the French side of the Spanish border. Although this location was at first temporary, Casals rejected offers from the United States and England, and thus Prades became his permanent home in 1939. Casals was a man of great personal dignity and conviction. As he had taken a stand against totalitarianism in Spain, he similarly felt responsible not to leave France during World War II. He supported the Red Cross with proceeds from his concerts, and he personally distributed supplies to fellow Catalans who were living in nearby refugee camps. Because Casals did not separate art from his personal convictions, he refused to play for audiences in Benito Mussolini's Italy or Adolf Hitler's Germany or Franco's Spain. After World War II, following a successful performance tour in England in 1945, Casals realized that no action was going to be taken against the Spanish regime. He thus decided to stop performing in public, believing it was wrong to accept money or even applause from people in democratic nations who, he felt, had abandoned the Spanish people.

This hiatus in public performance, which Casals termed a renunciation, ended in 1950 at the Bach Bicentenary when eminent musicians came to Prades to make music with Casals and he was featured as conductor and soloist. Thus began the annual summer Prades Festival, where many recordings have been made by the distinguished participating musicians. On January 28, 1956, in Veracruz, Mexico, Casals made his first concert appearance outside Prades in many years. In that same year, he finally settled in Puerto Rico, his mother's birthplace, where he established the Casals Festival in 1957. Like the festival in Prades, this too became an annual event, and it had a stimulating influence on Puerto Rican culture. In 1957, Casals also married for a third time, to Marta Montanez, a youthful Puerto Rican cello student, who was his companion for the rest of his life.

Casals maintained an impressive schedule of composing, conducting, and performing into his eighties and nineties and continued his efforts on behalf of global peace. In 1958, he gave a cello recital at the United Nations General Assembly to celebrate the thirteenth anniversary of the United Nations, a performance broadcast in many countries. In 1961, he played for President John F. Kennedy at the White House. In the early 1960's Casals made it a practice to conduct the chief choral work of the Casals Festival each year at Carnegie Hall in New York. There, in 1962, he initiated a worldwide peace campaign with the first international performance of his own oratorio *El Pesebre* (the manger), first performed in 1960. Traditionally, after his Carniegie Hall appearance each year, Casals went to the Marlboro School in Vermont, where he taught master classes and conducted the school's chamber orchestra as part of the Marlboro Music Festival. In October, 1971, Casals returned to the United Nations to conduct the premier of his *Hymn to the United Nations*. Performed to a text by W. H. Auden, this was the high point of the United Nations Day Celebration, and Casals was awarded the United Nations Peace Medal. His other honors included the United States Presidential Medal of Freedom, the French Legion of Honor, the Royal Philharmonic Society's Gold Medal, and an honorary doctorate from the University of Edinburgh. When in San Juan, Casals continued to work on the Casals Festival and also served as president of the Puerto Rico Conservatory of Music. Only four months before his death in 1973, Casals told a crowd after a New York concert, "I am an old man, but in many senses a young man. And this is what I want you to be, young, young all your life, and to say things to the world that are true." Two months later, he took part in the festival celebrating the twenty-fifth anniversary of the State of Israel, conducting the Festival Youth Orchestra in a Mozart symphony. Casals was active and happy—making music and receiving guests—until shortly before his death in San Juan on October 22, 1973.

Summary

Pablo Casals was an artist committed to humanity, and his life—as well as his music—serves as a source of inspiration to the world. Throughout his long and productive career, Casals used his music to enhance the spirit of international brotherhood in support of his goal of world peace. He held high standards for the world, maintaining an unwavering belief in democracy and human dignity, and refused even to perform in countries that suppressed individual rights through dictatorship. In protest against social and political injustice in his native Spain, Casals lived the latter half of his life in voluntary exile from his homeland.

A man of simplicity and integrity, Casals displayed focused attention that accepted no compromise in musical expression. He demanded much of himself and his musicians, believing that truth and beauty were the artist's responsibilities. Acclaimed as one of the greatest cellists of all time, Casals expanded the possibilities for cello in both performance and composition, and he is given major credit for international appreciation of this instrument. Probably his greatest influence occurred from 1950 onward, when Casals emerged—after years of silence—at the first Casals Festival in Prades and exposed an entire younger generation of musicians to interpretation and technique radically different from the sharp, more mechanistic brilliance then established as contemporary performance style.

Bibliography

Corredor, J. M. *Conversations with Casals*. Translated by André Mangeot. New York: E. P. Dutton, 1956. This 240-page volume of informal conversations with Casals presents his opinions on life and music in a question-and-answer format. Indexed for easy reference, it also includes an introduction by Casals, as well as tributes from people as diverse as Alfred Cortot, Albert Schweitzer, Albert Einstein, Isaac Stern, and Thomas Mann.

Forsee, Aylesa. *Pablo Casals: Cellist for Freedom*. New York: Thomas Y. Crowell, 1965. Written in a manner that is accessible to young people, this biography presents Casals' life until 1964 and includes a short annotated bibliography.

Gelatt, Roland. *Music Makers*. New York: Alfred A. Knopf, 1963. Reprint. New York: De Capo Press, 1972. Subtitled "Some Outstanding Musical Performers of Our Day," this volume includes twenty-one entries on musicians who interested the author and whose careers seemed appropriate for informed comment. The twenty-eight pages on Casals give a chronological overview of his life and work to the early 1950's, highlighting Casals' integrity and strength of character.

Kahn, Albert E. *Joys and Sorrows: Reflections by Pablo Casals*. New York: Simon & Schuster, 1970. This 314-page text grew out of the author's extended conversations with Casals. Although Kahn has assimilated Casals' recollections and observations into a first-person narrative written from Casals' perspective, he emphasizes that it is not intended to be an autobiography. Includes many photographs.

Kirk, H. L. *Pablo Casals*. New York: Holt, Rinehart and Winston, 1974. For this fascinating and extensive biography, Casals and his wife opened their personal archives to the author. A prime source for those interested in details, it also includes a compilation of Casals' discography, an extensive bibliography, and many photographic illustrations.

Littlehales, Lillian. *Pablo Casals: A Life*. 2d ed. London: J. M. Dent and Sons, 1949. This pioneer biography, by a cellist friend of Casals and Susan Metcalfe Casals, highlights the holistic and balanced nature of Casals' personality. Written in 1929 and updated in 1948, it also includes a list of Casals' recordings.

Nelson, James, ed. *Wisdom: Conversations with the Elder Wise Men of Our Day.* New York: W. W. Norton, 1958. This volume includes short conversations with twenty-four eminent men of the mid-twentieth century. Casals' interview was conducted by a former student, Madeline Foley, in 1955. Although the Casals chapter is only eight pages in length, it allows the reader an insightful glimpse of the man.

Taper, Bernard. *Cellist in Exile.* New York: McGraw-Hill, 1962. This tribute offers an intimate portrait of Casals—his daily life and work. Beautifully produced, the volume is an expanded version of a 1961 *New Yorker* profile written from a series of visits with Casals during the 1961 Casals Festival in Puerto Rico.

Jean C. Fulton

RENÉ CASSIN

Born: October 5, 1887; Bayonne, France
Died: February 20, 1976; Paris, France
Area of Achievement: Law
Contribution: Through his part in encouraging adoption of the Universal Declaration of Human Rights of the United Nations, as well as his activities on behalf of international organizations, Cassin promoted the recognition of an international plane of legal standards to support the rights of the individual.

Early Life

René-Samuel Cassin could point to a distinguished lineage that at times imparted a deeply personal dimension to the concerns that preoccupied him in later life. His father, Henri Cassin, was a Jewish merchant whose ancestors over many generations had been established in his native region; he had married Gabrielle Déborah Dreyfus, whose forebears among others included a dragoon from Alsace who had been celebrated for his service during the Napoleonic wars. René Cassin was born on October 5, 1887, in Bayonne, in the Basses Pyrénées near France's border with Spain. He was reared in a household that included his sister, Félice. He was educated at a *lycée* in Nice and completed a program of studies in humanities and law at the University of Aix-en-Provence in 1908. The following year, he was admitted to the bar in Paris; in 1914, he presented a thesis at the University of Paris dealing with exceptions for the failure of execution in synallagmatic—bilateral or reciprocal—contracts.

Cassin entered the French army when World War I, broke out, and he was commissioned as an infantry officer. He was severely wounded in fighting on the Meuse in October, 1914, when he was struck by German shrapnel. In spite of a remarkable recovery, he was declared 65 percent invalided in April, 1915; notwithstanding his own perseverance and determination, abdominal complications were to trouble him often in subsequent years. After some time in Paris and Provence, he began teaching law courses in Aix, and in 1917 he became an adjunct secretary of a local association for the benefit of war wounded. Later, in November, 1917, and February, 1918, he assisted in the foundation of the Federal Union, a larger organization devoted to social and humanitarian service on behalf of veterans, the disabled, and widows. In March, 1917, he married Simone Yzombard, whom he had known since his student days of 1908; though they had no children, they were to remain together during many difficult periods.

Life's Work

Cassin taught civil and international law at the University of Lille for a period of about ten years, and then, from 1929, he held an appointment at the University of Paris; he also taught during some terms at The Hague and Geneva. He formally retired from the academic profession in 1960. During the years following World War I, he was active in efforts to mobilize the support of former soldiers from many countries in the interests of peacekeeping. He took part in the work of the International Labor Organization, and in 1922 he became president of France's Federal Union. He also served as a delegate to the League of Nations between 1924 and 1938, and, when the Geneva Disarmament Conference began its deliberations in 1932, he attempted, but with little success, to secure the support of veterans throughout Europe for the promotion of arms reduction. For much of his life, Cassin was associated with the Alliance Israélite, and he evinced a profound sympathy toward the aims of political Zionism; his conviction that some satisfaction should be found for the aspirations of the Jewish people was reinforced both by his first visit to Jerusalem, in 1930, and by the menacing drift toward Fascism and militarism on the part of some European nations.

It would appear that Cassin had few illusions about the gravity of the challenge posed by Nazi and other authoritarian regimes. He opposed measures of appeasement, such as the Munich accords of 1938, and he seemed cognizant of the dangers that were posed by unchecked aggression and expansion on the part of Axis states and their allies. When France was defeated and overrun by German armies in 1940, Cassin went on to London; he served in the government-in-exile under General Charles de Gaulle and held positions such as secretary of the Council of Defense and commissioner for justice and public education. He drafted an instrument that would define relations between the Free French and Great Britain. He also wrote an opinion that attempted to show that the Vichy regime established under the sponsorship of German occupation forces was illegal and could not be the legitimate government of France. In letters and memoirs dealing with this period, de Gaulle praised Cassin's loyalty and maintained that he had been of real service to their cause. In December, 1942, a military tribunal in occupied France condemned Cassin to death in absentia. Undaunted, he assisted in the preparation of documentary files dealing with atrocities and acts against civilian populations in Europe. In 1943, Cassin became president of the Alliance Israélite, which essentially had ceased to function in France itself. After the Allied liberation of 1944, Cassin returned to his native country and became, for sixteen years, the vice president of the Council of State. He was named to other important public positions as well.

Those who worked with Cassin sometimes described him as dynamic and somewhat impetuous; though he was not unusually skilled as a debater, his public presentations seemed to evince an acute and finely honed intelligence that could be brought to bear extemporaneously upon matters of particular importance to him. During the later portions of his career, he presented a memorable figure: Though he was not tall and seemed somewhat wizened, he had large, thick features with dark, penetrating eyes. A broad, curved nose and wide mouth seemed to suggest a benevolent cast of mind. In later years, he became largely bald, but his appearance was rendered rather distinctive by his broad, full beard and mustache. It was for his efforts in connection with the work of the United Nations (U.N.) that he became well known throughout the world. He assisted in the foundation of the United Nations Educational, Scientific, and Cultural Organization (UNESCO), and he also served on that body as a delegate. The United Nations Charter had established a Commission on Human Rights, which was meant to determine means by which legal standards could be drafted to forestall further acts of state terrorism or oppression of the sort that had occurred during World War II. Eleanor Roosevelt of the United States held the chair for the commission. Cassin became vice president; a number of other important figures, including Charles Malik and Carlos Romulo, each of whom later were to become president of the U.N. General Assembly, also took part.

The drafting sessions began in January, 1947, and gave rise to numerous differences of opinion and philosophical clashes; for example, references to the Deity and issues regarding freedom of religion and expression seemed to allow limited basis for consensus, and other areas in which cultural differences existed tended to frustrate the composition of a precise legal document. From time to time as well there was opposition from those outside the commission; for example, some U.S. senators were unsettled at the possibility that race relations within the United States might come within the purview of the declaration. While the significance of Cassin's role in the actual composition of the document has been contested by some of those who were also present, it would appear that his work in revising and editing the declaration was vital. In December, 1948, after numerous meetings and prolonged consideration of many drafts, the Universal Declaration of Human Rights was adopted. The fundamental proposition of the first article was stated forthrightly: "All human beings are born free and equal in dignity and rights. They are endowed with reason and conscience and should act towards one another in a spirit of brotherhood." The articles concerning personal liberties prohibited torture, slavery, arbitrary arrest, detention, exile, and other abuses; some articles referred to economic and cultural rights, while other parts of the declaration dealt with the rights of criminal defendants and political rights. The declaration was not itself of binding legal force and was not regarded as such by many governments. Cassin himself maintained that the declaration was not a coercive legal instrument but could be considered as coming into force as an authoritative interpretation of the United Nations Charter. With the support of Cassin and a number of others, much later, in 1966, the U.N. General Assembly adopted two international covenants—the first on economic, social, and cultural rights, and the second on civil and political rights—which formally went into force in 1976.

Cassin also held judicial positions, which drew upon his international experience. From 1950 to 1960, he served on the Court of Arbitration in The Hague. The European Convention for the Protection of Human Rights and Fundamental Freedoms, which was adopted in 1950, had drawn major precepts from the Universal Declaration of Human Rights; between 1965 and 1968, Cassin served as president of the European Court of Human Rights. He was widely recognized as one of the world's outstanding exponents of the principle that human rights could be upheld through the rule of law, and in December, 1968, on the twentieth anniversary of the day that the Universal Declaration of Human Rights was adopted, he was awarded the Nobel Peace Prize. In his acceptance speech, Cassin contended that, in the light of the rights that every human being should enjoy, the jurisdiction of states could be regarded as fundamental but no longer exclusive. Other awards that Cassin received included the United Nations Prize, the Decalogue Society Award of Merit, and the Goethe Prize; Cassin also received honorary degrees from several institutions. Toward the end of his life, he also helped sponsor a conference that provided impetus, several years later, for the inclusion of human rights provisions in the Helsinki Declaration of 1975. While his previous writings generally had appeared in professional journals or as pamphlets, his ideas and experiences were made more accessible with the publication of *La Pensée et l'action* (1972), which deals with legal topics; he also wrote a book of memoirs, *Les Hommes partis de rien: Le Réveil de la France abattue 1940-41* (1975). His wife Simone died in 1969; at times Cassin was measurably affected by failing health. In November, 1975, after he had suffered a heart attack, he married Ghislaine Bru; rather soon thereafter, however, on February 20, 1976, Cassin died in Paris from heart complications and pneumonia.

Summary

The life and work of René Cassin has invariably been associated with the effort to establish fundamental norms of legal force that could uphold the rights and dignity of the individual notwithstanding the traditional place of state sovereignty in international law. While some authorities had regarded customary law as imposing such obligations upon states, others have maintained that no international order could come into existence without express treaty commitments on the part of states across the world. Other questions, in many regions, have concerned the standing of individuals to bring action on their own behalf to enforce humanitarian law. Even with the adoption of the international covenants, some skepticism as to the utility of such measures had remained, in view of continuing violations of human rights by various governments. On the other hand, relatively few alternatives have been considered more desirable and more appropriate from the standpoint of the prevailing international order. Although neither he nor any of his coworkers was able successfully to overcome doubts about enforceability in the modern world, it was the particular virtue of Cassin to have enunciated principles by which state actions could be scrutinized. For that matter, however admonitory actual agreements may appear, in fact or in law, it could be argued as well that the promotion of norms and ideals may have had some overall salutary effect upon the international system.

Bibliography
Claude, Richard Pierre, and Burns H. Weston, eds. *Human Rights in the World Community: Issues and Action*. Philadelphia: University of Pennsylvania Press, 1989. A wide-ranging series of articles that considers areas in which problems of international legal norms have arisen.

Henkin, Louis, ed. *The International Bill of Rights: The Covenant on Civil and Political Rights*. New York: Columbia University Press, 1981. This group of essays, by scholars and jurists, is helpful for the relationship between the Universal Declaration of Human Rights and subsequent agreements, such as the international covenants.

Humphrey, John P. *Human Rights and the United Nations: A Great Adventure*. Dobbs Ferry, N.Y.: Transnational, 1984. The author, a Canadian lawyer who was director of the division of human rights before the U.N. Secretariat, discusses his experiences of twenty years' work for the world body; he was present during work on the Universal Declaration of Human Rights and is inclined to regard Cassin's role at that time as seriously overstated by many writers.

Luard, Evan, ed. *The International Protection of Human Rights*. New York: Frederick A. Praeger, 1967. A collection of articles on this general topic, some of which deal with early work in humanitarian legislation by the United Nations and the European bodies.

Meron, Theodor. *Human Rights Law-Making in the United Nations: A Critique of Instruments and Process*. Oxford, England: Clarendon Press, 1986. This study by a leading specialist briefly mentions Cassin's efforts while delivering a reasoned assessment of problems in the world body's juridical position.

Newman, Ralph A., ed. *Equity in the World's Legal Systems: A Comparative Study Dedicated to René Cassin*. Brussels: Établissements Émile Bruylant, 1973. The depth and extent of Cassin's influence may be measured from this group of articles by students and colleagues from across the world, who deal here with legal conceptions of importance in many countries and regions.

Ramcharan, B. G., ed. *Human Rights: Thirty Years After the Universal Declaration*. The Hague: Martinus Nijhoff, 1979. Difficulties and prospects in the drafting and implementation of U.N. law are considered by the contributors to this commemorative volume.

Robertson A. H. *Human Rights in Europe.* 2d ed. Manchester, England: Manchester University Press, 1977. Useful for its treatment of the European court and its decisions. A number of individuals, including Cassin, who have been involved in the work of this body, are discussed at intervals.

_____. *Human Rights in the World: An Introduction to the Study of the International Protection of Human Rights.* 2d ed. New York: St. Martin's Press, 1982. A competent survey of the institutions, legislation, and cases that have been associated with humanitarian law on a regional and world basis, particularly since the United Nations was formed.

Sohn, Louis B., and Thomas Buergenthal, comps. *International Protection of Human Rights.* Indianapolis: Bobbs-Merrill, 1973. A basic textbook that deals in broad terms with international concerns under the United Nations and the European convention as well as other theories and topics generally pertinent to this area.

Tolley, Howard, Jr. *The U.N. Commission on Human Rights.* Boulder, Colo.: Westview Press, 1987. Helpful for the origins of the Universal Declaration of Human Rights, which the author also discusses in the light of subsequent agreements and practices.

Vasak, Karel, and Philip Alston, eds. *The International Dimensions of Human Rights.* 2 vols. Westport, Conn.: Greenwood Press, 1982. Salient historical, political, and legal factors are considered from scholarly perspectives by the various authors who have contributed to this work.

J. R. Broadus

ERNST CASSIRER

Born: July 28, 1874; Breslau, Germany
Died: April 13, 1945; New York, New York
Areas of Achievement: Historiography and philosophy
Contribution: Cassirer created an innovative and modified form of Kantian philosophy. He published a number of works on the history of philosophy that demonstrated the relevance of philosophy to scientific and humanistic knowledge.

Early Life

Ernst Cassirer was born in Breslau, a region called Silesia in Germany (now Wrocław, Poland), to a large middle-class Jewish family. His extended family was engaged in both publishing and commercial enterprises, with the result that Cassirer enjoyed financial independence throughout his life. He entered the German university system in 1892 and, over the next seven years, attended universities in Berlin, Leipzig, Heidelberg, and Marburg. At first, Cassirer lacked a clear direction for his intellectual pursuits; he sampled a number of subjects. In 1894, however, he took a course from Georg Simmel that set the direction for his future career. Simmel taught that conflicts between the individual and society are inevitable and unavoidable: Tension results from the conflict between the individual's desire for freedom and society's need to limit the individual through institutions, laws, and other encumbrances. Cassirer retained and refined these lessons throughout much of his productive life. While studying with Simmel, Cassirer found that his teacher admired the philosophical works of Hermann Cohen. Because of his high regard for Simmel, Cassirer went to the University of Marburg in 1896 to study under Cohen.

The philosophy department at Marburg was strongly influenced by the thought of Immanuel Kant. Indeed, neo-Kantian philosophy prevailed in many institutions of higher learning in Germany at the beginning of the twentieth century. Although Cohen focused much of his philosophical work on the objects of natural science, he believed that it is thought which provides the natural world with a coherent reality. Influenced by his teacher, Cassirer wrote a dissertation on René Descartes and his critique of mathematics and natural science. Completed in 1899, this early work of Cassirer revealed two key assumptions that were to inform his mature philosophy: first, that historical studies of philosophical problems provided insight into the problems of knowledge; and second, that reality is not static but must be reconstructed in order to be understood.

Life's Work

Cassirer returned from Marburg with his doctoral degree in hand and began a prolific half century during which he would produce 125 published works. Unencumbered by financial necessity, Cassirer pursued his studies of Descartes, science, and the problems of knowledge. In 1902, he married; he and his wife Toni eventually had three children. In 1903, the Cassirers moved to Berlin; as a result of anti-Semitism, however, Cassirer did not gain a teaching position until 1906, when he became an instructor at the University of Berlin. In the next twelve years, in fact, no European university offered him a professorship, despite his already significant achievements. It is ironic that during this time his contribution to philosophy was recognized by Harvard University, which offered him a two-year visiting professorship.

Cassirer's first major philosophical work was *Substanzbegriff und Funktionsbegriff* (1910; *Substance and Function*, 1923). In this work, he analyzed the development of concepts of chemistry in terms of the rational approach of science. Given a world of material substances, he argued, it is possible through logical thought to discover the theoretical framework that controls physical entities. In 1914, as Cassirer prepared himself for a study of Kant, he was interrupted by the outbreak of World War I. Although the war captured the imagination of a number of German Jews, Cassirer did not respond to this great surge of German nationalism. Rejected from military service for medical reasons, he was drafted to teach in a high school for the duration of the war. Thus, as it turned out, he was able to continue his study of Kant's philosophy. *Kants Lebun und Lehre* (1918; *Kant's Life and Thought*, 1981) marked a major turn in Cassirer's intellectual development. In his reinterpretation of Kant, Cassirer moved away from earlier concerns with science and the logical formulation of knowledge toward a larger vision of the humanities.

After the war, the Weimar Republic of Germany established several new universities. One of these, the University of Hamburg, offered Cassirer a professorship. Eventually, anti-Semitism reached Hamburg as well, but for a time Cassirer found a refuge there. In addition, Hamburg became the location of the Warburg Library. Aby Warburg, from a rich banking family, wanted to create a library containing a history of human civilization—a library that would reveal the secrets of the human spirit. Cassirer's interests had also moved in this direction during the war years. The first publications of the Warburg Library were two of Cassirer's essays on myths and symbolic forms. During these early years at Hamburg, Cassirer continued his work in the philosophy of science with an essay on Albert Einstein's theory of relativity and began his most significant work in the philosophy of symbolic forms.

In 1923, Cassirer published the first of three volumes of *Die Philosophie der symbolischen Formen* (*The Philosophy of Symbolic Forms*); the second and third volumes followed in 1925 and 1929, with the English translations of all three volumes appearing in 1955. This work was Cassirer's most significant contribution to philosophy and the humanities. Cassirer believed that consciousness imposes signs and symbols on the world and that as a result of these symbols the world has meaning. There are scientific symbols that bring about the objective world, mythic symbols that bring about myths and religion, and finally the symbols of language—which at first one is not inclined to perceive as symbols, since it is language that constitutes the commonsense world as one experiences it. For Cassirer, all human thought is symbolic.

To justify this philosophy of symbolic forms, Cassirer examined a vast amount of material taken from philosophy, history, science, languages, anthropology, and the humanities. The result was a work of remarkable erudition. Cassirer remains the only major philosopher of the twentieth century to place myth at the center of his philosophy.

Cassirer was appointed rector of the University of Hamburg in 1929, but, with the rise of National Socialism in Germany, he was able to serve in this position for one year only. In the following two years, Cassirer worked on *Die Philosophie der Aufklärung* (1932; *The Philosophy of the Enlightenment*, 1951), a study of law, state, and society during the Enlightenment. In this book, he contends that the heights of human achievement have been reached through rationality and reason. In 1933, Cassirer resigned his position at the university. In his letter of resignation he stated that a Jew could no longer be a part of the German educational system.

Cassirer taught at the University of Oxford for two years and in 1935 went to the University of Gothenburg in Sweden. In 1941, he emigrated to the United States, where he was a visiting professor at Yale University for three years before a final year at Columbia University in New York. After leaving Germany, Cassirer lost much of the liberal optimism that colored his historical and philosophical works. He began to have serious doubts about the ability of human culture to prevail against the irrational and violent elements that are also part of the human heritage. He shifted his concern from cultural symbols toward the individual human being, and his last publications, *An Essay on Man* (1944) and *The Myth of the State* (1946), reflect that change in orientation. Cassirer died in New York City in April, 1945.

Summary

Ernst Cassirer listened to the voices of rationality and science, yet he also understood the crisis that beset liberal institutions in the twentieth century. He understood that the rise of intolerance, lawlessness, and violence threatened to sweep aside those key elements of civilization that give meaning to individual existence. Cassirer clarified his position in one of the most interesting philosophical debates of the twentieth century. In 1929, Cassirer had recently published the third volume of his *Philosophy of Symbolic Forms*. Two years earlier, Martin Heidegger had published *Sein und Zeit* (1927;

Being and Time, 1962), which was already acclaimed as one of the more important works of the century. The two philosophers met on March 17, 1929, in Switzerland, to debate their respective views on reason and existence. Heidegger argued that reason must play a secondary role to existence because it is a part of the imagination. Cassirer replied that reason is independent of sensibilities and imagination, and that consequently philosophy has the power to liberate humanity from the finality of existence and provide room for individual freedom.

The debate in Switzerland was no ordinary disagreement between two philosophers, each pursuing his own intellectual path within the sheltered world of academia. In 1933, Cassirer fled Germany, and he was to spend the remainder of his life as an expatriate in various countries. During that same year, Heidegger became the rector of Freiburg University, where he gave a speech praising the Nazi regime. For Cassirer, the philosophical task does not exist in isolation but is nourished by the human spirit and the entire history of humanity.

Bibliography
Copelston, Frederick Charles. *A History of Philosophy*. Vol.7, part 2. Garden City, N.Y.: Doubleday, 1965. Copelston wrote a multivolume history of philosophy covering the ancient Greeks to the present. This volume deals with the twentieth century European philosophers and serves well both as a background work to this period and for information on Cassirer as well.

Ferretti, Silvia. *Cassirer, Panofsky, and Warburg: Symbol, Art, and History*. Translated by Richard Pierce. New Haven, Conn.: Yale University Press, 1989. First published in Italy in 1984, this study compares and contrasts the approachs to cultural history taken by Cassirer and the art historians Erwin Panofsky and Aby Warburg.

Gay, Peter. "The Social History of Ideas: Ernst Cassirer and After." In *The Critical Spirit*, edited by K. H. Wolff and B. Moore, Jr. Boston: Beacon Press, 1967. Gay is a sympathetic interpreter of Cassirer's philosophy; this essay serves to illustrate how Cassirer uses the historical past and cultural patterns.

Itzkoff, Seymour W. *Ernst Cassirer: Scientific Knowledge and the Concept of Man*. Notre Dame, Ind.: University of Notre Dame Press, 1971. All too often Cassirer's philosophy is associated exclusively with art, language, and the humanities. Cassirer believed that science is one of the three major forms of human expression. This book shows why Cassirer placed such emphasis on scientific knowledge.

Krois, John Michael. *Cassirer: Symbolic Forms and History*. New Haven, Conn.: Yale University Press, 1987. This is the most comprehensive study of Cassirer's thought available in English, covering the entire range of his work. Krois argues that the common view of Cassirer, as preoccupied with epistemological questions, is far too narrow; he emphasizes the importance of myth in Cassirer's philosophy.

Lipton, David R. *Ernst Cassirer: The Dilemma of a Liberal Intellectual in Germany, 1914-1933*. Toronto, Canada: University of Toronto Press, 1978. Lipton portrays Cassirer's life in terms of the growth and formation of his philosophy and against the background of rising anti-Semitism and political and social repression in Germany.

Schilpp, Paul A., ed. *The Philosophy of Ernst Cassirer*. Evanston, Ill.: Open Court, 1949. This massive volume (just under a thousand pages in length) in the Library of Living Philosophers series includes Cassirer's own account of his life's work, followed by critical responses from scholars and fellow philosophers. Volumes in this series customarily include the subject's reply to his critics, but Cassirer died before he was able to respond. Nevertheless, this is an indispensable resource.

Victor W. Chen

FIDEL CASTRO

Born: August 13, 1926; near Birán, Cuba

Areas of Achievement: Government and politics

Contribution: Castro led a successful revolutionary struggle against the Cuban dictatorship of Fulgencio Batista y Zaldívar in the late 1950's. The revolutionary leader subsequently implemented Latin America's third social revolution of the twentieth century and transformed Cuba into the first communist state of the hemisphere in defiance of the United States.

Early Life

Fidel Castro Ruz was born on a large cattle estate near the village of Birán in Cuba's Oriente Province. Fidel was the third of seven children sired by a prosperous Spanish immigrant landowner and his second wife. Between 1941 and 1945, Castro completed his secondary education at the Colegio Belén, a prestigious Jesuit institution in Havana. Taller in stature than most Latin males, Fidel was a natural athlete, excelling in many sports, especially basketball and baseball, which he played with near professional ability. Castro enrolled in the University of Havana's Law Faculty in 1945. There he became a student political activist in a frequently violent campus political setting. Castro joined one of the rival student political groups, became known for his speaking talent, and occasionally expressed nationalist and anti-imperialist sentiments, while condemning the exploitation of the poor by the rich.

While a university student, Castro became involved in two international incidents—first, an aborted attempt in 1947 to overthrow the Dominican Republic's dictator Rafael Leónidas Trujillo Molina, and then, in 1948, political disorders following the assassination of a prominent Colombian politician in Bogotá, where Castro was attending an anti-imperialist student congress. In spite of these extracurricular interruptions, Castro was graduated in 1950 with a doctor of laws degree. The politically ambitious graduate began his career as an attorney who litigated on behalf of underprivileged clients. Castro also became active in the Havana organization of the Ortodoxo Party, which championed reform and crusaded against corruption. Most recent presidential regimes had succumbed to graft and gangsterism, frustrating popular sentiment in favor of economic nationalist policies and profound social reform. The young attorney was selected to run as an Ortodoxo candidate for congress in the general elections scheduled for June, 1952.

Life's Work

Events soon propelled Castro into a revolutionary career. On March 10, 1952, former president and political strongman Fulgencio Batista y Zaldívar seized power in a coup and canceled the elections. When it became clear that peaceful tactics could not dislodge Batista, Castro and his younger brother Raúl organized an armed conspiracy. On July 26, 1953, the rebels attacked the Moncada military barracks in Santiago, hoping to set off a general uprising. The effort ended in disaster as about one-third of the one-hundred-seventy-man force survived the clash and reprisals that ensued. At Castro's trial, the young rebel delivered a five-hour address in defense of his actions, which became known by its closing statement, "History will absolve me."

The court sentenced Castro to fifteen years' imprisonment. Yet Castro was released in May, 1955, through a general political amnesty. In July, Castro departed for Mexico to organize a new armed effort to topple Batista. Castro broke all ties with traditional political parties and called his new independent organization the 26th of July Movement. Joining the rebel leader abroad were his brother Raúl, other Cuban political refugees including survivors of the Moncada attack, and an Argentine-born physician, Che Guevara. After a period of secret military training, Castro's force, numbering eighty-two men, sailed at the end of November, 1956, from the Yucatán coast for Cuba in an overloaded old yacht called the *Granma*. A few days after they landed in Oriente Province, an army unit nearly wiped out the small invading force. A remnant of only twelve survivors reached safety in the nearby Sierra Maestra mountains.

Eventually Castro's tiny force received the support of peasants and was also bolstered by recruits from the movement's urban organization. Publicity from journalistic interviews and news of rebel successes made Castro the focus of the popular resistance in Cuba. Moderate middle-class opposition groups signed an accord with the rebel leader on his terms in April, 1958. Shortly thereafter, the Cuban Communists, who had previously criticized Castro's tactics, secretly agreed to support him. Meanwhile, Batista's severe repression had alienated his government. The dictator's large but ineffective army failed in its campaigns to eliminate the guerrillas. Castro's Rebel Armed Forces, numbering fewer than one thousand, assumed the offensive in the summer of 1958, and the dictatorship collapsed as Batista fled Cuba on New Year's Day of 1959.

Now the most popular figure in Cuba and in control of the armed forces, Castro gradually pushed aside his moderate middle-class allies in the new government, who objected to his sweeping agrarian reform proposal and the growing influence of the Communists in the revolutionary process. After mid-1959, the government consisted solely of Castro's youthful 26th of July Movement, revolutionary student organizations, and veteran Communist politicians. As Cuba's prime minister, Castro sought a radical restructuring of Cuban society on behalf of the rural and urban lower classes and a diversified economy free from foreign dominance and dependency on sugar exports.

The question of whether Castro held but concealed Marxist and Communist views during the struggle against Batista is still a matter of controversy and conjecture. In any event, the radical nationalist and socioeconomic goals of Castro's revolutionary government facilitated a working alliance with the Cuban Communists.

United States-Cuban relations deteriorated steadily over the next two years. Castro reacted to Washington's hostility to his regime's orientation by nationalizing foreign-owned firms and seeking ever closer ties with Communist Bloc countries. The United States severed relations with Havana in January, 1960, while the Central Intelligence Agency plotted to assassinate the Cuban leader and organized an unsuccessful invasion by anti-Castro exiles in April, 1961. Strengthened by this victory, Castro openly labeled his revolution "socialist." Then, in an effort to secure Soviet economic and military commitment to his revolution, the Cuban prime minister declared himself a Marxist-Leninist in December, 1961. United States influence, once a dominant force in Cuba's economic, cultural, and political life, disappeared as Castro aligned his country with the Eastern Bloc states.

Castro established a one-party state amalgamating his movement and its political allies into a Marxist-Leninist party. The regime wiped out illiteracy, raised the living standards of rural laborers, and brought better health, educational benefits, and opportunities for social advancement to Cuba's masses. Castro's Cuba has also made strides toward ending racial and sexual discrimination. Cuba became more prominent on the international scene. Castro sponsored international conferences, spoke out frequently on Third World issues, dispatched Cuban medical personnel, teachers, and technicians to a number of countries, and provided direct military aid to Marxist regimes in Ethiopia and Angola. On the negative side, Castro did not succeed in achieving his original economic goals for Cuba. At an early date, industrialization efforts and attempts to diversify agricultural production failed and were set aside on Soviet advice in favor of renewed dependency on sugar exports. Production goals frequently fell short, and Cuba's economy became very dependent on Soviet subsidies and technical aid. Shortages of consumer items, suppression of public and organized dissent, and curbs on artistic freedoms caused a significant number of Cubans to leave their homeland as exiles.

Castro is noted for his flamboyant, personal style of leadership. The Cuban head-of-state, simply referred to as "Fidel" by most Cubans, has a powerful charismatic appeal and macho qualities which are valuable assets in Latin American political culture. Castro is charming and entertaining in his personal contacts with individual Cubans, mass audiences, or foreign visitors to Cuba. He has frequently toured the island, dealing directly with his countrymen and their problems. The Cuban leader annually makes many public speeches on revolutionary anniversaries to audiences that number in the hundreds of thousands. Although his speeches sometimes last several hours and may even cover mundane topics, Castro establishes a close rapport with listeners and mesmerizes crowds throughout the performance. Castro makes very effective use of television to convey his powerful personal touch in messages and appeals to the Cuban public. These political talents and qualities have enabled the Cuban leader to retain the support of many of Cuba's ten million inhabitants despite his regime's authoritarian nature and lagging economic performance.

Summary
Fidel Castro has made himself the central factor in contemporary Cuban history and has vigorously asserted his presence on the international scene. Twentieth century Latin America has witnessed three significant social revolutions: in Mexico (1910-1940), Bolivia (1952-1964), and Cuba. Furthermore, Castro personally directed his revolutionary movement to victory over the Batista dictatorship against great odds. In spite of Cuba's vulnerable geographic location within the United States' sphere of interest, the Cuban leader founded the first communist state in the Western Hemisphere and survived the United States' early attempts to isolate or topple him.

An interdependent relationship now exists between the Soviet Union and its small Latin American ally. Castro's freedom of action is somewhat limited by Cuba's dependence on vital Soviet aid. Moscow is similarly restrained from asserting its leverage to the point of suffering a major political reverse by allowing Castro's revolutionary experiment to collapse. Therefore, Castro has occasionally taken positions contrary to Soviet views on international and domestic issues.

Among contemporary world leaders, Castro is one of the better known. Few heads of state have held power longer than the Cuban leader. Contrary to the fact that Cuba is a small Caribbean nation whose influence in world affairs is relatively minor, Castro is an important although controversial world figure and statesman.

Bibliography
Bourne, Peter. *Fidel: A Biography of Fidel Castro.* New York: Dodd, Mead, 1986. One of the more recent biographical portraits of the Cuban leader. The author, a psychiatrist who met Castro while serving with the Carter presidential administration, attempts to explain some of Castro's actions and personality traits through psychoanalysis. The author is generally sympathetic to his subject.
Castro, Fidel. *Revolutionary Struggle, 1947-1958.* Edited by Rolando E. Bonachea and Nelson P. Valdés. Cambridge, Mass.: MIT Press, 1972. A collection of Castro's speeches, writings, and interviews during the period before he came to power. The long introduction provides a valuable por-

trait of the Cuban leader against the background of this era.

Guevara, Ernesto. *Reminiscences of the Cuban Revolutionary War*. Translated by·Victoria Ortiz. New York: Monthly Review Press, 1968. This is a good historical account of Castro's guerrilla struggle against the Batista regime; it is based on the careful first-hand observations of one of Castro's leading military and political collaborators.

Lockwood, Lee. *Castro's Cuba, Cuba's Fidel*. New York: Macmillan, 1967. Lockwood's book is one of the most useful works on Castro's personality and leadership style. A series of interviews and events show the Cuban leader in a variety of situations. Illustrated with many photographs.

Ruiz, Ramón Eduardo. *Cuba 1933-Prologue to Revolution*. Ithaca: Cornell University Press, 1972. An analysis of political and economic factors in the two decades preceding the start of Castro's revolutionary career which contributed to his nationalistic and Marxist social revolution.

Szulc, Tad. *Fidel: A Critical Portrait*. New York: William Morrow, 1986. The most comprehensive and detailed biographical study of Castro. Szulc utilizes extensive and detailed personal interviews with Castro and knowledgeable Cubans of varying political persuasions. This is a balanced and objective treatment of the subject, unlike most previous biographical studies.

Thomas, Hugh. *Cuba: The Pursuit of Freedom*. New York: Harper & Row, 1971. A lengthy history of Cuba that is useful for placing Castro in the context of Cuban historical development. The relevant period from the 1940's through the 1960's makes up about half of the book. An objective study.

David A. Crain

AIMÉ CÉSAIRE

Born: June 25, 1913; Basse-Pointe, Martinique

Areas of Achievement: Literature and colonial administration
Contribution: Césaire contributed to the spiritual foundation of a number of
Afro-American social, intellectual, and literary movements. His poetry
and plays embody the idea of *négritude*, a word he created, which became
the affirmative basis of the idea that one is black and proud of it. Although a renowned poet, playwright, and essayist, he has functioned as an
active politician in the government of his native Martinique.

Early Life

Aimé Césaire was born in 1913 in Basse-Pointe, a town on the northeast
coast of the West Indian island of Martinique. Although his family was poor,
they were not from the impoverished class of illiterate farm workers that
made up the majority of the black population of Martinique. Aimé's father
was a local tax inspector, while his mother contributed to the welfare of the
six children by making dresses. Aimé was the second eldest of the children.
It was his grandmother, Eugénie, who taught him to read and write French
by the time he was four. The family made a concerted effort to imbue their
children with French culture and literature; his father read stories to his
children, not in Creole, the primary language of black Martinicans, but in
French. He particularly favored the prose and poetry of Victor Hugo.

When Aimé was eleven, the family moved to the capital of Martinique,
Fort-de-France, where he attended the Lycée Schoelcher. It was during his
years at this school that the young Césaire came under the influence of
Eugène Revert, a teacher of geography, who introduced his students to the
specific richness of the Martinican botanical and geological landscape. Revert also encouraged Césaire to further his education by recommending him
for acceptance at a well-known preparatory school in Paris, the Lycée Louis-
le-Grand, where he readied himself for entrance to the distinguished École
Normale Supérieure, also in Paris.

During his time at the Lycée Louis-le-Grand, he met and developed a deep
friendship with a fellow classmate, Léopold Senghor of Senegal, who later
became both the president of that African republic and a highly respected
poet. Senghor then collaborated with a friend and fellow poet of Césaire, the
French Guianan, Léon-Gontran Damas, in forming a newspaper called
L'Étudiant noir (the black student), a publication that brought together
young blacks from Africa and the West Indies and created the opportunity
for an intercultural mix that eventually gave birth to the concept of *négritude*. In the group that formed around *L'Étudiant noir*, Aimé Césaire met a
Martinican woman, Suzanne Roussy, whom he married in 1937 and who

later helped him create and edit the well-known journal *Tropiques*.

During his time at the École Normale Supérieure, Césaire was introduced to the literary and anthropological works that would determine the direction of his artistic and political vision: the writing of James Joyce, Virginia Woolf, Marcel Proust, Arthur Rimbaud, Stéphane Mallarmé, the Black Poets of the Harlem Renaissance, and the anthropologists Maurice Delafosse and Leo Frobenius. The last two scholars revealed to Césaire that Africa possessed its own highly articulated history, art, and civilization, while one of his professors introduced him to the idea of a black cultural archetype that went beyond geographical borders.

With all these influences brewing within the imagination of the young Césaire, he began in 1936 the poem that was to make him famous throughout the world and upon which his literary reputation was permanently based. The long poem *Cahier d'un retour au pays natal* (1939, 1947; *Memorandum of My Martinique*, 1947; also known as *Return to My Native Land*, 1968) documented his spiritual journey from adolescence to adulthood through the various cultural, linguistic, and moral conflicts that he was forced to confront as a black Martinican educated in a Western, French colonial intellectual system. By the time he returned to Martinique after seven years of European schooling, he was already beginning both a literary and a political career that would establish him as one of the greatest black writers of the twentieth century.

Life's Work

Césaire combines a number of seemingly contradictory roles within a single career. All of them, however, stem from his overwhelming conviction that the political is always the personal and that a man's work, whether it be writing poems or running a city government, embodies his belief system. After earning his degree at the prestigious École Normale Supérieure in Paris, he returned in 1940 to teach languages and literature at his former school, the Lycée Schoelcher. He and his wife founded and edited their own West Indian version of *L'Étudiant noir*, calling it *Tropiques*, which helped promulgate the concept of *négritude* to the politically naive natives of the West Indies. Following World War II, Césaire decided that the only way to help his country improve its economic and political situation was to become an active member of the government. After retiring from teaching, he was sent to Paris as a deputy to the French Assembly, returned to become the mayor of Fort-de-France, and finally founded and became president of his own political party, the Progressive Party of Martinique. He has continued to hold a deputy's seat in the French Assembly for almost forty years. Concurrent with his exceptionally active political activities, he has also published five major volumes of poetry, four full-length plays, and three major political and historical prose works.

The key to understanding all of his multifaceted scholar's activities and production is the concept of *négritude*, a word that Césaire first used in his revolutionary long poem, *Return to My Native Land*. The word has come to represent the affirmation that one is black and proud of it, an idea that became in the sixties "Black Is Beautiful." This neologism was created by Césaire, Senghor, and Damas and referred to blacks who had been dominated and oppressed politically, culturally, and spiritually by Western values. The word expressed a total rejection of assimilation with white culture and urged an exploration into and a celebration of their unique racial roots. The Western values most antithetical to the values embodied in the idea of *négritude* were rationalism, Christianity, individualism, and technology. Césaire, particularly in his poetry, celebrates the ability of the black soul to participate in the energies of nature and not to control them by technology; he rejects the zeal of the Christian missionaries in their attempt to destroy ancient, pagan rituals. Most important, however, is his dismissal of the Western concept of individualism symbolized by its apotheosis of the hero to a semidivine status. He celebrates, rather, the loss of the individual ego in the collective effort toward a communal idea in which all may participate. In all of his poetry, plays, and prose works, Césaire expresses in varying degrees his loyalty to the tenets of *négritude* in one form or another.

The first and most influential work written by Césaire is his long poem, *Return to My Native Land*. It is a classic example of a writer who writes himself into political action by rejecting all the values that he has just spent seven years assimilating in France. He had recently received his degree from France's most distinguished university, the École Normale Supérieure, had mastered the French language and its literature, yet had also assimilated the techniques and visions of the prevailing European aesthetic movement, Surrealism. Indeed, André Breton, the founder of the Surrealist literary movement, declared that Césaire handled the French language "as no white man can handle it today." Jean-Paul Sartre theorized that Césaire used the techniques of Surrealism to liberate himself from the stuffy conventions of French literature, while other critics recognize Césaire's difficult, exuberant wordplay and unorthodox metaphors, mixed with African and Caribbean imagery and history as attempts to forge a new language that can express the violently chaotic nature of the black collective unconscious from which his imagination proceeds.

Three major themes dominate *Return to My Native Land* and chart the poem's spiritual journey while simultaneously embodying the principal tenets of *négritude*. Césaire identifies "suffering" as the primary mode through which blacks experience the world. From the recognition of this suffering, which becomes the agent of his awakening to consciousness, the fictive voice in the poem learns to hate and reject the white world of racism, colonialism, and slavery. The poem concludes with hope not only for black redemption and unity but also for worldwide celebration of the common values of all races. By celebrating his specifically black Martinican heritage, he celebrates the world in all its diversity.

Césaire's attempt to reject the values of a white, colonial European society led him to a lengthy flirtation with Communism. He and a number of his fellow poet-politicians found that Marxism gave them a revolutionary stance in the same way that Surrealism had given them a modernist perspective and, therefore, an individual voice in expressing the yearnings of their people. Césaire's famous *Lettre à Maurice Thorez* (1956; *Letter to Maurice Thorez*, 1957) announced his break with Communism, finding its goals as incompatible as French colonialism or any other foreign influence in relieving the poverty of his fellow Martinicans. He had returned, in effect, to the same conclusions of his earlier rejection of colonialism as a civilizing force that had been the major theme of his *Discours sur le colonialisme* (1950; *Discourse on Colonialism*, 1972). His next important prose work was a biographical and historical study of Toussaint-Louverture, the revolutionary liberator of Haiti called *Toussaint Louverture* (1960). From this documentary treatment of Haiti's earliest hero, Césaire's attention focused on specific black heroes rather than on theoretical treatises that only the well educated could comprehend, and he began a series of plays that had historical figures as their main characters and who would be recognized by the people of the West Indies.

By the early sixties, Césaire, whose poetry had become virtually inaccessible to the common man, made a conscious effort to reach a larger audience by choosing topics that would be recognizable and, more important, comprehensible both to the people of his own area and to the rest of the world. His choice of famous black figures and his treatment of them in rather straightforward dramatic structures demonstrated his dedication to propounding black causes. His first highly successful play was *La Tragédie du Roi Christophe* (1963; *The Tragedy of King Christopher*, 1969), which is the story of the rise of a young slave to the status of self-declared King of Haiti and his subsequent fall. Henri Christophe's tragic flaw was that once he attains his position of power, he loses sight of his primary reason for driving out the tyrannical French colonials and becomes obsessed with expanding his power base, thus becoming as cruel and greedy as the departed French.

Césaire's next play, *Une Saison au Congo* (1966; *A Season in the Congo*, 1968), treats the tragic career of the revolutionary leader Patrice Lumumba, the first president of the Republic of the Congo. His earlier ambitious dreams for his people collapsed into power struggles among competing black leaders and led to his assassination in 1961 in spite of heroic efforts by the United Nations. By the late 1960's, a number of literary critics declared Césaire the leading black dramatist writing in French. Both these plays are highly crafted, impeccably executed literary works that entertain audiences while at the same time registering their political points with subtlety, wit, and exquisite poetic language. His last play of this period, *Une Tempête* (1969; *The Tempest*, 1974), is an adaptation of William Shakespeare's play. In this play, Césaire uses Prospero as the white, colonial conqueror, or the "man of reason." Caliban becomes a metaphor for the black man, the instinctual, nature-loving slave, or victim of Prospero. Ariel becomes in this political allegory the mulatto, or man of science, a combination of the European and black sensibilities but equally repressed by the rationalistic Prospero.

After the writing and production of these three highly acclaimed plays of the 1960's, Césaire devoted himself to his political duties and responsibilities as the mayor of Fort-de-France and, more important, his role as deputy in the French National Assembly for Martinique for nearly forty years. As a result, he has spent much of his time in Paris, attending to his civic responsibilities as a participant in the governance of France and its international interests. He has also been reelected many times to head his own political party, the Progressive Party of Martinique.

Summary

Besides being an outstanding poet, playwright, and political figure, Aimé Césaire made a major contribution to the worldwide black movement in that he is recognized as one of its most honored spiritual leaders. He began to assume that spiritual leadership role with the publication of *Return to My Native Land*. In this poem, certainly one of the major long poems of the twentieth century, he charts the spiritual journey of a colonial black man through the abstractions of Western civilization to his return to the spiritual and instinctual sustenance of his native Martinique. Because of his concern for the welfare of his suffering people, he turned to a more accessible literary format and wrote three plays which eschew the former Surreal intellectuality and instead realistically document the tragic destinies of two actual black historical figures: Henri Christophe and Patrice Lumumba. Concurrent with both his poetic and dramatic productions is a consistent barrage of brilliantly scathing prose works condemning the pernicious effects of slavery, racism, and, most important, colonialism.

Some scholars of the Afro-American movement view Césaire's career as not within the mainstream of either American or African social transformation. While they include him as a major literary and spiritual leader, he is viewed by some as torn between the claims of his black identity and those of his French heritage. He is, obviously, committed to the French parliamentary system, having served as its Martinican deputy for almost forty years, and has never advocated any kind of revolutionary overthrow of any government in the West Indies or Africa. His writings demonstrate that he sees himself as heir to the great French intellectual poets, philosophers, and statesmen. To the dismay of more radical black leaders, he appears to believe in the humanistic principles inherent in the French political and social heritage. Though these ideas may appear paradoxical, they are not mutually exclusive, although they do seem to preclude him from ever being viewed as a serious revolutionary, activist leader. More than any of his literary or political achievements, Césaire will be most remembered and honored for his invention of the term *négritude* and his first use of it in one of the country's most compelling poems.

Bibliography
Arnold, A. James. *Modernism and Negritude: The Poetry and Poetics of Aimé Césaire*. Cambridge, Mass.: Harvard University Press, 1981. This work is certainly the definitive study of Césaire's poetry and its relationship to both *négritude* and modernism. Highly readable and elegantly written.
Frutkin, Susan. *Aimé Césaire: Black Between Worlds*. Coral Gables, Fla.: Center for Advanced International Studies, University of Miami, 1973. A short but clearly written document on Césaire's career. Frutkin covers the biographical, both actual and intellectual, in a thoroughly convincing manner. While pointing out Césaire's undeniable contribution to various Afro-American movements, she places him accurately between the two worlds of his French heritage and his black identity.
Gleason, Judith. "An Introduction to the Poetry of Aimé Césaire." *Negro Digest* 19 (January, 1970): 12-19, 64-65. An outstanding article showing Césaire's poetry and plays as documenting the spiritual dislocation of the black people but done within the specific boundaries of his native Martinique. An excellent guide through some of the more perplexing poems.
Kennedy, Ellen Conroy, ed. *The Negritude Poets*. New York: Viking Press, 1975. An excellent collection of translations of French poetry written by black writers from the Caribbean, Africa, and the Indian Ocean area. Kennedy's preface to Césaire's work serves as an informative introduction to his work, his career, and his literary significance. Although purists may wince, her abridgment and summary of *Return to My Native Land* might make Césaire's difficult work more accessible to the beginner.
Okam, Hilary. "Aspects of Imagery and Symbolism in the Poetry of Aimé Césaire." *Yale French Studies* 53 (1976): 175-196. Okam's lengthy article discusses the difficulties of Césaire's language, especially his poetic idiosyncrasies and sometimes complex syntax. One of the best literary analyses of the poetry.

Patrick Meanor

MARC CHAGALL

Born: July 7, 1887; Vitebsk, Russia
Died: March 28, 1985; Saint-Paul-de-Vence, France
Area of Achievement: Art
Contribution: Chagall was a master of several artistic media, including stained glass, printmaking, mosaic, stage design, mural, ceramic, and tapestry, but he is best known for his paintings that depict the fantastical states of dreams and memories. The distinctive Chagallian appearance of an artistic work portrays a world of vibrantly colored figures in incongruous juxtaposition and magical abrogation of natural law, the kind of vision that many people experience in their sleep.

Early Life

Marc Chagall was born Moishe Shagal in a village with a substantial Jewish population in what became the western Soviet republic of Belorussia. His family was active in the mystical Jewish sect called Hasidism. The quality of Chagall's childhood may be gauged by the presence of the huts of Vitebsk in almost all of his paintings, testifying to pleasant memories of his youth, a characteristic that sets Chagall apart from many twentieth century artists. This is especially surprising because Chagall grew up in a period when Russian life regularly was punctuated with brutal violence against Jews.

Young Marc received his early education from a synagogue cantor and then through a brief enrollment in a village school. He did not take well to school, so his parents apprenticed him to a photographer. That training did not suit him either. Painting attracted him, and he moved to St. Petersburg in 1907 to study in an art school. He did not do well as a student of art. Chagall explained the apparent futility of his varied experiences of learning as the result of the impossibility of his being taught anything. He said he could do only what was instinctive for him. Instinct led him to paint, and his work pleased one attorney well enough for him to buy two of Chagall's works and to send him to Paris with a monthly stipend.

Life's Work

In Paris, pictures flowed from Chagall's brush in a veritable torrent. In the course of hundreds of paintings, he found his personally distinguishing characteristics of colors with airy brilliance and figures without apparent weight. From this five-year period come some of his most famous and representative works, including *I and the Village* (1911), *Self Portrait with Seven Fingers* (1912), *The Fiddler* (1912), and *The Praying Jew*, or *Rabbi of Vitebsk* (1914).

Despite regular exhibition of his works, Chagall failed to find a market for

them. He returned to Russia in 1915, partly to escape his penurious existence in France and more so to persuade his childhood sweetheart, Bella
Rosenfeld, to marry him. The couple married on July 25, 1915. Their happy
and productive partnership lasted until her death in 1944. Chagall celebrated
the romance of the early years of marriage with tenderly affectionate paintings such as *Birthday, Double Portrait with a Glass of Wine* (1917), and
Over the Town (1917-1918). In the last one, for example, two figures in a
lovers' embrace float ecstatically above a cluster of Russian huts and fences
surmounted by the Orthodox Church of Vitebsk.

Chagall served the czarist state from 1915 to 1917 as a clerk in an army
office in the capital. He served the revolutionary Bolshevik state after the
November revolution of 1917 with much more enthusiasm as commissar of
the arts for his native Vitebsk province, assuming this post on September 12,
1918. There he worked diligently to establish a system of art education for
young people. His dedication to providing art for the people and not merely
for an elite was unqualified; he set aside his personal creative activity in
order to perform his service to society. Yet he faced continued frustration
from the unappreciative criticism of literalists who could not understand
green cows and levitated horses.

Chagall recruited to his school the artistic genius Kasimir Malevich,
whose employment backfired upon him. The point of conflict between Chagall and Malevich was symptomatic of the tension that remained throughout
his nearly seven decades of creative work, namely, the desirability of art's
representing objects. In 1919, Malevich carried the banner of suprematism,
which abjured representational art to concentrate on pure shape and color
independent of figures. Chagall had no hesitation about the inclusion of
figures in art; for him complete artistic representation must add to the three-
dimensional world of physical things a fourth dimension, the psychic. Chagall had no heart for battle over art style, and he left Vitebsk permanently in
May, 1920. Chagall moved to Moscow, but he found the conditions there
inhospitable to his artistic impulse. Moscow was receptive to two extremes
in painting with which Chagall was not comfortable, either objectless art or
strictly figurative reality. His topsy-turvy world of unfettered fantasy fit
badly in the revolutionary state of workers and peasants. With the help of
Commissar of Education Anatoly Lunacharsky, Chagall received permission
to leave the Soviet Union. He did not return for fifty years.

Chagall settled in France, with his wife and daughter, to begin a
seventeen-year stay during which his artistic fame slowly grew to grand
proportions. Shortly after his arrival in Paris in 1923, he took up a new
artistic medium, in which, like every one he tried, he soon produced a
prodigious quantity of works. This new medium was printmaking for books.
A Paris art dealer, Ambroise Vollard, commissioned etchings for an edition
of the novel *Myortvye dushi* (1842, 1855; *Dead Souls*, 1887) by the nine-

teenth century Russian novelist Nikolai Gogol. Working between 1923 and 1925, Chagall made 107 plates for this book. Then Vollard gave Chagall the major project of producing illustrations for an edition of the Bible, totaling 105 by the time the edition was finished in 1956. In his prints, Chagall was deprived of the vivid colors that radiate from his paintings, but these black-and-white engravings demonstrate his mastery of shape. Chagall's second stay in France was punctuated in 1931 with a trip to Palestine, where he saturated himself with the physical and human environments for his etchings for the Bible, and in 1932 with a trip to Holland, where he sought psychological affinity with Rembrandt. In 1935, he visited the Lithuanian town of Vilnius, in Poland, which was the nearest he returned to Vitebsk throughout his fifty years away from Russia.

Changes in the international climate cast a shadow over Chagall's life as the 1930's advanced. He expressed his fears for the world in the face of the rise of Fascism in *White Crucifixion* (1938), in which a central crucified figure stretches across the canvas, encompassing a world of suffering and terror in which a synagogue burns and a boatload of fugitives barely escapes the threatening mob. Above the suffering figure, both the Hebrew and Christian (INRI) inscriptions are displayed in ecumenical communion: "Jesus of Nazareth, King of the Jews." This painting does not speak a Christian message. The Christ figure suffers amidst the tortures of humanity. He does not take upon himself the evils of the world, as in Christian soteriology, but he is one victim alongside a multitude of other Jewish victims. The personal meaning of that tribulation transpired for Chagall in his flight from the anti-Semitic Nazi conquerors of France in July, 1941. He and his family sailed to New York, and he remained in North America, where Bella died in 1944, until 1948. In 1945, he produced remarkable stage sets for a major new production of Igor Stravinsky's ballet *Firebird*.

In 1948, Chagall returned to France, which became his home for the rest of his life. In 1952, he married Valentina (Vava) Brodsky. At sixty-five years of age he took up new media: ceramic sculpture, stained glass, and tapestry. Beginning in the late 1950's, he produced a succession of amazing windows for the Cathedral of Metz (1958, 1963), the synagogue of the University Medical Center in Jerusalem (*The Twelve Tribes of Israel*, 1960-1961), the United Nations, a church in Tarreyton, New York (1964), the Fraumünster of Zurich (1970), and the Cathedral of Reims (1974). In 1977, in celebration of the American bicentennial and in memory of Mayor Richard Daley, he unveiled a set of windows, which was displayed at the Art Institute of Chicago. Tapestries that Chagall designed on biblical themes were unveiled in the building of the Israeli Knesset in Jerusalem in 1969.

In 1973, a museum containing his works alone was opened in Nice, France. In the same year, he was permitted to visit the Soviet Union. Although his reception was formally polite, it was chilled by the anti-Semitic atmosphere that prevailed. Chagall's greatest disappointment was that paintings which he had left behind fifty years earlier were neither displayed in public nor released to his possession. Not until 1987 was the Soviet Union to grant him an exhibition on a grand scale in commemoration of the centenary of his birth. In his ninetieth year, 1977, the government of France bestowed on him the Grand Cross of the Legion of Honor. Italy, too, honored him with the highest award it had to give. In the same year, sixty-two of his paintings were hung in the Louvre, an extremely rare event for a living artist. Chagall died at the home where he spent the postwar years, less than three years short of his hundredth birthday.

Summary

Marc Chagall established himself as a leading artist of the twentieth century, displaying recognized talent and attracting a popular following. Yet he was an artist who defies easy classification. Although his works show signs of cubism, expressionism, symbolism, and even abstractionism, he does not stand out as a representative of any of these styles. Because his works depict the psychic dimension of reality, Chagall may be classified a surrealist, but the buoyancy and joyfulness of his works set them apart from those of most representatives of that fashion. Chagall's conviction was that the interior world of the human psyche is more real than the external world, and therefore to paint it is to paint realistically, not, as critics often suggest of his works, symbolically, fantastically, or surrealistically.

Although he was clearly an artist of the twentieth century, Chagall may be placed solidly within an artistic current flowing out of the Middle Ages. Vital artistic affinities to Chagall's work are to be found in the Russian tradition of religious icons. With figures of the physical world, he portrayed the world of the spirit and he made his canvases, like the wood of the icon, windows that opened onto that world. Religious themes permeate Chagall's productions, but his affirmation that he personally was not religious can be taken at face value. He confined himself to the world of the human spirit, while the spirit of the divine apparently eluded him.

Bibliography

Alexander, Sidney. *Marc Chagall: A Biography.* New York: G. P. Putnam's Sons, 1978. A warm and personal treatment of the life of Chagall that successfully incorporates the memoirs of Chagall, friends, and family members into a scholarly, but necessarily incomplete, account of his life. In keeping with the author's focus, only two works by Chagall are reproduced, and these are in black-and-white.
Amishai, Ziva. *Tapestries and Mosaics of Marc Chagall at the Knesset.* New York: Tudor, 1973. Includes simple text and acceptable color reproductions of the works in Jerusalem indicated by the title.

Chagall, Marc. *Chagall by Chagall*. Edited by Charles Sorlier. Translated by John Shepley. New York: Harry N. Abrams, 1979. A selection of almost three hundred works organized by subject matter and illuminated with text from Chagall's *My Life* and other writings. This book, edited by Chagall's assistant, Sorlier, updates Franz Meyer's work below. Includes a chronology and an annotated bibliography.

_____. *The Jersualem Window*. Translated by Elaine Desautels. Text by Jean Leymarie. 2d ed. New York: George Braziller, 1975. Displays color reproductions of the twelve stained-glass windows that Chagall did for the synagogue of the medical center in Jerusalem. The book has a sparse text by art critic Leymarie that interprets the contents of these beautiful translations of Chagall's painting style into stained glass.

_____. *My Life*. Translated by Elisabeth Abbott. London: Peter Owen, 1965. A translation of a charming book, written in Yiddish in the early 1920's, in which Chagall narrates the first thirty-three years of his life.

Compton, Susann. *Chagall*. New York: Harry N. Abrams, 1985. Prepared for an American exhibition of Chagall's work in the year of his death, this book gives a thorough introduction to his life and work by a historian who specializes in Russian art. Includes a helpful chronology, judicious bibliography, and more than one hundred color reproductions.

Keller, Horst. *Marc Chagall*. Translated by Roger Marcinik. Woodbury, N.Y.: Barron's Educational Series, 1980. A brief introduction to Chagall's art by a respected historian of European art. Contains almost one hundred small illustrations, one quarter of which are in color.

Meyer, Franz. *Marc Chagall*. Translated by Robert Allen. New York: Harry N. Abrams, 1964. Written by the husband of Chagall's daughter, Ida, this book gives much helpful detail about Chagall's works. Many of the reproductions are in excellent color. More than one hundred pages at the back of the book constitute a classified catalog, with black-and-white photographs, of works in the several media.

Paul D. Steeves

COCO CHANEL

Born: August 19, 1883; Saumur, France
Died: January 10, 1971; Paris, France
Areas of Achievement: Fashion, business, and industry
Contribution: Chanel was the first to dress women in a manner that reflected
   their increasing liberated status, which began in the first quarter of the
   twentieth century and she continued to do so for nearly six decades,
   reigning as queen of fashion in Paris. Her pioneering genius elevated her
   above the level of merely a great designer, allowing her to support independently her creative brilliance with a fashion empire that encompassed
   design, textiles, jewelry, and perfume.

Early Life

Little is known for certain, but much, often contradictory, has been written about Gabrielle "Coco" Chanel's early years. It is generally agreed that
she was born into poverty and that she tried all of her life, with lies and
silence, to keep her early life from being known. Chanel herself is probably
the least trustworthy source for accurate and truthful information on her
early existence. With Chanel, as with many artists who attempt to hide a past
of which they are ashamed, the truth comes out most clearly in her creations.
The almost peasant simplicity of her designs is complimented by a style that
can be seen to be influenced by the convent, the military, and equestrian
sportsmanship.

She was born into a poor family whose ancesters had come from the
uncompromising granite highlands of France's Massif Central. Driven from
their homeland by agricultural disasters in the middle of the nineteenth century, the Chanel clan became open-air market salesmen and women throughout central France, selling whatever they could, wherever and whenever
conditions seemed favorable. Gabrielle was, therefore, the product of the
union between an itinerant salesman and a young woman he had seduced and
only bothered to marry when Gabrielle and her older sister were joined by a
younger sister. Two more children, both boys, were to follow before their
devoted and long-suffering mother died of tuberculosis. Gabrielle was probably twelve. At some point she was given over to the care of nuns in a
convent, and this is where she received her only formal education. By the
time she was about twenty, she went to live with an aunt who had married
slightly above her station and had settled in the town of Moulins in the
center of France.

Café society was at its peak, and France's most popular stars were the
singers and entertainers of the "café concert." Gabrielle determined to join
their ranks. She was a lamentable singer, but her enthusiasm and style won
for her a small following as she traveled the circuit in and around Moulins.

One of the songs in her limited repertoire included the rooster's cry "koko-ri-ko," and she was called upon to sing this number by cries of "Coco! Coco!" which would become her nickname.

Coco's most ardent admirer was a wealthy young bourgeois named Étienne Balsan, who had great equestrian ambitions and who had purchased an estate in Compiegne to the north of Paris, where he raised race horses. It was there that he brought Chanel and there that she remained for nearly a decade as she added the stigma of being a "kept woman" to that of her humble origins. She slowly abandoned hope of stardom and resigned herself to live on the fringes of a society whose moral hypocrisy deemed her unacceptable.

Arthur "Boy" Capel was a dashing Englishman who had a past as dubious as Chanel but who had the advantage of being a man. He had one foot in Balsan's equestrian society, where he met Chanel, and another in the Parisian society that cultivated the artistic revolution of men such as Sergey Diaghilev, Jean Cocteau, and Igor Stravinsky. Boy had beauty, wit, and enterprising spirit to match Chanel, and the two fell in love. Capel set about nurturing his new mistress' latent talents. He introduced her to friends in Paris, where the women of his set admired and borrowed the hats that Chanel had always made for herself. The hats were simple but alluring, made from coarse materials that many milliners would consider rejects, and they possessed the great advantage of being free from the oppressive weight of extravagant adornment. Capel helped Chanel establish a business, and her hats proved so popular that, when fashionable society moved to Deauville for the summer holiday of 1913, she set up shop there. Her white awning set off, in black capital letters, her name, Chanel, advertising for the first time a business that was to become an industry that would outlive its founder.

Life's Work

The next year, 1914, saw the political chain reaction that plunged Europe into World War I. Deauville became deserted as everyone returned to Paris to prepare for the conflict. His instinct told Capel to encourage Chanel to remain in Deauville. She trusted him, and her tremendous success can be partially seen as the result of his advice. As the German juggernaut advanced with alarming speed on Paris, thousands of people from all walks of life, both military and civilian, fled westward. Deauville was inundated with potential clients who, in the confusion of their world turned upside-down, were more willing to be seduced by the unconventional simplicity of Chanel's designs. The men were at war, leaving women free to choose hats they might move about in with greater comfort.

With her milliner's business an unqualified success, Chanel went next, on Capel's advice, to another great French beach resort, Biarritz, so strangely populated in the off-season. It was there that she established her first full *maison de couture*, adding women's clothing to her hat collection. After securing a thriving business there, Chanel advanced closer to the enemy line, taking Paris by storm in the fall of 1915.

Chanel purchased from a textile manufacturer named Rodier a loose, machine-knit jersey wool that was a drab, utilitarian shade of beige. Previously unable to market it as material for men's undergarments, Rodier reluctantly supplied it to Chanel, who did with it the unimaginable: She made women's dresses of uncompromising grace and simplicity. The material was too loose to hold restrictive waist and bust lines, and Chanel took advantage of this recalcitrant quality to serve her innovative vision. She abandoned the traditional waistline, dropping it lower to the hips as she radically raised the hem of the skirt to somewhere just above the ankles. Thus she helped to pioneer a silhouette that announced the advent of the jazz age. So great was her success that she was able to pay back everything that Capel had invested to start her business. By 1916 she was independent, and she was only thirty-three years old.

Capel had himself prospered from the same foresight that had led him to encourage Chanel to remain in Deauville. Guided by this instinct, he had cultivated radicals such as Georges Clemenceau, sticking with them as they rose from oblivion to the forefront of French politics and business during the course of the war. These contacts helped Englishman Capel make his fortune by supplying France with coal during the conflict. With his newfound prestige, he began to think of an advantageous marriage, and Chanel's hopes of marrying him were destroyed as he chose a more "suitable" woman of noble birth. He was killed shortly thereafter in an auto accident, leaving Chanel emotionally shattered. Although there were to be a great many affairs with illustrious men in the future, Chanel was convinced, amidst her first successes in business, that she had failed as a woman. On the threshold of international success, the provincial rigidity of her peasant upbringing was to close Chanel's heart, leaving room for satisfaction only through her work and driving her to tremendous achievement during the years that separated the world wars.

Misia Sert, the thrice-married wife of artist José-Maria Sert, was a close friend of and muse to the group of avant-garde artists of the day that included Pablo Picasso, Cocteau, Stravinsky, Colette, and Diaghilev. During the time of her first triumphs and greatest grief, Chanel was taken under Misia's wing, introduced to this gilded collection of geniuses, and eventually considered their peer. These associations brought her into contact with a great many influential people, who helped her with her expanding empire. Beyond this, the excitement generated by the activities, both public and private, of these personages lent to Chanel's business a cachet that was worth more publicity than any fortune could buy.

The essence of Chanel's appeal was distilled, quite literally, in her first perfume, No. 5, which was introduced in 1922. Prior to No. 5, perfumes had each had an identifiable floral scent and were bottled in elaborate crystal flacons, which were purchased as much for their quality as sculptures as for the perfumes they contained. Chanel did not create, but commissioned and chose, a scent that allowed the perfume industry its first success with abstract, high-quality perfumes that were not restricted to any one flower or floral group. No. 5 is a blend of more than fifty natural and synthetic ingredients whose mystery is sealed by its equally enigmatic name. Not the fifth, but the first Chanel perfume, the logic or illogic behind its name was known only to Chanel. It was packaged, unlike any perfume before it, in a blunt, cubelike bottle with a rectangular stopper. Its white label bore, in simple black lettering, its name, and below it the name of its "creator," Chanel, in a manner that was reminiscent of the awning outside Chanel's first boutique in Deauville. Her growing legend fed its mystique, which in turn fed her own. No. 5 became the financial backbone of her entire empire. It revolutionized the perfume industry, making all other perfumes obsolete, and has been popular since the day it was introduced.

Chanel's industry grew and prospered uninterrupted until 1936. The spring of that year saw the general strikes that crippled French industries and brought unions to France. Chanel, by that time, was mistress of a fashion empire that employed nearly four thousand workers, mostly women. She thought her own industry, with its decidedly feminine accent, exempt from the strike, but was bitterly undeceived when her workers not only struck but also blocked her from entering her Paris salon. She negotiated with and met the workers' demands in time for the fall collection but was left embittered by what she considered her employees' betrayal. She continued for three more years, but in late 1939 she took advantage of the outbreak of World War II to fire all of her workers and shut down her industry. Chanel closed everything but her Paris boutique, severed relations with what was left of the family of which she was still ashamed, claimed poverty (she was in fact tremendously wealthy), and led a shadowy existence during the German Occupation.

She continued to live in the Ritz in Paris, despite the fact that the Nazis had requisitioned it. She took a lover who was in German intelligence, and through him either instigated or became involved in a plot to meet with Winston Churchill and sue for peace at a price considerably less than the unconditional surrender the great English leader had just declared would be the only way to end the war. Nothing came of the plot, but rumors of Chanel's Nazi collaboration led to her immediate arrest upon the liberation of Paris. She was released after twenty-four hours, it is thought on Churchill's personal orders, and was thus spared the great humiliation of having her head shaved and being paraded naked down the streets of Paris, as many unfortunate women who had had German connections were. Several years later, the former head of Nazi intelligence was paid a large sum of money to keep Chanel out of his memoirs. Worse than these ill-advised personal and political decisions was Chanel's cold-blooded attempt to wrest complete control of Chanel Perfumes from its co-owner and cofounder Pierre Wertheimer, who was Jewish and had fled to the United States. Their relationship had long been difficult and litigious because Chanel was unhappy that she was not in complete control of her enterprises. She tried to take advantage of her partner's reduced status, but his interests were fiercely protected in his absence, and she did not succeed. After the war, not wishing to sully the name on the bottles of perfume that he was selling, Wertheimer forgave her and they buried their differences, becoming friends in time for him to help her with her big comeback.

After the war and the liberation, a new breed of fashion designer (mostly men), led by Christian Dior, began to leave its mark on women's fashions. A new look, which found its inspiration in the pre-Chanel era, owed its popularity to a nostalgic desire to return to earlier days, before modernity had brought about horrific world conflict and the atomic age. Skirts were becoming longer, the material was heavier, and the styles were once again trying to squeeze and mold women's figures into exaggerated forms of themselves.

Chanel bided her time, correctly assessing the current trends as more fad than fashion. On February 5, 1954, after an absence of fifteen years, at the age of seventy, and with the press poised to attack, she launched "le comeback." It was a short-term failure and a long-term success, ensuring her legend and creating a "look" that is immediately identifiable as hers, even to those who have no especial interest in the history of fashion. What the press was so quick to savage, but which possessed qualities of grace and comfort sensed more than seen by a steadily growing, more youthful market, was the Chanel suit. A simple, collarless cardigan jacket worn over a blouse with a matching skirt that is neither tight nor loose, this highly copied design has never gone out of fashion. Buyers in the United States, trusting the label, had purchased it sight unseen, and, just when its failure seemed assured, a generation of American women that wartime had employed began to buy the suit for its businesslike qualities, its comfort, and its feminine chic. Slower to catch on in Europe, Chanel's new designs, along with the memory of her interwar triumphs, not only reinstated "La Grande Mademoiselle" as leader of feminine fashion but also earned for her a place far above and beyond any yet achieved by her predecessors or colleagues.

This vaunted position often left the peasant girl from Moulins who had never married alone and lonely. As monstrous as she could be charming, Chanel had never been easy to approach, and, until the day before she died at eighty-seven, she buried her solitude in her work. She died while taking a nap in her apartment in the Ritz on Sunday, January 10, 1971.

Summary

Coco Chanel never sketched her designs. She created by pinning, sewing, and cutting her garmets on live models. Her scissors were the most important tools of her trade, because what she did best was minimize. For her, luxury and elegance were best expressed with understatement and simplicity. That was half of her genius. The other half was the business acumen she used to sell her revolution. A descendant of salespersons, she knew how to charm and seduce, and she knew when to bully and scold. Most of all she knew herself. She knew what she could do best and how to capitalize on it. Hand-in-hand with selling her products, Chanel sold herself, lending her own unique charm to everything that came out of her workrooms and salons. She was suspected of designing everything with only herself in mind, no matter how illustrious or beautiful her client may have been. If that is so, she made it not only flattering but also, in her heyday, imperative to dress in Chanel. She replaced the individual monogram with the designer label, creating a style that could be worn by all women. She took what was simple and common, distilled the beauty she found there, and, with the guarantee of her own good name, sold it to a century of women whose changing needs it so well served.

Bibliography

Berman, Phyllis, and Zina Sawaya. "The Billionaires Behind Chanel." *Forbes* 143 (April 3, 1989): 104. This article, along with a companion article on Chanel Perfumes, is an in-depth look at the Chanel empire as it is today under the guidance of designer Karl Lagerfeld.

Charles-Roux, Edmonde. *Chanel: Her Life, Her World, and the Woman Behind the Legend She Herself Created.* New York: Alfred A. Knopf, 1975. This is probably the definitive biography of Chanel. The two stories of the public and private Chanel are made one by this fashion editor who knew the designer personally. Written with great style and imagination, the author also pays strict attention to accuracy and detail and is unafraid to reveal the sometimes ugly truth about her subject.

Fucini, Joseph J., and Suzy Fucini. "Gabrielle (Coco) Chanel." In *Entrepreneurs: The Men and Women Behind Famous Brand Names and How They Made It.* Boston: G. K. Hall, 1985. This is a fascinating backstage look at the business aspect of Chanel's empire. It brings to light many of the names that went into the creating of the Chanel label.

Galante, Pierre. *Mademoiselle Chanel.* Chicago: Regnery, 1973. Written shortly after the designer's death, this is perhaps the first account of Chanel's business as it could not have been written during her lifetime. It is thorough and accurate and reveals the inner workings of an empire that had been previously masked by the charisma and personality of its founder.

Haedrich, Marcel. *Coco Chanel: Her Life, Her Secrets*. Boston: Little, Brown, 1971. Haedrich published this account of Chanel's life based on a series of tape-recorded interviews he had with the designer shortly before she died. The book is full of misinformation and lies, and Haedrich, despite his occasional sycophantic attachment to the woman, seems to be aware of this. This book offers a revealing glimpse of the contradictory and fascinating elements of a personality without which the Chanel empire would not have been.

Pavlin Lange

CH'EN TU-HSIU

Born: October 8, 1879; Huaining District, Anhwei Province, China
Died: May 27, 1942; Chiangching, Szechwan Province, China
Areas of Achievement: Government, politics, and literature
Contribution: As the editor of a groundbreaking literary journal and Dean of
   Arts and Letters at Peking University, Ch'en Tu-hsiu was a central figure
   in the Chinese "literary renaissance" of 1915-1921 and in the May Fourth
   Movement of 1919. He founded the Chinese Communist Party with Li Ta-
   ch'ao in 1921 and served as its chairman from 1921 to 1927.

Early Life

Ch'en Tu-hsiu's formative years spanned a time of great political, social,
and intellectual ferment in the last decades of the Ch'ing Dynasty (1644-
1912). Foreign incursion, official corruption, and belated attempts at "self-
strengthening" and reform impressed the young Ch'en with the need for
China to become a cohesive and powerful nation-state. To a remarkable
degree, his life was a continual quest for the best method of effecting this
change.

Ch'en was born Ch'en Ch'ien-sheng to a modest gentry family in China's
northern Anhwei Province. His father, who died when Ch'en was two, had
served as an officer in Manchuria, and the Ch'en family reportedly boasted
ties to the powerful official Li Hung-chang. Following the practice of ambitious Chinese families, Tu-hsiu and his brother Meng-chi were provided
with a rigorous classical education in preparation for the examinations to
qualify for government service.

At the precocious age of seventeen, Ch'en passed the initial test but in
1897 failed to obtain the provincial or *chü-jen* degree. He was free to try
again, but this setback coincided with the aftermath of the humiliating war
with Japan (1894-1895) and the European "race for concessions," and Ch'en,
like many of China's young literati, now sought Western learning as a key to
China's salvation. Though the reform movement of K'ang Yu-wei and Liang
Ch'i-ch'ao was quashed in the Empress Dowager Tzu-hsi's *coup d'état* of
September, 1898, their attempted synthesis of Confucian and Western ideas
would provide an important model for Ch'en's thinking for most of the next
decade.

During the next five years, Ch'en studied English, French, and various
technical subjects at a school in Hangchow and rounded out his basic studies
at the Tokyo Higher Normal School. During this period, he formed the basis
of his beliefs in vernacular language as a tool of reform and the need for
China to be reconstituted by revolution. He also acquired a taste for the
bohemian habits of Chinese expatriate intellectuals, indulging in frequent
bouts of drinking and womanizing. Ch'en's revolutionary activities at this

point consisted of little more than flirting with romantic anarchism. Yet his literary accomplishments were considerably more advanced. In 1904, he founded the *Anhwei su-hua pao* (Anhwei common-speech journal), one of the first vernacular publications in China.

In 1906, he again left for Japan and briefly studied at the University of Waseda. There he came into contact with members of Sun Yat-sen's T'ung meng-hui, or Revolutionary Alliance. While generally enthusiastic about Sun's program, Ch'en's intellectual independence would not allow him to accept the alliance's call for the suppression of the Manchus. In a pattern that was to repeat itself in later life, Ch'en maintained ties to the revolutionaries but refused to be subject to their discipline.

Life's Work

Following the abdication of the Ch'ing in 1912, Ch'en's ties to the revolutionary government and his reputation as a scholar and editor secured him a position as head of the Anhwei Department of Education. Within a year, however, General Yüan Shih-k'ai, now president of the republic, moved against his parliamentary opposition, and Ch'en and his patron, Anhwei governor Po Wen-wei, fled to Japan. Following a brief stint as an editor of the opposition *Tiger Magazine* there, Ch'en moved to foreign controlled Shanghai, where he founded *Ch'ing-nien tsa-chih* (youth magazine) in September, 1915.

Though the immediate reason for the founding of *Ch'ing-nien tsa-chih*— or *La Jeunesse*, as it was rendered by the Francophile Ch'en—was to oppose Yüan Shih-k'ai's efforts to start a new imperial dynasty, it soon became a vehicle for articulating ideas on social reform. For Ch'en, the youth of a nation represented its potential for renewal and progress. In the West, he believed, the movements toward democracy and emancipation had drawn their impetus from this source. In China, however, the weight of the past retarded the progress of the nation in innumerable ways.

A dead classical language, accessible to only a fraction of the population, kept the people from reaping the fruits of their past, while it drained the time and energy of the few who could master it. The language ensured that Scholasticism rather than science would predominate in Chinese thought. Finally, it robbed the nation's youth of the independence of mind and will needed to remake the nation and culture in their own image. Instead it burdened them with a cult of age and a slavish worship of ancient learning.

Perhaps the most direct expression of Ch'en's iconoclasm may be found in his "Call to Youth" of 1915. Drawing liberally from such diverse thinkers as Friedrich Wilhelm Nietzsche, Leo Tolstoy, and Rabindranath Tagore, as well as the Chinese classics, he demanded that China's youth, "Be independent, not servile . . . progressive, not conservative . . . aggressive, not retiring . . . cosmopolitan, not isolationist . . . utilitarian, not formalistic . . .

[and] scientific, not imaginative. . . ." Ch'en's articles extolled Western pragmatism and democratic values as embodied in his characters "Mr. Science" and "Mr. Democracy," and his attacks on Confucianism grew increasingly pointed.

In 1917, Ch'en received an appointment as Dean of Arts and Letters at the University of Peking, which had become a center for politically active scholars. Under Ch'en's patronage, *Hsin ch'ing-nien* (new youth), as the journal was now called, ran articles by Peking professors Hu Shih, Ch'ien Hsuan-t'ung, and Li Ta-ch'ao that were written in vernacular Chinese. The prestige and eclecticism of its contributors made *Hsin ch'ing-nien* the most important publication of this Chinese "literary renaissance." Increasingly, however, the articles addressed political subjects.

In the wake of Yüan Shih-k'ai's death in 1916, China lapsed into a state of incessant warfare by competing warlord factions, which was exacerbated by the Japanese. The hopes of China's intellectuals had been kindled by the end of World War I in Europe, the Russian Revolutions, and the idealism of United States President Woodrow Wilson's Fourteen Points. Chinese delegates to the Versailles Peace Conference in 1919 had expected to regain the Japanese-occupied province of Shantung and hoped to modify relations with the Western powers. Instead, on May 4, 1919, it was revealed that Japan would be allowed to keep Shantung. The news caused widespread student demonstrations that rapidly grew into a nationwide anti-Japanese boycott. Ch'en, as an active supporter of the students, was briefly arrested by the Peking government. He soon despaired of the West providing any real help to China and became increasingly attracted to Marxism and the Bolshevik experiment in Russia. Through Li Ta-ch'ao, his Marxist study group was approached by Comintern, and a provisional central committee formed in May, 1920, with a national party officially founded in 1921.

Ch'en soon found himself at odds with Comintern direction of the party. In 1923, the Chinese Communist Party was directed to form a united front with Sun Yat-sen and join his Kuomintang (nationalist party) in order to unite China by force of arms and move the country into the "bourgeois-democratic" stage of development. Ch'en, however, considered this to be a costly abdication of his party's role as the vanguard of workers and peasants. The death of Sun in March, 1925, and the splintering of the Kuomintang into right and left factions contributed to Ch'en's misgivings about Comintern's long-term strategy in China.

The telling blow came in the wake of Chiang K'ai-shek's "White Terror" against the Communists. After consolidating Kuomintang control of South China and the Yangtze Valley in the spring of 1927, Chiang launched a six-month purge that decimated the newly strengthened party. A series of ill-conceived uprisings, belatedly ordered by Comintern, culminated in whole-sale massacre. A small remnant of the party escaped under the leadership of

Mao Tse-tung and established a base in remote Kiangsi Province. Other survivors, including Ch'en, settled in Shanghai, where they faced the prospect of extradition by the foreign authorities.

Ch'en excoriated the Central Committee and Comintern for the disaster in 1927 and, after being censured for his activities, was expelled from the Party on June 11, 1930. At about this time, Ch'en, who had been attracted to Leon Trotsky's ideas of compressing the stages of development leading to socialism and of the need for the proletariat to take the leading role over the peasants, became a full convert to Trotskyism. While struggling to establish his faction, however, he was arrested, tried by the Nationalists, and sentenced to fifteen years in prison in 1933.

Ch'en's four years in prison were devoted largely to researches into the origins of the classical written language and its relationship to the vernacular. Because he was still considered one of the nation's premier intellectuals, he was accorded lenient treatment and allowed books and visitors. The Second United Front between the Kuomintang and the Communists, and the war with Japan in 1937, brought Ch'en's release, but he remained a center of controversy. Though still highly critical of the Nationalists, he was accused by each side of secretly aiding the other, and even of being in the pay of the Japanese. In 1938, he retreated to China's wartime capital of Chungking, eventually settling in the village of Chiangching. There, his health declining and the nation's fortunes again at a low ebb, he died on May 27, 1942.

Summary

Ch'en Tu-hsiu's life embodied nearly all of the intellectual and cultural movements experienced by China in the twentieth century, and he is still considered a controversial figure in both China and the West. The nature of his iconoclastic approach to literature and his condemnation of Confucianism as a sterile orthodoxy has perplexed scholars as to whether his main influences were heterodox classical Chinese thinkers or Westerners. The exact provenance of his conversion to Marxism is obscured by his penchant for sampling widely from diverse ideologies. His importance as a catalyst and as an organizer is indisputable, yet his determination to go in his own direction continually separated him from potential allies and mainstream party members. Perhaps his significance was best expressed by Mao, who called him simply the "commander in chief" of the May Fourth Movement.

Ch'en's last writings, *Ch'en Tu'hsiu tsui hou tui yü min chu chêng chih ti chien chieh* (Ch'en Tu-hsiu's last opinions on democratic government), issued posthumously in 1950, complete the intellectual circle that began at the turn of the century. Divorcing himself from Leninism as well as Trotskyism, he raised questions about the relationship of political freedom and economics and about the limitations of totalitarianism as a moral system that would have tremendous relevance for China in subsequent decades. In the process, he groped back to a faith in political pluralism and science and democracy, tempered by economic justice. To the end, he railed at enforced orthodoxy of any kind, whether Confucian or Marxist.

Bibliography
Chow, Tse-tsung. *The May Fourth Movement*. Cambridge, Mass.: Harvard University Press, 1960. In terms of scholarship and accessibility to the general student, this remains the standard work on the May Fourth Movement. It contains extensive background material on Ch'en as well as a number of other intellectuals involved in the "literary renaissance."
Feigon, Lee. *Chen Duxiu: Founder of the Chinese Communist Party*. Princeton, N.J.: Princeton University Press, 1983. Utilizing materials previously unavailable to scholars, Feigon's work deftly traces the complicated evolution of Ch'en's ideas to Marxism and Trotskyism. Particularly valuable are his explorations of Ch'en's early vernacular writings.
Kuo, Thomas C. *Ch'en Tu-hsiu (1879-1942) and the Chinese Communist Movement*. South Orange, N.J.: Seton Hall University Press, 1975. Pioneering monographic treatment of Ch'en's intellectual progress toward Marxism and the founding of the Communist Party. Kuo lays great stress on developing a contextual foundation by means of examining Ch'en's personal experiences.
Meisner, Maurice. *Li Ta-ch'ao and the Origins of Chinese Marxism*. Cambridge, Mass.: Harvard University Press, 1967. This book remains a classic in the field of Chinese Communist intellectual history by one of the most respected scholars in the field. Provides an excellent complement to any study of Ch'en and contains abundant material on the interplay of his ideas with those of Li.
Sheridan, James E. *China in Disintegration: The Republican Era in Chinese History, 1912-1949*. New York: Free Press, 1975. The standard text on the republican period (1912-1949). The chapter on the new literature and the May Fourth Movement provides succinct accounts of Ch'en's role in the founding of the literary movement and the Communist Party.

Charles A. Desnoyers

CHIANG KAI-SHEK

Born: October 31, 1887; Ch'ik'ou, China
Died: April 5, 1975; Taipei, Taiwan
Areas of Achievement: Government and politics
Contribution: Chiang was the most important man in the Kuomintang government during the Nanking decade. He led the government and Chinese armed forces through eight years of war against Japan (1937-1945) until Allied victory, was elected president, but lost the civil war to the Chinese Communist Party. He and his Kuomintang followers fled in 1949 to Taiwan, where he ruled until his death.

Early Life

Chiang Kai-shek was born on October 31, 1887, in the town of Ch'ik'ou, in Fenghua county, Chekiang Province. Chiang's grandfather had begun a successful business as a salt merchant, which Chiang's father, Chiang Ch'ao-ts'ung, had continued. His mother, née Wang, was his father's third wife. Chiang had an elder half brother, half sister, a younger brother (who died as a child), and two young sisters by his mother. His schooling began at age five; his own and others' memory of his early years was that he was a mischievous boy. His grandfather's death in 1895, followed by that of his father in 1896, resulted in division of the family's property that left his mother in financially straitened circumstances for many years as she struggled to rear and educate her children.

At fourteen, Chiang married a girl chosen by his mother, née Mao. She bore him a son, Ching-kuo, in 1909, who became President of the Republic of China on Taiwan in 1978 and died in office in 1988. Chiang had a traditional Chinese education in the classics up to 1906, when he obtained his mother's permission to go to Japan to pursue a modern military education. Since he could not enter a military academy in Japan without Chinese government sponsorship, he first gained admission to a Chinese military academy, studied there for a year, then won a scholarship to study in Japan. There he met Ch'en Ch'i-mei, an associate of Sun Yat-sen, and joined the T'ung-meng hui (United League), which Sun had organized in 1906 with the goal of overthrowing the Ch'ing Dynasty in China. Chiang was graduated from the Shimbu Gakko (military preparatory school) in 1910 and served for a year in the 13th Field Artillery Regiment of the Japanese Army, until the outbreak of the revolution against the Ch'ing Dynasty in 1911. He then resigned from the Japanese army, sailed for Shanghai, and participated in military actions that overthrew the dynasty. With Sun's resignation as Provisional President of the Chinese Republic early in 1912 and the eclipse of the Kuomintang by strongman Yuan Shih-k'ai and warlords, Chiang spent much of his time until 1918 in Japan or in Shanghai.

Life's Work

In 1918, Chiang received a summons to join Sun in his new government in Canton. He assisted Sun in military affairs and became the rising star of the Kuomintang. In 1923, he headed a group that visited the Soviet Union to study its party and military and political organizations and to inspect its military schools and facilities. While there, Chiang met Leon Trotsky, Georgi Chicherin, and other Soviet leaders. He submitted a report to Sun upon his return in 1924. It showed his keen appreciation of some Soviet policies that contributed to the strength of the Red Army, but he was suspicious of Soviet Communism and its intentions in China. In 1924, Chiang was appointed commandant of the Whampoa Military Academy, which Sun had ordered him to establish to train officers dedicated to the Kuomintang cause. Chiang took personal command in the training of the first three classes of about two thousand cadets.

After Sun's death in 1925, Chiang took a centrist position in the party's ideological disputes and supported continued cooperation with the Soviet Union and the Chinese Communists. After securing Kwangtung and neighboring areas for the Kuomintang, Chiang was appointed commander in chief of the National Revolutionary Army in 1926 and launched the Northern Expedition to unify China under the Kuomintang. Victorious against numerically superior warlord armies, Chiang's troops quickly drove through south China and captured Nanking and Shanghai in early 1927. Chiang thereupon broke with the left-wing Kuomintang government in Wu-han that was headed by Wang Ching-wei but that was manipulated by Soviet advisers, established a rival govern-ment in Nanking with the support of right-wing Kuomintang leaders, expelled Soviet advisers, and purged Chinese Communists in areas under his control. The dissolution of the left-wing Kuomintang government in Wu-han in July, 1927, left the Nanking Kuomintang government without challengers as Chiang resumed leadership of the campaign to unify China in 1928. The Northern Expedition ended in triumph with the capture of Peking and the peaceful accession of the northeast (Manchuria) at the end of 1928. Thereupon the Kuomintang (Nationalist) government received international recognition.

Chiang dominated the Nationalist government politically and militarily during the Nanking decade (1928-1937) and survived all challenges mounted by dissident politicians and generals who vied for power. His government was, however, pinched between the Communists, who sought to launch their power in China through armed rebellion, and Japanese imperialism, which aimed to subjugate China before it could modernize and defend its sovereignty. Chiang believed that China must be unified and modernized before it could face Japan. Therefore, he launched campaigns to eliminate the Communists and dissident warlords, on the one hand, while on the other he sought German military advice to modernize his army; he created an air force and supported measures to build industries, roads, and railways.

Professing adherence to Sun's political program for China, the government proclaimed in 1929 the beginning of a period of political tutelage, in preparation for constitutional rule. During the next years, new law codes and other reforms to modernize the Chinese economy and infrastructure were put into effect, but no land reform took place.

Chiang's marriage to Mei-ling Soong in 1927 obtained for his government assistance from the modern financial community in which the Soong family was prominent. All the while he negotiated and made concessions to Japan, trading space (Manchuria and parts of northern China) for time. He was, however, compelled to halt his anticommunist campaign, which had much reduced but not eliminated that group as a result of the Sian Incident in December, 1936. Chiang was kidnapped and held for two weeks by a powerful subordinate general but was freed on his verbal promise to stop the anticommunist campaign and head a united front of all Chinese parties against Japan. During the Sian negotiations, the Soviet Union pressured the Chinese Communists to work for Chiang's release and support his leadership so that China could act as bulwark against Japanese designs on the Soviet Union. Japan's attack on China in July, 1937, which led to an eight-year war, sealed the United Front between the Kuomintang and the Chinese Communists and catapulted Chiang to the height of power as supreme military commander and party leader.

Chiang led China through eight years of war, at first heroically as it resisted a militarily superior and brutal enemy. Japan conquered the coastal regions but could not defeat a determined Chinese government that had retreated to Chungking in the inaccessible interior. The stalemated war of attrition and accompanying inflation and other sufferings led to the deterioration of Chinese morale. The government became increasingly authoritarian and corrupt. After the Japanese attack on Pearl Harbor and United States' and other Western colonies in Southeast Asia, the Chinese-Japanese War became part of World War II. The initial drubbing the Japanese gave to the Westerners earned for the Chinese, who had fought and held out alone, international respect. Limited United States aid after it entered World War II led to friction between the two governments. Meanwhile, the United Front with the Communists had long since broken down, as the Communists availed of opportunities provided by the war to increase vastly their territory and power. On his part, Chiang reserved some of his best units to blockade the Communists. Both the Kuomintang and the Chinese Communists prepared for the civil war to come.

Chiang's prestige peaked as the China he led won international equality in 1943, after a century of humiliations by Western powers, with the abrogation of remaining unequal treaties with Great Britain and the United States. He met British Prime Minister Winston Churchill and United States President Franklin D. Roosevelt at the Cairo Conference in 1943 to discuss Allied war goals; China was promised return of all Japanese conquests since 1895. When titular Chairman of the National Government Lin Sen died in 1943, Chiang was elevated to that position also. China was recognized as a Big Four Allied power, a founding member of the United Nations in 1945, and a holder of one of five permanent seats on its Security Council.

After victory against Japan on August 14, 1945, the government returned to Nanking. The National Assembly convened by the Kuomintang in 1946, but boycotted by the Communists, adopted a constitution that ended the period of political tutelage. Chiang was elected president by a new National Assembly under the terms of the constitution in 1948, but his vice presidential candidate was defeated by a rival Kuomintang general Li Tsung-jen. The real contest for control of China had resumed between the Kuomintang and the Communist Party in renewed civil war in 1946. United States special ambassador George Marshall had attempted but failed to mediate a truce that he had hoped would be followed by the formation of a coalition government. The Nationalists received economic and military aid from the United States up to 1948, and the Chinese Communists received from the Soviet Union Japanese weapons that it had captured in Manchuria. From seeming strength in the beginning, the Nationalist position deteriorated rapidly in 1948. Chiang resigned the presidency in January, 1949, to let vice president Li Tsung-jen salvage what he could of the Nationalist debacle. When Li also failed to stem the Communist advances, Chiang and his loyal supporters retreated to Taiwan. Mao proclaimed the establishment of the People's Republic of China on October 1, 1949.

Chiang resumed his presidency on Taiwan in March, 1950, but the precarious position of the Nationalist government did not improve until Communist North Korea attacked South Korea in June, 1950. This action, and Communist China's intervention on behalf of North Korea with more than a million "volunteers" led the United States to order its Seventh Fleet to patrol the Taiwan Strait and to sign a Mutual Defense Treaty with the Nationalist government in 1954. Taiwan received American military aid and economic aid until the mid-1960's to build up its war-ravaged economy. Meanwhile, Chiang supervised the reform of the Kuomintang and carried out a nonviolent land reform. These factors and a sound education system combined to bring about marked and sustained economic growth on Taiwan that has continued at an accelerated rate after Chiang's death. He was reelected to a second six-year term as president in 1954 by those members of the National Assembly who had been elected on the mainland seven years earlier and who had retreated to Taiwan with his government; suspending the constitutional provision that limited the presidency to two terms, he was elected to a third term in 1960, a fourth term in 1966, and a fifth one in 1972, dying in office in 1975.

Summary

Chiang Kai-shek was truly one of China's and the world's key history makers of the twentieth century. From the time he set out to unify China as commander in chief of the Northern Expeditionary Army in 1926 until the defeat of the Kuomintang by the Communists in 1949, he was the dominant person in Chinese politics and played a pivotal role in the government. His authority, however, was always challenged, by rival generals and politicians in the Kuomintang and by the Chinese Communists. Thus, while he was China to the world for two decades, he never was able to assert absolute dictatorial power as his critics claimed. Chiang was a complex person, a dedicated Chinese nationalist, follower of Sun Yat-sen, and, after his marriage to Mei-ling Soong and conversion, a sincere Christian. Above all, he was a soldier-politician. While his government was mired in corruption during its last years on the mainland, and while many of his relatives benefited from the corruption, he himself remained incorruptible and lived a sternly simple life. A man of monumental ego, he equated himself with China and could not brook a vision of China other than his own. Thus he was trapped by his own failings and by international circumstances beyond his control. He was caught in the vise of Japanese imperialism and Communist armed insurrection. Even though the Allied cause finally triumphed over Japanese imperialism, the China that he had led was destroyed in the process. Thus he ended his career in eclipse on Taiwan, while his archenemy, Mao Tse-tung, ruled mainland China.

Bibliography

Chang, Hsin-hai. *Chiang Kai-shek: Asia's Man of Destiny.* Garden City, N.Y.: Doubleday, Doran, 1944. Sympathetic biography of Chiang's life up to the date of publication, with background information about China since its first defeat by Great Britain in 1842.

Chi, Hsi-sheng. *Nationalist China at War: Military Defeats and Political Collapse, 1937-1945.* Ann Arbor: University of Michigan Press, 1982. An analysis of the weaknesses in the Chinese military and political systems and how they could not withstand the strains of an eight-year war.

Crozier, Brian, with Eric Chou. *The Man Who Lost China: The First Full Biography of Chiang Kai-shek.* New York: Charles Scribner's Sons, 1976. A generally unsympathetic analysis of Chiang's career and by no means a "full" biography.

Furuya, Keiji. *Chiang Kai-shek: His Life and Times.* New York: St. John's University Press, 1981. At almost a thousand pages, even this abridged edition gives a great deal of information. Many subheadings makes this a good reference book.

Linebarger, Paul M. *The China of Chiang Kai-shek: A Political Study.* Boston: World Peace Foundation, 1941. A sympathetic and laudatory study of

Chiang up to the time of publication.

Morwood, William. *Duel for the Middle Kingdom: The Struggle Between Chiang Kai-shek and Mao Tse-tung for Control of China.* New York: Everest House, 1979. An account of the Kuomintang-Communist struggle up to 1949, with emphasis on the two main protagonists.

Tong, Hollington K. *Chiang Kai-shek, Soldier and Statesman: Authorized Biography.* 2 vols. Shanghai: China Publishing, 1937. A detailed, fulsome, and laudatory account of Chiang up to the point of writing.

Jiu-Hwa Lo Upshur

CHOU EN-LAI

Born: March 5, 1898; Shao-hsing, Kiangsu Province, China
Died: January 8, 1976; Peking, China
Areas of Achievement: Diplomacy, government, and politics
Contribution: Chou En-lai was the premier of the new People's Republic of
China from its birth in 1949 until his death in 1976. He thereby guided the
new China in solidifying the new order, led in domestic reform toward
modernization, and was instrumental in having the new government ac-
cepted by the international community during trying times.

Early Life

Chou En-lai was born in Shao-hsing, Huai-an County, in China's Kiangsu
Province on March 5, 1898. Although the Chou family was part of the
aristocracy, it was in a state of decline. The increasingly impecunious position of the family made Chou's childhood most unstable and meandering.
Before age one, he was taken by an uncle and aunt as a foster son to be
nurtured and reared. His genteel and cultured foster mother was determined
to prepare him for the civil service examination, passage of which was the
ladder to success in imperial China. By age four, he was able to read; by age
ten, he was devouring classical Chinese literature. Yet these days of security
would end when his foster mother died. In 1910 and at age twelve, Chou
was dispatched to live with another uncle in the far northeast of China.
There he entered elementary school, which continued his learning of Chinese
tradition but which also added some of the new learning of mathematics and
science.

In 1913, Chou was enrolled at Nan-kai Middle School in Tientsin. This
school, founded only in 1906, emphasized a modern curriculum with the
goal of training Chinese to lead the country into modernization. Upon his
graduation from Nan-kai, Chou left to study in Japan, being fascinated by, as
were many other Chinese, Japan's great success in developing a modern
society. He did not, however, pass the entrance examination for study in a
Japanese university.

In 1917, the revolution in Russia "shook the world" and stirred Chou. He
began to study Marxism. While Russia was in revolution, civil war, and
tumult, China was to have her lesser, albeit societal, rattling upheaval as
well, in May, 1919. Chou rushed back to his homeland and to Tientsin to
participate. Students at Peking University demonstrated in the streets of their
nation's capital when they learned that China had gained nothing from her
participation in World War I. Disillusioned and disappointed, they expressed
condemnation of their government's ineptitude and the continued presence of
foreign imperialists on China's soil. Chou became a leader, organizer, and
even editor of a newspaper.

In 1920, Chou went on a work-study program to France, where he hoped to learn more about Marxism and about how it might be used to restore and reinvigorate China domestically and internationally. Chou studied Marxism assiduously, and he helped form Marxist groups among the other Chinese who were working and studying in Western Europe at the same time.

Back in China, a small group met and formed the Chinese Communist Party (CCP) in Shanghai in July, 1921. Chinese Marxists inside and outside the country were enlisted as full-fledged members of the Party. Chou was officially in the organization. Activities going on in China synchronized with his, and so he returned home in 1924.

Life's Work

Chou returned to China to find his country greatly divided. Yet he saw great hope for China's future; the nationalistic spirit loosed by the May Fourth upheaval was still widespread. Sun Yat-sen and his Kuomintang (KMT) had plans for the reunification of the Chinese homeland, and the fledgling CCP, small though it was, stood ready to contribute to the cause as best it could. Sun, although not a Marxist, could only receive the aid he needed for his plans of unifying China from the Soviet-dominated Comintern, and so he took it. The CCP would lend its support, and here Chou was to contribute crucially. This twenty-six-year-old suave and articulate Chinese Communist brought his reputation of successful leadership in France home with him when he returned. Immediately, he was selected for the prominent post of working to develop an army for the KMT. He was appointed the political adviser to Chiang K'ai-shek, the commandant of the newly founded Whampoa Academy for the training of officers. Chou gained great respect from many of the student officers during his tenure at Whampoa; many of these would defect to the Communists once the battle between the KMT and the CCP reached decision-making proportions in the civil war, 1946-1949.

By 1926, the KMT felt ready to tackle the warlords who were dividing China. Sun had died in 1925; Chiang had come to be the new leader, and he proclaimed a "northern expedition" from his southern base in moving militarily to restore China to a unified nation. Chou moved from the military academy in Canton to Shanghai to aid the plan, and he was assigned the role of organizing the labor force in this largest of China's cities and making it ready to accept the KMT as the new leader of a unified China. Chou did his work as assigned, but the outcome was not what he expected. Chiang had come to distrust the CCP totally, saw it as detrimental to China's unity, and attempted to destroy it. The KMT, instead of accepting Chou's delivery of Shanghai to its allegiance, tried to kill off all the Communists; most were massacred. Chou escaped that fate and fled to a haven of safety at a Communist camp in the hills of a rural base. At this base, Chou aided Communist military leader Chu Teh in founding a Red Army for the Party in order to survive. Chiang was determined to destroy the Communists and kept up the attack. The war went on for years, with the Communists mostly on the defensive, and culminated in the famous "Long March."

During the Long March, Mao Tse-tung had been selected to be the main spokesman and leader of the Chinese Communist Party. He would hold the title of leadership from that time until his death in September, 1976. Chou accepted Mao's leadership and would work hand-in-glove with the entitled chairman for the rest of his existence. Both were strong Chinese nationalists; both were Marxists. Both were determined to push forward to the success of Chinese nationalism with a Marxist society. Chou decided to work within the framework of the new society as an administrator and as a diplomat. He began his work almost immediately.

In 1936, Chiang reactivated his quest to rid China of what he viewed as the divisive Communists. He decided to attack them at their new base of Yen-an in Shensi Province. His generals, however, were more concerned about the presence of the Japanese in China. The Japanese had launched an attack on China's northeastern section in Manchuria, were successful, and had established a puppet government. After intense negotiations between the KMT and the Communists, the Communists decided it would be in everyone's best interest for them to join forces with the KMT to drive out the Japanese.

The united front came into full play when Japan launched an attack on China proper in July, 1937. Japan's successful military surges in China forced Chiang to abandon much of his domain to foreign occupation and to flee to Chungking. Chou moved to Chungking as the liaison of the CCP. Chou worked during most of the war in Chungking for the advantage of the Communists. Chou's many contacts with foreign diplomats and foreign journalists during the war allowed him to display his cosmopolitanism, his cordiality, and his diplomatic flair for the benefit of his Communist comrades. He did his work well, for those who had any association with him came away most impressed with his personal talents and came away believing that those in Yen-an were serving the war effort and Chinese society more adeptly and more energetically than were the KMT group in Chungking.

After World War II, the CCP-KMT cooperation came to an end, and old conflicts arose, creating civil war. Despite the material advantages of the KMT, it lost the support of the Chinese people, who saw the CCP as the organ to lead China to a better life and a more secure status internationally. On October 1, 1949, the Communists, through the mouth of Mao, announced the creation of the People's Republic of China (PRC). Chou became the premier as well as the foreign secretary. The former office he would hold until his death in 1976; the latter he would assign to another in 1958, but he would still be present at any major contact with a foreign dignitary.

Chou, as the premier and head administrator of the new nationwide government, held the responsibility for putting into order policies and instruments of rule. Policies, programs, and agencies that had been used effectively in the "liberated areas" (as the territory under rule of the Communist base in Yen-an was called) were now extended into all of China. The peasants were urged to form cooperatives and to attack the large landowners; Chinese entrepreneurs were asked to turn over their enterprises to public ownership; imperialist holdings were confiscated; Chinese intellectuals were cajoled and encouraged to support the "new." It was Chou who stood forth in making the pronouncements and the encouragements. He expounded the new laws for the equality of women. Chou used all the talents that he could muster through counseling, persuasion, encouragement, and force to rally Chinese of all classes and categories to support the new system of Chinese Communism and Chinese national unity. By 1951, when he was at the age of fifty-three, the premier then pronounced a new constitution and moved on to announce the start of Five Year Plans. Chou was instituting Marxism in China with finesse, flair, and success. The people's support expanded, agricultural and industrial production grew, diets improved, and diseases decreased.

Mao, ever the philosophical and revolutionary visionary, used his prominence to direct China toward major changes in 1957 and again in 1966. Chou, the ever-loyal administrator, made Mao's ideas public. In 1957, it was the Great Leap Forward; in 1966, it was the Great Proletarian Cultural Revolution. Both brought upheaval to Chinese society; both were formally announced and supported by Chou. Both saw major reorganizations of the Chinese power centers.

After the failure of the Great Leap Foward, Mao, although keeping his title and public eminence, had lost power. Others were able to wrest the control over policymaking, and Chou stood in support. Mao, however, would not stand by for long. In 1966, through the announcement by Chou, Mao launched the Great Proletarian Cultural Revolution. Leaders in communes, in factories, in art, in education, in government, and even in the Party were ousted, criticized publicly, and sent to live in the countryside. Mao led the upheaval; Chou joined the new crusade, but he tried to keep some semblance of order and stability as the disruption of the Cultural Revolution proceeded for ten years, 1966-1976. It seems that Chou's levelheadedness made a mark, for the system still survived when he died in January, 1976.

Chou's diplomatic talents were as demanding as his domestic administrative ones. Chou was not only the prime minister of the new republic but also the leading actor in the foreign ministry. He carried the title of foreign minister from 1949 until 1958; he continued to be China's leading spokesman in that area until his death, trying to gain for his country acceptance by the world community. Chou was able to make headway in this respect at the Geneva Conference in 1954 and the Bandung Conference in 1955.

From its foundation in 1949 and during the Cold War, the PRC had to rely on an alliance with the Soviet Union, an alliance that was not overly cordial from the start and one that devolved into a break and increased bitterness after 1961. Chou's diplomacy at Geneva and at Bandung did bring solid relationships for China from other countries, even though they were of lesser stature, and he tried to build on these bases by traveling to numerous countries. He continued in his attempts to gain China's entry into the United Nations and in having formal diplomatic recognition from the United States.

In 1971, the PRC was voted membership in the U.N.; in February, 1972, President Richard Nixon visited China, although full relationships were not established between the two countries until January, 1979. Chou did not live to see the outcome of these relations; he died on January 8, 1976.

Summary

Chou En-lai was a transitional figure in twentieth century Chinese society. He was born into a family of status and had been inculcated with the values of old China; however, early during his adolescence, he came to be educated in schools that taught modern subjects. Both of these exposures guided him for the rest of his life. He believed that China should reassert and reestablish itself as the "middle" country that it had been throughout most of its early and long history, and he decided that it could only be done via the communist route.

Although China had difficulties in finding the type of communism it would follow, Chou, as the head administrator and directing diplomat, tried to keep his society functioning during these oscillations and continued to press for China's acceptance in the world community. Chou's persistent and stabilizing influences left their mark during his lifetime and after. Mao was hailed as the "helmsman" in his later years; Chou was the ballast, although not so entitled. Where Mao was the domineering patriarch, Chou was the warm, loving, and stable matriarch, if viewed from the perspective of the traditional Chinese society.

Bibliography

Archer, Jules. *Chou En-lai*. New York: Hawthorne Books, 1973. This is a work written for the general public; it is interestingly written but with little new information.

Fang, Percy Jucheng, and Lucy Guinong J. Fang. *Zhou Enlai: A Profile*. Peking: Foreign Languages Press, 1986. The only complete biography in English coming from the PRC. It is mostly favorable, but it includes information on his private life not found elsewhere.

Fitzpatrick, Merrilyn. *Zhou Enlai*. St. Lucia, Australia: University of

Queensland Press, 1984. This work is forty-eight pages long and covers all major events of Chou's life.

Hsu, Kai-yu. *Chou En-lai: China's Gray Eminence*. Garden City, N.Y.: Doubleday, 1968. Hsu was the first of Chou's biographers. The book is well written and has an abundance of information from a favorable viewpoint.

Keith, Ronald C. *The Diplomacy of Zhou Enlai*. New York: St. Martin's Press, 1989. The only solid study of Chou's work in diplomacy, showing how he was a communist and a nationalist.

Li, Tien-min. *Chou En-Lai*. Taipei, Taiwan: Institute of International Relations, 1970. This is a highly critical work, but it contains valuable factual information.

Wilson, Dick. *Zhou Enlai: A Biography*. New York: Viking Penguin Press, 1984. This is a book written in the style of a journalist, with much emphasis on personal acts and foibles.

Zhou, Enlai. *Selected Works of Zhou Enlai*. Vol. 1. Peking: Foreign Languages Press, 1981. This is a collection of some of Chou's writings, 1926-1933. The only collection available in English.

Raymond M. Lorantas

444

CHU TEH

Born: November 30, 1886; Linglung Village, Yilung County, Szechwan
Province, China
Died: July 6, 1976; Peking, China
Areas of Achievement: The military, government, and politics
Contribution: Chu is one of the great military figures of the Communist
Revolution in modern China. He is acclaimed as the "Father of the Red
Army." His service as commander of the Communist Army in the 1930's
and 1940's attests that he was respected for his military ability as well as
for his unflagging commitment to the Communist movement. In addition
to his military contributions, Chu helped establish the Chinese soviets,
and he served in the Politburo and was Chairman of the Standing Committee of the National People's Congress.

Early Life

Chu Teh was born in Linglung Village, Yilung County, Szechwan Province, China, on November 30, 1886. He was the third son in a family of
thirteen children born to an impoverished tenant farmer. Hoping to escape
their dire circumstances, the family decided that Chu should be educated to
qualify for civil service in the Ch'ing imperial government. Consequently,
his formal education began in his fifth year in a private school in his village,
but his lack of funds allowed him to attend only half of each day. His
intellectual progress qualified him to pass the imperial examinations in 1906,
but he decided to attend the Normal School at Ch'engtu and become a
teacher. In 1908, he attended the School of Physical Training at Ch'engtu.
After completing his studies, he and other graduates started their own school
in Ilungshen, where Chu taught physical education and acted as business
manager. The new school was forced to close after the first year, however,
because the townspeople considered the courses too revolutionary and the
physical education courses indecent.

Having disappointed his family and with little recourse to any other profession, he chose to pursue a military career. He applied for admission to the
Military Academy in Yunnan but was refused entry, largely because he came
from outside Yunnan Province. Discouraged, he volunteered for military
service in the Szechwan Regiment; his natural leadership ability and personal
discipline won the attention of his superiors. They recommended him for
officer training, and the Military Academy accepted him the second time he
applied. While in the Military Academy, he was attracted to the teachings of
Sun Yat-sen and soon joined Sun's Revolutionary Alliance.

Life's Work

Commissioned a second lieutenant in July, 1911, Chu was attached to
General T'sai Ao's brigade. After the Wu-ch'ang Uprising, the T'ung Meng-

hui (Sun's secret society) requested that Chu carry on political agitation against the Manchus within the Yunnan army; he succeeded in this dangerous assignment. On October 11, 1911, three weeks after the Wu-ch'ang Uprising, which set off the 1911 Revolution, Chu took part as a company commander under T'sai Ao in the revolt at K'un-ming, which overthrew the Manchu authorities of Yunnan Province. Chu was commissioned captain and made commander of forces in both Szechwan and Yunnan provinces. In 1912, he returned to teaching as instructor at the Yunnan Military Academy. Chu was one of the first men to transfer his T'ung Meng-hui membership to the Kuomintang (KMT) when Yüan Shih-K'ai became China's president. For the next two years, his troops guarded the Tibet-Yunnan frontier against French-instigated incursions from Indochina. He was promoted to full colonel in December, 1915, and placed in command of the Tenth Yunnan Regiment. In January, 1916, after T'sai Ao's campaign against Yüan Shih-k'ai in Szechwan, Chu was promoted to brigadier general. In only five years, Chu had risen from second lieutenant to brigadier general because of circumstances and obvious ability to train and lead men.

In early 1922, Chu sought a new life through communism. He determined to break an addiction to opium he had formed after the deaths of his father and two brothers, to leave the warlord Yang Sen, for whom he had been working, and to travel abroad in order to study in Europe. In Shanghai, with proper medical care, he broke his addiction. At this point, the only meeting between Chu and Sun Yat-sen occurred. Sun requested that Chu return to his military post in Yunnan, but Chu refused. When he applied for membership in the Chinese Communist Party (CCP), his application was rejected because of his affiliation with and aid to the warlords. In September, Chu, then in his mid-thirties, left China intending to study in Germany or Russia. After a monthlong stay in Paris, he proceeded to Berlin, where he met Chou En-lai. With Chou's sponsorship, he was able to join the CCP in Germany, where he was among the eldest of the members and the only one with military experience. In Berlin, he was converted wholly to communism, but difficulty with the German language caused him to end his formal studies. In 1924, he became editor of the political weekly *Cheng-chi Chou-pao*, and that same year he was elected to alternate membership of the Central Executive Committee of the Berlin chapter of the KMT.

When Chu returned to China, the KMT and CCP were cooperating in their struggle against the warlords. Both sides hoped to win the minor warlords over to their side or to neutralize them. Because of his previous connection with Yang Sen, Chu was able to persuade Yang to join Chiang Kai-shek's Northern Expedition in 1926, and Chu served in the political department of Yang's Twentieth Army. General Yang, however, became suspicious and resentful of the communist influence among his troops and placed all the blame on Chu. Chu learned of Yang's plans to assassinate him, and he fled to Nan-ch'ang. There he was given command of an officer training regiment and made head of the military training school.

When the CCP voted to begin the Peasant Uprising against Chiang in July, 1927, it planned to rely heavily on the military school and its graduates. On the night of August 1, 1927, Chu was able to persuade the Kuomintang troops to mutiny and overthrow Nan-ch'ang. Chu was then voted deputy commander of the Chinese Workers and Peasant Revolutionary Army, still under the KMT banner. Chu and his Ninth Division, however, were forced to retreat from Nan-ch'ang to South Hunan. Following orders from the Communist Central Party to break with the KMT, Chu's troops then openly proclaimed themselves to be a Communist unit.

In the spring of 1928, Mao Tse-tung joined with Chu, and the two inaugurated the "base area," where troops were stationed to support the local rebel leaders. This merger laid the groundwork for the Red Army. The Communists officially united the armies of Chu and Mao and organized the Fourth Red Army with Chu as commander and Mao as political commissar in charge of political indoctrination. The Communists officially date the birth of the Red Army from the 1927 Nan-ch'ang uprising, when Chu induced the municipal garrison to defect to the CCP, but now the names of Chu and Mao were linked together. Once the Red Army had been formed, the troops under Chu waited for the Nationalist forces to attack. Using "mobile warfare," the Chu-Mao troops made daring strikes behind enemy lines and launched campaigns of disruption and surprise intended to weaken the enemy. Chu built the Red Army into a formidable force, which at its peak totaled more than 200,000 men.

In China's remote hinterland, the Communists organized the peasants into soviets and parceled out the land on an equal basis. Mao and Chu supported a rural-based peasant uprising in opposition to the Comintern, which favored a proletarian, urban revolution. When the Kiangsi Soviet was established in 1931, Chu was elected to the Central Executive Committee, and his role as Commander of the Red Army was confirmed. Two years later, he was elected to the Politburo, and then to the Presidium. From this time forward, Chu served on committees, in congresses, in the Politburo, and on military and executive councils.

When the Nationalists began their so-called Fifth Extermination Campaign, German military advisers devised a new "blockhouse" strategy for which the Red Army had no defense. In July, 1934, Chu and Mao announced a "northward march" for the ostensible purpose of defending China from the Japanese. By October, the Red Army was pared down to eighty thousand soldiers and twenty thousand administrative cadre and began the famed Long March with Chu as commander. During this period, Mao assumed effective control of the CCP, and Chu continued as commander of the Red Army.

China was eventually forced to form a united front against the Japanese, so Chu and Mao flew to Nanking to conclude an agreement that in theory placed the Red Army under the control of the National Government. Chu was appointed commander of the Second War Zone, and the Red Army was renamed the Eighth Route Army. The winter of 1939-1940 saw the collapse of the KMT-CCP alliance, and the United Front ceased to exist. Chiang alleged that the Eighth Route Army was merely playing "hide and seek" and not fighting the Japanese. As a result, supplies were withheld and a determined effort was made to starve Chu's forces. Isolated and pressed by the Japanese troops, the Eighth Route Army was forced to become self-sufficient. Crops were cultivated and other manual labor was performed collectively by the troops and leaders as well.

After Japan's surrender in August, 1945, Chu rushed his troops in to occupy those areas held by the Japanese and Chinese puppet troops to accept their surrender and disarm them. The Nationalists denounced this action as an attempt by the Communists to unite with Soviet troops. Chiang ordered the Japanese and Chinese troops to join together and fight if attacked by the Communists. A truce was finally arranged through the help of American General George C. Marshall in January, 1946, but it lasted only a few months. The two Chinese sides fought again, and by mid-1946 civil war raged in many parts of China. The Eighth Route Army and other Communist fighting units assumed the new name of the People's Liberation Army (PLA), with Chu and other leaders openly acknowledging a war of attrition against the Nationalists. The Nationalists were finally forced out of China in January, 1949.

After the fall of the Nationalists, Chu participated in preparations for the establishment of the People's Republic of China on October 1 and served on the special committee that drafted the Organic Law of the central government. In the new government, Chu received top posts in three key organs, each chaired by Mao. In addition, he remained as Commander in Chief of the PLA. Although he is often depicted as being inactive after 1954, Chu continued to serve in various political and military capacities.

From 1960 on, however, because of his age, Chu played a different role in China. He made "inspection tours" of the country, and, while he hosted delegates to Politburo conferences, he no longer attended them. By his eightieth birthday, his role appears to have been largely ceremonial as one of the prestigious "grand old men" of the Communist Party. He did enter the debate over modernizing the military and developing nuclear weapons, but he usually assumed a hard-line Party position and argued that such expenditures as were needed for new technologies could not be to the detriment of the masses. He also argued against a career military and stated that China's military operations should rely fully on the masses of the people and on the concerted efforts of the regular army, guerrillas, and militia to carry out a war by the whole people.

Chu was among the army leaders severely criticized during the Cultural Revolution. He was characterized as a "big warlord and careerist who had wormed his way into the Party." Chu refused to write letters in support of the Cultural Revolution, and he also refused to write a self-criticism for failing to support it. Chu must have retained considerable power during the revolution, because Mao could not have instigated it without the support of the armed forces. Whether he had power during the Cultural Revolution, Chu was elected only to the Politburo in 1969. By 1973, however, he was re-elected as a member of the Politburo's standing committee.

When the Fourth National People's Congress wrote a new constitution in 1975, ceremonial duties of China's formal head of state fell to the aged Chu in his capacity as Chairman of the Standing Committee of the National People's Congress. Chiang Ching, Mao's wife, reportedly pushed Chu forward in the Party structure as a possible heir to Mao, or perhaps to use his prestige to win over the military and other influential people to her side. He was not to enjoy the new position long, however, nor did he serve Chiang's purposes. Chu, father of the Red Army and a symbol of revolutionary legitimacy and unity, died on July 6, 1976, at the age of eighty-nine.

Summary

Chu Teh never forgot the grinding poverty and hardships of his early life. He developed a passionate concern for the Chinese peasants, who suffered similar deprivations. Angered by the actions of the wealthy and the government, which only worsened the plight of the peasants, he turned to the study of Marxism and espoused communism. He participated in the earliest stages of the Revolution and committed his life to the movement.

In 1940, Major Evan F. Carlson characterized Chu as one who had "the kindliness of a Robert E. Lee, the tenacity of a Grant, and the humility of a Lincoln." His concern for his soldiers caused him to stop corporal punishment, while the Japanese and Nationalists beat their troops with rifle butts. His troops did not come before his countrymen: Chu would not allow the Red Army to take from the peasants, even when Chiang attempted to starve the army into surrender. The Red Army soldiers went unfed rather than take food from the poor peasants. Chu helped to establish China's rural-based peasant armies, and he never abandoned the concept of a peasant conscript army. He taught his officers to respect the "armies of the masses." Shortly before his death, he warned against replacing the peasant armies with "military careerists" and professionals, for he was convinced that only a war of the whole people could successfully defend China.

Bibliography

Houn, Franklin W. *A Short History of Chinese Communism*. Englewood Cliffs, N.J.: Prentice-Hall, 1973. Presents the story of the first stages of the Chinese Communist Revolution and the emergence of the first Chinese guerrilla bases. Excellent general approach to the communist movement.

Hsüeh, Chün-tu, comp. *Revolutionary Leaders of Modern China*. New York: Oxford University Press, 1971. The article on Chu is an excellent but brief profile and shows his relationship to many other revolutionary leaders.

Klein, Donald W., and Anne B. Clark. *Biographic Dictionary of Chinese Communism, 1921-1965*. Vol. 1, *Ai Szu-Ch'i-Lo I-Nung*. Cambridge, Mass.: Harvard University Press, 1971. The article on Chu contains the most comprehensive biographical information from his birth to 1957. The emphasis is on the chronological developments.

Smedley, Agnes. *The Great Road: The Life and Times of Chu Teh*. New York: Monthly Review Press, 1956. This work is the most comprehensive and intimate biography available on Chu. The author knew her subject personally and included their shared experiences. The work is thorough and includes a fine chronology of Chu's life. Unfortunately, it ends with the death of the author in 1955.

Terrill, Ross. *Mao: A Biography*. New York: Harper & Row, 1980. Based on wide reading and filled with bold assertions in a first-hand style, the book is a good source for the relationship between Mao and Chu.

H. Christian Thorup

ANDRÉ-GUSTAVE CITROËN

Born: February 5, 1878; Paris, France
Died: July 3, 1935; Paris, France
Areas of Achievement: Engineering, industry, and exploration
Contribution: Citroën introduced Henry Ford's mass production techniques
to the European automobile industry and founded the company that produced the first car that was affordable to a broad cross section of consumers in Europe. He financed several scientific exhibitions and gave the
lighting of the Arc de Triomphe and the Place de la Concorde to the city
of Paris.

Early Life

André-Gustave Citroën was born in Paris on February 5, 1878, to a family
of wealthy Jewish diamond merchants of Dutch extraction. While he was
still a young child, Citroën's parents lost most of their assets in a complex
financial swindle, and, when André was six, his mother died. In the same
year, his father committed suicide. Despite these difficulties, Citroën entered
the Lycée Condorcet at seven and later attended the Lycée Louis le Grand,
where he performed quite well scholastically. In 1898, he began at the École
Polytechnique but ceased studies there in 1900.

Shortly after leaving school, he established a small shop to manufacture
herringbone or vee-shaped gears whose innovative form provided extra
strength. This undertaking achieved an annual sales volume of one million
francs by 1910. Known under the name Société Anonyme des Engrenages
Citroën, the firm's capital rose to three million francs in 1913. It produced
the steering gear for the Titanic, and, by 1913, more than five hundred gears
had been manufactured there. A new factory was opened on the Quai Gre-
nelle in Paris.

At the outbreak of hostilities in 1914, Citroën was called up into the
French artillery, where he became concerned about the paucity of French
munitions and men. In discussions with General Baquet, who was the defense ministry official responsible for ordnance, Citroën proposed building a
shop that would produce twenty thousand shells a day. In 1915, the government agreed to the plan, and in six weeks, Citroën built on Paris' Quai
Javel a munitions factory that ultimately manufactured more than fifty-five
thousand shells daily. Citroën assisted in the revitalization of all factories
involved in the war effort and was particularly instrumental in achieving
increased coal supplies for those factories as well as for gasworks and electrical generating stations. He reorganized the Roane arsenal on the same
mass-production lines as the Javel factory and arranged the equitable distribution of food supplies to wartime French civilians through the introduction of ration cards.

Life's Work

Much of Citroën's success in enhancing France's wartime output derived from his interest in mass production techniques. In 1912, Citroën visited the Ford works in the United States for the purpose of learning their methods and with the hope of applying them to the French automobile industry. Citroën had long been convinced that the European car industry could and needed to experience substantial expansion, and he considered cost to be the major obstacle to the automobile's widespread use by large numbers of consumers. The war interfered with his plans to produce such a vehicle. He applied the mass production techniques to the munitions industry during the war years, and, when hostilities ended, the armaments factory that the government had authorized him to build on the Quai Javel was adapted for automobile production.

Applying the standardized techniques of which he had become a major European proponent, Citroën began producing the 10 CV Type A on a large scale in 1919. Most automobile manufacturers of that time produced but one chassis and one engine, which had to be assembled in a specialist's workshop before it could be utilized. Citroën's Type A came from the factory fully assembled and ready for the road. Because all parts were produced and assembled in a standard series, costs were considerably reduced. Before the Type A had been seen by the general public, interest in the automobile was substantial. In a span of two weeks, sixteen thousand orders were received.

The Type A that came off the assembly line for the first time on May 28, 1919, featured a thrifty, four-cylinder engine and consistently achieved a speed of forty miles an hour. It was equipped with electric starter and lights. The Type A became available in several variations: the three- and four-seater Torpedos, the three-seater Coupé, the four-seater Limousine, the City Coupé, and a delivery van. Two thousand were built in 1919 and eight thousand in 1920. By that time, Type A was outproducing all other European automobiles. More than 150,000 had been built by 1924.

In order to facilitate production and meet the enormous demand for its small, economical cars, the Citroën company expanded. In 1922, a factory at Levallois-Perret was bought, part of the Mors Company was purchased, and a new plant was opened in Saint-Ouen. Citroën's French holdings involved two hundred acres of land and employed thirty-five thousand workers in the mid-1920's, and by 1927 the company was producing four hundred cars per day. The following year, Citroën commanded 36 percent of the French automobile market. Ultimately, Citroën was manufacturing automobiles in Great Britain, Germany, and Austria.

Other models followed the Type A. In 1922, the 5CV Type C appeared, a five-horsepower model conceived of as a young people's car. This model also achieved success as a popular means of transportation. Citroën later modified the Type C, lengthening the body and adding a back seat. After

1926, the firm also manufactured taxis, half-track vehicles, and one-ton commercial vehicles. Citroën manufactured its first six-cylinder vehicles in 1928: a car and a 1.8-ton commercial vehicle.

Citroën engaged in innovative advertising, insurance, and maintenance practices that increased public information concerning his product and reduced both psychological and financial obstacles associated with car ownership. By 1929, total sales had exceeded 100,000 vehicles, and, in 1932, the well-publicized 134-day endurance test of an 8CV affirmed the reliability of Citroën cars.

The best-known Citroën innovation in the passenger car industry came with the introduction of the Citroën "7" in 1934. Most noted for its front-wheel drive capability, the "7" contained many unique applications that combined to revolutionize design thinking in the automobile industry. This new model incorporated the overhead valve engine, removable liners, hydraulic brakes, torsion bar suspension, and a monocoque body, and it became the only popular front-wheel-drive car of its time. By 1934, however, Citroën's unsatisfactory financial practices caused his 2,450 creditors to petition for bankruptcy, and the automobile industrialist lost control of his firm. A French government commission assumed control of the company and persuaded one of the creditors, the Michelin Tire Company, to acquire the business in 1935.

In addition to innovative contributions to the automotive industry, Citroën sponsored pioneering scientific expeditions across Africa and Asia, extending funds as well as the technical knowledge of his staff. A Citroën caterpillar tractor convoy set a twenty-day record crossing the two-thousand-mile Sahara in December, 1922, and January, 1923. The Trans-Sahara Expedition consisted of a Citroën manager, several military representatives, one scientific observer, and other technical personnel. The tractors were specially equipped with rubber and canvas bands that worked successfully to overcome the varied terrain of the route. Similar expeditions followed, and, in 1924, eight ten-horsepower Citroën caterpillar tractors embarked upon a fifteen-thousand-mile, nine-month trip from Algeria through Central Africa, reaching as far as Cape Town, Mozambique, and Madagascar. The Central African Expedition included experts in the area of science and technology, amassing ninety thousand feet of motion-picture film, eight thousand photographs, and considerable original research on then-unknown parts of Africa. The Citroën Trans-Asiatic Expedition covered eight thousand miles from Beirut to Beijing, undertaking similar research between 1931 and 1932. Two of Citroën's caterpillar tractors traversed the arduous Himalayas, the first instance of a motorized crossing of those mountains.

Summary

André-Gustave Citroën and the automobile company he founded came to symbolize audacity and progress in Europe's advancement toward the technological age. Citroën himself possessed and was able to communicate a vision for the steps essential to the advancement of France's automobile industry, and his career parallels its developments. The financial crisis that the company faced in the mid-1930's emerged not only from the difficult world economic situation but also from the particular personality of French businessmen and their business practices. The individualist spirit of French firms combined with the aversion of French banks for long-term loans to undermine the stability and growth of French industry.

For inventor-industrialists such as Citroën, the lure of profits for their own sake, a distinguishing characteristic of financial institutions, was fundamentally unable to stimulate the great innovations of the kind Citroën pursued. These varied perspectives produced a mutual disdain that ultimately compromised the vigor of important French enterprises. The Citroën firm was among them. Despite reverses, however, Citroën cars continue to be regarded as unique among automobile manufacturers. Consistently subjugating form to function, Citroën cars are designed from the inside out: The driver is the first and most dominating element to be accommodated by the final product. This principle has produced an at times bizarre, but always harmonious, appearance that echoes the daring and vision of Citroën himself and his penchant for progressive and always useful experimentation.

Bibliography
Baldwin, Nick, et al. *The World Guide to Automobile Manufacturers*. New York: Facts on File, 1987. The article on Citroën is the most useful brief account of the company and its founder, including the major contributions and events in the history of the firm.
Broad, Raymond. *Citroën*. New York: St. Martin's Press, 1976. Broad presents the history of the Citroën company from the first Type A through the merger with Peugot in 1974. The twenty-nine short chapters deal with the successive innovations and explain the problems they resolved. The book is sufficiently illustrated.
Dumont, Pierre. *Citroën, the Great Marque of France: A Pictorial History*. Translated by Tom Ellaway. London: Interante, 1976. This work provides a description of the automobile industry before Citroën and a discussion of his contribution to it. Dumont provides a complete study of the evolution of Citroën cars from the Type A of 1919 to the SM and GS models. This book constitutes the most complete resource for specifications, production statistics, and general information concerning Citroën and his automobile business.
Haardt, Georges-Marie, and Louis Audouin-Dubreuil. *Across the Sahara by Motor Car: From Touggart to Timbuctoo*. Translated by E. E. Fournier d'Albe. New York: D. Appleton, 1924. This work describes the Trans-

Sahara expedition from the perspective of its leader and Citroën's business associate, Georges Marie Haardt. Citroën wrote the introduction, which provides insight into his personality and motivation.

_____. *The Black Journey.* New York: Cosmopolitan Book Corp., 1927. This book deals with the Citroën Central African Expedition, following its itinerary and providing details of its achievements.

Hackin, Joseph. "In Persia and Afghanistan with the Citroën Trans-Asiatic Expedition." *Geographic Journal* 83 (May, 1934): 353-363. This article contains some of the findings of the first phase of the Asian expedition as well as photographs collected along the route through Afghanistan.

LeFevre, Georges. *An Eastern Odyssey.* Translated by E. D. Swinton. Boston: Little, Brown, 1935. This is the story of the Citroën Trans-Asiatic Expedition by the expedition's historian. LeFevre provides a detailed account of the discoveries, obstacles, and successes of the trip. Citroën wrote the preface, which reflects the origins and purposes of such continental journeys and explains the development of half-track vehicles.

Schmittel, Wolfgang. *Design, Concept, Realisation.* Translated by M. J. Schärer-Wynne. Zurich: ABC-Edition, 1975. Schmittel includes a chapter on the contribution of Citroën and his company to the automobile industry. The piece discusses the design philosophy of the Citroën enterprise and concludes that its subordination of structure to function produced consistently harmonious designs and reflected the firm's commitment to progress and its daring approach to innovation.

Margaret B. Denning

GEORGES CLAUDE

Born: September 24, 1870; Paris, France
Died: May 23, 1960; St. Cloud, France
Areas of Achievement: Chemistry, invention, and technology
Contribution: Claude was the first successfully to liquefy air in quantity
  independent of Carl von Linde in 1902. A few years later, Claude's Liquid Air Company was separating the components of liquid air and producing high-quality oxygen. Founder of Claude Neon, he held a monopoly on
  the neon-tube industry in the 1920's.

Early Life

Georges Claude was the son of a modest family in Paris, France. His
father was the assistant director of the Manufactures des Glaces de Saint-
Gobin. Claude's education came principally from a municipal school of
physics and chemistry. He was graduated in 1889 and took his first job at the
Usines Municipales d'Électricité des Halles. In 1893, he married and later
had three children.

As the result of an almost-fatal accident with a high-tension wire, Claude
developed better safety procedures which he presented to the French bio-
physicist Arsène d'Arsonval, his teacher and collaborator. Ironically, this
would set the stage for some related inventions and a closer relationship with
d'Arsonval.

During the years from 1896 to 1902, Claude worked for the Compagnie
Française Houston-Thomson. In 1897, Claude discovered that acetylene gas
could be handled and transported safely by dissolving it in acetone. His
method was largely accepted and resulted in an expansion of the acetylene
industry. This was the first of Claude's discoveries that would trigger the
growth of new industrial technology.

In 1902, Claude and d'Arsonval worked on the industrial methods for the
liquefaction of gases; in 1903, Claude wrote his first book, *L'Air liquide*
(1903; *Liquid Air, Oxygen, Nitrogen*, 1913), and he asked d'Arsonval to
write the preface. In 1908, d'Arsonval established an international society
for cryogenic studies.

It was his work on the liquefaction of air and the subsequent separation of
the gases of air that made Georges Claude an industrial giant. Originally,
Claude was after inexpensive, high-quality oxygen, which was in demand by
hospitals and for oxyacetylene welding. After successfully separating oxygen
from liquid air, he also proposed the use of liquid oxygen in iron smelting as
early as 1910; his innovations in this process, however, would not be
adopted until after World War II. During World War II, he used liquid
oxygen in explosives and also produced liquid chlorine for poison-gas attacks. Faced with substantial leftover quantities of the rare gases neon and

argon, Claude cleverly built an entirely new technology which resulted in an industrial monopoly.

Life's Work

On December 24, 1877, Louis Cailletet had liquefied a few drops of oxygen before the Academy of Sciences in Paris. The skeptics of the time asked, "What purpose can the liquefaction of air serve?" Claude, unswayed by negative opinion, envisioned the continuous commercial production of liquid gases and the impact it would have on the metallurgy, chemical, and agriculture industries. Several attempts at large-scale liquefaction had not been entirely successful; Claude would be the first to succeed.

Theory provided Claude with two processes that would cool air sufficiently to liquefy it. The first process is based on the Joule-Thomson effect. The gas was expanded after compression so that work is done against internal forces. The second process is to expand the gas so that it does work against the external forces of an engine. Both processes are based on the principle that a gas cools when it expands. After the gas is allowed to expand, part of the cooler gas is compressed, and the remaining gas is used to carry the heat of compression away. The compressed gas is allowed to expand again. The cycle is repeated until the remaining gas becomes cold enough to form a liquid. In addition, the two processes require that the cooling effect be cumulative, so heat exchangers need to be incorporated in both systems. All the industrial air liquefaction is based on one of these two processes or a combination of them.

The first attempt to liquefy air with an expansion machine was made by Ernest Solvay. In 1887, a patent was granted to him that described three processes for the liquefaction of air. Only one of those processes was tried and resulted in little success. The Joule-Thomson effect was used for large-scale production of liquid air in 1895 by Carl von Linde in Germany and William Hampson in England. In 1902, subsequent work on adiabatic expansion of the gas in a cylinder, with the performance of external work, resulted in the liquefaction of air by Claude in France. This method is thermodynamically more efficient than the Joule-Thomson method, but there were two formidable technical problems for Claude to solve.

The first was that the expansion engine had to be well insulated, since its operating temperature was well below −150 degrees Celsius. In Claude's successful attempt to liquefy air, he introduced the principle of regenerative cooling. The air that had been cooled by expansion in the cylinder was used to precool the compressed air before it entered the cylinder. As the initial temperature nears the liquefaction point, however, the amount of cooling through expansion at a given pressure decreases. Also, liquid air in the cylinder causes "water-hammer" effects that could fracture the cylinder. The Claude cycle demanded that an optimal pressure and temperature be found for the gas entering the cylinder.

The second problem, since oil freezes at these low temperatures, was to find a method of lubricating the moving parts. Claude's first solution was to use petrol ether, which remains a liquid down to −140 degrees Celsius, but he achieved better results using pretreated leather in place of the metallic piston rings in the cylinder. This arrangement allowed a small amount of air to leak out between the piston and the cylinder wall; thus, the air is the real lubricant.

The ultimate goal was not simply the liquefaction of air but also the separation of air into its component parts. Linde was the first to achieve this goal with his introduction of a rectification column in 1903 that was capable of separating oxygen from liquefied air. Claude was to achieve the same result, but instead of separating totally liquefied air, he used a process called backward return. This process liquefies only a relatively small portion of the air to be treated in order to obtain without evaporation a highly oxygenated liquid. The Claude patented processes were put into practice by the Liquid Air Company in France. Over time, several modifications and improvements were added to the Claude cycle.

Claude also developed a process for the manufacture of ammonia in 1917 that was similar to the Fritz Haber process. Claude increased the production of ammonia by using a high operating pressure. Also, by transferring the heat of reaction to the incoming hydrogen and nitrogen mixture, he could more efficiently bring them to the reaction temperature.

Claude's success in separating the components of air left him with considerable quantities of rare gases. Searching for a way to use the leftover gases, Claude would start a million-dollar industry. In 1897, Sir William Ramsay discovered that when neon, a chemically inert and colorless gas, is placed in evacuated tubes and an electric current is passed through the tubes, the neon gas glows reddish-orange. Yet the cost of isolating the rare gases at that time was too expensive for a commercial product. The relatively cheap large-scale isolation of the components of air by both Linde and Claude in 1907 made possible a commercial product.

In 1910, Claude displayed his first neon sign at the Grand Palais in Paris. Neon-filled tubes produced a reddish-orange, and argon produced a grayish-blue. By coating the inside of the tubes, Claude found that he could expand his range of colors. Unfortunately, the first neon tubes had short lifetimes because of the corrosion of the electrodes. In 1915, Claude received a patent for an electrode that had high resistance to corrosion. Good neon tubes could now last up to thirty years.

The Claude Neon Company grew as a result of his patent, and Claude built a near monopoly in the neon-tube industry. The company's largest growth occurred during 1925-1929, reaching its peak after World War II. Expansion was inevitable, and Claude Neon became an international organization through an early form of franchising. In 1923, a United States Claude Neon franchise was bought for around 100,000 dollars plus royalties. During the Depression years, Claude neon lights could claim nine million dollars of an eleven-million-dollar industry. Claude Neon would survive the Depression, but when his patent expired in 1932 the competition flourished. Claude Neon would no longer have the monopoly on neon tubes.

A very rich man, Claude turned his attention to still another project in 1933. Claude believed that the generation of energy could be accomplished by transferring the heat of the warm surface water of the ocean to the lower temperature of the depths. Unfortunately, after eight years of effort the project ended in a costly failure.

Claude received many honors in his lifetime. Most important were the John Scott Medal of the Franklin Institute in 1903 and his membership in the Legion of Honor. Claude was also involved in politics, and he joined the Action Française in 1919. He ran, unsuccessfully, for public office in 1928. In the years from 1940 to 1945, he conducted "Conférences sous l'occupation allemande: Mes imprudences et mes malheurs," and after the war he was accused of being a supporter of the Vichy government. He pleaded guilty; his name was removed from the Legion of Honor; and, despite his age, he spent four and a half years in prison. Several of his friends arranged for his release, but he remained under police surveillance. He wrote many articles, patents, and books. Among his autobiographical books are *Souvenirs et enseignements d'une campagne électorale* (1932) and *Ma Vie et mes inventions* (1957).

Summary

In 1903, Georges Claude and Carl von Linde began a scientific revolution. Air could be inexpensively liquefied and separated into its components. Cryogenic (low-temperature) studies could flourish, and the world would soon be able to reach extremely low temperatures with ease. The practical liquefaction of air was more than a scientific revolution; it was an industrial, social, and economic revolution as well.

Pure nitrogen, either as a liquid or as a gas, is essential in the following endeavors: ammonia and fertilizer production, blanketing atmospheres for chemical processing, enhanced oil recovery, flash-freezing, electronic manufacture, and aerospace. Claude's main goal was the inexpensive production of oxygen. His success has changed the standard of living in the modern world. Oxygen is a very chemically reactive element. Pure oxygen, rather than air, can increase production and rates of reactions. There are at least twenty elements essential to life, and it would be hard to name the most essential element of life. Yet oxygen certainly would be on any list. Many people owe their lives to a tank of pure oxygen. The basics of the Claude process are used to separate life-giving oxygen from the air. Life support, be it medical, underwater, or space-related, is possible because of the pioneering work of Claude.

Claude not only enhanced the quality of modern life but also discovered a new form of art. Neon lighting has sold products and added color and excitement to the nightlife of the world's major cities.

Bibliography

Claude, Georges. *Liquid Air, Oxygen, Nitrogen.* Translated by Henry E. P. Cottrell. London: J. and A. Churchill, 1913. The first book Claude wrote. Describes the early work on air liquefaction, including the theoretical aspects. Gives the reader a good sense of Claude's struggle to achieve air liquefaction.

Hoare, F. E., L. C. Jackson, and N. Kurti, eds. *Experimental Cryophysics.* London: Butterworth, 1961. An excellent account of the development of low-temperature research and the historical development of commercial liquid-air production.

Mendelssohn, Kurt. *The Quest for Absolute Zero: The Meaning of Low Temperature Physics.* New York: McGraw-Hill, 1966. Mendelssohn concisely describes the development of both processes for air liquefaction and Claude's role in the development of the external work method of gas liquefaction.

Stern, Rudi. *Let There Be Neon.* New York: Harry N. Abrams, 1979. Stern gives one of the best historical accounts of the development of neon lights. Stern includes photographs of Claude in his laboratory as well as a copy of a front page of *Claude Neon News* from 1928.

Webb, M. *The Magic of Neon.* Layton, Utah: Gibbs M. Smith, 1986. Webb briefly describes the history of neon tubes and gives a clear and concise description of how neon tubes are constructed.

Michael J. Welsh

GEORGES CLEMENCEAU

Born: September 28, 1841; Mouilleron-en-Pareds, France
Died: November 24, 1929; Paris, France
Areas of Achievement: Government and politics
Contribution: Clemenceau was significant in French politics from 1871 to
1919. Although he influenced the nation's political course several times,
Clemenceau is best known for his role as premier during the last eighteen
months of World War I, when his determination to win inspired France
despite enormous adversity.

Early Life

Born in the Vendée in 1841, Georges Clemenceau was the eldest son of
Benjamin and Emma Gautreau Clemenceau. The family eventually consisted
of three sons and three daughters. Oddly, as the region was strongly Catholic, the patriarch was an atheist and his wife Protestant. Georges followed
his father in religion and in his leftist political views.

Clemenceau's early education was at home, but in 1853 he enrolled at the
lycée in Nantes. Upon graduation in 1858, he entered medical school there.
In 1861, he transferred to Paris. Although he was graduated in 1865, he
had spent so much time getting acquainted with leftist political circles—
participation in an 1862 demonstration cost him two months in jail—that he
got a poor residency. The articles he wrote in the early 1860's suggest that he
had more talent as a political journalist than as a physician.

In 1865, frustrated by unrequited love, Clemenceau went to the United
States for four years. At first he lived on a paternal allowance and the
proceeds of his articles about the United States sold to the Paris press. When
his father cut him off in an effort to get him home, he took a position
teaching French at a Connecticut academy. He fell in love with a student
named Mary Plummer, and, after some disagreement with her guardian over
Clemenceau's distaste for religion, the two married on June 23, 1869. The
match was unfortunate, for after the births of a son and two daughters the
two were estranged. Mary had little part in Clemenceau's life after 1875, and
they divorced in 1892. Tales of Clemenceau's callousness have circulated
ever since, but although his wife spent much of the rest of her life in some
isolation, there is no real evidence that he mistreated her.

Life's Work

Clemenceau's political career began in the turmoil of the Franco-Prussian
War (1870-1871). Personally he had no use for the Second Empire or Na-
poleon III, but, a determined patriot, he could hardly hope for a French
defeat. The disastrous defeat at Sedan, where the emperor himself was taken
prisoner, led to the creation of the Third Republic. On September 5, 1870,

Clemenceau was appointed mayor of Montmartre. Known for his leftist views, Clemenceau organized the National Guard in his district and forbade religious instruction in the schools. A gulf began to open between the Left and the government, and, when municipal elections agreed to in the face of riots were canceled, Clemenceau resigned his post. A national plebiscite supported the government, but Clemenceau was reelected on November 5. The Left believed that the National Guard was the equal of the professional forces of Prussia, and, when France was forced to accept an armistice on January 28, 1871, Leftists cried treachery.

In February, Clemenceau was elected to the new National Assembly and voted against a peace that was to give Alsace-Lorraine to the Prussians. In March, he attempted to defuse the violence that erupted when the army tried to confiscate some cannons that had been left in Montmartre. He was too late, and two officers were murdered. The Radical Republicans and Socialists formed the Paris Commune, intending it to be the nucleus of a national government. On March 19, 1871, the mayors of Paris, including Clemenceau, met with the Central Committee of the Commune; they were ready to represent the city's grievances before the national government, led by Adolphe Thiers, but not to rebel. Compromise failed, and Clemenceau was crushingly defeated in the ensuing communal elections. Pretending to be an American, he got out of the city for a conference of delegates from republican cities and was thus away during the bloody week of May 21-28, when the government crushed the Commune. For much of the rest of his career, however, he was damned by the Right as a supporter of the Commune and by the Left as a traitor for abandoning it.

For the first four years of the Third Republic, Clemenceau was in the political background. He served on the Paris Municipal Council, becoming president in 1875, and practiced medicine. In February, 1876, he was elected to the Chamber of Deputies, wherein his calls for amnesty for Communards and increased popular sovereignty quickly established him as one of the leaders of the Left. As Republicans gained more electoral strength, Clemenceau sought to offer the electorate a choice between radical and conservative Republican factions.

In the late 1870's, Clemenceau began a campaign for leadership of the Radical Republicans. He established a newspaper, *La Justice*, to express his views, created a party organization, and began making speeches in and out of Parliament. Like most political journals, Clemenceau's had a patron, Cornelius Herz, but, unlike many legislators, Clemenceau did not do favors in return for the money. The target of his campaign was a Radical Republican victory in 1885. The issues were constitutional reform, the condition of the working class, and colonial policy. Clemenceau wanted an elected judiciary and the abolition of the senate whose members served for life. Although the Senate was made an elective body, by 1885 Clemenceau found such reform was not of popular concern. Although not a collectivist, Clemenceau supported trade unions and improved conditions for workers. He became more conservative over time, but during the 1880's he inspired some of the younger French socialists, such as Jean Jaurès and Léon Blum. In the mid-1880's, however, the major issue was colonial expansion in Tunis and Indochina. Clemenceau argued that the profits of colonies did not offset their expenses; that colonial conflict would divert military resources from European preparedness; and that aggressive colonialism would produce friction with England, leaving France alone against Germany. In March, 1884, just as the premier Jules Ferry was making secret arrangements with China over Tonkin, Clemenceau, justifying his reputation as a brutal debater, crushed the government with information about military setbacks that later proved false. A caretaker government was appointed and a spirited electoral campaign followed, leading to elections in October of 1885. The Republicans, however, could not agree about issues or candidates, and the result of the first ballot was the biggest victory for the Right since the early 1870's. The feuding Republicans managed to combine their lists of candidates for the second ballot, resulting in a chamber divided in thirds: Right, Opportunists (moderate Republicans), and Radicals.

Clemenceau was perhaps lucky that his attacks on Ferry had angered enough Republicans that he got no office. The parliament of 1885-1889 was marked much more by scandal than reform. Efforts by Ferdinand de Lesseps to duplicate his Suez Canal building success in Panama led to failure and many bribes and special favors for legislators to ensure the profits of those at the top before the company fell. Also, in 1888, General Georges Boulanger, who had risen in politics as a protégé of Clemenceau, began to attack the failure of the republic to make reforms. A popular military hero, Boulanger, secretly in league with the royalists, seemed about to stage a coup. The Republican legislature, belatedly aware of the danger, trumped up charges against his lieutenants, causing Boulanger to panic and flee. Clemenceau then successfully initiated legislation that would force Boulanger's faction to form a structured party, which it lacked the unity to do. The Radicals had been forced to help the government without getting any reforms and lost much of their separate identity. The popular reaction was a drift to the Right, and so there would be no constitutional reforms before the defeat in World War II resulted in a new constitution.

The elections of 1889 reduced the influence of the Republicans and Clemenceau. Then three years later, the aftermath of the Panama Canal scandal virtually ruined him. No one ever directly charged Clemenceau with misconduct, but his longtime friend and backer Cornélius Herz was involved and had even attempted to blackmail government figures. Right-wing politicians, perhaps seeking revenge for the defeat of Boulanger, damned Clemenceau by association, using the charges to defeat him at the polls in August, 1893.

Clemenceau, forced out of politics, embarked on a career as a man of letters. He wrote almost daily for *La Justice*, until it failed in 1887, and often for other papers, and, before returning to politics, produced a novel and a play. His most important publications were the volumes of essays *La Mêleé sociale* (1895) and *Le Grand Pan* (1896).

The Dreyfus affair, which arose because of the indictment and hasty conviction for espionage of Alfred Dreyfus, the only Jew who had ever served on the French general staff, provided a cause that helped Clemenceau to focus his writing. His style improved markedly, and in the last years of the century he was writing almost daily about *l'affaire*. When Émile Zola, whose article "J'accuse" (1898) had made Dreyfus a national concern, was tried for libel, Clemenceau was allowed to join the defense team even though he was not a lawyer. Dreyfus was convicted largely because of anti-Semitism and sent to Devil's Island. Even after his innocence had been established, there was resistance to changing the verdict.

Clemenceau had once again become an influential figure, and in 1901 *Le Bloc*, a weekly newsletter written entirely by him, began to appear. Aimed at an elite audience, it was influential, but only a year later he gave it up to campaign for a senate seat, which he held for the rest of his political life. On March 14, 1906, he became minister of the interior. Clemenceau was quite influential from the beginning and became premier on October 9. The government has on occasion been criticized for failing to advance the program of the Left, but it accomplished much in adverse circumstances. Without battles over church-state relations and the Dreyfus affair, the Left had no unifying cause. There was no majority for a coalition of the far Left, and so the cabinet was made up of mostly moderate Republicans. Over its three years, this cabinet managed to nationalize the western railroad, get an income tax bill through the chamber (it failed in the Senate), and start work on an old-age pension bill that was finally passed in 1910. It was a respectable set of reform efforts for a government based on moderates.

The Clemenceau government had problems at home and abroad. During the Algeciras Conference (1906), which dealt with a German challenge over the growing French role in Morocco, Clemenceau's determination kept up French resolve. Ultimately, the *Entente cordiale*—the semiofficial connection between London and Paris—held firm, and the Germans backed down. When large-scale strikes led to violence, Clemenceau adroitly combined repression, using troops to keep order, and conciliation, blocking efforts to suppress the Confédération Générale du Travail and supporting reasonable wage and hour demands. Throughout his tenure Clemenceau was faced with labor problems, but, although the Socialists were not pleased, his policy was quite successful.

Clemenceau's fall from power came ostensibly over a question of naval preparedness but was actually a result of personality. He was challenged by

Théophile Delcassé, whose efforts to create an English alliance and resist Germany had made him very popular. Instead of defending his own program, Clemenceau attacked his foe, with whom he had previously had personal difficulties. The vote that brought down Clemenceau was really a vote of sympathy for Delcassé. It was difficult for Clemenceau to put personal feelings aside and react purely in political ways. The next few years were quiet. In 1911, Clemenceau spoke against concessions to Germany in the second Moroccan crisis and campaigned for extending the basic term of military service from two to three years, which was done in 1913. He also began to publish a new newspaper, *L'Homme libre*.

The outbreak of war in August, 1914, led to Clemenceau's finest hour. At first, however, he was a critic. In the senate and his newspaper, which he renamed *L'Homme enchaîné* in response to censorship, he demanded a more vigorous prosecution of the war while condemning the tactic of mass assaults. The Left was inclined to seek compromise, and the Right was loyal to the Sacred Union (the nonpartisan war government). By the time the horrendous butcher's bill from the Western front began to produce disillusionment, he was the only politician who had both criticized the handling of the war effort and demanded an all-out effort to win. His moment came in the summer of 1917 when the bloody failure of the Nivelle Offensive led to large-scale army mutinies. While General Philippe Pétain restored discipline, Clemenceau attacked the government for tolerating defeatist attitudes, which the army blamed rather than admitting that the horrors of the front, added to the disgusting conditions in rest camps, had been the real cause of the revolt. Governments failed in October and November, and Clemenceau was asked to form a cabinet. The members were mostly Republicans, but none of prominence. No one from the Right was included, but that side was strongly supportive in any case. The Socialists abandoned the Sacred Union and went into opposition. The result was that Clemenceau was completely dominant and, unlike his predecessors, had no reason to adjust his policy to accommodate the Socialists.

At seventy-six in 1917, Clemenceau, who was short and rotund, was still in good physical condition. Fitness had long been important to him, and he was an expert horseman and fencer. He was dapper, with a high forehead and walrus mustache, but his dominant feature was his piercing eyes. His appearance did not belie his nickname, "The Tiger," earned by the ferocity of his debating.

Russia's withdrawal from the war because of the Bolshevik Revolution freed large numbers of German troops for the Hindenburg offensives of early 1918, but Clemenceau's oratory helped maintain the French will to fight. By making it clear to unions that he would support wage and condition improvement but crush any hint of pacificism or defeatism, he got such cooperation that the number of days lost to strikes fell dramatically. He pressed the

English to increase the proportion of their young men drafted and promoted plans to make the aggressive Ferdinand Foch supreme Allied commander. When things went awry, he backed his generals, refusing to look for scapegoats. He frequently visited the front at considerable personal risk to show the *poilus* that he cared.

With the arrival of the Americans, the Germans were stopped and the tide ineluctably turned. Clemenceau worked for Allied unity and to ensure that peace arrangements would guarantee French security. He had to balance the idealism of Woodrow Wilson, the practical desires of English Prime Minister David Lloyd George for a revived Germany in European trade, and the demands of Foch and President Raymond Poincaré for the crushing of Germany. Clemenceau was very influential at the Paris Conference as chairman of the Council of Ten (later reduced to the heads of the major powers) and, despite being shot by an anarchist, was able to get much of what he wanted in the Versailles Treaty.

A key question for Clemenceau was security. Foch and Poincaré demanded major territorial cessions by Germany, but, when it was clear that the Allies would not agree, Clemenceau accepted a fifteen-year occupation of the Rhineland and the separation of the Saar from Germany for a similar period with a plebiscite in the latter region to determine its final fate. In return, France was to get an Anglo-American guarantee of its borders. The guarantee was voided by the refusal of the United States to ratify the Versailles Treaty, and Clemenceau had to defend the arrangement as adequate. It bought time to rearm. The other great concern was reparations, and Clemenceau was as guilty as the other negotiators for the impossible burden imposed on Germany. Although more vindictive than the other negotiators, Clemenceau was little more responsible for the treaty's failure. He had to satisfy the political demands of the electorate and compromise with France's allies. Even had he wished to, he could not have changed the treaty very much.

During the negotiations, Clemenceau was faced with labor unrest, financial problems, and an increasing Socialist challenge. There were some dramatic strikes, but on the whole the postwar boom prevented political danger. Although the government seemed in good shape, a change in electoral law made coalitions extremely important, and, since the Socialists refused any coalition, the result was a massive victory for the right-center Bloc National in 1919. Clemenceau, despite the prestige of having led the nation to victory, had to resign.

After 1919, Clemenceau took little part in politics, though he did make some effort to help his protégé, André Tardieu. For a decade he devoted most of his time to travel and writing. He composed biographies of Demosthenes and Claude Monet and, most important, *Grandeurs et misères d'une victoire* (1930; *The Grandeur and Misery of Victory*, 1930). The latter was in part memoirs but was more intended as a response to Foch, who had continued to criticize the peace settlement and Clemenceau for agreeing to it. He died very early in the morning of November 24, 1929, in Paris.

Summary

Georges Clemenceau was above all a politician. He was devoted to the liberal principles of separation of church and state, support for labor, and popular sovereignty. Although he became more conservative toward the end of his career, his support for those principles never wavered. Part of that conservatism came from his unyielding sense of patriotism, and his conviction that France had to be preparing to defend herself against Germany.

Present at the creation of the Third Republic in 1871, Clemenceau's combativeness slowed his political rise, for he made enemies more easily than friends. Guilt by association in the Panama Canal scandal also sidetracked his career. He carried on, using journalism to make his opinions known and to regain respect in the political arena. Getting a chance to serve in a government, he effectively furthered the program of the moderate Left. When he fell, he was an elderly man and could have retired with honor.

The summit of his career came in the darkest hours of World War I. Taking almost solo control of the government and war policy, Clemenceau's enormous willpower stiffened the resolve of the nation to make the final sacrifices and win. His importance to his nation was greater than that of any other war leader in any of the belligerents. His career ended with his influential role at the Paris Peace Conference, at which he did as much as was possible to protect the future interests of France.

Bibliography

Bruun, Geoffrey. *Clemenceau.* Cambridge, Mass.: Harvard University Press, 1943. Although in places outdated, Bruun's biography is a good, straightforward narrative that is still worth reading.

Churchill, Winston S. "Clemenceau." In *Great Contemporaries.* New York: G. P. Putnam's Sons, 1937. Churchill's eloquence and shrewd insights into human nature are evident in this biographical sketch. Churchill packs much information into a few pages.

Clemenceau, Georges. *Georges Clemenceau: The Events of His Life as Told to His Former Secretary Jean Martet.* Translated by Milton Waldman. New York: Longmans, Green, 1930. Although not always trustworthy, this book is one of the few sources available for the study of Clemenceau's early life. It is a must for any biographical research.

Douglas, L. "Clemenceau." In *The History Makers,* edited by Lord Longford and Sir John Wheeler-Bennett. New York: St. Martin's Press, 1973. Focused on Clemenceau's importance in the development of French history, this is a good introductory article for those interested in seeing the key elements of the subject's career.

Jackson, John Hampden. *Clemenceau and the Third Republic*. New York: Macmillan, 1948. A useful biography with a political slant. Jackson's judgments are judicious, and he is at times insightful.

King, Jere C. *Foch Versus Clemenceau: France and German Dismemberment, 1918-1919*. Historical Monographs series 44. Cambridge: Harvard University Press, 1960. Clemenceau was so intimately involved in the entire resolution of World War I that although this book is really about Franco-German diplomacy, anyone seeking an in-depth knowledge of him should read it.

Lansing, Robert. "Georges Clemenceau." In *The Big Four and Others of the Peace Conference*. Boston: Houghton Mifflin, 1921. An eyewitness, Lansing offers an impressionistic but valuable view of Clemenceau's dominating role at the 1919 Paris Peace Conference. Although short on biographical data, this article is a very good introduction to the administration of the peace talks.

Roberts, J. "Clemenceau the Politician." *History Today* 6 (September, 1956): 581-591. A popular article focused on Clemenceau's role in politics. Because so much emphasis is placed on his role in World War I, the article's emphasis is helpful in establishing a balanced view.

Watson, David Robin. *Georges Clemenceau: A Political Biography*. New York: David McKay, 1974. An excellent scholarly biography, Watson's volume is perhaps a little short on personal information and at times shows a tendency to be overly favorable to the subject.

_____. "Pillar of the Third Republic." *History Today* 18 (May, 1968): 314-320. By one of Clemenceau's biographers, this article is an effort to establish the subject's central role and importance in the development of the Third Republic of France. The popular approach makes it a valuable introduction to Clemenceau.

Fred R. van Hartesveldt

JEAN COCTEAU

Born: July 5, 1889; Maisons-Laffitte, France
Died: October 11, 1963; Milly-la-Forêt, France
Areas of Achievement: Literature, film, and art
Contribution: From the years before World War I until his death in 1963, Cocteau enriched the cultural life of France with his highly creative contributions to such diverse fields as literature, ballet, art, and cinema. His works express with great lucidity a pessimistic view of the world that continues to fascinate admirers of Cocteau's films, novels, plays, and poems.

Early Life

Jean Cocteau was born on July 5, 1889, in Maisons-Laffitte, a small town outside Paris. His father, Georges, was a wealthy businessman and his mother, Eugénie, was very interested in art and music. His maternal grandfather was both an avid art collector and a respected cellist. Art and music played an integral part in Cocteau's childhood and adolescence. After Georges Cocteau's death in 1899, his widow Eugénie moved to Paris with her two sons, Jean and Paul, and her daughter Marthe. During his adolescence, Cocteau frequented Parisian literary salons and composed well-crafted but rather conventional poems. He was not yet an original artist.

During the years before World War I, Cocteau met the eminent Russian ballet impresario Sergey Diaghilev and the composer Igor Stravinsky. Their creative transformations of musical conventions inspired Cocteau to seek equally imaginative and disciplined ways to express his own poetic vision. Lasting friendships with such poets as Max Jacob and Guillaume Apollinaire, with painters including Pablo Picasso and Georges Braque, and with the composers Darius Milhaud, Erik Satie, and Arthur Honegger encouraged Cocteau to develop profound relationships among these art forms. Cocteau produced drawings of excellent quality. He worked together with Picasso and Diaghilev on an experimental 1917 ballet entitled *Parade*, and he would later write the libretto for Stravinsky's 1925 oratorio *Oedipus Rex*. His extended contacts with important poets, painters, and composers helped to transform Cocteau from an urbane salon poet into a creative writer.

Life's Work

Although Cocteau did produce during the 1910's highly imaginative books such as his 1919 volume of poetry *Le Cap de Bonne-Espérance* (the Cape of Good Hope), which describes the world as seen from an airplane, there was no real unity or depth in his works from this decade. He was then an extremely eclectic writer who followed whichever literary movements were popular in Paris. In 1919, however, Cocteau met Raymond Radiguet. The four years that they spent together changed permanently Cocteau's understanding of his role as a writer. Radiguet became Cocteau's lover, but, more important for Cocteau, Radiguet became his intellectual mentor and the only real friend whom Cocteau ever had. He persuaded Cocteau to distrust all trendy and thus ephemeral literary movements. He wanted Cocteau to create a new French classicism that would stress aesthetic distance, clarity in style and thinking, and profound analyses of human emotions. Under Radiguet's guidance, Cocteau began to compose truly significant works such as *Thomas l'imposteur* (1923; *Thomas the Impostor*, 1925), a powerful psychological novel about an adolescent's personal suffering during World War I. Radiguet's death in December, 1923, of typhoid fever drove Cocteau into an extreme depression from which he never fully recovered. His acquaintances feared that Cocteau would kill himself. Louis Laloy, then director of the Monte-Carlo Opera House, believed that opium would help Cocteau. Cocteau began taking opium, and his drug addiction clearly exacerbated his emotional problems. Several times Cocteau entered drug rehabilitation programs, but his efforts never fully succeeded, largely because Cocteau enjoyed the illusory pleasures of consuming opium.

Despite his drug addiction, Cocteau remained a very prolific writer. Perhaps recalling Radiguet's passion for the classics, Cocteau now sought inspiration more and more frequently in classical literature. Cocteau adapted classical myths to modern sensibilities. In 1927, Cocteau completed a one-act play entitled *Orphée* (*Orpheus*, 1933). According to classical mythology, the poet Orpheus was a generous husband whose wife, Eurydice, truly loved him. Orpheus willingly risks his life in order to free Eurydice from Hades. Cocteau believed, however, that the great loss of life in World War I made it difficult for his contemporaries to identify with such an idealized representation of love. Cocteau depicts Orpheus as profoundly alienated from his insensitive and aggressive wife. His Orpheus becomes a lonely artist for whom happiness and love no longer exist. Orpheus can now use his poetic gifts only to express his deep sense of despair and frustration. *Orpheus* seems to express the emotional anguish and anger that Cocteau felt so acutely during the two years after Radiguet's death.

In 1934, Cocteau would express an equally pessimistic view of the world in his play *La Machine infernale* (*The Infernal Machine*, 1936). This work portrays Oedipus and Jocasta as totally helpless victims of fate. His Jocasta is not the dignified queen of classical mythology but rather a very vulnerable woman with whom the audience can identify. Spectators come to understand that Oedipus must go blind and Jocasta must die before either can become free. Although they both acted rashly, they did not deserve such cruel treatment by the gods. Jocasta and Oedipus were alienated not only from their subjects in Thebes but also from the gods who destroyed their lives.

Although alienation would remain the dominant theme in Cocteau's works for the last four decades of his life, he nevertheless portrayed the effects of alienation in many different ways. His 1929 novel *Les Enfants terribles* (*Enfants Terribles*, 1930; also as *Children of the Game*, 1955) is perhaps his most effective and yet disturbing book. *Children of the Game* describes four adolescents whose parents are conspicuously absent. As this novel opens, the father of Paul and Elisabeth is already dead, and their mother will soon die. No relative or social worker tries to determine if an adult is taking care of these young adolescents. Society acts irresponsibly by abandoning them. Elisabeth develops an incestuous love for her brother. She transforms their house into a terrifying fantasy world in which pseudoreligious rituals are performed. Elisabeth manipulates her sickly brother, whom she changes into a bitter and frustrated individual. Elisabeth's cruelty toward her brother seems totally gratuitous. Love for her equals domination, but it is not clear why. Paul himself is so unbelievably submissive to his sister's fantasies that readers feel no sympathy for him. This novel ends with two suicides. Readers have little hope that moral order can be reestablished in a society that does not protect children and adolescents from sexual and emotional exploitation.

Although Cocteau remained a prolific writer during the 1930's and 1940's, his works tended to become predictable. His characters were invariably frustrated and unhappy individuals who expressed a very pessimistic view of life. It is especially difficult for readers to identify with Cocteau's female characters. A modern critic, Bettina Knapp, has suggested that Cocteau portrayed women in a consistently negative manner because "he looked upon women in general as aggressive, possessive, and jealous." Such sexual stereotypes distort reality, but they do, unfortunately, describe quite accurately numerous female characters in Cocteau's plays and novels. It is reasonable to conclude, as Knapp did, that Cocteau could not identify with the feelings and needs of women.

Although the quality of his literary works generally declined after the early 1930's, Cocteau did write and direct several important films. In his 1932 art film *Le Sang d'un poète* (*The Blood of a Poet*, 1949), Cocteau used beautifully filmed images in order to suggest the many sacrifices that a poet must make for the sake of art. Charles Chaplin and many film critics praised the quality of Cocteau's cinematography. In his 1946 film *La Belle et la bête* (*Beauty and the Beast*, 1947), Cocteau transformed this famous fairy tale into a very intimate work that evokes quite effectively the loneliness and solitude of the title characters.

In 1947, Cocteau published his masterpiece, a volume of essays entitled *La Difficulté d'être* (*The Difficulty of Being*, 1966). It is a pity that these essays have not received the critical attention that they richly deserve. As he grew older, Cocteau began to see a great similarity between himself and the French essayist Michel de Montaigne (1533-1592). Like Cocteau, Montaigne had only one true friend, Étienne de La Boétie, a writer who, like

Radiguet, also died at a relatively young age. Neither Cocteau nor Montaigne ever fully recovered from the death of his friend. *The Difficulty of Being* imitates creatively Monaigne's *Essays* and contains profound essays on themes such as friendship and death, which Montaigne had also explored. Like Montaigne, Cocteau converses with his readers in an eloquent and yet direct style.

Cocteau remained a successful and prolific writer until his death and became an important film director. He was elected to the French Academy and to the Royal Belgian Academy in 1955. He died on October 11, 1963, at his home in the French town of Milly-la-Forêt.

Summary

Jean Cocteau's artistic development was quite extraordinary. Before he met Raymond Radiguet, Cocteau was little more than an elegant writer who explored themes and narrative techniques then popular with avant-garde French writers and artists. His writings from the 1910's are now only of historical interest. Radiguet transformed Cocteau into a profound thinker who learned to express clearly his own perception of the world. As a mature writer, Cocteau never belonged to any literary movement such as surrealism or existentialism, but his plays such as *Orpheus* and *The Infernal Machine* did encourage an entire generation of French playwrights and theatergoers to appreciate the eternal values of classical Greek tragedies.

His was an independent voice that expressed his own understanding of the human condition. After Radiguet's death, Cocteau developed a very pessimistic philosophy of life. His novels, plays, poems, and essays express quite clearly his intense loneliness and solitude. Although the significance of his literary works should not be underestimated, Cocteau's most important contribution was to the cinema. His 1932 film *The Blood of a Poet* was the first truly successful art film and his 1945 film *Beauty and the Beast* revealed the universal psychological truths in this famous fairy tale. The quality of his cinematography was quite extraordinary and his films continue to enrich the lives of film viewers many years after Cocteau's death.

Bibliography

Crosland, Margaret. *Jean Cocteau*. New York: Alfred A. Knopf, 1956. This is a very sympathetic study of Cocteau's artistic development. Margaret Crosland analyzes especially well Cocteau's major films *The Blood of a Poet* and *Beauty and the Beast*.

Fowlie, Wallace. *Jean Cocteau: The History of a Poet's Age*. Bloomington: Indiana University Press, 1966. This general study defines Cocteau's originality by comparing him to other French writers and film directors of his lifetime. Fowlie proposes a very sensible evaluation of Cocteau's real accomplishments.

472   *Great Lives from History*

Gilson, René. *Jean Cocteau*. Translated by Ciba Vaughan. New York:
    Crown, 1969. This thoughtful analysis of Cocteau's films also includes
    several insightful comments on Cocteau by actors whom he had directed
    in his films.
Knapp, Bettina A. *Jean Cocteau*. Rev. ed. Boston: Twayne, 1989. This is
    the best general introduction to Cocteau's works. Bettina Knapp describes
    quite judiciously the nature of Radiguet's extraordinary influence on Coc-
    teau's literary career.
Steegmuller, Francis. *Cocteau: A Biography*. Boston: Little, Brown, 1970.
    This is an extremely well-researched biography of Cocteau. It is a pity
    that his obvious disapproval of Cocteau's homosexuality prevents Steeg-
    muller from evaluating objectively Cocteau's contributions to literature
    and the cinema.

                                                          Edmund J. Campion

COLETTE
Sidonie-Gabrielle Colette

Born: January 28, 1873; Saint-Saveur-en-Puisaye, Burgundy, France
Died: August 3, 1954; Paris, France
Area of Achievement: Literature
Contribution: Colette's work has been called the finest naturalist expressionism of the early twentieth century. Her gift for conveying sensations, emotions, and ambience produces the very personal style that her nom de plume so immediately calls to mind.

Early Life

Sidonie-Gabrielle Colette was born in Saint-Saveur-en-Puisaye, France, a Burgundian village in the Yonne region, on January 28, 1873. Her father, Jules-Joseph Colette, a retired army captain and the local tax collector, was something of a village character. Her mother, Adèle-Eugénie-Sidonie (Sido) Landoy, was extremely fond of pets and books. Sidonie-Gabrielle (Colette) was the fourth of her mother's children (two were the issue of a previous marriage, to Jules Robineau-Duclos). A special relationship existed between mother and daughter. Until Sido's death in September, 1912, Colette wrote to her long letters, chronicling in detail her sometimes Bohemian activities. For this reason, the relationship has been characterized as literary as much as it was familial.

Colette spent the first two decades of her life in the provinces. In 1890, the family left Saint-Saveur-en-Puisaye, after experiencing a financial reversal, and moved to Châtillon-sur-Loing in the nearby Loiret district. There, the family took up residence in the house of Doctor Achille Robineau-Duclos, Sido's second child. The next year, Sidonie-Gabrielle became engaged to Henri Gauthier-Villars, who referred to her simply as "Colette." Thus, she gained what would become her famous pseudonym. In May, 1893, the couple were married at Châtillon-sur-Loing. Gauthier-Villars, nearly fifteen years Colette's senior, moved in Left Bank literary circles where he was known by his professional pseudonym of Willy. After honeymooning in the Jura, the couple settled in the Rue Jacob, Paris.

Colette always professed to hate writing, and her literary career was certainly launched under a form of coercion. Her husband came across a notebook of her schoolgirl reminiscences and astutely judged that with a little spice they would make a successful book. The result was *Claudine à l'école* (1900; *Claudine at School*, 1956). The novel, which was published under Willy's name, quickly sold fifty thousand copies.

Life's Work

So closely was Colette associated with her heroine—once, that is, she became known as the true author—that a reference work published in 1942 actually includes an entry for her under the name Gabrielle Claudine Colette. The success of *Claudine at School* led to a series of Claudine novels based upon Colette's memories of her childhood in Burgundy and her life immediately thereafter—*Claudine à Paris* (1901; *Claudine in Paris*, 1958), *Claudine en ménage* (1902; *The Indulgent Husband*, 1935; also as *Claudine Married*, 1960), and *Claudine s'en va* (1903; *The Innocent Wife*, 1934). Willy signed his name to these as well, giving no formal indication of collaboration (indeed, it was a collaboration in which one partner primarily did the work, and the other exploited it). For this reason, Willy and Colette Willy are sometimes listed as additional pen names for Colette. Willy was music critic for the *Écho de Paris*, and, in 1903, he and Colette wrote a music column called "Claudine au Concert" ("Claudine at the Concert"). In the same year, Colette received her first lessons in the art of mime. Colette and Willy were constantly in need of money, so, to increase her income, she went on the stage, miming in the suggestive melodramas then popular in the music halls. During one of these performances, she bared her bosom. As a result, tales of her "nude dancing" became a part of the Colette legend. At the turn of the century, books about the animal world were enjoying a vogue and, in 1904, Colette, always an animal lover, published a book entitled *Dialogues de bêtes* (*Creatures Great and Small*, 1957). The author's name appeared as Colette Willy, and, so far as the public knew, this was the first book she had ever written. In 1905, Colette left Willy, and they were divorced the following year. Willy had used her and been unfaithful to her. Colette had written those scabrous portions of the Claudine books, which caused some people to regard them as unfit for young readers, at Willy's insistence. Yet he had also introduced her to the literary world and forced her to write. She had discovered her great gift and had learned to use it.

Colette worked steadily as a performer from the age of about thirty-three until she was forty, touring across Europe while continuing to write a book a year. During this period, suggestions of lesbianism were associated with her name and persist to this day. She performed in several mime dramas with Madame de Morny (known as "Missy"), the divorced wife of the Marquis de Belboeuf. Missy would play the part of a man and was, in fact, masculine in appearance. After her separation from Willy, Colette often stayed with Missy at the latter's home in Paris and in her villa at Le Crotoy. In January, 1907, they acted together in a play, and their prolonged and passionate kiss during the premiere performance scandalized the audience at the Moulin-Rouge. There had been broad hints of homoeroticism in the Claudine books, but these were perhaps more the product of Willy's spice than of autobiography. Some biographers state flatly that Colette had lesbian relationships with Missy and other women as well. Other biographers suggest that these relationships were far too emotionally complex to be characterized adequately by that term. Although Colette wrote about her own life for all of her life, this, like so much else about her, remains problematical. One result of her theatrical experiences was *La Vagabonde* (1911; *The Vagabond*, 1955), which has been called her first masterpiece.

In 1909, she met Henri de Jouvenel, editor of *Le Matin*, and by the next year was regularly contributing articles to that newspaper. She fell in love with Jouvenel and was living with him in Passy, a suburb of Paris, when she discovered, in the autumn of 1912, that she was pregnant. As a result of this unexpected occurrence, the lovers were married the following December. In July, 1913, Colette, at the age of forty, gave birth to her only child, Colette de Jouvenel. When war came in 1914, Colette worked as a volunteer night nurse in Paris, then spent two months at the front, where her husband was serving. Afterward, she wrote a series of articles about the experience for *Le Matin*. Colette's only full-length novel from the war years was *Mitsou: Ou, Comment l'esprit vient aux filles* (1919; *Mitsou: Or, How Girls Grow Wise*, 1930). This sentimental story of an actress who falls in love with a soldier on leave was a great popular success.

In 1920, Colette published her greatest novel, *Chéri* (English translation, 1929). Chéri is an eighteen-year-old boy whose worldly education is directed by Léa, a fashionable Parisian courtesan and his mother's best friend. After a long relationship that they thought afforded only mutual pleasure, Chéri and Léa make the horrifying discovery that they are in love. The situation is an impossible one. Léa is middle-aged, on the very point of growing old, but she has made any other woman unthinkable for Chéri. Compared to her, his youthful bride seems bland and arouses no appetite in him. During the 1920's, with the help of Léopold Marchand, Colette adapted *Chéri* and *The Vagabond* for the stage. In 1922 and 1925, she acted the role of Léa, and in 1926 she appeared in *The Vagabond*. Also in 1926, she wrote the libretto for a Maurice Ravel opera, and *La Fin de Chéri* (*The Last of Chéri*, 1932) was published. In 1924, her marriage to Henri de Jouvenel had ended in divorce.

Colette continued to work tirelessly in journalism. She served for a time as literary editor of *Le Matin* and wrote dramatic criticism for *Le Journal*. Though never really comfortable in the world of the cinema, she wrote scenarios for films in 1933 and 1934. During this same period, she opened a beauty institute in Paris and conducted more than thirty demonstrations in provincial towns in the art of makeup. On April 3, 1936, she married her third husband, Maurice Goudeket, in Paris.

She had been for many years France's foremost woman of letters and a spate of public honors came to her. In September, 1920, she had been named Chevalier de la Légion d'Honneur; in November, 1928, she was promoted to Officier de la Légion d'Honneur and in February, 1936, to Commandeur de la Légion d'Honneur. Also in 1936, she was received into the Belgian Royal

Academy of Literature (Colette had long had Belgian ties; Sido's two brothers had settled in Belgium in 1840 and had made names for themselves in journalism). In May, 1934, she was elected to the famed Académie Goncourt, and in October, 1949, she was elected its president. In 1953, she became Grand Officier de la Légion d'Honneur.

Although her last work of fiction, *Gigi* (1944; English translation, 1952), appeared during the Occupation, Colette continued writing into old age. By the time of her death, she had been writing for more than fifty years and had produced at least that many books, of all sorts. On August 3, 1954, she died in Paris. The last great honor conferred by her countrymen was a state funeral, the first ever accorded a woman. A surprisingly large throng filed by the flag-draped catafalque, since Paris is traditionally abandoned by its inhabitants in August. The ceremonies were marred, however, by the nonparticipation of the Catholic church. The Cardinal-Archbishop of Paris denied Colette the Roman Catholic burial rite on three grounds: she was twice divorced, she had not practiced the faith for many years, and she had not received the last sacraments. For this decision, he received much criticism, the most notable coming from the Catholic convert Graham Greene. In an open letter in *Le Figaro littéraire*, Greene politely took the archbishop to task by reminding him that everyone baptized a Catholic had the right to be accompanied to the grave by a priest, and that right could not be forfeited. So Colette died as she had lived, passionately loved and admired by many thousands but the object of controversy.

Summary

Many who knew Colette have testified to her personal magnetism, citing particularly her triangular face, shrewd blue-gray eyes, and rich warm voice. She deflected questions about her writing and her life by saying that she had put her life into her books, and the books were there to be read. At first, she was considered an instinctive, natural writer. Her evocation of the details of provincial life—the soil, the plants, the animals—is highly sensuous and has a quality not commonly found in French writing about nature. She stated that a part of her had always remained provincial and bourgeois. The strong, vibrant women and weak men in her books are totally convincing, while giving no suggestion that they have been created for the purposes of feminist argument. *Chéri* is the great amatory novel in twentieth century French literature. By the middle of her career, this instinctive writer had developed a fine classical style, upon which critics have frequently commented. When she became the *grande dame* of French letters, she was, as a professional actress, well qualified to play the part. She was, in short, an original, whose writing cannot be described by means of stock phrases. In discussing *Chéri* and *The Last of Chéri*, the English novelist John Braine says to the aspiring writer: "Colette's domain is the world of the senses. . . . Most novelists, compared with her, seem to inhabit a sparse bare world where the only physical pleasure is sex. I can think of no other novelist from whom you can learn so much."

Bibliography

Crosland, Margaret. *Colette: A Provincial in Paris*. New York: British Book Centre, 1954. A very appreciative biography, written while Crosland was much under the spell of Colette's personality. During her preparation of the book, Crosland often visited Colette and her third husband in their Palais-Royal apartment. She states in the introduction that one of her purposes is to convince others of Colette's greatness.

_____. *Colette: The Difficulty of Loving*. Indianapolis: Bobbs-Merrill, 1973. A critical biography that analyzes the subject's work as well as her life. Janet Flanner, long a commentator on the French scene, contributes an interesting introduction. A chronology and a bibliography of works by and about Colette are appended.

Marks, Elaine. *Colette*. New Brunswick, N.J.: Rutgers University Press, 1960. An examination, insofar as possible, of the relationship of Colette's works to her life. Marks begins from the premise that Colette's books totally lack analogues in philosophy and politics. They are informed by a highly personal moral admonition, summed up in the term *regarde*—look, experience, feel.

Mitchell, Yvonne. *Colette: A Taste for Life*. New York: Harcourt Brace Jovanovich, 1975. This biography makes the argument that, although some of her readers found her choice of subject matter objectionable or even depraved, Colette was instinctively deeply moral. She accepted no arbitrary hierarchies, choosing instead to be led by the life force and her five senses. A chronology, a bibliography, notes, and an index—all extensive—are provided.

Richardson, Joanna. *Colette*. New York: Franklin Watts, 1984. Richardson represents hers as the first full-scale biography of Colette to be written in English. It is based upon Colette's published work, the mass of secondary sources, and the subject's papers, lately made available at the Bibliothèque Nationale.

Patrick Adcock

PIERRE DE COUBERTIN

Born: January 1, 1863; Paris, France
Died: September 2, 1937; Geneva, Switzerland
Areas of Achievement: Sports and diplomacy
Contribution: Coubertin was the driving force behind the revival of the
   Olympic Games on an international scale. Through his efforts, the International Olympic Committee (IOC) was established in 1894, and the first
   modern international Olympics were held in Athens in 1896; he also oversaw the difficult formative years of the Games until they reached maturity
   and success.

Early Life

Baron Pierre de Coubertin was born into a wealthy French aristocratic
family in Paris on New Year's Day, 1863. The third of four children, he
enjoyed a privileged upbringing. Serious beyond his years, he was an intense
young man of rather small stature and average appearance (later made more
distinguished by an enormous, carefully groomed mustache), who developed
attitudes much too liberal for his conservative, Catholic, royalist parents.
The disastrous defeat suffered by the French in the Franco-Prussian War
(1870-1871) was a disturbing reminder to him and other patriots of France's
decline and convinced the young man that the old values of his family were
no longer realistic in a "Bismarckian" world. The shaky beginnings of the
Third Republic made the country's future uncertain, but Coubertin became a
firm supporter of the new regime. He developed interests in social criticism,
journalism, history, and, most important, educational reform.

After completing a Jesuit education in Paris in 1880, the idealistic Coubertin embarked on a plan to reform French education along the lines of
England's privileged class—especially in regard to physical training. No
stranger to sport and competition (he had fenced, rowed, and boxed), he
believed that part of France's problems lay in the poor physical conditioning
and mental attitude of its youth. In the British style of upper-class amateur
athletics, he saw the seeds for English patriotism and a reason for England's
success. Becoming an unabashed Anglophile, Coubertin made the first of
many trips to Britain in 1883 to observe for himself the playing fields which
had nurtured the English elite.

Hoping to establish further his credentials as an expert in physical education and aiming to strengthen his control over French amateur athletics,
Coubertin organized and financed a Congress for Physical Education in June
of 1889. Besides the usual speeches and business meetings, there was music,
ceremony, and sporting events. While the congress had many of the ear-
marks that would later characterize the Olympics, it attracted little positive
attention. To expand his movement and give it a more international flavor,

Coubertin visited the United States and Canada on an educational fact-finding mission for the French government soon after the 1889 congress. On his return, he stopped in England, where he attended some annual local English "Olympic Games" in Shropshire, which, along with widespread publicity sparked by the recent excavations at Olympia in Greece, may have led Coubertin to think about a revival of the Olympic Games.

Life's Work

While Coubertin is credited with organizing the first modern international Olympics in 1896, others had proposed the idea earlier, and the Greeks had already held their own modern Olympic Games in Athens in 1859, 1870, 1875, and 1889. Coubertin first publicly proposed reviving the Olympic Games in 1892 at the "Jubilee" meeting of his organization of French athletic clubs, the Union des Sociétés Françaises des Sports Athlétique (USFSA). The idea received a cold reception.

In 1893, Coubertin was again in the United States as the Third Republic's representative to the Chicago World's Columbian Exposition. His main reason for being there was to attend an international congress of higher education, but he used the opportunity to travel extensively, speak at American Universities, visit athletic clubs (such as the Olympic Club in San Francisco), and look for allies sympathetic to his ideas about the Olympics. On this trip, he met William Sloane of Princeton, who would become his most fervent United States supporter and a member of the first international Olympic Committee.

Undaunted by his lack of success in generating sufficient interest in a modern Olympics, Coubertin organized an International Congress of Amateurs in 1894 at the Sorbonne and invited representatives from amateur athletic organizations in the United States and Europe to Paris, ostensibly to discuss the concept of amateurism in sport, one of the burning sports issues of the day. Contrary to the modern idea of amateurism, the term was being used by aristocratic sportsmen of the late nineteenth century to distinguish themselves from "professional" working-class athletes, with whom they had no desire to compete or associate.

It was at this conference that Coubertin and his circle of supporters, including Sloane, first confronted the unsuspecting international guests with the idea of reviving the Olympic Games—a modern, multinational athletic contest among the young elite of the world as a means to promote patriotism, peace, and mental and physical excellence. Before the assemblage had dispersed, they had been seduced by the wily, affable, and persuasive Frenchman into voting to reestablish the Olympics—for "amateurs" only. They had also accepted Coubertin's International Olympic Committee (largely titled nobility with little or no responsibility) as the administering body of the Games, and had confirmed his Greek cohort, Demetrius Vikelas, as its first president and him as secretary. At the closing session of the conference, Coubertin announced that there was no need to wait to hold the first Games in Paris at the 1900 Universal Exposition as he had originally proposed; they could be held in Greece, the land where the Games had originally begun, in Athens two years hence in 1896. The motion passed enthusiastically, and the modern international Olympics began to take shape.

Once the organization of the Games was under way, the Greeks did whatever they could to exclude Coubertin, whom they considered an interloper. Understandably, they saw these Olympics as an international edition of their own revived national Olympic festivals, and they intended to make Greece the permanent site for the Games. Consequently, while much of his organizational plan was incorporated, Coubertin was treated more like a visiting journalist than the founder of the IOC.

Despite these difficulties and others, the 1896 Athens Olympics were a success. The fully restored ancient stadium (the first modern athletic spectator facility and model for all subsequent stadiums) was the same one used for the earlier 1870 and 1875 Greek Olympics, the majority of attending athletes and spectators were Greek, and most of the medals were won by Greeks, but, still, there was enough multinational flavor and support to get the Olympics off on the right foot. It was now an international sports festival, but it had attracted little worldwide attention.

Coubertin was able to fend off the Greek challenge to be permanent hosts of the "official" Olympics, and, through his carefully calculated propaganda, would eventually make the world practically forget the Greek contribution to the revival of the Games. As president of the IOC, Coubertin now looked to the 1900 Games to be held in his beloved Paris. Unfortunately, they took place within the context of the Paris Exposition, and, while Coubertin expected to have a prominent place in organizing the athletic activities, he was virtually ignored and had no control. The 1900 Games were a failure. Coubertin became so dismayed at the carnival atmosphere of the 1904 St. Louis Games (held with the St. Louis Exposition) that he did not even attend. The Greeks, still hoping to advance their cause as the home of the Games, held an "Olympics" in Athens in 1906 which was well attended and was the most successful athletic gathering to date. The disgruntled Coubertin dismissed them as "unofficial" and made little of their impact. Ironically, the success of the "unofficial games" probably saved his faltering Olympic movement.

The 1908 London Olympics were again, to Coubertin's dismay, held in conjunction with an international fair, this time the Franco-British Exhibition. A 100,000-seat stadium was built to accommodate the growing athletic spectacle, but these Games were also marred. Finally, the Olympics came of age in Stockholm in 1912, ensuring their continuation and bringing Coubertin's dream to fruition; these Olympics were held solely for the sake of the

Olympics. They were not part of a larger spectacle, the facilities had been built specifically for the 1912 Games, and, for the first time, all five continents were represented. The world now recognized the Olympics as a legitimate international event, and, as it did, Coubertin began to lose his exclusive control over the IOC and the Olympic movement. Though he continued to express his views through vehicles such as the *Revue olympique* (1901-1914), a monthly newsletter of the Olympic movement that he edited and published, fewer and fewer people were listening to what he had to say.

Just at the time the Olympics were coming of age, the 1916 Berlin Games were canceled because of World War I, which caused great family tragedy for Coubertin. During this period, he turned the presidency of the IOC over to Baron de Blonay, who was Swiss and therefore neutral. In 1918, Coubertin moved to Switzerland and established the IOC headquarters at Lausanne. The war focused the world's attention on the need for international peace and harmony, and the only world festival which, on the surface at least, promoted these ideas was the Olympics. The Games of the Seventh Olympiad were quickly organized at Antwerp in 1920.

In 1924, the Olympics came to Paris for the second time. On this occasion, Coubertin probably came closest to receiving his country's appreciation for his life's work, though France never gave him the recognition he desired for his efforts in behalf of his native land. He was more appreciated outside France, where he was recognized solely as the father of the Olympic movement. By this juncture, the IOC had gone from an assemblage of influential dignitaries selected by Coubertin to reinforce his own decisions to a working body almost independent of his direction. He had become a symbol rather than a factor in the mechanics of the Games. The elitism of the early Olympics had passed, and they became the property and heritage of all the people of the world. Coubertin, who had become lonely, unhappy, bitter, and suspicious, did what he could to remind the world of his role as the reviver of the Games. He remained IOC president until 1925 and a member of the IOC until his death. He ultimately produced twenty books and hundreds of articles of uneven import and quality. Many of his projects ultimately came to nothing.

The Olympic movement continued to grow with successes at Amsterdam in 1928 and Los Angeles in 1932. The last Olympics of Coubertin's lifetime were, ironically, the Nazi Olympics in Berlin in 1936. By this time, the Olympics were an unimagined phenomenon already assuming social, economic, and political implications that even Coubertin could not have foreseen. His place in sports history had been ensured, and the process of mythologizing the Games and the man responsible for their revival had begun. The 110,000 spectators at the opening ceremony of the Berlin Olympics listened in reverence to a recording of Coubertin's voice, but the man himself was not even invited to attend. The real Coubertin was left almost forgotten and in poverty in Switzerland. He died the following year in Geneva of a heart attack when he was seventy-four. His heart was placed in a monument that can still be visited today on the grounds of the International Olympic Academy at Olympia, Greece. Perhaps the greatest irony of Coubertin's life was that the man who had done more than any other to create the world's greatest modern athletic spectacle rarely associated with athletes himself.

Summary

More than any other single individual, Pierre de Coubertin deserves credit for reestablishing the modern Olympics. Others had ideas and made proposals to revive athletic competitions along the lines of the ancient games in Greece, but none had the perseverance and wherewithal of Coubertin. Aggressive, dynamic, energetic, and persuasive, he was born in France during a difficult period. French fortunes were on the decline, accentuated by the recent defeat in the Franco-Prussian War, and it was a time of soul-searching for every Frenchman, particularly one of aristocratic background. A patriot and firm supporter of the Third Republic, he looked for an avenue to which to devote his energy and wealth and found it in educational reform, particularly in regard to physical fitness. This idea led to his ultimate proposal at the congress held at the Sorbonne in 1894 of reviving the Olympics on an international scale to promote patriotism, world peace, and mental and physical excellence. By the time of his death in 1937, the Berlin Games had established the Olympics as a world spectacle of unlimited dimensions, and Coubertin, never fully appreciated, had lost control of the movement he had begun. Mythologized by the world, he became part of the symbolism of the Olympic Games. The man himself was almost forgotten.

Bibliography

Lucas, John. *The Modern Olympic Games*. South Brunswick, N.J.: A. S. Barnes, 1980. An overview of the Olympics into the 1980's. The first chapter is on Coubertin, and the next six cover the Games and the growth, trials, and triumphs of the Olympic Movement during his lifetime.

MacAloon, John J. *This Great Symbol: Pierre de Coubertin and the Origins of the Modern Olympic Games*. Chicago: University of Chicago Press, 1981. A social scientist's intense, detailed study, which is at once a history of the origins of the modern Olympics and of the first Games in Athens, and a biography (focusing on the first half of Coubertin's life) of their founder.

Mandell, Richard D. *The First Modern Olympics*. Berkeley: University of California Press, 1976. A sports historian's general assessment of Coubertin's life and activities before, during, and after the first modern Olympic Games in Athens, as well as discussions on the Ancient Games, earlier proposals for revival, and a full treatment of the 1894 Games.

Yalouris, Nicolaos, ed. *The Olympic Games*. Athens: Ekdotike Athenon, 1976. The best illustrated survey for the general reader of the Olympic Games from ancient to modern times. In the second section, entitled "Modern Olympic Games," Coubertin's role in reviving the Olympics is discussed, and short accounts and photographs are included for the Olympiads with which he was associated and others up to 1976.

Young, David C. *The Olympic Myth of Greek Amateur Athletics*. Chicago: Ares Press, 1984. This book is not specifically on Coubertin, but it contains the most realistic assessment to date of his motives and methods in reinstituting the Olympic Games.

Robert B. Kebric

JACQUES-YVES COUSTEAU

Born: June 11, 1910; Saint-André-de-Cubzac, France

Areas of Achievement: Biology, zoology, and engineering

Contribution: Cousteau is the father of underwater exploration, having coin-vented (with Émile Gagnon) the self-contained underwater breathing ap-paratus (SCUBA) in 1943. Cousteau has shared his explorations of the underwater world with millions of people around the world through his films, books, and television productions. Cousteau has also directed the engineering of several underwater living structures and systems as well as the design of an oceangoing vessel using a rigid turbosail for propulsion.

Early Life

Elizabeth (Duranthon) Cousteau vowed that her second child would be born in her native village of Saint-André-de-Cubzac on the banks of the Dordogne River. Jacques-Yves Cousteau was born on June 11, 1910, son of Daniel P. Cousteau and Elizabeth, in her ancestral home in the heart of Bordeaux, as she had wanted. Jacques had a brother, Pierre, four years his senior. The Cousteaus were a family in constant motion. Daniel was an at-torney to wealthy American magnate James Hazen Hyde. Daniel and family followed Hyde until World War I. After the war, the elder Cousteau severed his relationship with Hyde to work for another wealthy American, Eugene Higgins, and the Cousteaus moved to New York when Jacques was ten.

As a young student, Jacques was bored by academics, although he held a fascination for mechanical devices of all kinds. When the family moved back to Paris in 1922, Jacques purchased his own motion-picture camera and became engrossed in making films. Yet Jacques's academic habits had not improved, and his parents impounded the camera. After breaking seventeen windows in his parent's apartment in a fit of boredom, his parents sent the young, roguish Jacques to a boarding school. The transformation at boarding school was notably remarkable. Three years later, he was graduated second in his class, a disciplined, interested student. He entered the French navy as a second lieutenant.

After completing a world tour on the ship *Jeanne d'Arc*, Cousteau volun-teered for duty as a naval aviator. Before graduation and the winning of his wings, however, he badly injured both arms in an automobile crash. During the ensuing days of hospitalization, doctors told him his right arm had be-come infected and would have to be amputated. Cousteau feverishly refused. He recovered from the infection to a right arm and hand that hung paralyzed and useless beside him. It required nearly a full year of rigorous physical therapy before Cousteau could move his right hand at all. To his extreme contrition, he missed his aviator's wings and graduation with his class, but three years later all but one of his classmates would be dead in the opening days of World War II.

Cousteau was assigned to the naval base at Toulon, a base on the Mediterranean Sea. At the suggestion of a friend, Philippe Tailliez, Cousteau began swimming in the waters of Toulon to strengthen his arms. On the beach, he met a civilian artist, Frédéric Dumas. The three men soon began to use aviator's goggles when diving underwater in order to obtain a better view of the submarine world. Said Cousteau of his first experience with the goggles, "Sometimes we are lucky enough to know that our lives have been changed."

Life's Work

Cousteau and Dumas became engrossed in exploration of the underwater world. In 1937, Cousteau found time to court and marry Simone Melchior, but he continued his diving. He remained frustrated at being able to remain submerged only for a single breath of air. He attempted to bring his air underwater with him in the form of tanks of compressed oxygen. Yet there was no known way to regulate how the air was fed to the diver, and Cousteau almost poisoned himself on the compressed oxygen.

As he was contemplating an assault on this new, alien underwater world, virtually unknown to humankind, Adolf Hitler assaulted France. Cousteau was made gunnery officer on board the cruiser *Dupleix*, and the war became all-encompassing. Cousteau sailed out of Toulon on the *Dupleix* leaving behind Simone and his infant son, Jean-Michel. Yet France surrendered to Germany before the end of 1940, the *Dupleix* was disarmed, and Cousteau was assigned to a shore unit. In December, Simone bore another son, Philippe, named for Cousteau's good friend, Tailliez.

While the war continued, Cousteau, now shore-bound, became a member of the French Resistance, while his brother Pierre had sided with the Axis powers. Yet Cousteau managed to develop the idea to make air available to underwater divers. Cousteau had assembled a system consisting of a tank of compressed air, air lines, and a mask. What he lacked was a regulator that would adjust the air pressure to match that of the ambient water pressure at depth.

Simone's father sat on the board of directors of the French company Air Liquide. Hence, Cousteau was able to persuade Air Liquide to fund a prototype regulator designed by French Air Liquide engineer Émile Gagnan. (Gagnan used a modified automobile natural gas regulator as a model.) Together with Gagnan, Cousteau designed the missing link for what had become known as an underwater lung by fitting the regulator with a hose and mouthpiece. In June, 1943, Cousteau successfully tested the device off the French Riviera. In the joint patent, Cousteau and Gagnan called their device the aqualung. Not wasting any time, Cousteau joined Dumas and Tailliez on the Mediterranean for a series of test dives. Cousteau used his motion picture camera, adapted for underwater use, to make short documentaries.

As the war ended, Air Liquide put the aqualung into full commercial production. Cousteau, still an active naval officer, convinced the French navy of the efficacy of using the new device to search for mines, and he was named director of the effort. The aqualung would later become known as SCUBA. While conducting mine searches, Cousteau and associates discovered and began to develop divers' tables that would prevent the occurrence of the bends, an affliction resulting from nitrogen bubbles forming in the bloodstream.

It was during this postwar period that Cousteau's brother, Pierre, was convicted and sentenced to death as a Nazi collaborator, an event that would haunt the Cousteau family. (His sentence was later commuted to life imprisonment.) Cousteau testified for Pierre, whom he sincerely loved, in a highly publicized trial, outfitted in full dress uniform and medals. This move was one his superiors advised strongly against, but Jacques did not see another alternative. The defense of his brother effectively limited his future military career, and Cousteau resigned at the rank of captain in 1957.

By the early 1950's, Cousteau founded the Campagnes Océanographiques Françaises and the Centre d'Études Marines Avancées to coordinate and finance his underwater work. In July, 1950, Cousteau obtained the retired Royal Navy minesweeper *Calypso*, backed by the English philanthropist, Thomas Loel Guinness. With the *Calypso*, newly refitted and commissioned in June, 1951, Cousteau was offered passage to the oceans of the world. Cousteau's first expedition aboard *Calypso* was under way by late 1951. Cousteau united his talents of underwater photography and his eye for documentaries to document his first expedition to the Red Sea. Meanwhile, he and Dumas had teamed to cowrite *The Silent World* (1953), a montage of their underwater experiences.

Cousteau's fame began to spread. By the mid-1950's, he had secured National Geographic Society sponsorship. Cousteau would find funding for a four-year worldwide expedition during which *The Silent World* was made into a film documentary and went on to win an Oscar in 1957 and the Grand Prize of the Cannes Film Festival. Cousteau followed his initial success from *The Silent World* with *The Living Sea*, written with James Dugan and published in 1963. In 1957, Cousteau was named director of the Oceanographic Institute in Monaco, helping to ensure a steady financial base and consistent backing.

In 1962, Cousteau made good on his promise to enable man to work and live beneath the sea. He constructed the first fully versatile, underwater habitat and set it on the floor of the Mediterranean, twelve meters below the surface. He called his habitat Conshelf, for Continental Shelf Station. By 1963, the simple Conshelf station had expanded to a multiple-wing habitat

(Conshelf II) and was placed twelve meters below the Red Sea. The documentary *Le Monde san soleil* (1964; *World Without Sun*) was completed, a film diary of this adventure. By 1965, the crew of the *Calypso* had developed Conshelf III and manned it 108 meters below the surface of the Mediterranean. Six men, including Philippe Cousteau, lived there for twenty-eight days. Conshelf III ended the underwater living experience for Cousteau and company, now heavily in debt from the project. By 1980, Cousteau would rescind his long-held belief that man would one day live on the ocean floor by declaring colonization of the sea as unrealistic.

The end of the Conshelf experiments found Cousteau hastening to find funding sources. He knew well that the sure path to more funds was film-making, which had made him an international celebrity. By the spring of 1966, he had presented *The World of Jacques Cousteau* to an American television audience, sponsored by the National Geographic Society. Cousteau would find an almost inexhaustible appeal for his work from the world audience.

By the early 1970's, Cousteau published a series of books on the underwater world. The American editions became instant successes. These works described in detail the behavior and range of sharks, dolphins, and coral seas among other things for the first time to a mass audience.

Cousteau had evolved from a simple explorer to a seafloor inhabitant to an unabashed popularizer. On July 21, 1969, Neil Armstrong became the first human to set foot on the moon, an event which deeply affected Cousteau. He became preoccupied with notions of ecology and of rescuing a polluted Earth that the Apollo photographs depicted as a beautiful but fragile oasis of life hanging in a hostile and alien space. He founded the Cousteau Society in 1974, an organization to protect and improve life on the earth.

Cousteau also embarked on an enterprise of another sort as he developed a motorized sailing ship with a revolutionary design. Dubbed *Alcyone*, the oddly configured craft featured dual wing-shaped, rigid sails called "turbosails." In 1985, Cousteau triumphantly sailed into New York Harbor at the helm of the *Alcyone* to a hero's welcome. Soon thereafter, President Ronald Reagan awarded him the highest civilian honor of the United States, the Medal of Freedom.

Summary

Jacques-Yves Cousteau represents a relentless curiosity, a driving need to explore and push back the limits of the frontier. One of the most productive men of the twentieth century, his life's work is a series of cyclic explorations: to simplify the ability of man to work freely and independently underwater, to live and work there, to enable everyone to learn about and enjoy the oceans through the media, to improve the plight of the seas and the world's ecology through education, and finally to reexplore the world through a more mature, more complete vision. He has been a relentless public relations master, knowing how to fund, how to publicize, and when to change his own ideas to meet the considerations of the world community, all to meet the demand of his explorations. He has often been criticized for craving too much publicity and attention, but no one can argue with his final achievements. Reagan described him as a "dominant figure in world history." Cousteau's legacy will be no less than the father of the free diver and the man who, almost singlehandledly and for the first time, imposed the underwater world on the vision of the earth's peoples with energy, compassion, and a remarkable insight.

Bibliography

Cousteau, Jacques-Yves, and Philippe Cousteau. *The Shark: Splendid Savage of the Sea*. New York: Doubleday, 1970. This book narrates one of the first accurate, popular accounts of the shark in his natural habitat. Cousteau narrates the book with actual accounts of his encounters with sharks, their habits, and dangers, and he discounts popular myths. He discusses their role in the ocean as an important predator.

Cousteau, Jacques-Yves, and Philippe Diole. *Life and Death in a Coral Sea*. New York: Doubleday, 1971. The book uncovers the ecology of a coral reef community and the predation and living balance of the reef. Also discusses the ecological consequences of pollution on the delicate life balance in a coral sea community.

Cousteau, Jacques-Yves, and James Dugan. *The Living Sea*. New York: Harper & Row, 1963. This work, coauthored by underwater explorer Dugan, has become a classic of the sea and was one of the elements of Cousteau's work that certified his fame with the people of the world. Details the first expedition of the *Calypso* through the Conshelf I trials.

Dugan, James. *World Beneath the Sea*. Washington, D.C.: National Geographic Society, 1967. This book details the exploration of the sea through the mid-1970's. Places the pioneering work of Cousteau in perspective with his peers. It is lavishly illustrated with photographs of Conshelf and other underwater habitats.

Limburg, Peter R., and James B. Sweeney. *Vessels for Underwater Exploration*. New York: Crown, 1973. This work concentrates on submersibles (including Cousteau's diving saucer) but reserves a chapter for habitats. Provides a chronological accounting of the habitats' evolution.

Madsen, Axel. *Cousteau: An Unauthorized Biography.* New York: Beaufort Books, 1986. This work details the life of Cousteau. It fairly and impartially devotes appropriate and compassionate accounting of the good and bad elements of Cousteau's life in a well-balanced, easy-to-read, and entertaining account of one of the most important explorers of the twentieth century.

Dennis Chamberland

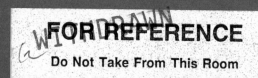